RADIANT MINDS

Scientists Explore the Dimensions of Consciousness

Edited by **Jean Millay**
Foreword by **Jeffrey Mishlove**

Revised and Updated Version of the 1993 PRG Anthology
SILVER THREADS: 25 Years of Parapsychology Research

Copyright © 2010 by Jean Millay

All rights reserved. No portion of this book may be reproduced, by any process or technique, without the express written consent of the publisher or of the individual authors.

Printed in the United States of America by Lightning Source, Inc.

Cover Design by James Dowlen
Book layout by Jean Millay

Library of Congress Cataloging-in-Publication Data

Millay, J., editor, publisher and one of the authors. Doyle, CA, 2010

Radiant Minds: Scientists Explore the Dimensions of Consciousness

Foreword by Jeffrey Mishlove

Fifty-five authors provide research, essays, biographies, and references
ISBN 978-0-615-29633-3

The paper used in this book complies with the Permanent Paper Standard issued by the National Information Standards Organization. (Z39.48--1984)

This is the first team to create an anthology for
the members of the Parapsychology Research Group:

SILVER THREADS:
25 Years of Parapsychology Research
Copyright © 1993 by Beverley Kane, Jean Millay, and Dean Brown
London, Westport, CN: Praeger—ISBN 0-275-94161-2

Editors — Beverley Kane, Dean Brown, and Jean Millay.
Back Row: Russell Targ — First president of the PRG.
He was among the original founders in 1966.
(The complete list of founders is in Section XI.)

Copyright Acknowledgments

The author and publisher gratefully acknowledge
permission to use the following materials:

Association for Humanistic Psychology, SF, CA. (1979 – 2001) Excerpts from several essays published in special issues devoted to education.

Dakin, Henry S. (1974, 1975 & 1978) Excerpts from *High-Voltage Photography*. SF, CA: Washington Research Institute (WRI).

Dowlen, James (2009) Cover design for *RADIANT MINDS: Scientists Explore the Dimensions of Consciousness.* Framed prints of the cover are available at www.dowlenartworks.com.

Harris, Sidney (Cartoon) – www.ScienceCartoonsPlus.com.
"I think you should be more explicit in step two."

Henningfield, J.E. (for NIDA) – published in NY Times by Hilts, P. (1992). www.DrugWarFacts.org and www.CommonSenseDrugPolicy.org.

Persinger, Michael & Krippner, Stanley (1989) "Dream ESP experiments and geomagnetic activity." In: *JASPR 1989*; 83;101-116.

Nelson, Roger. *Global Consciousness Project* at the Princeton Engineering Laboratory, Princeton, NJ.

www.shamanismconference.org/. Excerpts from several essays from these two conferences – third (1986) and fifth (1989) – published in the *Proceedings of the International Conf. on the Study of Shamanism and Alternate Modes of Healing.* R-I Heinze (Ed.) San Rafael, CA: Independent Scholars of Asia.

Radin, Dean (2004) "Psychophysiological studies of PSI and emotions." The Institute of Noetic Sciences, Petaluma, CA.

Rauscher, Elizabeth & Rubik, Beverly (1983) "Human volitional effects on a model bacterial system." In: *PSI Research Journal* 1983; 2, no. 1.

Schlitz, Marilyn & Radin, Dean (2007) "Prayer and intention in distant healing." In: *Whole Person Healthcare: Vol. 2: Psychology, Spirituality and Healthcare.* Ilene Ava Serlin (Ed.) Westport, CT: ADTR Praeger Publishers.

Targ, Russell (2004) *Limitless MIND: A guide to remote viewing and transformation of consciousness.* Novato, CA: New World Library.

Vallee, Jacques & Davis, Eric (2003) "Incommensurability, orthodoxy and the physics of high strangeness: A 6–level model for unidentified aerospace phenomena." Based on a presentation at the Forum on *"Science, Religion and Consciousness"* held at the University Fernando Pessoa, Porto (Portugal), October 23-24, 2003.

To Our Founders And Our Finders

*This work is dedicated to those who
Founded the Parapsychology Research Group
To those who continue the research in consciousness
And to those who will find this book
Where and when
It is most meaningful to them.*

CONTENTS

List of Illustrations, Graphs, Charts and Tables xii
Acknowledgments xvi
PROLOGUE (from the Epilogue of *Silver Threads*) xviii
Dean Brown (1993)
FOREWORD xxiii
Jeffrey Mishlove
INTRODUCTION xxxiii

SECTION I ~ DIMENSIONS OF PERCEPTION   1

1. A Decade of Remote Viewing Research 12
   Russell Targ (1993)
2. Psychophysiological Studies of
   PSI and Emotions 23
   Dean Radin
3. The Scientific Study of Anomalous Dreams 38
   Stanley Krippner (Excerpts)
4. National and Gender Differences in
   Reports of Extraordinary Dreams 43
   Stanley Krippner
5. Syntonics:
   Optometric Phototherapy 55
   Raymond Gottlieb

SECTION II ~ DIMENSIONS OF INTENTION   61

6. Psychoneuroimmunology — The Bridge
   Between Science and Spirit 65
   Sondra Barrett (1993)
7. Human Volitional Effects on a Model Bacterial System 80
   Beverly Rubik and Elizabeth Rauscher (1993)
8. A Study on Prayer and AIDS 90
   Russell Targ and Elisabeth Targ
9. Prayer and Intention in Distant Healing:
   Assessing the Evidence 95
   Marilyn Schlitz and Dean Radin

10. Firewalking: A New Look at an Old Enigma 110
    Larissa Vilenskaya (1993)

11. Psycholuminescent Effects 122
    Henry Dakin

12. The Biofield: Bridge Between
    Mind and Matter 127
    Beverly Rubik

SECTION III ~ BELIEF SYSTEMS ARE EVOLVING   133

13. Shifting Assumptions (Excerpts) 136
    Willis Harman (1993)

14. Parapsychology, Science and Intuition (Excerpts) 144
    William H. Kautz (1993)

15. The Nature of Personal Belief Systems (Excerpts) 154
    Beverley Kane (1993)

16. Playing with Ideas and Beliefs 161

SECTION IV ~ MIND AND BRAIN/BODY CHEMISTRY   165

17. The Evolution of Consciousness Intertwined
    With the Evolution of the Science of Plants 175
    Dean Brown (1993)

18. Alternate States of Consciousness:
    Access to Other Realities 178
    Ruth-Inge Heinze (1993)

19. Short Interviews with Independent
    Neurochemists and a Psychotherapist 189
        a) *Alexander (Sasha) Shulgin* 190
        b) *Ann Shulgin* 198
        c) *Hosteen Nez* 201
        d) *Tim Scully* 208

20. Psychic Gifts from Entheogens 217
    Jean Millay

21. Implications of Consciousness Research for
    Psychotherapy and Self-Exploration 227
    Stanislav Grof (1993)

SECTION V ~ MIND AND BRAIN/BODY ELECTRICITY   233

22. Brainwave Synchronization:
    Report on a Pilot Study 239
    James R. Johnston (Revised from 1993)

23. Our Intimate, Magnetic Connection to
    Our Living Planet and Its Bio-Diverse Life 255
    Elizabeth Rauscher and William Van Bise

24. Dream ESP Experiments and Geomagnetic Activity 259
    Michael A. Persinger and Stanley Krippner (1993)

25. The Interaction of Sonic Resonance with the
    Dynamics of Cerebral Spinal Fluid Relative to
    Focus of Attention and Alternate States 276
    Cheri Quincy and Joel Alter

SECTION VI ~ MATHEMATICAL MODELS   283

26. Longitudinal Comparison of Local and Long-Distance
    Remote-Perception Phenomena 288
    Elizabeth A. Rauscher (1993)

27. Investigation of a Complex Space-Time Metric to
    Describe Remote Perception and Precognition 305
    Elizabeth Rauscher and Russell Targ

SECTION VII ~ PHYSICS   335

28. Energy 342
    Saul-Paul Sirag (1993)

29. Hyperspace Reflections 355
    Saul-Paul Sirag (revised from 1993)

30. Quantum Reality and Consciousness 368
    Nick Herbert (1993)

31. Time, Consciousness and PSI 373
    Jean E. Burns (revised from 1993)

32. Individuality and Wholeness in
    Quantum Physics 387
    James R. Johnston

SECTION VIII ~ DIMENSIONS OF SPIRIT   407

33. Cells and the Sacred 411
    Sondra Barrett

34. A Journey:
    One Healer's Story 417
    Joel Alter

35. The Mist Wolf 425
    Stephan A. Schwartz

36. Research on an Approach to Bereavement
Using a Process with a Psychomanteum 431
Arthur Hastings

37. Messages from Spirit Friends 443
Transmissions from Different Spirits

SECTION IX ~ DIMENSIONS OF CONSCIOUSNESS   455

38. The Essence of Dean Brown's Cosmic Law 459
William C. Gough (Review, excerpts, and commentary)

39. The Global Consciousness Project:
Can a Meeting of Minds Structure Random Data? 469
Roger Nelson

40. Incommensurability, Orthodoxy and the Physics of
High Strangeness: A 6-Level Model for
Unidentified Aerospace Phenomena 492
Jacques Vallee and Eric Davis

SECTION X ~ EDUCATION: INCREASING INTELLIGENCE   509
(Through the Understanding and Application
Of the Dimensions of Consciousness)

41. Education: The Problems
Children Are Not Machine Parts 515
Alpha Quincy

42. Education: Solving The Problems
Outline for Change 518
Stanley Krippner

1st: Learning How to Learn: Training the Instrument
(Lesson Plans Included) 520
Ray Gottlieb

2nd: Learning the Language of the Senses to
Improve Communication of Nonverbal Intelligence 529
Jean Millay

3rd: Self-Discovery Science — Reports From Two Teachers
(Lesson Plans and Success Stories Included)
   A) Biofeedback and Neurofeedback 538
      Marge King
   B) Listen To Your Heart Talk 544
      Mara Mayo

4th: Exploring the Dimensions of Self 549
Sola Patricia

43. Holistic Education: A Statistically Significant Study 555
V. Louise Crawley Sample

SECTION XI ~ REFLECTING ON PARAPSYCHOLOGY — 557

Milestones in the History of the PRG
(Parapsychology Research Group) 559

44. Fifty-Five Years in Parapsychology:
Frustrations, Advances, Directions,
Meaning and an Interesting Life 564
Charles T. Tart

45. Additional Biographies, Statements and Websites
of PRG Members 589
   1) *Joe Kamiya* 590
   2) *Jon Klimo* 592
   3) *William Braud* 594
   4) *Brian McRae* 596
   5) *William Croft* 597
   6) *Kenneth Ring* 598
   7) *Barbara Honegger* 599

46. Additional Biographies, Statements, Examples and
Websites of Psi Sensitives 607
   9) *Gail Hayssen* 608
   10) *James Dowlen* 612
   11) *Tom Byrne* 614
   12) *Mark Harris* 616
   13) *Greg Schelkun* 618

EPILOGUE (2010) — 621

Envisioning the Global Mind 621
Roger Nelson

APPENDICES — 623

1) **Table of Contents Of The First PRG Anthology**
   Silver Threads: 25 Years of Parapsychology Research
   Published in 1993 625

2) **Glossary** 627
   a) General Terms 627
   b) Terms Commonly Used in Parapsychology 628
   c) Terms Used in Physiological Measurement 629
   e) Terms Used in the Global Consciousness Project 630

ILLUSTRATIONS

ILLUSTRATIONS, GRAPHS, CHARTS AND TABLES
Listed In Order

Order	Title	Page Number
> 1)	COVER – *"Radiant Minds"* – designed by James Dowlen	
2)	Kane, Brown, Millay & Targ, photo of the first PRG editors	iii
* 3)	Dean Brown, PhD, portrait and bio	xviii
* 4)	Jeffrey Mishlove, PhD, portrait and bio	xxiii
>	SECTION I – *"Does the Eye See?"* – drawing by Tom Byrne	1
6)	Harris & Winkler Telepathy from Marvel Comics	5
7)	Dowlen & Byrne, Local RV	6
8)	Schelkun, Long Distance RV—photo by C. Brush	7
9)	Dowlen, Long Distance RV in 4 places (1)	8
10)	Dowlen, Long Distance RV in 4 places (2)	9
11)	Rolling Thunder and Seucuicui – photos	9
12)	Dowlen, Precognition	10
* 13)	Russell Targ, portrait and bio	12
14)	Pat Price, Local RV	16
15)	Hella Hammid, Local RV	17
16)	SRI Physicist, Long Distance RV	18
17)	McMoneagle, Local RV	19
* 18)	Dean Radin, PhD, portrait and bio	23
	Graph – Douglas Dean, 1962	26
	Graph – Av. Electrogastrogram values	28
	Graph – Presentiment experiment	30
	Diagram of experimental layout (Eye-Trac)	31
	Diagram of sequence of events	32
	Graph – % of change in pupil dilation	33
* 19)	Stanley Krippner, PhD, portrait and bio	38
	Table – Extraordinary dreams by country and gender	47
	2 Tables – ESP-Type dreams	48
* 20)	Raymond Gottlieb, OD, PhD, portrait and bio	55

>	SECTION II – *"Firedancer in Bali"* – photo by Millay	61
*	22) Sondra Barrett, PhD, portrait and bio	65
	23) Rubik & Rauscher Flow Chart	83
	2 Graphs – Generation time	*85*
	2 Graphs – Generation time	*86*
	Table – Summary of results	*87*
*	24) Elisabeth Targ, MD, portrait and bio	90
*	25) Marilyn Schlitz, PhD, portrait and bio	95
*	26) Larissa Vilenskaya, LHD, portrait and bio	110
*	27) Henry S. Dakin, portrait and bio	122
	28) Hickman's Kirlian photos of Geller's finger	124
	29) Hickman's Kirlian photos of Geller's PK	125
*	30) Beverly Rubik, PhD, portrait and bio	127
	31) Biofield photos of Dean Brown, PhD, by Don Parker, PhD	130
	32) Dean Brown, PhD, exposes film through mental intention	131
>	SECTION III – *"Pot-Shot Logic"* – drawing by Ashleigh Brilliant	133
*	34) Willis Harman, PhD, portrait and bio	136
*	35) William Kautz, SCD, portrait and bio	144
*	36) Beverley Kane, MD, portrait and bio	154
>	SECTION IV – Brain / Body Chemicals	165
	Graph of drugs by P. Hilts in NY Times	*174*
*	38) Ruth-Inge Heinze, PhD, portrait and bio	178
	Diagram of states of consciousness	*181*
*	39) Alexander T. Shulgin, PhD, portrait and bio	190
*	40) Ann Shulgin, portrait and bio	198
*	41) Hosteen Nez, portrait and bio	201
	Chart of the Shulgin System	*206*
*	42) Timothy Scully, PhD, portrait and bio	208
*	43) Jean Millay, PhD, portrait and bio	217
*	44) Stanislav Grof, MD, PhD, portrait and bio	227
>	SECTION V – *"Think, Don't Think"* – drawing by Millay	233
*	46) James R. Johnston, PhD, portrait and bio	239
	Diagram of EEG hookup	*243*
	EEG chart recordings and a graph of IP Sync scores	*245*
	Graph of IP Sync and telepathy scores	*246*
	47) Brainwave light sculpture – photo by Krippner	249

48) Electromagnetic Spectrum – Extreme-Low-Frequencies only **254**
49) Robert O. Becker quote – *"Electrotherapy for Drug Addiction"* **258**
* 50) Michael Persinger, PhD, portrait and bio **259**
       Graph – Mean daily averages *264*
       2 Graphs – Log of mean daily values *267*
* 51) Cheri Quincy, DO, portrait and bio **276**
  52) Photo of Quincy during shamanic drumming **281**
> SECTION VI – **"Miracle"** – cartoon by Sidney Harris **283**
* 54) Elizabeth Rauscher, PhD, portrait and bio **288**
  55) G. Langford – Local RP **292**
  56) G. Langford – Long Distance RP (CA to Alabama) **293**
  57) Rauscher – Time delayed RP **294**
  58) A systems analyst – Long Distance RP **295**
  59) Rauscher – Long Distance RP (1,000 miles) **296**
  60) Hella Hammid – Precognitive RP **297**
       Graph – Comparison of local and long distance RP *300*
  61) Pat Price – Long Distance RV with No Outbound Team **308**
  62) Targ – Long Distance RV = CA to Colombia, SA **309**
       Graph – Location of 4 events in a complex plane *328*
> SECTION VII – Cartoons for the Physics Chapter **335**
* 64) Saul-Paul Sirag, portrait and bio **342**
       Graph – A-D-E Coxeter graphs (Dynkin diagrams) *365*
* 65) Nick Herbert, PhD, portrait and bio **368**
* 66) Jean Burns, PhD, portrait and bio **373**
       Diagrams – Double and single slit interference *391*
       Abstract and manifest layers *392*
       Delayed choice interferometer *398*
> SECTION VIII – **"Gramma's Spirit"** – photo by Echo Penrose **407**
  68) A) Photo of a cave painting. B) 9th C. medicine wheel **414**
  69) A) Barrett drawing of cell. B) Langridge graphic of DNA **415**
* 70) Joel Alter, DO, portrait and bio **417**
* 71) Stephan Schwartz, portrait and bio **425**
* 72) Arthur Hastings, PhD, portrait and bio **431**
       Table – Changes in bereavement *438*
  73) *"Spirit Face of the Heart Donor"* – Photos by Jack Stucki **445**

> SECTION IX – *"The Absolute"* – Image of Gough's and Brown's concept .. 455
* 75) William Gough, portrait and bio 459
* 76) Roger Nelson, PhD, portrait and bio 468
        Graph – GPC Egg (ElectroGaiaGram) world locations *474*
        Graph – Bombing in Kosovo –3, 24 – 1999 .... *476*
        Graph – Terrorist attacks – 9-11-2001 (A) *477*
        Graph – Terrorist attacks – 9-11-2001 (B) *478*
        Graph – TM yogic flyers – 2006 .... *479*
        Graph – Peace demonstrations – 2003 .... *480*
        Graph – New Years – 1999-2008 .... *481*
        Graph – Obama wins, Speech – 9-4-2008 .... *482*
        2 Graphs – Presidential approval – 1999-2007 .... *484*
        Graph – GCP results, Aug 1998-2008 .... *486*
* 77) Jacques Vallee, PhD, portrait and bio 491
* 78) Eric W. Davis, PhD, portrait and bio 492
> SECTION X – **"Holding Hands"** - Adapted from *Biomeditation* 509
  80) Child art develops visual intelligence (3 pages) 534
  81)   *2 Graphs of irregular heart rhythms* *546*
  82)   *Graph of coherent heart rhythms* *547*
> SECTION XI – **Reflection Photos** 557
* 84) Charles T. Tart, PhD, portrait and bio 564
* 85) Joe Kamiya, PhD, portrait and bio 590
* 86) Joe Kamiya, PhD, and Dean Radin, PhD *590*
* 88) Jon Klimo, PhD, portrait and bio 592
* 89) William Braud, PhD, portrait and bio 594
* 90) Brian McRae, portrait and bio 596
* 91) William Croft, portrait and bio 597
* 87) Barbara Honegger, MA, portrait and bio 599
* 92) Gail Hayssen, portrait and bio 608
  93) Hayssen's precognition 609
* 94) James Dowlen, portrait and bio 612
  95) Dowlen's precognition 613
* 96) Tom Byrne, portrait and bio 614
  97) Byrne's remote viewing 615
* 98) Mark Gurumukh Harris, portrait and bio 616
* 99) Greg Schelkun, portrait and bio 618
> APPENDICES – *"Real Magic"* – drawing by Millay 623

ACKNOWLEDGMENTS

On behalf of the Parapsychology Research Group, we thank our founders, members, and benefactors for their support of psi research. We are honored to have had Russell Targ followed by Charles Tart as our first two presidents. The rest in succession were Barbara Honegger, Elizabeth Rauscher, Saul-Paul Sirag, Jean Millay, Elisabeth Targ, Mark Cummings, and Ruth-Inge Heinze.

We gratefully acknowledge Jeffrey Smith and Nancy Keisling who hosted our meetings during those first years of PRG. Some of the later meetings were held at Elisabeth Targ's home, and the last were held at Ruth-Inge Heinze's apartment. Most of the rest of the meetings were held at the Washington Research Institute (WRI). Henry Dakin and his staff deserve special thanks and appreciation. Not only did the WRI generously provide comfort, hospitality, and inspiration through many long and lively meetings held there, but also Dakin provided closed-circuit television monitors, as well as audio and video recordings of our speakers, which are archived. We also thank our many distinguished visitors from around the world who shared their research and their ideas with us at our meetings.

We additionally thank the many people who have served on the board of directors over the years, and those who have spirited the first book along with technical, historical, and creative assistance: Jean Burns, Henry Dakin, Ruth-Inge Heinze, David Hurt, Bryan McRae, Charles Muses, Elizabeth Rauscher, Russell Targ, Dean Brown and Beverley Kane.

For this new edition, I wish to express everlasting gratitude to Carol Guion, the best and most altruistic editor of our time, for volunteering to help on this project. For many years, Carol was the editor of the *AHP Newsletter* for the Association for Humanistic Psychology. Later she served as associate editor with Barbara McNeill on the *IONS Review* for the Institute of Noetic Sciences. Over those years she became quite familiar with the writings of the authors in this book. More than that she has been my dearest friend for over fifty years. When additional editing of technical papers was required, Saul-Paul Sirag, Elizabeth Rauscher and Jim Johnston graciously volunteered to perform those jobs.

We are especially grateful for the generous cooperation of all the authors, whose contributions celebrate the memory of the PRG, and the more than 40-years some of our members have dedicated to the study of consciousness. All of us with our diverse ideas and perspectives, combined with those concepts that we share in common, have collectively provided the reader and ourselves with a comprehensive examination of the fundamental questions involved: How is remote viewing (RV) possible? (Can we really *"know the world without leaving the house,"*[1] as the Chinese philosopher Lao Tzu wrote in ancient times?) How does distant healing intention (DHI) work to help heal others? What can we know about the incomparable abilities of mind and consciousness?

Some of the answers are here. Many are yet to be answered. However, as we study the writings of all of these authors as a group (even though they don't all agree), we begin to appreciate the possibly limitless dimensions of mind. Our collective efforts to explore the unknown have expanded our awareness as we observe and support this historic shift in basic assumptions about the nature of life, consciousness and the cosmos.

This book would not be possible without the unconditional love and spiritual guidance of Darrell Lemaire. The peacefulness of his energy as a medicine man in this environment is truly inspiring. We enjoy expansive views of nature with uninterrupted hours of silence. This allows us both to maintain a coherent focus of attention for study, contemplation and communication with beings of light. Here in the high desert overlooking the Great Basin, we enjoy abundant solar power and clear spring water.

Roger Fein and Ashton Hawkins have kept my computer and email functional, and we all know how vital that is. I am deeply grateful for such noble activity that can only come from those who are experts in their different fields, and who, as exceptional friends, also volunteered to help with this long project. This song is true for me, *"I get by with the help of my friends,"* and I am grateful to all of them: Gail Hayssen, David Levitt, Jerry Tatton, Shoshi Morginn, Mylan Hawkins, Ellen Baker, Richard Donovan, Cheri Quincy, Joel Alter, Wanda and Herb Blumenthal, Jack and Judy Stucki, Celia Coates, Estee Tatton, Cheryl Wells, Sola Patricia, Alpha Quincy, Serena Mayo, and our incomparable teacher Stanley Krippner.

We offer an extra-special thanks to James Dowlen who volunteered to design the cover. A framed print of this cover in a limited edition will be available for purchase from his website: www.dowlenartworks.com.

We also give thanks to the reader, who cares enough about consciousness to question old assumptions and is flexible enough to confront an unknown future with creative ideas. We are part of a global village, and that means none of us is ever really isolated. Therefore, let us create our future on Earth with the increased optimism that comes with the knowledge that we are all in this together. This is certain:

Love helps. Hatred hurts.

Mind power works.

---

[1] Lao Tzu. *The Tao Te Ching.* (For various translations of this ancient text, see the list of references in Section III, Chapter 16.)

PROLOGUE

Dean Brown, PhD

Dean Brown was a theoretical physicist, metaphysicist, and Vedic scholar. In his youth, he worked at the Institute of Advanced Studies in Princeton, and was a friend and colleague of Albert Einstein. In his early career, he designed the fuel element for the Nautilus, the world's first nuclear submarine. In the late 1950s, he pioneered the use of interactive educational computing at Stanford Research Institute (SRI) and at UNESCO, designing educational computer programs for Spain, the Gold Coast and elsewhere.

Dr Brown was one of the founders of Zylog, Inc., and he was instrumental in designing the Z80 chip (one of the first microprocessors). When such chips made desktop computers possible, he continued to develop interactive educational programs, so even young children could learn to use computers as a natural part of their education for their future. He had many other interests, as well. He could actually name all of the plants in California (about 7,000) and in the United States, which he said was about 11,000. His essay in Chapter 17 reflects this intense interest.

Dr Brown became involved with the parapsychology research of physicists Russell Targ and Hal Puthoff in 1972 when they studied the psychic abilities of Uri Geller. Over the years, he and his wife Wendy became excellent remote viewers. (See Targ, Katra, Brown, Wiegand, 1995. "Viewing the Future: A Pilot Study with an Error-Detecting Protocol." In: *Journal of Scientific Exploration*. 9:3, 367-380.) He was one of 3 editors of our 1993 edition of *SILVER THREADS: 25 Years of Parapsychology Research*. The Philosophical Research Society published his Sanskrit translations in *The Upanishads* in 1996, including his translations of *The Yoga Sutras of Patanjali*. For Brown's final paper *Cosmic Law: Patterns in the Universe*, see website: www.fmbr.org/. Wm. Gough's summary is on page 175.

FROM THE EPILOGUE OF *SILVER THREADS*

Dean Brown

The contributions to this retrospective volume have taken us far afield, to topics as varied as medicine, physics, perception, and communication. But there is a pattern, an underlying common landscape that emerges from these seemingly diverse perspectives.

Are there other research groups with parallel interests in other cities, in other countries, in other cultures? Is there a commonality in seeing the world in this way? We believe that there is, and that this collection of insights matches up with those of other inquiring minds viewing the world from various centers. In a sense, our research is intensely intimate, based on personal interests, direct experience, and disciplined observation. It is expressed and shared by hammering out research designs and results within the group, in accord with our mutual concepts and vocabularies. It is reflected and shaped by our conviviality. It is to say what is going on here among thoughtful people.

Remote viewing has always been the main core of our group's thrust throughout the past [40 years]. Perhaps that is the area in which results are easier to get. Or is it that remote viewing is closer to the substrate of objective reality than the other domains of parapsychological research? Or could it be merely an expression of the zeitgeist of this particular place and time? Whatever the reason, I believe that a profound understanding of remote viewing can be the foundation on which the other so-called psychic phenomena ultimately will be mapped.

The dimensions of parapsychological research, as brought out in this compendium, are as follows:

- Viewing and otherwise experiencing remotely—in space, time, and states of consciousness (thought forms, precognition, clairvoyance, telepathy)
- Healing (shamanism, psychoneuroimmunology)
- Deep sharing, including perception of archetypes
- Channeling (spirit guides, artistic inspiration)
- Causation, including psychokinesis
- States of consciousness (hypnosis, near-death experiences)
- Possession and exorcism, poltergeists

- Intentionality (synchronicity and providential events, supply and demand)
- Innate intelligence (instinct, migration, plant and animal wisdom, genius, savants)

Parapsychological research is fundamentally based on mind processes. We can make good use of the 16-dimensional classification analyzed in the Aitareya Upanishad:

> Consciousness
> Instinct
> Discrimination
> Intelligence
> Wisdom
> Insight
> Perseverance
> Reason
> Genius
> Impulse
> Memory
> Conception
> Will
> Vitality
> Desire
> Drive

All these faculties combine and blend in the processes of perception, experience, and expression.

Parapsychology is the cutting edge of science, where experience is yet barely recognized, patterned, repeatable, subject to consensus – the horizon where the known meets the unknown. The unknown can mean that which is not yet understood or that which is not yet experienced. What is now the dead heartwood of science, holding up the tree of knowledge, was once parascience.

The etymology of the word science derives from the root *skei,* meaning to cut, to separate one thing from another (as in the words discern, conscience, conscious, prescient, schism, scissors) – to know by the process of making critical distinctions. Science is based on observation and critical reasoning, first personal and then consensual. Science is obliged to accept all data unless and until they can be invalidated by experiment. Data must be triangulated and crosschecked from every possible perspective.

Hypotheses come and go as matters of convenience. Theories arise from inductive insights, and are tentatively accepted (as intellectual scaffolding) until they can be rejected by contradicting data or by the principle of beauty or by the principle of economy (Occam's razor). The quality of a theory is superior if it is more comprehensive and more concise. The dynamic of science is to gather and confirm data, to infer theories, and then proceed with diligence to find ways to reject them.

We are living in an epoch of convergence between the physical and personal sciences, between external and internal, between observer and observed, between manifest and unmanifest. Quantum physics has become the most quantitative branch of science, able to compute states with 12-digit precision, yet it is centrally based on probabilities and intrinsically unmanifest realities such as virtual states, vacuum excitations, and indeterminancies.

Science is not necessarily expressed in mathematics, and it is rarely predictive. Their highest successes have been descriptive (as in geology and astronomy) or comprehensive (as in medicine and economics).

We understand the law, of nature as distillations, of reality. There are two coexistent definitions of reality. They are polar opposites:

- Reality is the pattern that is invariant and eternal, that remains fixed in a flux of change, that never varies under transformations to other situations.
- Reality is the pattern (gestalt) that you experience at this very instant.

Examples of the invariant kind of reality are fixed-point theorems in topology and standards of aesthetics in art. Examples of the now-and-here kind of reality are being in love and having a life-changing dream. Laws of nature are of the invariant kind.

Physics and psychology have many elemental laws in common. For example, they share the principle of least action, principles that involve energy, entropy, and chaos, symmetry and symmetry breaking, and principles that involve discrete states and state transitions.

Mihaly Csikszentmihalyi, in his book *Flow* (1990), identifies a set of parameters that can be used directly in formulating laws of psychology: purpose, quest, center, entropy and negentropy, chaos, control, goal, skill, mood, order, sensation, harmony, rules, game, intention, joy, play, rhythm, challenge, grace, effort, meaning, event, feedback, shaping experience, order, states of mind, concentration, motive, attention, ecstasy, faith, expectation, and the experience of time. And he goes on to derive algorithms using these parameters to achieve practical outcomes. Other modern psychologies are isomorphic to his. We are well on our way to enunciating laws that will provide a framework for designing experiments, obtaining verifiable and consensually acceptable data, and organizing the results in elegant formulations.

Perhaps the richest domain for future research in parapsychology is emerging from the classic boundary between the brain and the mind, at the interfaces between neuroscience, psychology, and immunology. Here is where our contributions on shamanism, healing, and body chemistry come to bear.

In an article, "Organization of the Human Brain," published in *Science* (1989; 245), Michael Gazzanaga, professor of psychiatry at Dartmouth, correlates discrete modules of brain activity with cognitive functions. For example, visual areas, the receptive language area (Wernicke's area), and the expressive motor language area (Broca's area) are distinguished. Gazzanaga has located a module in the dominant left verbal hemisphere that he terms the interpreter. The interpreter harmonizes and unifies discontinuities between internal and external reality. Gazzanaga's insight is shared by William Blake in his beautiful engraving on pewter, *"The Man Sweeping the Interpreter's Parlour"* (1822). Each of us is compelled by our biological circuitry to be a theoretician! A driving thrust of intelligence, of life itself, is to explain experience. The domain of parapsychology has an abundance of solid facts to work with and a drive to explain them.

The work presented here and similar works elsewhere have established the setting for the future. We can expect new understanding of the nature of space and time (which depend so much on biological and subjective considerations), the interconnectedness of observer and the observed, intelligence of plants and animals, and the influence of chemicals, set and setting on psychic processes.

Not only will the external universe be more understood as a projection of Mind, but also more of the personal universe will become clear. The cycle of conception → perception → sensation → cognition will become the basis for all science. The processes of intention, knowing, expression, and causation and the interplay of states of consciousness will come more within our grasp.

With the new understanding, a richer lifestyle will emerge with the goals of health (wholeness), joy of living, radiance, wealth, harmony within self and with nature, energy (action), purpose, and fulfillment. And (by one of the laws of the universe) the capabilities for evil will increase in lockstep. A profound understanding of ethics becomes urgent for us to cope responsibly with these new powers.

And so we arrive at the summation of our work, at the frontier of science, where we possess that most precious asset of humankind, the body of experience that cannot yet be honestly invalidated nor can it yet be explained – the zest and the lifeblood of true sciences. Its value? Remember that what you believe sculpts what you perceive. What we believe together forms what we perceive together. Let us proceed to broaden our horizons and expand our aliveness.

FOREWORD

~~~~~~

Jeffrey Mishlove, PhD

Jeffrey Mishlove holds a unique doctoral diploma in "Parapsychology" from the University of California at Berkeley. Awarded in 1980, it remains the only doctoral diploma in parapsychology ever awarded by an accredited American university. From 1988 to 2002, his weekly television program, *Thinking Allowed*, has been shown throughout North America, consisting of interviews with leading figures in psychology, philosophy, science, health and spirituality. This series of interviews included most of the authors in this book, as well.

Dr Mishlove currently serves as Dean of Transformational Psychology at The University of Philosophical Research. His newest book is called *The PK Man: A True Story of Mind Over Matter*. Mishlove conducted a 20-year field investigation with a man who had extraordinary psychokinetic and precognitive abilities. His three previous books are 1] *The Roots of Consciousness: Psychic Exploration Through History, Science and Experience* (originally published in 1975 by Random House); 2] *Psi Development Systems*, an evaluation of ancient and modern methods for training extrasensory abilities—based on his doctoral dissertation (published as a Ballantine paperback 1983); 3] *Thinking Allowed*, a collection of thirty-two interviews from the television series (released by Council Oak Books).

Dr Mishlove is past-president of the California Society for Psychical Study and past-vice-president of the Association for Humanistic Psychology. He is also past-president of the nonprofit Intuition Network.

www.thinkingallowed.com. -- http://www.mishlove.com/virtual.htm.

FOREWORD

Jeffrey Mishlove

I became a member and active participant in San Francisco's Parapsychology Research Group (PRG) in the early 1970s. For a time, I served as a board member of the organization. The community of support and encouragement that I found there was instrumental in my creation and completion of an interdisciplinary doctoral program at the University of California, Berkeley, from which I received my PhD in "Parapsychology" in 1980.

It was a time during which the field appeared to be making great strides. And the San Francisco Bay Area was, undoubtedly, a world center for this activity. Dozens of researchers and scholars, from diverse disciplines, were involved – physicists, computer scientists, biologists, engineers, philosophers, psychology researchers and psychotherapists. World-class psychics such as Uri Geller, Luiz Gasparetto and Matthew Manning were also regulars.

Nearby, in Orinda, California, the fledgling John F. Kennedy University (JFKU) had established a masters degree program in parapsychology – with a laboratory – where a coterie of very promising students were engaged in a variety of projects.

And, a two-hour drive down Highway 1, along the spectacular California coast, led to the world-famous Esalen Institute, a place revered for its instrumental role in establishing the human potential and consciousness movement of the 1960s.

It was an open secret, at that time, that the intelligence establishment of the US government was funding research, and other activities, in the field of remote viewing. This activity lasted for about twenty years, until 1996. PRG members Hal Puthoff, Russell Targ, Ed May and Keith Harary were central to this effort.

Psychic magazine began publishing in San Francisco in 1969. The magazine's editor, Alan Vaughan, was also a talented psychic and remote viewer with a specialty in precognition. He had achieved a measure of fame for his forecast concerning the assassination of Robert Kennedy in 1968. His prediction was quite specific. And, New York parapsychologist Charles Honorton, who took Vaughan seriously (for good reason as Vaughan had amply demonstrated his abilities in the famous Maimonides

Hospital dream telepathy study), informed me that he had actually been trying to warn Kennedy in June 1968 when the tragedy occurred.

Vaughan's prediction was based on an odd synchronicity he experienced. And it struck me at the time that Jungian psychology, with its theory of synchronicities, along with parapsychology research on remote viewing and precognition, combined with leading ideas on the frontiers of physics were converging to form a new "paradigm" that would have the power to completely change our understanding of reality. Neither science nor religion would remain the same for very long, I thought.

In 1973, the Institute for the Study of Consciousness opened its doors in Berkeley, CA, in a brown-shingle house located on Benvenue Avenue. The founder, cosmologist Arthur M. Young, was also famous for his invention of the Bell helicopter. I was invited to move into the Institute, to live with Arthur and his wife Ruth Forbes Young (founder of the World Peace Academy). Science writer Saul-Paul Sirag was also invited to live at the Institute. As a result of Arthur Young's mentoring, Sirag developed some exciting ideas of his own concerning the relationship between the mysteries of consciousness and those of theoretical physics.

In 1973, Sirag was commissioned by a magazine to write an article about the famous Israeli psychic Uri Geller who had recently visited the PRG group and performed what appeared to be credible demonstrations of psychokinesis, or mind-over-matter. Of course, Geller was then, and is now, quite controversial. Sirag, however, performed his own simple experiment with Geller that I regard as definitive evidence in favor of Geller's PK abilities. (I am sorry it was not videotaped. However, I do trust Sirag's account of the event.) Sirag choose to present Geller with a task for which he would be totally unprepared. He handed Geller a mung bean sprout and told him to "make the movie run backward." Geller closed his hand over the bean sprout and concentrated. When he opened his hand again, about a minute later, the sprout was no longer there. Instead there was a single mung bean. It would seem that time had reversed itself there in the palm of Geller's hand.

The San Francisco Bay Area was very instrumental in other major changes that were dramatically influencing society. The 1970s ushered in the age of the microprocessor and the computer revolution. In fact, physicist Dean Brown, a PRG member and one of the editors of the first edition of *Silver Threads*, actually was a founder of the Zilog corporation and helped design the Z80 microchip – a major workhorse of that era (that is still in production).

Another PRG member, Jacques Vallee, was a futurist whose writings on computer networking helped to pave the way for the internet that is now a universal feature of our lives today. And, of course, Vallee is also known for his work in the area of UFOlogy. In fact, he served as the model for the French scientist character Claude Lacombe played by Francois Truffaut, in Steven Spielberg's 1977 blockbuster movie *Close Encounters of the Third Kind*. Vallee has written his own account of his experiences in the 1970s that includes many references to the PRG and its members.*²

To add to the excitement of the era that I sometimes refer to as "the psychic seventies," I had conducted my own study in 1976 with an extraordinarily unruly psychic named Ted Owens who claimed to embody within himself the mysteries of both parapsychology and UFOlogy. He offered to demonstrate his abilities by causing a UFO to appear "before startled human eyes" near SF. He claimed that this event would be witnessed by multiple individuals, that it would be photographed, and that the photograph would be published on the front page of one of our local newspapers. This is, indeed, exactly what occurred on December 10, 1976. The entire affair is reported in a chapter titled "My San Francisco Experiment" in my book *The PK Man*.*³ I believe this was probably the most highly documented UFO sighting on record at that time. There were hundreds of witnesses, both on the ground and in a nearby airplane. The event was even videotaped and broadcast on the local KQED-TV news. PRG members were instrumental in organizing a group of scientists, including famed UFOlogist J. Allen Hynek, to meet and discuss the Owens case.

In 1981, when I was teaching in the parapsychology program at John F. Kennedy University, I received an unexpected visit from a Brazilian healer named Brother Macedo from the city of Recife. Macedo, a businessman who owned a factory that manufactured pajamas, claimed to have an energetic, healing ability that he referred to as "telergy." In an effort to validate this claim, I received help from PRG member Professor David Deamer, a biologist who was then teaching at UC Davis. Deamer set up a pilot study that I believe could serve as a model for students and other researchers who wish to experimentally test the abilities of ostensible psychic healers. We took fruit flies in a laboratory flask and anesthetized them with ether. Once they were anesthetized, we put an equal number into two different test tubes that were then sealed and placed on a counter next to each other – with a light nearby shining into the opposite end of the test tubes away from where the flies were. As the flies awakened from the effects of the ether, they instinctively crawled toward the light and could be counted.

One of these test tubes was randomly selected as our control group. Brother Macedo was then asked to apply his "telergy" to the other test tube

---

[*2] Jacques Vallee, *Forbidden Science, Volume Two: Journals 1970-1979*. SF, CA: Documata Research LLC, 2008.

[*3] Jeffrey Mishlove, *The PK Man: A True Story of Mind Over Matter*. Charlottesville, VA: Hampton Roads Publishing Co., 2000.

and cause the flies in that tube to awaken more rapidly than in the control tube. We repeated this pilot study six times. In five of these trials, the "telergy" apparently succeeded and more flies awakened in the experimental test tube. One of the trials was a tie. Overall, 261 of 417 (62.59%) flies treated with "telergy" recovered from the ether. In the control group, 210 of 440 (47.73%) of the flies recovered. This is a very large effect size as the "telergy" group flies outperformed the control group by more than 31%. If we eliminate the trial in which the results were, essentially, tied and apply simple binomial statistics to the remaining five successful trials, the probability that this pilot study yielded only chance results would be 0.03125. This result is more conservative than $p = 0.023$ of a simple, two-tailed t-test that includes all trials. More conservative, nonparametric tests of statistical significance yield a p value of approximately 0.10.[*4]

In my own mind, during this time, it seemed to me only logical that developments in parapsychology would progress and influence our culture in just the same way that the computer revolution seemed to be doing. As far as I could see, the evidence was equally impressive, substantial and convincing in both areas.

Of course, looking back more than three decades later, it is evident that I was wrong: Not a single doctoral diploma, for example, in parapsychology has been issued from an accredited American university since I received mine in 1980; the US government-sponsored remote viewing program was dissolved in 1996 – and has yet to be replaced by any similarly substantial effort in private industry; the parapsychology program at JFKU closed down in the mid-1980s and has never been replaced; parapsychology laboratories at UC Davis and Santa Barbara also closed down, along with the Maimonides Hospital laboratory in NY, Washington University in St. Louis and at Princeton University. At one time, more than a hundred colleges and universities offered parapsychology courses; now there are virtually none.

Naturally, having invested so many years of my life obtaining a degree in parapsychology, this lack of social acceptance for the field has been disheartening. I think I can take some comfort in the fact that William James, the founder of American psychology, who also was deeply committed to psychical research (as the field of parapsychology was known during his lifetime), experienced this same sense of disappointment over a century ago, when he sat down – as I am now – to evaluate the previous three decades of his involvement with this research. He wrote:

> It is hard to believe, however, that the Creator has really put any big array of

---

[*4] Jeffrey Mishlove, "Anesthetized Fruit Fly Experiment," paper presented to the Parapsychology Research Group, San Francisco, August 4, 1981.

phenomena into the world merely to defy and mock our scientific tendencies; so my deeper belief is that we psychical researchers have been too precipitate with our hopes, and that we must expect to mark progress not by quarter-centuries, but by half-centuries or whole centuries.*[5]

Clearly, James was correct. But, why? Statisticians such as PRG member Jessica Utts point out that the data in parapsychology are far stronger than that for many other well-accepted findings in the behavioral sciences and medicine.*[6] The example she often cites is the use of aspirin for preventing cardiovascular events (such as heart attack). This finding is well-established and non-controversial. It carries no stigma whatsoever. Yet, statistically speaking, it is no stronger than the data supporting the existence of what parapsychologists call extrasensory perception.

Contrary to the arguments of many skeptics, in my opinion, the failure of scientific parapsychology to achieve academic and social acceptance is best understood in sociological and psychological terms rather than strict, scientific considerations. Arguments concerning lack of replication, shoddy research, etc., simply do not square with the facts.

The psychological dynamics that support this state of affairs was, I believe, revealed to me in 1973 when the noted science and science fiction writer Arthur C. Clarke appeared on the campus of UC Berkeley, where I was then a student. Clarke had recently published a letter in *Time* magazine criticizing the recently published research of PRG members Hal Puthoff and Russell Targ concerning their work with Uri Geller. I was somewhat puzzled by this since his popular novels often make reference to psychic functioning. So, after his lecture, I stood up and posed the following question: *"Mr. Clarke, do you believe in ESP?"* His stark, and very blunt answer revealed what I believe to be a deep truth: *"No, I do not because I do not want anybody to read my mind."*

Upon reflection, this non sequitur made perfect sense. After all, the entire edifice of Freudian psychology, including the many psychodynamic schools that followed Freud, is built upon the premise that we exert a great deal of psychic energy in hiding the contents of our own minds from ourselves. In effect, the suppression of parapsychological science in western culture is directly analogous to the suppression of the contents of our own consciousness so deftly articulated by Freud in his elucidation of defense mechanisms. For many people like Arthur C. Clarke, the idea that others could use telepathy to sense hidden aspects of themselves is

---

*[5] William James, "What psychical research has accomplished." In: Gardner Murphy and Robert O. Ballou (Eds.), *William James on Psychical Research*. London: Chatto and Windus, 1961. Originally published in *The Will to Believe and Other Essays*. NY: Longmans, Green and Co., 1897.

*[6] Jessica Utts, "Replication and Meta-Analysis in Parapsychology." In: *Statistical Science*, 1991, Vol. 6, No. 4, 363-403.

certainly intolerable. This situation, in my opinion, is the basis for much of the emotional resistance to parapsychology.

But there is more. The subject of "fear of psi" (psi is the term used by parapsychologists to include extrasensory perception and psychokinesis) came up many years ago, in the context of an online debate among professional parapsychologists. One of my colleagues, PRG member Edwin May, a physicist, maintained that the objections of mainstream scientists to parapsychology were all based on logical and methodological grounds. He even went so far as to say he could not think of any reasons at all why people would be afraid of psi. I was amazed. So, in response, I quickly typed up a list of reasons that I thought people might have for fearing the subjects that parapsychologists study. Within a few minutes, I posted it to the discussion list:

- It is associated with diabolic forces, magic and witchcraft.
- It suggests the loss of normal ego boundaries.
- People might be able to read your mind and know that you secretly (or unconsciously) harbor sexual and aggressive thoughts, or worse.
- If you talk about it, people might think you're crazy.
- If you think you experience psi, maybe you are crazy.
- Your parents provided negative reinforcement for any demonstrations of your psychic ability (or past lives) when you were a child.
- Thinking about psi leads to a medieval superstitious mentality, which will in turn support a rising tide of dangerous, primitive thinking.
- With ESP, you might learn things that you do not want to know about yourself or other people – i.e., accidents that are about to happen, and things you would rather not be responsible for knowing about.
- If you are telepathic, how will you distinguish other people's thoughts from your own? Perhaps this will lead to mental illness.
- Many people have a self-destructive streak to their personality. What damage would result if psi were used in the service of this factor? Psychiatrist Jule Eisenbud wrote about this in his book *Parapsychology and the Unconscious.*[*7]
- If psi exists, how many of my other cherished beliefs will I have to give up?

[*7] Jule Eisenbud, *Parapsychology and the Unconscious.* Berkeley, CA: North Atlantic Books, 1992.

- Psi might interfere with the normal human process of ego separation and development. Therefore, we have devised subtle strategies for cultural inhibition.
- If psi exists, does that mean that a psychic could watch me while I am using bathroom facilities?
- If psi exists, then perhaps I cannot wall myself off so easily from from the pain and suffering in the world.

To my surprise, this list eventually became incorporated into the "Parapsychology FAQ" that has now been translated into German, Finnish, Portuguese and Spanish and is readily available on the internet.*[8]

It's very ironic then that as scientific parapsychology has shrunk in significance, popular interest in the field appears to be growing. This can be judged by the quantity of television and radio programs on the paranormal, as well as books written for the general public, websites, psychic hotlines and feature films. From the standpoint of scientific parapsychology, most of this can be considered "low-brow" in the sense that it is aimed at entertaining a large audience with very little, if any, emphasis on the careful sifting and winnowing of evidence and competing hypotheses that characterizes rigorous research and investigations.

If the psychological arguments for the fear of psi and the resistance to parapsychology are valid, why, then, is the popular interest in psychic phenomena so strong? The simple answer would be this: Virtually all parapsychologists are in substantial agreement with the skeptical argument that popular psychic fads are the result of public incredulity. One might even go so far as to suggest an inverse correlation between the rise of popular psychic fads and the influence of scientific parapsychology in our western culture. The truth is that – in spite of the claims by parapsychology's CSICOP debunkers – scientific parapsychology encourages critical thinking. While parapsychologists generally subscribe to the existence of extrasensory perception, psychokinesis, psychic healing, synchronicity and even reincarnation, they are exceedingly wary and critical of the claims made by a surfeit of popular promoters. In fact, my own doctoral dissertation at Berkeley was largely a critical look at dozens of popular claims concerning ESP training programs.*[9]

What are the societal factors that have most contributed to the marginalization of parapsychology? There are two obvious, large-scale social movements that regard parapsychology as a danger and impediment to human progress. The first of these is Christianity. Generally speaking,

---

*[8] "Parapsychology: Frequently Asked Questions." http://www.parapsych.org/faq_file1.html

*[9] Jeffrey Mishlove, *Psi Development Systems*. New York: Ballantine, 1987.

Christian churches regard manifestations of psychic phenomena that occur outside of their sanctified jurisdictions to be "the work of the devil." The second movement is something of a reverse mirror image of Christianity. I am referring to the organized debunkers, who often misleadingly refer to themselves as "skeptics." The main organization in this category is the Committee for the Scientific Investigation of Claims of the Paranormal (CSICOP). While this social grouping is certainly smaller, and less influential than Christianity, the philosophy of that it represents has substantial influence within academia. The debunkers have no fear of the devil. However, they associate parapsychology with the "rising tide of the irrational" – which is their equivalent.

In order to overcome the suspicions and stigmas generated by the aforementioned social groupings, parapsychology faces a daunting task. Good data exist. Good theories exist. Applications exist. Decade by decade, research methodology improves. The question, then, is: What will it take for society to accept and integrate these findings and applications?

In my opinion, this will require the psychological evolution of human beings – at least to the point where the Freudian premise (that we cannot tolerate awareness of the contents of our own minds) no longer pertains on a large scale. Contemporary society, in many ways, is engaged in a project of making the unconscious conscious. My belief is that this project will eventually reach a tipping point signified by the acceptance of parapsychology. Frankly, I do not believe this will happen in my own lifetime. But I think that, when this tipping point is reached, a copy of this book, *Radiant Minds: Scientists Explore the Dimensions of Consciousness* (the revised and updated version of the 1993 *Silver Threads: 25 Years of Parapsychology Research)*, will make its way into every college and university library.

INTRODUCTION

[*10] ...Years ago, a remarkable group of pioneers began organizing new discoveries into a rethinking, an updating, a refinement, a modernizing of the traditional concepts of the structures of consciousness.... [This group] has brought together doctors of philosophy, medicine, physics, biochemistry, anthropology, education, and psychology, both researchers and clinical practitioners. Among the group also are computer scientists, engineers, artists, writers, poets, shamans, and spiritual healers. All have experienced unexplained events that do not properly fit within the scope of religion or science.

In the PRG, the common thread running through the ineffable in each person's experiences has been the suspicion that at stake is a challenge to the most entrenched theories about the nature of reality. Our common goal has thus become an exploration of the nature of brain, mind, perception, and the physical and metaphysical universe.

We called ourselves the Parapsychology Research Group. The title is perhaps a misnomer, if one adheres to a strict definition of research as consisting of experimental activities and of parapsychology as consisting of the study of telepathy, clairvoyance, precognition, and psychokinesis. Although many members of the PRG are indeed internationally respected experimental parapsychologists, the PRG as an organization is a forum for ideas.

Over the years, we have insisted that it is the duty of any avowed scientist to maintain open-mindedness about all human experiences. Twentieth-century natural laws reflect not merely the absolute limits of our measuring instruments, but, as throughout history, prevailing politics and popular psychology.

The concepts of scientific law and scientific method are continually being refined and deepened. The laws of the universe, as expressed in the many sciences, can be applied to the study of mind. Conversely, it has been fruitful to apply the laws of the mind to the laws that govern the other sciences. In physics, as Herbert discusses in Chapter 30, the role of the observer in measurement bred new philosophies of reality. In other sciences as well, it becomes imperative to consider the psychological factors that introduce observer bias into experiments. After all, it is

---

[*10] Excerpt from Dr Beverley Kane's original introduction to the 1993 publication of *Silver Threads: 25 Years of Parapsychology Research*.

impossible to contemplate or to observe any object of science except through the instrument of the mind.

Despite the generally liberal milieu of the San Francisco Bay Area and its Silicon Valley, and often despite their high professional standing, PRG members frequently face a harsh climate of intellectual dogmatism. So we have given one another the permission and the conviction and the stamina to assail outdated conventions and patterns of thought, while maintaining our own flexibility. We must have the courage to restructure, when necessary, our own secure deep habits, beliefs, values, and realities.

Why do we do it? Because the subtle clues about the universe that we receive through experience compel us to investigate as scientists; because to reject these gifts, these glimpses, is to fragment our own psyches; because the study of mind is the consummate metascience, providing the ultimate road map for the attainment of a richer humanity.

Beverley Kane

~~~~~~

Introduction to the 2009 Revised Version

The members of the PRG did not always agree. A good open-minded lively discussion was fun and exciting. Unlike some "religions" or "scientific" research establishment and/or universities who adhered to dogma, we encouraged and insisted upon exploring paranormal experiences and our differing ideas about them. One of the areas that most of our members did agree upon was that the dimensions of consciousness had access to information from "nonlocal spacetime." This seems to be a new term for a very old concept. Physicist, and metaphysicist, Dean Brown found an ancient term to match it from his Sanskrit translations:

> <u>Ritam Bhara pragyam</u> is where the higher visions come from. Ritam means right...the level of consciousness where the ten thousand things exist before they are named. The naming of them, the 'nam,' brings them into manifestations. Manifestation means expressed through the four elements in the domain of mass, energy, space and time.... Precognition is possible because a person looks into the ritam bhara pragyam and gets out of spacetime entirely. You can look anywhere if you are looking through that field. Precognition and postcognition are identical processes.*[11]

---

*[11] Brown, D. (1983) "A conversation with Dean Brown." In: *Association for Humanistic Psychology Newsletter.* C. Guion (Ed.). March, SF, CA.

A debate that has raged for over a century has been on the question of the survival of consciousness after death.*[12] Here is a very short summary of the beliefs that each side supports:

1) The position of 20th century materialistic science is a definite "NO." Consciousness (as defined by that group as mind and personality) cannot survive because it is created by, and limited to, the matter and energy of the brain and body, as it exists in the four-dimensions of spacetime. The legal definition of the end of life is established at the time the energy (as measured by brainwaves and heartbeat) can no longer be detected in the body. Without electrical signals in the brain, or blood flow from the heart, the matter (brain and organs) begins to deteriorate. Therefore, neither the mind nor its personality can function. Death is final.

2) The position of 21st century multidimensional science is a definite "YES." Consciousness is rooted in the Essence of the Eternal Cosmic Consciousness. Our material brains and bodies are only the spacetime manifestation of our minds and personalities, which are animated by spirit. Spirit exists in four-dimensional spacetime, but can explore all dimensions, as it becomes aware of its Eternal Essence. For countless centuries, people around the world have maintained a reverent communication with the spirits of their ancestors. The spirits of our own teachers and ancestors may speak to us as well, if we listen. (Chapter 37)

Most of the authors in this book stand on the side of 21st century multidimensional science. They have addressed the fundamental questions about the dimensions of consciousness through their own careful scientific investigations. If the reader has questions, please contact any website listed. We encourage the discussion to keep the dialog going to advance creative thinking among different groups and individuals around the world. Be part of the change you want to happen to advance the study of consciousness and peaceful co-existence.

If the reader needs more information about a few specialized areas that are not covered here, the authors have provided references for them: Near-death experiences (NDE – p. 598), past lives and reincarnation (pp. 453, 585), out-of-body-experiences (OBE – p. 585). Electronic Voice Phenomena (EVP – pp. 443-444), psychokinesis (PK – pp. 124-125 and 609). (Reports of teleportation often seem to include the concept of poltergeist. *[13])

The table of contents of our 1993 PRG anthology (*Silver Threads: 25 Years of Parapsychology Research*) is included in Appendix 1. We included some chapters, since they formed the foundations for work that followed.

---

*[12] Myers, F.W.H. (1903) *Human Personality and Survival of Bodily Death*. 2 vols. London: Longmans, Green.

*[13] Manning, M. (1975) *The Link: Matthew Manning's Own Story of his Extraordinary Gifts*. NY: Holt, Rinehart & Winston.

This book has 46 chapters that are organized into 11 sections by subject matter. An additional section is devoted to the Appendices. Each of the 55 participants has expertise and proven ability in his/her field. Seventy-five percent of those who have written full chapters hold advanced degrees. As a group they represent a wide variety of disciplines.

Section I — ***Dimensions of Perception*** — introduce us to some of the wide-ranging abilities of human perceptions. Examples of the different types of remote viewing that can provide statistical analysis are illustrated in the introduction.*[14] In addition, some astonishing and spontaneous psi events are illustrated that defy statistical analysis.

Three of the best know researchers in the field of parapsychology — Russell Targ, Dean Radin and Stanley Krippner — demonstrate a range of the dimensions of perception and suggest further explorations. Their work sets the stage for the theoretical discussions in Sections VI (math) and VII (physics). However, sometimes certain visual limitations inhibit a person's ability to think. Developmental optometrist Raymond Gottlieb explains how these limitations can be corrected with a special light therapy.

Psi perception also includes interaction between animals and humans. Beverley Kane, MD, the first editor of our 1993 anthology, has developed an award-winning program to teach nurses to become more sensitive to the needs of nonverbal patients by having them work with horses. Her book *The Manual of Medicine and Horsemanship – Transforming the Doctor-Patient Relationship with Equine-Assisted Learning* – is available at:
http://www.authorhouse.com/bookstsore/ItemDetail.aspx?bookid=49669.

Additional information about her innovative program to advance the quality of healthcare – *Horsensei Equine-Assisted Learning & Therapy* – can be found on her own website: http://www.horsensei.com.

Section II — ***Dimensions of Intention*** — examine the potential power of human intention. Sondra Barrett begins the discussion of the power of intention with psychoneuroimmunology (PNI) (e.g., the patient's belief in a placebo indicates that the patient's mind must be doing most of the healing). Beverly Rubik and Elizabeth Rauscher studied the effect of spiritual healing beyond the "placebo" effect, by examining bacteria before and after the spiritual healer Olga Worrall attempted to "heal" them, which she did successfully in a double blind study. (See also Mishlove's reference to his study of Brother Macedo's effect on fruit flies – pp. xxvi-xxvii.) Elisabeth Targ found that the intention of distant healers helped to relieve discomfort among AIDS patients significantly.

---

*[14] Some members of the PRG and the International Remote Viewing Association teach advanced classes in RV, ARV, CRV, etc. See www.irva.org for their newsletter.)

Marilyn Schlitz and Dean Radin analyzed a large number of independent studies of distant healing (DHI) to determine their efficacy.

Many people have done remarkable things, because their *intention* to do them was stronger than the belief of others that such could not be done. Larissa Vilenskaya conducted firewalking ceremonies, after walking the fire pit herself many times. She has provided an analysis of the different ways that participants responded to this dramatic experience. Henry Dakin wrote about human "psycholuminescence," and included a Kirlian photo of Uri Geller's intentional PK ability. Beverly Rubik continues to study the human biofield with modern equipment. Dean Brown was able to project his own biofield intentionally onto both Polaroid film and 35-mm. indoor color film.

Section III – *Belief Systems are Evolving*. – In 1988, Willis Harman wrote the need for *Global Mind Change: The Promise of the Last Years of the Twentieth Century*. Excerpts from these insights of 20 years ago predicted how the prevailing concepts of "reality" could begin to evolve. (In 2009, Charles Tart expanded Harman's predictions – p. 564) Because of the cultural taboo at the time, William Kautz successfully counseled clients by substituting the word "intuition" for the word "psychic." Beverley Kane examined the nature of personal belief systems, and why it is important to acknowledge one's own personal experiences during this time of inevitable expansion. Some people choose the "reality" they like, based on emotional attachment to dogma, rather than on any logic. So, we suggest a way to "play" with many ideas without emotion, along with your own belief system.

Section IV – *Mind and Brain/Body Chemistry*. – Cheri Quincy describes the various chemicals of the brain and body, and some of the foods, plants or drugs that increase the neurotransmitters or hormones that affect consciousness. Dean Brown suggests that humans evolved together with the plants they gathered and later cultivated. Ruth-Inge Heinze studied native cultures that used plants (called "entheogens") to enhance healing through communication with gods, spirits, animals or plants. Scientists who studied different entheogens include Sasha and Ann Shulgin (MDMA or "ecstasy"), Hosteen Nez ("smart pills") and Tim Scully (LSD). Scully believed that LSD could expand the rigid ideas prevalent in the culture of the early 1960s (it did – including his own). He then turned from exploring mind chemistry to mind electricity and by 1970 he had created the first inexpensive portable EEG biofeedback instruments for personal use and research (see pp. 235-254). Millay summarizes her experiences using entheogens for spiritual guidance, telepathy, and psychotherapy. When LSD became illegal, Stanislav Grof and his wife Christina developed new therapies (e.g., holotropic breathing, hypnosis, and spiritual emergencies) so more people could experience those mental states that enhance increased self-awareness.

Section V — ***Mind and Brain/Body Electricity.*** James Johnston describes the study he did with Scully's EEG equipment to see if phase-coherent brainwaves between two people might be a measure of rapport. Rauscher and her husband William Van Bise wrote about their studies of brain and heart rhythms in relation to the magnetic properties of the Earth. Krippner and Persinger discovered that strong geomagnetic activity can and does interfere with reception of telepathic dreams. Quincy and Alter explain why the rhythm of shamanic drumming can evoke alternate states of consciousness through the entrainment of cerebral spinal fluid. Musical frequencies entrain brainwaves as well, so a list of websites of musicians who have created music to enhance meditation and creativity is provided.

Sections VI and VII — ***Mathematical Models*** and ***Physics***. Elizabeth Rauscher offers her own mathematical model that will include the psi phenomena of precognition within the main body of physics. The many experiments that she and Russell Targ conducted over the years provided enough data for a comprehensive analysis. In the Physics Section PRG members Saul-Paul Sirag, Nick Herbert, Jean Burns and James Johnston share their different concepts about quantum reality and our multidimensional universe.

Section VIII — ***Dimensions of Spirit.*** — Ruth-Inge Heinze begins with a statement about the importance of honoring our connection to the sacred. Barrett contemplates the sacredness of cells. Alter writes about his own long journey in the field of medicine, beginning as a surgeon, moving to alternative methods (including resonating energies), and ultimately into a spiritual practice. Stephan Schwartz describes an amazing healing that he observed directly as Rolling Thunder performed it. Arthur Hastings, one of the founders of the PRG, developed an innovative way to help people who are grieving over the loss of a loved one. Finally, spirit guides and friends, who have graduated from Earth School, share their experiences in the Spirit World through different transmissions.

Section IX — ***Dimensions of Consciousness.*** — What if the cosmos and our own consciousness are of the same essence? Dean Brown asked William Gough to publish his last major work, *Cosmic Law: Patterns in the Universe* on www.fmbr.org, instead of in a book. Since Gough worked closely with Brown during his illness, he reviews *Cosmic Law* for us here. Roger Nelson reports on *The Global Consciousness Project (GCP)*, which found that random number generators across the world cease to be random when millions of people all "care" about the same event. Jacques Vallee and Eric Davis explain why it is necessary to re-evaluate our concepts of reality, because the Unidentified Aerospace Phenomena (UAP) suggest they are from "other-dimensions." Vallee and Davis analyzed all of the data from years of reports of UAP, and suggest that we must now take this "high-strangeness phenomena" very seriously.

Section X — *Education: Increasing Intelligence Through Understanding and Application of the Dimensions of Consciousness.* Several experienced teachers supply theories and lesson plans to apply what we know about the multiple dimensions of consciousness to enhance intelligence, beginning, as it should, in the early years. Even though retired teacher Alpha Quincy had no interest in psi phenomena (or in the PRG), her solid background and understanding about the ongoing severe problems of public education provide us with a clear look at what has gone very wrong in our schools. (*Education: The Problems.*)

Next is a series of suggestions by Stanley Krippner for *"Solving The Problems,"* though changes in the gargantuan institution of public education are either ignored or move very slowly. Developmental optometrist Gottlieb illustrates the first suggestion: *Learning How to Learn*, along with learning to focus attention. Retired art teacher Millay illustrates the second suggestion: Teach children to expand their awareness of all of their senses, especially vision and the power of visualization for creativity and healing. Parents and sitters need to encourage the art of children from their first scribbles to the way they create images of the life they see around them. Marge King and Mara Mayo offer the third suggestion: Provide the technology of bio/neurofeedback and HeartMath in classes designed to teach *Self-Discovery Science*. When students experience directly the relationship between their thoughts and their own health, the future cost of healthcare for stress related illnesses would diminish dramatically. Sola Patricia outlines the fourth suggestion in 2 parts: 1] Create teacher supervised games that allow students to release emotions safely, and that encourage them to express those emotions creatively. (This is in contrast to the discipline of suppression, which just prolongs the angry and destructive activity that afflicts education.) Creativity builds the self-confidence and inner power to face the changing world. 2] Establish games that validate students' understanding and practice of their own natural psi sensitivity.

Louise Samples, a 5th grade teacher, used these holistic methods in her class, while other classes in the same school did not. Final tests: The GPA and emotional levels of her 5th grade students were much higher than those of the students in the other 5th grades. This significant study shows that holistic education can work within some public school environments.

Section XI — *Reflecting On Parapsychology.* Since the first brave scientists established the PRG in 1966, the resulting creative zeitgeist of innovative thinkers expanded the concepts about psi and consciousness. Their list of milestones of notable events—up to the 1993 date of the first publication—is reprinted here. Though the PRG disbanded in 2004, many of our members are still active, and their own individual advances in the field are included in each chapter along with their biographies and websites. The open meetings of the PRG made it easier for others to "come out of the psi closet," and acknowledge their psychic experiences. We want to encourage the readers to do the same.

Charles T. Tart, one of PRG's founders and former president, reflects on that long strange trip of psi research through his own fascinating life experiences.

We have included additional biographies, statements and websites, to enlarge the ring of information about former members and their associates: Joe Kamiya, Jon Klimo, William Braud, Brian McRae, William Croft, Kenneth Ring, Barbara Honegger, and Charles Honorton.

Parapsychology research is possible because of the ability of psi sensitives. We have included biographies, statements and websites, from: Gail Hayssen, James Dowlen, Tom Byrne, Mark Harris and Greg Schelkun.

<u>Epilogue</u> — Envisioning Global Mind
Roger Nelson

<u>Appendices</u> — (1) and (2)

1) The 1993 "Table of Contents" of *Silver Threads: 25 Years of Parapsychology Research* is listed for comparison with the studies done since, which are included in this revised PRG anthology of 2010. Both are published as a tribute to that unique organization.

2) Glossary
   a) General Terms
   b) Terms Commonly Used in Parapsychology
   c) Terms Used in Physiological Measurement
   e) Terms Used in the Global Consciousness Project

~~~~~~

Dr Jeffrey Mishlove's archives of both radio and TV interviews provide additional information. He hosted a TV series – filmed by Arthur Bloch – called *Thinking Aloud*. This series included conversations with most of our PRG members. He also hosted the *"Virtual U"* radio program for the Wisdom Network, on which Dean Brown was a regular guest. Brown did fifteen two-hour interviews together that are still preserved on tape:

www.thinkingallowed.com – http://www.mishlove.com/virtual.htm

--- Jean Millay

xli

xlii

SECTION I

Page 1

DIMENSIONS OF PERCEPTION

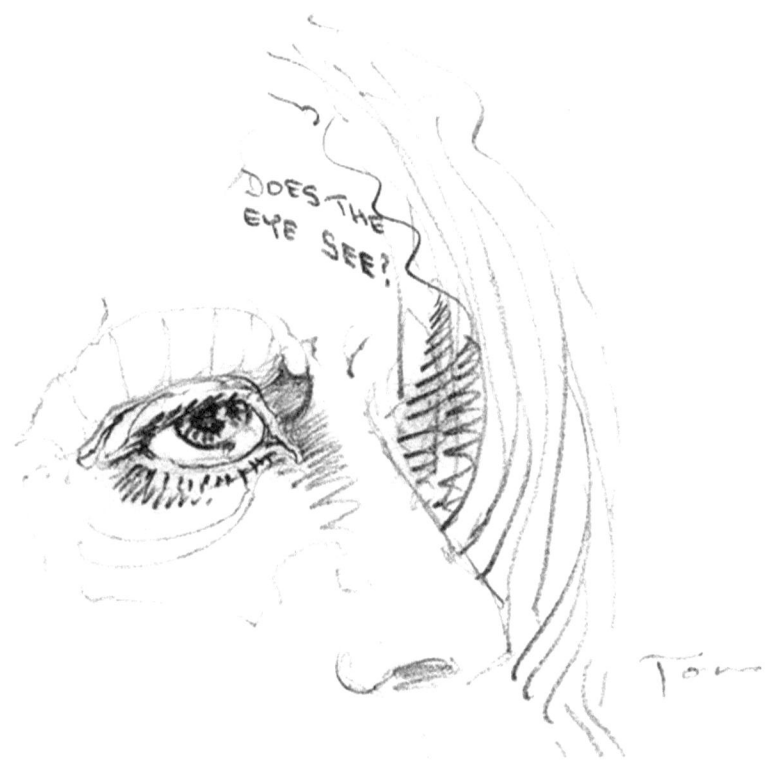

* Commercial artist Tom Byrne created this drawing in 1976 at the end of a very successful remote viewing experiment. He expressed what we all wondered at the time. What aspect of the vision system can provide an accurate image from 10 miles away?

2

SECTION I
~~~~~~

DIMENSIONS OF PERCEPTION

When we think of our sense organs, we usually think of these five: tasting, smelling, touching, hearing and seeing. There are more than that, though, since touch includes temperature, pressure, texture and pain, the heart and the gut respond to emotions, and the hair on the back of the neck might react to an unknown fear. The dimensions of perception include all the abilities of all of our senses, whether we experience them at close range, or remotely from miles away, as in what has been called "ESP" (extra-sensory perception), "telepathy," "clairvoyance," "gut feeling," "remote perception" (RP), or "remote viewing" (RV—includes ARV and CRV). (1) All of these are included here under the label of "psi perception."

From Webster's New World Dictionary (2)

Per-cep-tion *(par sep'shan) n. [L perceptio < pp. of percipere: see PERCEIVE]* **1.** *a) the act of perceiving or the ability to perceive; mental grasp of objects, qualities, etc., by means of the senses; awareness; comprehension; b) insight or intuition, or the faculty for these.* **2.** *the understanding, knowledge, etc. gotten by perceiving....*

Russell Targ and Elizabeth Rauscher discuss these issues of perception at length in Chapters 1, 26 and 27. Dean Radin's study in Chapter 2 demonstrates that the body perceives and responds to emotional telepathic stimuli before the conscious mind is aware of them. Stanley Krippner and colleagues began publishing research forty years ago (3, 4) proving that messages and images "sent" telepathically to a dreamer in the lab were included in the dream reports. Krippner summarizes this in Chapter 3, and in Chapter 4, he reports on the differences in extraordinary dreams by gender and nationality. Most of the psi perceptions discussed here were conducted in the same time frame, though separated by varying distances. However, psi perception can access unknown information from both past (5) and future time. (Illustrations of precognition are on pages 297-298 and page 609.) Visualization for creativity and healing is in Section X, pp. 536 and 552. Developmental optometrist Ray Gottlieb works to expand the perceptions and thinking of children by clearing up vision problems. Another important aspect of the dimensions of perception is the nonverbal communication between humans and animals. Beverley Kane has developed a program to train nurses to work with horses, so they can understand nonverbal patients better. For more information about this program and about her book, see her bio in Section III, page 154, and her website: www.horsensei.com.

EXAMPLES OF DIFFERENT TYPES OF PSI PERCEPTION

A psi sensitive may "sense" a distant smell, taste, feeling, sound or "emotion" and attempt to describe that in words. However when a person "sees" a distant image, the viewer needs to add a drawing, or represent it in some 3-D form. Some unusual images are difficult to describe in words alone, except to compare them with something that is already known. However, words may misrepresent the accuracy of what the viewer actually "saw" (e.g., One viewer's drawing showed the same shape and color as the target picture of a hat, but he named it "UFO." The judge called it a miss, based on the word, rather than on the image). Shape and color are often the most common similarities between RV image and target. (7, 8) Whereas the initial psi search for the target produced a direct response, naming involved memory association (a secondary mental process). Targ, Puthoff and Rauscher noticed this also and discouraged viewers from naming a target. (p. 14)

Targ and Rauscher rightly claim that anyone can do RV successfully. However, those (whether artist or scientist) who have trained themselves to "see" more when they "look" are at an advantage as remote viewers because they can more easily draw an accurate image of a target (or of a dream), whether it is of a flat picture or the space of an entire environment.

The following is a partial list of some of the different types of psi research that have been organized around visual responses. (All targets are chosen randomly. Psi sensitives prefer a target to be totally unknown.)

1) Mind-to-mind (or telepathy) studies are often done with flat images used as the "target," which a person attempts to "send" to a partner who is either awake or dreaming. (See Figures 1a, 1b, 1c.)
    a) The target is a picture on paper, or displayed on a computer.
    b) Computer targets may have DVD sound and action included.

2) Basic Remote Viewing studies use a whole environment as a target.
    a) The outbound team records their impressions while at the target site, and gives feedback to the viewer after his/her response is completed. (Figures 2a, 2b, 2c, 2d and 3a, 3b.)
    b) No one is at the target environment, and feedback may or may not be provided later. (Illustrated by Pat Price on page 308.)
    c) The remote viewer is only given a set of coordinates, or numbers. Feedback may or may not be provided later for some RV or CRV experiments.

3) Associative Remote Viewing (ARV) involves an object that stands for future information and will not be chosen until after the viewing. (CRV and ARV are not illustrated here – see IRVA ref. 1.)

Examples of these different types of psi perceptions are shown here to help the reader (who is unfamiliar with RV) understand the various tasks.

Between 1974-1975 (and again in 1980) I (Millay) collected 355 telepathy trials from 16 teams comprised of one "sender" and one "viewer." The first 11 teams were chosen from students who volunteered. Those accepted had already developed a rapport as close friends or as a couple, and had a personal need to know about their own telepathy. Targets were pictures cut from a wide variety of magazines, pasted on 3" X 5" cards, and placed in envelopes. The monitor asked the "sender" chose a target randomly out of a stack of 80 to 100, to redraw the image on another card and to write about it. This recorded the sender's thoughts, as well. The isolated "viewer" put his responses on his card. Both partners had 10 colored pens to use, since color was assumed to be important. (8)

Figures 1a, 1b and 1c. Team 4 Telepathy Trial #9 (one of five in a series)
Figure 1a. Target (From Marvel Comics)   Figure 1b. Sender's Drawing

Figure 1c. Viewer's Response   Sender's Text

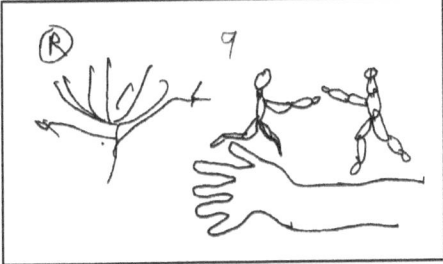

"Colorful, Oh, My! Nasty, Poor Lady, Mean, Beastly, Ogrely." *1

Viewer's Text

"Branching, Reaching out.
Antlers, Hand.
Attraction between opposites." *2

Each team did 5 such trials in a row before they received feedback to compare thoughts about their experiences. Then they did 5 more. On a different day, the team practiced EEG phase-coherence neurofeedback, and later they did 10 more trials. A comparison of the EEG and telepathy scores for 16 teams gave a correlation coefficient of $p > .001$. (Chapter 22)

---

*1 Drawing and text by Russell Winkler (February 26, 1975).
*2 Drawing and text by Mark (Gurumukh) Harris (February 26, 1975). (See also Chapter 46.)

Professional artists James Dowlen and Tom Byrne provided some of the most extraordinary images of accurate RV when they participated in my RV series in 1976 and in 1984. (More illustrations are in Chapter 46 — Biographies.) Figures 2a, 2b are my rough sketches of the target — the biology building at Santa Rosa Junior College (inside and out). This target was chosen randomly from ten possible targets within 5 miles. Figure 2c shows Byrne's more detailed RV response to the target. Figure 2d is one of Dowlen's RV responses. Both artists were working separately in the enclosed audio-visual studio, since the director Bob Budereaux and crew were videotaping them while they were drawing during this RV session. This videotape shows the progression of all of these drawings in real time. (7) Both admit they were nervous under the lights and cameras.

Figures 2a and 2b. Millay's sketches of the SRJC biology building

The first sketch was made of the outside of the biology building.

The second set of sketches from inside the building included stuffed and live birds.

Figure 2c. Byrne's RV response

Byrne spent his entire time during this session drawing the details of his first RV image of the target. Since he was a student there, he was very familiar with the design of the building, and he could draw it from memory.

Figure 2d. Dowlen's RV response

Dowlen drew two pages of curved lines and arches, wondering what they were. When Millay started drawing the birds inside, his drawings included this bird, a face with wings and the arches.

Spiritual healer Greg Schelkun drew this at his home in San Rafael, CA, across the Pacific Ocean from the target in Maui, HI. All reports from the "viewer" and the outbound team were mailed the same day to Saul-Paul Sirag in SF, CA, for security. (Schelkun's biography is in Chapter 46.)

Figures 3a and 3b. Long Distance Remote Viewing—Almost 3,000 Miles
Target: The 7 Sacred Pools in Maui, Hawaii

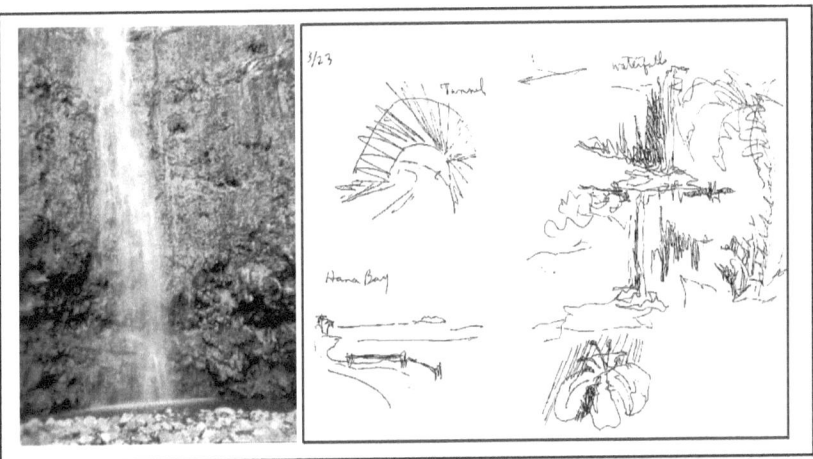

Dr Charles Brush offered to participate with me as the outbound team for this Hawaiian series. The Seven Sacred Pools was the randomly selected target in Maui. Brush took this photograph of the falls while we were there, and then he drove the winding road to Hana Bay, while I used a tape recorder to tell about each area as we experienced it, including the tall trees that touched above us as though we were driving through a tunnel. At that same time Greg Schelkun was making this page of drawings in CA. Greg wrote: *"Tunnel, Waterfalls and Hana Bay."*

Extraordinary Psi Perceptions by James Dowlen

In August 1975, I was invited to Bogotá, Colombia, to demonstrate our *Stereo Brainwave Biofeedback Light Sculpture* at the *Congress of Sorcery*. At the same time the Association for Humanistic Psychology (AHP) was holding its annual conference in Estes Park, Colorado, so I decided to attempt a long distance RV session between those two places. The idea of first tuning in to the frequency of the earth (7.8 Hz), which is in brainwave range, might enhance the resonance for communication across the continents. This idea also appealed to Rolling Thunder, a Native American Medicine Man, who led his group in a sunrise ceremony every morning at his Metatantay Center near Carlin, NV. James Dowlen agreed to draw whatever came to mind during that same time, and since he would be in Santa Rosa, CA, he had to get up at around 4:00 a.m. to participate, since each of the sunrises began in a much earlier sequence.

Stanley Krippner, Walter Houston Clark, (9) Susan Engelman and my sister Marge King (with 18 people altogether) were asked to build a fire on the hill nearest the AHP conference, form a circle and throw the *I Ching* coins for the random message to "send" to us in South America. As I arrived in Bogotá, Colombia, I realized that much of this idea was to go very differently than planned. Nevertheless, after we "tuned in," Lee Sannella, MD, (10) received the first trigram *"FIRE,"* and I received the other trigram *"MOUNTAIN."* Both were accurate. However, both of us independently "saw" a shadowy image of the trigram for the *"CREATIVE,"* which created confusion about the actual hexagram of the real target.

Meanwhile in CA, Dowlen drew two pages of images that could be seen as a record of the event in all three places — all mixed into a psychic soup. He describes *"A man with thick dark spectacles..."* [Spelled with "i"] Such a man was there, but only to ask the Abinticua medicine man to help him find his kidnapped son. This medicine man led our meditation with his brother and translator and they did indeed sit *"highest in a circle of friends."* The rest of our group sat on lower ground, as the drawing shows. *"The sympathetic traveler with unconscious direction...."* could be a translation of *"The Wanderer,"* which was the actual hexagram the group in Colorado obtained from the coins — formed by the two trigrams *"FIRE"* over *"MOUNTAIN."* Later, when Rolling Thunder saw these drawings, he acknowledged the eagle as a symbol of his own participation. Andrew Weil, MD, also in our circle, wrote a funny story for *Rolling Stone*. (11)

Figure 4a. The first full-page of remote viewing drawings by James Dowlen as he "saw" them from three widely separated places simultaneously.

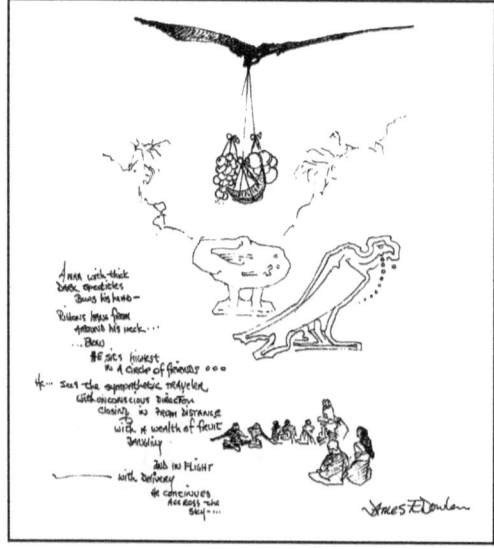

James Dowlen RV

At 4:00 am, August 27, 1975 artist James Dowlen began this first full-page of his remote viewing images during Millay's intercontinental long distance RV experiment held in four different places during the same time frame.

Dowlen was in the fourth place as an additional remote viewer—totally independent and unknown by the others, yet he combines all images in a psychic soup. His results are amazing, and enlightening about the unlimited range of the dimensions of perception.

Figure 4b. Dowlen's second full-page of RV drawings (8-27-1975) includes:

1] The unexpected rain: Rain continued on the drive from Bogotá, but stopped as the group reached Lake Guatavita in Colombia. 2] Seucucui, the Abinticua medicine man: He guided the meditation joining the groups together. (Neither Dowlen nor I had any idea that I would meet him at the Congress of Sorcery.) 3] The coins for the *I Ching*: Marge King and I decided at the last minute to let the coins determine the random message, and told no one else. 4] A deer with elaborate horns: Some indigenous people ask a *"deer spirit"* to carry messages between distant places. (None of us knew about that then. We only learned about it later at a shaman conference.)

Figure 4c. Seucucui, the Abinticua medicine man (called a Mamu) (12)

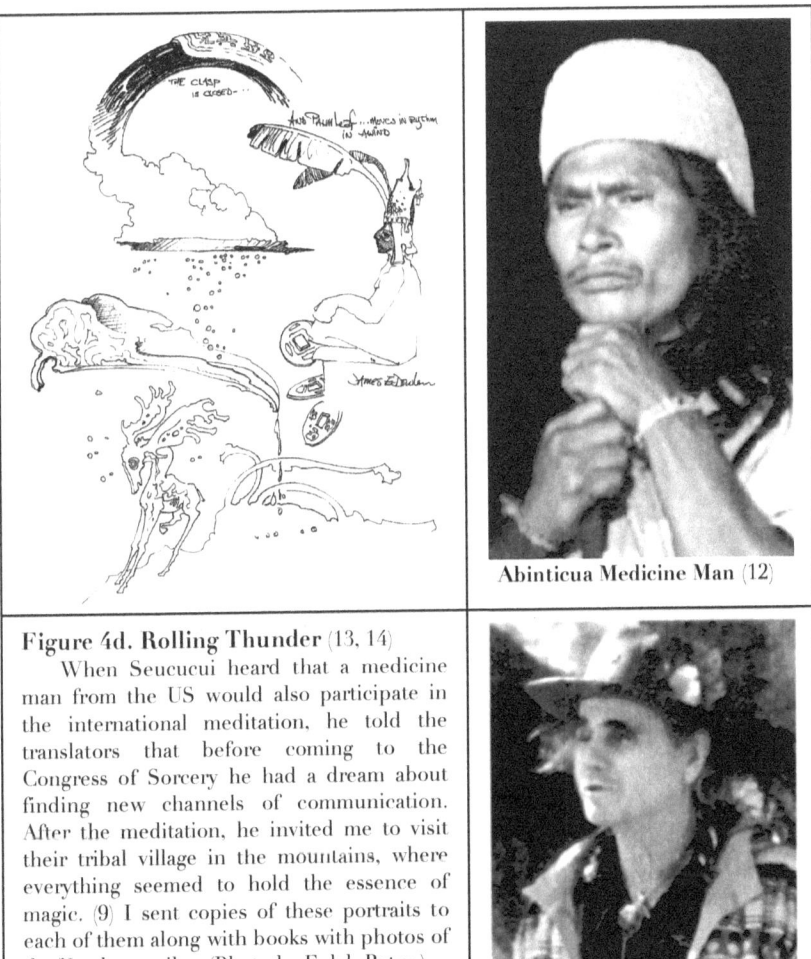

Abinticua Medicine Man (12)

Figure 4d. Rolling Thunder (13, 14)

When Seucucui heard that a medicine man from the US would also participate in the international meditation, he told the translators that before coming to the Congress of Sorcery he had a dream about finding new channels of communication. After the meditation, he invited me to visit their tribal village in the mountains, where everything seemed to hold the essence of magic. (9) I sent copies of these portraits to each of them along with books with photos of the Northern tribes (Photo by Eolah Bates.)

At the end of my 1976 series of ten RV sessions, I had invited both artists Dowlen and Byrne to my small apartment for dinner about two hours later. Neither of them had ever been there. Even though the last session was over, Dowlen kept drawing, and among the drawings he brought with him was this one of a room with high windows — similar to the high windows in my apartment. He said his drawing looked more like his mother's table than mine. However, his words amazed me, *"A letter of importance & opened — on the floor."* This surpassed any of the previous classifications of psi phenomena listed here, but I would not know that for a year.

I looked for such a letter and found one under my desk. I was an announcement of a parapsychology conference in Brazil during the summer, which I had ignored. By the time it was forwarded from my former address, it was too late to submit a paper, and I couldn't afford the trip. Anyway, I was trying to finish my dissertation before all my money ran out. Unnoticed and forgotten, the letter fell to the floor, and slid under the desk.

Nevertheless, because Dowlen had "viewed" it, I wrote a response. Next year, though I had moved again, a telegram was sent (to the address on my response) to invite me (expenses paid) to the 1977 Brazilian parapsychology conference. The organizers wanted me to show the *Brainwave Biofeedback Light Sculpture*. If I had not answered that letter, even a telegram couldn't have found me, since I had moved as often as rents and inflation increased.

A whole year passed before I discovered the personal significance of this precognitive psi perception.

How do we interpret this level of remote viewing? Did his or my spirit guides influence him to draw the *"letter on the floor"*? Was it my "destiny" to go to Brazil where a whole culture would confirm my experiences of communication with light beings and the spirits of the ancestors?

I wonder if anyone could design a repeatable study of this type of information with statistical significance? This demonstrates that there are still many unknown and unexplained dimensions of perception.

That trip to Brazil greatly increased my understanding and appreciation of the Spirit World. I was still uncertain how to relate to those experiences, even though over the years I have felt that grandparents gave me dreams and advice, and that a "guide" helped me design the *First Stereo Brainwave Biofeedback Light Sculpture*. Our educational system does not tolerate even a discussion of such things. In Brazil, one of the religions devoted to spirit communication (Espiritistas) operate many "healing" clinics. Psychiatrists and psychologists consulted with mediums. I watched mediums help clients by teaching them to channel loving spirits, and how to avoid being possessed by the negative spirits that may possibly cause illness.

At an Espiritista meeting, spirits gave a message to the group in Portuguese, but I actually "heard" it in my own head in English, *"the mind is a light energy form that has been radiating for billions of years."* (15) We have yet to discover the full extent of the possible dimensions of perceptions.

--- Jean Millay

REFERENCES AND NOTES

1) Buchanan, L. (2009) "Successful associative remote viewing." In: *Aperture: The Official Publication of the International Remote Viewing Association.* CT: Vol. 4, No. 4; 15.
2) (1988 & 1991) *Webster's New World Dictionary: 3rd College Ed.* NY: Simon & Schuster.
3) Ullman, M. & Krippner, S. (1970) "Dream studies and telepathy: An experimental approach." In: *Parapsychological Monographs* No. 12. NY: Parapsychology Foundation.
4) Krippner, S. (1975) *Song of the Siren.* NY: Harper & Row.
5) Schwartz, S. (1978, 2006) *The Secret Vaults of Time: Psychic Archeology and the Quest for Man's Beginnings.* NY: Grosset & Dunlap.
6) Galyean, B. (1983) Workshops and classes in *Visualization for Creativity.*
7) Millay, J. (1978) "The Relationship Between Phase Synchronization of Brainwaves & Success in Attempts to Communicate Telepathically: A Pilot Study." Doctoral Dissertation. SF, CA: Saybrook Graduate School and Research Center.
8) Millay, J. (1999) *Multidimensional Mind: Remote Viewing in Hyperspace.* Berkeley, CA: A Universal Dialogues Book, North Atlantic Books.
9) Clark, W.H. (1977) "Parapsychology and religion." In: B.B. Wolman, et al. (Eds.) *Handbook of Parapsychology.* NY: Van Norstrand Reinhold, 769-780.
10) Sannella, L. (1976-1987) *The Kundalini Experience.* Lower Lake, CA: Integral Publishing.
11) Weil, A. (1975) "A bunch of the brujos were whooping it up." In: *Rolling Stone.* NY: October 23, 1975. 56-58.
12) Congress of Sorcery Conference photo by Foto Pontón.
13) Photo by Eolah Bates. (1975) Rolling Thunder speaking to students at Sonoma State.
14) Boyd, D. (1974) *Rolling Thunder.* NY: Dell Publishing Co.
15) Millay, J. (2009) "Explorations and gifts from the spirit world." In: *Bridges* 2009 –1. C. Coates & L. Thornton (Eds.)

CHAPTER 1 — A DECADE OF REMOTE VIEWING RESEARCH

Russell Targ

Russell Targ conducted pioneering research on the development of the laser, and published numerous articles on plasma physics, microwaves and lasers. As a physicist he was also a senior staff scientist at Lockheed Research and Development Laboratories in Palo Alto, CA. He was cofounder of the psychic research program at SRI International (formerly Stanford Research Institute) in 1972. Beginning in 1974, this unique SRI remote viewing research was published in *Nature*. Additional papers were published in the *IEEE* and the *Proceedings of the AAAS* (American Association for the Advancement of Science). In 1982, he carried out the first remote viewing experiments between Moscow and SF, CA.

Among his many published works are **1)** 1977, *Mind Reach: Scientists Look at Psychic Ability* with Harold Puthoff; **2)** 1979 & 2002, *Mind at Large: Institute of Electrical and Electronics Engineers Symposium on the Nature of Extra-sensory Perception* with Charles Tart and Harold Puthoff; **3)** 1998, *Miracles of Mind: Exploring Nonlocal Consciousness and Spiritual Healing* with Jane Katra; **4)** 2004, *Limitless Mind: A Guide to Remote Viewing and Transformation of Consciousness*; **5)** 2006, *The End of Suffering: Fearless Living in Troubled Times* with J. J. Hurtak; **6)** 2008, *Do You See What I See? Memoirs of a Blind Biker*, an autobiography.

Russell Targ was one of the founders of the Parapsychology Research Group in 1966, and its first president, when meetings were held in Palo Alto. He continued to be active in the group when it met at the WRI (Washington Research Institute) in SF.

Website: www.espresearch.com.

CHAPTER 1

A DECADE OF REMOTE VIEWING RESEARCH
(1993 Version Plus an Update)

Russell Targ

Psychic functioning was not invented in the laboratory; rather, it was naturally occurring in the field. When we founded the Parapsychology Research Group in January 1966, we talked about how important it would be, if we were to progress in psychic research, to have some sort of a psychic "battery" to charge us up for a high level of psychic functioning when and where we needed it. Psychologist Charles Tart proposed that progress in understanding electricity, which had been studied for some twenty-five hundred years, became possible only around the end of the eighteenth century, when an actual electrical battery was made. Then progress was rapid. Demonstrations could go beyond the weak but reliable creation of static electricity by rubbing an amber rod with silk, and beyond merely observing the rare but powerful results of electricity in the field – lightning and thunder.

We needed to set up tests that were reliable and repeatable, that would fit in with ordinary human experience, yet could mold themselves to experimentation in the laboratory. We knew you could demonstrate psychic functioning in a fairly uninteresting and declining way, as with the Zener cards with the five familiar symbols used by J. B. Rhine and L. Rhine in the 1930s. Then there's the spectacular kind of ESP, such as the precognitive dream, that, like the lightning bolt, is not easily repeatable in the laboratory. We wanted to create experiments that a person could do at any time, developing and using intuition rather than the analytical approach that is attempted for card guessing.

How could we make a battery for a steady source of psychic abilities, for furthering our own psychical research? In 1972, when Hal Puthoff and I pioneered experiments in remote viewing — the ability to describe what is going on in some distant place to which you have no ordinary access — we took the first steps toward making an ESP battery. In fact, we were probably among the first people to articulate what the problems in psychic research were in a relatively jargon-free way and to set about correcting these problems, which were really simple ones.

First, we had to overcome people's fear or distrust of psychic phenomena. This began with our choosing the term *"remote viewing,"* picking a neutral descriptive phrase that was free of past prejudices and occult assumptions. We then set up rigorous scientific protocols, including a random protocol for target selection. Next we created an environment in which it was safe to be psychic. Just walking through the entry of SRI International, where the experiments took place, we impressed prospective viewers with the atmosphere of respectability and the multimillion-dollar layout of high-technology equipment. We conveyed the feeling that in a sense, SRI was giving its blessing, and that even though being psychic is a slightly forbidden activity in society, we give you permission to do it now.

In the laboratory itself, the viewers were made to feel at ease — no white lab coats were in evidence. The activities were always happy occasions that we *expected* to be successful. We were not examining people under a microscope to see whether they were part of a weird species of psychics. Rather, we were investigating the remote viewing phenomenon together; we were partners in research.

In our decade of research at SRI, throughout hundreds of experimental trials, we used no drugs, hypnosis, strobe lights, sensory deprivation, or meditative techniques, nor did we even require belief. In fact, to overcome the problem that Arthur Koestler called the *"Ink Fish (Octopus) Effect,"* in which a skeptic may view a clearly successful ESP demonstration one day and have doubts about its clarity — or even honesty — the next, (1) we encouraged any willing skeptic to take part in a remote viewing experiment. We found that with patience and encouragement, almost anyone can experience remote viewing.

Everyone seemed to have his own way of "seeing," and we encouraged participants to prepare to "see" in any way they chose. What works for one may not work for another; what works, works.

My role evolved as a sort of psychic travel agent, guiding the viewer to learn to distinguish psychic signals from mental noises. I encouraged viewers to stick to descriptive, impressionistic images of the target, and not try to guess at what it might specifically be. In steering viewers clear of analytical judgments — naming the object or describing its function and relating other incidental things about it — I kept them focused on what they were experiencing. We had found that analysis is a source of mental noise and, along with memory and imagination, is the enemy of psychic perception. Because psychic abilities correspond to the intuitive side of life, the more the viewer could be coaxed out of "naming" and the analytic mode, the more successful the experiment would be.

We also showed that it is much easier to close your eyes and describe a target place that you haven't been to than to guess a star or circle on a card. If you close your eyes and see your own house, for example, you'll know that's not the right answer. But if you see some peculiar, hard-to-describe thing of unknown origin, you're more likely to accept it as the target and not confuse it with some kind of mental noise or imagination or memory. It is the *surprising* character that allows you to get in touch with the psychic image, and the less you know about the target, the more likely you are to see it correctly. So we tried to maximize the surprise element and minimize educated guessing.

We refrained from assigning boring, repetitious tasks so that viewers would remain fresh and interested, thus avoiding a decline effect — the extinguishing of correct responses over time, another disadvantage of the classic card-guessing experiments.

Finally, we gave our viewers feedback and reinforcement so each trial was a learning experience. In our experiments, we found that almost anyone who is assured that it is safe to experience paranormal functioning can learn to do so. Almost anyone could perceive scenes, including buildings, roads, and people, even when the targets were at great distances and blocked from ordinary perception. We concluded that the ability for remote viewing is natural and innate, and anyone who feels comfortable with the idea of having paranormal ability can have it. Our "psychic battery" — the scientific methods and psychological environment we developed in our laboratory — helps to facilitate psychic functioning. We ultimately found that people improved their skills and incorporated them into their lives.

TESTING THE BATTERY

Pat Price

Pat Price was a likable, crafty ex-police commissioner and an ex-vice-mayor of Burbank, CA. When he first tried an informal remote viewing experiment with us, he was astoundingly accurate, down to reading (correctly) the labels on file folders in locked file cabinets. With our protocol firmly in place, we invited him to take part in a controlled series of nine remote viewings.

On the first viewing, he not only described the site, he named it (Hoover Tower on the Stanford University campus). As Hal Puthoff said, *"It may sound strange, but we still find ourselves burdened to a large degree by the collective conditioning of our society, wondering before every experiment how it could possibly work, and surprised every time it does. We have, however, satisfied ourselves by exhaustive investigation that the result is genuine, and not an artifact of a flawed protocol."*

The fourth experiment was a classic example of the *"fraud and collusion"* paranoia that can creep into research. This time the director of the division himself took the experimenters to the site to be viewed, rather than offering them a sealed envelope, as was the protocol. Was there some flaw in our protocol? He wanted to find out.

Figure 1.

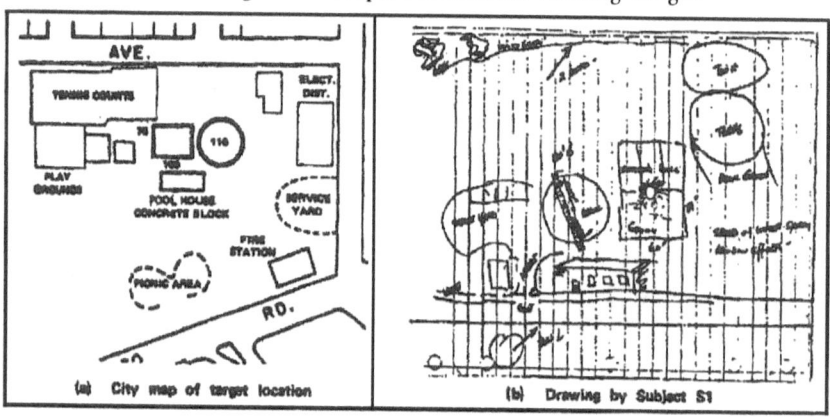

Figure 1. Subject Pat Price correctly described a park-like area containing two pools of water. Note an apparent left-right reversal, often observed in psi experiments.

While they were away, Price described the site so accurately that Puthoff was to say, *"The excellent quality of the transcript began to raise a paranoid fear in me that perhaps Price and the division director were in collusion on this experiment to see if I could detect chicanery! Only the concern shown by our director as he tried to figure out how we could have fooled him brought me back to equilibrium."*

Sometimes Price's stunning accuracies were mixed with inaccuracies, as shown in an experiment in which Price correctly detailed two pools of water in a park, one round and one rectangular (his dimensions were off by only 10 percent); but he was totally incorrect in describing the pools as used for water purification, not swimming, as was the case. (Figure 1) Puthoff remarked, *"With further experimentation, we began to realize that the occurrence of essentially correct descriptions of basic elements and patterns coupled with incomplete or erroneous analysis of function was to be a continuing thread throughout the remote viewing work. This observation eventually led to a major breakthrough with regard to understanding the connection between remote viewing and brain functioning."* (In 1998 I learned that seventy-five years ago the pool area, called Rinconada Park, used to be the city's water purification plant, and the two tanks shown in the top right of Price's drawing were water storage tanks — the tallest structures in the city.)

Hella Hammid

Hella Hammid was a professional photographer and an early participant in our experiments who demonstrated to us the importance of feedback. In a 1978 series of six experiments, she gave clear descriptions of three sites that she physically visited after each viewing. For the three sites she did not visit, her descriptions were not accurate. Because she wanted to end on a success, we threw in an extra target, which she described as a *"tower-like building...square...from the top it looks like it has wing-like projections on either side of it...with something mechanical that needs to be visible from the sky, and that's directional; definitely a kind of marker...some technical installation, like a weather station, or an airport tower, or a radar installation or radio. No, it's not radio. It is not that high, and it is not metal."* (Figure 2)

Hammid correctly identified the target as an airport tower and accurately surmised that it could not have been a radio tower. She could not clearly see what was at the base of the tower, which were both trees and airplanes. Here we have the combination of both the analytical and the nonanalytical.

By 1976, we had carried out highly significant experimental series with Price and Hammid that were published in *Nature* and the *Proceedings of the IEEE*.

Figure 2.

Palo Alto Airport Tower as Remote Viewing Target

Local remote viewing experiment:

Figure 2. Palo Alto Airport tower (above) and drawing made by viewer Hella Hammid during local remote viewing experiments. Viewer describes site in a "square tower... some technical installation."

An SRI Physicist

The target was the Louisiana Superdome, to be viewed from the distance of 1,500 miles by a physicist in California. He accurately described the scene as *"a large circular building with a white dome"* but was hesitant to report his sighting because he felt it looked too much like a *"flying saucer."* (Figure 3)

Figure 3.

Louisiana Superdome as Remote Viewing Target

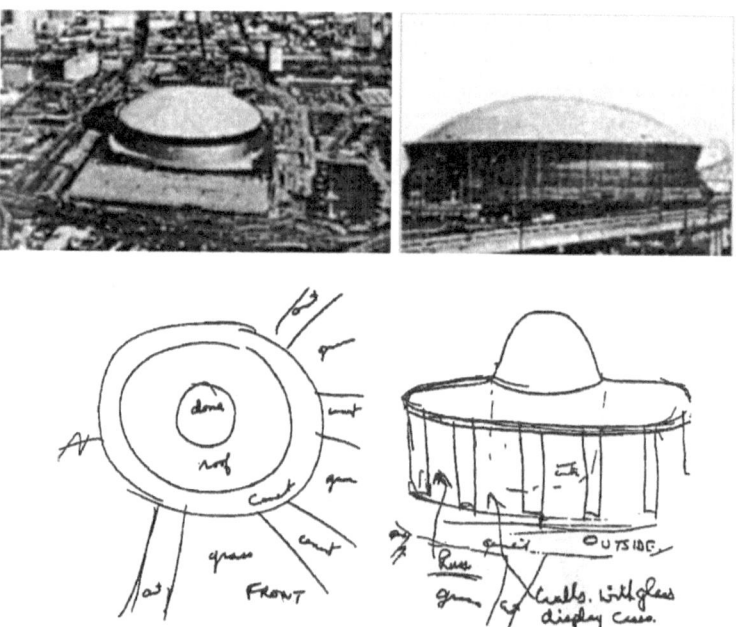

Long-distance remote viewing experiment:

Figure 3. SRI, Menlo Park, to Louisiana superdome. Subject described large circular building with a white dome. October 31, 1976.

In another experiment, we were working with Joe McMoneagle, a US Army intelligence officer and photo interpreter. This time the outbound team had been sent to the Stanford University Art Museum a few miles from SRI. As I interviewed our participant in his first remote viewing exercise, he drew fragmentary images around the edge of his page. He then said that the image *"sort of coalesced into two geometric solids,"* which he drew as the building shown in Figure 4. You can compare his drawing with the photograph taken by the experimenters at the site.

Figure 4.
Stanford Art Museum As Remote Viewing Target

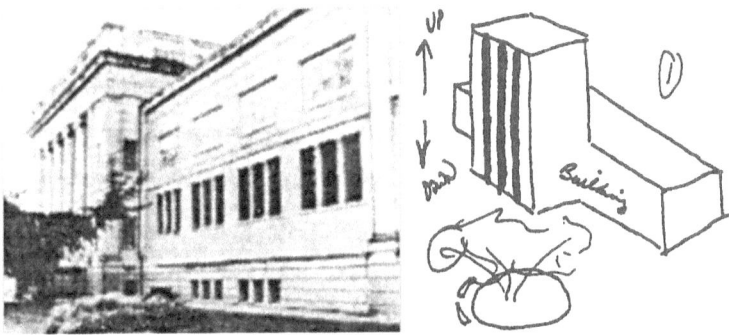

Local remote viewing experiment:

Figure 4. Subject described a building made of two rectangular solids. Note the circular planter in subject's drawing that corresponds to the circular planter in front of the museum.

~~~~~~

WHAT WE'VE LEARNED ABUT PARAPSYCHOLOGY IN THE PAST TWENTY-FIVE YEARS. (1993 Version)

In our ESP research, particularly in the remote viewing experiments at SRI, we had (and still have) no idea of the physical mechanisms behind the experiments we were doing. That's a great disappointment for us as physicists. But we learned a good deal about the psychology of the phenomenon. In our day-to-day activity doing these trials, at one trial per day, it was almost as though we were carrying out a sacrament to the powers controlling the psychic functioning that we were asking to manifest. The sacrament might involve lunch and ice cream, general play and great lightheartedness, with the assumption that when the scheduled experiment time came, we would do the experiment, and we could accept success. As a remarkable outcome of this acceptance, outstanding success is what we often found.

We learned that people with the right degree of acceptance could be taught what they need to know about psychic function in a few days. Hella Hammid, for example, came to us as a control subject. She had never done any psychic work, and yet from the first trial, her work was extraordinary. Typically, four out of six of her trials would be correct. That is like four miracles out of six attempts, or to put it another way, for every six times she tried to walk across the bay on the surface of the water, four times were successful. So to say that it is simply four rights and two wrongs greatly understates the quality of what she did. But that is just one of the frustrations of the research.

I suggest that the way to increase the reliability of psychic functioning, of increasing the juice in the psychic battery is to try to carry out each experiment in what I would call a state of grace in which experimenters, judges, subjects, everybody in the environment has reached some kind of harmonious agreement with the universe that what we are doing makes sense and can be accomplished.

STATE OF THE ART IN REMOTE VIEWING

In the bibliography to *The Mind Race*, researchers George Hansen, Charles Tart, and Marilyn Schlitz report results of their survey of all the published and unpublished remote viewing experiments at the time (1973-1982). They found that *"more than half (fifteen out of twenty-eight) of the published formal experiments have been successful, where only one in twenty would be expected by chance."* They also located eighteen unpublished studies, with eight reporting statistical significance. They concluded from this *"the success of remote viewing is not due to reporting bias, in which vast numbers of unsuccessful experiments go unreported."*

Given the data from remote viewing in the SRI experiments and others throughout the world over the past twenty years, we have greatly increased our knowledge about this ability. The illustrations in this chapter show the results of some of this work. We have produced three books and more than fifty technical articles describing this work. (2-4) These findings, described by Hal Puthoff and Russell Targ in *Mind at Large* (and most recently in *Miracles of Mind* by Russell Targ and Jane Katra), may be summarized as follows:

1) *Target acquisition.* Remote-viewers can acquire and describe target locations based on the presence of a cooperative experimenter at a distant site or from maps, pictures, or geographical or arbitrary coordinates related to the targets in question. It does not matter whether the person ("beacon") at the distant site is known or unknown by the viewer.

2) *Target attribute perceptions.* Descriptive aspects, such as shape, form, color, or material, are much better described than analytic concepts, such as function or name. At times, analytical data can come through.

3) *Simultaneity and precognition.* Information access appears to be available essentially in real time. Activities at the target site are also often perceived in advance of their occurrence.

4) *Spatial resolution.* Resolution appears to be accurate for targets less than a millimeter in diameter. A pin was correctly described at a quarter-

mile distance, and a quarter-inch upholstery button was described at ten thousand miles.

5) *Distance effects.* The accuracy and resolution of remote viewing are not sensitive functions of the distance between a viewer and the target over terrestrial distances. In 1984, we had excellent results in experiments carried out between Moscow and San Francisco.

6) *Shielding.* Faraday cage or seawater electrical shielding is not effective in blocking remote viewing perceptions. (Electrical shielding may improve psi functioning.)

7) *Sensory modalities.* In addition to visually observable details, viewers often correctly describe sounds, smells, and tactile information that can be verified as existing at the target location.

8) *Inhibitory factors.* A viewer's prior knowledge of target possibilities as well as certain psychological and environmental factors may inhibit viewer capabilities by increasing the level of mental noise relative to information signal.

9) *Enhancement factors.* Psychological interest for a viewer together with the necessity and relevance for obtaining the information, seriousness of purpose, training in overcoming and avoiding mental noise, and the presence of a facilitating interviewer to ask questions and help direct the viewer's attention to acquiring relevant information enhance accuracy in remote viewing.

10) *Accuracy.* An analysis of remote viewing transcripts generated by experienced viewers indicates that roughly two-thirds of viewer-generated material constitutes an accurate description of the target, and about one-third is ambiguous, general, or incorrect. Sometimes near-perfect results are obtained.

11) *Use of redundancy to increase signal-noise ratio.* Redundancy, whereby more than one person attempts to collect data on a given target, has been shown to improve reliability by reducing the effects of individual viewer biases.

12) *Replicability of remote viewing.* Continuing demonstration and replications of remote viewing at laboratories throughout the world indicate that this is a robust human perceptual ability. More than half of all published experimental papers report independent statistical significance.

13) *Distribution of remote viewing in the general population.* The ability appears to be widespread, although latent. Volunteers with no previous history of remote viewing exhibit the ability, indicating that special subjects are not necessary.

14) *Improvement potential.* Viewers trained over a several-year period have shown improved performance in both accuracy and reliability. Viewer reliability tends to improve with practice.

15) *Theoretical considerations.* Because viewers often are able to obtain information that is blocked from traditional means of perceptual access by both space and time, research in remote viewing suggests that modern physics cannot as yet satisfactorily deal with the observed data. These data suggest that the current description of the spacetime metric in which we live is inaccurate or incomplete.

NOTES

1) This term refers to how an octopus escapes by secreting a cloud of ink, thus leaving doubt that he was ever there.

REFERENCES

2) Targ, R. & Puthoff, H.E. (1977) *Mind Reach: Scientists Look at Psychic Ability.* NY: Delacorte.
3) Tart, C.T., Puthoff, H.E. & Targ, R. (Eds.) (1979) *Mind at Large.* NY: Praeger.
4) Targ, R. & Harary, K. (1984) *The Mind Race: Understanding and Using Psychic Abilities.* NY: Villard Books.

> *However, we are confident that two factors will remain: Namely that these phenomena are not a result of an energetic transmission, but rather they are an interaction of our awareness with a nonlocal hyper-dimensional space-time in which we live.*
>
> --- *Russell Targ & Elizabeth Rauscher*
> --- 2008

CHAPTER 2 PSYCHOPHYSIOLOGICAL STUDIES OF PSI AND EMOTIONS

Dean Radin, PhD

Dean Radin is Senior Scientist at the Institute of Noetic Sciences (IONS). His early career as a concert violinist shifted into science after he earned a masters degree in electrical engineering (1975) and a PhD in psychology (1979) from the University of Illinois, Champaign-Urbana. Prior to joining the IONS research staff, he worked on advanced telecommunications systems at AT&T Bell Labs and GTE Labs, then conducted parapsychological research at Princeton, Edinburgh, and Nevada U, and at three Silicon Valley thinktanks, including SRI International.

Dr Radin is author or coauthor of over 200 articles, a dozen book chapters, and several books including the bestselling *The Conscious Universe* (HarperOne, 1997) and *Entangled Minds* (Simon & Schuster, 2006). His popular writings have appeared in magazines like *Psychology Today* and his technical articles in journals such as *Foundations of Physics* and *Psychological Bulletin*. He was the subject of a feature article in the *New York Times Magazine*, he has been interviewed on dozens of television shows, including Oprah, Larry King Live and the History Channel, and he has presented over a hundred invited lectures in venues ranging from Harvard, Stanford and Princeton Universities, to Google, DARPA and the Naval War College. In 2008, the University of Illinois' Department of Electrical and Computer Engineering selected Dean Radin as "Alumni Leader."

Find more information at http://www.ions.org/.

PSYCHOPHYSIOLOGICAL STUDIES OF PSI AND EMOTIONS

Dean Radin

Case studies of spontaneous psi experiences show that these experiences are often associated with emotional events. Consider the following example, one of thousands of such reports collected by Louisa Rhine and others: (1- 2)

> One Thursday morning about 4 a.m., I jumped out of bed, feeling as if I was dying. I felt as if blood or something was pouring down from my head choking me and I was trying desperately to get my breath. My husband got up to help me. He tried to get me to the bathroom for some water to drink to stop the terrible choking spasms I seemed to be having. They soon diminished and I grew very weak. I thought I must be really dying. My husband put me down on the bed where I rested but felt so "all gone." Then I thought my son had called, saying "Oh, Mama help me," in such anguish. Later in the day I went to the doctor for an X-ray of my chest. I thought with such acute pain that something must be wrong. But the doctor could find nothing. That was February 10th and on the 12th we received a telegram saying our son was killed by gunshot in the head at one o'clock on February 10th. There is a nine-hour difference in time. I feel he called me as it happened, and I heard his groan and felt his dying. (1, p. 138)

This type of experience is dubbed a case of *"crisis telepathy,"* usually involving an emotional episode amplified by deep emotional bonding between the individuals involved. (3, 4) A second class of psi experience associated with high emotion is the precognitive dream, (5) and a third is called recurrent spontaneous psychokinesis, also known as poltergeist activity. (6) The latter cases involve anomalous movement of objects often associated with a prepubescent "agent," typically one whose hormones are raging but whose emotional expression is suppressed.

While reports of such experiences are common, and at face value the link with emotion is plausible, to gain better confidence that these phenomena are what they appear to be, over the past few decades investigators have conducted controlled laboratory investigations of the psi-emotion relationship. Many of these studies have focused on unconscious emotional responses as detected by changes in the autonomic or central nervous system. What follows is a brief review of three classes of such experiments.

EMOTIONAL NAMES

Douglas Dean was one of the first investigators to use a psychophysiological method of studying the effects of emotions in modulating psi perception. (7-8) Dean asked a percipient (acting the role of a telepathic "receiver") to write down emotionally meaningful names on cards, names known only to the percipient. These cards were later shuffled randomly into a deck containing an equal number of blank cards. The percipient was then asked to relax while his or her fingertip blood flow was continuously monitored using a photo-plethsymograph. Meanwhile, a distant agent (acting the role of a telepathic "sender") was also asked to write down names on cards, names known only to him or her, and those cards were randomly shuffled into that deck as well. Now the agent was asked to look at and mentally "send" each card for 30 seconds, one at a time, to the percipient.

The telepathy hypothesis predicted that when the agent was sending names only known to him or her, or blank cards, that the percipient would remain calm. But when sending emotionally charged names known only to the percipient, then the percipient would experience an emotional response resulting in sympathetic arousal, which in turn would stimulate vasoconstriction in the periphery, and thus fingertip blood flow would decline.

Two decades after Dean's publication, Haraldsson reviewed conceptually similar experiments, all using plethsymographic recordings as detectors of psi responses, and most using emotional stimuli (names, auditory or visual stimuli, electric shock, etc.). (9) He found 11 replications reported by 10 investigators, of which seven were reportedly significant at $p < 0.05$. An unweighted Stouffer Z of this group of studies results in $z = 4.99$, $p = 2.96 - 10^{-7}$. The extent to which selective reporting may be biasing this replication rate is unknown, but based on meta-analyses which have examined the "file-drawer" effect in other classes of psi experiments, it seems unlikely that this outcome can be entirely attributed to a file-drawer effect. (10) This suggests that emotions may indeed act as modulators, or perhaps as attentional amplifiers, of psi perceptions.

Figure 1. Douglas Dean found this in repeated trials (7)

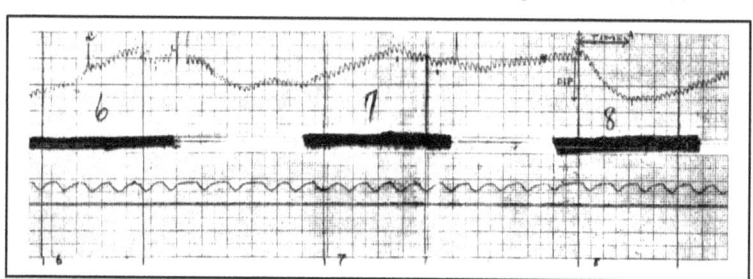

Figure 1. From Dean (1962) During stimulus period 6 the agent looked at a name known only to himself. Period 7 was a blank card control, and during period 8 the agent looked at a name known only to the distant percipient.

GUT FEELINGS

Over time, experiments involving emotional names became subsumed into a larger class of psychophysiological studies known as Direct Mental Interactions with Living Systems (DMILS). Most DMILS studies have not explicitly involved modulation of emotions, but rather sending calming or activating intentions, or merely directing attention, toward another person. In an exception to this rule, Marilyn Schlitz and I studied the commonly reported experience of viscerally experienced intuitive hunches, or "gut feelings," about the emotional state of another person at a distance. The experiment tested whether a percipient's gut, as measured with an electrogastrogram, would respond to a distant agent's emotions. (11)

In this study, 25 pairs of volunteers were recruited. Each pair mutually decided who would take the role of agent (or sender, S) and percipient (or receiver, R). R was invited to relax in a reclining chair in an electromagnetically and acoustically shielded room. Three Ag/AgCl electrodes were applied to R's abdomen. The resulting electrogastrogram (EGG) signals were amplified by a Biopac EGG amplifier and digitized by a Biopac MP150 physiological monitor. After confirming that R's EGG was recording properly, the experimenter (E) focused a video camera on R's face, and R was asked to relax while attempting to maintain a "mental connection" with S. R knew that S would be watching him or her periodically over closed circuit video, but R did not know the timing, length, or frequency of those periods. R listened to a meditative tone over headphones to encourage relaxation and to provide additional acoustic masking. To encourage a mutually shared state of mental connection, before S left for the sender's room, the two participants were asked to exchange a personal, meaningful item, like a watch or ring. They were each instructed to hold this item in their right hand during the remainder of the experimental session. Then S was led to a room about 15 meters away.

S was invited to sit in front of two video monitors and asked to wear a set of noise-canceling headphones to block external sounds. One video monitor periodically displayed R's live image; the other displayed a sequence of pictures. The stimulus pictures were selected from the International Affective Picture System, a standardized pool of color digital photographs with pre-assessed ratings for emotional arousal and valence. (12) Music was selected from popular songs and movie soundtracks to evoke emotions, as described below.

Digitized signals from the R & S physiological monitors were transmitted over a local area network to two Windows-based personal computers (PCs). The experiment was controlled by a third PC that ran a program that randomly selected one of two counterbalanced sequences of emotional conditions. Each sequence consisted of a 30-second inter-epoch rest period, followed by a two-minute epoch presenting one of four emotions: positive, negative, calming, or neutral. After four epochs were presented, the same sequence was repeated using new pictures and sound for the positive and negative conditions, and the same pictures and sound for the calm and neutral conditions.

To avoid psychological and physiological habituation to the emotional stimuli, S viewed a series of 20 different pictures during each sending epoch. Each picture was displayed for 6 seconds, and each picture within a given sending epoch was selected to have approximately the same IAPS-standard valence and arousal level. At the beginning of each sending epoch, the computer switched R's video image to one monitor in S's room, sent electrical marker signals to the R and S Biopac systems to synchronize the two sets of physiological recordings, started playing music to S that was appropriate to the emotional condition, and also displayed the stimulus pictures to S on the second video monitor. During the inter-epoch rest periods, one monitor was black and the other presented the word "relax" in green on a black background.

Positive emotional stimuli included photos of smiling babies and kittens. Positive epoch 1 was accompanied by the Beatles' rendition of the song *Twist and Shout*, and positive epoch 2 by Little Richard's song *Long Tall Sally*. The negative emotion epochs included a sad theme, which used pictures such as a graveyard accompanied by Samuel Barber's *Adagio for Strings*, and an angry theme, using pictures such as an atomic bomb explosion and accompanied by the song *Feuer Frei*, by the German heavy metal rock band Rammstein. The calming epoch consisted of low-arousal IAPS pictures transformed into gray-scale images, accompanied by the song *May It Be*, by the New Age artist Enya. The neutral epoch pictures were all gray-hued rectangles accompanied by pink noise. The inter-epoch rest periods were accompanied by the same pink noise.

The eight epochs presented in each session could appear in one of two orders: Order I consisted of calm, negative-sad, neutral, positive–2, calm, negative-angry, neutral, and positive–1. Order II was the reverse of Order I. The order assigned to a given session was determined randomly by the controlling program. Two orders were provided to keep both E and R blind to the emotional condition sequence during each recording session, and to allow an assessment of potential EGG baseline drifts. Each experimental session thus consisted of eight two-minute sending epochs, each separated by a 30-second rest period, plus a two-minute cool-down period before the session began, for a total of 22 minutes. R and S were allowed to relax with the electrodes in place for about 10 minutes before the session began. During sending epochs, S was instructed to periodically gaze at the video image of R with intention to send the emotions evoked by the stimuli. Between epochs, when the video screen went black, S was instructed to withdraw his or her attention from R and relax.

A total of 26 sessions were conducted, resulting in a total of 208 epochs, 52 in each of the four emotional conditions. Five of the 208 epochs were only partially recorded due to equipment failures, resulting in 52 positive, 51 negative, 51 neutral, and 49 calm usable epochs.

Figure 2 shows the average maximum EGG values

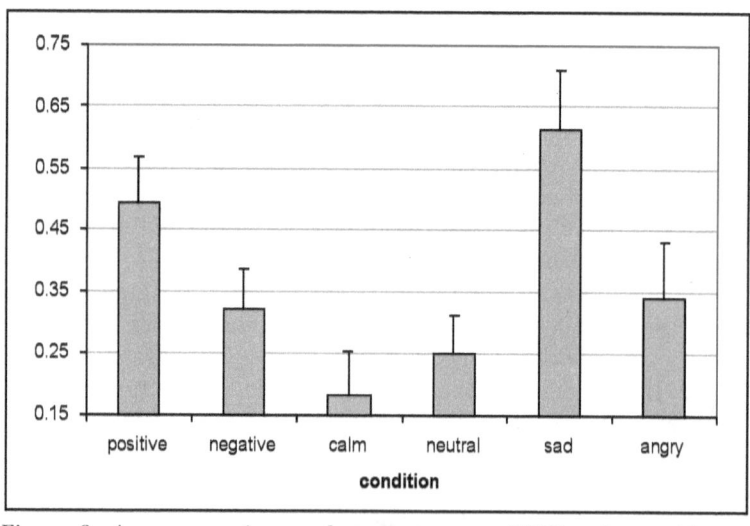

Figure 2. Average maximum electrogastrogram (EGG) values, with one standard error bars, pooled across all participants, for positive, negative, calm, and neutral epochs, and for the two components of the negative emotional epochs.

Among Rs there were five males and 21 females (mean age 45), and among Ss there were 12 males and 14 females (mean age 44). Participants in all cases knew each other, some as friends and others as long-term partners. Two pairs were run twice with the S/R roles reversed, and two individuals participated in four sessions, each taking S and R roles twice.

Figure 2 shows the average maximum EGG values recorded during the different emotional epochs pooled across all participants, with one standard error bars. Comparison of the emotional and calm means with respect to the neutral mean revealed that overall the positive emotion was significantly larger ($z = 2.54$, $p < 0.006$), the negative emotion was larger (nonsignificantly), and the calm was smaller (nonsignificantly). When the negative emotion epochs were partitioned into their sad and angry components, the sad emotion was found to be significantly larger than the neutral ($z = 3.13$, $p < 0.0009$), and the angry emotion nonsignificantly larger. The significant effects withstand correction for multiple testing.

These findings are consistent with the spontaneous case studies, suggesting that the emotions of one person, whether positive or negative, can be viscerally "felt" by a distant partner, and thus that the commonly used phrase "gut feelings" may reflect a genuine form of intuitive perception.

PRESENTIMENT

The two classes of experiments discussed so far explored interconnections occurring at the same time between two isolated people, as detected by a percipient's physiological response to a distant sender's emotions or to an activity like looking at cards with names meaningful to the percipient. A third class of phenomena also involves interconnections, and also associated with emotion, but occurring within the same individual separated *in time*.

The experimental design is based on experiences often described as a foreboding that something meaningful is about to unfold. In the laboratory this effect is referred to as a *presentiment* experience. To detect such effects, one or more measurements of nervous system activity are collected before, during and after a participant is exposed to randomly selected stimuli of varying emotional affect. Presentiment predicts that the nervous system will respond differently before emotional vs. calm events under conditions that exclude sensory cues and anticipatory biases.

Presentiment experiments have been conducted while monitoring skin conductance level, (13-21) nonspecific skin conductance response, (22-23) heart rate, (26-27) brain electrical activity, (24-27) and blood oxygenation levels in the brain as measured with fMRI. (28) Stimuli have included emotional vs. calm photographs, stylized happy vs. sad faces, auditory startle tones vs. silence, and electrical shock vs. no-shock. In some studies participants initiated trials of fixed lengths at will, in others stimuli appeared spontaneously at random times (called "nonaging foreperiods" in the psychophysiological literature.) (29) As of mid-2008, at least 14 investigators have reported 19 experiments of this type, of which 17 were in the predicted direction and 10 were significantly positive. (30)

Figure 3 shows the outcome of a presentiment experiment using skin conductance as the physiological measure (31)

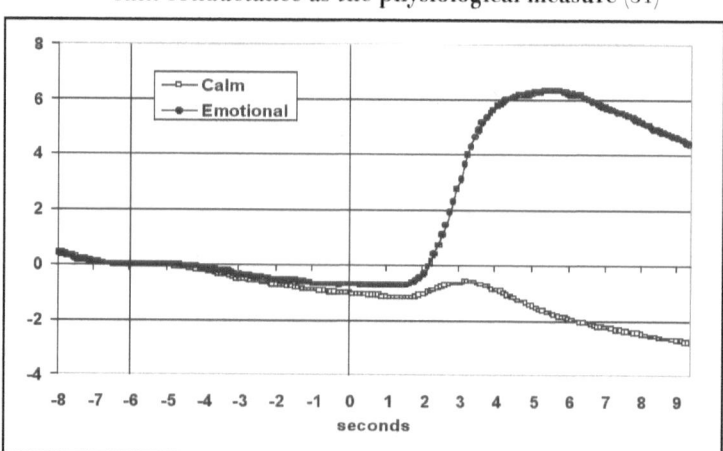

Figure 3. Presentiment experiment using skin conductance measures, showing normalized change in skin conductance level (SCL) from the moment (-6 seconds in this case) that the participants initiated a trial with a button press. This shows pooled results of 47 participants who together contributed 1,410 trials. A nonparametric test of the difference in SCL prior to the stimulus (at time 0) resulted in $z = 3.34$, $p = 0.0004$.

The principal critique to date of the presentiment studies is that the results might be explainable by anticipatory strategies developed through implicit learning. Simulations of idealized strategies suggest that outcomes resembling presentiment effects can be produced when the experiment involves asymmetric distributions of dichotomous stimuli, combined with the assumption that nervous system activity between successive emotional stimuli becomes progressively increased. (31) Analyses of actual data collected in these experiments have put this idea to the test, and they have uniformly failed to support the anticipatory hypothesis. To date, no artifacts have been found that can adequately explain these effects by conventional means.

To illustrate the presentiment experiment in more detail, a recent design based on pupillary dilation is described. This measure provides a convenient psychophysiological measure that reflects attention, cognitive processing load, emotional response, anticipation, and the degree of balance between sympathetic and parasympathetic activation. (32-33) The experiment assumed that presentiment effects are largely mediated by the sympathetic nervous system, which, if true, would cause the eye to dilate more before emotional events than before calm events.

Participants in this study were recruited by convenience among staff members and visitors to IONS, and among adult attendees at an IONS conference. Eye data were collected using a video eyetracking system that provided eye movement and pupil diameter measures at 60 samples per second (Applied Science Laboratories' model Eye-Trac 6000). A computer program controlled the random selection and display of emotional picture stimuli, and it coordinated two computers used to control the experiment. A program running on a "stimulus PC" responded to the participant's interactions, randomly selected and displayed the pictures, communicated with the Eye-Trac 6000 to inform it about the on-going experimental condition (between trials, prestimulus period, etc.), and retrieved random numbers as needed by a true random number generator. Another program running on an "eyetrack PC" continuously collected eye data from the Eye-Trac 6000. (Figure 4)

Figure 4. An illustration of the experimental layout

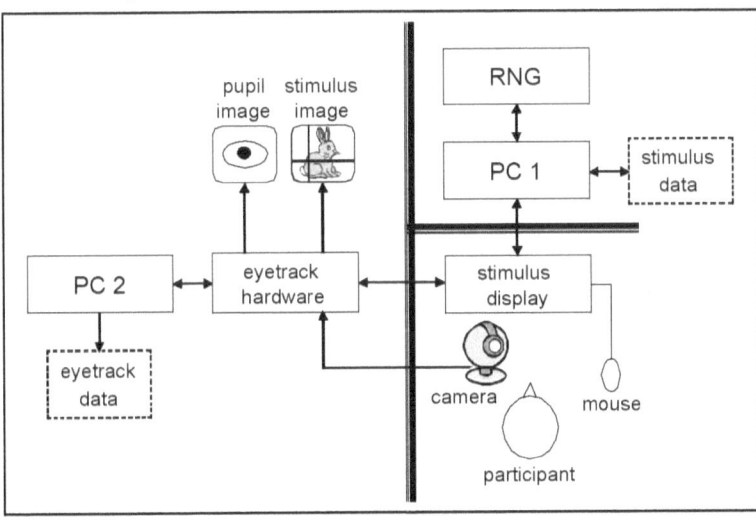

Figure 4. Participants in the eyetracking presentiment study contributed data in a cubicle containing the stimulus display, a mouse and keyboard, and a camera used to image the participant's eye. The other equipment included a computer (PC1) used to select, display and record the picture stimuli, a random number generator circuit used to select the stimuli, eyetracking hardware (Eye-Trac 6000 control unit), one video monitor displaying the pupil and a second displaying the stimulus overlaid with crosshairs indicating where the eye was looking, and a second computer (PC 2) used to collect the eyetracking data.

Emotional stimuli used in this study were a pool of 592 IAPS images, with standardized arousal scores ranging from 1.72 (low affect) to 7.35 (high affect), and standardized valence scores ranging from 1.31 (negative affect) to 8.34 (positive affect). The experimental procedure was as follows: When a participant (P) arrived at the lab, the experimenter (E) asked P to rest his or her chin on the Eye-Trac 6000's head and chin rest apparatus. After adjusting the apparatus and focusing the camera on P's left pupil, E dimmed the lights and ran an eye calibration procedure on P. Then E advanced the computer display to a screen showing a gray rectangle on a black background.

E told P that when a gray screen appeared, that was a signal to click the mouse button at will to begin each trial. As shown in Figure 5, after the button press the screen remained dark for 3 seconds, then an image was randomly selected from the stimulus set, displayed for 3 seconds, and then the screen returned to dark for 3 seconds. At this point a message appeared on the screen alerting P to advance to the next trial at will. Before beginning the session, E asked P to attempt to feel the emotions evoked by each successive image, if any, and to allow his or her eyes to freely wander over the display screen both before and during stimulus exposure.

Figure 5. A diagram of the sequence of events

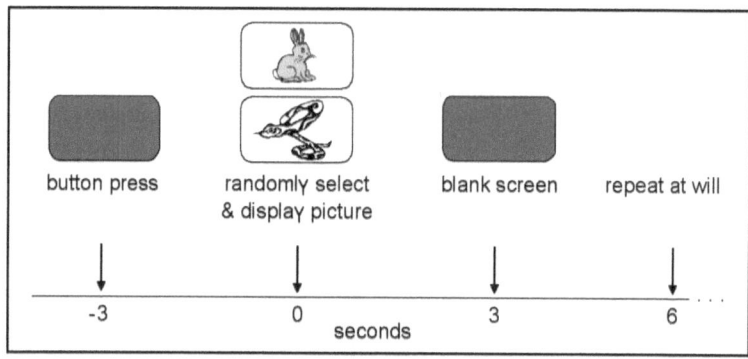

Figure 5. Each eyetracking trial began with a button press at will (at -3 seconds). Then the computer randomly selected an IAPS photo and showed it at stimulus onset (0 seconds). At +3 seconds the screen went black, and three seconds later the next trial could begin.

The eye data of interest per trial consisted of 1 second of baseline data, 3 seconds prestimulus, 3 seconds during stimulus display, and 3 seconds of postdisplay. The stimulus pictures were selected uniformly at random, with replacement, from the 592 picture IAPS set. Eye data were collected on the left eye.

The presentiment hypothesis predicted that change in pupillary dilation would be larger before randomly selected emotional vs. calm pictures. For purposes of this test "emotional" was prespecified as the 5% of contributed trials having the highest IAPS arousal scores, and "calm" as the 5% of trials with the lowest IAPS arousal scores. This ± 5% emotional contrast threshold was selected based on results of previous presentiment experiments using IAPS targets. (29)

A total of 33 volunteers contributed 37 sessions and a total of 1,438 usable trials. Of the 33 participants, 31 were righthanded and two were ambidextrous; their ages ranged from 20 – 83 (mean 47.5), 14 were male and 19 were female. At the planned 5% level of emotional contrast (72 calmest trials, average IAPS arousal of 2.43 vs. 72 most emotional trials, average IAPS arousal of 7.05), the differential change in pupillary dilation during the prestimulus period, as determined using nonparametric randomized permutation methods, was significantly positive as predicted by the presentiment hypothesis, $z = 3.17$, $p = 0.0008$ (one-tailed, see Figure 6). (34)

Figure 6. The percent of change in pupil dilation

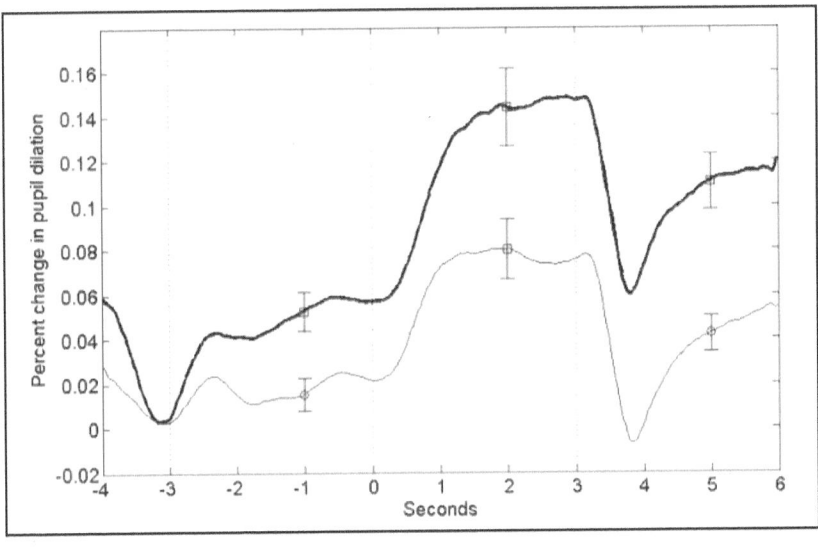

Figure 6. The bold (top) line shows average proportional change in pupillary dilation for the 5% most emotional targets across all 1,438 usable trials; the thin (bottom) line shows the same for the 5% most calm targets. Both lines are baseline adjusted to the average pupillary dilation value per trial during the 167 msec before the trial-initiating button press (at second -3). Stimulus onset is shown at second 0 and stimulus offset at second +3. Confidence intervals are plus and minus one standard error, and curves are smoothed 500 msec to clarify the figure. Analyses were conducted on raw data.

DISCUSSION

The studies described here are examples of experiments conducted to explore the psychophysiological relationships between psi and emotions. The results support the idea that strong emotions modulate psi perception, as suggested by the spontaneous case literature. It is clear, of course, from many other experiments as well as spontaneous experiences, that emotions are not *necessary* for psi perception, but they do seem to play a meaningful role in bringing them to awareness.

Why do emotions modulate psi perception? Perhaps for the same reason that emotions modulate ordinary attention. We are constantly negotiating a flood of sensory inputs, far more than we can consciously process. Something is required to direct how attention is allocated, and many studies indicate that emotion is a principal source of that modulation. (35) The amygdala plays a central role in this capacity, through both direct and indirect signals into the sensory pathways. These signals influence the representation of emotional events, especially threatening events.

From an evolutionary viewpoint, we are markedly sensitive to emotional events because our survival depends on fast allocation of attention towards dangerous or threatening circumstances. In the modern world we need not be wary of marauding tigers, but we are faced with the occasional drunk driver swerving on the highway. So we are fortunate that our hardwired emotional responses still prioritize our allocation of attention, which in turn provides privileged access to our awareness.

Using emotion to modulate attention seems pregnant with possibilities for future psi research. Douglas Dean's design using emotional names is ripe for replication because his method offered a way of distinguishing the nominal "source of psi"—percipient vs. agent. (36) His studies suggested a form of clairvoyance on the part of the percipient, in that the percipient's blood flow was modulated by emotional names that were not known to the agent. Other studies, such as the "gut feelings" experiment, suggest a form of telepathy, in that the percipient appeared to be influenced by the agent's emotions. Would an experiment using emotional names known by both percipient and agent result in effects that are stronger than names known only to one party?

Experiments employing strongly arousing stimuli, including erotic pictures, stimulating music, and pleasant odors, would be fruitful to explore in more detail. Most spontaneous psi cases do not involve pleasant events, but the "gut feelings" study did show that an agent's positive emotions evoked a significant change in the distant percipient, so this is a direction worth exploring. It is also much easier to recruit and retain human subjects in experiments using pleasant vs. unpleasant stimuli.

The search for the parapsychological Holy Grail — the trivially easy to replicate experiment — is unlikely to be established in the domain of emotion-psi research without paying close attention to individual differences. Both personality and baseline anxiety probably influence the degree to which emotion modulates attention. Thus, if one intends to use emotion as a psi modulator, it would be useful to partition percipients on the basis of their affective responses.

It is not yet clear whether attention overrides emotional processing, or vice versa, nor to what extent these modes of processing may interfere or be additive. Indeed, the distinction might be more semantic than substantive. But if focused attention can override emotional responses, then it should be possible to devise a psi-emotion experiment in which the psi effect is "switched" on and off via modulation of voluntary attention. Emotional responses also modulate memory and learning, suggesting that psi effects using emotional stimuli might show improved learning vs. using the same design with neutral stimuli.

In conclusion, the evidence from these classes of experiments suggests that we can sense others' emotions at a distance and our own emotions from the future. From an experimental perspective the fact that we can detect these emotions as psychophysiological fluctuations is not particularly surprising because emotions strongly push the body's autonomic and central nervous system in predictable ways. What is surprising is that the emotions are perceived in the first place. How this occurs remains an open and intriguing question.

ACKNOWLEDGMENTS

I am indebted to the Bial Foundation for generously supporting the electrogastrogram and pupil dilation experiments described in this paper, and for their continuing support of the field of parapsychology. I also thank Marilyn Schlitz, Dick Bierman, Edwin May, Russell Targ and Richard Shoup for many discussions about the design, analysis and interpretation of these experiments.

REFERENCES AND NOTES

1) Rhine, L.E. (1981) *The invisible picture: A study of psychic experiences.* Jefferson, NC: McFarland.
2) Feather, S. & Schmicker, M. (2006) *The gift: The extraordinary experiences of ordinary people.* NY: St. Martins Press.
3) Schouten, S.A. (1980) "Emotions as targets in ESP studies." In: *European Journal of Parapsychology,* 3, 264-283.
4) Lumsden-Cook, J. (2005) "Mind-matter and emotion." In: *Journal of the Society for Psychical Research,* 69. 1-17.
5) Besterman, T. (1933) "Report of inquiry into precognitive dreams." In: *Proceedings of the Society for Psychical Research,* 41, 186-204.
6) Gauld, A. & Cornell, T. (1979) *Poltergeists.* London: Routledge.

7) Dean, E.D. (1962) "The plethysmograph as an indicator of ESP." In: *Journal of the Society for Psychical Research*, 41, 351-353.
8) Dean, E.D. (1966) "Plethysmograph recordings as ESP responses." In: *International Journal of Neuropsychiatry*, 2, 439-446.
9) Haraldsson, E. (1980) "Confirmation of the percipient-order effect in a plethysmographic study of ESP." In: *Journal of Parapsychology*, 44, 105-124.
10) Schmidt, S., Schneider, R., Utts, J. & Walach, H. (2004) "Distant intentionality and the feeling of being stared at: Two meta-analyses." In: *British Journal of Psychology*, 95, 235-247.
11) Radin, D.I. & Schlitz, M.J. (2005) "Gut feelings, intuition, and emotions: An exploratory study." In: *Journal of Alternative and Complementary Medicine*, 11, 85-91.
12) Lang, P.J., Bradley, M.M., Cuthbert, B.N. (1999) *International affective picture system (IAPS): Technical manual and affective ratings*. Gainesville, Florida: University of Florida, Center for Research in Psychophysiology.
13) Bierman, D.J., Radin, D.I. (1997) "Anomalous anticipatory response on randomized future conditions." In: *Perceptual and Motor Skills*, 84: 689-690.
14) Vassy, Z. (1978) "Method of measuring the probability of 1-bit extrasensory information transfer between living organisms." In: *Journal of Parapsychology*. 1978: 43(2), 58-160.
15) Bierman, D.J., Radin, D.I. (1999) "Conscious and anomalous nonconscious emotional processes: A reversal of the arrow of time?" In: *Toward a Science of Consciousness*, Tucson III. Cambridge, MA: MIT Press. 367-386.
16) Radin, D.I. (1997) "Unconscious perception of future emotions: An experiment in presentiment." In: *Journal of Scientific Exploration*, 11: 163–180.
17) Wildey, C. (2001) *Impulse response of biological systems*. Master's Thesis, Department of Electrical Engineering, University of Texas at Arlington.
18) McCraty, R., Atkinson, M., Bradley, R.T. (2004) "Electrophysiological evidence of intuition: Part 2. A system-wide process?" In: *Journal of Alternative and Complementary Medicine*, 10: 325–336.
19) McCraty, R., Atkinson, M., Bradley, R.T. (2004) "Electrophysiological evidence of intuition: Part 1. The surprising role of the heart." In: *Journal of Alternative and Complementary Medicine*, 10: 133–143.
20) Parkhomtchouk, D.V., Kotake, J., Zhang, T., Chen, W., Kokubo, H., Yamamoto, M. (2002) "An attempt to reproduce the presentiment EDA response." In: *Journal of the International Society of Life Information Science*, 20 (1): 190-194.
21) Radin, D.I. (2004) "Electrodermal presentiments of future emotions." In: *Journal of Scientific Exploration*, 18: 253-274.
22) Spottiswoode, S.J.P., May, E.C. (2003) "Skin conductance prestimulus response: Analyses, artifacts and a pilot study." In: *Journal of Scientific Exploration*, 17: 617–641.
23) May, E.C., Paulinyi, T., Vassy, Z. (2005) "Anomalous anticipatory skin conductance response to acoustic stimuli: Experimental results and speculation about a mechanism." In: *Journal of Alternative and Complementary Medicine*, 11: 695-702
24) Levin, J., Kennedy, J. (1975) "The relationship of slow cortical potentials to psi information in man." In: *Journal of Parapsychology*, 39: 25-26.
25) Hartwell, J.W. (1978) "Contingent negative variation as an index of precognitive information." In: *European Journal of Parapsychology*, 83-102.
26) Radin, D.I., Lobach, E. (2007) "Toward understanding the placebo effect: Investigating a possible retrocausal factor." In: *Journal of Alternative and Complementary Medicine*, 13: 733–739.

27) Hinterberger T., Studer P., Jäger, M., Haverty-Stacke, C., Walach, H. (2007) "Can a slide-show presentiment effect be discovered in the brain electrical activity?" In: *Journal of the Society for Psychical Research*, 71: 148-166.
28) Bierman, D.J., Scholte, H.S. (2002) "Anomalous anticipatory brain activation preceding exposure of emotional and neutral pictures." Paper presented at *Toward a Science of Consciousness*, Tucson IV.
29) Jennings, J.R., van der Molen, M.W., Steinhauer, S.R. (1998) "Preparing the heart, eye, and brain: Foreperiod length effects in a non-aging paradigm." In: *Psychophysiology*, 35: 90-98.
30) Five of these experiments were student projects at the U of Edinburgh, as described in Watt, C. (2007) "A peek in the file-drawer: Review of 96 undergraduate student projects at the Koestler Parapsychology Unit." In: *Proceedings of Presented Papers*, 50th Annual Convention of the Parapsychological Association, Petaluma, CA: Parapsychological Association; 133-142.
31) Dalkvist, J., Westerlund, J., Bierman, D.J. (2002) "A computational expectation bias as revealed by simulations of presentiment experiments." In: *Proceedings of Presented Papers*, 45th Annual Convention of the Parapsychological Association, Cary, NC: Parapsychological Association, 62–79.
32) Steinhauer, S.R., Hakerem, G. (1992) "The pupillary response in cognitive psychophysiology and schizophrenia." In: Friedman, D., Bruder, G., Eds. *Psychophysiology and experimental psychopathology: A tribute to Samuel Sutton.* Annals of the New York Academy of Sciences; 658: 182-204.
33) Bitsios, P., Szabadi, E., Bradshaw, C.M. (2004) "The fear-inhibited light reflex: Importance of the anticipation of an aversive event." In: *International Journal of Psychophysiology*, 52: 87–95.
34) The randomized permutation technique estimates a p-value; an inverse normal function is used to obtain a z score.
35) Vuilleumier, P. (2005) "How brains beware: Neural mechanisms of emotional attention." In: *Trends in Cognitive Sciences*, 9, 587-594.
36) The experimenter is always another possible source of psi in these experiments.

Reality and How it Works

In our time, in our very years, is coming to be experienced a formula for new ways of being. What we are now coming to suspect about the way reality works grants a perspective on our humanity, which up till now would have seemed more mythic than real. This it does within a sturdy background of scientific research and years of conclusive studies by physicists, biologists, anthropologists, parapsychologists, spiritual seekers and just about anyone interested in opening themselves to the deeper reaches of human nature.

--- Jean Houston
--- Excerpts www.jeanhouston.com

CHAPTER 3   THE SCIENTIFIC STUDY OF ANOMALOUS DREAMS

Stanley Krippner, PhD

Stanley Krippner directed the Kent Sate University Child Study Center (Kent, OH), and the Maimonides Medical Center Dream Laboratory (Brooklyn, NY, 1964-1973) where he advanced the science of parapsychology substantially by joining Montague Ullman in studying anomalous dreams; they coauthored the classic book *Dream Telepathy: Experiments in Nocturnal ESP* in 1974. That same year he was invited to be the Alan Watts Professor of Psychology at Saybrook Graduate School and Research Center (SF, CA). He received Lifetime Achievement Awards from the Parapsychological Association (for his studies and experiments on anomalous effects in dreams) and from the International Association for the Study of Dreams. The Ashley Montagu Peace Award honored his writings on the psychological effects of war trauma on civilians, as well as his investigation of PTSD in US veterans of six wars. The American Psychological Association gave Krippner its 2002 award for Distinguished Contributions to the Advancement of International Psychology, which recognized his seminars in hypnosis, his fieldwork in shamanic practices, and his organization of conferences in humanistic and transpersonal psychology. He is "Distinguished Professor" in institutes in Mexico and Brazil, and "Lecturer" at Academies of Science in China and Russia, and has given workshops and seminars in 27 countries around the world.

Dr Krippner has authored, coauthored or edited over 40 books, and published hundreds of papers in scientific journals.

Website: http://www.Stanleykrippner.weebly.com/.

THE SCIENTIFIC STUDY OF ANOMALOUS DREAMS *[1]

Stanley Krippner

Anomalous dreams have been reported throughout history from various cultural groups throughout the world. Parapsychologists usually classify these dreams as "telepathic," "clairvoyant," and "precognitive," with considerable overlap. Together, reports of these three phenomena are referred to as possible "extrasensory perception" or ESP, in contrast to "psychokinesis" or PK, the alleged influence of volition on distant objects or events. All of these reported phenomena are "anomalous" in the sense that if verified, they are difficult to explain within the framework of modern science's concepts of time, space, and motion. As a result, scientists usually offer such explanations as coincidence, faulty memory, delusional thinking, self-fulfilling prophecies, unconscious sensory cues, and outright fraud. As a result, the attempt to verify or falsify these reports has been a crucial one for parapsychology and for interested scientists from other disciplines. As K. R. Rao (1978) has noted, parapsychological phenomena *"contradict...the basic limiting principles that are assumed to govern our cognitions and actions."* (p. 245)

For example, a survey of more than 7,000 self-reported anecdotal telepathic experiences was tabulated by Louisa Rhine (1961). Two out of three of these experiences were said to have occurred in dreams. But anecdotes of this nature are unreliable; by themselves they merely indicate that there are phenomena that deserve more rigorous scrutiny. An additional body of literature involves psychotherapists' reports of anomalous dream reports; Sigmund Freud observed such phenomena, Carl Jung often integrated them into psychotherapy, and Montague Ullman (1986) proposed a theoretical model for dreaming that encompassed them.

The first attempt to study anomalous dreams in a disciplined manner was made by G. B. Ermacora (1895) who worked with an Italian medium who attempted to influence the dreams of a child by telepathic (i. e., "mind-to-mind") communications. This attempt was flawed by contemporary standards because the child was the medium's cousin; however, it launched serious work in this area.

---

*[1] These excerpts are taken from Dr Krippner's original detailed studies of anomalous dreams.

THE MAIMONIDES EXPERIMENTS

In the 1960s, Ullman had the opportunity to organize a dream laboratory at the Maimonides Community Mental Health Center in Brooklyn, New York, where he served as the director. I joined Ullman shortly after these experiments were initiated; between 1966 and 1972, Ullman and his colleagues published over 100 research articles discussing these experiments in referred psychological and psychiatric journals. To reproduce the real life circumstances of the anomalous dream in a controlled laboratory setting, an agent (i.e., a person who attempted to influence the dreamer at a distance) and a research participant (i.e., a person who attempted to incorporate the distant target material into his or her dreams) were utilized. For clairvoyant and precognitive dream studies, the agent was not needed. For all three types of experiments, the target material most generally was an art print containing vivid, emotionally arousing material. Experimental procedures were developed that attempted to rule out sensory cues; statistical procedures were employed that attempted to rule out coincidence as an explanation for the correspondences between the dream reports and the target material.

When the research participant entered the dream laboratory for the night, electrodes were glued to his or her head for the monitoring of brain waves and rapid eye movement (REM) activity. Participants were awakened during REM activity in order to harvest dream reports, which were tape recorded and transcribed. Judges, who were never present during the experimental sessions, attempted blind matchings of the dream transcripts and the pool of target material from which one art print had been randomly selected once the research participant had entered the soundproof room for the duration of the night. We developed these procedures to imitate the emotion and interpersonal connections that mark most of the spontaneous cases reported by Rhine and the psychotherapists, but putting them into a laboratory setting where various controls could be implemented.

To evaluate whether or not our target/transcript correspondences were due to chance, we sent copies of the dream reports and post-sleep associations to three outside judges who worked blind and independently. All judges had worked previously with dream reports and/or with "free response" parapsychological material (in which the variety of potential targets is unlimited rather than circumscribed). Each judge was sent copies or duplicate sets of the targets used in the study; no judge was sent the actual target that had been used as it might have been possible that a smudge or written note on the picture would have cued the judge that someone had been concentrating upon that particular item. The averages of the judges' evaluations were used as data for statistical analysis.

Some critics of our work have admitted that they are baffled by the results. For example, Hyman (1986) states that *"attempts to replicate the Maimonides research have either failed or provided questionable results."* He grants, *"Many of the parapsychologists have been well trained in one of the sciences.... They...know how to produce appropriately controlled and analyzed experiments. A fair and honest review of their reports indicates that they are more sophisticated and 'scientific' than many of their critics give them credit for."* Hyman concludes, *"Something peculiar, in my opinion, is going on. But I do not believe it has anything to do with PK or ESP. Rather, I think it will turn out that there are subtle and previously unknown ways that humans, no matter how sincere and dedicated, can become convinced of things that are not so"* (pp. 91-92).

I disagree with the tenor of Hyman's conclusions but agree with him that "something peculiar" is going on. Unconscious bias appears to play an important role in human behavior, even among individuals with scientific training. Both those sympathetic to the psi hypothesis and those who are skeptical are vulnerable to bias, and this fact alone justifies the importance of studying presumptively anomalous phenomena. We do not completely understand how bias operates but there is ample evidence that interpersonal expectancy effects play an important role in the study of human behavior (Rosenthal & Rubin, 1978). As the Parapsychological Association has stated, *"A commitment to the study of psi phenomena does not require assuming the reality of 'non-ordinary' factors or processes. Regardless of what form the final explanations may take, however, the study of these phenomena is likely to expand our understanding of the processes often referred to as 'consciousness' and 'mind' and of the nature of disciplined inquiry (e.g., the effect of the investigator upon the phenomenon being investigated)." (8)* There is a possibility that psi may turn out to be hitherto undetected interpersonal expectancy effects, subtle statistical artifacts of which we are currently unaware, and/or extended sense perceptions that have eluded our attempts at sensory shielding. Personally, I doubt that the anomalous effects we observed at Maimonides could be explained in this fashion. Yet, if these explanations did suffice, parapsychological researchers would deserve credit for enhancing the understanding of behavior and experience. In the meantime, there is no lack of theoretical models (e. g., cognitive, psychodynamic, electromagnetic, quantum mechanical) that can be utilized to generate hypotheses that are both testable and falsifiable (Rao, 1978; Stokes, 1987). Ullman (1986), for example, has subsumed psi effects in his vigilance theory of dreaming.

The scientific study of anomalous dreams has played a small but vital role in parapsychological inquiry and the search for knowledge. Perhaps this database will be a continuing source of material for serious researchers who are attempting to encompass the study of anomalous phenomena within the scientific enterprise.

REFERENCES

1) Ermacora, G.B. (1895) "Telepathic dreams experimentally induced." In: *Proceedings, Society for Psychical Research*, 11, 235-308.
2) Hyman, R. (1986) "Maimonides dream-telepathy experiments." In: *Skeptical Inquirer*, 11(1), 91-92.
3) Rao, K.R. (1978) "Theories of psi." In: S. Krippner (Ed.), *Advances in Parapsychological Research: Vol. 2.* (pp. 245-295). NY: Plenum.
4) Rhine, L.E. (1961) *Hidden Channels of the Mind.* NY: Sloane.
5) Rosenthal, R. & Rubin, D.B. (1978) "Interpersonal expectancy effects: The first 345 studies." In: *Behavioral and Brain Sciences*, 3, 377-415.
6) Stokes, D.M. (1987) "Theoretical parapsychology." In: S. Krippner (Ed.), *Advances in Parapsychological Research: Vol. 5.* (pp. 77-189).
7) Ullman, M. (1986) "Vigilance theory and psi. Part II: Physiological, psychological, and parapsychological aspects." In: *Journal of the American Society for Psychical Research*, 80, 375-390.

As I began studying psi, I was compelled to explore the main body of physics and reconcile it with psychic phenomena. After I pondered this issue, <u>I had a dream</u> in which I saw what is called the Minkowski space-time metric in a hyperdimensional space. I saw that a hyperdimensional geometry was necessary to explain precognition. I knew from my dream I had the correct answer.... The dream led to my complex eight-space model of psychic phenomena in Chapter 27.

<u>I had another dream</u> about the stress energy tensor and Einstein field equations. I saw an equation for force where $F = c^4 / G$. I felt that this force term was very significant in describing cosmogenesis. This vision ultimately resulted in ten years of research, numerous publications, and a textbook. On awakening, I was sure it was correct.

--- E.A. Rauscher

NATIONAL AND GENDER DIFFERENCES IN REPORTS OF EXTRAORDINARY DREAMS

Stanley Krippner

In the English language, one of the definitions of the word *"extraordinary"* is *"beyond what is common or usual."* This term can be applied to those dreams that are so rarely reported that they resemble *"extraordinary"* specimens of plants, animals, or gemstones. (12) Despite their unusual nature, dreamers often find extraordinary dreams filled with meaning and direction.

Among these unusual, extraordinary dreams are *creative dreams* that assist dreamers' attempts to solve problems or bring something new into being. Also extraordinary are those dreams described as *"lucid."* In *lucid dreams,* in which the dreamer is aware that he or she is dreaming while the dream is going on, sometimes the dreamer can change the direction of these dreams in ways that are entertaining and instructive.

Healing dreams can alert the dreamer to an oncoming health problem or can give suggestions as to preventive or remedial action. Dreams within dreams are extraordinary because the dreamer has a dream or dream-like experience within the dream. Dreamers may dream about having a dream, or about having a vision, drug experience, or other dream-like episode. In *out-of-body dreams,* dreamers have the sensation of leaving their body while the dream is going on; sometimes this impression persists upon awakening and they have an impression that they are floating near the ceiling of their room for a few seconds.

In *telepathic dreams* it is the dreamer's impression that a dream correctly identified the thoughts of someone in waking life at the time of the dream. *Mutual dreams* are those in which the dreamer and someone else report having had similar dreams on the same night. *Clairvoyant dreams* concern distant events about which the dreamer has had no ordinary way of obtaining information.

In *precognitive dreams,* a dream is said to provide information about an event that has not taken place at the time of the dream. A *past-life dream* concerns past events in which the dreamer participated, but with a different identity than characterizes his or her current life. Some of these dreams are said to include events that the dreamer would not have known about unless they had been there at the time.

Initiation dreams introduce the dreamer to a new worldview, or a new mission in life. Sometimes these dreams take place in the interior of an unidentified flying object; sometimes they involve being admitted to membership in a secret society; sometimes they are a "call" to a new vocational path—such as one concerned with spiritual healing, protecting the Earth, or fighting for social betterment. In *visitation dreams,* the dreamer is greeted by ancestors, spirits, or deities, and is given messages or counsel by them.

PURPOSE

The purpose of this study was to investigate the incidence of a selected number of extraordinary dreams from a large sample of dream reports. What is extraordinary in one culture might not be especially strange in another culture, and what is extraordinary for one gender may be less extraordinary for the other gender. Studies of spontaneous ostensible psi experiences indicate cross-cultural differences in the incidence of such reports. (e. g., 11, 15, 16) In addition, a number of studies indicate that gender, age, education, religion, ethnic background and socioeconomic status influence the likelihood of reporting unusual experiences. (13) It was hoped that this study would expand the cross-cultural literature of dreams and the data regarding gender and dream reports to include those dream reports that can be described as extraordinary.

PROCEDURE

The research participants for this study were members of dream seminars that I conducted between 1990 and 1998. These events were held in various parts of Argentina, Brazil, Russia, Japan, Ukraine, and the United States. The age span ranged from people in their 20s to their 70s (as determined from registration information and informal conversations), with a few individuals even younger or older. Middle and upper-middle income groups were over-represented because there were entrance fees for most of the seminars; however, a few scholarships were available for lower income individuals. Because most of the events were held at colleges, universities, and cultural centers, the educational level of the participants was higher than would have been found in the general population. Many ethnic groups were represented in the sample. Dreams of expatriates were excluded from this study.

It was ascertained, whenever possible, that research participants had lived for at least three years in the country to which they were assigned for comparative purposes. Only one dream from each of the research participants was utilized. There were 212 dream reports (111 female, 101 male) from Argentina, 239 (136 female, 103 male) from Brazil, 136 (66 female, 70 male) from Japan, 245 (140 female, 105 male) from Russia, 204 (104 female, 100 male) from Ukraine, and 630 (353 female, 277 male) from the United States. The total number of dreams collected for analysis was 1,666 — 910 from women and 756 from men.

LIMITATIONS

These samples had particular characteristics that were both advantageous and disadvantageous for a study of gender and national differences. The participants were self-selected. This fact limits the generalizability of our findings. Even though participants were merely asked for a "recent dream," it is possible that they selected an especially extraordinary, dramatic, or puzzling dream, hoping it would be selected for group discussion. But it is also possible that they selected an ordinary dream that would not be personally revealing. Therefore, no claim is made that these dreams are representative of this sample.

The samples were not directly comparable. The Ukraine sample was largely composed of university students while the samples from the United States and Argentina were almost entirely professional workers. The samples from the United States and Brazil were distributed from around the country, while those from Argentina and Japan represented large urban centers.

Hall and Van de Castle (10) obtained 5 dreams from each of their 200 research participants in an attempt to counter selectivity. (4) It was not possible to follow this practice in the current investigation, and so the possibility of selectivity is a serious limitation of this study.

DELIMITATIONS

This study was delimited to self-selected participants from six countries. No attempt was made to generalize these findings to the population of these countries as a whole, or to other parts of the world.

This study was also delimited to only twelve types of extraordinary dreams, those discussed by Krippner and de Carvalho (12) in their book by the same name. There are other dream categories that could be described as "fascinating," "unfamiliar," and "enticing," and perhaps this study will encourage future investigation of them. Examples would include sexual dreams, incubated dreams, and "numinous" dreams, i.e., those in which there is an encounter with *"that which is beyond the sphere of the usual, the intelligible, and the familiar."* (2, p. 2)

It was kept in mind that these were dream reports, not the experienced dreams themselves.

Any number of distortions and omissions can occur between the time a dream is experienced and the time the dream is reported. As a result, I made no attempt to determine whether a purported clairvoyant dream actually matched the event in waking life about which the dreamer claimed to dream. No attempt was made to verify precognitive or telepathic dreams. These attempts have been made under controlled conditions (e.g., 22), but were considered beyond the scope of this study.

SCORING GUIDELINES

For a dream report to be scored as a creative dream an actual problem from waking life had to be solved or a new product had to be brought into actuality. There are various degrees of lucidity in lucid dreams, but to be scored as such the dream report had to specifically state that the dreamer was aware that he or she was dreaming before awakening from the dream.

To be scored as a healing dream, the dream report had to contain a statement that the dream content assisted in ameliorating or preventing physical, emotional, or spiritual distress at a point in time following the dream experience. To be scored as a dream within a dream, the dream report mentioned entering a different state of consciousness within the dream itself, or appearing to wake up from the dream only to discover that the dream was still going on.

To be scored as an out-of-body dream, the dreamer needed to report the sensation of leaving his or her body while the dream was going on. For scoring as a telepathic dream, the dreamer claimed that a dream matched the mental content of a distant person in external reality; in the latter instance, there was a purported match that was confirmed sometime after the dreamer awoke. For a dream report to be scored as a mutual or shared dream, the dreamer and someone else claimed that they had experienced similar dreams on the same night. These dreams have apparent telepathic elements but were scored as mutual dreams, not telepathic dreams, for the purpose of this study.

For a dream report to be scored as a clairvoyant dream, it needed to match a distant event, and that a purported confirmation of this match was made during wakefulness. A precognitive dream report was one that provided specific information about a future event that purportedly matched information later gleaned about that event. To be scored as a past-life dream, the dreamer had to report taking on a different identity than his or her ordinary identity, one subjectively associated with a purported former lifetime or "incarnation."

To be scored as an initiation dream, the dream report had to describe the introduction of the dreamer to a nonordinary reality, to membership in an esoteric social group, or to a previously unexplored vocational path; in each case, this initiation needed to be agreeable and meaningful.

It is not unusual for people to dream about dead friends and relatives, but to be scored as a visitation dream, the deceased person or an entity from another reality had to provide counsel or direction that the dreamer found of comfort or value.

When a dream contained elements of two categories, it was scored for both categories; for tabulation purposes, half a point was given for each category.

RESULTS

The results of this study appear in Table 1. There were 4.5 (0.3% of the total dream reports) creative dreams, 28.5 (1.7%) lucid, 3 (0.2%) healing, 9.5 (0.6%) dreams within dreams, 24 (1.4%) out-of-body, 2 (0.1%) telepathic, 2 (0.1%) shared, 5 (0.3%) clairvoyant, 17 (1.0%) precognitive, 5.5 (0.3%) past-life, 15 (0.9%) initiation, and 19 (1.1%) visitation dreams.

Table 1. The Incidence of Extraordinary Dream Reports Listed by Dreamer's Country and Gender (presented as percentages of the total dream reports for respective country and gender)

	ARGENTINA		BRAZIL		JAPAN		RUSSIA		UKRAINE		USA	
	F	M	F	M	F	M	F	M	F	M	F	M
Creative	0	1.0	0	1.0	0.8	0	0	0	0	1.0	0.3	0
Lucid	2.7	1.0	2	1.5	0	0	2.1	3.3	0	1.0	1.3	2.9
Healing	0	0	0	0	0	0	0.7	0	0	0	0.6	0
Within dream	0.9	0	0.7	1.0	1.5	0	0.7	1.4	0	2.0	0	0.4
Out-of-body	2.7	2.0	1.1	3.4	1.5	1.4	2.9	1.0	1.0	1.0	1.1	0.4
Telepathic	0	0	1.5	0	0	0	0	0	0	0	0	0
Shared	0	0	0	0	3.0	0	0	0	0	0	0	0
Clairvoyant	0.9	0	0	0	0	0	0	2.9	0	0	0.3	0
Precognitive	0	3.0	0	0	1.5	2.8	0.7	2.9	1.0	1.0	0.8	0.7
Past-life	0	0	1.1	0	1.5	0	0.7	0.9	0	0	0.3	0
Initiation	0.9	0	2.9	2.9	0	0	0	2.9	1.0	0	0.6	0.4
Visitation	1.8	1.0	1.5	1.0	2.3	0	2.9	0	1.9	1.0	1.3	0

Female dreamers reported 77 extraordinary dreams (8.5% of all female dream reports), while male dreamers reported 58 extraordinary dreams (7.7% of all male reports).

The country with the highest percentage of extraordinary dreams was Russia (12.7%), followed by Brazil (10.9%), Argentina (8.6%), Japan (8.1%), Ukraine (5.9%), and the United States (5.7%). It would be tempting to offer explanations for these differences, but the lack of standardization among sample populations forestalls this option.

Data from an additional analysis of reported ESP-type (i.e., telepathic, clairvoyant and precognitive) 24 dream reports (1.4% of total reports) regarding the type of event in the dream and the relationship between the dreamer and the target person (i.e., the person to whom the ostensible psi message refers) by country are presented in Tables 2 and 3 respectively.

Table 2. Type of Event in Reported ESP-Type Dreams by Country

	Death/Serious Illness/Injury	Trivial Event	Positive Event
Argentina	2	2	0
Brazil	2	a	a
Japan	a	2	1
Russia	1	5	1
Ukraine	1	a	1
USA	3	2	1
Total	9	11	4

Table 3. Target Person in Reported ESP-Type Dreams by Country

	Personal (Self)	Family	Friend/Acquaintance	Stranger/Impersonal
Argentina	a	1	1	2
Brazil	a	a	2	a
Japan	1	1	1	a
Russia	a	2	3	2
Ukraine	a	2	a	a
USA	3	a	2	1
Total	4	6	9	5

The term "ESP-type dreams" is used here conditionally, because by definition ESP may be involved in other types of psi-related dreams as well. However, the dreams scored as telepathic, clairvoyant and precognitive are amenable to such an analysis, while other types of psi-related dreams discussed in this study are not.

As seen from Table 2, ESP-type dreams included four positive events, a rarity in existing surveys of psi-related dreams. Twenty dreams were either negative or trivial (i.e., related to insignificant, commonplace events), echoing Priestly's (1964) statement that dreams about future events tend to be either "terrible" or "trivial." Table 3 shows that, in over half of the ESP-type dreams, purported psi messages referred to the dreamers' friends and acquaintances, strangers and impersonal events, while only one-quarter of the ESP-type dreams involved the dreamers' family members. These findings are tentative due to a small number of ESP-type dreams in this sample.

EXAMPLES

One of the dreamers whose dream report was scored as a creative dream was a Japanese woman: My father, who died in World War II, appears to me. He gives me advice about my artwork. He gives me specific advice on what to paint and how to do it. He tells me the topics, what brushes to use, and what colors to use. *(When I wake up, I follow his advice, and I sell the pictures!)*

An Argentine woman reported a lucid dream: I was passing through a large house with my two daughters.... We went into a salon, which was a part of the complex. It was very modern with windows that opened into a garden where there was an arbor of trees. Suddenly I encountered a door to a workshop and saw a student walking down a long corridor.... When I arrived at this corridor, I realized that I was sleeping and dreaming. I was totally aware of this during the rest of the dream.

Another Argentine woman submitted a dream report that was scored as an out-of-body dream: It was almost twilight. I was suspended from something white. It seemed to be near a cloud. I steered into that part of the cloud, and the movement enabled me to get out, surging out of the center of my body and surging with a high velocity until I was able to observe the scene below. I did not like the sensations. I perceived a man I had known before the dream. My impulse was to go toward him, but my velocity was so strong that my hope of seeing him more closely disappeared. *(I was frightened when I woke up.)*

A Russian woman rendered a report that was scored as a healing dream: In my dream, I'm walking along the road and see a man coming toward me. When he comes closer, I recognize him. He is my husband. We look at each other carefully. Suddenly, a small black snake appears and bites me on the right side of my neck. I squeeze it with three fingers and it opens its mouth. I squeeze the poison out of it, and try to find a place to put the snake. I find a glass box and open it with great difficulty. I put the snake in. *(When I wake up, I am still squeezing my hands. But that action decreases my recurring headaches. I still use that squeeze when I have headaches, but they have almost disappeared.)*

A Brazilian woman reported a dream-within-a-dream: I dream that I see an Indian man who is running. He has a knife in his hand, and is being chased by a leopard. I watch him fight with the leopard and I am frightened. But then I stop being a witness and become the Indian in the exact moment that the leopard jumps on him. I think I wake up, and recall the dream, but actually I am still in the dream. But this time I am the leopard and I attack the Indian!

Another Brazilian woman dreamed: A man told me he was interested in the course I teach on neurolinguistic programming. He said that there were going to be many changes in his life, and that he would take the course so that I could help him out. The man seemed to be the brother of a woman I know, and he said he was dying of cancer. *(Later, I talked with this woman and described the man in my dream. The description fit her brother exactly, and he does have cancer.)* This was scored as a telepathic dream.

Two Japanese women reported dreams from the same night; these were scored as mutual dreams. The first woman dreamed: I am in the lobby of a big hotel. There is a large pillar made of marble. My friend Aiko is there and I stab her with a knife. I don't know why I stab her. Nobody seems to notice what I have done.

The second woman reported: I am in a hotel lobby. There is a big pillar there and I am standing by it. My younger sister comes in. She walks right up to me and stabs me with a knife. My younger sister's name is Tomoko. I died from the stabbing.

The dream report of a Russian man was scored as a clairvoyant dream: I am in an empty room.... I try to pass through the wall. It is solid and I cannot go through it. This wall divided two spaces.... There is a slogan on the wall, "If you are brave, come through it." Mr. Gorin, a business associate of mine, appears. Then I wake up. *(Later, I ask Mr. Gorin if I can visit his house. When I enter, I see the same wall-but with no slogan on it.)*

An American woman's dream was scored as precognitive: I had a vivid precognitive dream about a valued colleague. I dreamed that he was rushed in an ambulance, to the hospital with heart trouble, even though he was in good health the last time I saw him. But when I called the hospital–in the dream–they told me that he was in bad shape and they were preparing him for immediate surgery. *(When I woke up, I telephoned and he told me he was preparing to enter the hospital for major heart surgery.)*

A Russian man's report was scored as an initiation dream: I dreamed about some deities who told me that I needed to transform myself to become a healer. It seemed as if I had died, and then I was reborn again. The deities told me that I needed to advance one more level, to learn about external kindness but also to be kind to myself. Once I learned this lesson, I would be able to start healing people. I went through three cycles of death and rebirth, and when I awakened, I felt that my initiation was complete.

A Brazilian woman dreamed: I'm in a bedroom and I look at a man who is kneeling by a bed that is between the two of us. He doesn't look at me. Then I say to myself that he doesn't care about me as a person, he only wants sex from me. So I am about to go away when he asks me if I am going to see a doctor. Before I can answer him, he says that it is no use to see a doctor because there is no treatment for what is wrong with me. He asks me if I want to know why I am so ashamed. I say "yes" and he says, "dive in me to see your life before this one." So I kneel by the bed in front of him, go out of my body, and dive into his chest. At this moment, I am upside down and in a dark area. I feel a stroke on my back at the heart level and realize that I am in another life. In this past life, I wanted to hurt a man. To provoke him, I got into an accident and paralyzed myself. So I was in a wheelchair. I couldn't move and had no control of the lower part of my body. *(And that is why I am still ashamed of that part of my body and that area of my life.)* This report was scored as a past-life dream.

A Ukrainian woman reported: In this dream, I am afraid of dying because my neighbors start to die, one by one. I think of what a short period of time it took for so many of them to die, both men and women. I would like to live a more spiritual life, but the conditions around me do not permit it, as I must work very hard each day. Then one of my dead neighbors comes to see me and tells me that I can lead a spiritual life through my work. This was scored as a visitation dream.

Sometimes dreams represent two categories. A Brazilian man dreamed: I was sleeping when I suddenly awoke. I was thirsty and went to the door. When I reached it, I looked behind me and saw my own body lying there on the bed. But I went to the kitchen to get some water. When I was passing through the hall, I suddenly saw three women and two men walking in the yard. They were talking and laughing. I thought they were thieves so I ran to the laundry room to close the doors and windows to keep them from entering the house. The woman seemed to be the leader. She saw me, and suddenly all of them passed through the wall and got into the kitchen. I was scared, but decided to talk with them. Their clothes were colorful and bright. One man wore blue jeans. The leader's clothes were old-fashioned. They said they were only passing through. They had to help the family of the man in jeans. I asked if there was life after death; she said there was no death. She had lived a long time ago. They communicated telepathically. I saw that she was pregnant. She said pregnancy was completely natural, but the time was different. She said they lived in a peaceful, beautiful place, and asked me not to tell anyone about this matter. I tried to avoid saying goodbye but they needed to go. When they disappeared, I felt a different energy in the air. I could not keep this secret. It was too exciting. This was scored both as a dream-within-a-dream and as an out-of-body dream.

DISCUSSION

An inspection of the examples suggests that some extraordinary dreams fall into more than one category. The Japanese woman who dreamed about her father giving her advice about her painting put his suggestions into practice with positive results. Hence, this report qualifies as a creative dream, a category accurately described as "rare" by the psychiatrist Jules Eisenbud. (9, p. 254) However, it was also scored as a visitation dream because her father, dead at the time of the dream, gave valuable counsel to the dreamer. The Brazilian woman who dreamed about a man who resembled the brother of a friend discovered that he actually was suffering from cancer, just as in the dream. This report was scored as telepathic instead of clairvoyant because of the communication described in the dream. Even under laboratory conditions, it is often difficult to separate purported telepathic effects from purported clairvoyant effects.

It is possible that telepathic, clairvoyant, and precognitive dreams represent coincidental matches, unless they are gathered under tightly controlled conditions or include extremely precise descriptive material. A precognitive dream may also represent a premonition, i.e., that it gives one a chance to actually change the future, as if the dreamed events do not have to happen or can be modified in some way. In other words, some precognitive dreams appear to represent mutable premonitions (warnings) rather than immutable "destiny," over which one does not seem to have much control. Some evidence does point to a possibility of the dreamer's intervention to prevent the event he or she was "forewarned" about. For example, in her study of spontaneous (self-reported) ostensibly precognitive dream and waking experiences, Louisa E. Rhine (18) selected 191 apparently precognitive experiences in which people attempted to prevent a foreseen event from taking place. In 131 cases (69%) people were successful in taking steps to avoid the undesirable consequences of whatever appeared to have been "foretold" in their experiences. In our database of dream reports, we have found that even if the dreamer is convinced that they are premonitory in nature, dreams about death do not always have a tragic ending.

A Ukrainian man dreamed: **I saw a funeral procession. Many people had come for this funeral. Close relatives went in a file by the coffin of the dead person. I got in line. When I went by the coffin, I was really scared because it was my mother who was lying in the coffin!** *(In two days my mother fell seriously ill, but she recovered.)*

Several precognitive dreams involved positive events, which appear to have appreciable (perhaps life-long) significance to the dreamer, as the following dream of a Ukrainian woman: **I am sitting at the mirror, speculating about the future. In the mirror I see a glass of water. On the bottom of it I notice a ring. There are two men standing on the ring. One of them is taller and one is shorter. I am acquainted with the short man. He is looking at me.** *(In a few months we were engaged to be married in waking life!)* This dream involves a cultural symbol divination with a glass of water, a mirror placed on the bottom of the glass and a ring placed on the mirror is a widespread folk tradition in Russia and the Ukraine.

Some precognitive dreams reportedly resulted in the dreamer's practical gain. A Japanese man dreamed: **I am at a dog racetrack, about to watch the dog races. I see the numbers "1-78." I see these numbers on the scoreboard. I think that perhaps I should bet on these numbers. I see a man at a betting stand and walk over in that direction.** *(In my waking life, I went to the dog racetrack and bet on "1-7-8." Then I actually won $500.00. I often have dreams that come true in my waking life.)*

As shown in Table 3, about 17 percent of reported ESP-type dreams involved positive events and nearly 46 percent were related to trivial occurrences — a much higher percentage than was reported in collections of spontaneous psi experiences (21, p. 35), although the total number of ESP-type dream reports is too small to warrant definite conclusions. Still, the prevalence of trivial events in our sample is consistent with Rhine's (19) hypothesis that a barrier between the unconscious and conscious mind is relaxed in the dream state, allowing more trivial psi messages (as compared to emotionally charged premonitions of negative events — death, serious illness, or injury) to emerge into consciousness.

Not all extraordinary dreams are pleasant. The Argentine woman who reported an out-of-body dream said that she "did not like the sensations," that she could not control the velocity of her travel, and that she "was frightened" when she awakened. Some precognitive dreams leave dreamers with a sense of dread. But in other cases, dreamers are grateful that they were prepared for a tragic event, or relieved when the event does not occur.

In the meantime, there are several books, most of them popular rather than professional, which discuss extraordinary dreams (e.g., 8, 23), including creative dreams (3), lucid dreams (5), healing dreams (1, 6); mutual dreams (14) and precognitive dreams. (20) Kelly Bulkeley's (2) book *Spiritual Dreaming* contains separate chapters on creative dreams, lucid dreams, healing dreams, precognitive dreams, initiation dreams and visitation dreams.

This study has shown that Russian participants reported twice as high incidence of extraordinary dreams as dreamers from the United States, while the difference between percentages of extraordinary dreams reported by Brazilian and Argentine participants was relatively small. On the other hand, the percentage of extraordinary dreams in the Ukraine was much closer to that in the United States rather than in Russia, despite the geographic proximity of Ukraine and Russia. The question arises as to what characteristics of a particular culture may be associated with the incidence of extraordinary dreams. It is of interest that Joseph Glicksohn (7) found a correlation between participants' belief systems and the incidence of occurrence of various types of unusual subjective experiences, such as lucid dreaming and out-of-body experience. In this connection, cultural belief systems appear to be the most likely parameters to be explored in future studies about the consequences of extraordinary dreams.

Finally it should be noted that female dreamers reported more extraordinary dreams than did male dreamers. Do women actually have more of these dreams, or are they simply more able to recall them and more willing to report them? Those questions, among others, need to be addressed in future studies.

REFERENCES

1) Barasch, M.I. (2000) *Healing Dreams: Exploring the dreams that can transform your life.* NY: Riverhead/Penguin.
2) Bulkeley, K. (1995) *Spiritual Dreaming: A cross-cultural and historical journey.* Mahwah, NJ: Paulist Press.
3) Delaney, G. (1991) *Breakthrough Dreaming.* NY: Bantam Books.
4) Domhoff, W.C. (1997) *Finding Meaning in Dreams.* NY: Plenum.
5) Gackenbach, J. & Bosveld, J. (1989) *Control Your Dreams.* NY: Harper & Row.
6) Garfield, P. (1991) *The Healing Power Of Dreams.* NY: Simon & Schuster.
7) Glicksohn, J. (1990) "Belief in the paranormal and subjective paranormal experience." In: *Personality and Individual Differences,* 11(7), 675-683
8) Guiley, R.E. (1998) *Dream Work For The Soul: A spiritual guide to dream interpretation.* NY: Berkeley Books.
9) Eisenbud, J. (1973) "Appendix A." In: M. Ullman & S. Krippner with A. Vaughan, *Dream Telepathy* (pp. 253-259). NY: McMillan.
10) Hall, C. & Van de Castle, R. (1966) *The Content Analysis Of Dreams.* NY: Appleton Century Crofts.
11) Haraldsson, E. & Houtkooper, J.M. (1991) "Psychic experiences in the multinational human values study: Who reports them?" In: *Journal of the American Society for Psychical Research,* 85, 145165.
12) Krippner, S. & de Carvalho, A.P. (1998) *Sonhos Exoticos [Exotic Dreams].* Sao Paulo: Summus.
13) MacDonald, W.L. (1994) "The popularity of paranormal experiences in the United States." In: *Journal of American Culture,* 1, 35-42.
14) Magallon, L.L. (1997) *Mutual Dreaming: When two or more people share the same dream.* NY: Pocket Books.
15) McClenon, J. (1990) "A preliminary report on African-American anomalous experiences in northeast North Carolina." In: *Parapsychology Review,* 21(1), 1-4.
16) McClenon, J. (1994) "Surveys of anomalous experiences: A cross cultural study." In: *Journal of the American Society for Psychical Research,* 88, 117-135.
17) Priestly, J.B. (1964) *Man and Time.* Garden City, NY: Doubleday.
18) Rhine, L.E. (1955) "Precognition and intervention." In: *Journal of Parapsychology,* 19, 1-34.
19) Rhine, L.E. (1981) *The Invisible Picture: A study of psychic experiences.* Jefferson, NC: McFarland.
20) Ryback, D. with Sweitzer, L. (1988) *Dreams That Come True.* NY: Dolphin/Doubleday.
21) Stokes, D.M. (1997) "Spontaneous psi phenomena." In: S. Krippner (Ed.), *Advances in parapsychological research.* (Vol 8, pp. 6-87) Jefferson, NC: McFarland.
22) Ullman, M. & Krippner, S. with Vaughan, A. (1989). *Dream Telepathy: Experiments in nocturnal ESP (2nd ed.).* Jefferson, NC: McFarland.
23) Van de Castle, R.L. (1994) *Our Dreaming Mind.* NY: Ballantine.

CHAPTER 5   SYNTONICS – OPTOMETRIC PHOTOTHERAPY

Ray Gottlieb, OD, PhD

Ray Gottlieb received his Optometry Degree from the UC School of Optometry in 1964 and a PhD in 1978 in humanistic science from Saybrook U Graduate College of Psychology and Humanistic Studies, SF, CA (Dissertation: *A Neuropsychology of Myopia*). In 1976 he invented an exercise for reversing and preventing presbyopia. These are available on a DVD at his website. The title is *The Read without Glasses Method*. In the 1980s he founded the Eye Gym in Santa Monica, where members of all ages learned to expand their ability to see more, correct their near-sightedness and focus attention. Even people with ADHD learned to improve, because as he discovered, "With practice and patience, lasting changes take place deep in the brain, in the chemistry and physiology of attention." Now he writes and lectures around the world on vision improvement, light therapy and education. He is an internationally known optometrist, who specializes in vision training and Syntonic Phototherapy to prevent and rehabilitate eye problems and brain injury and to improve and expand vision and brain performance in children and older adults. Since 1984, he has been the Dean of the College of Syntonic Optometry. Between 1983 and 1991, he was research editor for the *Brain/Mind Bulletin*.

Dr Gottlieb has been on the piano faculty of the Chautauqua Institution, Chautauqua, NY, since 1993, where he applies his vision training approach to help college and postgraduate piano students improve their learning and attention skills. He is the author of *Attention and Memory Training: Stress-point learning on the trampoline* and coauthor with his wife Rebecca Penneys of *The Fundamentals of Flow in Learning Music*.

Website: www/withoutglasses.com

SYNTONICS
Optometric Phototherapy

Ray Gottlieb

> Is there light in the brain? Yes, there is, according to scientists who've shown that DNA radiates measurable levels of coherent light, (1) and that photic energy can travel through brain matter outside of nerve pathways without dispersing or losing coherence. (2) As Richard Lipkin of Science News stated it: "As a means of carrying signals from one place to another nothing beats light. Fast and frictionless, photons trounce electrons as the ideal carriers of information."

Optometric phototherapy – <u>Syntonics</u> (3, 4, 5) – uses colored light, delivered through the eyes, as a fast-acting, non-invasive treatment for ocular and nervous disorders including stroke, traumatic brain injury, cognitive decline, learning and attention problems, mood and affective disturbances, strabismus and ocular pathology. Therapy devices use a white light source shined through colored absorption filters onto a frosted lens. Patients see a glowing dot of light 50mm in diameter from a distance of 50cm in a darkened room. They look at the colors for 20 minutes, once a day for three to five consecutive days per week, usually for a total of twenty sessions.

Specific colors prescriptions are based on the patient's medical history, symptom profile, and clinical measurements. Success of treatment is judged by improvements in signs and symptoms, personal and social behavior (mood/attitude, coping ability, and social/verbal skills), performance (academic, athletic and expressive) and functional vision test results. The most common syntonic diagnostic and treatment protocols are organized as syndromes called "Lazy Eye"; "Acute"; "Emotional Fatigue"; and "Chronic" and are treated respectively using red/orange, blue/green, deep red and yellow/green filter combinations.

Of special importance in syntonics are measurements of eye pupil fatigue and collapsed visual fields. Normally pupils constrict and stay small for at least ten seconds when tested by shining sustained light into the eye as the patient looks into the distance in a dim room. Fatigued pupils constrict but appear to fatigue and widen within a few seconds, even under sustained bright light stimulation. Pupil fatigue is not uncommon, especially in children showing weakness in functional optometric tests and in emotionally stressed, toxic or post-trauma patients. The severity of release (sluggish response, short latency dilation) correlates with reduced visual fields and autonomic nervous system imbalance.

Visual fields measure the awareness and sensitivity of central and peripheral vision of each eye as the patient looks at a central target. Blind areas are diagnostic for pathology due to damaged retina, vision tracks or visual cortex following retinal degeneration, glaucoma, brain tumor, retinal detachment, stroke, or head trauma. These are almost always permanent losses.

Visual fields can also be constricted because of fatigue, toxic, nutritional or emotional or physical distress. These patients often present with a history of head trauma, high fever or birth or pregnancy difficulties. Nerve tissue in these cases has not been destroyed but is stressed physiologically due to poor oxygen, edema, toxic or metabolic imbalance. These are called functional field constrictions. The patient looks with one eye covered at a central fixation spot. The practitioner monitors the patient's fixation while moving a small target from the periphery towards the center. The patient indicates when they first see the target. Syntonic practitioners measure the central 60 degrees of the field.

With appropriate treatment these fields expand fully and when they do, symptoms and other clinical measures improve. Fifteen to twenty percent of school children have fields of less than 15 degrees in diameter and some lose all but the central one or two degrees of vision. Generally, the more tunneled the field, the poorer are the child's learning, reading, social or performance abilities. Functional field testing, once a respected medical tool, is not part of modern medical practice and mainstream physicians do not use or consider them relevant. This may be because modern computerized visual field devices measure specific types of visual loss but are not sensitive to functional field constriction. Thus functional visual fields are rarely screened in schools and a substantial number of children with unexplained learning and emotional dysfunction suffer needlessly every day in our schools and for the rest of their lives.

EXAMPLES OF SYNTONIC TREATMENT
FOR THE EXPANSION OF PERCEPTION

The following are four cases that I treated. Not all cases are as dramatic and not all of my syntonic patients have shown such obvious success. The first patient was a 78-year-old woman who came for vision therapy because of double vision that began eight weeks earlier when she suddenly became cross-eyed. Ophthalmologists and neurologists could not determine the cause. In addition, she was mentally confused and emotionally distraught and had been since her husband died ten months earlier. After just twelve syntonic treatments, her eyes straightened and she became mentally sharp and emotionally balanced. When I asked her what had helped she answered, *"I know it was the green light. Every time I watched the green light I could feel waves of electricity or energy moving inside my head. Finally during one light session I felt a kind of energy shift in my brain and my vision and everything else became clear."*

Another patient, a 6-year-old girl, was being expelled from her public school class because she could not learn and was seriously disrupting class. Diagnosed as autistic and retarded from an early age, she was so hyperactive that even objective optometric testing was impossible. Her history included toxic pregnancy (pre-eclampsia), blue baby syndrome (hypoxia due to the umbilical cord wrapped around her neck, and her father was rundown and killed in a crosswalk a few feet in front of her when she was two. She started syntonic color therapy using yellow-green filters with the idea to eliminate any toxemia that might have transferred and remained from the pregnancy. The results were astounding. In five treatments, for the first time in her life she had become a calm, cooperative and communicative little girl who could learn and participate in her normal first grade class.

Lisa was ten years old. Her mother brought her for an eye examination because Lisa had suddenly stopped riding her bicycle. When asked why she said that she was afraid to ride because she couldn't see very well. Her history revealed a recent mild head injury. Three months earlier she had fallen down a flight of stairs and hit her head on the doorframe at the bottom. She had suffered a bump and slight headache that was gone by the next morning. No doctor examined her at the time. The visual field in each eye was constricted to 15 degrees and in her superior visual field, the test target appeared doubled even though one eye was covered. This acute problem required green/blue light. At the seven-day progress exam her field had enlarged to normal with no target doubling. Her vision and self-confidence had returned.

Nine-year-old Kristin fell off a fence at age five years. A month after that she became withdrawn, anxious, confused, completely unaffectionate and she refused to attend school. She could not move her eyes normally and her visual fields were collapsed to less than 2 degrees. Her mother told us that she failed to see things that were right in front of her, that she often banged into walls and tripped over obvious objects, and she could not follow directions because she forgot them as soon as she heard them. Syntonic treatments commenced and as her visual field expanded her personality totally changed. A week post-treatment, her mother wrote that the night before, Kristin had come to her, sat on her lap, hugged her and told her she loved her, the first affection in four years.

The College of Syntonic Optometry was started in 1933 based on theories that chronic ocular and systemic disease is caused by imbalance of the autonomic nervous system. Light was thought to restore health by bringing these into balance. Light from the blue side of the visible spectrum restores parasympathetic nervous activity and light from the red side increases sympathetic. In the decades following the discovery that red laser speeds wound healing and hair growth, photobiomodulation research has provided a solid scientific basis for light's role in health and healing. Depending on its frequency, light influences circulation, oxygen supply and immune function by stimulating photosensitive elements in the blood, alters mitochondrial metabolism, triggers non-visual eye-brain pathways to modulate circadian phase and amplitude, reverses depression, improves sleep in Alzheimer's patients and more. The accelerating volume and quality of light research is changing the medical and research paradigm.

Today a small but growing percentage of optometrists in many countries practice syntonic phototherapy. Syntonists have successfully treated many thousands of patients since 1933. The lives and health of children and adults with learning, reading and attention disabilities, people suffering the effects following head trauma and stroke, retinal diseases, cross eyes, headaches and senility have been greatly enhanced by syntonics when nothing else was helping.

More information is available at: www.syntonicphototherapy.com.

REFERENCES AND NOTES

1) *Popp, F.A.* (1984) "Biophoton emission: Evidence for coherence and DNA as source." In: *Cell Bioph;* V 6, 1984, pp. 33-52.
2) Adey, W.R. & Lawrence, A.F. *Nonlinear Electrodynamics in Biological Systems.* Plenum Press, NY.
3) Liberman, J. (1991) *Light, Medicine of the Future.* Santa Fe, NM: Bear and Co.
   This is the most current far-ranging text on the subject of light as a therapeutic tool. It covers medical and psychological uses of light and contains an extensive bibliography. It is a must-read for anyone interested in the subject.
4) Spitler, H.R. (1941) *The Syntonic Principle.* The College of Syntonic Optometry.
   The thesis from which the practice of phototherapy by way of the eyes known as syntonics was established, this is available through the Optometric Extension Program www.oepf.org.
5) Breiling, B. (Ed.) (1990) *Light Years Ahead.* San Jose, CA: Celestial Press.
   This is a compilation of a 1990s conference of all the various light therapies being practiced around the world at that time. It is one of the best texts to get an overview of all the different light therapies and light technologies now in current use.

   [EDITOR'S NOTE ABOUT REF. #5: PRG member William Croft's work is mentioned in *Light Years Ahead.* See www.lightfield.com, and Biographies in Chapter 46.]

SECTION II

DIMENSIONS OF INTENTION

* Firedancer   Photographed in Bali by Millay in October 2001
(with the assistance of Ronnie Whitman Shepard).

SECTION II

DIMENSIONS OF INTENTION

The dimensions of intention include such an astounding capability as walking on fire without burning your feet, bending metal with mind power alone, and most importantly, self-healing and spiritual healing of others.

In 1971 Patty Westerbeke was one of the first to study the relationship between the strength of a person's belief in a spiritual healing method and the success of the recovery.*[1] Added to that and the growing realization that the "placebo" was a major factor in healing, a new field of study developed called "psycho-neuro-immunology." Dr Sondra Barrett made substantial contributions to that field, as she realized this model of healing created a bridge between science and spirit. (Chapter 6) In an effort to study spiritual healing separately from a patient's belief in a "placebo," B. Rubik and E. Rauscher asked the well-known spiritual healer Olga Worrall to attempt to "heal" bacteria placed in unmarked jars in a double-blind study. The rate of success is reported in Chapter 7. (See also p. xxvi.)

Psychiatrist Elisabeth Targ enlisted the intention of 40 healers from Christian, Jewish, Buddhist, Native American and shamanic traditions to participate in an outstanding double blind study of the effects of distant prayer on healing. This compassionate intention produced measurably positive therapeutic results. (Chapter 8) In Chapter 9, M. Schlitz and D. Radin provide an extensive review of different studies of prayer and healing to compare the methods and efficacy of such attempts.

Such studies published by IONS encouraged other types of intentional healing. In 1993, Dr John Hagelin gathered 2,500 meditators to sit in the park across the lawn from the White House in Washington, DC, to demonstrate the effect of peacefulness on the larger community.*[2] These attracted other meditators increasing the group to 4,000. Following is a brief excerpt from Hagelin's report:

> ...There was a distinct and highly statistically significant drop in crime compared to expected rates based on previous data, weather conditions,

---

*[1] Westerbeke, P. & Krippner, S. (1980) "Subjective reactions to Filipino healers." In: *International Journal of Paraphysics*, 14-9-17.

*[2] Hagelin, J. (2007) "The power of the collective." In: *Shift at the Frontiers of Consciousness*. Petaluma, CA: Institute of Noetic Sciences (IONS) No. 15, June.

and a variety of other factors. We collaborated with the local police department, the FBI, and 24 leading, independent criminologists and social scientists from major institutions.... We predicted a 20 percent drop in crime, and we achieved a 25 percent drop.... We have also found in other studies that in the geographic vicinity of such a meditating group, people experienced physiological changes—increased EEG coherence, reduced plasma cortisol, increased blood levels of serotonin, biochemical changes, and neurophysiological changes—as if they were meditating.

But how we do have such an influence on one another at a distance? There are no clear answers yet, but I believe that the clue lies in the notion that beneath the physical levels of human existence—our bodies and the quantum realm of molecules, atoms, quarks, and leptons—is a unified field of pure, abstract, universal consciousness. It's at this level of reality, this level of nonlocal mind, where you discover that the qualities of space are, at least in theory, capable of accommodating extraordinary experiences.

The full potential of the dimensions of intention are yet to be revealed. The photograph of a firedancer in Bali on page 61 is one example. His faith is so strong, even the cloth of his garment does not burn. L. Vilenskaya tested her own ability when she participated in firewalking ceremonies. Since she did so successfully, she decided to share her experience with others, and led several groups through firewalking ceremonies. Her report of their responses is in Chapter 10.

Another example is psychokinesis (PK)—the ability to exert mental intention over material things, such as bending metal, moving objects, or causing changes in objects at a distance. The members of the PRG were naturally interested, and invited Jack Houck to conduct "Spoon-bending Parties" at the WRI. (It is a weird sensation to feel the metal become pliable in your hand, before it freezes up again.) Many of us watched Uri Geller perform such feats when he visited meetings, so J. Hickman and H. Dakin wanted to see what Uri's biofield looked like in a Kirlian photo. The results are seen in Dakin's Chapter 11. (At the PRG we watched Geller cause a small seed to sprout in his hand. Later, Sirag reported that Geller was able to cause the sprout to be reversed – p. xxv.) In Chapter 12, Rubik studies types of *biofield* measurements for a link to mind-matter interactions. Dean Brown projects the "light" of his own biofield onto film.

Understanding and using the power of intention is the next step in human evolution. When we consider that the emotions of millions can even affect random number generators (Nelson's GCP in Chapter 39), we might create a time for millions of us to intend peace; to intend that exclusionary religions look beyond prejudice and war; to intend that humanity choose to live in harmony with the earth and its life; to intend our democracy triumph over the challenge of corporate control.

--- Jean Millay

CHAPTER 6   PSYCHONEUROIMMUNOLOGY

Sondra Barrett, PhD

Sondra Barrett *has followed a variety of interests leading to her important work in psychoneuroimmunology. Her degree in biochemistry from the U of Illinois (1968) was followed by a post-doctoral fellowship in immunology-hematology at UC Medical School (1972) where she remained on the faculty for a decade. Her research to develop tools to diagnose leukemia and follow treatment was funded by NIH and the American Cancer Society. While exploring the benefits of imagery, shamanic and energy traditions, she began teaching bodymind strategies and expressive arts to children with cancer. Later she developed patient support and graduate programs in the emerging field of psychoneuroimmunology.*

The beauty of the invisible world of cells, molecules, and wine inspired her to use the microscope as an art tool. Her photography has won awards from Olympus and Nikon and has appeared in publications such as Scientific American and The World of Fine Wine. One of her images was in the 2009 Bioscapes Museum Tour. Her trained eye had her unwittingly deciphering patterns of information among molecules for taste, minerals, and drops of wine. This surprisingly instilled within her the idea of a mystical code hidden in our molecules.

Dr Barrett *now sees cells as sacred with life lessons to teach us. She asks—are our cells templates for spiritual practices and ancient sacred art? (See Chapter 33.) She loves to teach and has blended the new biology, art, science, wine and food into nourishing programs for children and adults. Her first book, The Soul of Wine, was released in 2009.*

Her website is http://www.SondraBarrett.com.

PSYCHONEUROIMMUNOLOGY:
The Bridge Between Science and Spirit

Sondra Barrett

A field of science and medicine, psychoneuroimmunology (PNI), has evolved out of the interaction of psychology, neurobiology, immunology, theology, yoga, shamanism, and the space program. The union has not been an easy one, nor is it totally embraced by mainstream medicine. Yet. PNI started off on the shaky ground of psychosomatic medicine, which claimed that emotions and stress influence illnesses such as asthma, allergies, and rheumatoid arthritis. That the psyche could influence the soma was not a popular idea in academic medicine forty years ago. Now, some "accidents" of science, corroborated by the unprejudiced observations of astute investigators, add impetus to PNI's theories of mind-body connectivity.

ANATOMICAL CONNECTIONS

Underlying the beginnings of this once infant discipline was the quest to identify biological links between the nervous system and the immune system. (1-3) It must be kept in mind that it was once believed that the immune system operated independently of any other system in the body. Because immune cells could function normally in the test tube, it was assumed that they were outside of regulation by any internal or external factors.

Initial studies showed that there were nerves connected to the thymus, the primary organ of the immune system. Damage or changes to the brain, specifically the hypothalamus and left cerebral hemisphere, was shown to damage or alter immune functions. (4) Similarly, vaccination, which stimulates an immune response, accelerated electrical firing of noradrenergic neurons in the hypothalamus. (5) In other words, growing anatomical evidence confirmed that the nervous and immune systems could communicate with each other. Further evidence came when it was demonstrated that lymphocytes, the cells of the immune system, have receptors for many of the chemicals synthesized in the nervous system, such as growth hormone, adrenalin and noradrenalin, prolactin, endorphins, acetylcholine, substance P, and enkephalins. (6-9) In addition, lymphocytes also can synthesize some of the same substances made by the nervous system, such as corticotropin and endorphins. (10) An effector of immune reactivity, interleukin-1, once thought to be made only by immune cells, can be produced by brain cells. (11) Not only are there anatomical connections between nervous and immune systems, they also share many of the same biochemical properties.

CONDITIONING THE IMMUNE SYSTEM

The coup de grace that launched PNI into legitimate interdisciplinary dimensions was the controversial discovery by Robert Ader, a psychologist, and Nicholas Cohen, an immunologist, that the immune system could be trained just like a reflex. In other words, immune cells could be conditioned to do new things with sensory input. (12) A new assumption and branch of medicine—PNI—came to modern science: If the immune system could learn behaviorally, then it must be part of or at least influenced by the mind. (13, 14) Conditioning often occurs without conscious perception of the process. Sensory conditioning can trigger an automatic, unconscious physiologic response.

Pavlov's classical conditioning of salivation in a dog with the sound of a dinner bell set the stage for the scientific protocol to study learning and the immune system. (15) To discover how animals are conditioned to adverse stimuli, Ader fed rats saccharin-sweetened water paired simultaneously with a one-time injection of a drug that would cause gastrointestinal upset—the adverse response. The association of the ill feeling with the unusual taste resulted in subsequent aversion to the saccharin-sweetened water. However, when thirst overpowered the aversion, the rats were obliged to drink the saccharin water. Unexpectedly, after about thirty days some animals began dying of infections; those that died had consumed the most saccharin-sweetened water. What was happening? Ader, in discussing the experiment with immunologist Nick Cohen, learned that the drug he used to cause GI upset (cyclophosphamide—Cytoxan), a cancer chemotherapeutic agent known to cause nausea, also suppresses the immune system. In this experiment, the rats were exposed to Cytoxan once and even though the rats were no longer exposed to immunosuppressive Cytoxan, they continued to suppress their immune systems by drinking the saccharin-sweetened water. Ader and Cohen went on to confirm the unexpected, that the immune system could be suppressed through a classical conditioning paradigm. Subsequently many investigators have substantiated and expanded their work.

Other studies have shown that all the physical senses are powerful triggers for conditioning the immune system as well as other autonomic behaviors. In the 1920s and 1930s, Metal'nikov, at the Pasteur Institute, injected bacteria into animals while simultaneously massaging their skin. Later, that touch alone evoked an immune response showing a large increase in white blood cell count and antibodies to the bacteria previously injected. (16) Besides taste and touch, smell (of camphor) and visual cues have been used in association with agents to suppress or enhance immune capabilities. (15, 17) In a series of experiments, Spector and associates conditioned the production of interferon and natural killer cell activity by pairing a synthetic immuno-stimulant, Poly I:C, with the smell of camphor. Conditioning occurred after nine sessions. Poly I:C mimics the action of a virus, which rapidly raises levels of interferon and natural killer cell activity. The odor of camphor alone, before conditioning, had no effect on immune functions. (17)

Jeanne Achterberg, author of *Imagery and Healing* (18) and *Bridges of the Bodymind*, (19) once suggested that perhaps someday people with cancer could take a mint paired with an anti-tumor drug, Eventually they could stop taking the drug and get the same beneficial anti-tumor effects with the mint alone, eliminating any toxic side effects of the drug.

PLACEBO EFFECT

Any effect produced in the absence of an identifiable causal agent raises the question of whether a placebo (from the Latin for "I shall please") response is being triggered. The placebo effect has long been a nuisance to drug companies doing placebo-controlled studies to test new pharmaceutical agents. After all, how can a new sleeping pill be proven effective and commercially viable, if experimental subjects who are strong placebo-responders sleep even better with an inert pill?

Although the mechanisms of the placebo response are not yet well understood, factors that influence the effects include physician-patient relationship, the person's belief system, and environmental and cultural components. The existence of the placebo response implies that beliefs about one's own curative abilities can stimulate the necessary physiological systems that mediate healing. The psychological factors most commonly implicated are suggestion, expectation, anxiety reduction, and the hope and will to live. Ader, Wickramasckera, and others suggested that conditioning also might account for the placebo effect. (20, 21) Wickramasckera says: *"All effective interventions have the potential for Pavlovian conditioning and triggering a placebo response. The response to any active ingredient includes two components: a placebo and an active component."*

Virtually every physiological response in the body, including blood flow pain control, and cancer cytotoxicity has been subject to a placebo effect, and in many studies, the placebo accounts for at least 30% of all observed effects. (22) Changes can be positive or negative, producing the same expected effect as the active drug and the same unpleasant side effects. In one area of placebo studies—pain control—a biological mechanism is understood. Jon Levine and his colleagues at University of California San Francisco reported that placebos appear to modulate pain relief by releasing endorphins, the brain's opiate-like pain-killing substances. (23)

ATTITUDES AND SURVIVAL

The existence of the placebo effect opened the door for seeking to understand if and how belief, attitude, and states of mind affect the physical body. Much of the initial work in this area looked epidemiologically at the psychological differences between those people who stayed well and those who got sick. An excellent overview of the historical work is found in Blair Justice's book *Who Gets Sick*. (24) Suzanne Kobasa, a pioneer in attitudes and health, studied executives from Illinois Bell Telephone Company during the stressful job-changing time of federal deregulation. She showed that certain mental states contributed to health and hardiness. (25) In these executives, the factors most predictive of healthy coping were the three Cs: Challenge—the perception of a threat or change as a challenge, a problem looking for a solution; Control—the ability to do something about the situation versus a feeling of victimization or helplessness; and Commitment—the sense of purpose in life or to family, that there is something important to accomplish. Those executives who faced the crisis at work with the three Cs stayed healthy. Kobasa calls the three Cs the hardiness factor; these same factors have been shown to be the basis for resilience and survival in brutal circumstances, such as during the Holocaust and in prisoner-of-war camps. The hardiness factor also plays a role in survival from HIV and AIDS. (26) One biochemical explanation for this effect on health—when people feel challenged rather than threatened, they produce far less immune-suppressing cortisol. In addition, an attitude of hardiness means being able to take action; mental states influence behaviors.

Many attitudes, such as trust and feeling nurtured, that contribute to health and well-being are formed, for the most part, during childhood. It is widely known that loving touch is essential for survival and growth of babies, both human and other animals. In addition, touch in newborns alters the stress response. One study showed when baby rats were gently handled every day from birth to weaning twenty-two days later, they had lower stress hormone released than rats not touched, an effect that lasted until "old age" of twenty-four months. (27) Baby rats licked by their moms thrived long after the grooming practice was over. New epigenetic studies indicate that future offspring of the nurtured rats also thrive. (28)

Childhood upbringing is implicated in how attitudes and emotions affect later health particularly in the relationship between hostility and heart disease. Cultural differences between American and Japanese children shed some light on how attitudes learned as children influence later adult health and behavior. Child–rearing practices in Japan include close physical contact, little separation from the mother, and preference for maternal–child closeness over strict discipline. A feature of the "typical" Japanese personality is *amae*, the expectation of being treated well with kindness. Child abuse, unfortunately so common in the United States, is virtually nonexistent in Japan. (29) Traditional Japanese mothers avoid expressing negative emotions toward the child and take care to spare the child embarrassment. The parental attitude toward the child is that he or she is good, wonderful, and clever. (30) The early nurturing environment coupled with preliminary research findings of lower hostility scores among urban Japanese men led Redford Williams and coworkers to postulate that the attitude the Japanese have toward their children is a contributing factor to lower rates of coronary heart disease in Japan compared with the United States. (29) As discussed below, hostility has been identified as a key psychological factor in coronary artery disease.

A challenge for our society and practitioners of PNI is to find ways to learn and teach healthful attitudes to those who haven't learned them as children. One specific goal is to help people shift from a helpless mode to one in which they experience control and mastery. We learned that animals subjected to uncontrollable stress from which they could not escape were more likely to experience infections, increased tumor growth, and other experimentally induced diseases. (31, 32) This led to the understanding that in people, helplessness and lack of control have long-range negative effects on mental and physical health. As suggested by Martin Seligman, helplessness in one stressful situation often is carried over to others. (33) Furthermore, helplessness and optimism can be learned. (34)

The importance of having a sense of control rather than helplessness to overall health increases as we age. (35) Research in the area of aging, attitudes and autonomy has suggested that the ability to choose one's environmental surroundings is important in healthy aging. Adverse effects on health after admission to a nursing home were, in part, a function of the amount of individual control over the move. Prospective residents given a choice about when and where they moved, as well as about specifics of the living arrangements, showed little decline in level of health and psychological well-being. (35) Conversely, lack of control has adverse effects on emotional states, subjective well-being, and longevity. (36) As we age, the locus of control often changes from internal, or directed from within, to external, or imposed from without.

PNI provides a scientific framework for understanding how attitudes like optimism, emotional states, or a sense of control impact the immune system, quality of life, and longevity. (37, 38) It also provides us with the rational incentives to search for empirical ways to alter consciousness to improve health and quality of life. Emotional states, such as depression, (39) loneliness, (40) hopelessness, (41) suppress immune function, making a person more prone to illness. Depression and stress also put people more at risk for coronary artery disease. (42) Inappropriate anger, another so-called negative emotion, appears to have its first effects on the cardiovascular system rather than immune functions. In the 1950s, Meyer Friedman and Ray Rosenman introduced the concept of coronary-prone or Type A behavior – the fast-paced, impatient, competitive "hyper" person – to help explain the increased incidence in coronary artery disease (CAD) in twentieth-century Western societies. (43) Redford Williams and others showed that not all Type A behaviors were negative or life-threatening. (44, 45) Hostility, lack of trust, and cynicism seem to be the damaging components of Type A behavior. Yet our culture still holds to Type As having more heart disease; the data don't support that. Now it's about Type H, the hostile, cynical character.

Dr Dean Ornish added another piece to the mind-body puzzle of heart disease by initiating for people at risk for CAD a lifestyle program of meditation, yoga, support group, and vegetarian diet with only 10% calories from fat. By engaging in a year-long program, many people reversed their cardiac blockages by simple lifestyle strategies. (47, 48) On long-term follow-up, stress reduction and group support appeared to be the most important features. (49)

Are there ways a person can counterbalance or change self-defeating attitudes and emotions and continue in a state of health despite great upheavals? It is the mandate of PNI to search for and develop these behaviors. With the benefit of early Soviet science, we find clues to altering emotional behavior and physical responses via an effective mind-body dialogue.

THE SPACE PROGRAM, ATHLETICS, AND YOGA

Pioneering work on stress by Nobel laureate Hans Selye established that our emotions and mental states dramatically influence the autonomic nervous system, such as hormonal activity and blood flow. (50-52) Excitement and anxiety can increase blood pressure, heart rate and blood vessel constriction, resulting in tell-tale stress signs of cold hands and feet. Worry, depression, or performance anxiety can slow body and brain functions.

We all experience emotional ups and downs, yet this kind of emotional instability was totally unacceptable in the Soviet and American space programs. In the early 1950s, initial efforts of the Soviet space program were aimed at exploring the possibility of using yoga techniques to teach cosmonauts to control psychological and physiological processes while in space. Yoga is an ancient Eastern mental and spiritual system in which the practitioner can learn to regulate functions such as temperature, heart rate, and mental concentration. Using these traditional teachings, the Russians developed methods of control that depended on feedback signals between the body and the mind. The successful training emphasized intentional control of heart rate, muscle tension, and emotional reactions to stressful situations like zero gravity. Before this work, most scientists, unfamiliar with or skeptical of yoga, believed that these autonomic, automatic processes were outside conscious control. (53)

Similarly, in the early phases of the American space program, National Aeronautics and Space Administration (NASA) scientists predicted that astronauts during prolonged lunar spaceflights would experience irregular blood pressure and heart rate along with emotional instability. To combat these effects, rather than risk drugs that had never been tested at zero gravity, NASA explored self-regulation through meditation and biofeedback. In a spaceflight simulator, the astronauts were taught how to preprogram their minds and bodies for optimal space performance. (53)

Space projects, like Apollo, taught us that the disciplined use of self-regulatory methods such as imagination, mental rehearsal, and biofeedback could be effective in reversing the negative effects of stress, emotions, and thoughts.

From their success in the cosmonauts with controlling automatic responses, like heart rate, Soviet scientists set out to discover whether emotional reactions, detrimental to peak athletic performance, could be consciously controlled before competition. In fact, they were able to translate mental training techniques for the cosmonauts to help combat stress and enhance physical abilities in their athletes. The power of visualization and imagery to alter physical performance was successful for weight lifting, golf, skiing, running, and tennis. The result, in the 1970s, many books – "Inner Games of" – were written using imagery, mental rehearsal, and relaxation of the astro-cosmonauts to improve athletic performance.

Outstanding athletic performance brought to the public awareness that stress, attitude, and mental training affect physical training and competence. In his book *Peak Performance*, Dr Charles Garfield describes how athletes can identify signs of stress and negative emotions as shortness of breath, lost coordination, cramped muscles, and the inability to perform optimally. (53) When an athlete is worried about performance, and doesn't deal with the worry, the body responds in ways that makes performance less successful.

The body-mind methods perfected for optimal performance in astronauts and athletes began to enter the health arena. From visualization by cancer patients to the practice of yoga and meditation for chronic pain, health consumers and medical research are finding that many of the "old ways" work. New body-mind technologies are achieving scientific respectability and proving to be useful "medicine" in many health-promoting settings.

RELAXATION RESPONSE, MEDITATION, AND PRAYER

Harvard physician Herbert Benson studied yogis and other people engaged in meditation practices for biological clues to possible health benefits. His work contributed substantially to integrating meditation with a modern understanding of stress. Central to Benson's definition of the "relaxation response" was his idea that the body operates in a yin-yang, off-on manner. For every "on" reaction, or stress response, he believes that there had to be a corresponding "off" response. (54, 55)

Benson showed that the relaxation response, exemplified by the practice of transcendental meditation, improves hypertension and irregular heart rhythms. Since his initial studies, it has been learned that meditation is effective in alleviating pre-surgery anxiety and adverse effects of cancer chemotherapy, and decrease a diabetic's need for insulin. By putting the body in a state of altered consciousness and lowered biochemical arousal, a more balanced metabolic state is achieved. Jon Kabat-Zinn and colleagues went on to achieve groundbreaking results teaching yoga and mindfulness meditation to people with unresponsive pain. People who committed to the 8-week program showed decreased pain even two to five years later if they continued practicing meditation. (56, 57) Now these practices are being taught in hospitals and health care settings throughout the United States; many are even covered by insurance.

It turns out that meditation does more than alter physiology; it influences relationships and spirituality. After years of study, Benson saw a relationship between meditation and prayer. Though the study of prayer seems to have no place in science, its tangible results are growing. A seminal study by cardiologist Randy Byrd at San Francisco General Hospital looked at the effect of prayer on 393 persons who had suffered a myocardial infarction (heart attack). About half of the patients were prayed for, the others weren't. The prayed-for group had five to seven people of different religions (Protestants, Catholics, and Jews across the United States) praying for them each day. Those praying were given the patient's name, diagnosis, and condition, and prayed for the beneficial healing and quick recovery. (58) The prayed for patients had fewer complications while in the cardiac care unit compared with the control group. The patients were not told of the prayers, nor did the people praying personally know those whom they were praying for. Byrd's unusual results launched many prayer studies since including those of Dr Larry Dossey and the late Dr Elisabeth Targ (See Chapter 8).

SOCIAL TIES THAT BIND
People and Our Health

Like prayer, the potential for personal relationships to benefit physical health and longevity seemed implausible as a scientific experiment. However, work by dedicated investigators is showing what we intuitively might expect: that the kinds and number of relationships we have affect our risk of disease. One of the initial studies was an epidemiological look at the residents of Roseto, Pennsylvania, who had the lowest incidence of heart disease in the United States. Yet it turned out they had most of the accepted risk factors for heart disease. They ate high-fat diets, smoked, didn't exercise, and many were obese. So why didn't they have heart disease? (59) The researchers concluded that the advantageous factor was personal relationship. Roseto was a close-knit Italian-American community in which social ties were very strong. When the next generation started moving away and adopted better health behaviors – they stopped smoking, changed their diets, and began exercising – their health declined; the incidence of heart disease increased dramatically. The breakdown in close social ties was said to contribute to their increased heart disease

Groundbreaking work on the importance of the quality of relationships, intimacy, and health came from both epidemiological studies and research by Seymour Cohen and others. Prospective epidemiological stories showed greater morbidity and mortality in people with fewer close relationships. (60) In controlled human experiments, people exposed to rhinoviruses showed cold symptoms if they had fewer than six social contacts a week. Here the number of relationships influenced health. Cohen et al. didn't even account for quality or intimacy. (61) Divorce, how spouses fought, and the quality of relationships affected immune functions more in women than men. (62) Furthermore, James Pennebaker, Janice Kiecolt-Glaser, and Richard Glaser showed that being able to express emotions from past traumatic events improves immune function in the test tube as well as physical health. (62) In Pennebaker's original experiments, college students who had been sexually or physically abused as children spent fifteen minutes a day writing about their early traumas. (63) In their journals, they emphasized their feelings rather than the narrative of the events. After a trial of only four consecutive days of writing, long-range effects were apparent. The students had stronger lymphocyte reactivity, used the student health service significantly less frequently for illness, and had less subjective distress than a control group of students who only wrote about random, nonemotional events. The researchers' explanation for these interesting results—failure to confront a buried trauma forces the person to live with it in an unresolved manner exacerbating the stress response; actively confronting it, through writing, allows for understanding, assimilation, and release of the held-in stress. Pennebaker and colleagues went on to use this strategy with people with asthma or rheumatoid arthritis (RA) showing it to improve lung function in those with asthma and decrease pain in the people with RA. What's amazing about this—they wrote thoughts and emotions about an emotional trauma four days for only fifteen minutes. They enjoyed the benefits for more than six months. (64)

The salutary effects of intimate relationships and the ability to disclose emotional traumas were further demonstrated in support groups for breast cancer patients in research by Stanford psychiatrist David Spiegel. (65) After one year in the group, patients reported mood improvement and pain-reduction. Unexpectedly, in a ten-year follow-up, a difference in survival time was discovered in patients who had been in the support group. Such compelling evidence of prolonged survival from participating in a support group suggests that one major change in the practice of medicine should be the inclusion of psychosocial support as an integral part of any cancer therapy or health-enhancing program.

Looking at this material fifteen years later, the history still speaks for itself with substantial evidence supporting how the mind, attitudes and stress influence risk factors and healing from disease. The one area I think relevant for our troubling times is the importance of supportive relationships to our well-being. Human contact and support is essential for any kind of health-changing program, be it for losing weight or changing the course of an illness. (66)

Kiecolt-Glaser showed that caregivers of parents with Alzheimer's Disease suffered considerable unrelenting stress; their health suffered as well. However if they had supportive relationships, their well-being and health improved considerably. (67, 68)

FUTURE HEALTH AND MEDICINE

PNI is in a position to create a solid theoretical framework for preventive medicine. By continuing to provide experimental data on the mind-body connection, PNI will clarify how mental states, stress and relationships confer susceptibility to and protection from illness. Concomitantly, PNI clinicians will define practical means to strengthen the internal environment. Many successful strategies have been put into play in health-care settings throughout the world. (69)

The clinical applications of this information may be of profound value for people with AIDS (acquired immune deficiency syndrome), cancer, and autoimmune diseases such as rheumatoid arthritis. Even in the absence of unequivocal laboratory data on the beneficial effects of imagery, meditation, yoga and relaxation, these modalities are effectively being used for improving the subjective quality of life in people with illness or stress. (70) Fortunately, the relatively new National Center for Complementary and Alternative Medicine (NCCAM) now provides funding for such studies. They may even show how to improve quality of life and longevity. (71)

This chapter has focused on the objective aspects of PNI. It provides a context in which to interpret future work on the effects on health of consciousness-altering modalities. Medical science tends to emphasize quantitative, reproducible outcomes by exercising concrete, measurable interventions. Yet many of the interventions used for reducing stress and anxiety cannot be tested by the conventional placebo–controlled double blind study. We must develop new models for research. In our efforts to seek out the hard facts, we also must acknowledge the role of the individual and spirit in healing. The effects of immeasurable energies may be more elusive, less concrete than that of penicillin. Yet the results for the individual are no less dramatic. There is no "one size fits all" for healing or diminishing risk factors.

Medically, PNI offers insight into how, beyond the chemical changes, mental, emotional, and spiritual states of consciousness affect the body. Philosophically, PNI promises to leap from formal proofs to an elucidation of the human and spiritual component of healing; an individual's quest for purpose is essential for health and quality of life. Personally, PNI offers the individual options and choices that began in ancient times with the underpinnings of modern science. All people must be their own testing ground for choosing, exploring and discovering what works best for their own well-being, whether they are challenged by an illness or life. It is only when we each make choices to change, that we may discover what works for us.

To learn more, see this website: www.SondraBarrett.com.
For direct contact email Dr Barrett at sondra@SondraBarrett.com.

REFERENCES AND NOTES

1) Bulloch, K. & Pomeranz, W. (1984) "ANS innervation of thymic–related lymphoid tissue in wild–type and nude mice." In: *J. Compo Neurol.,* 228:57-68.
2) Cabanac, J. (1931) "Les nerfs du thymus." In: *Bull. Assoc. Anal.,* 25:92-100.
3) Bulloch, K. (1985) "Neuroanatomy of lymphoid tissues: A review." In: Guillemin, R. et al. (Eds.) *Neural Modulation of Immunity.* NY: Raven Press, 49-85.
4) Cross, R.J., Markesbery, W.R., Brooks, W.H., Rozman, T.L. (1980) "Hypothalamic-immune interactions." In: *Brain Res.,* 196:79-87.
5) Besedovsky, H.O., Sorkin, E., Felix, D., Haas, H. (1977) "Hypothalamic changes during immune response." In: *Eur. J. Immunol.,* 7: 323-325.
6) Pert, C.B., Ruff, M.R., Weber, R.J., Herkenham, M. (1985) "Neuropeptides and their receptors: A psychosomatic network." In: *J. Immunol.,* 135:118-122.
7) Malinski, W., Grabezewska, E. & Ryzewski, J. (1980) "Acetylcholine receptors of rat lymphocytes." In: *Biochem. Biophys. Acta.,* 663:269-273.
8) Payan, D.G. & Goetzl, E.J. (1985) "Modulation of lymphocyte function by sensory neuropeptides." In: *J. Immunol.,* 1 35:783-785.
9) Hazum, E., Chang, K.J. & Cuatrecasas, P. (1970) "Specific non-opiate receptors for β-endorphins on human lymphocytes." In: *Science,* 205:1033-1035.
10) Smith, E.M. & Blalock, J.E. (1981) "Human leukocyte production of corticotropin and endorphin-like substances." In: *Proc. Nat. Acad. Sci.,* 789;7530-7534.
11) Fontana, A., et al. (1983) "Biological and biochemical characterization of interleukin-l from glioma cells." In: *Eur. J. Immunol.,* 13:685~688.
12) Ader, R. & Cohen, N. (1975) "Behaviorally conditioned immunosuppression." In: *Psychosom. Med.,* 37:333-340.
13) Ader, R., Felten, D. & Cohen, N. (2001) *Psychoneuroimmunology.* Academic Press.
14) Newman, M.G. (1990) "Can an immune response be conditioned?" In: *JNCI* 82:1543-45.
15) In Pavlov's experiment, a dog was given food at the same time a bell rang. The dog would salivate in response to the food while hearing the bell. Eventually the dog would salivate at the sound of the bell alone, when no food was presented.
16) Ghanta, V., Miramoto, R., & Spector, H.N. (1986) "Neural and environmental influences on neoplasia and conditioning NK activity." In: *J. Immunol 1986:*135;848-852.
17) Metal'nikov, S., & Chorine, V. (1926) "Role des reflexes conditionnels dans l'immunite." In: *Ann. Inst. Pasteur.* 1926; 40:893-900.
18) Achterberg, J. (1985) *Imagery and Healing.* Boston: Shambhala.
19) Achterberg, J. & Lawlis, F. (1980) *Bridges of the Bodymind.* Champaign, IL: Institute for Personality and Ability Testing.
20) Ader, R. (1985) "Conditioned immuno-pharmacological effects in animals: Implications for conditioning model of pharmacotherapy." In: White, L., et al., *Placebo: Theory, Research and Mechanisms.* NY: Guillford Press; 306-323.
21) Wickramasekera, I. (1985) "A conditioned response model of the placebo effect." In: White, L., et al. In: *Placebo: Theory, Research and Mechanisms,* pp. 255-287.
22) O'Regan, B. (1988) "Placebo effects: Investigations." In: *Institute of Noetic Sciences,* 2:1-3l.
23) Levine, J. & Fields, H.L. (1988) "Mechanism of placebo analgesia." In: *Lancet,* 2:654-657.
24) Justicem, B. (1988) *Who Gets Sick.* LA: Jeremy Tarcher.

25) Kobasa, S. (1982) "The hardy personality: Toward a social psychology of stress and health." In: Sanders, G.S., *Social Psychology of Health and Illness*. Erlbaum.
26) Nicholas, P. & Webster, A. (1993) "Hardiness and social support in HIV." In: *Arch. Gen. Psychiatry*, 6: 132-135.
27) Schaneberg, S.M. & Field, T.M. (1987) "Sensory deprivation, stress & stimulation in rat pup & preterm human neonate." In: *Child Development*, 58:766-68.
28) Watters, Ethan. (2006) "The new science of epigenetics rewrites the rules of disease, heredity, and identity." In: *Discover*, November 2006.
29) Doba, N., Hinohara, S. & Williams, R.B. (1983) "Type A behavior pattern and hostility in Japanese males with reference to CHD." In: *Japan J. Psychosom.*, 23:321-328.
30) Stevenson, H., Azuma, H. & Hakuta, K. (1986) *Child Development and Education in Japan*. NY: WH Freeman.
31) Riley, V. "Psychoneuroendocrine influences on immunocompetence and neoplasia." In: *Science*, 212:1100-1109.
32) Laundens-Jager, M.L., et al. (1983) "Coping with immune suppression: Inescapable but not escapable shock suppresses lymphocyte proliferation." In: *Science*, 221:565-570.
33) Seligman, M. (1975) *Helplessness: On Depression, Development and Death*. SF: WH Freeman.
34) Seligman, Martin. (1990) *Learned Optimism*.
35) Ostir, G.V., et al. (2000) "Emotional well-being predicts functional independence and survival." In: *J. Amer. Geriatric Soc.*, 48: 473-78.
36) Rowe, J. & Kohn, R. (1987) "Human aging: Usual and successful." In: *Science*, 237:1439.
37) Krantz, D. & Schulz, R. (1980) "Application of personal control." In: *Adv. Environ. Psychology*, 2:23-57.
38) Pelletier, K.R. & Herzig, D. (1988) "PNI: A mind-body model." In: *Advances*, 5:27-56.
39) Schleifer, S., et al, (1984) "Lymphocyte function in major depressive disorders." In: *Arch. Gen. Psychiatry*, 41:484-486.
40) Kiecolt-Glaser, J., Garner, W., et al. (1984) "Psychosocial modifiers of immunocompetence." In: *Psychosom. Medicine*, 46:7-14.
41) Goodkin, K., Antoni, M.H., Laney, B. (1986) "Stress and hopelessness in the promotion of cervical neoplasia." In: *J. Psychosom. Res.*, 30:67-76.
42) Glassman, A.H. & Shapiro, P. (1998) "Depression & course of CAD." In: *Amer. J. Psychiatry*, 155:4-11.
43) Friedman, M. & Rosenman, R. (1959) "Association of specific overt behavior patterns with blood and cardiovascular findings." In: *JAMA*, 169:1286-1290.
44) Blumenthal, P., Williams, R.B., Kong, Y., et al. (1978) "Type A behavior patterns and coronary atherosclerosis." In: *Circulation*, 58:634-639.
45) Matthews, K.A. & Haynes, S.G. (1986) "Type A behavior patterns and coronary risk: Update and critical evaluation." In: *Am. J. Epidemiol.*, 123:23-96.
46) Williams, R.B., Barefoot, J.C., et al. (1988) "Type A behavior and documented coronary atherosclerosis in 2287 patients." In: *Psychosom. Med.*, 50: 139-152.
47) Ornish, D., Brown, S.E., Scherwitz, L.W., et al. (1990) "Can lifestyle changes reverse coronary atherosclerosis? Lifestyle Heart Trial." In: *Lancet*, 336: 129-133.
48) Daubenmier, J.J. & Ornish, D. (2007) "Contribution of changes in diet, exercise, and stress to changes in coronary risk in the Multisite Cardiac Lifestyle Intervention Program." In: *Annals Behavior Medicine*, 33: 57-68.

49) Schulz, U., Daubenmier, J.J., Scherwitz, L., Ornish, D. (2007) "Social support group attendance is related to blood pressure, health behaviors, and quality of life in the Multicenter Lifestyle Demonstration Project." In: *Psychology, Health, and Medicine*, 2008.
50) Selye, H. (1956) *The Stress of Life*. NY: McGraw-Hill.
51) Selye, H. (1975) *The Physiology And Pathology Of Exposure To Stress*. NY: McGraw-Hill.
52) Marx, J. (1995) "How the glucocorticoids suprpress immunity." In: *Science*, pp. 232-233.
53) Garfield, C.A., with Bennet, H.Z. (1984) *Peak Performance. Mental Training Techniques from the World's Greatest Athletes*. NY: Warner Books.
54) Benson, H., with Klipper, M.Z. (1975) *The Relaxation Response*. NY: Morrow.
55) Benson, H., Beary, J., Carol, M. (1974) "The relaxation response." In: *Psychiatry*, 37:3746.
56) Kabat-Zinn, Jon. *Full Catastrophe Living: Using the Wisdom of Your Body and Mind to Face Stress, Pain, and Illness*.
57) Davidson, R.J., Kabat-Zinn, J., Schumacher, J., et al. (2003) "Alterations in brain and immune function produced by mindfulness meditation." In: *Psychosomatic Medicine*, 65(4):564-570.
58) *Brain Mind Bulletin*. 1986;11:7.
59) Bruhn, J.G. (1965) "Epidemiological study of myocardial infarctions in an Italian-American community." In: *J. Chronic Dis.*, 18:353-365.
60) Cohen, S. & Syme, S.L. (1985) *Social Support in Health*. NY: Academic Press.
61) Cohen, S., et al. (1997) "Human relationships & infectious disease." In: *JAMA*, 277:1940-45.
62) Kiecolt-Glaser, J., et al. (1987) "Marital quality, marital disruption and immune function." In: *Psychosomatic Medicine*, 49:13-34.
63) Pennebaker, J., Kiecolt-Glaser, J., Glaser, R. (1988) "Disclosure of traumas and immune function: Health implications." In: *J. Consult. Clinical Psycholology*, 56:239-245.
64) Smyth, J.K., et al. (1999) "Effects of writing about stressful experiences on symptom reduction in patients with asthma or rheumatoid arthritis." In: *JAMA*, 281:1304-1309.
65) Spiegel, D., et al. (1989) "Psychological support for cancer patients." In: *Lancet*, 2:1447-49.
66) Sobel, D. (1995) "Rethinking medicine: Improving health outcomes with psychosocial interventions." In: *Psychosomatic Medicine*, 57:234-237.
67) Kiecolt-Glaser, J., et al. (1995) "Slowing of wound healing by psychological stress." In: *Lancet*, 346: 1194-96.
68) Uchino, B.N., Cacioppo, J.T. & Kiecolt-Glaser, J.K. (1996) "The relationship between social support and physiological processes: A review with emphasis on underlying mechanisms." In: *Psychological Bulletin*, 119:488-531.
69) Rutledge, J.C., Hyson, D.A., Garduno, D., et al. (1999) "Lifestyle program in management of patients with coronary artery disease: Clinical experience in a tertiary care hospital." In: *J. Cardiopulmonary Rehab.*, 19(4):226-234.
70) Astin, J.A., Eisenberg, D.M., et al. (2003) "Mind-body medicine: State of the science, implications for practice." In: *J. Amer. Board Family Practice*, 16(2):131-147.
71) http://nccam.nih.gov/.

HUMAN VOLITIONAL EFFECTS ON A MODEL BACTERIAL SYSTEM

Beverly Rubik
Elizabeth A. Rauscher

BACKGROUND

What are the dynamics of healing and health? What is the purpose of illness and death? Are all living systems interconnected in some fundamental manner? Does such a fundamental connectedness involve a fundamental nonlocal aspect of human consciousness? Is this interconnectedness mediated by an energy or an informational process?

In this study, we address these and other vital issues that relate to a better comprehension of the nature and properties of living systems and life in general. We examine healing as a restoring phenomenon that involves fundamental and natural processes of living systems.

Health is everything; it is a positive, glowing state of mental, physical, and spiritual well-being. It is wholeness in function and not simply the absence of disease. The term "dys-ease" only provides a contrast to the state of ease or wholeness or health. It is readily apparent that there is a natural healing property or restoring force, an innate intelligence that all living things appear to possess. Small afflictions of the human body, ignored, soon heal without action of the conscious mind. Only when the wound or disease is severe or permanently disabling does the impetus to understand the process of healing and how it can be implemented come to the fore.

Historically, the practitioners of healing in our Western tradition have shifted from the practice of an art to the practice of science. Most modern physicians would agree that they are only assisting in the natural healing process of the body, rather than effecting any cure. As one practicing physician said, *"note the word* practice *connected with the word* medicine."* The healing process today remains largely a mystery. Yet modern scientific methodology and knowledge give us tools to scientifically explore healing and apply this knowledge to alleviate suffering and amplify health. To date, most medical research has been based on the study of the invasion of the physical body, the alleviation of disease, and symptomatic relief, sometimes by means of drastic chemical and surgical intervention. An alternative and complementary approach would be to focus on health itself — how to obtain it and how to maintain it naturally. Health is manifest at the physical, emotional, and mental levels as a wholism such that understanding this vital resource may involve exploring spiritual and psychic health as well. (1)

Can one only heal one's self, according to the saying, *"Physician, heal thyself"?* Or can others aid in the process? The methodology of Western medicine assumes that others can assist the patient in regaining his or her health. It appears that one can determine one's own movement toward or away from health by one's attitude, as is evidenced by psychosomatic illnesses, and from studies in psychoneuroimmunology. Some accidents, or the state of being accident prone, may be attributed to one's own state of mind. How much does one's attitude and self-awareness govern one's health, and how much can be induced and amplified by another person?

The laying-on of hands is an age-old tradition and is portrayed, for example, in art of ancient Egypt and Babylon. It has since been part of all cultures and has its place in our science-dominated culture as well, as evidenced by the work of Olga and Ambrose Worrall and others. (2) It is largely considered to be paranormal, however, and outside orthodox science and medicine. Section 3 of the American Medical Association Principles of Medical Ethics states that *"a physician should practice a method of healing founded on scientific basis and should not voluntarily associate professionally with anyone who violates this principle."*

The scientific methodology exists to test the effects of laying-on of hands under controlled laboratory conditions. Therefore, to test this method, Drs Rubik, Rauscher and Van Bise designed careful double blind experiments. This series of research experiments to study a healer's laying-on of hands on a model bacterial system was extensive. In addition, Van Bise and Rauscher have examined the interaction of electromagnetic fields with biological systems in healing, and Rubik is well known for her research in biofield science and energy medicine.

OBJECTIVES

Regarding the possibility of an energy exchange between living organisms, we conducted three comprehensive studies in which we examined the intentional effects of a well-known healer, Dr Olga Worrall, on the growth and motility of a model bacterial system, *Salmonella typhimurium*, which Rubik has studied for six years. (1) These three studies were conducted in February 1979, April 1980, and December 1981. A fourth study was done in November 1982.

The purpose of this work is to (a) investigate the fundamental process of the laying-on of hands; (b) elucidate the mechanism of a healing process on a well-characterized organism; and (c) demonstrate that our methodology yields a strong and persistent phenomenon that we and others can replicate. Thus we envision our work as an important contribution to the increased credibility and scientific acceptance of the effects of healers on the healing process.

Our experimental design involves the following criteria: (a) that the organism used to study healer effects be previously well characterized and experimentally familiar to us; (b) that real-time control (healer-untreated) samples, identical to test samples (healer-treated), be used; (c) that it be possible for the healer to obtain immediate feedback as to her effects on the system; (d) that the parameters used to measure the viability of the target organism vary relatively rapidly, are quantifiable, and hence are subject to statistical analysis; (e) that permanent records of both test and control samples are made; and (f) that after the healer treatment, data are gathered under double-blind conditions, such that any conscious bias on behalf of the experimenters may be eliminated.

Bacterial motility (swimming behavior), measured by means of a stroboscopic microscope with attached camera, and bacterial culture growth, measured by means of light absorption in a spectrophotometer, are the two parameters we used that satisfy all these criteria. (3, 4)

METHODS

S. typhimurium was grown at 37° C. on a gyratory shaker in flasks that contained a liquid medium designed for the species, Vogal-Bonner citrate, with 1% glycerol added as a carbon source (food supply). The bacteria were actively growing and used directly for experimentation.

In the growth experiments, identical samples were prepared by means of sterile technique transferring 15-milliliter portions of the culture to sterile capped test tubes. (5) For the motility studies, glass microscope slides containing 3 microliters of bacterial suspension under a coverslip were prepared in the presence of the healer. Chemical agents used to damage either motility or growth of the bacteria were diluted with bacterial media and added to the samples before any healer treatment.

Healer treatment consisted of Dr Worrall holding her hands near, but not touching, the test tubes or slides containing the bacteria for about two minutes. As a control, we had a laboratory technician, who was uninformed about the purpose of our experiments hold sample test tubes for two minutes. During healer treatment, control samples were removed from the room to eliminate possible healer effects at moderate distances. After treatment, samples were labeled and data gathered. In the motility experiments, the bacteria were observed and photographed immediately after healer treatment and at intervals up to 20 minutes post healing. In the growth experiments, light absorption of the cultures at a wavelength of 620 nanometers was monitored in a spectrophotometer up to 48 hours post healing treatment, as were the control samples.

Quantification of healer effect was based on measuring differences in the viability curves (numbers of bacterial survivors over time) between treated and control samples.

Table 1.

FLOW CHART SCHEMA FOR THE HEALER TREATMENT OF BACTERIA

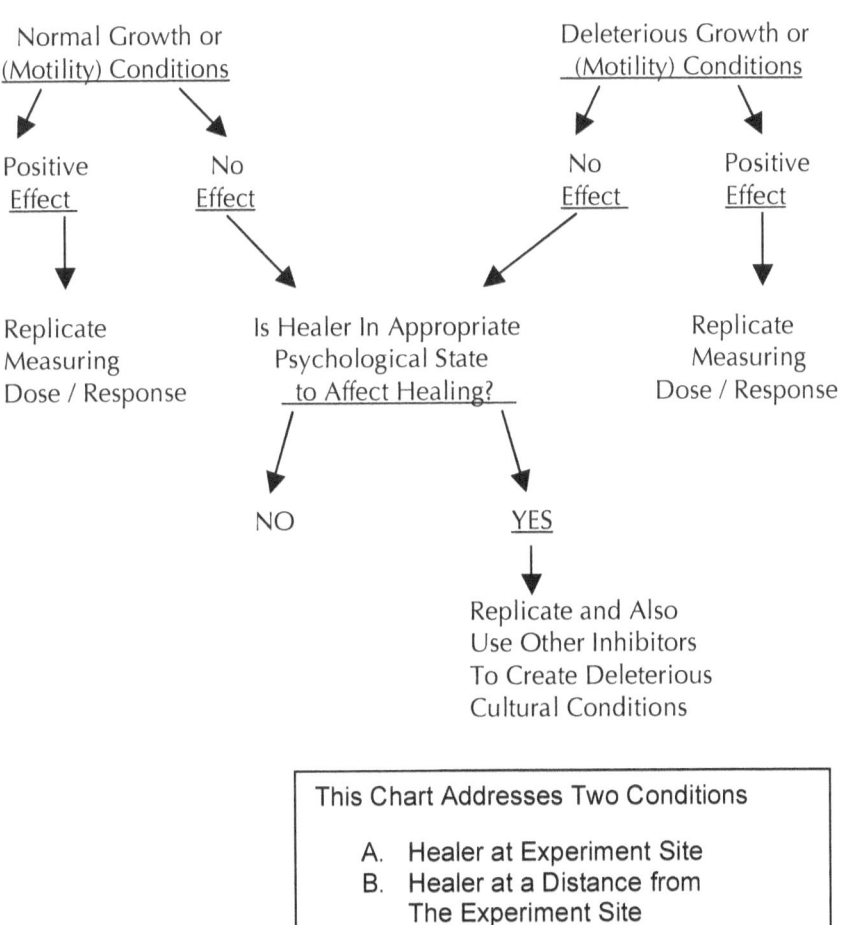

Positive Effect = An effect observed over that of naive participant or blank control

No Effect = No observed effect over that of blank control

RESULTS

We found similar trends in the data of each of the bacterial growth experiments for each antibiotic (growth inhibitor) used, as well as a dose–response effect. That is, for smaller concentrations of the antibiotic, the healer treatment produces a greater positive effect on bacterial growth than that resulting from healer treatment of bacteria in larger concentrations of the antibiotic. A dose–response effect is one criterion for a real and definite effect in medical research. It appears that the bacteria respond more positively to healer treatment when they are less damaged by an antibiotic.

We also found that in each of the three major studies, the time course of the effects of healer treatment on bacterial growth rate is relatively constant and depends on the specific antibiotic. For each healer–treated bacterial sample, the viability curve features are similar for each antibiotic used. These characteristic curves are one indicator of consistency in and reproducibility of our experimental data, rendering them more valid.

A summary of the conditions and results of all our experiments is presented in Table 2 – Human volitional effects. The data are expressed as the percentage of difference of healer–treated samples over control and are calculated from the numbers of bacterial survivors (bacteria per milliliter x 10^9) at equivalent numbers of bacterial generation times (time for a bacterium to divide in two).

Each experiment consists of about 30 data points that measure the number of bacteria at time intervals in control and treated cultures. The bacterial generation time was determined by examining the light absorbance of cultures incubated at a constant temperature and measuring the time at which the culture had doubled in opacity. At 37° C., a bacterial generation time is about one hour. Spectrophotometric absorbance is a standard methodology for determining the number of viable cells, and at 620 nanometers, an absorbance of 0.03 corresponds to a concentration of 3.0 X 10^8 S. *typhimurium* per milliliter.

In figures 1 and 2 we plot the viability growth curves for the comparison of control growth and healer-treated growth under the influence of the antibiotic tetracycline. Note the growth rate of the healer-treated sample occurs over time particularly for the lower concentration of the antibiotic in figure 1. In figures 3 and 4 we display two different experiments with the same concentration of the antibiotic chloramphenicol. Note the similarity in the two runs between healer-treated and control samples. Note there is a cross over point between the first and third hours after treatment and again the healer treatment effect appears to increase over time from the controls.

Figures 1 and 2.

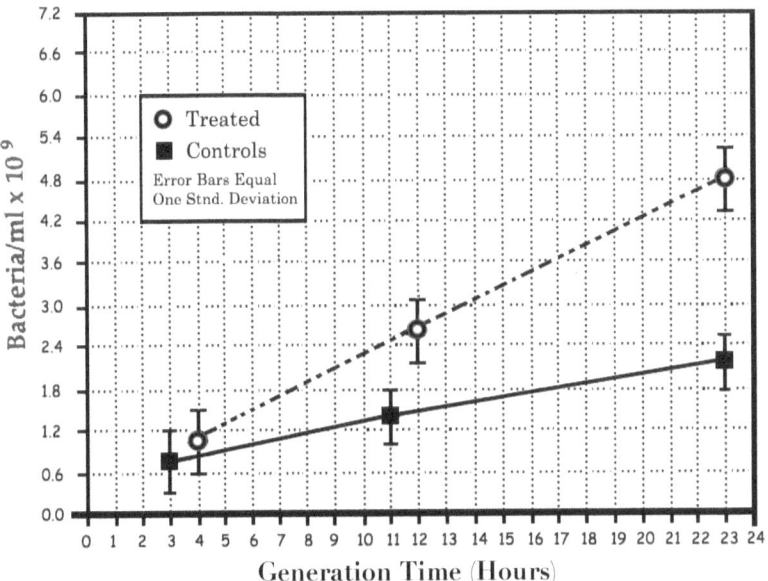

Figure 1. Viability curve for bacteria in presence of
1mg/ml of tetracycline (1981)

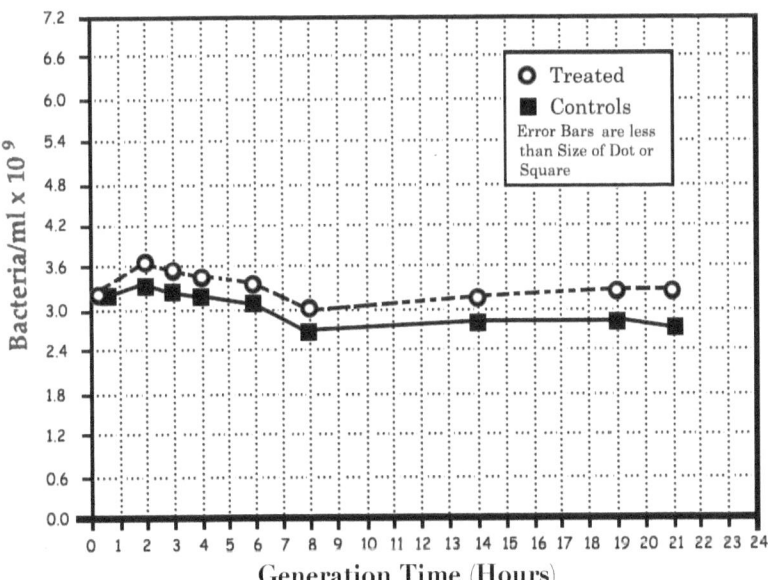

Figure 2. Viability curve for bacteria in presence of
10 mg/ml of tetracycline (1980)

Figures 3 and 4.

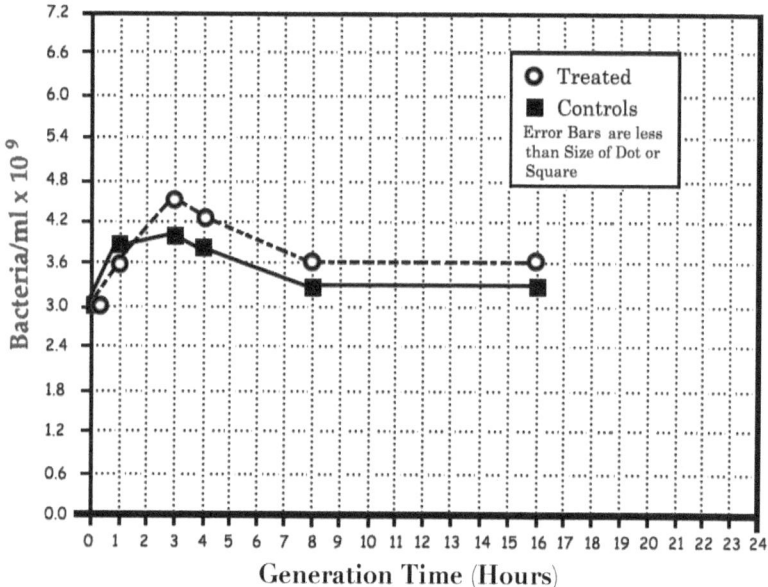

Figure 3. Viability curve for bacteria in presence of
100 mg/ml of chloramphenicol (1979)

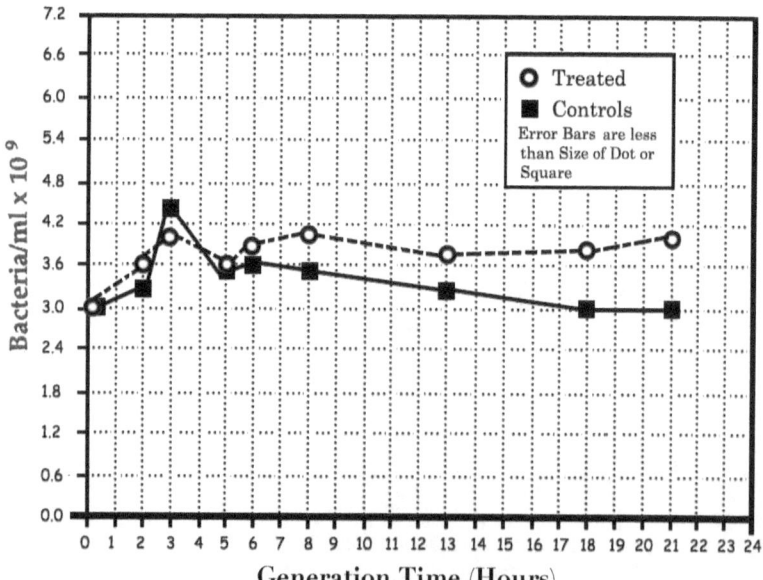

Figure 4. Viability curve for bacteria in presence of
100 mg/ml of chloramphenicol (1980)

HUMAN VOLITIONAL EFFECTS

Table 2.

Summary of Results from Healer-Influenced Bacterial Growth Experiments 1979, 1980, and 1981

Bacterial Culture Conditions	Generation Time (Hours)	% Average Difference Over Controls * of Healer-Treated
Normal, 1981	24	+23%
Normal, 1979	16	0%
Growth Inhibition Using Antibiotics:		
1 mg/ml Tetracycline, 1981	23	+121%
10 mg/ml Tetracycline, 1980	21	+28%
10 mg/ml Chloramphenicol, 1981	22	+70%
100 mg/ml Chloramphenicol, 1979	16	+22%
100 mg/ml Chloramphenicol, 1980	21	+34%
100 mg/ml Chloramphenicol, with naive participant acting as healer	23	+0%
Mutagens Present, 1981:		
0.05 M Sodium nitrite	31	-57%
0.05 M sodium nitrite plus 10 mg/ml Tetracycline	23	+50%
0.05 M sodium nitrite plus 100 mg/ml Chloramphenicol	23.5	+76%
Nutrient starved by removal of methionine to methionine auxotroph, 1980	23	0%
Motility inhibitor 50 mg/ml phenol present, 1979		+7%

* Percent difference is defined as (T -C)/C x 100%, where T = average number of bacteria in healer-treated samples, and C = average number of bacteria in control samples.

In the control sample exposed to the laboratory technician control, the nonhealer with nonhealing intentions had no effect on treated samples versus controls.

On two occasions during the experiments, Olga Worrall spontaneously volunteered unsolicited information that subsequently or contemporaneously proved to be correct. In one instance, on placing her hands near the growth-inhibited bacterial samples, she exclaimed that these were *"like starving children."* These samples in fact contained the methionine–minus mutagens. Because all the samples appeared identical, there were no clues to lead her to this information. On other occasions, Worrall placed her hands around a test tube labeled #20 and stated that it was anomalous and that she felt much "energy" associated with it. Data gathered subsequently on the growth of sample #20 indeed proved that it was an anomaly showing growth several times faster than all other samples. Such unplanned occurrences seem to hold no place in the scientific literature, but we believe them to be highly significant.

DISCUSSION

There is an apparent exchange of energy and information between living organisms. This process appears to involve a form of mind-matter interaction that may be related to both psychic healing (or so-called laying-on of hands on living systems), and psychokinetic interaction with inanimate systems.

Our results indicate that healer treatment produces significant growth and motility increases over control cultures in the presence of various chemical inhibitors. This leads us to hypothesize a general effect of healer intervention on cells, consistent, for example, with the possibility of field effects. One possibility is the existence of specific electromagnetic frequencies associated with laying-on of hands that enhances vitality. In subsequent studies, we plan to replicate some of our previous experiments and examine field characteristics associated with Worrall during her treatment. Theoretical studies and planned additional experiments are now in progress based on earlier research spanning four years. (6 – 12)

We would like to conduct future work to determine the level of cellular activity at which healing occurs, that is, whether it is at, for example, the level of extranuclear organelles, transfer ribonucleic acid, or deoxyribonucleic acid. We also plan to monitor certain physiological parameters of the healer, such as GSR (Galvanomic skin response), EEG (electroencephalography) and electrocardiography. We also plan to examine ambient electromagnetic, magnetic, and electrostatic fields before, during, and after an experimental session. In addition, we plan to examine pulsed, low intensity-specific frequency and waveform effects on the bacteria cultures in the absence of a healer. Different healers will participate in our experiments. The mechanism of healing, blastimal cell formation, and regeneration of tissue will be examined in theory and by experimental examination. (10, 11, 12)

REFERENCES

1) Rubik, B.A. (1979) *A Systems Approach to Bacterial Chemotaxis. UC Berkeley*: 1979. Dissertation.
2) Worrall, A. & Worrall, O. (1970) *The Healing-Touch*. NY: Harper & Row.
3) Rauscher, E.A. & Rubik, B.A. (1980) "Effects of motility behavior and growth rate of *Salmonella typhimurium* in the presence of Olga Worrall." In: *Research in Parapsychology*. Metuchen, NJ: Scarecrow Press, 1980: pp. 140-142.
4) Rauscher, E.A. & Rubik, B.A. (1983) "Human volitional effects on a model bacterial system." In: *Psi Research*. 1983: 2(1): pp. 38-40.
5) Spudich, J.L. & Koshland, D.E., Jr. (1975) "Quantitative assay for bacterial chemotaxis." In: *Proceedings of the National Academy of Science USA*. 1975: 72: pp. 710-713.
6) Rauscher, E.A. (1990) "Human volitional effects on a model bacterial system." In: *Subtle Energies*. ISSSEEM 1990: 1, pp. 21-41.
7) Rauscher, E.A. (1983) "The physics of psi phenomena in space and time." In: *Psi Research*. 1983; 2: pp. 87-102.
8) Rauscher, E.A. (1984) "Application of human volition mind-matter interactions." In: *Applied Psi*. 1984; 9 9-14 and *Archaeus*: 1984: 2: pp. 71-75.
9) Rauscher, E.A. (1979) "Some physical models potentially applicable to remote perception." In: *The Iceland Papers: Frontiers of physics conference; Select Papers on Experimental and Theoretical Research on the physics of consciousness*. Amherst, WI: Essentia Research Association. 1996; pp. 49-93. 2nd edition. PACE, Ottawa, Canada.
10) Rauscher, E.A. & Van Bise, W. (1984) "The dynamics of electromagnetic healing effects on in vitro and in vivo biological systems." Preprint *PSRL-I0796*; 1984.
11) Rauscher, E.A. & Van Bise, W. (1990) *Theoretical Models and Experimental Data Concerning the Space-time Properties of Consciousness and Remote Mental Influence*. PSRL– 60788; 1990: pp.1-220. Buck Fine Arts Grant, San Leandro, CA.
12) Rauscher, E.A. & Van Bise, W. (1999) *"Experimental Detection and Determination of the Properties and Characteristics of Human Remote Volitional Intentional Psychokinetic Effects on a Remote Electronic Sensor System."* Grant from Ditron, LLC. Tecnic Research Laboratory, Apache Junction, AZ. Rev.

Reality is unbroken wholeness in unending flow.

--- David Bohm

CHAPTER 8 A STUDY ON PRAYER AND AIDS

Elisabeth Targ, MD

Elisabeth F. Targ was president of the PRG beginning in 1992. She received her MD and Russian language translator's certificate from Stanford U, where she also received an MA degree in neuropharmacology, and two BA degrees (biology and Slavic languages). She was a practicing physician, Professor of Medicine at UCSF, and Director of The Complementary Medicine Research Inst. at CA Pacific Medical Center in SF. Her studies drew her to probe the possible role of the mind-body-spirit connection involved in medical healing early in her career. She began her formal inquiry through a peer-reviewed study on the complementary use of alternative medicine in the treatment of women with late-stage breast cancer. Based upon the success of the study, she helped create a center sponsored by the Department of Defense at UCSF, which she helped direct. Through randomized double-blind clinical trials, she and her colleagues found strong evidence that HIV positive AIDS patients who received prayers from distant healers of a variety of faiths had significantly better medical outcomes than patients who did not receive supportive prayers. This groundbreaking study was published in the Western Journal of Medicine in 1999, and was discussed in Time magazine, the Wall Street Journal, and The News Hour with Jim Lehrer.

Dr Targ designed a study (funded by the NIH) to explore prayer and healing as skills for health professionals to integrate into their healing work. Principally, the study examines the efficacy of prayer on patients with glioblastoma brain cancer. Shortly after receiving the funding, she was diagnosed with this same form of cancer, and moved peacefully beyond "this plane of illusion" in 2002.   www.etarg.net and www.etarg.org

A STUDY ON PRAYER AND AIDS [*3]

Russell Targ
Elisabeth Targ

Energy from the universal field of energy becomes available to the healer through the act of tuning his personal energy field to a harmonious relationship with the universal field of energy....
He acts in this way as a conductor between the universal field of energy and the patient.

--- Olga Worrall (1)

In his 1993 book *Healing Research* psychiatrist Daniel Benor examined over fifty controlled studies from around the world. He reviewed psychic, mental, and spiritual healing experiments performed on a variety of living organisms: enzymes, cell cultures, bacteria, yeasts, plants, animals, and humans. More than half the studies demonstrated significant healing. His 2001 book, *Spiritual Healing*, describes more than 120 scientific studies. (2)

PRAYER FOR AIDS PATIENTS

A landmark study by Fred Sicher, psychiatrist Elisabeth Targ, and others was published in the December 1998 issue of the *Western Journal of Medicine*, describing healing research carried out at California Pacific Medical Center (CPMC). (3) This research details and describes the positive therapeutic effects of distant healing, or healing intentionality, on men with advanced AIDS.

In this mainstream medical journal, the researchers defined nonlocal, or distant, healing as "a conscious dedicated act of mentation intended to benefit another person's physical and/or emotional well-being at a distance," adding that it has been found in some form in nearly every culture in history. Their research hypothesized that an intensive ten-week distant-healing intervention by experienced healers located around the US would benefit the medical outcomes for a population of advanced AIDS patients in the San Francisco Bay Area.

[*3] Targ R. (2004) *Limitless MIND: A Guide To Remote Viewing And Transformation Of Consciousness.* Novato, CA: New World Library.

The researchers performed two separate, randomized, double-blind studies: a pilot study involving twenty male subjects paired by number of AIDS-defining illnesses, and a replication study of forty men carefully matched into pairs by age, T-cell count, and number of AIDS-defining illnesses. The participants' conditions were assessed by psychometric testing and blood testing at their enrollment, after the distant healing intervention, and again six months later, when physicians reviewed their medical charts.

In the pilot study, four of the ten control subjects died, while all of the subjects in the treatment group survived. But this result was possibly confounded by unequal age distributions in the two groups.

In the application study, forty men with AIDS were again recruited from the San Francisco Bay Area. This time, they were paired more thoroughly, as described above. They were told that they had a fifty-fifty chance of being in the treatment group or the control group.

Forty distant healers from all parts of the country took part in the study. Each of them had more than five years of experience with their particular form of healing. They were from Christian, Jewish, Buddhist, Native American, and shamanic traditions, as well as from secular "bioenergetic" schools. Each patient in the healing group was treated by a total of ten different healers on a rotating schedule. Healers were asked to work on their assigned subject for approximately one hour per day for six consecutive days, with instructions to "direct an intention of health and well-being" to the subject. None of the forty subjects in the study ever met the healers, nor did they or the experimenters know into which group anyone had been randomly assigned.

After five weeks, at the midpoint of the study, neither group of subjects was able to guess whether they were the healing group. By the end of the study, however, there were many fewer opportunistic illnesses in the healing group, allowing the group's members to identify themselves as such — with significant odds against chance. Since all subjects were being treated with Triple-Drug Therapy, there were no deaths in either group. The healing group experienced significantly better medical and quality-of-life outcomes (odds of 100 to 1) on many quantitative measures, including fewer outpatient doctor visits (185 vs. 260); fewer days of hospitalization (10 vs. 68); less severe illnesses acquired during the study, as measured by illness severity scores (16 vs. 43); and significantly less emotional distress. In her summary, Elisabeth Targ concluded, *"Decreased hospital visits, fewer new severe diseases, and greatly improved subjective health supports the hypothesis of positive therapeutic effects of distant healing."*

The editor of the journal introduced the paper thus:

> *The paper published below is meant to advance science and debate. It has been reviewed, revised, and re-reviewed by nationally known experts*

in biostatistics and complementary medicine. We have chosen to publish this provocative paper to stimulate other studies of distant healing, and other complementary practices and agents. It is time for more light, less dark, less heat (fewer arguments).

OTHER CLINICAL DEMONSTRATIONS OF DISTANT HEALING

Two other balanced, double-blind studies of distant healing have been published in prestigious medical journals. In 1988, physician Randolph Byrd published, in the *Southern Medical Journal*, a successful double-blind demonstration of distant healing. The study involved 393 cardiac patients at San Francisco General Hospital. (4) In 1999, cardiologist William Harris of the University of Missouri in Kansas City published a similar successful study with 990 heart patients. (5)

The outcomes of all three clinical experiments departed significantly from chance expectation. The work of Sicher and Targ, however, required less than one-tenth the number of patients involved in the other studies to achieve this significance. One possible explanation for this greater effect size $[Z/(N)^{1/2}]$ is the fact that Sicher and Targ worked with healers who each had more than five years of healing experience, whereas the others worked with well-intentioned but much less experienced people. (6)

A detailed analysis of twenty-three clinical studies of intercessory prayer and distant healing has recently been published by John Astin, et al. in the *Annals of Internal Medicine*. (7) An examination of sixteen studies that they found to have adequate double-blind designs showed a relatively large effect size of 0.4, with an overall significance of 1 in 10,000 for 2,139 patients. In addition, two excellent analyses of the mechanisms for distant intentionality and distant healing studies have been published in *Alternative Therapies in Health and Medicine* by Marilyn Schlitz and William Braud, (8) and by Elisabeth Targ. (9)

REFERENCES

1) Worrall, O. In: Cerutti, E. (1975) *Olga Worrall: Mystic with the Healing Hands*. NY: Harper & Row.
2) Benar, D.J. (2001) *Spiritual Healing: Scientific Validation for a Healing Revolution*. Southfield, Mich.: Vision Publications.
3) Sicher, F., Targ, E., Moore, D. & Smith, H. (1998) "A randomized double-blind study of the effect of distant healing in a population with advanced AIDS." In: *Western Journal of Medicine*, vol. 169, December 1998, pp. 356-36.
4) Byrd, R.C. (1988) "Positive therapeutic effects of intercessory prayer in a Coronary Care Unit population." In: *Southern Medical Journal*, vol. 8r, no. 7, July 1988, pp. 826-829.

5) Harris, W.S., et al. (1999) "A randomized, controlled trial of the effects of remote intercessory prayer on outcomes in patients admitted to the Coronary Care Unit." In: *Archives of Internal Medicine*, vol. 159, October 25,1999, pp. 2273-2278.
6) The *effect size* measures the efficiency, or strength, of the phenomenon under investigation. It is equal to the number of observed standard deviations from chance, divided by the square root of the number of trials performed in order to achieve that level of significance.
7) Astin, J.A., Harkness, E. & Ernst, E. (2000) "The efficacy of 'distant healing': A systematic review of randomized trials." In: *Annals of Internal Medicine*, vol. 132, no. 11, June 2000, pp. 903-910.
8) Schlitz, M. & Braud, W. (1997) "Distant intentionality and healing: Assessing the evidence." In: *Alternative Therapies in Health and Medicine*, vol. 3, no. 6, November 1997.
9) Targ, E. (1977) "Evaluating distant healing: A research review." In: *Alternative Therapies in Health and Medicine*, vol. 3, no. 6, November 1977.

> *A natural question arises: how can one explain from the position of science such important, scientifically confirmed facts as remote influence of healers? If it is a kind of radiation emanation, it must comply with physical laws - it must diminish at a distance, have its own frequency range, be recorded by an instrument. But it turns out that this mysterious power, field, energy, emanation or signal, does not reduce in its influence at any distances and causes in a human organism directed reactions in accordance with the healer's desire and intention....*
>
> *In all cases a common denominator in DMH (Distant Mental Healing) is the mental directedness of the healer's consciousness. At the same time there appears to occur a harmonization of two systems of consciousness - the healer's and that of the living organism, as a result of which they become mentally congruent in relation to each other. Consequently, consciousness, as the main controlling, and regulating, and coordinating center of the organism invigoration, appears to be the basis of living systems' self-regulation.*
>
> *--- Alexander P. Dubrov*
>
> (Author of over 300 articles and 10 books published in Russia, USA, UK, and Japan, he is a world known biophysicist and lecturer. In 2005, he finished writing Cognitive Psychophysics - published in Moscow-Berlin.)
> His website is http://www.apdubrov.inc.ru.

CHAPTER 9 PRAYER AND INTENTION IN HEALING WITH DEAN RADIN

Marilyn Schlitz, PhD

Marilyn Mandala Schlitz received her PhD in anthropology from the University of Texas, Austin in 1992. She is a clinical research scientist, medical anthropologist, writer, and thought leader. Her work over the past three decades explores the interface of consciousness, science, and healing. She has taught at Trinity University, Stanford University, and Harvard Medical Center. Marilyn possesses a rare ability to translate complex ideas into a common sense language that excites the imaginations of audiences worldwide.

Dr Schlitz is the President and CEO for the Institute of Noetic Sciences (IONS), Senior Scientist at the Research Institute, California Pacific Medical Center, and cofounder of Heallio.

She has published numerous articles on consciousness studies in scholarly and popular journals and has given talks at the United Nations, the Smithsonian Institution, and the Explorers Club. Her books include: *Consciousness and Healing: Integral Approaches to Mind Body Medicine* (Churchill Livingston/Elsevier, 2005) and *Living Deeply: The Art and Science of Transformation in Everyday Life* (New Harbinger/Noetic, 2008).

The website for the Institute of Noetic Sciences is www.noetic.org.

PRAYER AND INTENTION IN DISTANT HEALING: ASSESSING THE EVIDENCE

Marilyn Schlitz
Dean Radin

The authors would like to thank Jenny Mathews, Charlene Farrell, and Cassandra Vieten for their help on the production of this chapter.

INTRODUCTION

Throughout history and in almost all cultures, people have claimed they were healed by another person's caring intention or will. (39) From botanic as in Mexico, to street markets in Senegal, the desert of the Kalahari, healing shrines in Japan, and suburban neighborhoods in the United States, we find settings in which people attempt to help others by consciously intending their well-being, even at a distance. (24)

Distant healing intention is often associated with the religious practice of prayer, and rituals for fostering such intentions can be found in all the major religions. Some individuals spend their lives in contemplative prayer, such as Carmelite nuns, and some monks and nuns devote a substantial proportion of their prayers to requests for healing. For example, the Unity Church has offered prayers on behalf of anyone who requests it, 24 hours a day and 365 days a year, for over a century. In Jerusalem, an Internet prayer service allows people around the globe to request prayer at the Wailing Wall. During the holy month of Ramadan, millions of Moslems gather at Mecca to engage in group prayer several times each day.

In contemporary US culture it is difficult to determine the precise prevalence of the use of distant healing intention as a complementary and alternative medicine (CAM) therapy, not because it is rarely used but because it is so popular that surveys have had to focus on finding the exceptions. We do know that distant intention is the most common healing practice used outside of conventional medicine. In a recent survey of adult Americans, conducted by the Centers for Disease Control and Prevention's National Center for Health Statistics, of the top five most popular CAM healing practices, three involved prayer and spirituality, (2) the most popular CAM practice was prayer for self, and the third most popular was prayer for others.

An earlier national survey found that 82 percent of Americans believed in the healing power of prayer, and 64 percent felt that physicians should pray with patients who request it. (38) Another survey found that 19 percent of cancer patients reported that they augmented their conventional medical care with prayer or spiritual healing. (8) And a survey of American Cancer Society support groups for women with breast cancer showed that 88 percent found spiritual or religious practice to be important in coping with their illness, (11) although the extent to which specific prayers or intentions of healing were part of their activities was not clear. In acute illnesses, such as cardiac events, these numbers are higher. For example, Saudia, Kinney, Brown, and Young-Ward (22) found that 96 percent of patients stated that they prayed for their health before undergoing surgery. Some 33 percent of Hispanic patients with AIDS reportedly sought such prayer assistance. (34) And in the United Kingdom, there are more distant healers (approximately 14,000) than therapists from any other branch of CAM, (1) indicating the widespread practice and use of distant healing.

Among medical professionals, the concepts of spiritual healing, energy healing, and prayer are slowly gaining acceptance as well. In a 1996 survey of northern California physicians, (38) thirteen percent of practitioners reported using or recommending prayer or religious healing as an adjunct to conventional interventions. Therapeutic touch, which can be performed at a distance, is used by nurses in at least 80 hospitals in the United States (16) and has been taught to more than 43,000 healthcare professionals. (13) Among the lay public, Reiki International, the largest training organization for "subtle-energy healing," reports having certified more than 500,000 practitioners worldwide. While Reiki healing is frequently performed through physical contact, it is also regularly practiced over distances of thousands of miles. (23)

Many terms have been used to describe intentional interventions. They include intercessory prayer, spiritual healing, nondirected prayer, intentionality, energy healing, shamanic healing, nonlocal healing, noncontact therapeutic touch, and level III Reiki. Each of these modalities describes a particular theoretical, cultural, and pragmatic approach toward mediating a healing or biological change through mental intention of one person toward another. (24) Those who engage in distant healing often share the conviction that their process involves contact with an ineffable spiritual realm.

While many patients and healthcare providers regard intention and prayer as vitally important, what support is there that distant intention extends beyond mundane psychological and sociological explanations? From a psychological perspective, all forms of intentional therapy may be thought of as employing a simple coping mechanism in the face of uncertainty or dire need. In addition, the concept that prayer for self promotes healing is no longer considered radical because of the growing literature on the salutary effects of meditation and placebo and, perhaps more importantly, the plausibility of psychoneuroimmunological*[4] models of self-regulation. (12)

Likewise, prayer for others is understandable as a practical coping mechanism, but the idea that it might be efficacious remains controversial. Distant healing effects are considered scientifically doubtful because the term distant in this context means shielded from all known causal interactions. (31, 37) Science is slowly coming to grips with the concept of "spooky action at a distance" in fundamental physics, (36) but so far the idea that nonlocal effects might also be important in the behavior of living systems evokes as much scorn as it does interest. Because the mechanisms underlying distant healing are unknown, most experiments studying the hypothesized effects have been concerned with the more straightforward empirical question: Does it work?

THE SCIENCE OF DISTANT HEALING

Distant healing intention (DHI) may be defined as "a compassionate mental act intended to improve the health and well-being of another person at a distance." (30)*[5] The fundamental assumption in DHI is that the intentions of one person can affect the physiological state of another person who is distant from the healer.

Over the past half-century, researchers have developed techniques for measuring possible distant healing effects on living systems. (4, 9, 17, 28, 29, 33) The goal of these experiments has been to see whether an individual's intentions can produce a measurable response in a distant living system. The best experiments have employed rigorously controlled designs that rule out all known conventional sources of influence, including environmental factors, physical manipulations, suggestion, and expectancy. (28)

A relatively small but compelling body of experimental literature supports the DHI effect in organisms ranging from bacteria*[6] (18) to laboratory animals (32) to randomized clinical trials with human patients. (7, 30) As of 1992, at least 131 controlled DHI studies had been published, of which 56 found a statistically significant effect. (3) More recent review, of subsets of these experiments continues to show positive trends. (1, 29) We will review a few of these experiments to illustrate the research and its relevance to assessing the plausibility of genuine distant healing.

---

*[4] Barrett, S. in Chapter 6.
*[5] Targ, R. & Targ, E. in Chapter 8.
*[6] Rubik, B. & Rauscher, E.A. in Chapter 7, also J. Mishlove, pages xxvi-xxvii.

DISTANT HEALING INTENTIONS IN A BASIC SCIENCE PARADIGM

Numerous studies have addressed the question of whether physiological measures — specifically autonomic nervous system activity in humans — might be susceptible to distant intentions. In the majority of these experiments, electrodermal activity (EDA) was used as the physiological measure. EDA provides a sensitive, noninvasive measure of the degree of activation in the autonomic nervous system.

Beginning in the 1970s, Braud and Schlitz conducted a series of experiments in which skin conductance was measured in the target person (a "receiver"), while a "sender" in an isolated, distant room attempted to interact with him or her by means of calming or activating thoughts, images, or intentions. (6, 24, 26) In these studies, the sender's intentions were not necessarily aimed toward distant healing, but the experimental task was consistent with a distant mental influence as proposed by DHI.

In 2004, psychologist Stefan Schmidt and his colleagues from the University of Freiburg Hospital, Germany, published a meta-analysis of these EDA-based experiments in the *British Journal of Psychology* by Schmidt et al. (29) Schmidt's team found 40 experiments conducted between 1977 and 2000. Overall the results were in favor of replicable DHI-like interactions ($p < 0.001$, Cohen's d weighted effect size $d = 0.11$). The possibility of inflated statistical results due to selective reporting practices was investigated, and no such biases were found. In addition, no significant relationships were found between experimental methods and the resulting outcomes, so the results were not explainable as design flaws. In a second set of EDA-based experiments focusing on an effect conceptually similar to distant intention, namely "the sense of being stared at" (over closed circuit television to avoid sensory interactions), Schmidt's team found 15 experiments conducted between 1989 and 1998. The meta-analysis again found a significant overall effect ($p = 0.01$, Cohen's $d = 0.13$), no evidence of selective reporting biases, and no relationship between study quality and outcome. In discussing their findings, Schmidt's group noted that: *"Because of the unconventional claim of the studies under research, we always chose a more conservative strategy whenever such a decision had to be made."* They concluded that, for both classes of experiments: *"There is a small, but significant effect. This result corresponds to the recent findings of studies on distant healing and the 'feeling of being stared at.' Therefore, the existence of some anomaly related to distant intentions cannot be ruled out."*

With decades of repeatable, statistically significant findings reported from different laboratories, confidence is increasing that DHI effects are real. The absolute magnitude of the effects observed in the laboratory is small, but this is true for many other medically relevant effects. For example, a major clinical study on the use of aspirin to prevent second heart attacks was stopped early because researchers decided it was unethical to withhold the drug from the control group given its observed, positive effects. The effect size for the aspirin effect was 0.03-nearly four times smaller than the equivalent distant intention effect size of 0.11. (25)

A recent experiment attempted to build a bridge between basic science investigations of distant healing using healthy volunteers and clinical studies on distant healing under conditions of genuine need. (20) The study investigated what would happen when the powerful motivations associated with clinical trials of DHI were combined with the controlled context and objective measures offered by laboratory protocols. It also explored the role of training in potentially modulating DHI effects. In the "trained group," the sender of distant healing (the healthy partner) attended a daylong training program involving discussion and practice of a secular DHI technique based on the Tibetan Buddhism practice of Tonglen meditation, Judeo-Christian forms of meditation, and therapeutic touch.

After attending the training session and practicing the DHI meditation daily for three months, each healthy partner and his or her spouse or friend undergoing treatment for cancer were tested in the laboratory. In a wait group condition, the couple was tested before the healthy partner attended the training. A third control group condition consisted of healthy couples who received no training. The results of this experiment showed that the overall effect size for the motivated condition was 0.74, nearly 7 times larger than the earlier DHI meta-analytic estimate of 0.11, and over 24 times larger than the aspirin study mentioned above. This suggests that distant healing practiced with very high motivation and training may be far more robust than previously observed in laboratory studies.

DHI IN CLINICAL STUDIES: ADDRESSING THE "SO WHAT?" QUESTION

Although there appears to be evidence to support proof of principle for the hypothesis that the intentions of one person have a measurable effect on the biology of another living system, we are still left with the question: Does DHI have clinical relevance? Can focused intention affect the course of healing within real patient populations? To date, only a small number of scientific studies have directly addressed this important question. So far, these clinical studies provide conflicting evidence that DHI can improve medically relevant outcomes in people suffering from conditions including arthritis, cardiac problems, hernia surgery, and AIDS. Interpretation of these clinical studies is complicated by lack of homogeneity in patient populations, lack of control and documentation of current medications, lack of consistency in healer background and intervention (30) and uncertainty about the role of patient expectancies and belief in DHI outcomes. However, this is not to say that there is no evidence. The majority of randomized, double blind investigations to date support the clinical efficacy of DHI. (21, 27) In a systematic review published in the *Annals of Internal Medicine*, John Astin and colleagues (1) found that 57 percent (13 of 23) of the published randomized, controlled clinical trials (RCTs) on DHI showed a positive treatment effect in a wide range of human populations, including both genders and a wide range of ages and ethnicities. As noted by Astin and colleagues (2000, p. 910):

> We believe that additional studies of distant healing that address the methodological issues outlined above are now called for to help resolve some of the discrepant finding in the literature and shed further light on the potential efficacy of these approaches.

Clinical trials of DHI were initiated in a seminal study by cardiologist Randolph C. Byrd. (7) In the 1980s, Byrd, then a cardiologist at San Francisco General Hospital, conducted an RCT to assess the effects of intercessory prayer on health outcomes in 393 patients admitted to the coronary care unit. Patients were randomly assigned to a prayed-for group or a control group; both groups underwent comparable conventional medical treatment. The healers Byrd chose were people with an active Christian life manifested by daily devotional prayer and an active fellowship with a local church. Each person prayed daily, that the cardiac patients would achieve specific outcomes, including rapid recovery, prevention of complications and death, and any other areas they believed helpful to the patient.

The study results showed that members of the group receiving healing prayer were five times less likely to require antibiotics and three times less likely to develop pulmonary edema compared to the control group. In addition, fewer among them died compared to the control group, and none of the prayed-for group required endotracheal intubation, while 12 in the control group did.

These results were intriguing, but the study was not without problems. Byrd did not assess the psychological health of those entering the study; thus, it is possible that the treated and control groups differed in this regard. Nevertheless, the results of this experiment have been quoted from pulpits to podiums and hailed enthusiastically as proof that prayer really works.

Given the scientific, social, and possible spiritual relevance of Byrd's findings, it is surprising that it took another dozen years for other researchers to conduct a more rigorously controlled replication. Finally Harris and colleagues, (10) working with 999 patients admitted to a hospital coronary care unit, found that the medical course of his patients was better in those who were prayed for than in the control group. Harris's study, unlike Byrd's, used distant healers from a variety of Christian traditions (35 percent were listed as nondenominational, 27 percent Episcopalian, and the remainder were either Protestant or Roman Catholic). Harris also chose a more global score to assess the outcome of prayer on coronary recovery. Like Byrd, Harris concluded that his patients significantly benefited from the intercessory prayer they received.

Together, these two studies provided preliminary evidence that the intention of people engaged in healing prayer can affect the physical well-being of people at a distance. A few years after the Harris study, another study of DHI was reported in the *Western Journal of Medicine* by Fred Sicher and his colleagues. (30) These observations included a small pilot and a larger confirmation study involving the effects of intercessory (petitionary) prayer on patients with advanced AIDS. Their choice of healers was interesting. Because it is not known whether one form of distant healing is more effective than another, Sicher incorporated a wide range of self-identified healing practitioners, representing many different healing, spiritual, and religious traditions. They reasoned that by combining DHI efforts they would be more likely to see a positive effect rather than relying on a fortuitous choice of one particular practice that might be effective. Healers received a photograph of their patient, his or her last name and first initial, and sometimes the T-cell count (an index of immune system functioning). The healers provided DHI to each patient for seven days, and at six months the prayed-for patients had acquired significantly fewer new AIDS-defining illnesses, had lower illness severity, fewer doctor visits, fewer hospitalizations, fewer days of hospitalizations, and improved mood as compared to the control patients. These were highly significant outcomes, given that AIDS at the time of this study had a grim prognosis and no effective treatments.

After the systematic review by Astin et al. (1) was completed, an additional three DHI RCTs have been published; none found significant evidence for a DHI effect. In the first, an NIH-funded clinical trial initiated by Elisabeth Targ and others at California Pacific Medical Center (later completed by John Astin), distant prayer had no effect on outcomes for AIDS patients. However, there was a surprising outcome: The treated patients correctly guessed that they were assigned to the treatment group to a highly statistically significant degree, unlike the control patients, who guessed at chance. This suggests that the treated patients accurately sensed the healers' distant intentions, but those perceptions did not correlate with medically relevant outcomes. This finding is consistent with laboratory DHI studies, which also indicate that one person's intentions can influence the nervous system of a distant person, without implying a healing effect.

The second DHI study was conducted under the direction of cardiologist Mitchell Krucoff of Duke University Medical Center. Earlier in his career, Dr Krucoff was a volunteer in a spiritually based hospital in an ashram in rural India. There he observed that, despite sometimes primitive facilities (it was the only place he had ever seen bare feet in an operating room) and poor prognoses, patients appeared relaxed and calm, filled with a sense of well-being. He wondered what created the "healing space" he had experienced? Could the same atmosphere in the ashram's hospital be translated into a state-of-the-art hospital in the United States, and would the combination of modern medical care and attention to spiritual well-being help patients more than standard medical care alone?

To test these questions, Krucoff conducted a pilot project on 150 cardiology patients scheduled for angioplasty at the Durham Veterans Affairs Medical Center from April 1997 to April 1998. Before the procedure, each patient was randomly assigned to either standard care or to an intervention involving guided imagery, stress relaxation, healing touch—all performed at patients' bedsides—or to intercessory prayer, which was distributed among prayer groups including Buddhists, Roman Catholics, Moravians, Jews, Baptists, and the Unity School of Christianity. The results showed that all of the interventions were helpful, and patients in the prayer group did the best. (15) However, a larger and more recent follow-up study involving 748 cardiac patients (14) found no overall result on the primary study outcome. A surprisingly strong effect was observed in one condition in which a group of people was assigned to pray for the prayers. This potential additive or "booster" effect leaves researchers intrigued despite the failure of the primary outcome to support the DHI hypothesis.

In the third recent clinical study involving cardiac patients, conducted by Herbert Benson and his colleagues (5) at Harvard Medical School, a group who received intercessory prayer without knowing that they were in the treatment group showed no improvement. But the group who did know that they were the object of distant prayer showed results that were significantly worse than the control group. This new experimental condition, which combines expectation plus DHI, had not been studied before, and it implies that, under some conditions, knowledge of receiving prayer may have a detrimental effect. Some researchers speculate that this might have occurred because patients with such knowledge may have feared that they were receiving prayer because their health had a particularly poor prognosis.

Based on all clinical trials conducted so far, we are left with more questions than answers. Should we conclude that DHI does not influence healing based on recent experiments that failed to show an effect? Or should the weight of all published clinical and experimental studies influence our decision in a more positive direction? Should we draw conclusions from the Harvard study that knowing someone is praying for us might cause harm? Does it make sense that DHI can be effective independent of any personal relationship between the person who prays and the person who is prayed for?

Researchers are faced with these and other challenges in designing and establishing scientific protocols to objectively measure, whether a particular medical problem may be helped by prayer or intention. Some of the most significant and still unresolved experimental questions include what type of prayer to use, how often to pray, how to describe what healers did so that others may reproduce the results, and how to match the belief systems of the patient with that of the healer. Investigators also face sociological constraints from both scientists and theists, neither of whom wants this research to take place at all. The former assert that prayer is nonscientific, and the latter maintain that testing prayer is blasphemous.

None of the clinical trials conducted so far has made use of what scientists call "ecological validity." This means the trials were not designed to model what happens in real life, where people often know the person for whom they are praying and with whom they have a meaningful relationship. In the Harvard study, for example, prayer groups were instructed for the sake of standardization to use a pre-scripted prayer that was different from what the prayers used in their normal practice. So the Harvard experiment did not really test what the healers claimed works for them. In addition, in most of the clinical studies, the investigators were tightly focused on medical outcomes, and hardly any attention was paid to the inner experiences of the healers and the patients.

THEORETICAL CONTEXT FOR DISTANT HEALING

One of the primary reasons that mainstream science and medical researchers doubt that distant healing is effective is that it seems to violate what might he called folklore physics—the physics of everyday experience. Sloan and Ramakrishnan (31) assert that:

> Nothing in our contemporary scientific views of the universe or consciousness can account for how the 'healing intentions' or prayers of distant intercessors could possibly influence the [physiology] of patients even nearby let alone at a great distance. (See pp. 1769-1770.)

But is it true that nothing in science suggests the presence of connections between apparently isolated objects? Quantum entanglement, a far from common sense effect predicted by quantum theory—described by Einstein as "spooky action at a distance" and later demonstrated as fact (36) in the laboratory—shows that, under certain conditions, particles that interact remain instantaneously connected after they separate regardless of distance in space or time. If this property is truly as fundamental as it appears to be, then in principle everything in the universe might be entangled to some degree. (19) Everyday objects do not appear to show such entanglements, and there are arguments why quantum entanglement would be difficult to sustain at the human scale.

But one cannot help wondering, what if this concept *did* apply to humans. Between an indifferent, unmotivated couple, entanglements between their minds and bodies may be difficult to detect. But in a highly motivated couple, such as a dedicated healer and a patient in great need, the underlying correlations might become more evident. Such a relational model is appealing because it does not require anything (force, energy, or signals) to pass between the healer and the patient. Instead, it postulates a physical correlation that is always present between people (and everything else) due to the "nonlocal threads" from which the fabric of reality is woven. (19, 36)

COMMON ELEMENTS ACROSS HEALING PRACTICES

Many spiritual practitioners maintain that anyone can be a healer. All that is required is a compassionate heart. At the other end of the spectrum, some traditions believe that only a special few have the gift of healing. Meanwhile, research by Elisabeth Targ and others suggests that most people have inherent healing capacities but that special training, motivation, and practice are required to bring these gifts to fruition. In our studies of healing practices across many traditions, we have found a few common guidelines. These include:

Set an intention: Bring one's awareness, with purpose and a sense of efficacy, toward a healing response in the distant person.

Focus attention: Cultivate a state of concentration on the intention. For healing, this requires a mind focused on the act of intending a healing outcome.

Cultivate love and compassion: Compassion is one person's selfless love and care for another's suffering. Experience a sense of connection to others.

Suspend disbelief: Confidence and openness to the healing method is associated with the ability to give and receive distant healing.

Take time: Professional healers often set aside at least an hour a day to provide healing intention.

CONCLUSION

Surveys consistently show that distant healing intention (in a secular sense) and prayer (in a religious sense) are very commonly used. The question is whether these practices and beliefs are efficacious beyond acting as psychological coping strategies. We have addressed this question by splitting the relevant evidence into basic science, which seeks a proof-of-principle answer, and clinical research, which seeks to understand possible applications. The answer to the first question appears to be yes. The laboratory studies have been successfully replicated by numerous researchers around the world, and meta-analyses continue to provide significant evidence for these effects.

The answer to the second question – do these influences produce medically efficacious outcomes? – is more complex. Overall, the clinical trials suggest that DHI occasionally improves some patients' health under some circumstances. However, the effects are not easy to reproduce, and they appear to interact strongly with many factors that are difficult to control. These include variables such as who is praying, for what exactly are they praying, how did they pray, what is their usual mode or style of prayer, what are the relationships among the healers, the patients, and the investigators, and so on. Dozens of such factors make studying the effects of intention on healing exceptionally challenging.

In her book, *Kitchen Table Wisdom*, oncologist Rachel Remen observes, *"An unanswered question is a fine traveling companion. It sharpens your eye for the road."* (40) DHI researchers have discovered over the last few decades that their collective eyes are becoming increasingly sharpened. What we've learned so far is that there is something interesting about the role of distant intention in healing, and that this something appears to be highly sensitive to the questions being asked about it. Undoubtedly, as new questions are posed, surprising new answers will patiently await us.

TOOL KIT FOR CHANGE

Role and Perspective of the Healthcare Professional

1. Prayer and compassionate intention are vital aspects of many patients' practice. As such, it is important for healthcare professionals to have knowledge and sensitivity about what is known about these modalities.
2. Many patients today want their practitioners to pray with them; an informed opinion on the role of prayer in healing is vital to effective communication and increased compliance.
3. Attending to their own spiritual care is an important part of health professional wellness.

Role and Perspective of the Participant

1. One way in which patients take an active role in their management of pain or suffering is the use of compassionate intention and prayer for self and others.
2. Distant healing is a sought-after form of healing intervention by many patients and has been shown to reduce stress and anxiety.
3. Data from laboratory studies support the usefulness of distant healing as a component of an integral program—one with which patients can be actively involved.

Interconnection: The Global Perspective

1. Prayer and healing are part of a worldview that includes dimensions that are not included in standard medical education.
2. Gaining knowledge of other worldviews is useful for enhanced communication between patients, health professionals, and the family and society in which they live.

REFERENCES

1) Astin, J.A., Harkness, E. & Ernst, E. (2000). "The efficacy of distant healing: A systematic review of randomized trial." In: *Annals of Internal Medicine.* 132(11), 903-910.
2) Barnes, P.M., Powell-Griner, E., McFann, K. & Nahin, R.L. (2004) "Complementary and alternative medicine use among adults" (Advance Data Report #343). Bethesda, MD: National Center for Complementary and Alternative Medicine.
3) Benor, D.J. (1992) *Healing research, Vol.1.* In: (Vol. Chapters 1-2). Deddington, United Kingdom: Helix Editions.
4) Benor, D.J. (1993). *Healing Research: Holistic Medicine and Spiritual Healing.* Munich, Germany: Helix Verlag.
5) Benson, H., Dusek, J.A., Sherwood, J.B., Lam, P., Bethea, C.F., Carpenter, W., et al. (2006) "Study of the therapeutic effects of intercessory prayer (STEP) in cardiac bypass patients: A multicenter randomized trial of uncertainty and certainty of receiving intercessory prayer." In: *American Heart Journal, 151*(4), 934–942.
6) Braud, W. & Schlitz, M. (1983) "Psychokinetic influence on electrodermal activity." In: *Journal of Parapsychology, 47,* 95–119.
7) Byrd, R.C. (1988) "Positive therapeutic effects of intercessory prayer in a coronary care unit population." In: *Southern Medical Journal, 81*(7), 826–829.
8) Cassileth, B.R. (1984) "Contemporary unorthodox treatment in cancer medicine." In: *Annals of Internal Medicine, 101,* 105–112.
9) Dossey, L. (1993) *Healing Words: The Power Of Prayer And The Practice Of Medicine.* SF: Harper.
10) Harris, W.S., Gowda, M., Kolb, J.W., Strachacz, C.P., Vacek, J.L., Jones, P.G., et al. (1999) "A randomized, controlled trial of the effects of remote intercessory prayer on outcomes in patients admitted to the coronary care unit." In: *Archives of Internal Medicine, 159*(19), 2273–2278.
11) Johnson, S.C. & Spilka, B. (1991). "Coping with breast cancer: The roles of clergy and faith." In: *Journal of Religion and Health, 30,* 21–33.

12) Kiecolt-Glaser, J., McGuire, L., Robles, T. & Glaser, R. (2002) "Psychoneuroimmunology and psychosomatic medicine: Back to the future." In: *Psychosomatic Medicine, 64,*15-28.
13) Krieger, D. (1979). *The Therapeutic Touch: How To Use Your Hands To Help Or Heal.* Englewood Cliffs, NJ: Prentice-Hall.
14) Krucoff, M., Crater, S., Gallup, D., Blankenship, J., Cuffe, M., Guarneri, M., et al. (2005). "Music, imagery, touch, and prayer as adjuncts to interventional cardiac care: The monitoring and actualization of noetic trainings (mantra) II randomized study." In: *Lancet, 366*(9481), 211-217.
15) Krucoff, M., Crater, S. & Green, C. (2001) "Integrative noetic therapies as adjuncts to percutaneous intervention during unstable coronary syndromes: Monitoring and actualization of noetic training (mantra) feasibility pilot." In: *American Heart Journal, 142*(5), 760-767.
16) Maxwell, J. (1996) "Nursing's new age?" In: *Christianity Today, 40*(3), 96-99.
17) May, E. & Vilenskaya, L. (1994) "Some aspects of parapsychological research in the former Soviet Union." In: *Subtle Energies, 3,* 1-24.
18) Nash, C.B. (1982) "ESP of present and future targets." In: *Journal of the Society for Psychical Research, 51*(792), 374-377.
19) Radin, D.I. (2006) *Entangled Minds: Extrasensory Experiences In A Quantum Reality.* NY: Simon & Schuster.
20) Radin, D.I., Stone, J., Levine, E., Eskandarnejad, S., Schlitz, M., Kozak, L., Mandel, D., Hayssen, G. (2008) "Compassionate intention as a therapeutic intervention by partners of cancer patients: Effects of distant intention on the patients autonomic nervous system." In: *Explore: The Journal of Science and Healing.* July/Aug,, V. 4. 235.
21) Roberts, L., Ahmed, I. & Hall, S. (2000) "Intercessory prayer for the alleviation of ill health." In: *Cochrane Database Systematic Reviews, 2.*
22) Saudia, T.L., Kinney, M.R., Brown, K.C. & Young-Ward, L. (1991) "Health locus of control and helpfulness of prayer." In: *Heart Lung, 20*(1), 60-65.
23) Schlitz, M. & Braud, W. (1985) "Reiki plus natural healing: An ethnographic and experimental study." In: *Psi Research, 4,* 100-123.
24) Schlitz, M. & Braud, W. (1997a) "Distant intentionality and healing: Assessing the evidence." In: *Alternative Therapies in Health and Medicine, 3*(6), 62-73.
25) Schlitz, M.J. & Braud, W.G. (1997b) "Distant intentionality and healing: Assessing the evidence." In: *Alternative Therapies, 3*(6), 62-73.
26) Schlitz, M.J. & LaBerge, S. (1997) "Covert observation increases skin conductance in subjects unaware of when they are being observed: A replication." In: *Journal of Parapsychology, 61,* 185-196.
27) Schlitz, M. & Lewis, N. (1996) "The healing powers of prayer." In: *Noetic Sciences Review,* Summer, 29-33.
28) Schlitz, M., Radin, D., Malle, B.F., Schmidt, S., Utts, J. & Yount, G.L. (2003) "Distant healing intention: Definitions and evolving guidelines for laboratory studies." In: *Alternative Therapies in Health and Medicine, 9*(Suppl. 3), A31-A43.
29) Schmidt, S., Schneider, R., Utts, J. & Walach, H. (2004) "Distant intentionality and the feeling of being stared at." In: *British Journal of Psychology, 95,* 235-247.
30) Sicher, F., Targ, E., Moore, D. & Smith, H.S. (1998) "A randomized double-blind study of the effect of distant healing in a population with advanced AIDS. Report of a small scale study." In: *Western Journal of Medicine, 169*(6), 356-363.
31) Sloan, R. & Ramakrishnan, R. (2005) "The mantra II study." In: *Lancet, 366,* 1769-1770.

32) Snel, F.W.J.J., van der Sijde, P.C. & Wiegant, F.A.C. (1995) "Cognitive styles of believers and disbelievers in paranormal phenomena." In: *Journal of the Society for Psychical Research*, 60(839), 251–257.
33) Solfvin, J. (1984) "Mental healing." In: S. Krippner (Ed.), *Advances in Parapsychological Research*, 4, 31–63.
34) Suarez, M. (1996) *AIDS Care*, 8(6), 685–690.
35) Targ, R.P., Puthoff, H.E. & May, E.C. (1977, September) "State of the art in remote viewing studies at SRI." Paper presented at the Institute of Electronic and Electrical Engineering International Conference on Cybernetics and Society, Washington, DC.
36) Walach, H. (2005) "Generalized entanglement: A new theoretical model for understanding the effects of complementary and alternative medicine." In: *Journal of Alternative and Complementary Medicine*, 11(3), 549–559.
37) Wallis, C. (1996a) "Faith and healing." In: *Time/CNN poll*, 58–64.
38) Wallis, C. (1996b, June 24) "Faith and healing." In: *Time*, 58–64.
39) Whitmont, E.C. (1993) *The Alchemy of Healing*. Berkeley, CA: North Atlantic Books.
40) Remen, R.N. (1996) *Kitchen Table Wisdom: Stories that Heal*. NY: Berkley Publishing Group, pg. 293

What seems to be true, however, is that by changing consciousness, we can experience more profound patterns of the universe. I find, for example, that when we alter awareness on the continuum of states of consciousness towards more meditative or spiritual states, we become citizens of a larger universe with regard to perception, time, space, dimensionality, and possibility. We are operating at larger frequencies within the electromagnetic spectrum of the light domain. This is because we are operating from the higher patterns themselves—what I am calling the archetypal domain. It is then, too, that our psychological makeup has more source hooks in it, is less traumatized by past experience, is more capacious and capricious, and we feel extended into a mutlidimensional universe. Thus, among many other things, we are able to cause action at a distance. There have been millennia of observations of these phenomena. Were not prayer to have produced some positive results, religion would have been abandoned centuries ago. That we ascribed these results to a supernatural agency rather than nonlocality is simply, again, another mode of description.

--- Jean Houston
--- Excerpts from www.jeanhouseton.com

CHAPTER 10 — FIREWALKING

Larissa Vilenskaya, LHD

Larissa Vilenskaya received her master's degree in engineering in the former Soviet Union (her country of birth), and worked with many psychics, healers, and researchers in that country. Later, she received her LHD from the College of Spiritual and Psychic Sciences in Montreal, Canada. In 1980, she moved to Israel, where she became an active member of the Israeli Parapsychology Society. In 1981, she emigrated to the US, where (with the sponsorship of Henry Dakin at the Washington Research Institute (WRI), she founded the *Psi Research Review*, a journal devoted to parapsychology research in the Soviet Union (USSR), Israel, Eastern Europe and the US. Since she was able to translate many languages, she also translated information for the foreign broadcasts of the *Voice of America* during the cold war.

Dr Vilenskaya learned how to walk on fire in 1983. That intense experience was so profound for her that she began conducting seminars to teach others how to exert mind-over-matter so they could also feel that personal power of accomplishment.

In the 1990s she continued to work in group research projects, achieving statistically significant results with her ability in precognition. She was a past member of the board of directors of the PRG (Parapsychology Research Group). She was a regular participant in Dr Heinze's *International Conferences on the Study of Shamanism and Alternate Modes of Healing*, providing important information about international psychic research.

All of her presentations to that group are available on their website.
www.shamanismconference.org

FIREWALKING:
A NEW LOOK AT AN OLD ENIGMA

Larissa Vilenskaya

In 1983, I met Tolly Burkan, a Californian who had learned the art of firewalking from a student of a Tibetan yogi. Tolly claimed that within three to four hours, he could teach any person to walk on red-hot coals unharmed. At one of Tolly's workshops, I was inspired to firewalk and found it to be an elating, exhilarating, and profound experience. I went on to teach firewalking and gave several dozen workshops in the United States and Europe. As I taught, I discovered firewalking to be not only a deep personal experience, but also an excellent tool for healing, spiritual growth, and psychological development.

As I continued teaching and performing firewalks, my interest changed to a deep curiosity about the whole phenomenon. I have written elsewhere about the implications of the nature of firewalking. (1-6) Whereas the ancients and many contemporary firewalkers have attributed their abilities to spiritual powers, scientists look to commonly understood properties of human physiology and the physical universe to explain the mystery.

In this chapter, I will discuss various hypotheses that have been made to explain this phenomenon: physical hypotheses, psychophysiologic hypotheses, belief systems, altered states of consciousness, and mind over matter. These hypotheses are not mutually exclusive, and more than one may be a significant factor in understanding this ancient enigma.

PHYSICAL HYPOTHESIS

The firewalking phenomenon can be formulated as follows: Certain people apparently possess immunity to the influence of temperatures sufficiently high enough to be detrimental for the human organism. The tissues of mammals cannot stand temperatures higher than 60° C. (140° F.), since protein begins breaking down, and skin exposed to a temperature of 75° C. (167° F.) will blister within one second of contact. At a temperature of 250° C., the effect on the protein, muscles, fatty tissue, and nerves of the foot would be devastating in only a fraction of a second.

Although most research to date has examined the physical aspects of firewalking (7-10) and has offered *physiological* hypotheses, (11) other ideas have been advanced to explain the phenomenon. Alternative hypotheses concerning firewalking and fire immunity include psychological, psychophysiological, and religious theories and must be thoughtfully considered.

Within the framework of classical physics, three primary propositions attempt to explain firewalking. The first and most simplistic belief is that the firewalkers have callouses on their feet. The second is that the surface across that individuals pass during firewalking ceremonies (hot stones or the hot coals of a wood fire) provide low heat conductivity, and therefore any person making quick, even steps can perform a short firewalk without injury. (12-17) A third position is that the natural moisture of the foot protects a person while passing across the coals. (7, 9)

Because there were a number of Europeans with noncalloused feet who participated in firewalking ceremonies without harm to themselves, the first explanation can be easily rejected. (18-20) Furthermore, although some participants may walk quickly and take only a few steps, this appears to be insufficient to explain the lack of burns, given the extremely high temperatures involved (21, 22) and the fact that 60-foot-long firewalks have been performed without injuries to the participants. (23, 24)

The low thermal conductivity hypothesis has been widely publicized in terms understandable by nonphysicists. (25, 26) The main proponents, Leikind and McCarthy, stress the distinction between thermal conductivity and heat. They explain that even though the coals seem hot, the firewalkers will be burned only over an extended period, not instantaneously, because of the low thermal conductivity of the coals. Leikind and McCarthy have not submitted quantitative data to suggest a maximum tolerance time.

Furthermore, chemist Mayn Reid Coe walked on hot iron, a surface that is a much better conductor of heat than basaltic stones or wood coals, without injury. (7) Friedbert Karger, a West German nuclear physicist who studied firewalking in Fiji using temperature-sensitive paints, reported that a firewalker stood for seven seconds on a rock with a temperature over 600° F. (8 p. 58) During his study of firehandlers, anthropologist Steven Kane observed instances when a person held each hand stationary at the midpoint of a torch flame for ten to fifteen seconds without injury. (27) Such reports provide evidence that refutes the hypothesis of low thermal conductivity as the major explanation of fire immunity.

The auxiliary hypothesis of classical physics, that the feet of firewalkers are protected because of natural moisture on them, often is referred to as the Leidenfrost effect. (7, 9) The name derives from the eighteenth-century physician Johann Leidenfrost, who noted that at temperatures lower than 200° C., water droplets on a smooth, heated surface will evaporate quickly. At higher temperatures, a vapor barrier builds up around each droplet, and it vaporizes much more slowly. At temperatures about 500° C., the droplets again vanish rapidly.

Enlisting this information to explain firewalking, proponents of the Leidenfrost view state that the natural moisture on the walker's foot partially vaporizes at high temperatures and provides a primary protection. This depends on the ability of water to achieve a spheroid state. (7, 28) The phenomenon is encountered by the breakfast chef who sprinkles water on the pancake griddle and sees that when the temperature is high, the droplets do not vaporize immediately, but turn to spheres and remain a moment dancing on the griddle. (One can easily surmise that a coal bed is a far cry from the smooth, nonporous griddle surface required for such effects. 29) According to this theory, the sweat on the feet of the firewalker enters the spheroid state of water. In doing so, the sweat does not vaporize instantaneously, but serves to protect the firewalker from burn.

Yet, since the Leidenfrost effect is stated to occur only within a fixed temperature range, how can we explain successful firewalks outside that range? The temperature of the coal bed (ranging from 100° to 800° C.) has been both above and below the Leidenfrost limits, without the occurrence of burns. (20 p. 27) Temperatures at the lower end of the Leidenfrost range for water or sweat (about 200° C.) are still more than sufficient to produce a painful burn in a short time. Furthermore, burns have occurred within the Leidenfrost range. (16) McClenon pointed out that the Leidenfrost effect does not occur at temperatures lower than 200° C. (390° F.). Because this temperature is still high enough to cause burns, it does not explain firewalks performed over "cool" firebeds, including one firewalk performed by James McClenon during cold and rainy weather in Japan. (20)

As far as the higher end of the Leidenfrost range is concerned, the *Guinness Book of World Records* indicates that during the firewalk of "Komar" (Vernon E. Craig of Wooster, Ohio), performed at the International Festival of Yoga and Esoteric Sciences, Maidenhead, England, on August 14, 1976, the temperature of the coals recorded by a pyrometer was 1494° F. (812° C.) (30) A group of eleven persons led by Steven Neil Bisyak of Redmond, Washington, participated in a firewalk with an average temperature of 1546° F. (841° C.) on December 19, 1987, at Redmond. (31)

In discussing the Leidenfrost hypothesis, Ingalls pointed out that moisture on the feet would present a disadvantage: It would cause hot embers to adhere to the soles and increase the time of contact with the hot surface and the danger of injury. (28) Ironically, James Randi, who is known for his debunking of extraordinary phenomena, notes that Sri Lankan firewalkers believe that foot moisture causes embers to stick and carefully dry their feet before walking. (14 p. 31)

Jearl Walker, from the Department of Physics of Cleveland State University, has been a proponent of the Leidenfrost hypothesis of firewalking. Walker himself attempted firewalking several times until he suffered third-degree burns on both feet. Walker warned that his explanation is sufficient for a short firewalk *"unless the walker has an unusual tolerance for pain."* (9 p. 131) He did not specify how short the "short" is. Therefore, one has no way to tell whether standing on a hot surface for 7 seconds, observed by Karger, (8) or holding a hand stationary in a torch flame for 10 to 15 seconds (27) falls into the "short" category.

In addition, the Leidenfrost hypothesis requires that the steps not be too fast, so that sufficient sweat can build up on the foot while in the air, midstride. In actual practice, the time range of steps varies considerably between, for example, the firedancers of Greece and the firewalkers of America. (1, 10, 31) An account of Greek firedancing emphasized that the firedancer's time of contact with the burning coals was "extremely variable." (32) Another account stated *"Thracian firewalkers somehow dance over...white-hot beds, and sometimes kneel down in the center for several minutes."* (33)

Finally, the laws of physics do not, by themselves, satisfactorily explain the numerous cases in which some firewalkers have been burned, while others remained unharmed. (19, 22, 27, 34-36) Feinberg describes a mass firewalk in Sri Lanka (Kataragama) in which about 100 devotees crossed a 20-by-6-foot fire pit: *"On the night we watched the firewalking at Kataragama, twelve people were burned badly enough to go to the hospital, and one of them died.... A young English clergyman who visited Ceylon a few years ago... volunteered to walk the fire with others. He...spent the next six months in a hospital, where doctors barely managed to save his life."* (37)

The hypothesis that explains firewalking strictly according to known physical properties, then, cannot give a satisfactory answer as to why some people are burned during the same firewalk when others are not.

PSYCHOLOGICAL HYPOTHESES

Recent attempts to understand the interrelation of mind and body have begun to shed light on the phenomenon of altered states of consciousness and fire immunity. Andrew Weil summarized a psychophysiologic perspective as follows:

> *Several different mechanisms may take part. Changes in blood circulation might help conduct heat away from body surfaces or reduce the flow of heat to vulnerable tissues. Changes in the functions of local nerves might suppress the activity of neuro-chemicals that mediate pain and inflammatory reaction to strong stimulation.... A more hypothetical*

possibility is some as-yet-undiscovered capacity of the nervous system to absorb potentially harmful forms of energy, transform them, and conduct them away from the body surface....

I think the abilities are quite natural, the results of using the mind in certain ways (or not using it in ordinary ways) and so allowing the brain and nerves to alter the body's responsiveness to heat. (11 p. 249)

In Weil's opinion, psychoneurological mechanisms that may contribute to successful firewalking include the following: (a) absence of fear or any effort at defense that produces neuromuscular tension; (b) deep relaxation; (c) the presence of someone experienced and unafraid; (d) concentration, produced by techniques such as chanting or hypnosis. (38 p. 253) (11 p. 254) In current research, within these categories, only (c), the presence of an experienced firewalker, and (d), concentration, were apparent in a significant measure.

The emergence of the relatively new field of psychoneuroimmunology may augment knowledge of the mind-body interaction as it relates to fire immunity. Recent research has documented correlations among psychological events, endocrine secretion, and modulation of immunity. (39-46) The studies indicate a connection between the hypothalamus, the limbic system, and the most evolved part of the cortex, the frontal lobes, which may affect certain aspects of immunity. (47, 48) Such findings may lead to further information about an interface between the mind-body interaction and extraordinary practices such as firewalking.

BELIEF SYSTEMS

The *power of belief* refers to the individual's relinquishing some degree of personal power to forces greater than himself, be they the natural forces of the universe, the power of a placebo, or the power of God. Although contemporary firewalk instructors strengthen the power to believe in the possibility of safety, Stillings has stated: *"No firewalk instructor that I know of claims that any one belief system is necessary for success."* (29 p. 58) Thus the specific belief system held by the firewalker is not as important as the fact that there is a belief system in place.

One example of the power of belief is from Leikind, who gave a physics lecture about the low thermal conductivity of the coals and then led a group of people through the firewalk unharmed. In his own way, Leikind used a well-ensconced belief system with appropriate imagery, *"a system with some 300 years of paradigm support behind it."* (29 p. 58) In other words, Leikind acted as a firewalk instructor by using the basic belief principle of firewalk preparation—in this case, belief in the laws of physics.

The most common conviction expressed by firewalkers is the attribution of their firewalking abilities to a belief in the power of God or "friendly spirits" that protect the participant. Similar to the magical thinking described in the literature of anthropology and mythology, the firewalking literature contains numerous references to firewalking adepts who believe in mysterious forces and supernatural powers that protect them from ordinary harmful external influences.

In India, the *devtias* who perform firewalking claim to be protected by their personal deity, or *Isht*, who is invited to come into and act through them during the firewalk. (49) In Greece, the firedancing Anastenarides are believed to possess *dinami* (spiritual or supernatural power to perform miracles), which enables them both to firewalk and to *"gain access to supernatural knowledge"* and perform diagnoses and healing. (50 p. 124)

Within our own culture, devotees of the Free Pentecostal Holiness Church, who participate in numerous feats of firehandling, (27, 51) evoke a biblical passage to explain their ritual use of fire without harm: *"When thou walkest through the fire, thou shalt not be burned; neither shall the flame kindle upon thee."* (Isaiah 43:2)

The essential concept is the belief that the Holy Ghost moves into the worshipers and takes possession of their faculties, rendering them capable of carrying out works of God, that is, firehandling, snakehandling, healing the sick, prophecy, and so forth.

Physician Andrew Weil says that extraordinary abilities are natural to all human beings, and that the question of how mind and body interact is the next frontier of medical research. Yet both Weil and Pearce conclude (11, 52, 53), that belief is the key—that the power of belief accounts for all the anomalies of innate healing, the placebo effect, and such extraordinary phenomena as firewalking. Weil (11 p. 253) specifies that:

> ...Belief that counts is gut-level belief that stirs emotions and connects to the body through the centers of the deep brain. It is based on experience as well as thought and must be psychosomatic to begin with, bridging the barrier between modern cortex and primitive brainstem.

In addition, Weil addresses the universal human tendency to externalize belief in saints and deities, rather than recognize one's own spiritual power. (11 p. 250) He postulates that we may need to project belief onto external objects, such as placebos or gods, to reap the benefits of our innate power, since there is an apparent barrier between the cortex and the deep brain centers that control psychosomatic events.

Regardless of the universality of the power of belief or the belief system utilized to protect one from injury, Evaggelou suggests that this hypothesis may not pertain to noninjurious firewalks by nonbelievers. (54) But Evaggelou does not consider that belief in natural forces may be as effective as belief in deities. One might conjecture that every firewalker believes in something, regardless how disparate the belief systems may be.

ALTERED STATES OF CONSCIOUSNESS

Spiritual or other beliefs could result in an altered state of consciousness, and the contention that firewalkers and firehandlers are in a trance or an altered state of consciousness has frequently been expressed in the literature. (21,23,27,55,56) There have been few attempts to assess experimentally the states of consciousness involved. After interviewing participants of firewalking workshops, Blake found that of 52 respondents, 38% reported perceptions inconsistent with consensual reality (i.e., the coals felt cool or wet), 67% described their experience as euphoric, 54% expressed a feeling of timelessness, and 81% described a shift in their energy while firewalking. (55 p. 57)

A Greek Anastenarides firedancer has described the experience (50 p. 281) in the following way:

> If the Saint [Constantine] calls you to go into the fire, then you don't feel the fire as if it were your enemy, but you feel it as if it were your husband or your wife. You feel love for the fire.... You go into the fire freely.... When the Saint gives you courage, you feel love for the fire. You feel hope. You have a longing to enter the fire.

Devotees of the Free Pentecostal Holiness Church claim to achieve the state of *"anointing,"* which they describe (27 pp. 376-377) as follows:

> "It makes a different person out of you"; "I about lose sight of the world for a while"; "It's like a good cold shower"; "You feel just like your hands are in a block of ice. I've had it all over me"; "You feel queer all over, like you stick your finger in electricity"; "It's like a bolt of lightnin' goes through you"; "It's so wonderful. You can feel it in your flesh. You're conscious, but everything looks just beautiful to you."

Stillings suggests that simply looking at the hot coals glowing bright orange and knowing that one will step on them in a few seconds can lead to an altered state of consciousness because this action is outside our ordinary behavior. (29) The underlying issue in this case concerns those factors that cause a person to enter an altered state, and how radical a shift in attention must be before one's state is considered to have been *"altered."*

Because there have been insufficient studies of the relation between firewalking and altered states of consciousness, the role of hypnosis, trance, and other kinds of altered states remains a topic for further study.

MIND OVER MATTER

The final assumption, the hypothesis of mind over matter, however loosely defined, is proffered by both advocates of psychokinesis (PK) and those writers who postulate that physical reality is mutable and that people, through their minds, are capable of changing physical laws. (52,53,57) Psychics have been touting this approach for ages. In contemporary terms, parapsychologists define PK as *"the direct influence of mind on a physical system without the mediation of any known physical energy or instrumentation—that is, the extra-motor aspect of psi."* (58 p. 191) Firewalking might involve a mind-over-matter effect that is a heretofore undiscovered electrostatic cooling mechanism. Stillings suggests that cooling effects produced by strong electrostatic fields can be quite dramatic, as in the cool winds that reputedly may blow across the séance table. He believes that *"the mind and body, in certain altered states, are capable of mentally producing strong electrostatic fields surrounding the legs and feet of firewalkers and can then protect the subject by cooling the coals."* (29 p. 17)

Interestingly enough, many firewalkers report tingling sensations, like slight electric shocks, on the bottoms of their feet during and after firewalking. (18, 22, 59, 60) There has been no research reported to date and no known attempts to measure electrostatic fields during firewalking or firehandling.

LeShan suggests that firewalking may not be possible in our ordinary reality, but it can probably be done in an alternate reality. (61) Similarly, Pearce proposes that we can create our own reality, even one that entails a change in physical laws. (53)

SUMMARY

The hypotheses that have been advanced through the ages to account for the phenomenon of firewalking range from the esoteric to the mundane and come full circle with the overlap between ancient spiritual beliefs and contemporary parapsychological hypotheses.

Hypothesis–builders tend to fall into two general categories: (1) Those who explain firewalking within a framework defined by the currently understood properties of the known physical universe and (2) those whose hypotheses fall outside the commonly accepted scientific laws. In the latter category are those who ascribe the mysterious phenomenon to external agencies, and those who believe that the human mind is capable of powers that are not yet fully understood. Controversy abounds and further research is necessary.

Several writers invoke natural processes to explain what might allow some people to cross burning coals unharmed: the low conductivity of the embers, which will radiate heat without burning skin, and the protection offered by sweat on the feet. Some psychologists postulate a fear of failure that inhibits firewalkers from reporting blisters they sustained while firewalking.

Psychophysiologists meanwhile study the mind-body relationship, and sometimes profess that the power of an altered state of consciousness provides protection—whether that state is induced by the hypnotic skills of a firewalk leader or the social reinforcement of the group. Physiologists also may study the role of endorphins, the hypothalamus, and the limbic system in fire immunity.

Psychologists, anthropologists, and contemporary firewalking instructors all agree on the importance of a strong belief system in enacting the firewalk. Trust in the power of belief, as evidenced in the ability of the belief in spirits and deities to protect the *"faithful,"* thus characterizes the most widespread consensus about firewalking.

There also is a strong possibility that several factors may operate simultaneously. A Fijian firewalker, who believes that his spiritual deity protects him from the fire, adeptly summarizes the overlapping of several hypotheses: *"It's really mind over matter.... There are ... endless incantations until each man is prepared to do just about anything. It's like hypnosis."* (62 p. 68)

Spiritual and physical hypotheses for firewalking may blend, each gracefully allowing for and including the precepts of the other. If so, the basis for a multilevel explanation of this phenomenon emerges: Belief can build on some natural phenomenon and can evoke other natural processes. Further research is needed, but from what is already known about fire immunity, we must support Steven Kane's conclusion that *"there appears to be more than a little objective truth in the communicants' assertion that 'it takes faith' to handle fire."* (27 p. 82)

REFERENCES AND NOTES

1) Vilenskaya, L. (1984) "Firewalking: A new fad, a scientific riddle, or an excellent tool for healing, spiritual growth and psychological development?" In: *Psi Research.* 1984:3(2):102-118.

2) Vilenskaya, L. (1985) "Firewalking: Renewing an old tradition to raise consciousness." In: Heinze, R-I. (Ed.) *Proceedings of the Second International Conference on Shamanism.* Berkeley, CA: Independent Scholars of Asia; 1985:58-65.

3) Vilenskaya, L. (1985) "Firewalking and beyond." In: *Psi Research.* 1985;4(2);91-109.

4) Vilenskaya, L. (1985) "Psi in mental healing, with observations from firewalking." Presented at the Panel Discussion *States of Mind in Psychic Healing,* 28th Convention of the Parapsychological Association, August 1985; Medford, Massachusetts. (Abstract in Weiner, D.H. & Radin, D.I. (Eds.) *Research in Parapsychology.* 1985:158.

5) Vilenskaya, L. (1989) "Symbolism of fire, firewalking and individual belief systems: Do we create our own reality?" In: Heinze, R-I. (Ed.) *Proceedings of the Sixth International Conference on Shamanism.* Berkeley, CA: Independent Scholars of Asia; 1989.
6) Vilenskaya, L. & Steffy, J. (1991) *Firewalking: A New Look at an Old Enigma.* Falls Village, CT: Bramble Company.
7) Coe, M.R. (1957) "Fire-walking and related behaviors." In: *Psychological Record.* 1957; 7(2):101-110.
8) Doherty, J. (1982) "Hot feat: Firewalkers of the world." In: *Science Digest.* August 1982; 6771.
9) Walker, J. (1977) "The amateur scientist: Drops of water dance on a hot skillet and the experimenter walks on hot coals." In: *Scientific American.* 1977;237:126-131.
10) Xenakis, C., Larbig, W., Tsarouchas, E. (1977) "Zur psychophysiologie des Feuerlaufers" [To psychophysiology of firewalkers]. *Archiv für Psychiatrie und Nervenkrankheiten.* 1977:223:309-322.
11) Weil, A. (1983) *Health and Healing: Understanding Conventional and Alternative Medicine.* Boston: Houghton Mifflin.
12) Langley, S.P. (1901) "The fire walk ceremony in Tahiti." In: *Nature.* 1901;64:397-399.
13) Fulton, R. (1902) "An account of the Fiji fire-walking ceremony, or vilavilairevo with a probable explanation of the mystery." In: *Transactions and Proceedings of the New Zealand Institute.* 1902;35: 187-201.
14) Leikind, B.J. & McCarthy, W.J. (1985) "An investigation of firewalking." *Skeptical Inquirer.* 1985;10(I):23-34.
15) Price, H. (1939) "A report on two experimental fire-walks." *Bulletin II.* London: University of London, Council for Psychical Investigation.
16) Price, H. (1939) *Fifty Years of Psychical Research.* London: Longmans, Green.
17) Roth, K. (1933) "The fire-walk in Fiji." In: . *1933;33;44-49.*
18) Gudgeon, W.E. (1899) Te umu-ti, or firewalking ceremony. In: *Journal of the Polynesian Society.* 1899;8(29):58-60.
19) Freeman, J.M. (1974) "Trial by fire." In: *Natural History.* 1974;83(1):54-62.
29) Mclennon, J. (1983) "Firewalking at Mount Takao." In: *Archaeus.* 1983;1(1):25-28.
21) Ianuzzo, G. (1983) "Fire-immunity: psi ability or psychophysiological phenomenon." In: *Psi Research.* 1983;2(4):68-74.
22) Kenn, C.W. (1949) *Arii-Peu Tama-Iti: Fire-walking from the Inside.* LA: Franklin Thomas.
23) Coe, M.R. (1978) "Safely across the fiery pit." In: *Fate.* June 1978;84-86.
24) Hopkins, E.W. (1913 - 1951) "Fire-walking." In: Hastings, J. (Ed.) *Encyclopedia of Religion and Ethics, Vol.* 34. NY Charles Scribner & Sons. 1951. (First printing 1913):30-31.
25) Baker, B. (1985) "A skeptical view: Doubting academics wage a flamboyant battle to debunk society's fascination with popular theories." In: *Los Angeles Times*; April 21.
26) Garrison, P. (1985) "Kindling courage." In: *Omni.* April 1985;44-48, 84-85.
27) Kane, S.M. (1982) "Holiness ritual fire handling: Ethnographic and psychophysiological considerations." In: *Ethos.* 1982;10:369-384.
28) Ingalls, A.G. (1939) "Fire-walking." In: *Scientific American.* 1939;160:135-138,173-178.
29) Stillings, D. (1985) "Observations on firewalking." In: *Psi Research.* 1985;4(2):51-60.
30) *Guinness Book of World Records* 1988. NY: Sterling Publishing; 1987:83.
31) *Guinness Book of World Records* 1989. NY: Sterling Publishing; 1988:31.

32) Ballis, T., Beaumanoir, A., Xenakis, C. Anastenaria. (1979) In: *Hellenic Armed Force Medical Review*. 1979;13:2.
33) (1978) "The mystery of firewalking." In: *Human Behavior*. 1978;7(3):51.
34) Darling, C.R. (1935) "Fire-walking." In: *Nature*. 1935;136:251.
35) Feigen, G.M. (1969) "Bucky Fuller and the firewalk." In: *Saturday Review*. July 12, 1969:22-23.
36) McClenan, J. (1983) "Firewalking in Sri Lanka." In: *Psi Research*. 1983;2(4):99-100.
37) Feinberg, L. (1959) "Fire walking in Ceylon." In: *Atlantic Monthly*. May 1959;73-76.
38) Weil, A. (1980) *The Marriage of the Sun and Moon*. Boston: Houghton Mifflin.
39) Ader, R, (Ed.) (1981) *Psychoneuroimmunology*. NY: Academic Press.
40) Borysenko, J. (1984) "Psychoneuroimmunology: Behavioral factors and the immune response." In: *ReVision*. 1984:7(1):56-65.
41) Locke, S.E. & Colligan, D. (1986) "Mind cures." In: *Omni*. March,1986:51-54, 112-114.
42) Locke, S.E. & Horning-Rohan, M. (1983) *Mind and Immunity: Behavioral Immunology, an Annotated Bibliography 1976-1982*. NY: Institute for the Advancement of Health.
43) Oubre, A. (1986) "Shamanic trance and the placebo effect: The case for a study in psychophysiological anthropology." In: *Psi Research*. 1986;5(1/2): 116-144.
44) Prince, R. (1982) "The endorphins: A review for psychological anthropologists." In: *Ethos*. 1982:10(4):303-316.
45) Prince, R.(1982) "Shamans and endorphins: Hypotheses for a synthesis." In: *Ethos*. 1982: 10(4):409-423.
46) Rogers, M.P., Dubey, D., Reich, P. "The influence of the psyche and the brain on immunity and disease susceptibility: A critical review." In: *Psychosomatic Medicine*. 1979:41:147-165.
47) Achterberg, J. (1985) *Imagery in Healing: Shamanism and Modern Medicine*. Boston: Shambhala, New Science Library.
48) Geschwind, N. & Behan, P. (1982) "Left-handedness: Association with immune disease, migraine, and developmental learning disorder." *Proceedings of the National Academy of Sciences*. 1982:79:5097-5100.
49) Pathak, R. (1970) "The India devtia: Fire-walking deity." In: *Fate*. June 1970:90-99.
50) Danforth, L.M. (1978) *The Anastenaria: A Study in Greek Ritual Therapy*. Princeton, NJ: Princeton University. Dissertation.
51) Schwarz, B.E. (1960) "Ordeal by serpents, fire and strychnine." In: *Psychiatric Quarterly*. 1960;34:405-429.
52) Pearce, J.C. (1973) *The Crack in the Cosmic Egg*. NY: Pocket Books.
53) Pearce, J.C. (1985) *Magical Child Matures*. NY: E. P. Dutton.
54) Evaggelou, I. (1971) *I Goiteta Tou Mistiriou (The Fascination of Mystery)*. Athens: Dodoni.
55) Blake, J. (1985) "Attribution of power and the transformation of fear: An empirical study of firewalking." In: *Psi Research*. 1985;4(2):64-90.
56) Gaddis, V.H. (1967) *Mysterious Fires and Lights*. NY: David McKay.
57) LeShan, L. (1975) *The Medium, the Mystic and the Physicist*. NY: Ballantine Books.
58) Mir, M. & Vilenskaya, L. (1986) *The Golden Chalice*. SF, CA: H.S. Dakin.
59) Menard, W. (1949) "Firewalkers of the South Seas." In: *Natural History*. 1949;58:8-15,48.
60) Ross, I. (1966) "I joined the firewalkers." In: *Fate*. April 1966:46-50.
61) LeShan, L. (1976) *Alternate Realities*. NY: M. Evans.
62) Breci, S. (1982) "Fire walking has its pitfalls." In: *Fate*. October 1982:67-69.

CHAPTER 11   PSYCHOLUMINESCENT EFFECTS

Henry S. Dakin

Henry S. Dakin is a graduate of Harvard College in Engineering and Applied Sciences. From 1985 to 2004 he operated business and nonprofit incubation facilities and participated in the many research projects of the Washington Research Institute (WRI) in SF, CA.

WRI became a meeting place for people involved in the growing field of consciousness studies. The facilities of WRI created a nourishing environment for new ideas to flourish in lively discussions, and provided computers, copiers, and audio-visual equipment for use by nonprofit groups. Dakin encouraged all participants to learn to use them, as they were becoming more and more essential to any writing that resulted from the research.

Henry Dakin served on the boards of several Bay Area organizations including the Institute of Noetic Sciences (IONS), Parapsychology Research Group (PRG), and San Francisco Waldorf School. He participated in the work of the Soviet-American Exchange Program, Center for Citizen Initiatives, and other organizations, which helped break down the information gap between the USA and the USSR during the cold war.

When Larissa Vilenskaya was finally able to immigrate to the US (from the USSR through Israel), Dakin made an office available to her so she could publish the journal *PSI Research*. Since she was able to translate parapsychology research from several languages, she provided the whole group with important work being done in other countries. Dakin's own book *High-Voltage Photography* was published in 1974. Dakin is currently a publication consultant in Ukiah, CA.

PSYCHOLUMINESCENT EFFECTS *7

Henry Dakin

The formation or shaping of luminous high-voltage photographic images by conscious mental effort occurs so rarely, if at all, that for most practical purposes it may be considered as impossible. The few apparent exceptions to this rule, which have been reported by V. Inyushin, (1) V. Krivorotov, (2) D. Dean, and others (3) are described in reports, which do not give enough information to allow a technical evaluation of the experimental apparatus and procedures. In general, these reports refer to work with very unusual and highly bioenergetic subjects, not to ordinary individuals.

Experimental work by James Hickman (4) using [Kirlian photographic]*8 equipment...and witnessed by technically competent observers, will be described here, because it meets at least some of the requirements of controlled experiment design, and because comprehensive technical information is available.*9 But because these experiments were done under less than ideal experimental conditions, any conclusions that might be drawn from them should be considered as tentative, not conclusive, until confirmed or refuted by further tests using more delicate methods of observation and measurement.

> [Uri Geller was available as a subject for this experiment in the winter of 1973, during the time that he was working with R. Targ and H. Puthoff in the now famous study that was done at SRI International and published in *Nature* in 1974.] (5)

Uri Geller is already well known for having confounded physicists and psychologists with displays of apparent mental-physical energy interactions, causing metal objects to bend and break, and magnetic field strength meters to show noticeable deflection accompanying his intense concentration and muscle tension.

Physical measurements and observations of such phenomena have been described by E. Mitchell, R. Targ, and H. Puthoff. (6) This work has

---

*6 Excerpts from Dakin, H.S. (1974, 1975 & 1978) *High-Voltage Photography*. SF, CA: Washington Research Institute (WRI).

*8 [Editor's Note: All words in square brackets like this are those added by the editor to clarify or to connect the separate excerpts from the original report.]

*9 All the technical information can be found in *High-Voltage Photography*.

been criticized by some commentators who claim that the reported experimental results could have been produced by "magic tricks" or deception unknown to the experimenters. However the evidence supporting such objections is circumstantial rather than conclusive. The fact that some of these phenomena may be duplicated by trickery does not necessarily mean that this was the case in the experiments reported.

This experiment took place in a hotel room in Palo Alto, CA...at 9:00 p. m. on an evening in December 1973. The experimenter (J. L. Hickman), the subject (Uri Geller) and observers (J. Mayo [7], H. S. Dakin, W. Westerbeke, S. Kenny) were present. The apparatus used was a timer-controlled high-voltage supply...with an 8" X 10" aluminum plate electrode separated from the object to be photographed by 11" X 14" X 1/8" glass insulator plate. The subject had no previous contact with the apparatus. Photographs...(d) and (e) are prints made from high-voltage contact exposures of the subject's right index fingertip, showing, in each case, control or normal exposures at the top, and unexplained apparent psycho-luminescent effects at the bottom of the photograph.

Kirlian Photos with Uri Geller (Part 1)

Figures 1 & 2. Top – Uri's Fingertips – Normal and Control

Figure 1. Bottom – Uri "Projects" a Circle Image into his Fingertip.

Figure 2. Bottom – Uri "Projects" a Triangle Image into his Fingertip.

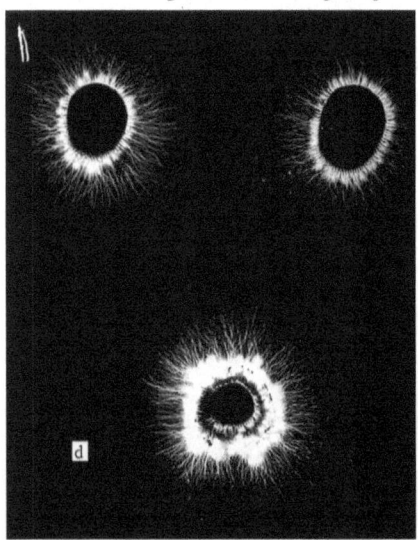
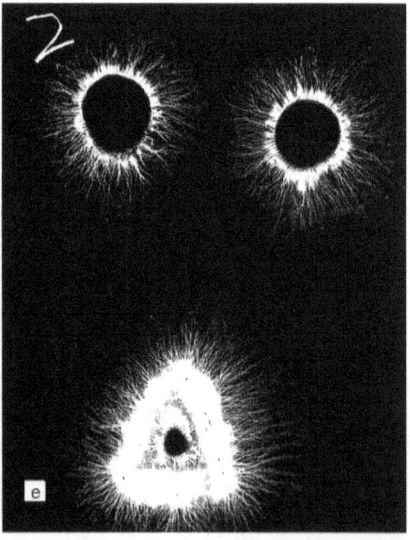

The experimental procedure was the following: {1} The experimenter and the observers chose an arbitrary geometric figure — for (d), a circle; for (e), a triangle; {2} the experimenter [asked an observer] to turn off the lights and then placed a sheet of 4" x 5" [Polaroid] film on the glass plate insulator, emulsion side up; {3} the experimenter [James Hickman] guided the tip of the subject's right forefinger to the film surface, while feeling carefully for any foreign material that might influence the image; {4} one or two control exposures were taken; {5} [Hickman] moved the subject's fingertip to another film (right), again feeling for foreign material, and keeping his own hands near the subject's hands to be able to detect any movement; {6} [all participants] concentrated on the target image, and on the subject's command, one of the observers activated the high-voltage supply; {7} the exposed film was placed in a light-tight box, and the lights were turned on.

Kirlian Photos with Uri Geller (Part 2)

Figure 3. Control exposure of Uri's Fingertip with wristwatch.   Figure 4. Uri Geller projects mental energy to the wristwatch.

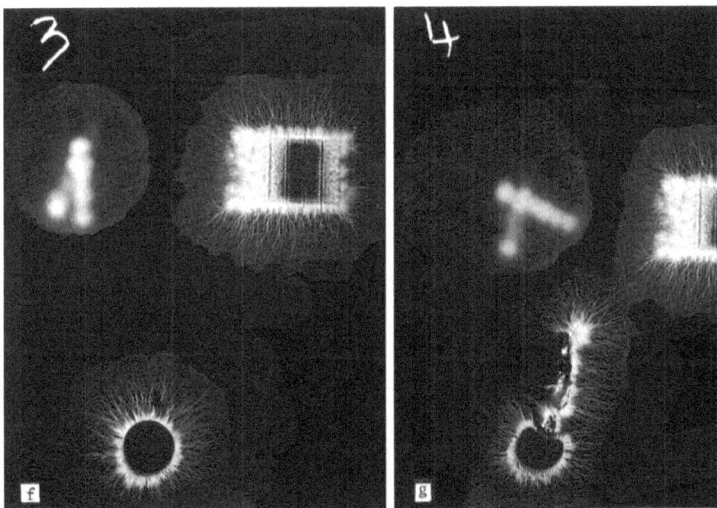

Exposures (f) and (g) were made following the same procedures, except Uri was asked to project mental energy from his finger to a luminous watch lying on the surface of the film.

[Polaroid prints of Kirlian images (f) & (g) are] of simultaneous exposures of a Japanese "Seiko" wristwatch at the top [with luminous dial] and subject's fingertip on the bottom. Streak of light in (g) occurred when [Geller intended] to transfer mental energy from his finger to the watch, during the high-voltage exposure [$1/30^{th}$ of a second]. [No one touched the watch, but you can see that the watch lost ten minutes.]

CONCLUSION

High-voltage photography — also known as Kirlian photography or electrophotography — is a method of making photographic prints or visual observations of electrically conductive objects, using as a light source the luminous corona discharge which appears around such objects in a high-voltage, high-frequency electric field.

Living organisms can be made luminous by this method. Tissue damage and electric shock hazard are minimized by the use of high frequencies and 10K currents, and by the careful design of experimental apparatus.

REFERENCES AND NOTES

1) Dombrovsky, B.A., Sergeev, G.A., Inyushin, V. (Eds.) (1972) *Bioenergetics Questions Material of the Scientific Methodological Seminar in Alma Alta.* (USSR) translated by G. Schepak, Southern California Society for Psychical Research, Beverly Hills, CA.
2) Krivorotov, V., et al. (1974) "Bioenergy therapy and healing." In: *Psychoenergetic Systems.* 1974, Vol. 1, No. 1.
3) Krippner, S., Rubin, D. (Eds.) (1973-1974) *Galaxies of Life, The Human Aura in Acupuncture and Kirlian Photography.* NY: Gordon and Breach. Revised as *The Kirlian Aura: Photographing the Galaxies of Life.* NY: Doubleday.
4) Hickman, J.L. (1973) *High-Voltage Photography Experiments with Selected Subjects.* SF, CA: Washington Research Institute (WRI).
5) Targ, R. & Puthoff, H. (1974) "Information transfer under conditions of sensory shielding." In: *Nature* 252 (1974), 602-607.
6) Mitchell, E. & White, J. (1974) *Psychic Exploration, A Challenge for Science.* NY: G. P. Putnam's Sons.
7) Millay, J. (1999) *Multidimensional Mind: Remote Viewing in Hyperspace.* Berkeley, CA: A Universal Dialogues Book, by North Atlantic Books.
8) One of the witnesses that night was J. Mayo (now Millay). Below is an excerpt of her report about an important part of that event Dakin did not mention in his book because there was no scientific explanation. In reference 7, she reported:

> While Geller was working at SRI, I showed him one of Hickman's beautifully colored Kirlian images of a hand, and asked him if he wanted one of his own hand. Geller agreed, so a meeting was set up in Geller's small hotel room. We all sat close to each other on available seating, while two of us sat on the floor. When Dakin made the first attempt to photograph Geller's whole hand, the energy interaction was so strong that Geller received a shock. Since I was one of those on the floor, and happened to be touching his foot, I also felt the shock. When Dakin began to put the equipment away, Geller asked why. Dakin said the shock was so strong that the transformer was no longer working. Geller asked Dakin to show him the transformer so he could focus his mental energy on it. He put his hand over the transformer, and soon it was working again. The Kirlian pictures shown here were those that could be taken only after Uri Geller 'fixed' the transformer.

[Editor's Note: Since those early days of Kirlian photography in the 1970s, the study of human energy has continued with advanced computers and newer systems, both in the US and in Russia. Dr Beverly Rubik worked with this technology to measure the human energy biofield, and she contributed a chapter about it in Mosby's *Complementary and Alternative Medicine* textbook published in 2009. Lynn Freeman (Ed.). Her explanation of biofields continues in Chapter 12, followed by a series of photographs of Dr Dean Brown's biofield.]

CHAPTER 12   THE BIOFIELD

Beverly Rubik, PhD

Beverly Rubik earned her PhD degree in 1979 in biophysics from UC Berkeley. She is internationally renowned for her pioneering research on subtle energies and energy medicine at the Institute for Frontier Science in Emeryville, CA, a nonprofit research and educational laboratory that she founded. She was one of 18 Congressionally appointed members of the Program Advisory Board to the Office of Alternative Medicine at the US National Institutes of Health (NIH) from 1992-1997, and chaired the NIH panels on electromagnetic medicine and manual healing. She serves on the editorial boards of the *Journal of Alternative & Complementary Medicine, Evidence-Based Integrative Medicine, ReVision: Integrative Medicine Insights,* and has published over 80 papers and 2 books. She is core professor in the PhD program in Interdisciplinary Studies at Union Institute and University, as well as adjunct professor in Integrative Health Studies at CA Inst. of Integral Studies and also at Saybrook Graduate School. In 1996, she founded the Inst. for Frontier Science (IFS), a nonprofit corporation, and serves as its president.

Dr Rubik has appeared on many TV programs throughout the US and worldwide, including "Good Morning America" (ABC-TV on Dec. 2000), where she presented her findings on the human energy field. She has authored a book, *Life at the Edge of Science* (1996), and edited an anthology, *The Interrelationship Between Mind and Matter* (1990). In 2007, her chapter on qigong was included in a peer-reviewed book *Whole Person Healthcare,* Ilene Serlin, ed., and a chapter on measuring the human energy field in Mosby's *Complementary and Alternative Medicine* textbook, Lynn Freeman, ed. (2009). She maintains a practice as holistic health educator and practitioner at Health Medicine Center in Walnut Creek, CA.   www.frontiersciences.org

THE BIOFIELD:
BRIDGE BETWEEN MIND AND MATTER

Beverly Rubik

The concept of a vital force or subtle energy is the quintessence of life and central to integrative medicine and all indigenous healing. A modern scientific term for this is the biofield, which is now a medical subject search term on MEDLINE, at the US National Library of Medicine, and the subject of increasing investigation in frontier science and medicine. The biofield is thought to permeate the human body and extend into the surrounding space. It entangles each person with one another, the biosphere, and the cosmos. I have hypothesized the biofield to be a super-organizer of development and healing and master regulator of the organism's physiology and biochemistry. (1) Mechanisms of action involving the biofield may also lie at the scientific basis of many types of alternative therapies, including laying-on-of-hands by energy healers, energy psychology, homeopathy, and other energy medicine diagnostics and therapeutics.

What Role, If Any, Does The Biofield Play In Psi Phenomena?

Contemporary parapsychologists have largely dismissed the concept of the biofield or other putative subtle energy field to be involved in the *modus operandi* of psi, because psi is observed to be independent of distance. Of course, parapsychologists' rejection of subtle energy is based on their understanding of conventional fields in physics such as the electromagnetic field, which diminishes inversely with distance, and the impossibility that such fields could mediate psi phenomena over long distances. However, some energy fields, such as the zero point energy (ZPE) field of the quantum vacuum are present everywhere and do not diminish whatsoever with distance.

As an intimate property of life, the biofield is not just the property of a single organism, but interactive with and possibly sustained by other fields, including geocosmic fields such as the earth's magnetic field, among others. Some scientists have considered that the biofield may even interact with the ZPE, in that life as a whole seems to have an intimate relationship with the universe, for example, in light of the Anthropic Principle.

Eastern philosophy and medicine holds notions of the biofield that are worth psi researchers investigating. The central premise of Oriental medicine is that where mind goes, *qi* (subtle energy) flows. So, subtle energy interactions would indeed follow intent, according to this Eastern viewpoint. This is also the basis of *qigong*, mind-body practices that originated in China designed to cultivate a mastery of *qi*, the universal life energy, and to cause qi to move according to will and intent. Qigong is also a form of biofield therapy according to the US National Center for Complementary and Alternative Medicine, and increasingly the subject of serious scientific research.

Some of the amazing stunts performed by qigong masters that I have witnessed over the years are not magic tricks whatsoever, but impressive examples of psychokinesis. For example, one man with a shaven head shattered a 1 cm thick iron slab on the crown of his head without leaving a mark, for as he explained, he was able to break it with his energy field. Another master threw chopsticks into butcher-block tables so as to cause them to penetrate the table like knives. Still another was able to pull a truck full of people using a rope tied between the truck and his male organs. Other stunts involve amazing physiological feats, too, such as sticking swords through one's tongue without any flinching, pain, bleeding, or apparent wound. In the case of the latter, the master told me that he put the sword in the space between the cells and the molecules of his tongue to avoid all injury.

There is evidence that certain qigong masters can project *qi* or otherwise influence the growth and physiology of cell cultures and other organisms across large distances; i.e., perform distant healing. Other Eastern practices, such as Reiki healing, which is another form of biofield therapy, can be performed *in situ* on a patient or over any distance, apparently bringing the power of universal life energy to mitigate pain, anxiety, as well as to produce other beneficial effects, as have been shown in various controlled scientific studies. (2)

With these findings and also new theory emerging from the frontiers of science and medicine, I think that it is timely that psi researchers reconsider the role of subtle energies and the biofield in studies on psi. That which mediates between mind and matter must be a phenomenon that has one foot in the metaphysical realm, and the other foot in the physical realm. The concept of a field is precisely that.

REFERENCES

1) Rubik, B. (2002). "The Biofield Hypothesis: Its biophysical basis and role in medicine." In: *Journal of Alternative and Complementary Med.*, December 2002, 8(6), 703-710.

2) Rubik, B., Brooks, Audrey & Schwartz, Gary (2006). "In vitro effect of Reiki treatment on bacterial cultures: Role of experimental context and practitioner wellbeing." In: *Journal of Alternative and Complementary Med.*, 2006; 12(1):7-13.

TWO EXAMPLES OF THE BIOFIELD

1) Both photos were taken of the biofield lights around Dean Brown, PhD, by Don Parker, PhD, with a Polaroid camera, using normal color film.

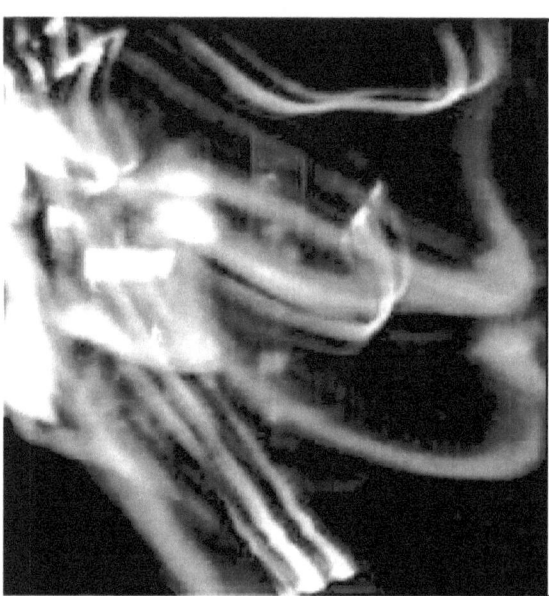

Dr Dean Brown was designing one of the 1st interactive programs for creative writing and reading comprehension for elementary students on the Apple computer. This was to be used by Parker's SRA Reading Labs in 1980. Dean was working in Don's living room under the only light, which was overhead—not moving. Don saw this image; thought there might be something wrong with his camera, so he took the next picture below.

In this picture, Dean's biofield has shrunk, as Dean becomes aware of the attention directed at him. Now we can see his head and shoulders, though the lights still move in many directions during one click of a camera. (In the background, a faint image of a chair shows that the camera is not moving.)

The next morning, Don was able to take normal pictures with the same camera and the same pack of film.

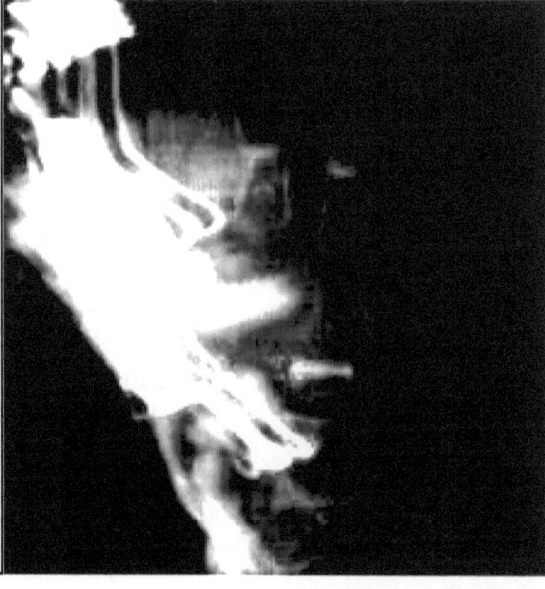

2) Both of these photos were taken of Dean Brown by Jean Millay with an ordinary 35 mm camera using fast color film for slides.

When Dean Brown showed Don's amazing photos to me (Millay) we discussed what they might represent in terms of human energy. I asked Dean if he could create a light on film through his own direct intention. He said "yes." We met at the WRI to test the results with a portrait lens. First, he closed his eyes, as in meditation. While he was still in that peaceful state of mind, I took this first picture.

As soon as Dean opened his eyes, I took this next picture. The brightest lines of light emanating from both of his eyes are white on the 35mm slide (though the artificial light in the room casts a warm tone on the other colors.)

The white light seems to form a curve of brightness, which fades gradually into the strong golden band of light across the image at the bottom. The light of this biofield shows his power of intention.

SECTION III

BELIEF SYSTEMS ARE EVOLVING

THE FACT THAT SOME THINGS HAVE NO RATIONAL EXPLANATION OUGHT TO STOP THEM HAPPENING — BUT IT DOESN'T.

* Copyright © 1995 by Ashleigh Brilliant
www.ashleighbrilliant.com

SECTION III

BELIEF SYSTEMS ARE EVOLVING

The 1993 anthology *Silver Threads: 25 Years of Parapsychology Research* began with these words by editor and author Dr Beverley Kane:

> *In essence, our Foreword and our Foundations sections are morphing old beliefs into new at three complementary levels.*
>
> *At the most general level, Harman reviewed the philosophy of science and initiated the reevaluation of our most fundamental concepts of science, philosophy, and the mind.*
>
> *At the next, more solidified level, William Kautz delved further into the elements of scientific praxis. Kautz' valuable contribution was to demystify terms like paranormal and psychic. By reframing these concepts to the more familiar notion of intuition, Kautz orients us to the unusual concepts in subsequent chapters.*
>
> *At ground level, Kane focused the broader discussion of philosophy, science, and society in an examination of the individual's everyday experience. Her thesis is that although the scientific method will continue to be appropriate for some types of formal investigations, it was never intended to disqualify the personal events of the individual's everyday experience that it cannot contain.*
>
> *Silver Threads is about the science of the possible. In a colorful, fluid melting of images, Harman morphed the dominant conservative philosophy into a liberal and visionary one. Kautz was able to morph skepticism about the paranormal into certainty about the intuitive. Kane morphed the common over-reliance on formal proof systems into validation of personal experience.*

Harman's writings on the need to shift our assumptions from the limits imposed by materialism were prophetic, since this shift is now expanding. Twenty years later we are observing how that morphing process has (and continues to) evolve as we find that the power of mind may be limited only by the belief it adopts.

To expand on Harman's vision, we encourage the reader to *"play"* with ideas. When we consider different belief systems, as though we were "playing a role" this becomes a "game" that can facilitate the release of irrational attachments to fixed, and possibly outdated, concepts of reality. Questioning all beliefs freely opens the mind to the expansion of consciousness.

--- Jean Millay

CHAPTER 13   SHIFTING ASSUMPTIONS

Willis Harman, PhD

Willis Harman was a US Navy officer at Pearl Harbor when it was attacked on December 7, 1941. He earned a BS in Electrical Engineering at the U of WA, and then moved to CA to attend Stanford, where he earned his MS in Physics and a PhD in Electrical Engineering. In 1952, he joined the faculty at Stanford, and taught engineering systems for many years. For the next 16 years, he became Senior Social Scientist at SRI International of Menlo Park, CA, where he was Director of the Educational Policy Research Center within the Stanford Research Inst. (SRI) of Stanford U. There he developed the Alternative Futures Project, which performed long-term strategic planning for corporations and government agencies. This group provided carefully guided LSD experiences to executives for enhancing creativity, until political pressure made the activity illegal.

Dr Harman was emeritus professor on Engineering-Economic Systems at Stanford, and was also a member of the Board of Regents of UC. In 1977, the Institute of Noetic Sciences (IONS) invited him to serve as their president. This is a nonprofit organization founded by astronaut Dr Edgar Mitchell to expand knowledge of the nature and potentials of the mind. Dr Harman believed the single most powerful means of bringing about social change is through challenges to the legitimacy of institutions and their behaviors. These institutions include the political, the corporate, the social, and the scientific. He was the founder of the World Business Academy, author of *Global Mind Change* (1988), and coauthor of *Changing Images of Man* (1982), *Higher Creativity* (1984), *Creative Work: Constructive Role of Business in a Transforming Society* (1990), *New Metaphysical Foundations of Modern Science* (1994).

(Photo by Victoria Rouse.)   Website: http://www.ions.org/

CHAPTER 13

SHIFTING ASSUMPTIONS [*1]

Willis Harman

> The research explored in this book is phenomena that are considered "paranormal." These explorations into the paranormal not only appear to transcend the boundaries of discovered knowledge; they apparently amount to a scientific revolution surpassing in its breadth and fundamental nature the Darwinian or quantum revolutions.

One needs to place this claim in the context of a reassessment that is already taking place within science. The extreme positivism and reductionism of science at mid-century have given way to more relaxed attitudes. Scientists exhibit growing appreciation of the need for more holistic and organismic models in the biological sciences and for a more participative methodology. Many scientists are seeking appropriate ways to include subjective experience as relevant data in the creation of our pictures of reality; others, including Nobel laureate neuroscientist Roger Sperry, argue that a complete science must include consciousness as agency.

The phenomena and experiences that are the stuff of parapsychological research occupy a crucial position in this contemporary reevaluation of the scientific method. They are of interest to scientists because they challenge accepted paradigms; at the same time, these experiences are, in the main, familiar in the contexts of diverse spiritual traditions — and comprise a conspicuous focus of interest in the "New Age" subcultures that in some sense seem to be a modern surrogate for religion.

Three of these overlap areas stand out as of particular significance:

(1) The origin of the universe and the evolution or creation of humankind;

(2) Altered states of consciousness, including near-death and other transcendent experiences; and

(3) The area of *"meaningful coincidences."*

Why do these experiences and phenomena seem to be so incongruous with the view of reality given us by mainstream science? One possibility is that the reports can all be dismissed as illusions, laboratory artifacts, or deliberate deceptions. Another is that the phenomena exist but are not really

---

[*1] Excerpts from Dr Harman's paper published in *Silver Threads: 25 Years of Parapsychology Research.* (1993)

paranormal; that is, they will in good time turn out to be explainable through the normal concepts of science, including those mysterious concepts of quantum physics. A third possibility is that there has been something wrong with science that precluded acceptance of these phenomena.

THE PRESENT CHALLENGE TO SCIENCE

It has not only been people's other-states-of-consciousness and paranormal experiences that challenge the worldview of modern science. Among the areas in which there are major failures of the prevailing scientific worldview to accommodate well-established evidence are the following:

1. The fundamental inquiry within physics into the ultimate nature of things does not appear to be convergent. The search for fundamental particles seems to lead to still more fundamental particles; the search for the ultimate reductionist explanation seems to point to a wholeness. But with Bell's theorem, quantum physics now displays an inherent contradiction; particles originally assumed separate turn out, apparently, to be connected.

2. There appears to be evidence for a fundamental self-organizing force in living systems, from the smallest to the largest known organisms that remains unexplained by physical principles. Living systems exhibit a tendency toward self-organization (e.g., homeostasis; intricate patterns in flowers and butterfly wings), toward preservation of integrity (e.g., healing and regeneration; ontogenesis from a single fertilized egg to an adult organism), and toward survival of the organism and the species (e.g., complex instinctual patterns for protection and reproduction). The evidences of a cumulative effect, over time, of this self-organizing tendency in evolution cast doubt on the adequacy of the neo-Darwinist orthodox view.

3. There is a persistent puzzle of "action at a distance" or nonlocal causality. This shows up, as we have already observed, in the far reaches of quantum physics. It also appears in the area that John Beloff calls "meaningful coincidences," referring to two or more events in which there appears to be a meaningful connection although there is no physical connection. (1) Here "meaningful" may refer either to the subjective judgment of the observer or to a judgment based in historical data (as in the case of astrology or the I Ching). The term "meaningful coincidences" includes Carl Jung's "synchronicity" and most of the range of the paranormal. (2) Examples include apparently telepathic communication, seemingly clairvoyant remote viewing, and the coincidence between the

act of prayer and the occurrence of the prayed–for, such as healing. Another example is the feeling of having a guardian angel when a person feels warned about a danger or provided with a particularly fortuitous circumstance in life. A host of historical and anecdotal examples fall into the categories of *"miracles"* and *"psi phenomena."*

4. Our scientific knowledge about the universe appears to be incomplete in that there is no place in it for the consciousness of the observer — nor, in general, for volition (free will) or any of the other attributes of consciousness. Sperry insists that no science can be complete that does not include downward causation, from the higher level of consciousness to the lower, physicochemical level. (3)

5. One of the most perplexing aspects of this consciousness challenge to science is the concept of the self. The conscious self is ineluctably involved in observation; yet the science constructed from those observations contains no place for the self. Psychologist Gordon Allport wrote in 1955, in a little volume entitled *Becoming* (New Haven, Ct: Yale University Press), *"For two generations, psychologists have tried every conceivable way of accounting for the integration, organization and striving of the human person without having recourse to the postulate of a self."* The battle is still going on.

6. Related, but worthy of separate mention, is the area of altered states of consciousness, including particularly those states traditionally sought out in a spiritual or mystical context.

To understand what it means for science to be presented with such a broad challenge, we need to review some basic aspects of scientific inquiry.

There ultimately is no such thing as a crucial experiment to prove a scientific hypothesis. Hypotheses and conceptual models are useful or not useful—not true or false. When experience contradicts scientific theory, the theory must be changed, but there is no infallible logic for determining what to change. It is precisely to that point that present-day scientific paradoxes have brought us.

In arguing that the areas of human experience listed above constitute a fundamental challenge to the adequacy of modern science, we are in no way attacking the fundamental spirit of scientific inquiry. We are, rather, suggesting that it is time for science to take a major step in its own evolution.

This point can be made more clear by considering the three basic aspects of scientific inquiry: (4)

1. *The activity of constructing, testing, and using conceptual models.* Creating, testing, and applying conceptual models make up the chief

activity of scientists. It is not unique to science; the main way little children learn about their environment is to create mental models and test them by experience. The uniqueness of scientific inquiry lies in the other two aspects.

2. *The distinguishing values of science.* Chief among these are openness of inquiry, healthy skepticism, and public validation of knowledge.

3. *Adopted assumptions.* Modern science is characterized by certain basic ontological and epistemological assumptions that are the result of both the longstanding characteristics of Western culture and the tension between science and the Church around the seventeenth century. It is in these basic assumptions that the current form of science is most vulnerable to challenge.

Western science by the eighteenth century had adopted an *ontological assumption of separateness:* The assumption of separateness leads to the hubris that we as humans can pursue our own objectives as though the earth and the other creatures are here for our benefit, to the myth of the objective observer, to reductionist explanations, and to the ethic of competition. It implies the locality of causes; that is, it precludes action at a distance, in either space or time. It implies the *epistemological assumption* that our sole empirical basis for constructing a science is the data from our physical senses.

From these two metaphysical assumptions follow others that have been assumed intrinsic to modern science; perhaps the most important of these are *objectivism,* the assumption of an objective world that the observer can hold at a distance and study separately from himself; *positivism,* the assumption that the real world is what is physically measurable; and *reductionism,* the assumption that we come to really understand a phenomenon through studying the behavior of its elemental parts (e.g., fundamental particles). These are essentially the assumptions of *logical empiricism.*

Having started with a limiting set of assumptions, science has then found it necessary to deny the validity and even the possibility of a host of reported phenomena that don't fit within those limits. A tremendous amount of effort has gone on within science to defend the barricades against (or to explain away) these outcasts, such as miraculous healings and psi phenomena, as well as more ordinary experiences, such as volition, selective attention, and the hunger for meaning. If there is validity to the subject matter of this collection of essays, we are talking now about far more fundamental change — actual replacement of these underlying assumptions by dramatically different assumptions.

TOWARD A MORE HOLISTIC SCIENCE

There is increasingly widespread agreement that science must develop the ability to look at things holistically. In a holistic view, everything, including physical and mental, is connected to everything, and a change in any part affects the whole.

One of the main implications of a science based on oneness is the epistemological assumption that we *contact reality in not one, but two ways.* One of these is through physical sense data, which form the basis of normal science. The other is through being ourselves part of the oneness – through a deep, intuitive *"inner knowing."*

There is much to be said in favor of this proposition that science be restructured on the basis of an *ontological assumption of oneness and wholeness and an epistemological choice to include as input both physical sense data and subjective experience,* in particular the experience of such trained *"inner explorers"* as are found in the various esoteric and spiritual traditions.

Such an extended science would meet many of the criteria of the current attempts to reform science. It would not invalidate any of the physical and biological science we now have; it would, rather, be more inclusive.

It would include and emphasize more participative kinds of methodologies; it would assume that whereas we learn certain kinds of things by distancing ourselves from the subject studied, we get another kind of knowledge from intuitively becoming one with the subject. In such research, the experience of observing brings about sensitization and other changes in the observer. A *willingness to be transformed* one's self is an essential characteristic of the participatory scientist.

This extended science would be concerned with downward causation, including causation from consciousness, as well as the reductionistic upward causation that currently dominates the scientific world. In such a science, conscious awareness, unconscious processes, volition, and the concept of the self do not present any fundamental contradiction. Nor does the recommendation, in the perennial wisdom of the world's spiritual traditions, of an inner search involving some sort of meditative or yogic discipline and the discovery of and identification with a higher or true Self that is beyond the physical realm but is nevertheless real.

Openness to alternative theories and explanations as well as healthy skepticism would be at least as important in this extended science as they are in modern science. Consensual validation of findings also would remain of central importance, but it would be accomplished in a different way.

Rather than having to defend against the anomalous, wholeness science permits the assumption that any class of inner experiences that have been reported or of phenomena that have been observed through the ages and across cultures apparently in some sense exist and have a face validity that cannot be denied. We seek, in other words, a science that can accommodate all that exists. (There are many subtleties. Whole societies can perceive things that observers from other societies do not, so it is necessary to be cautious about claiming that some class of experiences is universal, even in potential. There is a tendency among some people to regard it as a mark of New Age distinction to be willing to believe almost anything. Total gullibility is not a useful objective.)

The phenomena and experiences that are the stuff of parapsychological research, which are considered paranormal with respect to modern science, would fit comfortably in such a restructured science.

Some of the more radical implications of a wholeness science are not immediately apparent. Imagine starting from the holistic assumption that everything — not only physical things, but all things experienced, including sensations, emotions, feelings, motivations, thoughts — is really part of a single unity. If things are so interconnected that a change in any one can affect all, then *any accounting for cause is within a specific context, for a specific purpose*. In the broadest sense, *there are not cause and effect, but only a whole system evolving*. What normal science does, in this view, is to study relatively isolable systems in which causal factors can be considered limited and, in particular, in which no volitional factors need be taken into account. (To recall how special this is, note that the judicial setting comprises another special case, wherein volition and motivation are considered central.) Starting from the holistic assumption, there is no ultimate separation of observer from observed. Action at a distance does not pose a particular problem; we don't even have to hypothesize fields or particle exchanges to account for it. We don't find volition, other states of consciousness, teleological influences, meaningful coincidences, and so forth to be anomalous. To reemphasize the point, none of modern science is invalidated in the limited domains in which it was generated. However, some of the common extrapolations of scientific findings into the larger area of human affairs become questionable.

SUMMARY

The point of all this discussion is that what is paranormal is a function of choice of the foundation assumptions of science. If the current metaphysical foundations are retained, it appears likely that the sorts of phenomena described in this book will remain paranormal and more or less ostracized from the halls of science. But there is another path: to recognize that the problem is not with the paranormal, but with our concept of science — more specifically with the metaphysical foundations adopted in the course of modern science's evolution.

If science were to be recast by building on the oneness assumption rather than on separability, it would appear not only to accommodate the paranormal, but also to respond to other complaints. For one thing, although the reductionistic science would still be available for the purposes to which it is suited, it would no longer have the authority to insist that we are here, solely through random causes, in a meaningless universe or that our consciousness is merely the chemical and physical processes of the brain. Lynn Margulis, professor of botany at the University of Massachusetts Amherst, told an audience at the 1991 annual meeting of the American Association for the Advancement of Science that bacteria and other one-celled animals react as though they involve something akin to consciousness in the human being. If something like consciousness is to be found in all living organisms, is it utterly preposterous to postulate a substratum of consciousness that pervades the entire physical universe? Or, for that matter, a superstratum?

The time is ripe to insist on a reexamination of the metaphysical foundations of modern science. Until this is done, research on consciousness will continue to miss the mark because it will continue to be distorted by the misguided attempt to fit it into a basically reductionistic and positivistic framework. We cannot let legitimate experimental results be excluded by the tyranny of founding assumptions that masquerade as ineluctable axioms or valid scientific findings.

The true significance of the subject matter of this collection of essays is that it points to this paradox of experience that doesn't fit in, and thus hastens the day when we may have a more adequate science: one that includes all the findings and powers of reductionistic science but puts them in a different context in which everything in human experience is validated and affirmed.

REFERENCES AND NOTES

1) Beloff, J. (1977) "Psi phenomena: Causal versus acausal interpretation." In: *Journal of the Society of Psychical Research.* 1977; 49:773.

2) Peat, F.D. (1987) *Synchronicity: The Bridge Between Matter and Mind.* NY: Bantam.

3) Sperry, R.W. (1987) "Structure and significance of the consciousness revolution." In: *Journal of Mind and Behavior.* 1987; 8:1.

4) Rubenstein, R.A., Laughlin, C.D., Jr., McManus, J. (1984) *Science as Cognitive Process: Toward an Empirical Philosophy of Science.* Philadelphia: U of Pennsylvania Press.

ADDITIONAL REFERENCES IN ORIGINAL 1993 ESSAY

Quine, W.V.O. (1962) *From a Logical Point of View.* 2nd ed. Cambridge, MA; Harvard University Press.

Lincoln, Y.S. & Guba, E.S. (1985) *Naturalistic Inquiry.* Troy, NY: Sage Publications.

Goodwin, B. (1987) "A science of qualities." In: Hilary, B.T. & Peat, F.D. (Eds.) *Quantum Implications: Festschrift for David Bohm.* London: Routledge & Kegan Paul.

CHAPTER 14   PARAPSYCHOLOGY, SCIENCE, AND INTUITION

William Kautz, ScD

William Kautz earned his undergraduate and graduate degrees (BS, MA, MS and ScD) from the Massachusetts Institute of Technology (MIT) in electrical engineering and mathematics. He was the Founder and Director of *The Center for Applied Intuition* (CAI), a nonprofit organization in San Francisco, CA, devoted to research, training, counseling, consulting and public education in the area of intuition and its practical applications in many fields.

At the time of his formal retirement (1985) he was Staff Scientist at SRI International (Stanford Research Institute), where for thirty-four years he conducted or contributed to research projects in computer science, communications, geophysics and mathematics, for a variety of US and foreign clients.

For the next fifteen years he explored the role of intuitive processes in science and technology, with emphasis on the enhancement of creativity through the deliberate development of intuitive skills. CAI has been especially active in the direct application of intuitively derived information to personal self-enhancement (counseling) and the solution of socially significant technical problems.

He lectured and taught at several institutions throughout the world, including Stanford University, the Technical University of Denmark, and the Tata Institute of Fundamental Research. He now lives in Prague, Czech Republic, and Tucson, Arizona.

Website: http://www.appliedintuition.net/   Email: williamkautz@seznam.cz

CHAPTER 14

PARAPSYCHOLOGY, SCIENCE, AND INTUITION [*1]

William H. Kautz

Parapsychology is proudly called a science by some, and is considered *not* a science at all by many others. Are these differing views just a dispute over a definition, or is there a substantial basis for them?

IS SCIENCE TOTALLY RATIONAL? WELL, NOT QUITE

Most of the stages of scientific discovery are completely systematic and rational, but two appear to depend strongly on another faculty of the human mind. Let us examine these.

The scientific method is essentially cyclic. At one point of each cycle a hypothesis is formed: a statement that *might* be true. Some kind of experiment or a plan of observation is then devised in an attempt to substantiate or refute the hypothesis. The experiment or observations are carried out; the data are collected, processed, and analyzed; and deductions are then drawn, using the tools of logic and mathematics. These deductions then permit the formulation of a new and better hypothesis. The cyclic process continues. Eventually a chain of validated hypotheses combine to create a theory, which is a kind of model that expresses how the natural world appears to be working.

Every step of this process is perfectly linear and logical — except one: Within the methodology of science there is no fully systematic way to formulate the next hypothesis. At this step, the human being has to make an irrational leap to generate the next one. He is aided by the rest of the spiral, but a totally mechanistic method of hypothesis generation is impossible. Therefore the scientific method must rely on another part of the human mind besides the cognitive, reasoning part.

A second way in which science is not rational occurs in the selection of which problems are to be investigated in the first place. Scientific research is biased in the direction of problems that can be studied with available methods and tools. Scientists do not talk much about these limitations. They have a quiet fascination for the hidden essence of

---

[*1] Excerpts from Dr Kautz's paper published in *Silver Threads: 25 Years of Parapsychology Research.* (1993)

creativity, which they regard respectfully as a kind of spontaneous magic not to be tampered with. On the whole, they behave as if all their work is entirely systematic and logical, even though they know very well that it is not so.

The history of science itself provides abundant evidence that its great breakthroughs did not occur as a result of rational thinking alone. Science could not have moved forward as it did were it not for great insights that went beyond the reasoning process. In fact, these insights were the essential factor responsible for many important discoveries. (1-4)

This observation is supported in the biographies of many great scientists, who revealed (often late in life, when they cared little for what their peers thought of them) just how they obtained their breakthroughs.

The discoverers typically have attributed their success not to careful reasoning and analysis, but to a sudden impulse, a quantum of new knowledge that entered their minds. The result might be attributed to unconscious reasoning were it not for the fact that in many cases, their discovery did not follow logically from what preceded it. Clearly, then, there must be a process in the human mind whereby totally new information can enter under the right conditions.

The name for this process is *intuition.*

THE INTUITIVE PROCESS

Intuition and reasoning are the principal components of what we call thinking and almost all thinking involves both. Intuition is the mind process of direct apperception of knowledge, as distinct from knowledge acquisition by the senses, from reasoning or even from memory. (5-7) Intuitive perception is an inner process. Like reasoning, it is not inherently a type of behavior, but it underlies behavior. Belief in the capacity of the mind to acquire new knowledge directly is the crucial credibility gap to be transcended in appreciating intuition.

The source of direct knowledge may not have a *where* or even a *when* but may be simply omnipresent — as a property of reality, like the force fields of physics and abstract qualities of human life such as love and joy, which we accept without question. Is it such a stretch of faith to believe that all knowledge, past, present, and potential — already exists, ready to be accessed by the human mind?

The *conscious* mind represents that part of all reality we are *aware* of. It is largely an attention focuser; it directs our sensory input and motor output and draws as needed from memory banks within the unconscious. It has little or no memory of its own.

The *subconscious* mind is the part of the unconscious that contains the personal record of one's experiences throughout life. Most of these memories are irrelevant to conscious life, most of the time; they simply reside in the subconscious. Some are available through hypnosis and can be probed when there is a need to do so. (8) However, many of the experiences stored in the subconscious have been pushed (repressed) there because they were frightening or just irrelevant when they occurred and could not readily be dealt with at that time.

After a while, it is difficult to retrieve them, yet they exert their influence on thought and feelings, especially on one's emotional life. If sufficiently serious they can adversely affect mental and physical health. They may be returned to consciousness for completion, either deliberately through psychotherapy, hypnosis, meditative or remembering exercises, drugs or incidentally through peak experiences or "accidents," life-threatening illnesses, or similar personal crises.

In the *superconscious* mind lies a reservoir of the entire domain of human experience, past and potential. It is not solely personal but shared by all humanity. We may think of it as a bank of unlimited information, although it is much more than that. Here lies the deepest knowledge of who we are, where we are going in our lives, individually and collectively, and why: the answers to all our questions. One finds various names for this portion in all of the world's major religious and spiritual traditions: the Great Book, the Book of God's Remembrance, the Akashic Records, and so on. The great psychologist Carl Jung called it the collective unconscious. (9)

In these terms, the superconscious mind is the source of intuitive knowledge, and intuition is the process by which information or knowledge passes from the superconscious, through the subconscious, to the conscious mind. Thus, intuition may be thought of as the communication channel that allows the conscious mind access to the superconscious.

DEVELOPMENT OF INTUITIVE SKILL

Intuition is not the rare gift of a few people. Everyone has the basic ability or capacity to function intuitively. We all use our intuition continually, even though we may be unaware of doing so and credit the results of our thoughts to a rational process. Few people choose to deliberately develop this native capacity into a useful skill.

Young children are strong intuitives, but with disapproving parental and societal reactions they quickly learn to distrust their insights and push them into the background. The situation is quite different in some non-Western cultures, in which a direct — knowing capacity is taken for granted and even encouraged. Opening oneself to intuition is a matter of undoing prior conditioning and getting rid of blocks, such as inappropriate beliefs and fears that are impeding a natural development that is trying to take place. Thus, learning intuition is really a kind of *un*learning.

Most intuitive trainees receive intuitive information through one of their senses — certainly the most familiar way we all receive information—although with practice the communication may bypass the senses and just manifest in the mind as new knowledge, not necessarily even describable in words.

At *The Center for Applied Intuition* (CAI), we worked with a staff of expert *intuitives*, individuals who had successfully developed their intuitive faculties to such a high level that they could consciously and deliberately provide totally new information on demand, independent of what they already consciously knew from prior education and experience.

Expert intuitives function in various modes. For some, the intuitively received information is communicated in an ordinary conversational manner and from a fully conscious state. Others appear to go to sleep but speak clearly and coherently from this state; when they "wake up" later, they have little or no recollection of what has transpired. This latter mode is called *mediumship* in traditional parapsychology, or *channeling* in modern parlance. (10-12) Sometimes the voice quality of the intuitive changes while asleep, and what seems to be another personality emerges, but this feature does not always occur. In fact most expert intuitives function somewhere between these two extremes. The various modes appear to arise, as individual means for lifting the intuitive's conscious mind and personality out of the path of the intuitive flow so that clear information can flow through.

CAI's experience suggests that there is no limit to the depth and breadth of the information received, so long as the inquirer can comprehend it. This claim includes information that is highly technical or deeply personal, explanatory or inspirational, factual or mystical, historical or contemporary, and even part of the future. With few exceptions, the record indicates that all information requested has been provided fully and accurately as long as a few simple rules are followed.

SUCCESS IN INTUITIVE INQUIRIES

A number of conditions must be satisfied if the intuitive inquiry process is to work smoothly and effectively. The most important of these conditions is the motivation for conducting the inquiry. If one seeks information that is harmful to someone or that may reduce someone's freedom of thought or action in some way, the reception will probably be blocked. If information is sought that is already known or could easily be found by conventional means, the flow is weakened, the responses tend to be vague, and the process slows down and sometimes stops entirely.

A second important requirement is that the questions for the inquiry need to be stated clearly and unambiguously. CAI began its intuitive inquiries in science in order to generate new hypotheses for research in areas that had stubbornly resisted progress by conventional means. (13,14) The formulation of the questions turned out to be critically important. Unlike ordinary discourse, the questions must be specific, unambiguous, and free of biases. When these qualities are present, then accurate, complete, and relevant answers can be expected.

For inquiries on scientific and technical topics, a procedure called *intuitive consensus* was developed. (13, 15, 16) Intuitive consensus is a kind of multi-psychic inquiry technique in which the carefully formulated questions are posed to several intuitives independently. The answers are then combined into a common response. After a period of early experimentation, this technique was found to yield excellent agreement among the sources. It has been applied to more than a dozen scientific, parascientific, and societal problem areas, chosen because they were previously unexplored or because they appeared to have resisted the quest for solutions by traditional means. For example, an investigation was undertaken into the triggering of earthquakes: What is happening in the ground just hours or days before an earthquake occurs? The goal in this study was not to predict specific earthquakes, but to understand the physical process underlying earthquakes sufficiently well to permit the intelligent development of an earthquake prediction technology. The resulting consensus was excellent and contained many surprises. Some of the particular results were later verified through experiments, some conducted by CAI staff and some fortuitously by researchers who were not aware of our findings.

Other areas similarly explored using intuitive consensus were crib death, manic depression, human fertility, the detoxification of nuclear waste, levitation, the biographies of certain historical figures, and topics in archeology.

Intuition was also used to investigate the future, not strictly as prediction (although some prediction was included), but rather as prophecy in the biblical sense; that is understanding the personal and social processes in progress so that one may improve the future by making better decisions in the present. Although much of the course of human history can be predicted once the laws of social development are understood, other portions cannot be predicted because they depend critically on human decisions, which are never fully predictable. Thus, responsible intuitive prophecy consists almost entirely of identifying decision points and issues, describing the consequences of the various options, and then leaving the decision up to the user of the information. In this way, the user can make a conscious and responsible choice instead of fatalistically accepting a predicted outcome as inevitable or by blindly following "orders." Projections and predictions are typically given in the form of "if—then" statements: *"If man does not cut back on the use of chlorofluorocarbons, then the temperature of the earth's atmosphere will rise and coastal cities will be flooded!"* Two large and several small prophecy studies were completed. (17)

About 25 companies enlisted CAI expert intuitives for business consulting. In a typical scenario, the intuitive met with the company president, board of directors, or a project team for a half or full day. Company representatives posed their questions, with little or no explanation of background details. The expert intuitive provided the answers. It was apparent to those present that the intuitive was tapping a deep and broad source of information, well beyond what is normally accessed by most people, and certainly beyond the personal knowledge and experience of the intuitive. Opportunities for follow-up and confirmation are not always possible in the business world, but in no case was the information provided found to be downright wrong.

INTUITION AND PARAPSYCHOLOGY

What does the CAI's experience with intuitive process say about parapsychology and how parapsychologists conduct their work?

Most of the phenomena studied in parapsychology consist of the reception of novel information. This is obviously the case for clairvoyance, clairaudience, precognition, psychometry, and telepathy, all of which are situations in which the subject or experimenter receives information presumed to be inaccessible through ordinary sensory channels.

These psi processes are examples of the intuitive process at work. The names of these categories indicate how the information appears to be *received*: through sight or hearing, or from an object or another person. These different forms appear to be an artifact of the individual intuitive or psychic and are not in themselves significant. In the case of psychometry, for instance, it is commonly assumed that the information provided is somehow carried by the object through some kind of nonphysical energy field and that the sensitive is reading this field. There is no separate evidence for the existence of such a field, and contrary evidence is provided by experiments in clairvoyance and remote viewing that obtain the desired information without use of the objects. (8) In present terms, the information is drawn directly from the super-conscious, and the object simply serves as a point of focus. The need for the object to be present is therefore doubtful, though if the psychic believes its presence is essential, his belief may make it so. CAI's experience with expert intuitives and many psychics suggests that artifacts such as candles, incense, or crystals are also not fundamentally necessary, although an individual intuitive may believe that they are. After all, we are not dealing here with a rare phenomenon that requires special conditions, but with a natural human capacity.

Apparitions, near-death experiences, and out-of-body travel may be included as manifestations of intuition, but models for these are lacking, and existing explanations are surely stretching the intuitive hypothesis too far at this point. Faith healing (except the diagnostic component), firewalking, and psychokinesis apparently cannot be explained as instances of intuition, but we may legitimately ask here how all these phenomena came to be included in parapsychology in the first place. Indeed, the field has come to be a catch-all for unexplained events, including cattle mutilations, crop circles, UFOs, yetis/sasquatches and many others. It is surely a mistake to presume that all such phenomena have a common explanation. At the least, the passive, receptive sensory areas of parapsychology should probably be regarded as distinct from the active motor areas such as psychokinesis.

In summary, the foregoing indicates that the human awareness process that is taking place in many parapsychological phenomena can be explained (if I may use that term) as instances of intuition. Intuition thus emerges as the larger concept, the mind process, which underlies and is responsible for receptive parapsychological performance. Moreover, intuition opens the doorway to an even greater range of knowledge and mind-experience than has typically been investigated within the relatively narrow confines of parapsychology.

In establishing this explanation, are we just replacing one unknown with another? This is so in part because intuition is no better understood in scientific terms than parapsychology. But we already know the limitations of science for such studies. Moreover, intuition is offered here as the more fundamental and unifying process, and the one more directly connected to everyday experience. Finally, intuition is a much more acceptable and plausible concept to the informed public and even to the scientific community. Thus the research needed to enable us to understand intuition better may be less unfamiliar and less formidable, and therefore more readily compelling and supported.

A CHANGING SCIENCE, A CHANGING WORLDVIEW

To accommodate the changes presaged for science, and necessitated for and by parapsychology, we must somehow find a way to transcend the established scientific method and the social paradigm on which it rests. We are being forced beyond the models we have been using and must create new ones. What one might call the nonlinearization of science is taking place.

In effect, we are now in the midst of evolving a broader definition of what it means to be a human being — a grander model than our predecessors assumed. Naturally, this new definition affects how we interface with our physical and social realities. It leads us to what some call the spiritual side of life — a loaded term, to be sure, because it means such different things to different people. But it is a way of acknowledging that there is more to life than what can be seen, heard, and figured out, and that this unacknowledged part of the mind is behind and controlling all thought, hence crucially important in all we think and do.

We are saying, among other things, that a human being is not so much a body and a brain that has evolved to the point of generating consciousness, but by nature an evolving consciousness that has embodied itself in a body and a brain.

This alternative view implies a greater human purpose than assumed heretofore. It implies that human consciousness transcends the body, and the essence of who or what we are lies beyond the materialist model.

We are gradually realizing that we are more than our bodies and our brains. The next question is: What is this *more*? Each of us needs to inquire seriously into this matter. Intuition is a means for this inquiry. It is proffered as the communicative link for understanding who we really are, what in the world we are doing here and where we are going. Intuition can provide information, knowledge, understanding, and even direct experience that we can readily utilize in our personal lives, in our professional activities, and in our comprehension of the world.

AFTERWORD (Added in 2008)

In the years since the above was first written we have seen a modest strengthening of parapsychology as a research discipline, a little more acceptance of it within science itself, an increased attention to it in popular culture and media, and significant recognition in the newly emerging field of consciousness studies. The latter is perhaps the most hopeful reward for more than one hundred years of relative obscurity, though even here it is not yet clear where this new field is going. It has attracted scholars and researchers from a wide range of fields: neurophysiology, transpersonal psychology, physics, cognitive studies, Eastern spirituality, perceptual studies, philosophy and others. Many large conferences have been convened and several university departments have been established.

Still, good definitions are still lacking and no integrative consensus has yet appeared upon the horizon. It is anyone's guess whether and how parapsychology will fit itself into this still dynamic multidisciplinary milieu. One emergent theme is the recognition that the boundaries of conventional science are being transcended, and understanding mind and consciousness may call for new research methods and a revised scientific paradigm.

REFERENCES AND NOTES

1) Brewster, G. (1952) *The Creative Process*. NY: Mentor/New American Library; 1952:937.
2) Koestler, A. (1964) *The Act of Creation*. NY: Dell; 1964:ch 5.
3) Hadamard, J. (1949) *The Psychology of Invention in the Mathematical Field*. Princeton, NJ: Princeton University Press.
4) Shapiro, G. (1986) *A Skeleton in the Darkroom: Stories of Serendipity in Science*. SF: Harper & Row.
5) Vaughn, F.E. (1979) *Awakening Intuition*. NY: Anchor/Doubleday.
6) Goldberg, P. (1983) *The Intuitive Edge: Understanding and Developing Intuition*. LA: Tarcher.
7) Nadel, L. (1990) *Sixth Sense: The Whole-Brain Book of Intuition, Hunches, Gut Feelings. and Their Place in Your Everyday Life*. Englewood Cliffs, NJ: Prentice-Hall.
8) Hilgard, E. (1986) *Divided Consciousness: Multiple Controls in Human Thought and Action*. NY: Wiley & Sons. (See any standard text on hypnosis. This is one.)
9) Jung, C.G. (1973) Winston, R., Winston, C., trans. *Memories, Dreams and Reflections*. NY: Random House.
10) Kautz, W. (1987) Branon, M. *Channeling: The Intuitive Connection*. SF: Harper & Row.
11) Hastings, A. (1991) *With the Tongues of Men and Angels: A Study of Channeling*. Fort Worth, TX: Holt, Rinehart & Winston.
12) Klimo, J. (1987) *Channeling: Investigations on Receiving Information from Paranormal Sources*. LA: Tarcher.
13) Kautz, W.H. & Branon, M. (1989) *Intuiting the Future: A New Age Vision of the 1990s*. SF: Harper & Row; 1989:37-39.
14) Most of work at CAI now takes the form of personal intuitive counseling for individuals.
15) Kautz, W.H. (1982) "Earthquake triggering: a psychic exploration." In: *Psi Research*. 1982;3: 117-112 and 4:101-116.
16) Kautz, W.H. & Kodera, M. (1985) *The Future of Japan: An Intuitive Scenario* (in Japanese). Tokyo: Tama Publishing Co.
17) Records on file at the Center for Applied Intuition, Fairfax, CA.
18) Targ, R. & Putoff, H. (1977) *Mind Reach: Scientists Look at Psychic Ability*. NY: Dell Publishing Co.

The answers I seek are all right here
Whenever I keep my vision clear

--- Shelby Parker

CHAPTER 15   THE NATURE OF PERSONAL BELIEF SYSTEMS

Beverley Kane, MD

Beverley Kane is currently Program Director, Medicine and Horsemanship at the Stanford School of Medicine in Palo Alto, CA. After completing her residency in family medicine at San Francisco General Hospital and a fellowship in sports medicine at the University of London, she joined the staff at the Stanford Center for Research in Disease Prevention, where she conducted studies of multiple risk factor intervention for coronary artery disease.

From Stanford, Dr Kane went to Apple Computer, where she worked as both a clinician and a software developer in medical informatics. As a medical informatician, she became the Chief Medical Officer of Philips Medical Systems MedGrid Division and later, a product manager and subject matter expert at WebMD, building professional-to-consumer portals for doctor-patient communication.

Dr Kane has now come full circle to Stanford, teaching doctor-patient (clinician-consumer) communication by employing horses in her practice, Horsensei Equine-Assisted Learning and Therapy (HEALTH). She was first of the original three editors of *Silver Threads* with Jean Millay and Dean Brown; her latest book, *The Manual of Medicine and Horsemanship: Transforming the Doctor-Patient Relationship With Equine-Assisted Learning*, was written for other practitioners of equine-assisted learning and equine-assisted psychotherapy. Her upcoming book is entitled *The Frog Prints — The Parapsychology of the Horse-Human Relationship*.

http://www.horsensei.com   http://horsensei.com/bkmdcomm/index.html

THE NATURE OF PERSONAL BELIEF SYSTEMS [*2]

Beverley Kane

Is psi more like physics or more like love?
Russell Targ

Immanuel Kant would arise in the morning, seat himself in his study and ask, *"[Does] the simple but empirically determined Consciousness of my own existence [prove] the existence of objects in space outside myself?"* (1) From this inner dialogue, Kant arrived at his theory on the nature of perception, a critique of idealism, speculation on the nature of space and time: in short his theory of reality.

Today's thoughtful person wakes up and merely asks, *"Black socks or brown?"*

For thousands of years, philosophers have speculated on, debated, and offered "axiomatic" proofs for the true nature of the universe. From Plato to Peirce, from dualism to deconstructionism, the "ists" and the "isms" have all strenuously pitched tiles into the mosaic of reality. Most such philosophies Eastern and Western are abstract and impersonal. They prescribe broadly formulated generalities in an abstruse, technical language. Philosophers seldom speak of their own anecdotal experiences or appeal to the everyday reality of the common person.

If psi phenomena can be proved to exist, "the proof is in the pudding," the personal experience. Since the 1930s, a number of scrupulously performed psi experiments have yielded highly significant positive results. (2) An intellectual appreciation of these data must be corroborated by personal experience for belief in psi to occur.

Despite the popular insistence that all "scientific" phenomena be objectively verified, we pursue most of life's activities in the realm of subjective experience. Our mental machinations are predominantly trivial (compared with, say, Kant's elaborate ontology) and derive largely from unconscious elements. Yet the reflex nature of our decisions leaves little uncertainty about what we know: long division, our political views, and whether black socks or brown go with a blue suit.

[*2] Adapted from the Panel Discussion on *The Nature of Reality*, Parapsychology Research Group (PRG) General Meeting, May 1988. (Excerpts)

Psychologist Lawrence LeShan confirms the pragmatic view of psychologist-philosopher William James by stating, in effect, that the benchmark of a reality program is how well it meets the specified goals of the organism. (3) In particular, the system must be self-consistent and must answer the reasonable questions it has posed for itself. Its validity is established only when we *act* in terms of the beliefs it has engendered. No one has yet stipulated — nor shall I — the definitive algorithm for a reality test.

Reality testing is the process of evaluating feedback from the results of our accomplishments in the observable world. With that stated, we may still ask, how do we arrive at a methodology for knowing what we know? How do we admit or reject new truths into our set of beliefs? We are largely unconscious of the implicit rules we have established for deciding what to believe. Do we rely heavily on rational processes? Do we trust our own irretrievable experiences, either literally or symbolically? Do we trust the unreproducible experiences of others? What is the process by which we revise our beliefs? People who convert to a different religion, change political parties, or "come out" in a new sexual orientation conduct a conscious dialogue with their beliefs, but the key ingredient in the ultimate decision may remain elusive.

Twentieth-century Western philosophical and scientific thinking is anchored in a rational materialistic value system. In this system, logic is the primary lens through which we are conditioned to view truth. Chief among the reasons for exalting the intellectual function is that it provides the apparent basis for scientific understanding, which in turn yields our technological achievements. Although we value subjective experience for the sense of aesthetics, we usually do not accord it the privilege of arbitrating scientific truths. In business, politics, and academia we are expected to fortify subjective opinions with rational arguments.

One of the first modern scientists to elucidate the balance of rational and nonrational functions in the human psyche was the Swiss psychiatrist Carl Jung. The foundation of Jung's psychology is the concept of individuation — the means by which a person achieves psychological wholeness to become a fulfilled and balanced individual. One way that Jung characterized the process of individuation was by classifying the primary forces in the psyche that contribute to an individual's character. In his paper on psychological types, Jung established two personality types:

introvert and extrovert;
and four character functions:
intellect — the rational, analytic function;
sensation — sensory input from touch, taste, smell, sight, hearing;
feeling — emotional stirrings.
intuition — imagination, hunches, dreams. (4)

Jung did not originate this scheme; its antecedents are found in the legends of the Druids, in the records of the early Greeks, and in the writings of the alchemists in the Middle Ages.

Apart from the personality factors and cultural prejudices that influence judgment, belief systems are rooted in psychological and physical needs. Conclusions based on the *need to believe* are not necessarily incorrect. In fact, the logical extension of James' pragmatism and LeShan's goal attainment criterion is that the confirmation of a valid belief lies in whether it helps us meet our needs. In Abraham Maslow's hierarchy of drives for self-actualization are survival, emotional satisfaction, meaning, and transcendence. (5) In its most general form, Maslow's principle amounts to the need to increase one's sense of personal power. From that perspective, we can reframe the primary needs: to promote physical and emotional pleasure and fulfillment, to minimize cognitive dissonance, and to remove fear (especially of death).

One of the most denaturing perversities of our intellectual orthodoxy is our reliance on statistics. Our insurance risk, marriage prospects, and future health seem to be determined by a probability system that, by design, ignores the variables that make us unique and uniquely qualified to master our fate.

Statistical reality works well up to a point. It is comforting to know that, statistically, every time one drops a heavy object, it should indeed fall down, or that because the sun has risen 100% of our time on earth, the probability is high that it will do so tomorrow. Most applications of statistics, however, give probabilities far from unity. And out past the 95% confidence interval lies the power of the individual.

By focusing on the reproducible and statistically most likely outcomes in our experiments, we often ignore valuable clues to human potential. A major criticism of psi research is that much of the phenomena it purports to study, such as poltergeists and peak experiences, cannot be duplicated, much less reproduced a statistically significant number of times. Even individuals who want to recapitulate an anomalous experience may face the impossibility of being able to do so.

Ironically, the most valued human abilities are those that, like psi events, show incomplete penetrance in the general population and are statistically most improbable. For instance, most people can run a few stodgy laps around the track. Only a few can capture gold medals in the Olympic 800-meter. Like a world-class athlete, gifted (and practiced) psychics can repeatedly demonstrate superior abilities. Others, including animals, exhibit less dramatic, but observable, evidence of intuitive ability. Hundreds of athletes are now performing at the level that won gold medals in the past. Only one anomalous performance is necessary to show what is possible for the human race. (6)

Statistical reasoning (and even the idea of statistical immunity) promotes the fallacy that a certain number of people must suffer if others are to flourish, that there must be a certain percentage of poor versus rich, winners versus losers. This erroneous presumption that we live in a zero-sum universe is not a natural law, but one that is man-made from a pessimism (itself *a choice of belief*) that can be traced to myths of original sin and of good and evil.

In a like manner, beliefs about illness are inextricably linked to metaphors about reward and punishment, karma, demons, and other cultural and religious idiosyncrasies. The parapsychological approach to healing, and, in effect, to all reality, encourages people to assert *individual* strengths and abilities to overcome both statistical and religious determinism. Psychokinetic manipulation of one's own body, fate, and fortune is the most empowering consequence of recognizing and using psi abilities. When we seek to go beyond our limitations and have exhausted the repertoire of old truths, we become open to new ideas.

In achieving wholeness and maintaining sanity, we seek to meet all our needs without creating conflicting beliefs and values. For instance, material needs do not prompt most people to believe that it is ethical to steal. Resolving contradictions between old and new beliefs and between one's individuality and one's social conformity is the foundation of psychological growth. The most divisive conflict is the contradiction between logic and sensory (or extrasensory) experience.

LeShan (3) provides an eloquent analysis of how beliefs are formed and what instigates new beliefs in individuals and in societies. His most important observation, arising in the context of his belief in ESP, concerns the two ways we begin to realize that a thought system is no longer adequate.

The first clue is when social problems, such as nuclear weapons, threaten to overwhelm us. The second set of ways in which we are informed that a change is imminent are the small discrepancies, the little things that do not fit in that tell us there is something wrong with a large system of explanation. These discrepancies are not important in themselves — we can always adapt to them, individually argue them away — but they are the clues, the signposts that tell us that something is not right, that the system of explanation does not quite fit reality. When the exceptions (things that cannot be explained in the system) grow to be too many and too clear, the cultural picture of reality begins to break down and make room for the next picture to be developed and accepted. (p. 98-3)

The "little things that do not fit in" are invariably events in personal experience. The conflict between objectivity and subjectivity is intensified as we are forced to either integrate an anomalous experience or deceive ourselves that nothing out of the ordinary has happened. It can seem less nerve-racking to dismiss a few experiences than to topple a whole logical framework.

Although experience offers the most tangible influence for liberalization of beliefs, much of what we believe is taken on faith. We believe that physicists have detected atoms; although most of us have never seen one, the evidence for atoms seems logical to us. In the realm of psi, also, some things are taken on faith, by appeal either to logic or to empathy.

No one believes that we live, pragmatically speaking, in an anything-goes universe. We all have limits to our credulity through some process of elimination. LeShan says: *"The perceptions we have are not entirely up to us.... Whatever is 'out there' plays a part in our perception and response. The way we perceive the outside world is determined by a combination of 'us' and 'it,' no explanation that is either all one or all the other will stand up very long. I can perceive Beethoven's Ninth Symphony in a variety of ways ... I cannot, however, perceive it as God Save the Queen or as an automobile."* (p. 25 - 3)

On the other hand, there comes a point at which one cannot perceive a psi experience as indigestion or as an optical illusion. At this point, the exertion of clinging to old beliefs becomes more stressful and more untenable than accepting the validity of new experience. Under these circumstances, after the personal revolution has begun, one looks for confirmation in the annals of experimental science and in the experience of others.

From a historical perspective, we can be certain that many of our truths will become as obsolete as the geocentric model of the solar system. If we consider what reality will appear like a thousand years from now, we must concede, like British biologist J.B.S. Haldane, that not only is the universe stranger than we imagine, but it is stranger than we *can* imagine. We can logically assume that we are not the last conscious animal to evolve. We can predict, logically and psychically, that the next species will exhibit unimaginable physical and mental abilities that we now call, respectively, world class and paranormal.

CONCLUSIONS

Beliefs are the net effect of our consensus observations and our private experience. When the former is at odds with the latter, the conflicts are mediated with the Jungian character function we each habitually adopt as the arbiter of disparate information. We strive for the subjective feeling of being right and being sane, of embracing a self-consistent reality that is as substantive as the shirts on our backs. When we censor valid data, whatever their source, we sever the thread that connects us to our wisdom. The thread that runs by way of our experience through our faculties of discrimination is strung to the marionette of Belief, which dances for us on the stage of Reality.

Parapsychology seeks to integrate all dimensions of human experience into a cogent whole. To do so, anomalous experiences must initially be accepted at face value and then be subjected to the scrutiny of our intelligence. Parapsychology is not an anti-intellectual science. Rather, it seeks to elevate all abilities to the standard of our intellectual genius. Intelligence is neither synonymous with nor solely a function of the intellect. All modes of experience constitute a unified intelligence. Rejecting one's experience or failing to recognize the hidden dimensions of existence fragments the psyche and alienates the Self from a holistic reality.

In the history of evolution, consciousness afforded survival value initially on the strength of instinct and sensation and then on the basis of intellect. Now it is conceivable that the extrasensory, extrarational functions will accelerate us to the next phase.

For us as physical beings, psi experiences must be made pragmatically useful while we seek to extract from them clues to the transcendent nature of consciousness. These clues, which are segues to the next stage of evolution, are to be found in the subtle anomalous experiences that our consciousness — at once primitive and overcivilized — is just learning to perceive. Reality testing is a Panel Discussion on Individual Experience, conducted among all modes of information processing.

We conclude with Jung:

> At any level of meaning, reconciliation of the opposites is not a matter of logic and reason. Generations of men have struggled to reconcile the search for meaning exemplified in religion, and the search for fact, embodied in science, to no avail. The supposed dichotomy between these two basic urges in men cannot be reconciled through the intellect. Like all opposites, they cannot be resolved by logic; they can only come together at the point of experience. (4)

NOTES

1) Kant, I. (1966) *Critique of Pure Reason*. Muller, F.M, trans. Garden City, NY: Doubleday.
2) Edge, H.L., Morris, R.L., Rush, J.H., Palmer, J.O (1986) *Foundations of Parapsychology*. Boston: Routledge & Kegan Paul; 1986:87-93.
3) LeShan, L. (1976) *Alternate Realities: The Search for the Full Human Being*. NY: Ballantine Books.
4) Jung, C. (1920-1971) *Psychological Types. Collected Works*. Vol 6. Hull REC, trans. Princeton, NJ: Princeton University Press, Bollingen Series; 1971: par. 556. Original work published in 1920.
5) Maslow, A. (1962) *Toward a Psychology of Being*. Princeton, NJ: Van Nostrand.
6) The analogy admittedly breaks down when we consider that athletic performance is measurable and quantifiable. It is the poorly quantifiable aspect of psi that keeps it in a category apart from the 800-meter hurdle.
7) Nichols, S. (1980) *Jung and Tarot*. NY: Samuel Weiser.

PLAYING WITH IDEAS AND BELIEFS

To expand on Harman's vision, we suggest "playing a game." For example, we all experience the fundamental needs of life—Sun, Moon, Earth, air, fire, water—and over the centuries, different civilizations have established unique belief systems about them. For example: The Sun is God (for whom great stone temples are built); the Sun is our Father and the Earth is our mother; our Sun is a medium star, which can provide energy for our machines. The logic of the customs of every age is built on that primary belief. Question that, and logical people may become emotional. At this writing in 2010, we are watching the evolution of ideas begin to blossom again—in a new era in which all beliefs might be questioned. By simply playing with different ideas, we can perhaps prevent emotions from distorting the openness of thinking and discussion. Try playing with these:

First ancient premise:
The universe was created in past time, and will end in future time.
"In the beginning, God created the heavens and the earth.... And God said, 'Let there be Light,' and there was light." (1) **[One Initial Big Bang]**

In 1925, a huge new telescope at the Mt. Wilson Observatory allowed Edwin Hubble to see a galaxy other than our own <u>for the first time</u>. (2) He and other astronomers then agreed — the more distant a galaxy seemed to be, the faster it would seem to be moving away. The logic of that assumption established the math formula, which seemed to confirm the first premise.

Second ancient premise:
The universe is Eternal and Infinite. There was no beginning.
"There was something mysterious, without beginning without end, that is The Essence of the heavens and the earth." (3) **[This Essence is Eternal.]**

Scientists, who follow this second premise, might be called "crackpots" (4) by those who follow the first one. Yet even Einstein was at first uncomfortable (5) with the Big Bang Theory (BBT) that asserted the whole universe exploded 13 billion years ago (maybe 18) out of something unimaginably small, and in some future time it may collapse. Now, just imagine that the current cosmological beliefs could change for some reason unknown. For example, Radin reports in *Entangled Minds:* (6)

Cosmologists have learned that we might have accidentally overlooked 96% of the universe. The missing majority of the universe has been dubbed *'dark' energy and matter. We know next to nothing about it, and it's spawning whole new concepts about the structure and evolution of the universe.... Theories of cosmology are being reconsidered.... (7)*

But what if we imagine that the background radiation (used to "prove" the BBT) was only from the explosion of our own galaxy. That would be a big—though a somewhat smaller—bang. The Hubble Space Telescope can't "see" through to the opposite side of our own galaxy. Galaxies and stars are exploding throughout the changing universe we do see, so today's concept of an infinite universe would be very dynamic. It would not be at all like the old "steady state" concept that was replaced by the BBT.

This mysterious Essence that is *"without beginning or end"* means it is an Eternal Essence. That it might also be the foundation of "Cosmic Consciousness" is a pervasive idea held by meditators and psi sensitives, who may also believe that it is intrinsic to each individual consciousness.

The second idea to consider: PRG physicists agree that our individual consciousness does not fit into the four dimensions that also describe a simple box with no intrinsic energy or ability to reproduce. (8) They discuss a multidimensional consciousness in Sections VI and VII. (9)

The third idea is suggested by a scientist from the Spirit World: He questions why we count only <u>four</u> forces among the basic ones that make up the universe, (e.g., electromagnetism, gravity, the weak and strong nuclear forces). He would like you to consider the idea that a <u>fifth</u> basic universal force exists—LIFE and its Consciousness. Many living scientists will dispute this idea, but just remember that life comes from life. Scientists may modify cells in a test tube, but they have to start with something alive. By playing with ideas, open-minded discussions are possible. This enjoyable activity occurred often at PRG meetings—consensus was never a requirement.

REFERENCES

1) *The Holy Bible.* (Ancient) - *The New King James Version.* (1982) Nashville, TN: Thomas Nelson Publishers.
2) Bartusiak, M. (2009) *The Day We Found the Universe.* Pantheon Books
3) *The Tao Te Ching.* (Ancient) - Mitchell, S. (Trans.) *Tao Te Ching: A New English Version.* NY: Harper & Row, 1988. (There have been many translations over the years.)
4) Steinhardt, P.J. & Turok, N. (2007) *Endless Universe: Beyond the Big Bang.*
5) Panek, R. (2005) "Einstein." In: *Smithsonian,* June (2005)
6) Radin, D. (2006) *Entangled Minds: Extrasensory Experiences in a Quantum Reality.* NY: Paraview pocket books.
7) Clark, S. (March 12, 2005) "Did we miss dark energy first time around?" In: *New Scientist.*
8) Rauscher, E.A. & Targ, R. (2002) "Why only four dimensions will not explain the relationship of the perceived and perceiver in precognition." In: *Journal of Scientific Exploration. 2002, 16:655-658.*
9) Sirag, S-P. (1993) "Hyperspace Reflections." In *Silver Threads: 25 Years of Parapsychology Research.* Kane, Millay, Brown (Eds.) Newport CT: Praeger, pp. 156-165. [Update in Chapter 29.]

...The truth expressed in *The Upanishads* is now finding its way into science....

As scientists began studying consciousness, a few of them began to notice the "hard" questions: the question of free will, or what is now called downward causation—the idea of a causally potent consciousness that affects matter.... Although the majority of brain scientists continue to believe in material models of consciousness, there is a growing awareness that the hard questions may be too hard for the material models to crack. How can a causally potent consciousness be a mere epiphenomenon?

Vedanta says that consciousness is the ground of all being and that the material reality around us is the epiphenomenon. So here, finally, is how material science and the philosophy of Vedanta come together....

The quantum physicist, in resolving the measurement paradox, is positing that consciousness is the ground of being, consciousness is transcendent, unitive, and self-referent in us. It is the same picture of consciousness that Vedanta gives us. This cannot be simple coincidence....

So the upshot of all this is a new way of doing science within consciousness, within the philosophy of Vedanta.... Science supports Vedanta, science is incorporated within Vedanta, this is good.

--- **Amit Goswami**
--- Foreword from *The Upanishads*
--- Translated by Dean Brown, 1996.

SECTION IV

Page 165

MIND
AND
BRAIN/BODY CHEMISTRY*

SEROTONIN

ADRENALINE

DOPAMINE

MELATONIN

THEOBROMINE

* This chapter is included for scientific and historical information only. It is not intended to advocate the use of illegal substances.

SECTION IV

MIND AND BRAIN/BODY CHEMISTRY

For centuries, our forefathers and foremothers have sought ways to enhance sexual behavior. Much of this quest has focused on some chemistry—from ancient love potions to modern patent medicines. Our ancestors have also used other chemicals for sleeping aids, energy enhancers and pain relief. Whatever we experience happens on a background of molecular chemistry. Many states of consciousness can be characterized by their associated chemical events.

The chemistry of our moods and behaviors is extremely complex and can be thought of as both reflecting and creating the electrical activity within our nerve networks. But some generalizations can be made, based on both objective and subjective observation.

NEUROTRANSMITTERS

Chemical exchanges between the cells of our nervous system are part of the language of mental events. The major neurotransmitters (dopamine, serotonin, adrenalin, acetylcholine, endorphins, and many others) as well as hormones drive our daily lives, influencing movement, thinking, mood, reactions, pain, sleep, hunger, and thirst.

Adrenalin States

The adrenalin state commonly is recognized as a state of fight or flight. At the chemical level, we clearly have a cause-and-effect molecular process, but the mental interpretation of that message varies with individual experience and a person's ability to develop useful alternative behaviors. If we exercise no creativity, we repeat the behavior that succeeded first. In most personal histories, our first adrenalin state was birth, and our first adrenalin-associated behaviors may have been fear, anger, and rejection, or they may have been excitement and love.

Adrenalin itself does not *determine* any behavior. Our *interpretation* of the meaning of our detection, consciously or unconsciously, of the molecule adrenalin leads to our choosing a behavioral response. David Bohm has said that meaning is the link between mind and matter. (1)

Is it possible to *decide* that an adrenalin rush means excitement rather than threat? We can observe our responses and evaluate them by paying attention. By exposing ourselves to novel stimuli and creating new ways of responding, we can expand our chemical language. Creating a new behavior requires the ability to extinguish a habit by decoupling a stimulus-response loop.

> [Editor's Note: Neurofeedback helps us understand our fear-anger-pain memories and provides a way to disconnect our negative physiological responses to them. Suppressed memories create time bombs to future health. See Section X—*EDUCATION: INCREASING INTELLIGENCE.*]

Many people actively seek the adrenalin state by riding roller coasters, skydiving, or watching scary movies. When the adrenalin rush is interpreted as excitement and exhilaration, the body may generate interleukins, extremely potent immunoprotective molecules, some with antiviral and anticancer properties. Medically, a hyper-adrenergic state is associated with Type A behavior, overachieving, anxiety and panic attacks.

An adrenalin level interpreted as fear results in the production of corticosteroids, which suppress the immune system. Adrenalin can be blocked by the prescription drug propranolol (Inderal). Inderal can decrease stage fright, test-taking anxiety, panic attacks, palpitations, migraine headaches, angina, and hypertension, but prolonged use may lead to slow heart rates, depression, anhedonia, and low-energy complaints.

The relative activity of our adrenergic system regulates the amount and kind of information we select to notice. (This is clearly demonstrated by the selective perception of a person in a state of paranoia: Everything he or she notices is threatening.) What is the optimal level of adrenalin for the perception of paranormal events? Sometimes hyperactive or highly emotional states seem to empower telepathic communication—many spontaneous reports involve an emergency—but controlled telepathy experiments have not required intense hyper-adrenergic states. (2 - IRVA)

Dopamine States

Dopamine is another potent neurotransmitter. Its activity is increased by cocaine. The resulting state is similar to that induced by the related chemical family–amphetamine (crystal, ice) and some diet pills. Amphetamine stimulation usually is associated with high—energy feelings, a very directed and narrow focus of attention, self-centeredness, and egotistic, compulsive, hyperactive, hypersexual, and anorexic behavior states. Some evidence has led to the hypothesis that schizophrenia results from an excess of dopaminergic transmission. (3) Again, the chemistry produces a range of behavior but does not coerce.

In treating the selective dopamine deficiency condition Parkinson's disease, for example, there is a narrow range of balance in dopamine stimulation below which there is immobility and above which lies mania, insomnia, and hallucination.

Serotonin States

Operating in a delicate balance with the dopamine—language neurons are those that use serotonin for communication. Serotonin augmentation leads to effects suggesting that the serotonin receptor family is involved in the chemistry of feelings of well-being, anxiety, depression, and appetite. Medicines like fluoxetine (Prozac) that enhance serotonin levels are used in the treatment of depression and anxiety. In the setting of empathic interpersonal counseling situations, phenethylamines (MDA, MDMA, etc.) were widely used until they became illegal. (4) L–Tryptophan, a serotonin precursor, was used as a relaxation and sleep–inducing dietary supplement (until tainted synthetic preparations caused a Food and Drug Administration ban). D–Lysergic acid (LSD) also interacts with serotonergic synapses, among its other neurotransmitter effects. (5) Serotonin states of consciousness are associated with deeply empathic feelings in religious contemplation and meditative states. The serotonin state seems to promote truthfulness and intimacy with decreased fear of emotional upset. These serotonergic chemicals are discussed at length in this section by Shulgin, Scully, and Nez.

Endorphin States

Endorphin and enkephalin chemistry usually is introduced as the body's own internal morphine system, the opioid peptides. Endurance athletes, near-death accident survivors, conscious natural childbirthers, and warriors are some who understand this state experientially. It can be characterized as a state of (mental) ecstasy resulting from the dissociation of the mind from the body. This naturally occurs under the onslaught of overwhelming information overload associated with pain and a threat to physical survival (often manifested as out-of-body experiences). Endorphins abolish pain and other bodily sensations. Is a lack of pain awareness a prerequisite for paranormal states? If so, how much? In morphine–, heroin–, or other opiate–associated states of consciousness, there is a decrease in blood flow to the brain, metabolism, and electrical activity across the entire sensory–motor cortex that correlates with progressive loss of attention, focus, and memory. With larger amounts, unconsciousness, coma, and death may occur, as complete mind–brain–body dissociation occurs.

Natural Psychotropic Agents

Many kinds of neurotransmitters or their chemical precursors exist in our ecosystem naturally. They include the chemicals in plants such as marihuana, caffeine, nicotine, psilocybin, mescaline, coca, belladonna, and ergot or derivatives such as alcohol. In addition, many common foodstuffs (the psychoactive or mood foods), milk, peppers (and other nightshades), cheeses (and other tyramine–containing foods), chocolate, sugar, and others have behavioral effects through their action on endogenous (internal) neurotransmitters. Others are cognitively active because of habituation or associations (placebo effects and cultural expectations).

HORMONES

Other kinds of molecules—hormones—mediate the various repeating cycles of our physiology. Cortisones, sex hormones (e.g., estrogen, prolactin, testosterone), thyroid, and the releasing factors have major effects on the local or general eigenstate, or local baseline, of the nervous system. It is rather remarkable that they have only recently been popularly recognized as major psychoactive molecules as well. Admittedly, we have long recognized that a pregnant woman behaves differently. Even folk wisdom presumes that this is due to major hormonal shifts. Similarly, the use of male hormones—anabolic steroids—by athletes is associated with a dramatic increase in overtly aggressive behaviors and violence. An epidemic in the number of women complaining of premenstrual syndrome (PMS) has again brought endocrinology to the public eye. Studies suggest that PMS may be a disease of imbalanced interpersonal communication on a pheromonal level. (The interpersonal effects of secreted molecules used to be considered magic or paranormal.) Decreased endorphin sensitivity also may be involved in PMS.

We are on the verge of recognizing that we are truly animals who live in the world of seasons and reproduction, growth, and involution cycles. It is presumed that the major life cycle changes of conception, birth, puberty, menopause, and life span are probably under hormonal control or influence. How do these molecules interact with our states of consciousness, and further, do we have any conscious way of interacting with them?

Perhaps it might be better to consider that we are already altering and interfering with our endocrinology on a global scale. We have added synthetic hormones to increase food production, and we prescribe synthetic hormones for a multiplicity of conditions, such as the often over–diagnosed hypothyroidism. In the West, it is not unusual for a woman to start taking hormones at puberty, add progesterone for PMS, change to estrogen plus progesterone at menopause, and continue until she dies. Does this affect the range of states of consciousness available to women in this culture?

One of the effects of taking exogenous hormones is to alter the composition of the molecules secreted by our adult sweat glands. That is, hormones change our pheromones. That and other denials of our chemical identities have possibly limited our ability to respond to smells and odors, our molecular communication with others. The olfactory richness of communal or tribal life has nearly been eliminated from urban *Homo sapiens* (although other odors have filled the airspace). Cumulative transgenerational and inter-generational skills and information are being lost with every migration and refugee camp. Any experience with *telepathic communication* as a function of the "what's in the air" is being lost. In truth, such communication is sensory; we're just not sensing it anymore.

UNCONSCIOUS PERCEPTION

Conscious perception occurs through special senses: the skin and associated specialized nerve receptors, the retina of the eye, taste, smell, and hearing. But not all perception is noted consciously. Most is not conscious. Immune perception, the ability to distinguish one molecule from another, is incredibly precise. The process takes place throughout the entire body, seldom enters the realm of consciousness, and simultaneously handles hundreds of microorganisms from viruses to parasites, often without causing symptoms or awareness. In addition, humans also are affected by vibratory, electromagnetic, gravitational, meteorological, and paranormal stimuli. [*See Section V: Mind and Brain/Body Electricity.*]

EMOTIONAL STATES:
Accessible And Controllable

As anyone who has ever been overcome by the baser urges knows, drives emanating from the hypothalamic–pituitary axis are extremely difficult to ignore.

Thirst, hunger, sleep, warmth, mothering, and lust are only a few of the behaviors seemingly hard-wired into our physiology. But adrenalin will override many of these in the short term, as will other powerful endogenous or exogenous psychoactive agents. Some (stressful) states of consciousness are known to have effects on our endocrinology—for instance, the miscarriage or irregular menstruation that results from an emotional shock or loss.

Clearly, then, if the chemistry works both ways, which comes first? The extreme emotions associated with near–death states seem to catalyze major changes in both the behaviors and the mood of those who have experienced them. Alternatively, a convincing (near) death experience seems to be just as effective in catalyzing long-term behavioral and emotional–spiritual changes. (6) In either case, these changes in states of consciousness take place within a few seconds or minutes and sometimes involve remote viewing, telepathy, and spiritual contacts.

If these states are truly accessible to us, then only education in alternative states of consciousness and recognition of their power will save us from the helplessness implicit in a "Twinkie defense" or other violent acts committed while in a state of "temporary insanity." Powerful, yes, but uncontrollable, no. We must always be willing to consider our chemistry as only one of the factors involved in our decisions and actions.

In addition, almost all sensory data are filtered through a judgmental cortex that frequently refuses to recognize what it doesn't expect. The patterning resulting in optical illusion can be generalized to belief systems and is one of the drawbacks of socialization to a consensus state of consciousness. This unconscious or automatic filtering of information by the cerebral cortex also is an efficient way to reduce information overload, habituate behaviors, and resist new ideas.

CHOOSING STATES OF CONSCIOUSNESS

We seem to be in a state of destabilization of our molecular, hormonal, and temporal rhythms. Irregular work and sleep schedules, increased use of synthetic foods and medicines, and ubiquitous, accidental toxic exposures yield new chemical experiences both beneficial and detrimental. Increased interpersonal density results in increased stimulus density. The number of messages we must respond to may overwhelm anomalous or more unusual messages of the paranormal variety. Finding our personal *eigenstate* or center has become more difficult. We have destabilized and overloaded our input systems, and the result is *stress* (evolutionary pressure). People who can select new, useful information by conscious tuning of their neurochemical state may have a survival advantage.

With increased input to all our sensory systems and with stress, we have two of the preconditions for a jump in our level of understanding or the intelligent creation of new states of consciousness. Note that intelligence is not a particular state of consciousness, but the ability to access or create states of consciousness when it is useful to do so to most effectively interact with the universe. Changing circumstances require innovative solutions: We are limited only by the tools (chemicals, foods, sounds, lights, emotions, sensations, movements, thoughts) we use and how we intentionally use them together. Use them for a purpose. At this point, we are limited only by our models of the possible and the preconceptions that limit our perceptions. To be able to consciously recognize what we now call paranormal or to use altered states or voluntary control of internal states, we must integrate them into our models of reality. *"There is no monolithic, external, objective set of facts to which we can appeal in determining what is medically real.... Meanings and metaphors are powerful determinants not only of what we observe, but of what we* can *observe."* (7) I suggest that the process will involve metaphors of sensitivity, recognition, relationship, and responsibility and the redefinition of acceptable social relationships and states of consciousness.

How do we consciously interact or assist in the process of growth? We tend to remain in the first state that *"works"* or in a previously learned compromise, rather than selecting a state of consciousness that is optimum after a careful exploration of multiple options using chemical tools (hormones, food, and other psychoactive molecules), rhythmic mechanical tools (sound, biofeedback, ecstatic dance, yoga, massage, hypnosis, and television), intellectual tools (verbal, written, virtual), visual arts and spiritual practices.

Human beings have a remarkable capacity for creating states of consciousness that facilitate complex behaviors and relationship interactions. The experiences that we have come to call *parapsychological* may represent the edges of our electro–mechanical–chemical receptor interpretation system. Many of these paranormal events could represent the results of novel states of consciousness that allow perceptual expansion. Rather than discard input that doesn't fit, we may have discovered new information access skills to cope with the challenges of our society. Many of these experiences depend on interpersonal connection and trust. Our challenge is to develop models that validate this information and to teach this skill for our continued survival—as a species and as individuals—and for continued creative growth.

--- Cheri Quincy

I believe the possibility to have a psychedelic experience is inborn.... All the compounds you find in the plant kingdom—all those psychedelics are so closely related chemically to the brain compounds, which you already have.

--- Albert Hofmann

REFERENCES AND NOTES

1) Bohm, D. (1985) quoted in *Brain/Mind Bulletin*. 1985:10:1-2.
2) Smith, P. (2002) *Aperture: The Newsletter of the International Remote Viewing Association* (IRVA)
3) Kandel, E.R. & Schwartz, J.H. (1985) *Principles of Neural Science*. 2nd ed. NY: Elsevier. 1985:22.
4) Shulgin, A. & Shulgin, A. (1991) *Pihkal: A Chemical Love Story*. Berkeley, CA: Transform Press.
5) Osmond, H. (1957) "A review of the clinic effects of psychotomimetic agents." In: *Ann NY Academy of Science*. 1957, 66, 418-434.
6) Grof, S. (1985) *Beyond the Brain*. Albany: State University of NY Press.
7) (1982) In the famous *"Twinkie defense,"* Dan White, convicted killer of San Francisco Mayor George Moscone and Supervisor Harvey Milk, argued that he was a victim of temporary insanity brought about by eating junk food.
8) Dossey, L. (1991) *Meaning and Medicine*. NY: Bantam Books. 1991:132.

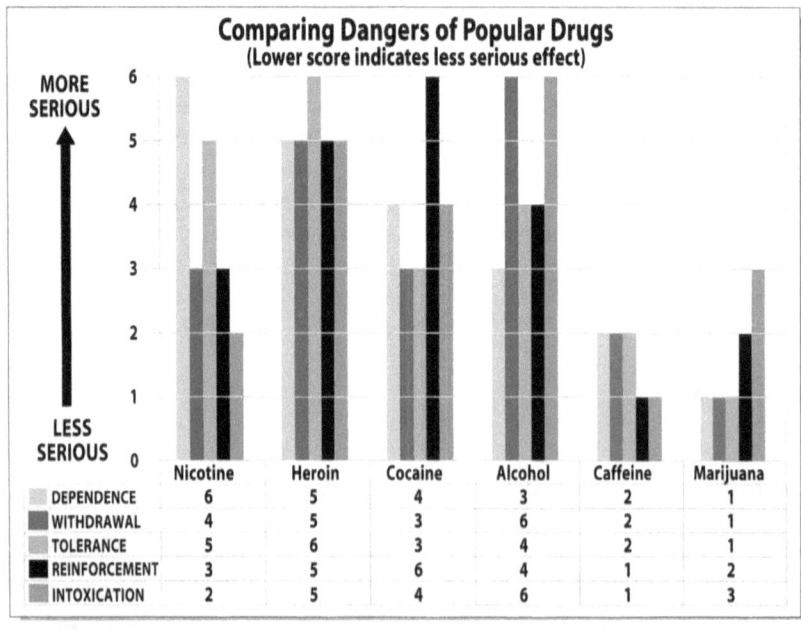

* Hilts, P. (Aug 2, 1992) New York Times.
Source: Dr Henningfield, J.E. for NIDA.
www.CommonSenseDrugPolicy.org and www.DrugWarFacts.org

THE EVOLUTION OF CONSCIOUSNESS INTERTWINED WITH THE EVOLUTION OF THE SCIENCE OF PLANTS

Dean Brown

. . . in media res. . .

The evolutionist Lucretius, in his monograph *De Rerum Naturum*, reminds us that we are always in the middle of things. When we consider the progression of consciousness, we look backward in time to the beginning and forward in time to the end. Today, at the precise center of this very moment, we stand in the middle of that progression.

From the beginning of time up to this moment, all life has evolved symbiotically—each living entity has emerged in harmony with one another. In particular, it is impossible to contemplate humankind, both socially and as individuals, without accepting our interdependence with all living creatures, especially the plants. We and our food plants have genetically modified each other from the beginning. The same holds for our fabrics, poisons, medicines, and mental states. Even oxygen, the primal source of our mental and bodily energy, derives from the plants. We have all come along together.

Our scientific understanding of the interplay between plants and civilization has developed in a tendential sequence, as a vector of increasing sophistication, pointing from plant origins to domestication to foods to beverages to commerce to medicines to psychoactives to ethnobotany. I here expand that magnificent vision.

Perhaps there are a million species of plants altogether. Lynn Margulis, in her book *Five Kingdoms*, estimates that about 500,000 have been classified. About 3,000 are known to be edible, palatable, and nutritious. Eating habits worldwide are generally restricted to only six: corn, wheat, rice, beans, cabbage, and potatoes. Among the million plants that might be set upon our table, we live on only six!

What a long way we have to go. Many new foods (even many old foods) await us in our future. Surely in their own future time some of them will be preferred to what we eat today.

Reasoning statistically, there may be perhaps 5,000 plants with consciousness-affecting properties. Humankind knows and uses about 300. In common use, there are less than 10, particularly tobacco, opium, coca, cannabis, *Psilocybe*, and peyote. Add several socially acceptable plant products—sugar, alcohol, and caffeine. Many new consciousness plants lie in our future. Surely some of them will be preferred.

Before I proceed with ingested plants, consider the importance of other plants and plant materials in the everyday elevation and diversification of consciousness.

- *Fabrics*. I (and many others) require cotton as the sole fabric allowed to be in contact with my skin. My clothing, in soft, breathing, humankind-evolved cotton, is essential to my ability to feel, think, and act in comfort. It enhances my senses, my being, and my functioning. I insist on it.

- *Flavors*. Food seasonings are not important in nutrition, but they elevate the intensity and the qualities of my sensitivities—my moods and the efficacy of the incarnation of my lunch.

- *Aesthetics*. Our peace of mind depends on being with plants in landscaping, plants at home, in the office, in the hospital, at the airport, ubiquitous in our works of art. Their presence is essential to the quality of consciousness.

In one of those mysteries of nature, most of the psychoactive chemicals from the plant world fall into two vast and complex categories, alkaloids and glycosides. Alkaloids and glycosides contain rings and radicals that are isomorphs to those that carry on the processing in our central nervous systems.

Is it only an accident that plants produce chemicals so intimately aligned to animals' complex makeups? Continuing study of these strange molecules fails to reveal any value that they could possibly have for the plants that produce them. But their value for humans and their impact on consciousness has been interwoven with us throughout the entire track of our evolution.

William Blake, in *The Marriage of Heaven and Hell*, says: *"If the doors of perception were cleansed every thing would appear to man as it is, infinite."* The alkaloids and glycosides present us with a vast spectrum in many dimensions for experiencing and exploring the *"many mansions in our Father's house."*

It is difficult to grasp the profound and subtle influences that plants have already made on consciousness, modifications of perception that have accreted through countless generations. The greatest effects are buried deeply in our behavior and ways of thought—genetically, socially, and aesthetically. They are embedded organically in the invisible substrate of our reality.

In the future, how much more so! Consciousness up to this point has largely evolved spontaneously, without much overt intervention on our part with organic chemistry, genetic engineering, or applied psychology.

But now, suddenly, the situation has become qualitatively different. Now we are manipulating the symbiosis of humans and plants with awareness, intentionality, purpose, and skill. Now, in this late twentieth century, we have passed a critical turning point.

In the flow of time from past to future, things occur at an exponentially increasing rate. In a historical context, we enjoy living on the cusp of intelligence. With modern science, information, attitudes, and perspectives, progress in the adaptation and synthesis of plant chemicals in the next twenty years will equal that of all history up to this point. Extrapolate that to 100 years, to 10,000!

Every food and medicine that we ingest has side effects, most of them undesirable, sometimes discovered much later. Take, for example, Bayer heroin (made around the turn of the last century for heroes!) and aspirin. Plant chemists with sharper tools, greater command of their science, and better focus of their efforts will progressively manage the adverse effects and intensify the desired ones. Most significantly, they will lead us to refine our paradigms on precisely what it is that is desired. Here is the point at which genetics, biology, psychology, aesthetics, philosophy, and religion converge.

Here is the place to confront and examine our underlying subliminal beliefs, values, and goals. Here is the place to express and fulfill our humanness. Here is the precise center of the discipline of ethnobotany. Here is the vortex where the moral and ethical dimensions of science come into focus. Here culminates our ultimate existential question: When these materials will have been identified and produced, distilled to their ideal quintessences, how shall we choose to use them?

The answers will reveal the profiles and contours of the human mind and its thrust into the future, into its ultimate fulfillment. We will have produced a snapshot of the elements of consciousness. We do not have the option to do otherwise.

Coda: And so we come full circle from the future back to that most ancient wisdom, the tantras and the vedas—with their quest for that revered plant, soma—today unknown.

CHAPTER 18   ALTERNATE STATES OF CONSCIOUSNESS

Ruth-Inge Heinze, PhD

Ruth-Inge Heinze was born in Berlin, Germany, in 1919. After Hitler came to power, she studied acting, and when she recited the lines "Give freedom of thought" from a play by Schiller, she spoke with such power that the audience gave her a standing ovation. She survived the bombing by the US, and the invasion and looting by the Soviet Army. In 1955, she came to the US and worked as a translator, while she took courses at the U of Chicago. In 1960, she moved to SF, CA, worked as a translator, and began holding bimonthly meetings for literary readings — the start of *The Universal Dialogues*. She became an American citizen and volunteered for the Peace Corps, training for work in Thailand. From UC Berkeley, she earned her BA (1969), her MA (1971) in anthropology, and her PhD (1974) in Asian studies. That year she founded the Independent Scholars of Asia, and taught Indian religions at Mills College in Oakland, CA. She traveled the world, spoke eight languages, and translated Sanskrit. In 1978, she received a Fulbright Award to study shamanism in Southeast Asia.

Dr Heinze was an adjunct faculty at: UC Berkeley; the CA Inst. of Integral Studies; The Institute for Transpersonal Psychology; and Saybrook Graduate School. Beginning in 1984, and for 23 years, she convened *The Annual International Conferences on the Study of Shamanism and Alternate Modes of Healing*. In 2006, the President of Mongolia honored her with a medal for advancing the study of shamanism. Dr Heinze also served as president of the PRG. She was a major teacher of our age. After her passing in 2007, Jurgen Kramer was elected director to continue the shaman conferences. All the papers from her 23 Conference Journals are found on www.shamanismconference.org/.

ALTERNATE STATES OF CONSCIOUSNESS: ACCESS TO OTHER REALITIES

Ruth-Inge Heinze

Whether we admit it or not, we all experience different states of consciousness. If we are sleeping, for example, our consciousness appears to be at rest, dreams arise and we cross thresholds and enter different realities not easily accessible during so-called ordinary, *consensus* reality. There are other occasions when access to different realities opens up spontaneously, even while we are awake. Such openings may occur when conditions and prerequisites coincide naturally. When we begin to look for the causes and conditions of these sudden shifts in consciousness, we may discover that shamans have been able access other realities at will for thousands of years and that everybody else can develop these faculties as well.

Do we have a general consensus of what consciousness is? Most of us know whether we *are* conscious of one thing or not and, most of all, do register when we *become* conscious of something. The latter usually happens when a need and the intention to expand our consciousness arise. The need and the intention then create the basis for the expansion of consciousness.

In this chapter, I want to prove that we have the capability of accessing different states of consciousness and do so for various purposes. Knowing how will enable us to speak more professionally of the different states of consciousness experienced by most of us, especially by shamans.

Research in the fields of comparative religion, anthropology, and psychology informs us that when we enter a specific state of consciousness, the characteristics and especially the quality of our perceptions and, consequently, our way of thinking and feeling change. For example, comparing waking consciousness with the state our consciousness is in when we are dreaming, we have to admit that the quality of what we are experiencing in dreams differs considerably from the quality of what we are aware of in ordinary, consensus reality.

In the following, I want to concentrate on available techniques to open doorways to other realities. Shamans have used all of them for more than 15,000 years. Meditation manuals, documentation on shamanic trances, and scientific reports (e.g., of hypnotists) tell us that non-ordinary realities can be accessed and influenced through thoughts, words, and actions on the material level. Mystics speak of a reversed process, that is, that non-ordinary realities can influence the material world.

Looking at the available data, it is important to recognize the state-specific set of rules operating on each level. One major difference between realities is that, as has been said above, when our consciousness transcends the ordinary level of consciousness, the commonly agreed on rules of time and space no longer apply. On the experiential level, we then begin to see the possibilities that quantum physics, mysticism, science, and religion may find ways to bridge what at one time split apart.

Before discussing the different techniques to access other realities, I want to clarify that I use the term *alternate* states of consciousness instead of *altered* states of consciousness (1) to avoid the implication that a state has been artificially altered. I maintain that each of the different states, accessed by the techniques described below, does not coexist, but alternates with other states of consciousness.

Looking closer, we may recognize a movement toward hyperactivity or hypoactivity, mind expansion or dissociation, increased control or increasing loss of control. Even when we occasionally observe areas of overlap and sometimes even flooding, a certain state of consciousness becomes distinguishable when it has reached its peak and demonstrates all its state-specific properties.

Tart speaks of

> ...A unique configuration or system of psychological structures or sub-systems. The parts or aspects of the mind that we can distinguish for analytical purposes (such as memory, evaluation processes, and the sense of identity function) are arranged in a certain kind of pattern or system.... The nature of the pattern and the elements that make up the pattern determine what you can and cannot do in that state. In dreaming, flying by an act of will is possible. I wouldn't want to say that is totally impossible in consensus consciousness, but it certainly is not easy. (2)

And Ludwig speaks of *"alterations in thinking, change in sense of time and body image, loss of control, change in emotional expression, perceptual distortion, change in meaning and significance, a sense of ineffability, feelings of rejuvenation and hypersuggestibility."* (3) Both findings confirm my hypothesis.

The range of possible alternate states appears to be almost infinite. We are just starting to map out states that we have learned to access for certain purposes. (1,4-6) Our "hidden observer" (7) watches the fluctuations of our consciousness between ordinary and non-ordinary realities but may not always be present when we enter certain states of consciousness. For example, in cases of deep dissociation, which I call *flooding*, people may lose control temporarily or for longer periods, depending on the depth of the dissociation. The diagram in Figure 1 shows these differences. Here **X** represents the state of consensus reality, and the range between intuitive knowledge and complete dissociation illustrates this point.

Figure 1.

Fluctuations of Consciousness between Ordinary and Alternate States

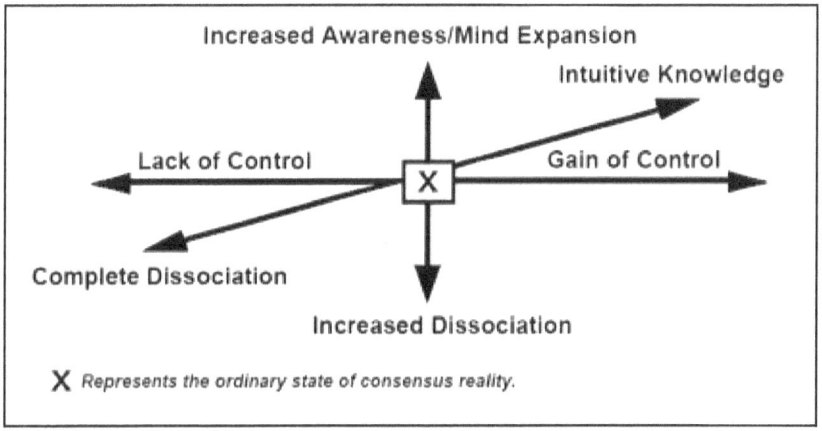

When we begin to cultivate awareness and control, we progress on the diagonal toward *intuitive knowledge*, which is the highest point in the upper right quadrant. This state indicates full control and complete awareness (i.e., being and knowing without objectification and discursive thinking). The lowest point on the diagonal, in the lower left quadrant, is *complete dissociation*, multiple personality, or possession. With respect to this lowest point, Jung spoke of *"unconscious, autonomic complexes,"* which appear in such a state *"as projections because they are not associated with the ego."* (8) Possession either has to be exorcised or is professionally utilized by shamans and mediums.

To give an example for how cautious we have to be when we want to define a certain state let us consider shamans who call a spirit into their bodies and surrender their consciousness to the spirit who begins to act through them. They must be plotted in the lower right quadrant because although they enter possession, which is a dissociative state and a state of temporary flooding, they have at least partial control over consciously accessing and leaving this state after its purpose has been fulfilled. Schizophrenics belong to the lowest point in the lower left quadrant because they have neither recall nor control over this state of consciousness. When going on a "magical flight," meditators and shamans have to be plotted in the upper right quadrant because they experience and control the expansion of their consciousness at all times to the point where they enter intuitive knowledge and just "be."

The following techniques and conditions facilitate access to states of consciousness other than the present state of my readers.

1. *Extreme Temperature Conditions.* The heat of a sweat lodge, for example, increases pulse rate and induces nausea, dizziness, and syncope (fainting). As with fevers, high body temperatures seem to activate the immune system, detoxify the body, and release emotional and cognitive blockages, facilitating spiritual experiences. Spiritual exercises (e.g., meditation, prayer, evocation of saints in Christianity or Wakan–Tankan in Native American tradition), on the other hand, do not only calm down the mind, but also result in a calming of the bodily functions, which allows a different kind of heat to arise.

We have, therefore, to distinguish between physical heat that penetrates our bodies from the outside, leading to increased physical functions (also influencing our emotional, mental, and spiritual levels of experience), and spiritual heat generated during meditation and prayer by stilling physical functions, which allows quiet transcendence and entry into a different reality. I predict that future research will yield more conclusive results toward the quality of states that can be entered through consciously induced changes in temperature from either the outside or the inside.

2. *Physical or Sensory Deprivation.* In the flotation tank, for example, the boundaries between self and non-self dissolve. The body is not restricted by clothing. Neither sensory nor motor systems are in play. At this point, unusual shifts into slower alpha activity have been reported by Heron and Zubek, Welch, and Saunders. (9)

Aside from restricted mobility and visual-sensory deprivation, sleep deprivation and seclusion also lead to alterations in consciousness. Food and water deprivation have an effect on the pituitary and adrenal glands that directly affects the hypothalamus and hippocampal-septal systems. (10)

On a vision quest, individuals fast, do not drink, and forgo sleep for three or more days and nights. Through abstinence, the life energy is "redirected toward healing, or to produce states of bliss." (9, 11)

3. *Pilgrimages.* Many oral traditions around sacred places—the sacred mountains of the Taoists, sacred trees, tombs of saints, sites of revelations (e.g., Lourdes, France; Fatima, Portugal; Medjugorge, Yugoslavia)—speak of religious trances occurring at these sites. Such trances cause a shift of attention and activate the pilgrims' self-healing powers. The question of whether these miraculous shifts are the result of the placebo effect, the pilgrim's expectations, geographical and meteorological conditions, or outside intervention cannot be answered conclusively because we don't have the tools to prove whether a single one of these agents or all the

above caused the shift. We can, however, establish medical records that document the physical condition of individuals before and after their pilgrimage. We also should continue with our research of sacred sites that have been and are still used by shamans (e.g., Sedona in Arizona and Mount Shasta in California).

4. *Sonic Driving*. We have archaeological documentation (e.g., petroglyphs) that the effect of drumming and rattling on the central nervous system was known already in prehistoric times. Whether in religious or nonreligious context, chanting also seems to produce shifts in consciousness. (See Chapter 25, pp. 277-281)

Research on rhythmic sensory stimulation was first conducted in the 1930s. The Walters then found in the 1940s that *"stimulation of other receptors gives even more convincing results, particularly when a very large group of sensory units can be excited simultaneously and rhythmically, for then the central electrical response is correspondingly larger."* (12)

Jilek elicited responses to auditory driving at the fundamental of each stimulus frequency (usually three to four beats per second). (12) When Neher exposed clinically normal people to low-frequency, high-amplitude acoustic stimulations produced by instruments similar to the deerskin drums used by North American Indians, he observed on the electroencephalograph that different sound frequencies were transmitted along different nerve pathways in the brain. (12) (He had, however, reinforced the acoustic effects by flashing lights; that means he did not control for all variables.) With the rise of neoshamanic groups, we now have the opportunity to conduct more accurate fieldwork on the use of *sonic driving* without becoming intrusive to shamans who practice in traditional societies.

5. *Kinetic Stimulation and Hyperventilation*. Extensive running and dancing result in overbreathing and oxygen depletion, which, coupled with hypoglycemia, causes the appearance of slow wave activity (2 to 3 cycles per second) and hallucinatory experiences, as do other forms of exertion. (10) I witnessed, for example, in India and Southeast Asia ritual dancing that produced dissociative states before firewalking and other physical feats.

I observed, especially with spirit mediums, who do not always use kinetic stimulation, that a change in breathing patterns occurs. Noteworthy also is the *energy darshan* practiced in Asia (e.g., during the ritual initiation of disciples).

To compare these practices with those in the United States, rebirthing comes to mind in which the desired state is activated with the help of quick breathing. Energy stimulations also can be observed in the use of

Reiki. Apprentices report that they experience a strong surge of energy during initiation.

Dance, rhythmic music, lights, and several breathing techniques, used by many psychotherapists today, are indeed techniques that combine elements from various shamanic traditions. Stanislav Grof, for example, uses holotropic breathing, certain body postures, lights, and music, and Felicitas Goodman found that certain postures, assumed during rattling, produce specific imagery, even in individuals not ethnically related whether they lived in prehistoric times or in contemporary societies. (13, 14)

   6. *Use of Chemical and Hallucinogenic Substances.* Weston La Barre wrote about the peyote cult, and Harner discussed extensively the use of hallucinogenics in shamanic and other religious ceremonies. (15, 16) Shifts in states of consciousness that produce chemical changes in the brain need not be activated by hallucinogenic substances; the intention and concentration of an individual may suffice without any outside help. Research to investigate the latter possibility has begun, and we anxiously await the first results.

Jilek talks about the endogenous opioid agents enkephalin and beta-endorphin and possibly other neuroendocrine peptides, such as neurotensin and bradykinin, which, for example, may play an important role in the integration of pain information. (12) Beta-endorphin injections have antidysphoric, antidepressant, anxiolytic, analgesic, and disinhibiting effects within five to ten minutes after injection that last from one to six hours. Kline speculates that beta-endorphin, produced by the anterior pituitary, may be the body's own way of producing and controlling affective states. (12)

The endorphins can be found in the limbic system, the thalamus, the peri-aqueductal gray matter, and the substantia gelatinosa of the spinal cord. They also are in areas of the brain that regulate respiration, motor activity, endocrine control, and mood.

Achterberg points to the role of the enkephalins as *"endogenous immunomodulators"* that assist the immune system in fighting disease. (9) The entire natural pharmacopoeia can indeed be reinforced. Achterberg added consciously used imagery, which also plays a role in the placebo effect. (9)

   7. *Hypnosis and Deep Sleep.* These are well-documented means to access different states of consciousness. Historically, sleep therapy has been used already (e.g., in classical Greece at Epidauros).

Tart recorded brainwaves (EEG), galvanic skin resistance responses, and heart rate in a woman who frequently had out-of-body experiences during sleep. (9) During these experiences, alpha activity was $1^{1/2}$ cycles per second slower than the subject's normal alpha, and there were no rapid eye movements, which normally accompany dreaming. There also was no physiological arousal despite her heightened mental activity.

Hypnotherapy and other techniques of focused attention are effectively used today by trained professionals. Hypnotism has proved to be a technique to bypass an individual's "erroneously limited belief system" and to circumvent "the all too narrow limits of ordinary everyday consciousness." (17) This statement alerts us to the wide area of unexplored territory. Extreme deprivation during a vision quest often is reinforced by hypnotic suggestions with which individuals prepare themselves for the visionary states. (18) The visions then signal, illuminate, and provide guidance for the transformative process of a shaman-to-be. I did not find any study that explored in depth the use of hypnosis by shamans, either self-hypnosis to bring about and enhance their trance states, or their use of hypnosis to shift the attention of their clients to put them into a healing frame of mind, which includes posthypnotic suggestions. I observed at numerous occasions the conditioning of shamans that showed similarities to the preparations of actors who condition themselves before each performance for the role they are going to play.

8. *Meditation*. In my book *Trance and Healing in Southeast Asia Today*, I discuss research on wakeful relaxed states in which reduction in oxygen consumption occurs together with changes in carbon dioxide elimination. (12) The rate and volume of respiration, when reduced, causes a slight increase in the acidity of arterial blood, marked by a decrease in blood lactate level. The heartbeat slows down, and there is a considerable increase in skin resistance and alpha brainwave patterns with occasional theta waves.

We have numerous manuals on different kinds of meditation, from Patanjali's *Yoga Sutras* (19) in Hinduism to the "insight meditation" *(satipatthana sutta)* (20) in early Buddhism as well as the tantric meditation systems of Hinduism and Mahayana Buddhism; the meditations of Taoist, Sufi, and Hasidic masters; and the *Exercises of St. Ignatius* (21) in Christianity. They all use breathing techniques and suggest focusing the mind; some use specific forms of visualization. The *Visuddhimagga*, for example, suggests forty subjects of meditation (*kammatthana*). All these meditation techniques additionally prescribe certain body postures. (14) When mental and spiritual health is the purpose of all these meditation techniques, do we find similar ultimate goals? The Abhidhamma speaks of 121 mental states that can be cultivated through meditation until practitioners reach *nirvana* (complete extinction of material attachments), whereas Hindu, Sufi, and Hasidic masters talk about the union with the Divine. There seems to be a difference between nirvana, the Void, and the union with the Divine. Shamans usually maintain that they communicate with the world of spirits, closer to our human world. Only a few speak of a High God (e.g., Wankan–Tankan of the Sioux). Chinese shamans expressedly communicate with mediators between the High Gods and the human world (e.g., Kuan Yin, generals of the Three Kingdoms, etc.).

9. *Ritualization.* Access to alternate states of consciousness is facilitated by ritualization, which (after all participants agreed on the purpose of the ritual) requires the following seven steps:

- *(1)* Preparation of the environment. Since time immemorial, it has been the task of shamans and priests to create a safe place where the unusual can happen. Visible boundaries are established—for example, by placing *sima* stones around the *bot* (ordination hall in Thai monasteries) or by forming a circle in shamanic practices. Such preparations create a state of readiness and raise the expectations; they also prepare practitioners for the experience of the unusual, the meeting with the supernatural world.
- *(2)* Purification of the site and all participants (with incense, sage, or water).
- *(3)* Separation. The ordinary reality has to be left behind and non-ordinary reality is entered ritually.
- *(4)* Entrance into the alternate state. In this *liminal* state, ordinary rules are suspended, and spiritual forces can be invoked. (22)
- *(5)* Communion. Participants come indeed into the presence of the Divine and experience the mystical union of being connected with everybody and everything else.
- *(6)* Celebration. The presence of the Divine is celebrated with food and often dance.
- *(7)* Closure. After having expressed gratitude for its manifestation, the Divine is sent off and a ritual closure protects, on the one hand, the spiritual world from pollution and on the other hand, participants from emotional overload.
- *(8)* Integration. After participants have returned to ordinary reality, ritualists facilitate the integration of the experience into daily life. (23, 24)

CONCLUSIONS

Michael Winkelman has provided us with a survey of psychophysiological research on the effects of trance-inducing procedures that lead *"to a state of parasympathetic dominance in which the frontal cortex is dominated by slow wave patterns originating in the limbic system and related projections into the frontal parts of the brain."* (10) Such investigations are helpful for distinguishing pathological from nonpathological cases. The main criterion appears to be the faculty to consciously access and exit alternate states of consciousness and to be able to recall the experience.

Science has to establish new categories for individuals who are capable of monitoring their shifts of attention and who can access other realities at will, a faculty that not only is of benefit to practitioners, but also serves the community. The conscious evocation of alternate states of consciousness has already proved to be beneficial in setting the self-healing process in motion and increasing our state of well-being. (9)

It is important to note that despite their excursions into other realities, masters of different states of consciousness function well in their communities in contrast to individuals who have no control over the different states of consciousness they are experiencing, and therefore fit the pathology suggested in the DSM-III (*Diagnostic and Statistical Manual of Mental Disorders, Third Edition*). (23, 25) More detailed results about alternate states of consciousness can be expected from ongoing and future research.

REFERENCES AND NOTES

1) Tart, C.T. (1969) *Altered States of Consciousness*. NY: John Wiley & Sons.
2) Tart, C.T. (1986) *Waking Up: Overcoming the Obstacles of Human Potential*. Boston: Shambhala, New Science Library.
3) Ludwig, A. (1960) "Altered states of consciousness." In: *Archives of General Psychiatry*. 1960; 15; 225-234.
4) Fischer, R.W. (1974) "A cartography of the ecstatic and meditative states." In: *Science*. 1974:89- 904.
5) Fischer, R.W. (1980) "A cartography of the ecstatic and meditative states." In: Woode, R. (Ed.) *Understanding Mysticism, Its Methodology, Interpretation in World Religions, Psychological Evaluations, Philosophical and Theological Appraisal*. Garden City, NY: Image Books; 1980:286-305.
6) Krippner, S. (1972) "Altered states of consciousness." In: White, J. (Ed.) *The Highest State of Consciousness*. NY: Doubleday; 1972:1-5.
7) Hilgard, E.R. (1977) *Divided Consciousness: Multiple Controls in Human Thoughts and Action*. NY: John Wiley & Sons.
8) Jung, C.G., Hull, R.F.C. (1960) trans. *The Structure and Dynamics of the Psyche*. Bollingen Series VI. NY: Pantheon Books.
9) Achterberg, J. (1985) *Imagery in Healing, Shamanism and Modern Medicine*. Boston: Shambhala, New Science Library.
10) Winkelman, M. (1986) "Trance states: A theoretical model and cross-cultural analysis." In: *Ethos*. 1986;14(2):174-203.
11) Foster, S. (1987) "Crying for a vision, the purpose circle, and emergence." In: Heinze, R-I (Ed.) *Proceedings of the Third International Conference on the Study of Shamanism and Alternate Modes of Healing*. Madison, WI: A-R Editions, Inc.; 1987:264-271.
12) Heinze, R-I. (1988) *Trance and Healing in Southeast Asia Today*. Berkeley/Bangkok: Independent Scholars of Asia, Inc. White Lotus.

13) Grof, S. (1985) *Beyond the Brain–Birth, Death and Transcendence in Psychotherapy*. NY: State University of NY Press.
14) Goodman, F.D. (1986) "Body posture and the religious altered state of consciousness: An experimental investigation." In: *Journal of Humanistic Psychology*. 1986;26(3):81-118.
15) La Barre, W. (1971) *The Peyote Cult*. NY: Schocken Books.
16) Harner, M.J. (1973) *Hallucinogens and Shamanism*. NY: Oxford University Press.
17) Erickson, M., Rossi, E., Rossi, S. (1976) *Hypnotic Realities: The Induction of Clinical Hypnosis and Forms of Indirect Suggestion*. NY: Irvington.
18) Rogers, S.I. (1982) *The Shaman: His Symbols and His Healing Power*. Springfield, IL: Charles Thomas.
19) Prabhavananda, S. & Isherwood, C. trans. (1969) *How to Know God, The Yoga Aphorisms of Patanjali*. NY: New American Library.
20) Ven, U. Silananda, & Heinze, R-I. (Eds.) (1990) *The Four Foundations of Mindfulness*. Boston: Wisdom Publications.
21) Mottola, A. (1964) trans. *The Spiritual Exercises of St. Ignatius*. NY: Doubleday.
22) Van Gennep, A. (1960) *The Rites of Passage*. Vizedom, M.B. & Cafees, G.L. trans. Chicago, IL: University of Chicago Press.
23) Heinze, R-I. (1991) *Shamans of the Twentieth Century*. NY: Irvington.
24) Heinze, R-I. (1991) "The ritual process: Translating the ineffable into ritual language." In: Heinze, R-I. (Ed.) *Proceedings of the Seventh International Conference on the Study of Shamanism and Alternate Modes of Healing*. Berkeley, CA: Independent Scholars of Asia, Inc.; 1991:1-17.
25) (1980) *Diagnostic and Statistical Manual of Mental Disorders, 3rd ed.* Washington, DC: American Psychiatric Association.

When we want to talk about shamanism and alternate modes of healing, it seems to be necessary to work with clear definitions...

1) Shamans can access alternate states of consciousness at will.

2) Shamans fulfill needs of their community, which otherwise are not met.

3) Shamans are mediators between the sacred and the profane.

--- Ruth-Inge Heinze

SHORT INTERVIEWS
With Independent Neurochemists and a Psychotherapist

Alexander T. (Sasha) Shulgin, PhD, and his wife Ann Shulgin have become cultural heroes over recent years. Both joined the PRG when they were invited to speak to the group about their experiences with MDMA before it became illegal. He wrote the formulas and recipes for a long list of psychoactive entheogens and published them in their books *PIHKAL* and *TIHKAL*. They also collaborated with other chemists, including Hosteen Nez, whose major addition to that long list is one that students will seek to find more about in the future. It is several compounds enthusiastically called *"Smart Pills."* While only a short study was done with these while they were still legal, the results were extremely promising. (For example, a graduate student was able to study enough in a few weeks using smart pills to pass his language requirement.*[1]) Since new interest is growing about compounds that can enhance focus of attention, memory and intelligence, perhaps *"smart pills"* could again become legally available. Though one wonders if students would ever be required to pass a drug test before they are even allowed to take an SAT exam.

Another neurochemist, who is an electronics engineer as well and a member of the PRG, is Tim Scully, PhD. Currently he is writing the history of underground LSD, along with the political suppression of it and the suppression of the scientific studies proving its potential use for therapy and spiritual awakening.*[2]

The careful scientific work by these brave pioneers has given us all very important insights about our minds, our memories, and the essence of spirit. This information is so very important to the evolution of our knowledge of mental processes, that it should be available to all, not kept just for some politically, or economically, privileged few.

---

*[1]   Nez, Hosteen. (1985) *Smart Pills: Compounds that Increase the Capacity for Mental Work in Humans*. Berkeley, CA: Published by Mind States in 2001, Jon Hanna (Ed.)

*[2]   Littlefield, C. (2002) *Hofmann's Potion (short excerpt below)*. Canada: National Film Board of Canada.

...*By the mid **1950s**, LSD research was being published in medical and academic journals all over the world. It showed potential benefits in the treatment of alcoholism, drug addiction and other mental illnesses.... The prevailing psychoanalytic model of mental illness was about to give way to one based on brain chemistry...*

CHAPTER 19-a CHEMISTRY AND MEMORY

Sasha Shulgin, PhD

Alexander T. Shulgin *has been in the business of exploring mind chemistry for over 60 years. He took an important chemistry book with him to read while he was in the US Navy during WW II, so when he attended chemistry classes at UC Berkeley later, he already knew the material, and he didn't like the way it was being taught. This is his story:*

"A lot of the people in chemistry were getting more deeply involved in the technical aspect of these, the loopholes in those—and the positions between this ring and that ring. So I dropped in on a biochemistry course. That was really about the chemistry of life, not a lot of technical stuff. I discovered it was very interesting that chemistry was used to try to find out how the body works. Since none of the people in biochemistry were into chemistry, and I knew my chemistry inside out, I got my PhD in biochemistry in 1952. I went to work for Dow Chemical for ten years, from the middle '50s to the middle '60s. After I was there for a couple of years, they showed me an unknown compound that they could make easily, and asked me what they could use it for. I changed it slightly so it could be a successful commercial insecticide. After that, they agreed to let me work on anything I wanted to, so I started working on psychedelic drugs, though they didn't want me to publish, except at my home address, and later, not even there. After that I built a lab at home, and decided to become an independent consultant. I had two properties:

1) I knew my subject well.
2) The disadvantage for some lawyers in court cases was that I was honest."

Sasha and Ann Shulgin's books are available at www.erowid.org.
PIHKAL (Phenethylamines I Have Known and Loved.)
TIHKAL (Tryptamines I Have Known and Loved.)

CHEMISTRY AND MEMORY
(Excerpts from tape-recorded interviews with
Sasha and Ann Shulgin in September 2008)

Sasha Shulgin

SS: Frankly, I was exploring all types of chemicals affecting the mind, from stimulants to suppressants to depressants though I ignored the opiates, heroin, all those types, as nonsense. I was introduced back then to mescaline and that was an entirely different world. It got my attention totally.

Mescaline does something that actually did not affect the brain as much as it affected the mind, and I began drawing the distinction between the brain and the mind. For a long while I functioned under the assumption that these drugs affected the mind, doing something to it and creating something new, creating something different, and I explored all different types of chemicals – changing them, checking them out. In all cases I was looking for effects on my mind/mental process – what they were doing in the mental direction, and then with the minds of the people I was working with – theirs collectively. Then my goal was to find new chemicals, determine their behavior in the mental process – confirm it with a number of different people – and then publish it in the literature – and make it become public information. I did not apply for any more patents in the meantime. I was dedicated to moving this information from the unknown to publically known material.

And then sometime ago, it began occurring to me that these chemicals were not affecting the mental process, they were allowing a new mental process to become available – ones that train mental transformation. It was a little hard to handle until I realized just what I was dealing with.

The chemicals are not acting on the brain; the chemicals are merely catalyzing the brain to act upon itself. And all the stuff that is being revealed by these chemicals is in the mind all the time. It is all a part of the brain function. We can choose to take the time to have access to it. We can choose a time to understand what the heck is going on in our heads.

And this gave me that chance to sit back and explore what was going on with my own childhood memories. How could a few good milligrams of a white powder contain a childhood memory of a strange adventure? It is not the chemical, it is in the mind, not the brain – and this material allows a mind to access itself. That's a huge research tool for the greatest understanding for self-exploration.

JM: That is most important. When people have suppressed old disturbing memories, which are then revealed, they may blame the drug, instead of their own natural process of self-discovery.

SS: They have access again to unhappy memories of the past that have been in there all the time. The brain has just found convenient ways of closing the shades on the window and not having access to it. A lot of what psychedelics do is to open up these windows, to remove these shades, allowing you access to what has been there all the time. It is just a strange way of looking at it, but it is the way I feel with great confidence – this is correct.

That's why "**a**" has a different response to this drug, than "**b**." For both, the drug is doing different things. The drug is merely allowing "**a**" and "**b**" to re-access what's in there all the time. And they have different memories and experiences in there – different backgrounds, different childhood behavior patterns. Take a 2- or 3-year-old baby, and the world is bouncing in all directions and everywhere. And as the child get older, he learns patterns that are socially acceptable, or if he is committed to not being socially acceptable, at least they are pleasing to him. People end up in similar adulthoods in many ways, having completely different childhoods.

Psychedelics are catalyzing that re-experiencing what was very real and totally forgotten, or not wanted – and sometimes the experiences on psychedelics are not very happy, because they bring back part of your life that hasn't changed. My father grew up speaking Russian, and later learned English. When he was quite old, he lost the ability to speak English. In old age, often there is a completion of the circle, going back to the earliest memories.

JM: When I was doing therapy with a friend, and I used either psychedelics or hypnosis, I learned to tell the person that it was important to *"know your drama. You mustn't reject your drama, because of repressed fear or anger, or else you are stuck to replay it. Enjoy it as though you were watching a TV drama full of emotional material."*

SS: Yes, that's right. Frequently we are at the end of the hallway, and we have successfully come down that hallway and are now a mature individual, adult, grown-up child, young/old person, who knows what? But when you turn around and look back up that hallway, you have any number of doors, all of them closed, and to go back up that hallway and open THIS door – by golly and you look inside of it – and very often you open up this other doorway and find it opens up to a hallway filled with closed doors. And you can go in there. Once you go in, you are already starting on a trail into your life. And you can find yourself in a fascinating area of re-discovery. This ideal is what the psychedelics mean. You arrive at a new discovery, aspects of your life of your past, that you have repressed out of sheer laziness, reward, fear, who knows what? You had closed them, but they are re-opened. The world I experience in many ways with the psychedelic culture is to re-open the doors, not the opening of new doors.

JM: I feel that once you change your reaction to the past, you change your future as well. You have a fear reaction to an old event, and if you continuously respond to that in the same fearful way, you will keep re-experiencing it as fear. But when you go into the past and recognize it as the past and think of a different way to respond to that past memory, that is more positive, then your future is also more positive.

SS: That is true in a number of ways. The future – how you are going to respond to something in the future – is not committed to where you are now. If you re-explore how you got there, you have opened up different doorways for the future. It is all about how you got where you are, about the re-experiencing of that which is past, and changing your reaction to it. The people who use psychedelics are not using words of chemistry or words of biochemistry or words of pharmacology. The words they're using: *"I met this person, or I discovered where I came from or where I was going..."* And it occurred to me that I did not understand where I was from, but if I see where I am going, I don't want to go there. Or I don't understand how I got here, but my path here might have been interesting, and I learn how very fascinating this trip can be.

It's the matter of opening up the doorways to what is in there all the time. You don't remember having closed them: You are unaware of them, but they are all real.

JM: Once you've closed the door, you no longer know it's there. So we know we are dealing with mind more than chemistry, but one thing I wanted to ask you especially: Are there different reactions to different chemicals, or do they open the doors differently, for instance with tryptamines or phenethylamines?

SS: In a very specific sense, no. Once you turn the doorknob and enter your own door, you see what is on the other side, whether you do it with your right hand or your left hand. On the other hand, you may be picking the doorknob by some aspect of memory that you are not aware of. You might choose the phenethylamines, because they are a benign trip to *"let it be where you are, enjoy who you are, enjoy what you recover."* Tryptamines are a lot more provocative in a critical way, and cause you more self-evaluation. When you turn this self-exploration over to a chemist or a bunch of white powder, you decide truthfully where you want to go. Where would I really like to go? Why I am curious about this area in the first place? Sometimes we say we needed that adventure, other times it could happen anyway. There is no path or map <u>in</u> the chemical compound. The map comes from you. The compound merely opens you up to reading the map.

When the mescaline triggered a description of what was in my brain, it occurred to me to take the structure of mescaline and make small changes. One little change had already been made at one time, and nothing else had been made since the beginning of the century – mescaline and THC (tetrahydrocannabinols – marijuana) were the only psychedelics known in northern hemisphere in text books. It's true that in South America, a few were known, but in the USA only the two of them were known. Albert Hofmann discovered LSD accidentally and a few clinics began to use it in the '50s. In the 1950s and 1960s I ran the numbers up from those two to ten times that – to about 20. In the year 2000 they had gone from 20 to 200. We now have three or four hundred. And I will say with no hesitation in the year 2050 there will be 2,000 psychedelics. It's a marvelous increase in rate of growth.

So I did make some small changes to the mescaline, and I ingested the compound again. It was slightly more potent, or less potent, depending on how much material I took, but not the experience I got. But with that first mescaline experience, for example, I was sitting at the end of the living room where I was living, and there were some flowers there, and I got transformed into the beauty of small flowers, and I looked at them, and I almost couldn't touch them, because they were just absolutely gorgeous. And they had voices, they almost spoke to me, they had honesty, they had integrity and I was entranced by the flowers.

About two months later, I changed the chemistry on another small part of the molecule: I put sulfur groups on the fourth position of the ring – and I ingested that. At some point, I came into the same living room and the same flowers, and I looked at them. This time, I just took them apart to see what was inside. That was something I never could have done with the first experience, but with a different chemical, my curiosity was expressed in a different way – from examining the flower to taking it apart. And even to study the science of the flower – the entire process – can be expressed in so many different ways each time you turn around.

And the same thing is true with what happens to yourself when you get into the psychedelic drug experience, there is no best, there is no better, there is no good, there is no bad, they are all different. Some have a personality background that allows them to feel comfortable, but the same substance used by another person, and the experience may be totally uncomfortable – just totally inappropriate. It is all you and your memory and your background and your personal likes and personal dislikes. But you are not aware of it, until you get in the middle of a psychedelic experience. The value of psychedelics is to show you where you are now.

To find why you went into this area, instead of some other area. Sometimes we need that bridge. You can actually re-live things that you had once lived, and for that you discover twists like that to find out how they really were. They are fun to re-live, and you say, *"Oh, wow, is that what happened?"*

I remember one time I had a friend who said he had never tried scopolamine, and he asked me to be his "babysitter" for it. I have no use for scopolamine, myself, but he was a fairly experienced druggy, so I agreed. He sat in the comfortable chair and listened to the radio, and as the drug was coming on, he said the radio had a strange sound to it, and since he never had heard this sound, it was not a memory recall. Then he was looking over at the door as though someone was coming into the room — nothing to cause him to be paranoid. He got up to follow – and walked into the door because it wasn't open. *"Whooh! That hurt"*

I asked him, *"Who were you following?"*

He said, *"I just had never seen her before. She came in that door and went out that door, and I was just going to see who she was, and the door wasn't open."*

This was a complete true hallucination. I asked, *"Do you think she was really here?"*

"I saw her."

"Well, what did she look like?"

"She had long curly hair and I don't remember having met her before."

He began exploring his memory, until he realized she didn't exist. Let's try other things, and then he began to explore this whole relationship, and after about an hour and a half or so, he said, *"I think I would like to go into the other room and lie down and maybe sleep for awhile."* He went back into the bedroom, and I don't know how many times I had to stop him from going out into the street. I kept him inside the house. He remembered nothing of getting out of the bed and going down the stairs. His complete world of imagination on top of these vivid hallucinations went beyond anything he had ever experienced before. And he had never experienced anything like this before in his memory.

When he said he was pretty well back to baseline, I asked him how he knew that. He told me to ask him a question. I did, and he answered it well. He could articulate fairly well.

After another hour, he drove from Berkeley to his home in SF. But two weeks later, he told me that the hallucinations continued while he was driving across to the San Francisco side of the bay bridge.

> *While driving between the towers a student from medical school was sitting next to me. We talked for a while, and all of a sudden, for some*

reason, he hopped into the back seat. So I turned around to the back seat to continue a conversation. But he wasn't there. "Oh shit, I'm not out of my hallucinations yet." Then I became aware of a tinkling on the radio. So I turned the volume up a bit to have more of a "real" reality around me, but I discovered that the radio had not been on. "Oh, shit, I am going to get off this bridge and out of this car." So I took the off ramp, parked my car and took a taxi home.

JM: What is scopolamine? It sounds dangerous.

SS: Scopolamine is generally known as an amnesia-releasing drug, that allows you to live a life that is not real, and you don't remember it, you don't remember having lived it or not having lived it. It is used as a poisoner. Don't ever let anyone get you involved with scopolamine or atropine. It is confusing, and if you get a little bit too much of it, you are unconscious – a bit less of it and you are conscious, but you don't have conscious memory of it.

JM: So this is a drug that actually does something **to** your brain, as different from the psychedelics.

SS: It takes you out of your brain, so you don't have access to it.

JM: If I understand you correctly – the phenethylamines and the tryptamines evoke what is already there, while scopolamine gives you something that is not there.

SS: Well, if you are observing an event, and you have what I call "babysitters" who are around to protect you – and they are seeing the same event – a car pulling out of a parking space down the street, and the car is red and it pulls out without signaling. There is no questioning on that. They say so and you saw it that way. You saw it and interpreted it differently. You say that person actually came out of that bank and looked over his shoulder, I bet he was a thief – the interpretation may be a matter of experiential, judgment and understanding, but the event is pretty well documented. In the case of scopolamine, the event did not exist. It was a true hallucination. And you have no way to get a confirmation, because no one else saw it. I have no patience (and do not care) about amnesia things, and imaginative creations. When you go into your own early consciousness, they may be your creations, but they aren't imaginative, they are quite real. And they are coming from you. I see the scopolamine world as hallucination and the psychedelic world as the real deal.

JM: What about uppers and downers and cocaine?

SS: There are physical changes. One may help you sleep, the other keeps you awake. You can't sleep if you are stimulated. You get a rush on your blood pressure. Your whole heart system is going at a different rate. There is a distinction on the heartbeat. And I know when someone comes here who is stoned on amphetamine; his eyes contract with light, they don't expand. Take a person whose eyes are diffused, not because of stimulations, but because of optical, retinal paralysis, that is something in the scopolamine world. The eyes do not contract and then re-expand; they stay expanded. A few physical monitors can pin it down correctly.

JM: I have seen major changes in brainwaves on people who use cocaine. My portable EEG equipment (designed by Tim Scully in the 1970s) did a great job in training people to produce alpha / theta rhythms. However, it didn't measure the frequencies above 20Hz or below 6Hz so it did not register that first cocaine rush. Several young men, who had learned voluntary control of some EEG frequencies, asked to be hooked up to my equipment while they snorted cocaine. They wanted to check out the results in their EEG. After that first rush, which registered on my brainwave analyzers only as noise (similar to 60 Hz interference), each of them seemed to have more voluntary control than before – but only for about 30 to 45 minutes. After that, each of them lost some of the voluntary control they had learned earlier when they were straight. It meant that over time with continued or habitual use, they would lose some mental function. Then as they lost more control, it would take more and more of the chemistry to feel those few minutes of being "in control." When they realized how much the cocaine changed their EEG, they stopped using it.

SS: There is a profound reality, guarantee, certainty, and confidence, with the psychedelics. And that is why I love the idea of introducing people to psychedelics – communication between people can flower. But for one who is not really quite willing to open himself up to be honest and candid, and the other person is willing to try to fool around with that, the MDMA can really help bring them in closer communication.

When a person goes to a doctor for therapy, and the doc gives a stimulant, or some other mild drug, the time for therapy may be reduced from four weeks or six weeks of introduction to two weeks. With MDMA, the time is cut down to 15 minutes. Immediately, the person is willing to trust, and in turn be trusted. These are the changes in individual personality with psychedelics. MDMA is not really a psychedelic, it is more of a stimulant, but that is immaterial. It allows for fusion therapy because of the opening of the personality. These are fascinating things. You get into yourself. With the chemistry, you are letting the chemistry allow the brain to tell you what it needs to know. So that is why all those things are really different.

Yes. There is a chemical difference. But then every material is different with different people, too. So you can't put anything on the structure of the specific chemical compound or the person. Without the compound, the person might not have the experience. The whole is blended together in nice ways.

CHAPTER 19-b   MDMA AS THERAPY

Ann Shulgin

Ann Shulgin was born in Wellington, New Zealand, the child of a New Zealand mother and an American father who was in the American Foreign Service there. When she was two the family moved to Sicily, where her father had been transferred by the US State Department. Two years later, they were moved to a suburb of Trieste, Italy, where they stayed 6 years until Italy was about to join the German Axis on the eve of World War II. They managed to leave on the last refugee ship. The family was subsequently posted to Cuba (2 years) and Canada (3 years) where Ann went to boarding school. Later she went to school in New Hampshire, where she fell in love. Her father retired and the family moved to the SF Bay Area, where Ann took classes in typing and commercial art and married an art student. They moved to LA, where she had her first child and her first divorce. Then Ann moved back to SF with her son and became a medical transcriber at UC Med. Center. Ann then married her first love and supported him through medical school before divorce. For 8 years she was married to a Jungian psychiatrist and they had three children.

Ann and Alexander (Sasha) Shulgin, finding a real soul mate in each other, were married in 1981. Ann has been in the forefront of MDMA psychotherapy ever since. Together, they produced *PIHKAL* and *TIHKAL*, both books widely considered to be fundamental to the basic understanding of entheogens. They are presently working together on a third book, tentatively titled *BOOK THREE*. Available from Transform Press, Erowid Library, P.O. Box 13675, Berkeley, CA, 94701; or at the website: www.erowid.org.

MDMA AS THERAPY

Ann Shulgin

Generally speaking MDMA has great use as the insight drug. That is the main value of MDMA (*"Ecstasy"* is the popular name). It allows insight without self-rejection or self-hatred. That is an incredibly important thing in any kind of psychotherapy, because avoidance is the normal human reaction to the idea of looking deeply into oneself. The psyche wants to avoid too much pain, too much self-disgust, or too much self-hatred, so it is hard to get insight, because people want to avoid what they unconsciously believe is a very nasty something down in the deepest part of the soul, what Jung calls *"the Shadow."*

With MDMA, in a way we absolutely cannot understand, it's possible for 99% of the people who take it to obtain important insights. (I should say the usual dose is 120 Mg. for the average person.) Taking the drug produces the ability to see into oneself — not just the negative things, but also the positive — without any anger at oneself or rejection of oneself because of what is being seen. This means that the most extraordinary results can be had even after just the first session. There have been many patients or clients that have had one session of MDMA and accomplished so much that they did not need or express a need for a second session.

It is a most valuable drug for Post-Traumatic Stress Disorder (PTSD). I have always thought, and obviously other people have come to the same conclusion, that for PTSD, this is the one most beneficial drug, because it helps the solders to release the terrible experiences of wars. For example, there is a tendency to react to a stimulus that sounds like a gunshot, and that suddenly brings back a whole scene from their times in combat. I think most people understand that. Post-Traumatic Stress Disorder may take many forms.

But there are other things that are much deeper and more harmful — especially to 18- or 20-year-old young men, who probably come from rather average families where they have been that taught certain things are good and certain things are bad.

For example   it is not just that such a man found himself killing somebody whom he had never met before, and who was certainly trying to kill him, also. And it is not just the horror of having actually taking a life.

But what can happen in some cases is that after he has been involved in a very long and involved fight, he can emerge from it realizing (in some part of himself), that he actually enjoyed killing. And that is the intolerable thing, because that means that, to the unconscious, his inner self — the real person that he is — has become something bestial or monstrous.

This is what will cause a real shying away from attempts at insight. But with MDMA the *former soldier* can see what he has done and how he felt then and be able to have the insight and understanding of the situation—and himself—at that moment in time. At no time does he feel he is being drowned in a sea of horror and self-negation, which if he did feel that, this might otherwise bring a good therapeutic session to an abrupt end. He is able to handle it because along with the insight is this continuing state of feeling of being a person of great value in the world. (The most important thing to most of us on this Earth is to feel that we are worth something.) It is not just insight, but it is insight with self-acceptance that happens. This is what makes MDMA one of the most valuable psycho-therapeutic adjuncts. This makes it an extraordinarily valuable drug.

Now, comparing the effects of MDMA with any other drug I can think of, there is no other drug that produces this effect. If you are a very intelligent person, blessed with a higher than average IQ, then you might be able to use any drug of this "entheogenic" type to find insight for yourself, but MDMA is, so far, the best we have.

The average person is very frightened of working through the stress of that much anxiety. I think of the other drugs that I have worked with, beside MDMA, are 2CB — and that would not be for PTSD. What it is for would have nothing to do with war or PTSD. When working with somebody for some time with MDMA, if they have achieved a change from what the original problem seemed to be, then the 2CB becomes a further step in an effort to achieve some kind of spiritual maturity.

The people who do this work with psychedelics are people who have gained a certain amount of insight into themselves. 2CB is a completely different experience from MDMA. It opens up the emotions and it opens up concepts in a way that gives access to the sources of anger and love and fear. It is a very valuable drug in a very practical sense, because 2CB doesn't last tremendously long (usually 6 to 8 hours), whereas something like LSD can last 12 hours. I have only used 2CB occasionally, not very often, so I can't speak for the value of tryptamines in psychotherapy. (LSD is not actually a tryptamine, but it is used for therapy. It is often used as a very good aid for inspiration, and spiritual awareness, but it is not for everybody.)

Almost everybody can get something out of MDMA. It is amazingly consistent. If MDMA is available, why not use the best there is?

Chapter 19-c   NOTES ABOUT PSYCHOACTIVE COMPOUNDS

Hosteen Nez

Hosteen Nez turned to the study of Native American plant medicine after he earned a BS in chemistry, an MS in metallurgy. These studies eventually led to a PhD in neurochemistry. Before that time, in the 1950s, Nez invented important tools for the mining industry. After a period of manufacturing and marketing his inventions, he sold the company he had started and retired in 1968. The success of his inventions supported his new research interests, so he would be free to guide all aspects of any of his projects without external influences or restrictions.

By 1969, he began researching synthetic psychoactive compounds, as well as plant compounds, and that is when he became an apprentice "medicine man." Psychiatrists used many of his compounds, because they were very useful in the facilitation of long lasting therapy.

However, in October of 1986, the US Congress passed sweeping laws prohibiting such research in both the known and as yet unknown therapeutic materials. (The political debate declared that recreational use led to "drug abuse." However the debate may have come from powerful lobbyists protecting pharmaceutical interests.) Nez stopped developing psychoactive compounds then. He has continued his "medicine man" studies developing other legal herbs and compounds to prevent flu and to lessen the effects of asthma. In recent years he collaborated with others to find and develop a homeopathic treatment to eliminate the tumors of cancer patients. This material, known as Salicinium, is now being tested on patients in Stage IV. So far, the results have shown great promise.

Websites: www.metabolicresearch.com and www.cancerhopecenter.com

NOTES ABOUT PSYCHOACTIVE COMPOUNDS

Hosteen Nez

In 1958, while living on the Navaho reservation in Arizona, I became interested in plant-based psychoactive materials. I was working at a uranium ore processing facility where most of the workers were Navaho, except for a few supervisory personnel. The main psychoactive used by the Navaho was peyote, and I noticed that those who used it as part of their religious ceremonies were the most intelligent, caring, good people in the work force. On the other hand, many of the others would get drunk on their days off and lose efficiency because of hangovers. I was not able to try peyote during the four years I was there, and several years later, I was still interested in exploring this substance.

It is always best to do a good literature search before engaging in any physical trials, as this will provide more information and direction to guide you in your endeavors. I made use of the chemistry library at the local university and spent many evenings there. I found a great deal of information on plant-based psychoactives, along with a large number of publications on synthetics. In looking through these publications, one author's name kept showing up. Not only was he very busy in the laboratory, he was also a prodigious writer. He wrote articles that described in detail the chemical synthesis of new compounds, the dosage range and the effects in humans plus some comments; his name is Alexander T. Shulgin, PhD.

A couple of his simpler compounds that he felt had use as adjuncts for psychotherapy were easy for me to synthesize, and I found them to be exceptional. Such a main focus of research made a great deal of sense to me and I felt it would be a good direction for me to follow. Shortly thereafter, I was able to meet Dr Shulgin.

Over the next fifteen years, I explored this fascinating field of research on compounds that could be used as adjuncts in psychotherapy. Not all the new compounds made during this period were suitable for use in psychotherapy, some were not active at all, and others showed some promise as materials that would increase the capacity for mental work in humans. We called this last group *"Smart Pills."* (1) We conducted a small pilot study for volunteers who wanted to try these Smart Pills for a wide variety of intellectual, physical and musical activity. Most all reported that their ability to function in their chosen field was greatly improved. During this time of initial exploration, it was noted that these compounds worked best on individuals who were inclined to be serious about their study habits. Those who were not serious about learning, but preferred a more full-on psychedelic recreational experience to the mildness of smart pills, did not find them to be as helpful as they anticipated.

All of this positive exploration was halted in 1986 with the passage by the US Congress of *"The Controlled Substances Analog Law."* (2) The draconian penalties made it prudent to stop the research on these materials. However, someday when those elected officials are more informed and less judgmental, we may see a resurgence of this type of research. When this happens, researchers will discover a treasure trove of information in two books by Sasha and Ann Shulgin, called *PIHKAL* (3) and *TIHKAL.* (4) These books contain all of their research, plus that of several others who were working in this fascinating area, also. So the genie is out of the bottle, and will not go back in.

During this period of synthesizing, testing, using and evaluating these new compounds, I was able to meet a number of psychiatrists and therapists using MDMA (Methylene Dioxy Methyl Amphetamine). All were interested in new psychoactives that could be used in their practices. Many of these doctors and therapists would visit me so they could evaluate first hand the effects of these new materials along with the person who had developed them. The results were nearly all very satisfactory and the therapist would leave with a generous sample of the compound in question. I never charged for these initial samples, but would charge a modest fee if they ordered a larger quantity and then only to cover the cost of the chemicals involved. Often while personally testing or tasting the compound in question, the therapist would unload his or her problems on me; I felt as though I was the therapist and the tester was on the couch (actually, I used a hot tub as it was friendlier and allowed deeper relaxation).

One therapist told me he had an older couple (past middle age) that had just sort of grown apart over the years and he had them on MDMA therapy once a month. After several months, there was no improvement and he felt something else was needed. He contacted me to see if I might have something that might help, so I sent him two 60 milligram tablets of **2CD-2 EtO** (*PIHKAL*, p. 514) to be used by the couple on an outpatient basis (no therapist present). At that level, the material engenders a feeling of closeness between couples without imposing a state of unacceptable intoxication. The duration is approximately 4 hours. The therapist told me that the couple renewed their feelings of closeness, and even several years later showed no diminishing of their feelings for each other.

As the years of testing these new compounds slipped by, I noticed that certain ones seemed to have rather specific effects on most of the testers and recreational users (yes, some of that occurred also).

Most of the active compounds showed some sort of (more or less) specific action on the user. A few examples of this specific action are as follows:

2CD-5EtO (*PIHKAL*, p. 515) allowed openness that led to easy talk, humor, and what might be described as a "museum tour" where one could spend considerable time examining in great detail various objects of art found in the immediate surroundings. The duration was about 10-12 hours and was followed by a ravenous appetite and a great appreciation of the food offered.

2CB and **2CI** (*PIHKAL*, p. 503 and p. 539). Both of these compounds could be considered to be aphrodisiacs for some, but not all, people. (These are some of Shulgin's compounds and I have included them here to round out the field.)

2CT2-5EtO (*PIHKAL* p. 561). At a dosage of 20 milligrams, there was a gentle climb to full effect of +3 at the third or fourth hour. (5) Easy thoughts and conversation lasted for many hours and a sedative was generally needed at the 16th hour. Some intoxication was noted the next day, together with a drained feeling. The nickname of *"Forever Yours"* has been used for this compound and its insights, but is quite too long in duration.

2CT4-2EtO (*PIHKAL* p. 564). At a dosage of 15 Mg., this material produced a +2 level of alteration that lasted some 10 hours. It was called *"Tenderness"* by many as there was a peaceful inner receptiveness and clarity with a sincere connection reported by those present. Uncomfortable sleep was noted afterwards.

My apprenticeship as a medicine man began in 1970, through which I learned a great deal about herbs in the following years. I was testing and evaluating synthetic psychoactive compounds at the time and my mentor was in favor of this and encouraged me to continue. He also introduced me to a number of plant psychoactives that I tried. He said that it was necessary for a medicine man to become familiar with the plant "medicine" and in my case with the synthetics (phenethylamines) as well, so the mind can change over time and reveal mental abilities one was not aware of having. We all have these exceptional abilities and are not aware of them, or we may feel that *"I can't do that."* If you feel that you cannot do something, then you truly cannot.

One of the major things my mentor introduced to me was the ability to communicate with plants. He said this was necessary to find out how a particular plant might be used to treat various problems. There was no verbalization involved with the plant, only mental concepts in their entirety. Later on, I was able to access the knowledge of the *"Great Spirit"* to get a broader picture and then to learn to do what is known as distant healing. In this healing method, the healer attains a deep meditative or alpha awareness state, and then *"sends healing energies,"* or specific interventions if the cause was known, to the persons involved. This is done once or twice daily for about one half hour. The term *"distant healing"* can mean anything from sitting across from someone in the tipi, or to be separated from him or her by hundreds or even thousands of miles. I find that actually knowing the person seems to give stronger results than having just a name and/or a picture. Also I find that my healing meditations seem to work much better on others than on myself. When using the meditations in my problems, the results are not as fast as with other subjects. My mentor told me that the healing meditations are reserved for serious health problems and minor ones are usually treated with herbal preparations.

The period of treatment may last for up to a month or more for serious problems, such as cancers, and perhaps a week for cuts and wounds. I feel that I would not have been able to do the things necessary for healing others without the use of psychoactive plants and the important synthetic compounds. I used the protocol of Dr Shulgin in testing these new compounds. (5) By using this protocol, I felt very safe in bio-testing these new materials and evaluating them.

There were some materials that could have caused serious problems if large amounts had been taken in the initial test. By starting at a very low dosage and incrementally increasing it over time and carefully observing any effects, one could avoid any potentially dangerous situations. If at any level there seemed to be negative effects, testing was stopped on that particular compound. Very few negative effects were noted; the most prominent was a precipitous lowering of blood pressure, then by negative mood alteration and then by what felt to be a condition that might lead to convulsions.

The human mind is the most marvelous structure that we as humans possess. It has vast potential to assist us in the complex reality of living as true humans. It is my feeling that certain kinds of psychoactive materials can, if properly used, allow us to expand our vision of life on this planet. Looking back on the number of things that I have done in my life so far, I make this statement to all: THERE ARE NO LIMITS.

The Shulgin protocol is this: For the first bioassay of a new compound, take only an amount that would seem to be below baseline. Wait three days for the material to leave your system, and then increase the amount by 1.5 times. Continue this process until reaching a +3 level. If any more is taken, and it only extends the time, not the level, then the amount before that is considered maximum dose.

SHULGIN SYSTEM
For Evaluating Level of Alteration of Consciousness

[—] Baseline — ordinary state.

[+/−] Move from baseline to alert or aware.

Each subject has his or her own individual body related signal, or (+0.5) = barely noticeable. Imagination can also produce a false positive.

[+ 1] This is a real effect.

There may be nausea or light-headedness, or a wish to remain motionless. Most physical complaints are dissipated within the first hour. One can still do almost everything one would ordinarily be able to do, even drive a car, if necessary.

[+ 2] This is the level where there is no doubt that the altered experience has begun.

Sensory awareness (vision, hearing, tactile, taste, smell) may be greatly enhanced. Cognitive faculties are largely intact, and much of the effects of the material could be suppressed if the need should arise. One could drive a car, but only for a life-and-death emergency.

[+ 3] This is the maximum intensity of the effect of the material.

This is the stay at home level, with the phone turned off. Innocent bystanders might get a contact high, or become alarmed at your appearance or behavior.

[+ 4] This symbol is occasionally needed for the "peak experience" in the terminology of Abe Maslow. (6)

This is a serene mystical state never to be forgotten. It can be independent of what material was used or not used. It is a gift, and often thought to be a *"State of Grace."*

REFERENCES AND NOTES:

1) Nez, Hosteen. (1985) *Smart Pills: Or compounds that increase the capacity for mental work in humans.* Berkeley, CA: Published by Mind States 2001. Jon Hanna (Ed.)
2) US Congress. (1986) *"The controlled substances analog law."*
3) Shulgin, A.T. & Shulgin, A. (1991) *Pihkal: a Chemical Love Story.* Berkeley, CA: Transform Press.
4) Shulgin, A.T. & Shulgin, A. (1997) *Tihkal: The Continuation.* Berkeley, CA: Transform Press.
5) Shulgin, A.T. & Shulgin, A., Jacob, P. III. (1986) "A protocol for psychoactive drug evaluation." In: *Methods and Findings in Experimental and Clinical Pharmacology.* (6): pp. 313-320.
6) Maslow, A. (1964) *Religions, Values and Peak-Experiences.* Ohio State University Press.

Rolling Thunder told me that when visiting an area for the first time, he will go into the woods and speak to the plants. They will answer him, he claims, by "singing me their song." In that way, the herbs and flowers will tell Rolling Thunder if they have healing power and how they can be used effectively.

--- Stanley Krippner
Proceedings of the 3rd annual Conference on the Study of Shamanism And Alternate Modes of Healing, 1986

CHAPTER 19-d   LSD, BIOFEEDBACK AND CONSCIOUSNESS

Timothy Scully, PhD

Tim Scully won honorable mention in the San Francisco Bay Area science fair for the design and construction of a small computer at age 14. At age 16 (after his junior year in HS), he was admitted as an undergraduate by examination to study math and physics at UC Berkeley. At the same time he worked as a lab assistant at the Lawrence Berkeley Laboratory. He dropped out to travel with Ken Kesey and the Acid Test, doing electronics for the Grateful Dead followed by several years as an underground chemist. In the 1970s–1980s he designed unique biofeedback instruments and computerized physiological monitoring systems for Aquarius Electronics and Mendocino Microcomputers, taking a few years out to serve a term at McNeil Island Penitentiary for his work making LSD in the 1960s. While in prison, he worked as the prison psychologist's research assistant, and designed a communication system for the non-vocal handicapped, and was named "Outstanding Young Man of the Year" by the Washington State JAYCEES. In 1979, he received his PhD in psychology from Saybrook Graduate School, based on his analysis of physiological patterns and events in consciousness. In 1980, he was appointed Assistant Research Psychologist II at UC SF Langley Porter Institute in Dr Joe Kamiya's lab. He designed computerized physiological monitoring systems and wrote software for education. Between 1987 and 2005 he was a senior software developer for Autodesk, Inc., until retiring. He holds two US patents: 1] Unique software 2] A biofeedback instrument. He is now researching and writing about the history of underground LSD manufacturing.

SOME ANECDOTES REGARDING LSD, BIOFEEDBACK AND CONSCIOUSNESS

Tim Scully

I was initially given the topic "LSD and paranormal phenomena" when I was asked to write something for this collection, but I only have a few 40-year-old anecdotes relevant to that subject.

Since then the focus of this book broadened and I was asked to also explain a bit about why I manufactured LSD for a few years during the 1960s and how that work segued into designing and making biofeedback instruments in the 1970s and 1980s.

In 1960, because of my intense interest in science, the University of California Berkeley Lawrence Radiation Laboratory hired me as a lab assistant when I was 16 years old. In 1961 I was admitted to UC Berkeley as an undergraduate student (by examination at the end of my junior year of high school) to study math and physics.

I was drawn to work at the Radiation Lab and to study physics because I hoped to help find the solution to controlled fusion, which would provide cheap and abundant power for everyone. Though I learned a lot at the Radiation Lab, I was somewhat discouraged by some of the tales of woe from graduate students at the lab. Because I was working my way through college, I started also doing electronic consulting work which grew so successful that I eventually left the Radiation Lab to spend more time with the better paying work doing electronic design consulting.

Between 1963 and early 1965 I was employed by Atomic Laboratories Inc. as electronics design consultant, where I designed radiation detection and measurement systems and various other instruments for educational applications. This work grew so intense that I took time off from studying math and physics in 1964 to work full time.

After a few years at UC Berkeley and exposure to the turbulent political debates there, I began to be more concerned that our rapid progress in technology was outstripping our ability to make wise choices in its use. Meanwhile, a childhood friend was studying oriental philosophy. He interested me in the Tao Te Ching (1) and Aldous Huxley's writings about psychedelic drugs. (2, 3) I was fascinated by the idea of expanded states of consciousness and wondered if they might help us to make better choices.

When I first took LSD in April 1965, I was captivated by the numinosity of the LSD experience. For a while I felt at one with the universe. From that time on I was much more sensitive to the beauty of the world around me and to the feelings of others around me. I wanted to share this peak experience with everyone, and I believed that if enough people took LSD, the world would change for the better. This was a fairly common belief among people who took LSD. (4) For many of us the experience was religious. (5) The psychedelic experience usually included a very deep sense of oneness with everyone and with the natural world. Because of this I thought LSD might help end racial and sexual discrimination, promote environmental consciousness and temper rampant consumerism in addition to promoting spiritual awareness. I also hoped it might bring an end to the Vietnam War. I wasn't thinking in terms of promoting paranormal experiences.

I wanted to make LSD and give it away. When I researched the problems involved in making enough LSD to turn on the world, I rapidly learned that Bear (Owsley) Stanley had both the know-how and a substantial amount of the essential raw material, lysergic acid. In late 1965 I became interested in working as his apprentice. At the time he had become fascinated by the Grateful Dead and Ken Kesey's Acid Test. (24) He offered me a job doing electronics work for the Grateful Dead while they traveled with the Acid Test. I looked on this work as an extended job interview for the position of sorcerer's apprentice. For several months in the first half of 1966 I lived and traveled with Bear Stanley and the band while doing electronics work on their sound system

During that time I had quite a few paranormal experiences, always associated with times when we took LSD together. These included several intense "gestalt mind" experiences that went far beyond the sense of oneness associated with most LSD experiences, one event that appeared at the time to be psychokinetic and several experiences of "conventional" telepathy.

In 1966 the Grateful Dead household took LSD frequently, often (at Acid Tests) with the Pranksters who made up the remainder of the Acid Test troupe. Many of the people in the group had read *More than Human* by Theodore Sturgeon. (6) This science fiction novel describes a group of outcast and seemingly defective youngsters who have paranormal abilities such as telepathy and telekinesis. Individually they can barely survive in the world but when they are together they form a gestalt entity much greater than the sum of their parts.

Sometimes when the Pranksters and Dead took acid together and the Dead played, it felt to us as though a similar gestalt organism was formed, including many of the Dead, Pranksters and other folks who came to the Acid Test to get high with us. The intensity of this experience varied from mild to very strong. In its strongest form, we experienced a single consciousness, which could use any of the group's bodies. The experiences lasted for an hour or more at a time.

In Sturgeon's story, the group of kids could tell that there were still some essential parts of their gestalt being that were missing. They searched for recruits to fill in the missing pieces.

Likewise, one of the reasons for Acid Tests was for the group to get high with lots of people to find missing parts of the gestalt that sometimes formed. One joke was that we'd all leave the planet together when we found the right people.

When the Dead and Pranksters parted ways, the gestalt phenomenon wasn't discussed much any longer, but we discovered that it still happened, at least to some extent, when the Dead played while taking acid and the audience was stoned too. This may have contributed to the intense sense of community, which developed among Deadheads. (7)

I can recall one incident that took place at an Acid Test in Los Angeles in 1966, which we believed at the time to be psychokinetic. The group was "linked up" in the group mind described above. (8) The Grateful Dead were playing. The band used large Altec Lansing theatre speakers at the time. These included exponential horns for the mid-range sounds. At one Acid Test one or more of the "drivers" for the exponential horns exploded (in a small way) at the same time when the group experienced a jolt of energy. Looking back, it seems impossible to assign cause and effect, but at the time we thought it was a psychokinetic effect.

I had several experiences of telepathy (distinct from the "gestalt" group mind mentioned above) where I was the sender (during an LSD experience) and Jean Millay was the receiver. In one case I was in Berkeley and Jean was in Southern California. I took LSD with a small group of friends and we had an event-filled experience. Jean telephoned me the next morning and described some of the events we experienced, from her telepathic impressions, unprompted by me or anyone else.

My overall impression is that paranormal abilities may be amplified or facilitated during LSD experiences. But investigating this possibility would present many challenges to researchers. (9)

After Bear Stanley decided that I had passed the *Acid Test*, he took me on as an apprentice in a lab he set up in Pt. Richmond. We worked there in the fall of 1966 making LSD, which was eventually distributed as *White Lightning*. From the fall of 1966 through 1968 the psychedelic scene in the Bay Area flowered, producing art, music, spirituality and social innovation. (10) Forty years later, scientific studies of the social impact of the Grateful Dead are still being conducted and presented at an annual conference of the *Grateful Dead Caucus,* and published in *The Grateful Dead in Concert: Essays on Live Improvisation*. (11, 12)

Nobel laureate in chemistry Kary B. Mullis, PhD, told the audience at the Third International Conference on Entheobotany: (13)

> ...I was at Berkeley and taking acid every week. That's what people did for entertainment: drink beer **or** go out into Tilden Park and take 500 micrograms of LSD and sit all day thinking about the universe, time going backward and forward....

Even in early 1966 there were sensational reports in the popular press about the dangers of taking LSD in a nonmedical setting. (14, 15) Why did I, and most young people experimenting with LSD, ignore or discount these reports?

One answer is that many LSD users also smoked marijuana and were aware of wildly inaccurate reports of the dangers (e.g., *Reefer Madness*) of marijuana dating back to Harry Anslinger's years as Commissioner of the Federal Bureau of Narcotics. (16) Another answer might be the disparity between our own experiences, the reports of friends who used LSD and the sensational press reports.

Over time this credibility gap grew wider and wider as new myths were reported and then debunked. (17) A series of reports claimed that LSD caused chromosome damage and caused women to have deformed babies. This also proved to be false. (18, 19, 20)

The vast majority of people had very positive experiences with LSD. (21, 22) With the help of selective attention, it was easy to see only the positive effects of LSD and to overlook the negative ones.

Because LSD was banned, it was pushed into the same distribution channels as other illegal drugs.*[3] (23) Anti-drug legislation and propaganda made no real distinction between psychedelics and hard narcotics, (24) encouraging young people to become color blind to the distinctions among drugs, with often-tragic results. All too many young people decided that, considering their experiences with LSD and marijuana, the other "dangerous drugs" were probably not very dangerous and were worth a try. This was a fatal error for some people. Even among the people who only took psychedelics some very bad trips and a few deaths occurred. (25)

In recent years I've been researching the history of underground LSD manufacturing, learning about many different underground chemists and I think it is safe to say that *making* LSD is often addictive. The work brought with it a sense of great significance; most of us believed that we were trying to save the world. At the same time, it conferred high social status among young people, including beautiful women. For some people, the money involved was also an increasingly significant factor.

---

*[3] Possession, sale or manufacture of LSD became illegal in California in October 1966.

By mid 1970 I had worked in several LSD labs, was in serious legal trouble and under heavy surveillance likely to lead to still more legal woes. At the same time, I was finally beginning to doubt that making LSD widely available was the panacea it had seemed to be. I still believed that extraordinary states of consciousness could be highly beneficial, but I wanted to find a more socially acceptable technology for achieving them.

I was aware of studies that associated unusually copious alpha brainwave patterns with Yoga and Zen masters (26, 27) and of research that had been done with brainwave biofeedback, teaching people to control alpha brainwave production (28) and I'd been a subject in one of Barbara Brown's early studies on EEG. (29) This led me to explore brainwave biofeedback as an alternative to psychedelic drugs. I was able to transfer some of my fervor for turning the world on with LSD to turning on with alpha brainwaves.

By 1971 I was working full time running Aquarius Electronics, making simple EEG biofeedback instruments. These were initially used mainly by people seeking to produce more alpha brainwaves with the goal of rapidly achieving meditative states. (30) It slowly became clear that although a large number of people did find single channel EEG biofeedback to be an aid to meditation, many others found that it was possible to produce lots of single channel alpha without a calm mind.

As a result of suggestions from Jean Millay, I designed a two-channel brainwave comparator in late 1973. It was configurable to train for coherence (both channels close to the same dominant EEG frequency) or phase synchronization (in addition to coherence, the two channels are close to zero degrees phase angle). (31) The first instrument was completed while I was in prison for my work in the 1960s. Millay used it to experiment with interpersonal EEG synchronization and interhemispheric EEG synchronization. (32, 33) Later, Johnston adjusted the program for the PDP 13 computers at Kamiya's Psychophysiology Lab at UCSF Langley Porter, in order to continue the experiment where EEG chart recorders were available. (34) (See also Chapter 22 – James Johnston's *Brainwave Synchronization: A Pilot Study.)* In 1977, Tod Mikuriya, MD, used our phase comparator to provide biofeedback training in bilateral synchronization with his schizophrenic patients, who then developed more voluntary control over attacks of anxiety. (35)

We learned that bilateral phase synchronized alpha was much more reliably associated with meditative states. This started me down the path to explore physiological patterns and eventually led to the topic of my PhD dissertation, *The Analysis of Physiological Patterns Associated with Events in Consciousness.* (36)

REFERENCES AND NOTES

1) Lao Tzu. (Ancient) *The Tao Te Ching*. Various translations, including:
   A) Mitchell, S. (1988) *Tao Te Ching: A New English Version with Foreword and Notes*. NY: Harper & Row Publishers. (Translation, 1943.)
   B) Frank J. MacHovec. (1962) *The Book of Tao: The Key to the Mastery of Life*. Mount Vernon, NY: The Peter Pauper Press.
2) Huxley, A. (1963) *Doors of Perception & Heaven and Hell*. NY: Harper & Row.
3) Huxley, A. (1962) *Island*. London: Chatto & Windus.
4) Ungerleider, J. Thomas & Fisher, Duke D. (1967) "LSD today." In: *Medical Digest*, 1967, <u>13</u>, 33-37, 40-42.
5) Pahnke, Walter N. (1967). "LSD and religious experience." In: *LSD, Man and Society*, DeBold, R.C & Leaf, R.C. (Eds.) Middletown, CN: Wesleyan University Press.
6) Sturgeon, T. (1953) *More than Human*. NY, NY: Ballantine Books.
7) Adams, R.A. & Sardiello, R. (Eds.) (2000) *Deadhead Social Science*. Lanham, MD: Rowman Altmira.
8) Douglas, D. (Excerpts from his poem about the Grateful Dead.)

"A Sign of Greeting"

...It calls up free playin' down on Haight Street, where they
had 'em dancin' on the rooftops... dancing from the telephone
poles, anything they could find.
There were free flowin' bodies in motion, it looked like a human ocean
and the Bear got 'em all connected up among their minds.
But that's long before the turtles danced down at the train tracks
yeah, but even the band was dancin' out in the street.
That scullbone lightning yet to come from Thomas' hand
and only Jerry gave the wave
as a sign of greeting

I saw more people manning concessions
than they used to have comin' to the dances.
They'd stop the traffic on the freeway 'bout every time they'd hold a show.
Some called 'em 'longest living relics,' a reminder of a high time that passed,
and others called 'em 'harbingers of a higher time to come.'
And in their world the turtles danced down at the train tracks
yes, and the people danced out in the streets...

9) Luke, D. & Kittenis, M. "A preliminary survey of paranormal experiences with psychoactive drugs." In: *The Journal of Parapsychology*
10) Lee, M.A, Shlain, B. (1985) *ACID Dreams: The Complete Social History of LSD: The CIA, The Sixties, and Beyond*. NY: Grove Weidenfeld.
11) Spector, S. & Tuedio, J. (2009) *The Grateful Dead in Concert: Essays on Live Improvisation*. CA: McFarland Publishers.
12) The *Grateful Dead Caucus* has met annually as part of the Southwest/Texas American/Popular Culture Association Conference in Albuquerque, New Mexico. Members of the Caucus represent a wide variety of disciplines, which they claim are not multidisciplinary, cross-disciplinary, nor interdisciplinary, but transdisciplinary — representing a discipline of its own.
13) Mullis, K.B. "The great gene machine." In: *Omni* April 1993. (Interviewer Liversibge, A.)
14) "The dangers of LSD." In: *Time*, April 22, 1966.

15) "The exploding threat of the mind drug that got out of control: LSD." In: *LIFE.* March, 1966.
16) Grinspoon, L. (1994) "Marijuana reconsidered." In: *Quick American Archives*, Oakland, CA.
17) http://www.snopes.com/horrors/drugs/lsdsun.asp.
18) Cohen, M.M., Marinello, M.J. &, Back, N. (1967) "Chromosomal damage in human leukocytes induced by lysergic acid diethylamide." In: *Science,* 1967; 155:141719. LSD #1506.
19) Davidson, B. (1967) "The hidden evils of LSD." In: *Saturday Evening Post,* Aug 12, 1967, p. 19.
20) Grof, S. (1980-1994) "The effects of LSD on chromosomes, genetic mutation, fetal development and malignancy." In: Appendix II of *LSD Psychotherapy.* Alameda, CA: Hunter House Publishers.
21) Grof. S. (1976) *Realms of Human Unconscious: Observations from LSD Research.* NY: E.P. Dutton.
22) Tart, C. (1969). *Altered States of Consciousness: A Book of Readings.* NY: John Wiley & Sons.
23) Leary, T. (1975) Excerpts from "Seeds of the Sixties." In: *Spit in the Ocean,* Kesey (Ed.)

...The inevitable backlash from this new message of individual power began in 1966 when various legislatures and Congress began considering bills to criminalize LSD and similar drugs. In this year, I testified before two Senate committees urging that control of all mind-changing drugs be assigned to the medical profession supervised by Federal and State health agencies. I predicted that if control of drugs were administered by law enforcement agencies, the result would be a black market more irrational and widespread than prohibition and the growth of enormous police-state repressive bureaucracy. And who, indeed, wanted that?

My own political position then was by no means radical or solitary. Indeed, during the Johnson administration, a bitter battle was fought on this issue. Medical and scientific people (backed by the Kennedys) urged that drugs be administered by the Department of Health, Education and Welfare while law-and-order people politicked for the Department of Justice. History may well decide that the second great, belligerent disaster of the Johnson years was the decision to turn drug control over to the police. LSD was made illegal and most of the top drug scientists began their steady exit from government responsibility. Another war on heresy had been declared....

24) The federal law governing LSD between 1966-1968 was Public Law 89-74, *The Drug Abuse Control Amendments of 1965.* This law lumped LSD with amphetamines and barbiturates and was enforced by the Federal Bureau of Drug Abuse Control (BDAC). In 1968 President Johnson merged the BDAC with the Bureau of Narcotics (which handled marijuana and heroin) into a new Bureau of Narcotics and Dangerous Drugs (BNDD). In California, the Bureau of Narcotics Enforcement (BNE) handled LSD along with heroin and other drugs. In 1969 the Nixon administration sent new drug legislation to Congress which established four "schedules" for drugs with Schedule 1 containing LSD, Marijuana and Heroin (an interesting grouping).
25) Wolfe, T. (1968) *The Electric Kool-Aid Acid Test.* NY: Farrar, Straus & Giroux.
26) Kasamatsu, A. & Hirai, T. (1963) "Science of Zazen." In: *Physiologica*, 6:86-91.
27) Anand, B., Chhina, G.S. & Shing, B. (1961) "Some aspects of electroencephalographic studies in yogis." In: *EEG Clin Neurophysiol.* 13; 452-456. Reprinted in *Altered States of Consciousness*, Charles Tart (Ed.) John Wiley and Sons, 1969.

28) Kamiya, J. (1969) "Operant control of the EEG alpha rhythm and some of its reported effects on consciousness." In: *Altered States of Consciousness: A Book of Readings.* Tart, C.T. (Ed.) NY: John Wiley & Sons.
29) Brown, B. (1974) *New Mind, New Body.* NY: Bantam.
30) Zimmerman, J. (1970) "Turning on with alpha waves." In: *LIFE* 69:8 p60-61.
31) See Appendix B of Johnston's Chapter 22 for Scully's full technical description of the Aquarius Electronics Brainwave Analyzers and Phase-comparator.
32) Millay, J. (1978) *The Relationship Between Phase Synchronization of Brainwaves and Success in Attempts to Communicate Telepathically: A Pilot Study.* SF, CA: Saybrook University—Graduate College of Psychology and Humanistic Studies. (PhD dissertation)
33) Millay, J. (1999) *Multidimensional Mind: Remote Viewing in Hyperspace.* Berkeley, CA: A Universal Dialogues Book, North Atlantic Books.
34) Johnston, J.R. & Millay, J. (1983) "A pilot study in brainwave synchrony." In: *Psi Research,* Vol. 2, No. 1 March. SF, CA.
35) Mikuriya, T. (1977) Personal communication.
36) Scully, T. (1978) *The Analysis of Physiological Patterns Associated with Events in Consciousness.* SF, CA: Saybrook University—Graduate College of Psychology and Humanistic Studies. (PhD dissertation)

> *You don't have hallucinations with LSD. In a hallucination you see something that does not exist. But under LSD, you see things, but which are transformed. It is a different view, or a different experience of our existence.*
>
> *--- Albert Hofmann*
> *--- Hofmann's Potion*
> *--- Canadian Film Board*

Jean Millay, PhD

Jean Millay studied at the SF Art Inst. in 1949-1952 (photography with Ansel Adams and painting with David Park), while working in a silkscreen-printing studio. In 1963, her BA in art and 2 teaching credentials were from UC Berkeley. She taught arts and crafts in grades 7 to 12 until 1965, when she and Allen Willis won a *Film as Art Award* at a SF Film Festival. In 1968 Dr Barbara Brown introduced her to EEG biofeedback. In 1969 Millay volunteered as a subject in Dr Krippner's dream telepathy research. In 1970 Dr Scully built a portable EEG so she could create visual feedback—The First Stereo Brainwave Biofeedback Light Sculpture—demonstrated in 1972 at the Metropolitan Museum of Art in NYC. In 1973, she participated in RV experiments at SRI, International with Targ, Puthoff and Geller. By 1974, the sculpture was a teaching tool for her college classes in biofeedback and parapsychology, and a research tool for her PhD in human science (Saybrook, 1978). However, all such public supported classes were cancelled across the USA after Carl Sagan declared, "parapsychology is pseudoscience." So, in 1980, Millay taught herself to create computer images for Dr Dean Brown's interactive educational programs, starting with the Apple (64k). In 1986, Brown, Scully and Millay created *Integration*—the first biofeedback stress management game for the IBM computers (256k). From 1984 on, she participated in Dr Heinze's *Conferences on the Study of Shamanism and Alternate Modes of Healing*. Millay was president of the PRG and helped Kane and Brown edit *Silver Threads*. In 1994, she retired with Darrell Lemaire to his mile-high, solar powered, retreat. In that clear environment, she completed *MULTIDIMENSIONAL MIND: Remote Viewing in Hyperspace* (1999). She and Marge King believed that classes in *Self-Discovery Science* could transform health education. So she posted their lesson plans for using simple bio/neurofeedback tools in grades 5-12 free on the web, at www.fmbr.org/millay.

PSYCHIC GIFTS FROM ENTHEOGENS

Jean Millay

When my grandfather made the ultimate transition from life to pure spirit, he was 250 miles away. At that same moment I thought about him so strongly, that I wanted to talk to him, and dialed his phone. Earlier that evening, my baby had become fussy, so we left the noisy family room to seek the serenity of our favorite rocking chair. These were special moments for us, and soon she was sleeping peacefully. It was then, in those lingering moments of stillness, that I became aware of my grandfather's presence, as though he were standing in the shadowy corner. When I phoned him at his ranch in Wabuska, NV, I was told that he had suffered a heart attack and was taken to a hospital in Reno. In those days, the telephone company hired real people to help when you called person-to-person, including finding the right hospital. The receptionist there informed me directly, *"He just expired."* Then she found my mother, who had arrived about the same time as the ambulance. The first thing mom asked me was, *"How did you know to call just now?"* I wanted to tell her, *"Grampa told me,"* but I was concerned that this was not the right time for her to consider the implications. But I knew his spirit had come to tell me goodbye. The next day, I tucked my baby into the traveling bassinette, and drove the 300 miles to help with the large family gathering. This was my first major psychic event over 50 years ago, and it was a gift of love from grampa. (1)

Over the next ten years, I experienced a few events I thought were psychic, though no one else believed me. During those years, I went through divorce, tried to support my children by painting murals and portraits while attending UC Berkeley for a teaching credential. This was before I learned that psychedelics/entheogens intensified psychic activity.

Then I read *The Doors of Perception*, (2) a life changing experience. The famous author Aldous Huxley described his heightened perception of color from ingesting mescaline—a derivative of peyote. At that time I was preparing a lesson for my art classes about the relationship between primary colors in pigment and primary colors in light. If there was more I could learn about color, I needed to know what that would be. A friend provided the peyote so I could check it out. My generation had been filled with government lies and propaganda about the dangers of marijuana *"because it caused one to become addicted to other bad drugs and wicked behavior."*

Naturally, since I was a properly educated high school teacher, I would *never* use such things, not even alcohol or cigarettes. However, since I had not heard of peyote I didn't know the FDA declared it to be illegal and dangerous. The question never crossed my mind about whether or not I should try it. I desired to experience Huxley's heightened perception.

It took considerable courage and determination to eat something that tasted that dreadful and caused the body to want to throw it all up. But after the worst was over, I went outside and was amazed to see the stars in motion—just the way Van Gogh painted them. I saw colors swirling through the air around my companions. At first I was fascinated by the colors in an abstract way, (3) until I realized that the colors and the direction of their paths represented the thoughts and emotions of the people around me. We confirmed that this was true. This was the second major psychic event in my life. The precious gift from Grandfather Peyote was the perception of the biofield—what psychics have always referred to as the "human aura."

After that I met Timothy Leary, Ralph Metzner and Richard Alpert at a conference at Esalen. They introduced us to *The Psychedelic Experience: A Manual based on the Tibetan Book of the Dead*. (4) Leary also introduced us to *The Tao Te Ching*, (5) and the *I Ching*. (6) This was the third major psychic event in my life—this gift revealed to me that my visions were not hallucinations, but had been described by Tibetans thousands of years ago.

Fifty years have passed since I studied those books and memorized the instructions, which were designed to keep one from being trapped in any of the Third Bardos. Such experiences were not uncommon during an acid trip. That book was the only really useful information available at the time. I totally believed the books would help me to realize the power and true nature of Mind, and I followed them carefully with one exception.

During those extraordinary times, while my friends and I were under the influence of one of these entheogens (mescaline, LSD, psilocybin mushrooms, hashish or marijuana), we often experienced spontaneous telepathic events that were unmistakable because of their clarity and accuracy. My dilemma was that, even though I believed in the Third Bardo guidance, I was concerned over whether or not I wanted to follow this one instruction: (4)

> *You may now feel the power to perform miraculous feats,*
> **to perceive and communicate with extrasensory power,**
> *to change shape, size and number, to traverse space and time instantly.*
> *These feelings come to you naturally, not through any merit on your part.*
> **Do not desire them. Do not attempt to exercise them.**
> *Recognize them as signs that you are in the Third Bardo,*
> *in the period of re-entry into the normal world.*

For me this was sacred knowledge, so I struggled for a long time with its prohibition against telepathy. The entheogens had shown me that my path must include the study of psi phenomena. The sacred plants had become my teachers. They revealed their power to evoke my own power. The stronger

LSD also showed me more of the world than I ever wanted to see—the war, the CIA, the FBI and the corruption in high places.*4 After that I only used the sacred plant Cannabis for my personal *"shamanic type"* of practice. (7)

We began to play telepathic and clairvoyant games when we had ingested or smoked the same substance, and paid close attention to the dreams we experienced afterward. Years later the SRI team created the term *"remote viewing"* (RV) for clairvoyance to avoid the prejudice of any terms previously related to the *"occult."* (Chapter 1 by R. Targ.) Eventually, we discovered there was much more to learn about space, time and the range of human abilities, no matter what they were called.

Meanwhile back in 1963, I was still dreaming about the delightful visions of that first peyote experience. The luminous colors in motion in the air inspired the artist in me to want show others what I experienced. Since my longtime friend Allen Willis was a film photographer who was interested in art films, I asked him to help, though he had no interest whatsoever in psychedelics. My children Mara and Mitchell Mayo and I had great fun creating reflection and refraction designs with colored lights, and filming them with a 16 mm camera that I had borrowed. After showing a few feet of film to Leary in 1964, he gave us permission to use the name of their book, (4) and he recorded the voice-over introduction for the film. (3) Ravi Shankar and Alla Rakha were willing to compose the sound track—which they did while watching the film when it was finished. The realization that I couldn't show a film called *"The Psychedelic Experience"* and still teach high school in that small town didn't occur to me, until the sound track was finished. Ooops!

The decision whether to show the film or quit that job was not too difficult, since the teaching salary was the lowest in the state, and basic living expenses were increasing. There had to be a better paying job somewhere, so I left while I could still get a good recommendation. We entered the film in the 1965 San Francisco International Film Festival, and won a *"Film as Art award."* Willis was promoted to *"Film Director"* for KQED. I just barely escaped being fired, even though LSD was still legal.

My sister Marge King, who lived in a different small town, also lost her job because the aerospace company she worked for as a literature chemist had lost its government contract. Desperate, we decided to combine our families and move to LA to look for work, though we knew our 6 kids (her four and my two) would not like a big city. They were used to open spaces to ride their bikes anywhere safely. We rented a house in Venice on Ocean Front Walk (no big buildings near the beach then, as now). Marge was hired to be a literature chemist right away, and I was hired as a substitute teacher of remedial reading at a jr. high in east LA, north of Watts just after

---

*4 Four of these heavy older visions of war and assassinations are detailed in End Notes.

the 1965 riots there—tensions were high. My students had new school clothes, perhaps for the first time, from looting the stores during the riots.

We lived a quiet life on the beach—as quietly as possible with six kids between the ages of 8 to 15 years, and surrounded by people taking acid and passing out pot cookies for *"trick or treat"* on Halloween. The local police were friendly to our children and to us—a librarian and a schoolteacher.

Since LA was a big place, I thought I might get away with showing the movie, and also pick up some extra change doing it. The *L.A. Free Press* announced a showing of the movie at a small auditorium. Later when I thought I might show it again, Bear (Owsley) asked if the Grateful Dead could play at this event, also. We agreed. (However, the Dead were the weirdest looking people this country girl had ever seen, and this was before they became famous.) After the show, while packing up, I heard (with horror) that Marge had invited them all to come visit us at the beach sometime. And without more warning than a phone call from Bear, they all showed up one day—twenty people and a jar full of a fresh batch of LSD.

For me to take LSD, I preferred the expanse of nature, or the quiet of the meditation room with candles and soft music. As a teacher with two children I was always very nervous about the psychedelic scene, unless I could keep it under some kind of control, and protect them from weirdness. With twenty or so people at our house taking acid, this was obviously not going to be one of those times. The afternoon was warm and sunny, so the Dead and their friends played on the beach. After a glorious sunset, they began returning to the house. As the noise increased, I encouraged the kids to watch TV with their dinner on trays, and suggested strongly that they stay in their rooms upstairs. I gave them permission for the first time to watch even the late shows, if they wanted to do so.

Then I felt a disturbance outside, so I went out to find two policemen trying to save us from two hippy-looking types sitting on the front steps. After I assured the police that these two were my guests, Bob Weir and Phil Lesh[5] both said, *"Thanks, Aunt Jeannie,"* and instantly disappeared into the sanctuary of the meditation room. (8)

After that, I went up to our large flat roof, to center myself, and under a vast starry sky, I asked for guidance to keep myself from freaking out under the circumstances. By then the effects of the LSD were beginning to take full hold, and soon I actually felt the strength of inner light.

When someone started screaming, I went to the edge of the roof to look. It was a friend of the Dead. He was a marine just back from Viet Nam, and was now screaming and running up and down Ocean Front Walk. This had to be dealt with NOW. I found Marge and Owsley in an

---

[5] Phil Lesh included his own version of this event in his book *Searching for the Sound, My Life with the Grateful Dead.* (8)

intense conversation about chemistry, with the auras of their radiant intellects filling the room. I said I could handle the situation, so Bear told his people to bring him in. The man was wild and out of control, and it took four strong men to carry him into the center room. He did not know anything about acid, but took it because everyone else did. Now he was in need of serious help. I grabbed the Leary, Metzner, and Alpert book (4) to find the *"Bardo"* that had trapped him. He screamed *"AIR, AIR, AIR"* for a time, and then, *"FOOD, FOOD,"* and then *"MOTHER, MOTHER,"* and then *"FUCK, FUCK"* and finally, *"DIE, DIE."* After that he stopped and said something about *"EONS AND EONS OF TIME."* At first, we gave him some food when he was screaming for it, but he crammed it into his mouth all at once, letting it spill all over the furniture and floor. Then when he screamed *"Fuck"* he lunged for me, but Don Douglas intercepted him. The man was unaware that he had kissed Don instead. (Don's version in ref. 9.)

By then I realized that he was suffering through *"eons"* of deaths and rebirths. When he cycled into that one part of his cycle in which he could receive a communication, he looked at me and pleaded, *"Help me."* We looked at each other deeply, eye to eye. I said only, *"Trust me."* He nodded and before the cycle of screaming started again, two police officers came to the door. The neighbors had called them. The police offered to take him away for us. In those days, the emergency room staff had no idea what to do with such people. Generally they gave Thorazine to calm them without any help to resolve the cosmic drama. Those who suffered this treatment might remain disturbed for a time. We had no intention to allow that to happen. Ordinarily, having the police at the door would have been enough to make me very nervous, but I was in a very different state of consciousness, and I could see that Marge would handle it easily.

In any case, so much energy was coursing through me at that time that I felt locked into position with my left hand receiving light and my right hand transmitting it to the man lying on the floor. For the first time in my life, I was experiencing a surge of light energy flowing through me directly to him, and that he was comforted because he was actually receiving it. The cops left and said we should call them if we couldn't handle it. Marge thanked them and assured them that we would do that if it were necessary.

Now it was time to exert control over the nonverbal environment. Anyone feeling anxiety might interfere with the promise of trust, so they were directed to the meditation room. Our two daughters chose to stay to offer calm support (as adults both earned professional degrees to help people get well). I had a recording of North Indian Classical Music that was capable of causing entrainment into meditative states, and asked that it be played into our speakers. Gradually the energy level settled down before the screaming cycle started again. By the next time he screamed, *"DIE,"* I was ready for him, and poked my finger into his soft belly, extemporizing the essence of the instructions for release from any Bardo: *"Your blood is flowing into the ocean of all life. You are passing into the place of perfect peace. Use this temporary death to be released from all pain and confusion. Go into the pure light of consciousness."* I continued to speak softly in this way, until he became totally quiet. After about 20 minutes of silence, he sat up and asked, *"What happened?"*

The two of us went up to the roof to discuss his experience in the fresh ocean air. Under that vast sky of majestic stars, we gave thanks to the Great Spirit. After that we joined the others in the meditation room.

Finding that such energy could be channeled like that was the fourth most important psychic experience of my life. The psychedelic/entheogen cleared my mind of analysis, judgment, and attachment, so the light could dominate beyond thought. The profound gift to channel light for healing was given from the multidimensional spirit of the sacred light, and connected to the person in need though me. (10)

When my daughter Mara was twelve years old, she was invited to spend the summer with her father and his Polynesian family in the Caroline Islands. On the day she was scheduled to return, there was not even a letter. I had no way to call her nearly half the planet away. Our whole family was quite worried. The next day, I stayed home from work to find out what happened, using the proven *"psychic booster entheogen"* mescaline. I sat on the roof deck where I could see the ocean, and focus my entire attention on Mara. I kept visualizing her face, but she kept turning away. I knew that until she looked me in the eye, we were not yet in communication. In my mind, I was hugging *"my little girl."* After a few hours, with no information, I finally realized that to receive a message from her, I would have to see her as *"my teacher"* instead. At that point, she looked me in the eye, and gave me this message: *"There was a problem about shots and transportation, and a letter would come in a week and a half."* Then the greatest gift from Mara was sharing a golden light from third eye to third eye with her words, *"pray, don't worry, mother."* Worry sends negative energy. Prayer means to surround her with love and light, which is psychically useful if she is really experiencing a crisis at the time. (11)

I let the rest of the family know she was OK (but not how I knew it). The promised letter came with her arrival time included. Both families (8 of us) met her at the airport, thrilled to see her and how beautiful she was, now 1/2" taller than her mother. The added psychic gift was to know that mind is not limited by space or time. (Physicists use the term "nonlocal spacetime.")

In 1975, we held the first intercontinental telepathic attempt between a group from the Congress of Sorcery in Colombia, SA, and a group from the Assn. for Humanistic Psychology (AHP) at Estes Park, CO, USA. (12) Marge harvested and rolled her home-grown cannabis for those *"senders"* who chose to smoke it. In Colombia, an Abínticua medicine man, (p. 9) called a "*mamu,*" agreed to lead the meditation for our group (his mouth was full of coca leaves and crushed seashells). A Venezuelan priestess smoked a very large entheogenic cigar. (13) I had brought LSD to share, but only one other person used it. The image of the two *I Ching* trigrams that were "sent" from Colorado was received clearly thousands of miles away in Colombia. (See Section 1, pages 8 - 9.) Then I tried to fit them into the right target hexagram. This error was the gift of learning—my analytical mind was useless in remote viewing. (IRVA now calls this error "AOL" for analytic overlay.)

In 1976, I decided to use LSD to "explore" Mars before the NASA landing. In the dry riverbed of the Marinara Valley, fine grey sand swirled around me, while stronger winds churned coarse red dirt above the unbelievably high cliffs. A large recess in the cliff face protected an icy swamp in the deepest part of the valley that had a well deep enough to connect to the top of a vast underground watery cavern. The top seemed mostly mud sprinkled with blowing sand. Strange primitive life survived there by using a different exchange of chemicals than those used by most life forms on Earth. (13)

It has been many years now since I have used any of the major entheogens, though now at my advanced age, I find the legal sacred herb marijuana still offers pain relief, gentle comfort, and some creative ideas.

REFERENCES AND NOTES

1) Millay, J. (2004) Excerpts from "Psi and Entheogens." In: *The Proceedings of the 21st International Conference on the Study of Shamanism and Alternate Modes of Healing.* Heinze, R.I. (Ed.) Berkeley: Independent Scholars of Asia, Inc.
2) Huxley, A. (1954) *The Doors of Perception.* NY: Harper & Row Publishers.
3) Willis, A. & Millay, J. (1965) *The Psychedelic Experience.* SF/Mendocino, CA. Originally a 16 mm film. Available on DVD since 2001 from www.eastbaymediacenter.com.
4) Leary, T., Alpert, R. & Metzner, R. (1964) *The Psychedelic Experience: A Manual Based on the Tibetan Book of the Dead.* New Hyde Park, NY: University Books.
5) Among the many different translations of the ancient Tao, are these:
    5a) MacHovec, Frank J. (1962) *The Book of Tao: The Key to the Mastery of Life.* Mount Vernon, NY: The Peter Pauper Press.
    5b) Mitchell, Stephen (1943 & 1988) *Tao Te Ching: A New English Version.* NY, NY: HarperPerennial
    5c) Leary, Timothy (1966 & 1997) *Psychedelic Prayers: and Other Meditations.* Berkeley, CA: Ronin Publishing.
6) Bollingen Foundation, Inc. (1950) *The I Ching or Book of Changes* (ancient) The Wilhelm, R. translation rendered into English by Baynes, C.F. (1950) Princeton, NJ: Princeton University Press.
7) Millay, J. (2001) "Some effects that smoking Cannabis has on the brainwaves of volunteers." In: *The Entheogen Review.* Vol. X, No.4. pp. 140-146.
8) Lesh, P. (2005) *Searching for the Sound: My Life with the Grateful Dead.* NY: Little Brown & Co.

9) Douglas, Don (private communication). The draft board asked Don if he were gay. He said he was not. They asked him if he ever kissed a man. Remembering the marine, he answered honestly. They promptly excused him from the draft.
10) A photo of the lights that I felt indicated the presence of my great-grandmother is illustrated on the title page of Section VIII, p. 407. My cousin, her grandson, was seriously injured, but he recovered and lived to be 89. (Photo by Echo Penrose.)
11) Mayo, M. "Listen to your heart talk." (See Chapter 42c – Education.) Mayo worked as a school therapist. She is an artist in many mediums, see: www.maramayo.com.
12) Millay, J. (1999) *Multidimensional Mind: Remote Viewing in Hyperspace*. A Universal Dialogues Book. Berkeley, CA: North Atlantic Books.
13) Weil, A. (1975) "A bunch of the Brujos were whooping it up." In: *The Rolling Stone*.

END NOTES

The following are three examples of extremely unpleasant visions that were given while I was using LSD, though they were educational. Since there was nothing I could do to change the situation, I stopped using LSD except on the rare occasions already mentioned. The entheogens allowed one to feel *"one with the universe."* However the oneness is a combination of both the light side and the dark side. At that time I still resisted the forced awareness of the dark side.

A) A full moon eclipse would happen on Friday. In order to see it without the smog in LA, CA, my sister Marge & I took our 6 kids and the dog camping about 100 miles away. (Somehow a sleeping bag usually got smeared with peanut butter and dog hair.) When the eclipse was over, and the kids were settled into their sleeping bags by the campfire, I climbed to the top of a hill of white rocks that glowed in the full moonlight and took LSD. I needed guidance from the Great Spirit. Gradually my mind cleared of all thought, and the essence of light filled me.

And then I *"saw"* a riot in the middle of a city, with the sounds of police sirens, storefronts smashing and people screaming.[*6] From there the visions jumped to an elegant cocktail lounge on the top floor of a NYC sky scraper. A woman in a red satin formal, with the fur of a white fox draped over her shoulder, turned to her tuxedoed companion, and with exaggerated superciliousness, remarked, *"It seems the natives are getting restless."* They laughed. Instantly the vision changed again—this time to an FBI office. There I saw only shadows, but I was filled with the realization that the order to murder Martin Luther King, Jr. had been given personally by J. Edgar Hoover. This was Good Friday when King's body was lying in state, and I *"saw"* the Christian symbolism creating a new positive self-awareness for my former remedial reading students near Watts. Pastors now praise Martin Luther King, Jr. as a spiritual teacher.

[*6] We were out in the country with no radio news. The riots I "saw" were in Memphis. Churches were filled with mourners.

Where could I report such a vision? Hoover was the biggest and most corrupt scoundrel in the country. He violated the Bill of Rights everyday. No one could touch him. He knew all the secrets that could blackmail not only politicians, but also errant judges and even a President. James Earl Ray was framed.

B) The trip that put a stop to my use of LSD for a long time was when I watched men clad in army gear (perhaps CIA?) drag a man through a jungle, tie him to a post, and thrust a long knife through him. Later the news reported that the election officials in Viet Nam had been murdered just that way. We were told that the US was there to assure a free election. The CIA knew the people might very well vote with the communists. By murdering the officials, elections were cancelled, so the war could continue as previously planned. War protestors were beaten and arrested.

C) Sometimes in the late '60s, when young men of draft age took LSD, they would have fearful visions and think they were going crazy. From my own experiences, I knew that LSD promoted spontaneous remote viewing (though such visions were not called that then). These images included fast planes bombing villages, explosions, screaming people burning with napalm and other horrors of the Viet Nam war, or any war. The few young people that I could explain this to learned to deal with it sensibly. Others took heavy downers and alcohol to suppress those terrifying visions, which also amplified their own unresolved internal problems.

D) In those years, if a psychology student used the word "consciousness," the professor would cross it out and substitute the word "behavior." So when college students took LSD, without a knowledgeable person to guide them through those hellish remote viewing images of war into an awareness that their own consciousness was connected to everything, grass roots guides (such as Wavy Gravy and his tribe) emerged to provide comfort and support. Nevertheless, millions of people who tried LSD found the experience of oneness with the universe to be transcendental the first time, and those who went directly into their creative process changed the way our civilization thinks (e.g., personal computers, internet, DNA, portable biofeedback machines, energy medicine, alternative healing).

> *I have tremendous respect for psychedelics as a tool. I have seen what they have done on the positive side. I also know the risk — I know what they can do if they are not properly used, and the more powerful the tool, the more powerful potential on both sides.*
>
> *--- Stanislav Grof*

CHAPTER 21   PSYCHOTHERAPY AND SELF- EXPLORATION

Stanislav Grof, MD, PhD

Stanislav Grof was born in Prague where he received an MD from Charles University, and a PhD in medicine from the Czechoslovakia Academy of Sciences. From 1960 to 1967, he was Principal Investigator in a psychedelic research program at the Psychiatric Research Inst. in Prague. In the US, he served as Chief of Psychiatric Research at the Maryland Psychiatric Research Center, and Assistant Professor at Johns Hopkins U in Baltimore, MD. He was also Scholar-in-Residence at Esalen Inst. His research includes experiential psychotherapy using psychedelics and nondrug techniques, especially the holotropic breathwork (a method he developed with his wife Christina) and a new understanding and treatment of psychosis as psychospiritual crises (spiritual emergencies). Dr Grof has more than fifty-years experience researching the healing and transformative potential of non-ordinary states of consciousness. His groundbreaking theories influenced the integration of Western science with his brilliant mapping of the transpersonal dimension. In 2007, he received the prestigious VISION 97 award granted by the Foundation of Dagmar and Vaclav Havel in Prague. He was the founding president of the International Transpersonal Assn (ITA) and served in this function for many years. In 2000, he received an Honorary Doctorate from Burlington College in Vermont.

Dr Grof has published 21 books. Among them are (1975) *Realms of the Human Unconscious: Observations from LSD Research;* (1980) *LSD Psychotherapy;* (1988) *Human Survival and Consciousness Evolution;* (2000) *Psychology of the Future: Lessons from Modern Consciousness Research;* (2006) *The Ultimate Journey: Consciousness and the Mystery of Death;* (2006) *When the Impossible Happens: Adventures in Non-Ordinary Realities.*

His website is http://www.stanislavgrof.com/.

IMPLICATIONS OF CONSCIOUSNESS RESEARCH FOR PSYCHOTHERAPY AND SELF-EXPLORATION

Stanislav Grof

Non-ordinary states of consciousness have long been of interest to me both for their extraordinary therapeutic applications and for their evolutionary potential. It is my firm belief that the new knowledge of the psyche brought by research into non-ordinary states has the potential to drastically change not only the future of psychiatry and psychotherapy, but also the basic philosophical assumptions of Western science.

When I began my research into psychedelic use in psychiatry, I was deeply influenced by my orthodox Freudian training and the fact that I was convinced of the value of psychoanalysis as a conceptual framework. I hoped that the use of LSD (lysergic acid diethylamide) as a catalyst would help to improve the highly disappointing therapeutic efficacy and practical results of his otherwise fascinating analytic approach.

The therapeutic modality combining analytically oriented psychotherapy with the administration of psychedelic drugs has become known as psycholytic treatment. Records from early research sessions are a rich source of information about the nature of the psychedelic state, the dynamics of psychopathological symptoms and syndromes, and the dimensions of the human psyche.

LSD and related substances can best be understood as catalysts and amplifiers of mental processes. They do not produce any specific contents in the psyche, but make its deep unconscious dynamics available for conscious experience and direct observation. It is therefore appropriate to compare the potential role of psychedelics in psychiatry and psychology to the role that the microscope has in medicine or the telescope in astronomy.

Research with these fascinating substances, shunned since the widespread nonmedical use of psychedelics made the continuation of this work difficult, is one of the most promising approaches to the study of the human mind. People who take LSD do not experience "toxic psychosis," but undertake a fantastic journey into the realms of their own unconscious that are not experientially accessible under normal conditions.

Knowledge about the psyche acquired in psychedelic sessions is directly applicable to a variety of situations in which non-ordinary states of consciousness occur spontaneously or are induced by different nondrug techniques. Such situations include aboriginal healing ceremonies and rites of passage, shamanic rituals, laboratory mind-altering techniques, traditional methods of spiritual practice and self-exploration, different forms of experiential psychotherapy, death and near-death experiences, and spontaneous evolutionary crises.

Since the 1980s my wife Christina and I have been developing what we call holotropic therapy. (The term holotropic is derived from the Greek holos meaning "whole" and trepein, "to move toward," it suggests aiming for totality and wholeness.) This is a technique of self-exploration that uses activation of the unconscious through a combination of controlled breathing, evocative music, and focused bodywork. Holotropic therapy mediates access to the entire spectrum of experiences that are available in psychedelic sessions and to powerful therapeutic mechanisms on the perinatal and transpersonal levels.

Traditional schools of psychotherapy see biography as the only source of psychogenic disorders. Modern consciousness research, however, has revealed beyond a doubt that emotional, psychosomatic, and interpersonal disorders also have important roots in the perinatal and transpersonal domains of the psyche. In this context, psychopathology represents as much an opportunity as a problem for the person involved.

Verbal (and sometimes even experiential) work limited to biography typically requires months or years to produce noticeable change. Yet deep experiences of death and rebirth, mystical and transcendental states, reliving of past incarnation sequences, or encounters with powerful archetypal figures, themes and energies can result in significant emotional and psychosomatic healing personality transformation, and consciousness evolution within a matter of hours or days.

The model that I had to construct to include the entire spectrum of experiences available to an average person with the use of psychedelics or powerful nondrug experiential techniques has four major levels or realms.

1. *Sensory experiences.* In the initial phase, techniques that activate the unconscious stimulate the sensory organs. This results in visions of geometric and architectural patterns and kaleidoscopic displays, hearing of various elementary sounds, and unusual body sensations and, sometimes, tastes or smells.

2. *Recollective–analytical experiences.* This is the only aspect of the new cartography of the psyche acknowledged and recognized by traditional psychiatry and psychotherapy. In therapy that is limited to verbal exchange, one may merely remember or reconstruct repressed material. In experiential therapy, it is possible not only to fully

reexperience the emotions and physical sensations from the past, but also to relive complex memories in complete age regression.

Experiential therapy also reveals the importance of physical traumas that are all but neglected in mainstream psychotherapeutic work. When the unconscious is activated, it will quite spontaneously disclose repressed memories, with all the emotions and physical sensations involved. While reliving these experiences, many clients are surprised to discover that these past events had a direct impact on their psychological development and played an important role in the genesis of the problems that they brought into therapy.

3. *Perinatal experiences.* The activation of the next level of the unconscious leads to powerful experiences that combine an authentic encounter with death and biological birth with elements of ego death and psychological and spiritual rebirth. The profound existential crisis that often accompanies sequences of dying and being (re)born leads to a spontaneous opening of intrinsic spiritual and mystical domains in the psyche, since the only way to resolve the crisis is through transcendence.

The phenomenology of the positive aspects of this process typically involves oceanic and cosmic experiences, a sense of mystical union, and radiant white or golden light. Negatively, one may have encounters with insidious demonic appearances, existential despair, and selective access to archetypal images of hells from the repertoire of the collective unconscious.

4. *Transpersonal experiences.* This domain of the new cartography of the unconscious contains a rich spectrum of experiences for which I coined the term transpersonal. They are characterized by transcendence of the person's usual ego boundaries (body image) and of the limitations of the Newtonian space and time. Here belong experiences of unity with other people, groups of people, or all humanity; authentic identification with animals, plants, or inorganic nature; and ancestral, phylogenetic, racial, and past-incarnation experiences. An important subgroup of transpersonal phenomena involves mythological sequences, archetypal figures and themes, and identification with the Universal Mind and the Supracosmic and Metacosmic Void.

NEW STRATEGY OF PSYCHOTHERAPY
AND SELF-EXPLORATION

Experiential therapy has revealed the far-reaching, self-healing potential of the psyche. As I have stated, the emergence of symptoms is seen in the new context not as the onset of disease, but as the beginning of a radical and powerful healing process — if properly understood and approached. The new therapeutic strategy based on this insight consists of using techniques that directly activate the unconscious (psychedelic drugs, various nondrug techniques of experiential psychotherapy, trance-inducing technology) and facilitate the emergence of biographical, perinatal, and transpersonal material. An essential part of this approach is deep trust in the autonomy and spontaneity of the healing process and willingness to encourage and support it, even if at times one must transcend rational understanding. This approach has its precedent in Carl Gustav Jung's shift of emphasis from the efforts of the therapist to change the dynamics of the psyche according to a particular conceptual system to reliance on the intrinsic wisdom of the collective unconscious.

INSIGHTS INTO THE NATURE OF REALITY AND THE NEED FOR A NEW PARADIGM

Observations from psychedelic sessions and holotropic therapy represent a serious challenge to current psychiatric theory and to the worldview of mechanistic science. This is particularly true with regard to the spectrum of transpersonal experiences whose existence is irreconcilable with philosophical materialism and with the Cartesian–Newtonian paradigm that has dominated Western science for the past 300 years.

In my book *Beyond the Brain*, I provide a detailed exploration of this fascinating aspect of modern consciousness research. The revolutionary data range from the various forms of extrasensory perception to the frequent occurrence of extraordinary synchronicities in Jung's sense. I offer the possibility of using intuitive channels to acquire new information about different domains of nature and the universe – by experiential identification with them.

Observations of this kind banish to the historical archives the myths of mechanistic science that portrays consciousness, life, and creative intelligence as epiphenomena of matter and as insignificant accidents in the evolution of the universe. In light of the new data, consciousness appears to be an equal partner of matter or even a principle supraordinated to it.

REFERENCES

1) Grof, S. (1976) *Realms of the Human Unconscious: Observations from LSD Research.* NY: EP Dutton.
2) -------- & Grof, C. (1980) *Beyond Death: The Gates of Consciousness.* London: Thames & Hudson.
3) --------. (1980) *LSD Psychotherapy.* Pomona, CA: Hunter House.
4) --------. (1985) *The Adventures of Self-Discovery.* Albany: State University NY Press.
5) --------. (1985) *Beyond the Brain.* Albany: State University NY Press.

SECTION V

MIND
AND
BRAIN/BODY ELECTRICITY

SECTION V

MIND AND BRAIN/BODY ELECTRICITY

*...Invisible waves stream out from our brains with
a wavelength of about 200 miles...*
--- David Bodanis, PhD.[1]

Every thought, feeling, emotion or movement is accompanied by electrical and chemical activity in the brain. As the illustration for the title of this section shows, the frequencies of brainwaves between different parts of the brain can be quite varied during different states of consciousness. People are rarely aware of the changes in this activity. However, in the late 1950s and early 1960s, Joe Kamiya showed that subjects could discriminate their alpha brainwaves from other frequencies. (1, 2, 3) Before that time he had studied EEG sleep patterns, since the EEG and eye movements demonstrate recognizable changes between known states of consciousness — deep sleep and dreaming. Then in the early 1960s, he developed a protocol for alpha training that involved the use of a feedback tone for instantaneous feedback of the strength of the alpha rhythm, with occasional display of an objective score indicating the average strength of alpha. This pioneering work set the stage for a new field of study – biofeedback. Researchers in other institutions began their own studies, organized societies and held conferences to share their information. (Brainwave biofeedback is now called neurofeedback.)

Through this work and that of others, Stanley Krippner who was working at the Maimonides Dream Lab in Brooklyn, NY, was able to track when a subject was dreaming and use that information to attempt to influence the content of the dream telepathically while the dream was occurring. (A summary of the many years of that research is in Chapter 3.)

In this section, Johnston, who worked with Kamiya for years, writes about using feedback to help people establish alpha phase coherence, not only between the two sides of the brain, but also between two people who have a close relationship.[2] (Chapter 22)

---

[1] Bodanis, David (2005). *Electric Universe: The Shocking True Story of Electricity.* NY: Crown Publishers. www.davidbodanis.com.

[2] [Note: When 6-7 Hz and 13-19 Hz are rhythmic "like alpha" they're called "alpha."]

Through the practice of meditation, and/or neurofeedback training, an individual can learn to increase the phase coherence and the amplitude of his/her alpha brainwave frequencies. That usually means one must stop thinking, because thinking involves other frequencies. Alpha coherence is maintained through a steady focus in the nonverbal hum of the present moment. When the mind wanders into thoughts — past or future — the feedback tone stops. Many have found that after a sustained period of meditation or of phase-coherent alpha/theta, they might suddenly announce, *"Oh, I just remembered..."* or *"I just figured out a solution to an old problem."* These spontaneous reports suggest that the phase-coherence of brainwaves encourages an integration of mental processes. The ability to shift one's focus from intellectual activity to the peace of no-thought and back again provides an enhancement of overall intelligence. (Section X — Education) Indeed, Kamiya has stated that:

> *Biofeedback presents ideal opportunities for the general education of children. Increasing all children's knowledge of physiology can start at all ages with biofeedback explorations. More important, helping them discover that states of consciousness are related to their physiology could be a long lasting contribution to their education. Letting the child learn, for example, that embarrassment, pleasure, surprise, anger and relaxed calmness have immediate effects on skin conductance, muscle tension, blood pressure, facial blood perfusion and many other measures is hard to top as a method of teaching body awareness. Many kinds of biofeedback equipment ought to be made available in the classroom, much like jungle gym equipment is made available on the playground at recess.*[*3]

Our brainwaves are also affected by the frequencies in our environment, whether we are aware of them or not. I found years ago, that it was impossible to practice voluntary control of my alpha rhythms (using the Scully portable brainwave analyzers for feedback) while sitting next to a refrigerator. The very loud scratchy feedback tone told me just how much more electrical interference was being measured from the refrigerator, than from my brainwaves. Then I wondered just what effect it had on my brain, as well as what other events in the environment might be influencing my brain's electrical activity, such as cell phones and TV.

Rauscher has studied magnetic field interactions with the brain and body, and is working with HeartMath to study the relationship between the Earth's magnetic field and heart rhythms. (Chapter 23)

Krippner and Persinger have found that heavy sunspot activity interferes with the accuracy of dream telepathy. It was only after many years of working independently (Krippner studying dream telepathy and Persinger studying sunspots) that they discovered this result. (Chapter 24)

[*3] Kamiya, J. (2002) "Introduction." In: *Self-Discovery Science*. www.fmbr.org/millay

Spottiswoode did an important study on the effect of the position of the planet on telepathic responses. (4) The most favorable time for more accurate telepathy is called Local Sidereal Time (LST). Though his work is not included here, it is important to bring it to your attention, because it significantly expands our concept of the possible range of environmental influence on consciousness. Spottiswoode explained this:

> The Earth rotates on its axis every 24 hours exactly with respect to the sun; this is known as a solar day. But due to the fact that the Earth is also orbiting the sun once per year, 24 hours is not the period of the Earth's rotation with respect to the distant stars. That period, called a sidereal day, is slightly shorter – 2 hours and 56 minutes long. It is the time required for the distant stars to return to exactly the same position when viewed by an observer at a fixed location on the Earth's surface. The time at any location with respect to the sidereal rotation period is known as Local Sidereal Time.

Sound can also entrain brain activity, which is why drumming is a standard part of tribal ceremonies. The repetitious rhythm can encourage a whole group to enter into a trance-like state of consciousness. Quincy and Alter, who have practiced alternative medicine for many years, have written about the direct relationship between the rhythms of sound affecting the rhythm of the cerebral spinal fluid. (Chapter 25.)

Music and the wide range of emotional effects it has on consciousness is not covered here. (5) The musicians listed below are among many who have created CDs to entrain brainwaves into specific brain frequencies.

  Steven Halpern   — at www.stevenhalpern.com
  Kelly Howell   — at www.brainsync.com
  Various artists — at www.Hemi-Sync.com
  Ali Akbar Khan and Zakir Hussain — at www.aakccm.com & AMMP
  George Deuter, Barry Osser and others at New Earth Records.

REFERENCES

1) Kamiya, J. (1962) "Conditioned discrimination of the EEG alpha rhythm in humans." Paper presented to the Western Psychological Association.
2) Kamiya, J. (1968) "Conscious control of brainwaves." In: *Psychology Today*. 1: 56-60.
3) Kamiya, J. (1969) "Operant control of the EEG alpha rhythm and some of its reported effects on consciousness." In: C. Tart (Ed.) *Altered States of Consciousness*. 507-556
4) Spottiswoode, S.J.P. (1997) "Apparent association between effect size of anomalous cognition experiments and local sidereal time." In: *Journal of Scientific Exploration*, Vol. 11, No. 2. (1997).
5) Campbell, D. (1997) *The Mozart Effect: Tapping the Power of Music to Heal the Body, Strengthen the Mind & Unlock the Creative Spirit*. NY: Avon Books.

--- Jean Millay

CHAPTER 22 BRAINWAVE PHASE SYNCHRONIZATION

James Johnston, PhD

James R. Johnston earned his BS (1960) and his PhD (1968) both in physics. In his early work in physics, he demonstrated the equivalence of coherence in laser radiation and macroscopic quantum coherence in superfluids. He taught graduate classes in quantum theory at Dalhousie University in Halifax and at San Diego State College (now University). From 1972 to 1980 he worked with Dr Joe Kamiya in his research in EEG feedback at Langley Porter Institute, UCSF, completed a post-doctoral Interdisciplinary Training Program, and conducted research regarding the correlation of interpersonal EEG phase-synchrony within the alpha frequency band and telepathy scores. After that he wrote and installed balance-of-plant software (all thermal and electrical balances, exclusive of the nuclear reactor) in the control rooms of nuclear power plants, in the US and in Switzerland. More recently he has developed a practice using EEG and peripheral biofeedback for enhancement of attention and improvement in responses to stress. During this time, he has benefited from an ongoing collaboration with Wm. G. Barton, PhD, and further collaboration with him and Erik Peper, PhD, in studying EEG of healers. Beginning in 2007, he is a research associate with Dr Peper at SF State University where he supports the Introduction to Biofeedback and Self-regulation class. He has authored and coauthored articles in physics and EEG synchrony, including: Peper, E., Wilson, V.E., Gunkelman, J., Kawakami, M. Sata, Barton, W. & Johnston, J. (2006). "Tongue Piercing by a Yogi: QEEG Observations." In: *Applied Psychophysiology and Biofeedback*. 34 (4), 331-338.

JRJohnston@ORION-Research.net – www.ORION-Research.net

CHAPTER 22   Page 240

BRAINWAVE PHASE SYNCHRONIZATION: REPORT ON A PILOT STUDY [*1]

James R. Johnston

INTRODUCTION

In 1980, Jean Millay and I did a pilot study in brainwave phase synchronization at the Washington Research Institute (WRI) in SF and at the Langley Porter Neuropsychiatric Institute, UCSF. (1) This was continuation of work that Millay had done on her PhD dissertation (2), where she discusses visual processing of subtle information. We were looking for the possibility that there might be some kind of brainwave resonance that corresponded to states of deep rapport between people.

Millay had experimented personally and with associates using equipment made especially for her by Tim Scully of Aquarius Electronics (AE), based on her requests for signal analysis features (Ref. 3 & Appendix B) and including her thoughtful and artistic design of visual and auditory feedback (p. 249). With this equipment – totally unique in 1972 – she later found correspondences between phase synchronization feedback and the experience of rapport as expressed by the participants in Appendix A.

My own motivation came from contemplation of issues in physics. While there has not been any significant disagreement between experience and quantum theory, there has been continual discussion and experimentation with respect to issues of our understanding or interpretation of unique quantum phenomena. It has become clear that these issues in understanding are related to our strong conceptual and perceptual bias toward perspectives of reality based on individual objects in interaction. These quantum phenomena, and the quantum theory that predicts/describes their behavior, indicate that reality is fundamentally a wholeness that manifests in discreet individualistic events. That fundamental quality of wholeness is "ontologically prior" to the individualistic events (or a seemingly continuum thereof) that make up our

---

[*1] Supported in part by the Institute of Noetic Sciences (IONS), the Washington Research Institute (WRI), SF, the Holmes Center, LA, and the researchers. Revised from the 1993 version in *SILVER THREADS: 25 Years of Parapsychology Research*, B. Kane, J. Millay & D. Brown (Eds.) Westport, CT: Praeger Publishers.

experience of reality. In this perspective, the "paradoxes" of quantum physics disappear, and the sense of mystery deepens (See addendum).

This perspective of individuality and wholeness, based entirely on consideration of quantum physics, is consistent with perennial wisdom that through the ages has described our being or consciousness similarly — particularly by those who believed the nature of our consciousness could be ascertained from direct experience of it and who participated in such practice. It is not unreasonable, then to treat the issue of individuality and wholeness as being fundamentally relevant to both domains. Thus, we are led to explore scientifically areas of experience that will inform and enhance our understanding of the relationship between individuality and wholeness, in physical reality and in our being.

This pilot project was aimed at exploring possible relationships between "mental/social rapport" and "physiological rapport" between the members of several pairs ("teams") of people. It was based on some "romantic notions" that were not validated, but led to some interesting and statistically significant results. Those notions are best described, perhaps, by excerpting a couple of introductory paragraphs from the report submitted to IONS: (2)

> This work is motivated by the belief that an increased awareness of self and our relationship to environment is crucial to our evolution, even becoming a matter of survival. There is a common thread in the problems presented to us by life on this planet, and in the perplexities of modern science as well: we are not just individuals, but also an inseparable part of the whole. The pretense that we are ever separate from the whole is at best an approximation. (This is as true for a hydrogen atom as it is for a sentient being.) Because it has served our industrialization, technology and science, the qualities of separateness and individuality have predominated our perspective of reality.
>
> Knowing is a process, not simply a collection of facts in a deductive logic. Knowing in its deepest sense involves a state of awareness in which there is a "resonance": There is no separation between "knower" and "known." This essential knowing (without separation) is somehow enhanced, or perhaps completed, by that part of awareness that pretends to "stand apart from" for the sake of an "outside" view. The latter has become so important in our technological evolution (it is the basis of our sense of scientific objectivity) that we seem to have forgotten the former. Special qualities of resonance in various arts (music, healing, dance, martial, etc.) have always been appreciated by practitioners of those arts, but are commonly relegated to the "esoteric." As a technological culture, we have developed little language and have very little consensus regarding those aspects of our being. It seems to us the problems we now face (as a civilization) are calling for a deeper knowing of our interconnectedness: with each other and with Earth. Thus, we find ourselves very interested in the possibility that resonance in physical or biological

dimensions may help tag and enhance resonance in subtler, subjective dimensions.

The "romantic notion" here was that we would find a resonance in alpha EEG brainwaves between pairs of individuals while they were in rapport during telepathic activity. Telepathic activities seemed particularly appropriate to me: I seldom consider access to "subtle information" as a special communication between individuals, but see it as an opening of awareness to our non-individualistic, or wholeness, aspect.

In this pilot project, we were not concerned with proof of the reality of telepathic phenomena, which we assume to be real. (4, 5) We explored the possibility of relationship between physiological rapport represented by brainwave phase synchronization and mental rapport represented by telepathic phenomena. Correlation between telepathic performance and physiology would open a rich arena for exploration of both. (We are also interested in subjective reports of participants responses to phase-sync training. (Appendix B)

We did not find evidence to support the idea that telepathic rapport would be accompanied by EEG phase synchrony, but we did find a solid correlation (.74, p < .001) between team-average interpersonal brainwave phase synchronization (IP phase sync) scores and team-average-telepathy scores. Our intent had been, for each team: [1] to compare learning trends in IP phase sync scores with variations in telepathy scores across training and laboratory testing sessions, and [2] to compare telepathy scores with IP phase sync scores taken during telepathy trials in three laboratory testing sessions. But, learning of IP phase sync across sessions was not significant, and there was very little interpersonal phase sync during laboratory testing-session telepathy tests. Thus, we looked instead at team-averages of telepathy scores versus team averages of IP phase sync scores across teams, for all training sessions, and found the significant correlated averages indicated above.

PILOT STUDY

The pilot project involved five male-female teams that we considered to have good rapport between the two members. (6) In order to reduce the traditional separation between subject and researcher/observer, Millay and I were one of the teams. We considered random sampling for subjects to be inferior to the use of a sample of adepts, and used our own judgment for subject selection.

The physiological resonance explored in this project was alpha phase synchronization. Here, alpha refers to a brainwave rhythm of 7 to 12 oscillations per second (Hz), often found to be stronger, for most people, when they close their eyes and relax, and are attentive with a wide or "soft" focus with minimal visual or mental processing of their perceptions. Phase synchronization refers to a kind of resonance between two brainwave signals: Both signals are at nearly the same frequency, with electrical oscillations moving nearly in unison. Personal rapport was represented by free-response telepathy scores.

Each team was given 15 telepathy trials, scored in groups of five. The targets were pictures of many disparate subjects cut from magazines and pasted on 3x5 cards (e.g., photos, cartoons – loving or violent – people, animals, objects, landscapes). One member of the team, the sender, concentrated on the target, and then drew her own rendition of it with colored pens, and wrote what came to mind. At the same time, in a remote room, the receiver drew and wrote what came to mind on his 3x5 card. The original picture and the sender's rendition of it were combined as a target to be matched to the receiver's 3x5 card. Five independent judges (not involved in the experiment) were asked to blind-match each set of trials (5 targets with the 5 receiver's cards). The average of the 5 separate judges' scores was used as a single score for each set of 5 telepathy trials.

Each team member was given feedback training for alpha phase synchronization between his/her left and right hemispheres (IH phase sync, or IH sync), and each team was given training in interpersonal phase synchronization between one hemisphere of each team member (IP phase sync, or IP sync). (As one might expect, allowing one's own brainwaves to resonate with another's is a delicate and subtle task.)

Figure 1. Subjects' EEG and Equipment Hookups

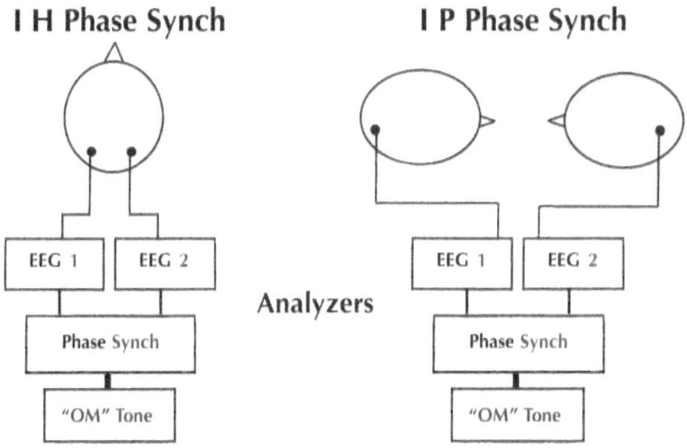

The term "two brainwave signals" refers to two situations:
[1] Left and right hemispheric EEG for a single subject (IH sync)
[2] One EEG signal from each member of a team (IP sync)

The phase synchronization analysis is the same for both situations.

The feedback training sessions employed Aquarius Electronics' (AE) brainwave analyzers and phase comparator (described in more detail in

Appendix B). A special feedback tone generated a pleasant *"OM"* (or *"AUM"*) sound (7) when the two brainwave signals were simultaneously producing alpha waves above a preset threshold. A gentle, harmonious buzz was added to the tone when, in addition, the two signals were in phase with each other to within 1/4 wavelength (+ or - 45 degrees). For each one-minute scoring period, the percent time of simultaneous alpha and the percent time of phase synchronized simultaneous alpha were each measured. The numeric scores for phase synchronization were based on the ratio of the two (alpha phase sync ratio, APSR):

$$APSR = \frac{\%\text{-Time of two-channel alpha phase synchronization}}{\%\text{-Time of two-channel (simultaneous) alpha}}$$

ASPR is the fraction of the time of simultaneous alpha that is also phase-synchronized. This provides a measure that allows comparison of phase synchronization among low and high alpha producers. (8)

Each team participated in several feedback-training sessions at the WRI. Each session consisted of training to increase (or control) IH phase sync for each team member followed by training in IP phase sync for the team, using the AE equipment. The total time in each mode of training was typically 1 to 1.5 hours for each person. In addition, three special testing runs were done on the laboratory PDP-15 computer, programmed to analyze each of the team's four EEG signals (left and right hemisphere for each subject), and to generate phase synchronization measures on each of the six pairs of EEG signals (two inter-hemispherical, four interpersonal combinations). The computer used the same analysis as the AE training equipment.

The testing data obtained on the laboratory (LPI) computer could not be combined with the training data as had been originally planned, but it provided us with EEG data during telepathy (not previously available) that generated a puzzle regarding the connection between EEG phase synchrony and telepathic performance.

Regarding training, some interhemispheric phase synchrony occurs naturally when both hemispheres produce alpha. Thus, once one learns to produce simultaneous alpha, there is usually a significant amount of feedback signal, enabling quick entry into learning IH phase sync. However, the scarcity of naturally occurring interpersonal phase sync between participants makes learning slower and more difficult. The amount of learning (increase in scores during this short project) in either IH or IP phase synch was not as high as we hoped for. Thus it was not possible to correlate changes in telepathy scores with changes in phase synch scores. However, the overall averages of the training sessions did show a relationship with success in telepathy. (See Figure 4.)

Below are some samples of laboratory polygraph recordings.

Figure 2. EEG traces

a) IH phase sync (early)
8.5-second trace

b) IH phase sync (later)
7.5-second trace

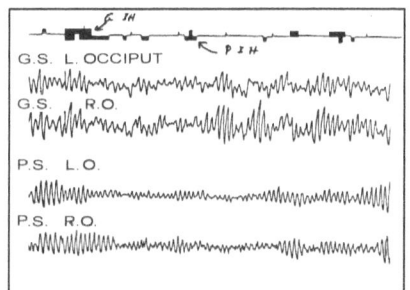
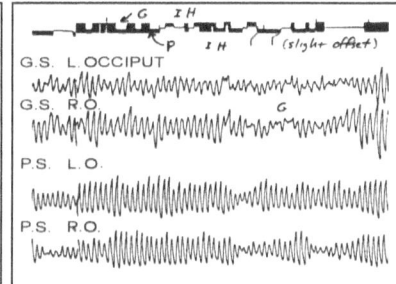

Figure 2-c) Enlargement of the event marker for Figure 2-b.

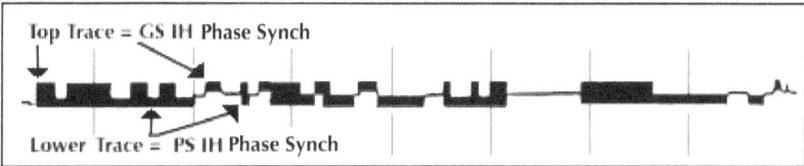

The black trace at the top is an event marker that shows when each member of the team achieves interhemispheric phase synchronization. The upper half of the event marker indicates when the first pair of channels (record of the EEG for G. S.) is in IH phase synch. The lower half of the event marker indicates when the second pair of channels (record of the EEG for P. S.) is in IH phase synch.

Figure 3. Interpersonal sync (IP sync) scores by 4 teams on the AE equipment. The graph shows the ratio between IP simultaneous alpha and phase coherence.

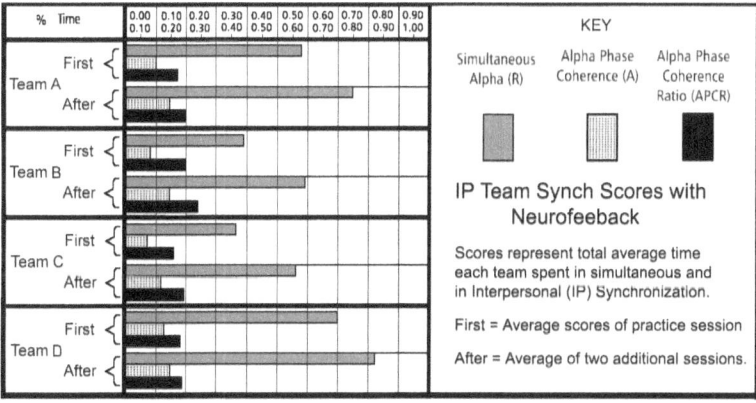

To make the data more robust, we combined the data for the 5 teams in this study with the data for the 11 teams Millay used in her PhD thesis – using only data obtained from similar training sessions on the same AE equipment with the same procedure for telepathy testing. The correlation of the 16 teams' average telepathy scores with their average IP sync scores, calculated over all the AE training sessions, was .74 (p< .001). The correlation between the team-average IH sync and telepathy scores was lower and also significant (r = .54, p < .0015). The team average IP phase sync scores varied from 10.8% to 30.6%. The team average telepathy scores ranged from 10% to 36%, where 20% represents chance. Visual inspection of a scatter plot of the data indicates a good correlation, with the major skew being due to the cluster of 3 subjects that scored significantly below chance on the telepathy scores (Figure 4).

Figure 4.

Interpersonal Alpha Phase Sync Ratio (APSR) Versus Telepathy Scores
(r = .74, p <= .001)

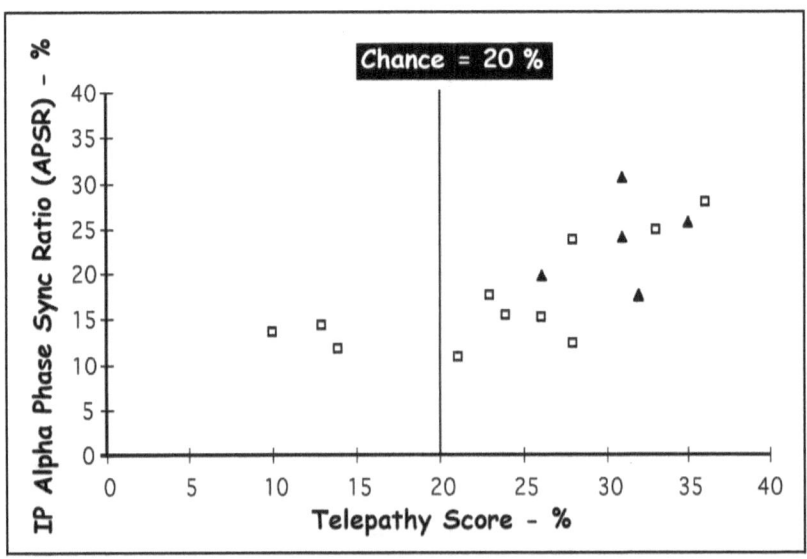

The black triangles represent team averages from the second study. The boxes represent team averages from the first study. (3) (Note the three telepathy scores below chance. If a line of zero slope is used for the below-chance region, the correlation is r = .81)

In summary, we believe this to be a plausible and important consideration; volitional maintenance of EEG phase synchronization and telepathic performance both involve skill in cognitive/attentional processes. Skill in one activity would imply skill in the other. This perspective puts emphasis on skills in attention and awareness.

SOME OBSERVATIONS ON EEG FEEDBACK

In the original study, Millay asked participants what they did to enhance the feedback tone. Those who were able to do that reported either that they *"put a light in the center of their head,"* or *"kept the feedback tone in the center of their head."* (For more on this, see reference 1.) In the IH sync, subjects were asked to try to keep the phase sync tone off occasionally, to help develop a sense of control.

Being both researcher and subject at Joe Kamiya's EEG/psychophysiological research laboratory at LPI for a number of years provided a lot of experience of single-channel alpha feedback. While the more complex task of generating alpha in both hemispheres in this project was more difficult at first, it soon became much easier than I had experienced with the less complex single-channel task at LPI. I think the focus on a more subtle and difficult phase sync task allowed skills in the secondary task (simultaneous alpha) to be integrated at a more automatic level. While it was an attentional skill, it felt somewhat like training a muscle.

While there are common strategies for achieving alpha production (and reliable "refined" strategies for achieving enhanced phase synchronization), there are interesting variations.

In an earlier alpha enhancement study at the LPI lab (in a room without sound-proofing), the occasional sound of a bus going by blocked alpha production. Intentionally blocking out the sound of the bus made things much worse. Then, after noticing a picture in my mind of a bus exhaust pipe accompanying the sound, staying with the sound only, without further mental or perceptual processing, led to abundant alpha. Discoveries like this are quite rewarding.

SUMMARY

We did not find evidence that interpersonal EEG phase synchronization accompanies telepathic rapport at the time of testing the latter. However, among 16 pairs of subjects, those pairs with higher average interpersonal phase synchrony scores tended strongly to have higher average telepathic performance scores ($r = .74$, $p < .001$). We believe this correlation indicates a similarity in the attentional skills required for the two tasks.

ADDENDUM

I want to speak more to the reason for including comments on quantum theory in this chapter, and try to give those scientifically oriented some sense of the scientific basis. During the time of this research project, I found myself not at all interested in an exploration of the possible transfer of psychic information via EEG alpha waves, and wondered why I was not attracted to something involving my two specialties: physics and EEG alpha. Holding that question for a while, I discovered a strong intuitive belief: (12) Psychic communication comes from our individual consciousness making contact with the "collective" aspect of our being – a place in which, perhaps, all history is, in principle, knowable. That is, a deeper aspect of subtle communication between individuals is an opening of individual awareness to our non-individualistic, or wholeness, aspect. And, the various mechanisms we attribute to psychic process are the ways we report that knowledge to our ordinary, individual consciousness. This is an intuitive belief; it may be poorly stated here, but I believe there is something fundamental in it.

As stated previously, fundamental issues of individuality and wholeness exist also in quantum theory. (The intention here is not to model one of the domains from the other, but to see the similarity in fundamental aspects of each.) The discussion of quantum physics in this regard is presented in the Physics Section VII, Chapter 32.

ACKNOWLEDGEMENTS

I would like to thank Joe Kamiya, PhD, (psychophysiology) for his steadfast counsel and support, and to thank Jean Millay, PhD, (Human Science) for inviting me into her research activities.

REFERENCES AND END NOTES

1) Millay, J. (1978), "The Relationship Between Phase Synchronization of Brainwaves and Success in Attempts to Communicate Telepathically: A Pilot Study," Doctoral Dissertation (SF, CA: Saybrook University); (Also published in: Millay, J. (1981) "Brainwave synchronization: A study of subtle forms of communication." In: *The Humanistic Psychology Institute Review*, 3, Spring.) This includes discussion of visual processing of subtle information. See also Millay, J. (1999) *Multidimensional Mind: Remote Viewing in Hyperspace*. Berkeley, CA: North Atlantic Books.

2) Johnston, J.R. & Millay, J. (1983) "A pilot study in brainwave synchrony," submitted to the Institute of Noetic Sciences, October, 1983. Copies may be obtained from IONS in Petaluma, CA. A preliminary version is in *Psi Research*, Vol. 2, No. 1 (3-'83).

3) Aquarius Electronics is now Mendocino Microcomputers, Albion, CA. The "Light Sculpture" had eight overlapping mandala patterns carved as dots in Plexiglas. These lit up in different colored lights corresponding to three standard EEG frequency bands (beta, alpha and theta), for both left and right hemispheres. The 4th pair of panels lit up in white for muscle artifact. This multidimensional display was unique, and was demonstrated at the NY Metropolitan Museum of Art in May 1972, and at the DeYoung Museum in SF, CA, in 1975. (See illustration on the next page.)

4) Jahn, R.G., Dunne B.J. & Nelson, R.D. (1987) "Engineering anomalies research." In: *Journal of Scientific Exploration*, Vol. 1, 21-50.

5) Targ, R. & Puthoff, H. (1974) "Information transmission under conditions of sensory shielding," In: *Nature*, Vol. 252, 602-607.

6) Anecdotal observations and technical details for this project, beyond that described below, and some observations of a few sessions with healers are included in the report available from   http://www.ions.org/.
7) Designed, built and contributed by Tom Etter, Mill Valley, California.
8) For those wanting a bit more detail, the EEG signals were measured from occiput (O1, O2) to prefrontal (Fpz), typical of much of the commercial home equipment). For each team member, the specific hemisphere used for IP feedback was chosen arbitrarily, after some "getting acquainted" runs, at the beginning of the project. The AE equipment used zero-cross analysis for dominant frequency determination and for cross-comparisons for phase synchronization analysis. (See Appendix B.)
9) The original work leading to research in operant conditioning of EEG was, in fact, a discrimination study asking the question: could subjects learn to discriminate two physiological states, high (A) and nearly zero (B) alpha production (unknown to them), if given yes/no feedback on their answers "A" or "B"? (Kamiya, J. (1969), "Conditioned discrimination of the EEG alpha rhythm in humans." In: Barber, T. et al. (Eds.). *Biofeedback & Self-Control*, p. 279, Aldine, NY.) The important original consideration of ability to discriminate got lost in the subsequent enthusiasm over the ability to control.
10) Stoyva, J. & Kamiya, J. (1968) "Electrophysiological studies of dreaming as the prototype of a new strategy in the study of consciousness." In: *Psychological Review,* Vol. 75.
11) Kamiya, J. (1984) "On the relationships among subjective experience, behavior, and physiological activity in biofeedback learning." In: *Self-Regulation of the Brain and Behavior.* Elbert T, Rockstroh B, Lutzenberger, W & Birbaumer N. (Eds.). NY: Springer-Verlag.
12) Nurtured by a practice in Aikido that involved dropping into a deeper space beyond personality in which "right action" and insight comes from a quiet place of receptivity and power, and associated group meditative exploration.

In 1972, Stanley Krippner, PhD, organized *The 1st Western Hemisphere Conference on Biofeedback, Acupuncture, Kirlian Photography and the Human Aura* in NYC, where Millay demonstrated this 1st Stereo Brainwave Biofeedback Light Sculpture. Krippner took this photo at the conference.

APPENDIX A

Comments on Brainwave Phase Synchronization And Telepathy Research[*4]

Jean Millay

Most of the participants in our biofeedback-training program did learn to identify some of their own personal mental processes in terms of the different frequency categories. Meditators claimed improvement in their understanding of meditation by practicing phase-sync alpha (or theta) feedback. Later, we found that those who had problems with focus of attention learned to sustain a stronger focus by practicing beta.[*5] For more than 30 years since then, neurofeedback therapists have alleviated ADD and ADHD. This therapy reduces or eliminates the need for the dangerous and expensive medication insurance companies prefer to prescribe for both children and adults, rather than prescribing the safer neurofeedback therapy, which gives the power back to the individual.

What I was most interested in was the possibility that two people might be able to synchronize their brainwaves with each other, and perhaps improve their telepathic attempts. Even though individual EEG records can be very different, some couples were able to identify the percent time of their *IP team synch* and then to raise it using the feedback tones. Some were not able to do this in the short time allowed. Comments made by those who were able to increase the scores of their *IP team synch* scores revealed the ways in which members of each team related to each other. The lovers related their experiences of synchrony to love, the musicians related their synchrony to music, and those who hoped to improve their communication and to enhance their relationship felt that biofeedback helped them to understand each other better. Below are some of their written responses to the training:

Don Kantor in the 1980 study said he felt the experience was:

> ...Similar to an Aikido exercise, projecting energy out of the forehead ... appreciation for the opportunity to explore deeper levels of communication together....

Greg Schelkun in the 1980 study wrote that he experienced:

> ...Intense focus at the heart level.... Afterwards it seems that maybe we converse more — or is it our differing opinions don't clash so much?

[*4] Millay, J. (1999) *Multidimensional Mind: Remote Viewing in Hyperspace.* Berkeley, CA: A Universal Dialogues Book & North Atlantic Books.

[*5] Green, G.H. (1997) *The A.D.D. Quest for Identity: Inside the Mind of Attention Deficit Disorder.* Reno, NV: The Biofeedback Center Press.

One couple that had been able to synchronize well was not nearly as successful during their next *sync* session. The woman wrote:
> *I couldn't sync well with [partner], probably because of an interpersonal problem...now resolved.*

She said later that she felt the phase-sync training helped them both to resolve that problem.

One couple was unable to establish phase-sync during their last session at the end of the semester for many reasons:
> *Hurried. Too many things to do before Christmas. About to move.*

Two couples told us that the *synch* training had helped them become more aware of each other's needs, and this carried over to other aspects of their relationships. Both couples got married after graduation. One wrote:
> *The experiment has put us in a good place together ... able to give each other our own space. I've gotten into paying more attention to my own various states. Been really good for both of us.*

This study indicated that both telepathy practice and IP Phase-Sync practice could become an excellent exercise for couples' therapy. Telepathy identified the different ways that each person "thinks," and the different memories that are stirred up by the target pictures. IP Phase-Sync practice is a very intimate exercise in focus of attention. It requires a serious <u>intention</u> to do so, and a <u>close attention</u> to one's partner. When those are not present, many of the other problems a couple may have are revealed. A therapist might then help them find the ways to work them out.

Mark Gurumukh Harris and his teammate Russell Winkler were musicians who had known each other since grade school. For them the EEG feedback *synch* training was similar to music. *Synch* training for them was play, not like a serious experiment. Their scores (telepathy and *IP team synch*) were the highest of the first eleven teams. Gurumukh reported:
> *Relative* [simultaneous alpha in IH Synch] *is like both of us nailing our alpha level at 100%. Then it's a matter of attuning — fine-tuning — micro-voltages and wave amplitudes. Experientially, once I get where we're both doing 100% alpha, then I get that he's higher or lower than I am. Then I can consciously do things like relax, deep breathe, and 'be' there and raise or lower my level. I'm not clear about what I can 'do' to do absolute* [IP team synch in phase-coherent alpha]. *I am clear that efforting, trying, or working does not work.*

Teammate Russell Winkler gave this humorous report:
> *Absolute Sync — where it is and how to get there. First, drain your mind. Then decide on a place to meet and be there. When we get together it's like perfect communion, comfortable, just exceedingly nice. It's powerful and safe. When we open our eyes we look at each other and say, 'YEP' we just both got something far-out. When we are connected we can travel together, play psychic tag, and hide and go Sikh.*

NOTES

My study of brainwave synchronization began in 1974 after my own extensive personal practice. I had seen energy patterns (auras) merge around couples who were in love, and I wanted to know if their brainwaves might also be harmonious. However, in 1979, the SRI team reported that electromagnetism (EM) could <u>not</u> be the carrier of remote viewing signals, because successful RV experiments had been completed in EM shielded rooms, and even in a submarine deep under water. (1) Physicists looking for what else might be the carrier of RV felt our EEG sync study to be "without value." On the other hand, we were looking for a connection between physiological and psychic rapport, not for a physical mechanism for RV. We found that all of us learned something important and useful through our EEG sync practice — the fundamental "<u>resonance</u>" of all beings. By establishing a steady frequency in our own brainwaves, we can resonate with our partners, or with someone far away. It is through that <u>internal EEG coherence</u> that RV information from <u>nonlocal</u> spacetime can be received more clearly. The earth itself vibrates constantly in the "Extreme-Low-Frequency" (ELF) range (7.8 – 7.4 Hz), and the alpha/theta EEG includes those frequencies. We are all resonating bodies between earth and sky. We live inside a standing wave between the surface of the earth and the edges of the ionosphere, since the ELF wavelengths are equal to the earth's circumference. (Ref. 2 and pp. 254-255) The ideas of Native Americans, — that you can be still and silent and receive information from the earth, trees, plants, directly — may have a basis in the physics of resonance.

REFERENCES

1) Tart, C.T., Puthoff, H. & Targ, R. (Eds.) (1979) *Mind at Large: Institute of Electrical and Electronic Engineers Symposia on the Nature of Extrasensory Perception.* C. NY: Praeger.
2) In 1975, we asked if groups of people in different parts of the earth could first tune-in to the earth's 7.8 Hz, and then to each other to send a randomly selected message. The message was successfully received thousands of miles away, whatever the actual "process" of transmission is finally determined to be. (See Section I.)

> *The unparalleled abilities of the human mind arise not from neurons but from the coherence of brainwaves.*
>
> --- *R. Douglas Fields, PhD.*
> --- *"Beyond the Neuron Doctrine."*
> --- In: *Scientific American Mind* **(2006)**

What Did Aquarius Electronics Mean By EEG Coherence And Phase Synchronization?

Tim Scully

The Aquarius Electronics brainwave analyzer (and subsequent Mendocino Microcomputers instruments) used zero crossing analysis to examine brainwave signals and you'll need to understand that before getting into coherence and phase synchronization.

Zero Crossing EEG Analysis

To understand zero crossing detectors, recall that the signals with which we are concerned are wavelike; they constantly vary. Once any steady (DC or direct current) component is eliminated, the signal varies up and down around zero. A zero crossing detector identifies the points at which the signal passes through zero, on its way up or down, as it must twice each cycle. The period of time between zero crossings is obviously closely related to the frequency of a monochromatic signal (one containing only one frequency component). The period between zero crossings is related to the dominant frequency in any mixture of frequencies.

This property of detecting the dominant signal is sometimes called "capture" and has both advantages and disadvantages. The advantage is that it can separate a dominant signal from rather strong competing signals (this is what makes FM radio have less static than AM radio), but the disadvantage is that information about the weaker signals is lost. A major and significant advantage of zero crossing analysis is that it is fast and well suited to real-time applications. It is also easily adaptable to varying epoch durations.

Both the circa 1971-1976 Aquarius Electronics "Brainwave Analyzer" and the later Mendocino Microcomputers "Biosystem" instruments used zero crossing detectors to classify EEG signals into frequency bins or categories.

These instruments also used peak hold circuits to capture and measure the peak amplitude of each half-cycle of EEG.

Coherence

Both the Aquarius Electronics phase-comparator and the Mendocino Microcomputers "Biosystem" are two channel systems – they analyze and compare two EEG signals. These might be one channel each from two people or they might be two EEG channels from different scalp locations on a single person's head.

In either case, the instruments define "coherence" as meaning that the two EEG signals have dominant frequencies that are similar.

In the case of the Aquarius Electronics 1510 Phase comparator, "similar" meant the two EEG signals had been sorted by the Brainwave Analyzer into the same frequency "category." If tunable brainwave analyzers were used, the width of each frequency category was adjustable.

The Mendocino Microcomputers Biosystem used software to classify EEG signals. It defined coherence as meaning that the period (and hence frequency) of the two EEG signals differed by less than 12.5% (1/8th).

Phase Synchronization

Both the Aquarius and Mendocino Microcomputers instruments require that the coherence criterion be met before examining phase angle. If the two EEG signals are coherent, then the relative timing of the two channel's zero crossings is measured to determine the phase angle.

The Aquarius Electronics 1510A Phase comparator uses a hybrid analog-digital circuit to measure the phase angle. The result of this measurement is displayed on an analog panel meter. Two concentric adjustable potentiometers allow the operator of the instrument to set a phase angle window criterion for synchronization.

The Mendocino Microcomputers Biosystem software requires the EEG signals to meet the coherence criterion and to be within + or – 45 degrees of zero phase angle. The phase angle is computed by comparing the difference in timing of the two channels' zero crossings with the period of the coherent signals.

The Extremely Low Frequencies (ELF) of the EM Spectrum

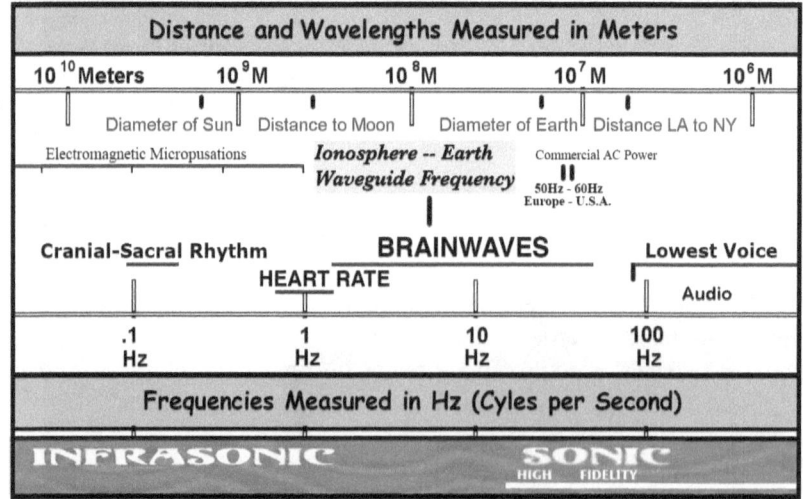

OUR INTIMATE, MAGNETIC CONNECTION TO OUR LIVING PLANET AND ITS BIO-DIVERSE LIFE

Elizabeth A. Rauscher
William Van Bise*[6]

From our joint research into geophysical and solar electromagnetic emissions, my husband William and I found fundamental common frequencies to those of the human brain and cardiovascular system. Not only are these fundamental frequencies common to the earth ionosphere system and human physiology but in fact active solar radiation and earth ionosphere activations entrain and affect our brain waves, cardiac and other systems of the human body. For example, coronal mass solar ejections of heavy particle protons interact with the upper ionosphere and produce an oscillation of 9.38 – 9.41 Hz. We identified over 50 such examples of how these frequencies affect and entrain our brainwaves. We are literally receiving a message from our sun!

One of the fundamental oscillations of the earth is the Schumann Resonance (or Ionosphere-Earth Waveguide). This frequency varies from about 7.4 – 7.8 Hz and has harmonics. Its center frequency is 7.6 Hz, which is the frequency of the Purkinje cells in the cardiac endocardium. This is also the standing wave oscillatory frequency of the iliac bifurcation where blood is pumped from the upper part of our bodies to our lower extremities. We also have found commonality and effects of our environmental detected frequencies on other species such as dogs, horses, and laboratory rats. These are just a few of the many interconnections between our environment that interact with us and perhaps suggests how we in turn relate to our environment.

One obvious correlation is the fact that we have evolved in these highly specific and fundamental fields and therefore would utilize these for our biological and perhaps psychological and emotional processes. Over 30 years of extensive research has validated how closely intertwined we are to the environment around us – not only for our physical needs but

---

*[6] William Van Bise (1931-2005) was a biomedical electrical engineer and spent many years studying signal and geophysical magnetic field detection, its monitoring and analysis. Together in the early 1980s, they started to study the dominant and very precise frequencies of natural electromagnetic, electric and magnetic field emissions from the earth, earth-ionosphere, and solar radiation system.

also to activate our basic biological processes. It is well known that changes in the solar emissions and high solar activity as well as fundamental earth vibrations affect our brain and nervous system activity. They also affect performance of athletes and other physical processes as well as our memory and conscious perceptions. Also these vibrations affect extrasensory perception experimental results (See Chapter 23). Some associations have been made to accidents and mental abnormalities as well as the changes in the number of heart attacks and strokes.

We have well documented these frequencies and their biological effects. We developed a unique non-superconducting magnetic and electromagnetic field detector, the T-1050, which has demonstrated these effects. Patents are held for this non-superconducting magnetometer, designed as a passive detector with a maximum sensitivity of 10^{-10} Gauss – or about 1000 fento Tesla. We primarily measure magnetic signatures between .01 – 300 Hz (cycles/ second). We can also measure up to 50,000 Hz using a slightly less sensitive measurement capability.

William and I have also discovered highly specific frequencies that act as precursor signatures to seismic and volcanic events. Signatures and their changes can be detected in different time frames. These are six weeks, three days, and about two hours before an impending event. Certain features of these signatures give the magnitude of the impending event. Each detector has three octagonal pickup axes. Directionality can be further determined by having multiple detection stations that allow us to identify the local region that the impending event will occur.

Some examples we have made of the many hundreds of correct predictions in terms of occurrence of seismic and volcanic events include: Detailed predictions of Mt. St. Helens in the early 1980s, the Mt. Pinatubo eruption in 1991, the Landers and Loma Prieta and many others. (1)

We have also made hundreds of measurements of ionospheric excitations due to natural volcanic activities and artificial excitations from space shuttle and rocket activity through the ionosphere. (2)

Another example of international prediction of seismicity is that of a major Greece-Turkey region earthquake in the fall of 1999. Predictions were registered with the US Library of Congress, and other international geophysical research groups including the UN Hazard Reduction Program where precursor signatures were recorded between 12 – 72 hours before the seismic event. These and previous statistically analyzed predictions had no false positives or negatives. These results had highly significant correlations between predictions and the actual occurrence of events. (3)

We are on the frontier of a wonderfully exciting global consciousness project that will use a worldwide network of detectors to correlate our intimate relationship with the earth, solar and lunar environment. I have joined with the Institute of HeartMath, who established a joint collaboration known as the Global Coherence Initiative (GCI). As part of this project HeartMath is utilizing our many years of data gathering to establish multiple detection stations throughout the planet. The purpose of these stations is to make measurements of the environmental natural frequencies and examine their influence on human cardiac and brain rhythm behaviors and other subjective impressions. This detection system that supports the GCI and includes detailed computer data acquisition and analysis from multiple stations is known as the Global Coherence Monitoring Systems ™ (GCMS). The mission of the GCMS is to monitor global environmental magnetic field changes, the manner in which these changes affect our brain and heart based intelligences, and to assess possible emotional-based collective interactions with the environmental frequencies that we are recording.

We are on a threshold of a new understanding of how our human physiology and emotions are influenced in both directions to our natural magnetic and electromagnetic pulsations from our living earth and our sun, earth, moon system. I have been profoundly interested in our relationship to our living cosmos and the multitude of species on our planet. As we further this work, we will explore our fundamental relationships between our environmental systems and each other. And I personally believe this direction of research will demonstrate and promote a more favorable, highly interconnected, synergistic relationship between our living environment and ourselves. (4, 5, 6)

REFERENCES

1) Van Bise, W.L. &. Rauscher, E.A. (1994) "Ambient electromagnetic fields as possible seismic and volcanic precursors." M. Hayakawa & Y. Fujinawa (Eds.) In: *TERRAPUB*. Tokyo, Japan: Terra Scientific Publishing Company, pp. 221-242.

2) Rauscher, E.A. & Van Bise, W.L. (1999) "The relationship of extremely low frequency and magnetic fields associated with volcanic natural activity and artificial ionospheric disturbances." M. Hayakawa (Ed.) In: *TERRAPUB*. Tokyo, Japan: Terra Scientific Publishing Company, pp. 459-487.

3) Van Bise, W.L. & Rauscher, E.A. (2003) "Detection and analysis of precursor magnetic signatures preceding the Turkey and Greece seismicity." In: *Geophysical Research Abstract*. Vol. 5, 14637.

4) www.HeartMath.org/GCMS/

5) Rauscher, E.A. *Fundamental Frequencies of the Sun, Earth, Moon System and Human EEG and EKG*. In progress for Institute of HeartMath.

6) Bentov, I. (1977) *Stalking the Wild Pendulum*. NY: E.P. Dutton.

THE ELECTRO-CHEMICAL PROCESSES
OF THE BRAIN WORK TOGETHER

Since all life is related to the energies of earth and sun, the idea that energy medicine might be more humane is obvious when we study the brain's natural electro-chemical processes together. Too many antibiotics lower the immune system; too many incompatible drugs cause negative reactions. From 1960, Robert O. Becker, MD, has studied and written about bioelectricity, and his book *The Body Electric* was a fundamental introduction to this field. In 1990, he wrote the following that should be seriously considered by the healthcare systems of the world, now that drug addiction has become such a health problem as well as a substantial component of the national economic crisis.

ELECTROTHERAPY FOR DRUG ADDICTION *[7]

The idea that electrical stimulation to the head could be beneficial in the treatment of drug addiction was derived primarily from the work of Dr Margaret Patterson, a British surgeon.... [In Hong Kong] a Chinese surgeon had shown her that auricular acupuncture... could be used in place of the usual large doses of narcotics to prevent withdrawal syndrome in postoperative drug addicts. ...

Later... Dr Patterson began using postoperative acupuncture... and patients began to consult her primarily for acupuncture treatment of drug addiction. ...

My sole contribution was to recommend that she stop using needle electrodes and instead use a flat, surface electrode of at least one square centimeter in size, applied to the skin just behind the ear....

I...examined a number of Dr Patterson's patients.... Even severely addicted patients could completely stop all drugs as soon as the electrodes were applied, and they showed no sign of withdrawal symptoms.... All of them believed that during the treatment time they had gone from being addictive to nonaddictive personality types.... The majority of her patients requires only one six-week treatment and remain drug-free thereafter....

First, it seems that very low levels of pulsed electrical current have major effects upon the highest functions of the brain. The personality alteration that follows the treatment is a most significant observation that urgently requires further study. Second, from all accounts this treatment is so superior to others for drug addiction that it certainly deserves a large-scale scientific study to determine its actual clinical utility.

---

*[7] Becker, Robert O. MD. (1990) *Cross Currents: The Perils of Electropollution: The Promise of Electromedicine.* LA, CA: Jeremy Tarcher, Inc.

CHAPTER 24 ESP AND GEOMAGNETIC ACTIVITY – with S. KRIPPNER

Michael Persinger, PhD

Michael Persinger earned his BA from the University of Wisconsin-Madison, (1967) his MA in physiological psychology from the University of Tennessee and his PhD from the University of Manitoba (1971). He organized the Behavioral Neuroscience Program at Laurentian University in Sudbury, Ontario, which became one of the first to integrate chemistry, biology and psychology. Because of the interdisciplinary nature of much of his work, Persinger insists on publishing his techniques and results within the public forum of the scientific literature.

Dr Persinger came to public attention in 1975 with his Tectonic Strain Theory (TST). Persinger argued that strain within the Earth's crust near seismic faults produces bodies of light that some interpret as glowing UFOs. This concept continues to generate much controversy. While some images of lights in the sky (reported as UFOs) do seem to correlate with subsequent earthquakes in the same area, others do not. This theory suggests more study is needed, though that would require a good method of earthquake prediction, which is not yet a solid science, though Dr Rauscher has found some magnetic anomalies that have predicted some earthquakes. During the 1980s, Dr Persinger artificially stimulated the temporal lobes of volunteers with a weak magnetic field to see if he could induce a religious state. He found that the field could generate hallucinations in the temporal lobe, based on images from popular culture. The field could also produce the sensation of "an ethereal presence in the room." This stimulated the debates about "reality," yet some insist that before <u>any</u> experience of the external world is perceived, the brain must already have the capacity to receive it.   See website: www.laurentian.ca.

DREAM ESP EXPERIMENTS AND GEOMAGNETIC ACTIVITY

Michael A. Persinger
Stanley Krippner

Determination of the mechanism by which telepathy occurs would facilitate its understanding and control. The first step to the isolation of mechanism requires the identification of some measurable variable that is systematically associated with the occurrence of telepathy. Spontaneous telepathic experiences concerning death or crises occur more frequently during days in which the global geomagnetic activity is significantly less than during the days before or after the experiences. A similar pattern has been shown for the Gurney, Myers, and Podmore (1) collection from the nineteenth century, (2) the Sidgwick collection from early in the 20th century (3, 4), and the unverified reports published in Fate magazine. (5, 6)

The systematic association between specific temporal patterns in daily average geomagnetic activity and the likelihood of a telepathic occurrence does not by itself reveal mechanism. There are at least three classes of explanations. Periods of sudden, relatively quieter geomagnetic activity facilitate telepathy by (a) producing environmental conditions that promote exchange of information between the agent and the percipient, (b) allowing normal telepathic factors already in the environment to be amplified between the agent and the percipient, and (c) evoking transient alterations in brain function such that normal telepathic factors (that do not change with geomagnetic activity) can affect the percipient's sensitized temporal lobes.

The association between geomagnetic activity and spontaneous telepathic experiences suggests the existence of a persistent factor that may serve as an empirical handle by which to study the phenomena. If this utilitarian objective is to be achieved, the geomagnetic activity pattern also should be observable in experimental cases of telepathy. This association also would support the presumption that spontaneous and experimental telepathy are indeed similar phenomena. Several studies have shown statistically significant relations between changes in daily geomagnetic activity and accuracy during remote viewing (7), the Circular Matching Abacus Test, and, more recently, both Ganzfeld sessions and restricted-choice computer games. (9)

One of the best-known examples of experimental telepathy involves the dream telepathy research inaugurated by Montague Ullman, Stanley Krippner, and Charles Honorton during the 1960s. (10-12) These studies were conducted at the Dream Laboratory of the Maimonides Medical Center in Brooklyn. To determine if the geomagnetic effect was evident in these data, the study was designed to examine three hypotheses.

1) Nights on which the strongest experimental telepathy occurred also would be nights that displayed the quietest geomagnetic activity compared with the days before and after (i.e., is the V-shape effect apparent?).

2) Cases that demonstrated weak or questionable telepathy should not demonstrate the V-shape effect.

3) Both the strongest cases of telepathy from the Maimonides studies and the most accurate cases from the spontaneous telepathic experiences from Gurney, Myers, and Podmore should demonstrate the same temporal pattern of daily geomagnetic activity (the V-shape).

PROCEDURE

Dream Telepathy Protocol

The typical procedure followed at Maimonides was for the percipient (or subject) to arrive at the laboratory in time to meet the agent—a person who would spend much of the night focusing on the contents of an art print. The percipient's task was to dream about this art print even though it would not be selected until the percipient was isolated from the agent. The percipient also would meet the two experimenters, who would explain the procedures. (On a few occasions in which possible clairvoyance was studied, the art print was selected randomly and was not removed from the sealed envelope, and no agent was used. The percipient was simply instructed to attempt to dream about the art print.)

After electrodes were attached to the percipient's head for the monitoring of brain waves and eye movements, the percipient would have no further contact with the agent until the next morning. An experimenter threw dice that, in combination with a random number table, provided a number that corresponded to a number on a sealed envelope that contained an art print. The envelope was opened once the agent reached his or her private room in a distant part of the building. This art print became the target on which the agent focused during the night. (11, 12)

The experimenters took turns monitoring the percipient's sleep. Toward the end of each period of rapid eye movement, the percipient was awakened by an experimenter by way of an intercom and described any dream content that could be recalled. These comments were tape-recorded, as was a morning interview in which the percipient associated to his or her dream recall. The interview was conducted double blind; neither the percipient nor the experimenters knew the identity of the target or the pool of art prints from which the target had been randomly selected.

The target for a given night and the dreams for the night often contained a number of striking similarities, suggesting that an anomaly (so-called telepathy) had occurred. For example, on May 23, 1966, the target was a print of a zebra painted by an unknown Indian artist. The percipient dreamed about a horse show, a horse race, and a striped tie. But it could have been the case that simply by chance any transcript of a night's dreams might have contained passages of striking similarity to any picture to which they might have been compared. (13)

To evaluate the chance hypothesis, the Maimonides team obtained judgments of similarity between the dream content and each of the other potential targets in the pool from which the actual target had been randomly selected. Typically, three judges were used who worked blind and independently from one another with materials that had been mailed to them. They had no information about which picture had been randomly selected as the target. Any extra-chance difference between targets and non-targets in their similarity to dream content was considered an apparent anomaly. The target pools typically used by the judges were duplicates that had never been handled by the agents.

Although sometimes percipients evaluated their own dreams against the target pool (before they discovered the identity of the actual target), and although some experiments required the judges to rate target-dream similarities on a 100 point scale, the only form in which data were available for all sessions was a count of judges' hits and misses. If the actual target had been ranked in the upper half of the target pool (e.g., #1, #2, or #3 in a pool of six) for similarity to the dreams and post sleep interview, the outcome was considered a hit. If the actual target had been ranked in the lower half of the pool (e.g., #4, #5, or #6 in a pool of six), the outcome was considered a miss. The median score of the three judges was selected to determine hits and misses.

For the purposes of this study, the ranks were divided into four categories. A "high hit" would be a rank in the top quartile (e.g., #1 or #2 in a pool of eight; # I in a pool of six); a "low hit" would be a rank in the second quartile (e.g., #3 or #4 in a pool of eight; #2 or #3 in a pool of six). A "high miss" would be a rank in the third quartile (e.g., #5 or #6 in a pool of eight; #4 or #5 in a pool of six); a "low miss" would be a rank in the fourth quartile (#7 or #8 in a pool of eight; #6 in a pool of six). In other words, these four groups represented judges' ranks of successive order from strongest hits to strongest misses.

The data from the first night each subject spent at the Maimonides Laboratory were utilized, and the data from any other nights were discarded. The rationale was quite simple: Some subjects spent only one night at Maimonides; to use the second or third night would have resulted in a smaller pool. If the last night had been utilized, there may well have been a built-in difference between subjects unfamiliar with the procedures (those spending only one night in the laboratory) and those quite familiar with laboratory procedures (those spending several nights). On the basis of this decision, 62 experimental nights were available for analysis—18 "high hits," 29 "low hits," 7 "high misses," and 8 "low misses." The 62 cases represent the total collection of subjects seen between 1964 and 1969 at Maimonides.

GEOMAGNETIC DATA AND ANALYSES

The daily average aa (antipodal) index (14) was selected as the measure of global or planetary geomagnetic activity. The aa index is the oldest continuous geomagnetic index (started in the year 1868) and was used as the measure of global geomagnetic activity for the Gurney, Myers, and Podmore (1886) cases that occurred between 1868 and 1886. (2) By using this index, direct comparisons could be made between the experimental cases from the Maimonides dream telepathy studies and the spontaneous telepathic experiences from *Phantasms of the Living*.

Although the aa values are based on data from only two stations (one in each of the hemispheres), the daily aa index is highly correlated (.95) with other, more well known daily global measures that utilize the magnetic activity from several geomagnetic observatories. The daily values correspond to the mean amplitude (in gammas or nanoTeslas, nT) of the displacement from a standardized baseline. Average daily aa values are derived from the eight 3-hour values (smallest temporal increment). The average daily value (the one used in our analyses) is considered a good indication of planetary activity, as defined by its near-continuous distribution. (15) Although local variations in the amplitude of geomagnetic activity do occur, the average daily temporal pattern of the changes in amplitude are relatively similar everywhere. The only exception to this statement occurs in areas that are subject to transient geomagnetic anomalies during geomagnetic storms in which the effects of stronger static components also can emerge.

Daily average aa values for the northern hemisphere were collected for each of the 7 days before, each of the 7 days after, and on the day each session began. Because most of the dreaming occurred during the early morning of the next day, it was selected as the key day. To be commensurate with previous studies that involved spontaneous experiences, (2, 5, 6) this twenty-four-hour period was selected as the key day instead of the (evening of the) day before, when the session was started. Mean monthly aa values for months in which the experiences occurred were also listed.

Figure 3.1

Mean Daily Average Values in Dream Telepathy Study

Maimonides Study

● High Hits (n= 18)   ○ Low Hits (n = 29)

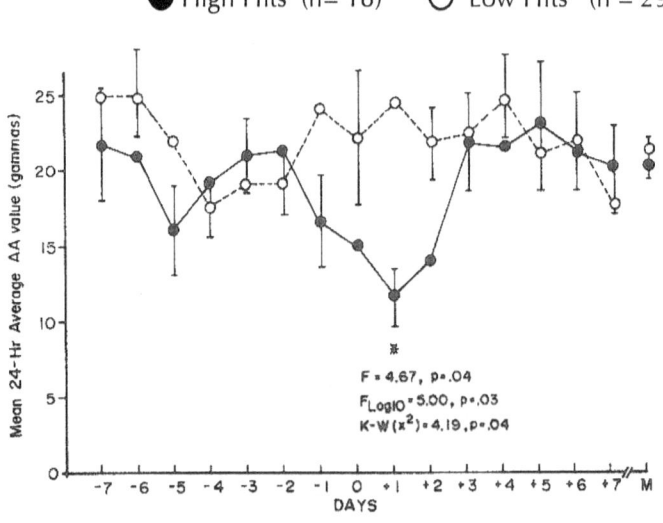

Mean average daily aa values (in gammas) for the days before (−), days after (+), and days of the beginning of the sessions for the high-hit (closed circles) and low-hit (open circles) dream telepathy groups. Vertical bars indicate standard errors (±1) of the means. M refers to the mean aa values for the months in which the experiences occurred.

We selected SPSSX MANOVA (multivariate analysis of variance) as the primary statistical procedure because of the statistically significant intercorrelation of geomagnetic activity levels during any 2 to 3 successive days. The basic design was daily geomagnetic activity by group, that is, the log (base of 10) of the daily aa values for 7 days (key day ±3 days) and the two groups (strong cases of telepathy versus the reference cases). Log values were used to reduce the contribution from days that contained extreme outlier values. (This procedure attenuated the problem within acceptable levels as defined by the lack of statistical significance displayed by the multivariate test for homogeneity of the dispersion matrices.) The total of 7 days (key day ±3 days) of geomagnetic activity was selected before the study began to be comparable and compatible with the analyses of spontaneous telepathic experiences. (2, 5, 6)

To test the first hypothesis, MANOVA was completed for the daily geomagnetic values (that served operationally as repeated measures) and two independent variables: groups (high-hit versus low-hit groups) and gender (male versus female). The latter variable was included because the possible differential sensitivity of females has been inferred from the markedly enhanced incidence of female percipients in spontaneous cases. (16)

The numbers of subjects for each group were high hit-male, 12; high hit-female, 6; low hit-male, 20; low hit-female, 9. Because of the small sample size for each of the other two categories (7 for high miss and 8 for low miss) and our reluctance to combine them, these cases were not included in this analysis. (Also, the issue of psi missing was considered to be an additional problem that would be best addressed elsewhere.) To test the second hypothesis, paired (correlated) t tests were completed between the geomagnetic activity for the key day and each of the other 6 days for the strongest telepathic cases (high hits) and weaker cases (low hits) separately.

To test the third hypothesis, the Gurney, Myers, and Podmore database (2) was combined with the Maimonides data. To specifically check the similarity in geomagnetic activity (the V-shape) around the days on which telepathy occurred, a MANOV A was completed as a function of 7 days of geomagnetic activity (key day ± 3 days) and the two databases: the strongest Maimonides cases ($n = 18$) versus the primary spontaneous cases ($n = 78$). To minimize the possible weighting from the larger number of cases in the latter group, we decided to compare the experimental cases with a subset of the spontaneous cases that contained a comparable number of subjects. By requesting all of the records that involved the dream modality (which was considered optimal in light of the Maimonides experiments) for one decade (1877 through 1886), a total of 22 cases was obtained. All analyses were completed using SPSSX software on a VAX computer.

RESULTS

Verification of Hypotheses

A simple plot of the average daily aa values for the 7 days before, the days of, and the 7 days after the beginning of the sessions for the high hit (11 = 18) and low hit (11 = 29) groups is shown in Figure 3.1. The only statistically significant difference between the two groups occurred on the day after the beginning of the session. This day (called the key day for all subsequent analyses) included the late evening and early morning hours during which time the dreaming and telepathic experiences occurred. The statistical significance of the quieter geomagnetic activity during the 24-hour period in which the strongest telepathy occurred was evident for the absolute aa values (F[1, 45] = 4.67, p = .04) (even with the statistically significant difference in group variances [Bartlett-Box = 21.29, p < .001]) and the log base 10 transformations (F[1, 45] = 5.00, p = .03) that eliminated the statistically significant difference in group variances; a nonparametric test (Kruskal–Wallis) also demonstrated the significant effect (c^2 = 4.19, p = .04).

The first MANOVA according to the two groups with different accuracy of dream telepathy (high hit versus low hit), gender, and the seven successive days of (log base 10) geomagnetic activity (key day ±3 days) did not reveal statistically significant group (F[1,43] = 1.19, p = .28), gender (F[1,43] = 0.20, p = .66), or group by gender (F[1,43], = 0.14, p = .71) interaction effects. Although there were no statistically significant interactions between gender and the geomagnetic activity on the different days during, before, and after the dreams, and gender (F[6,258] = 0.15, p = .99) or geomagnetic activity by gender by group (F[6,258] = .012, p = .99), there was a significant daily geomagnetic activity by group interaction (F[6,258] = 2.97, p = .008). The multivariate test for homogeneity of dispersion matrices was not significant (p >.05). (The geomagnetic activity by group interaction for the absolute aa values also was statistically significant (F[6,258] = 2.21, p = .04), even though the dispersion matrices were not homogeneous.)

As can be seen in Figure 3.2A, the source of the interaction was due primarily to the lower geomagnetic activity on the nights of the dreams that contained the greatest accuracy (high hit: strongest telepathy) compared with the nights of the dreams that contained less accuracy (low hit: weaker telepathy). Whereas the geomagnetic activity on the nights of the strong telepathic cases was significantly less (paired t[17] = 4.55, p = .00 1) than the monthly average of the months in which the dreams occurred, the geomagnetic activity on the nights of the weaker telepathy dreams was not significantly different from the monthly geomagnetic activity (paired t[28] = 1.49, p = .07).

These results supported hypothesis 1, which predicted that the geomagnetic activity should be significantly lower during 24-hour periods in which dream telepathy was strongest, as defined by the greater accuracy of target material. Paired t tests between the log base 10 of the aa values on the key day and for each of the other 6 days demonstrated statistically significant differences between the key day and 3 days before (t[17] = 3.14, p = .003), 2 days before (1[17] = 2.60, p = .009), and 3 days after (t[17] = 3.58, p =.001) for the high hit group only. There were no significant differences between the geomagnetic activity on the key day and each of the other 6 days for the group of telepathic dreams that were less accurate. These results supported hypothesis 2.

Figure 3.2

Log of Mean Daily Values for 24-Hour Periods in Dream Telepathy Study

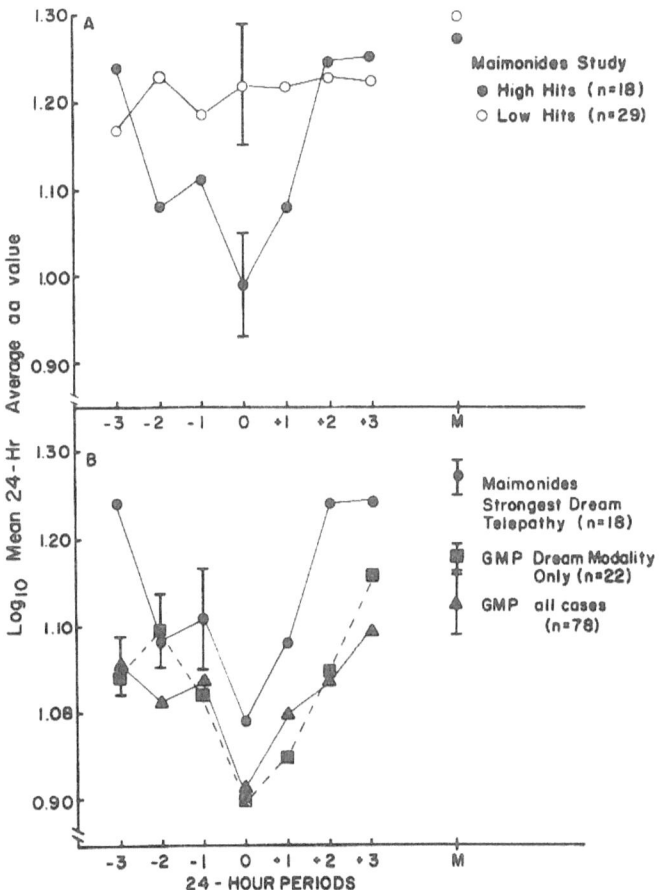

Log (base 10) of the mean daily aa values for the 24-hour periods during, before (—), and after (+) the key days (0) when (A) strong and weaker experimental telepathic dreams occurred during the Maimonides Series, and (B) spontaneous telepathic experiences (Gurney, Myers, & Podmore, 1886) occurred. M refers to the means of the monthly aa averages. Vertical bars indicate standard error of the mean.

The MANOVA between the two groups of data revealed that the strongest (high hit) telepathic cases ($n = 18$) from the Maimonides study and the spontaneous cases ($n = 78$) demonstrated that the log base 10 of the average geomagnetic activity (sec Figure 3.2B) was significantly lower during the week of the spontaneous cases (that occurred between 1868 and 1886) relative to the experimental cases (F[1, 94] = 5. 18, p = .025). Although there were no statistically significant days by group interaction (F[6,564] = 0.76, p = .06), there was a highly significant difference between the geomagnetic activity across the 7 days, regardless of group factors (F[6,564] = 4.29, p = .0003). Because paired t tests between the geomagnetic activity on the completed for the Maimonides strongest telepathy cases, paired t tests (all 77 df) were completed for the Gurney, Myers, and Podmore data. The geomagnetic activity on the key days was significantly lower than all of the other days (± 3 days) before or after (t values ranged from 2.41 to 4.29). In addition, the geomagnetic activity on the day of the spontaneous experiences was significantly lower than the average values for months in which they occurred (t[77] = 7.18, p <.001).

MANOVA with the Maimonides data and the 22 cases of *dream modality only* from the spontaneous cases (see Figure 3.2B) also showed a significant difference in geomagnetic activity between the days during, before, or after the experiences (F[6,228] = 4.00, p = .0008). Again, there was no significant interaction between the daily geomagnetic activity and the two groups of data (F[6,228] = 0.61, p = .72). The average geomagnetic activity for the week of the Gurney, Myers, and Podmore cases (dream modality only) also was lower than the week in which the contemporary cases occurred (F[1, 38] = 3.80, p = .059). The absence of significant interactions thus supported hypothesis 3 that the two groups should show (statistically) identical temporal patterns for mean daily geomagnetic activity on the days of, before, and after the experiences.

FURTHER EXPLORATION AND ANALYSIS

One obvious question that emerged from this research is, what is more important? (a) The *absolute values* of the geomagnetic activity (as defined by aa values), or (b) the *relative change* in geomagnetic activity on the day of the telepathic experience? To answer this question, T-score values (by definition a mean of 50 and standard deviation of 10) were computed for the non-transformed (i.e., absolute) aa values for each of the 7 days for each case for both sets of data. The T score for the aa values for each day for each case was calculated first by subtracting the value for that day from the mean of the scores for all 7 days and then dividing this value by the standard deviation for the 7 days. After multiplying this value (effectively the scores' standard deviation) by 10 and adding it to 50, the T score was obtained. Although outliers could still affect the analyses, the amplitude would be minimal because they would be expressed as standard deviations with respect to the mean of the week in which the experience occurred.

The T score allowed analysis of the relative change in geomagnetic activity on the key day and for each of the other days with respect to the mean value for the week. If the relative decrease in geomagnetic activity on the day of the telepathic experience was more critical than the absolute value of the geomagnetic activity (in aa units), then the *interaction* (even though the "repeated" measure would be invariant [i.e., singular variance–covariance matrix for each cell]) between the high-hit group (strongest telepathy) and the low-hit group (weaker telepathy) should be even more significant than determined in the previous analysis. MANOVA between the T scores of the aa values for the key day ± 3 days for the two Maimonides groups demonstrated no statistically significant day by group interactions ($F[6, 270] = 1.51$, $p = .17$). These results strongly suggested that the *absolute value* of the geomagnetic activity was more critical than the relative change of activity during the weeks of the dreams.

Comparison of the monthly aa values (log base 10) between the Gurney, Myers, and Podmore data and the 18 cases of the strongest experimental dream telepathy results indicated that the geomagnetic activity during the months of the 22 *dream modality cases* (years 1877 to 1886) was less than that during the months of the Maimonides studies ($F[1, 38] = 14.19$, $p < .001$). There was no statistically significant difference, however, between the geomagnetic activity during the 24-hour intervals of experimental and spontaneous telepathic experiences ($F[1, 38] = 1.03$, $p = .32$). The lack of a significant difference in geomagnetic activity on the days of the experiences for the two groups (even though monthly values differed) also supports the hypothesis that the *absolute amplitude of geomagnetic activity* rather than the relative change is the critical feature for facilitating telepathic experiences.

DISCUSSION

The results of this study indicate that the 24-hour periods during which experimental telepathic dreams were most accurate (strongest) were associated with significantly quieter planetary geomagnetic activity compared ± 3, 24-hour periods before and after. The V–shaped pattern of geomagnetic activity over days (with the trough occurring on the night of the telepathic dreams) was not observed in cases that were considered to be weaker indications of dream telepathy as defined by an objective ranking procedure. These results support the hypothesis that quieter periods of magnetic activity facilitate the occurrence of experimental telepathic experiences.

The pattern of the geomagnetic activity for the week (key day ± 3) of the strongest cases of dream telepathy also was identical (i.e., not statistically distinguishable) from the V–shaped pattern in geomagnetic activity that was observed in the spontaneous telepathic experiences from almost a century ago. This similarity suggests that some geomagnetic factor may influence the occurrence of both experimental and spontaneous telepathic experiences in a similar manner. Comparable V-shaped relations have been observed with other collections of spontaneous telepathic experiences. (5)

Persistence of a geomagnetic factor in telepathic experiences has theoretical and practical implications. First, the similarity of geomagnetic activity patterns around the days of both experimental and spontaneous telepathic experiences suggests that the two classes of phenomena are indeed related. Second, the occurrence of the geomagnetic V-shaped effect, assuming the sample size is appropriate, might be used as an indicator of the occurrence of telepathy within novel experimental designs. Significant differences within any experimental context, despite appropriate controls and valid statistical treatments, may not necessarily involve *traditional* telepathic processes. If the geomagnetic factor continues to be evident with well-established databases of both experimental and spontaneous telepathic cases, then its absence may serve as an indicator of the presence of some other factor that might be generating quasi-psi. Consequently, confusion about telepathy and argumentation between experimenters who use different procedures might be attenuated.

A preliminary answer to the question of whether or not the absolute level of geomagnetic activity rather than a relative decrease in geomagnetic activity is the critical factor was obtained in this study. When T-score transformations of the geomagnetic activity for each case were computed for each day with respect to its standard deviation from the week of activity, the differences between the strongest and the weaker experimental cases were not significant. In addition, there was no significant difference between the geomagnetic activity during the 24-hour periods of experiences for either the spontaneous telepathic experiences or the experimental dream reports, despite the elevated mean monthly aa values in the latter cases.

This pattern suggests that aa values of about 10 gammas (95% confidence interval of 8 to 13 gammas) are highly associated with the occurrence of a classic telepathic experience. If the aa values approach 25 gammas or more 95% confidence interval of 18 to 34 gammas), the mean value for the low-hit dream telepathy group, an (accurate) telepathic experience is less likely to occur. The reliability of the approximately 10 aa unit value is supported by the spontaneous cases from Gurney, Myers, and Podmore. The mean of the aa values for the 24-hour periods in which all verified experiences occurred (n = 78) was 10 gammas (95% confidence interval of 9 to 12 gammas), whereas the mean aa value for dream-only experiences was 12 gammas (confidence interval of 8 to 16 gammas). It is interesting that the mean aa values for the 24-hour period in which the 133 unverified telepathic experiences from *Fate* occurred was 14 gammas, (5) a value that is expected to be inflated because of poorer controls during case collection. For comparison, the means of the aa values for the days before the occurrence of these experiences ranged between 24 and 26 gammas.

The tendency for both spontaneous and experimental telepathic experiences to occur during the nights of 24-hour periods in which the mean aa amplitudes were about 10 gammas may facilitate the isolation of mechanism. It is not clear whether the optimal condition is the simple occurrence of geomagnetic activity within the range of 10 gammas, regardless of activity during the previous 3 days or whether the optimal condition occurs when there is a sudden change from some previous higher activity (aa 25 or greater) to within the range of 10 gammas within a 24-hour period. Both the spontaneous cases and the experiential telepathy data indicated that the actual absolute decrease in average daily geomagnetic activity was about 10 to 15 gammas.

The specification of this range of sudden decrease (by 10 to 15 gammas) in geomagnetic activity is important for precise isolation of mechanism. If, for example, some extremely low frequency magnetic field factor (17) is involved with the transmission of information, then its occurrence should be maximally correlated with the 24-hour periods in which the aa values are within the 10-unit range or those days in which the aa values approach 10 after a sudden decrease in activity. Whereas the first option would suggest a steady-state telepathic factor that is linearly related to the presence and duration of geomagnetic activity within the optimal range, the second option argues strongly in favor of a derivative solution that requires the optimal rate of change in magnetic activity within a specific temporal interval.

If, on the other hand, one assumes that the geomagnetic factor is coupled exclusively with its effect on the *sensitivity of the brains* of the people involved in the experience (agent or percipient, depending on the model), then the mechanism would involve some important neuroelectrical or neurohormonal alteration that is sensitive to (a) average daily magnetic activity in the range of 10 gammas or (b) a decrease in average daily geomagnetic activity by about 15 gammas to a value of about 10 gammas. That the human brain may be sensitive to subtle geomagnetic activity within this order of magnitude has been discussed previously. (5, 18)

A critique of the geomagnetic effect in traditional telepathic experiences has been developed by Hubbard and May. (19) They have attempted to indict the validity of these studies by implying that (a) there is no strong evidence for the biological effectiveness of either extremely low frequency or ultralow frequency magnetic fields and (b) the aa indices (and indeed magnetic indices in general) are not adequate indicators of geomagnetic activity for parapsychological studies. Although provocative and certainly worthy of consideration, their arguments are neither accurate nor relevant to this study.

First, there are both strong and consistent data that time-varying magnetic fields within the geomagnetic range affect living systems. (20, 21) Changes in specific behaviors (e.g., associated with circadian variations) and particular chemical pathways (e.g., indolamines) have been systematically associated with near-natural low-frequency magnetic field exposures. The variability and inconsistency that exist within the scientific literature are in large part associated with inappropriate conceptual aggregation of studies that involve different frequencies, intensities, and systems. To argue that effects of time-varying magnetic fields on living systems are inconsistent (and hence questionable) is equivalent to dismissing pharmacological effects because different drugs produce different responses. In addition, if the controversial nature of an effect was considered a criterion for its rejection, the subject matter of parapsychology would be totally excluded.

Hubbard's and May's second major argument involves the alleged decrease in coherence between mean daily geomagnetic activity in different localities. Hubbard and May fail to specify how much discoherence actually occurs and within what latitudinal boundaries. Extreme coherence in geomagnetic activity between stations is important for geophysical modeling. However, inter-correlations of even .80 between the average daily geomagnetic activity near all stations within the continental United States, for example, would be sufficient to demonstrate the geomagnetic field effect, considering the mean decrease of 10 to 15 gammas from a baseline of about 20 to 25 gammas (i.e., about 50% of the amplitude) that is associated with days of strong telepathic experiences. Indeed, even a random selection of two distant stations, such as between Fredericksburg, Virginia, and Anchorage, Alaska, during the last 6 months of 1987 demonstrates a Pearson correlation coefficient of .85 and a Spearman correlation of .92 between the average daily activity (A index) for the two stations. Even weaker interspatial correlations of geomagnetic activity would not necessarily contest the validity of the phenomenon if the shared variance of geomagnetic activity between loci was the same source with which telepathic experiences were associated.

From an operational perspective, technical discussion concerning the geomagnetic indices with respect to psi phenomena is analogous to an obsession with decimal points when the background fluctuations in the phenomenon involve a large range of integers. Compared with measures of telepathic experiences, the numerical reliability between geomagnetic indices is extremely robust. The arguments concerning precision may be discipline-specific (22) and of questionable relevance to the understanding of psi mechanisms. At most, the discrepancies noted by Bubenik and Fraser-Smith (15) as reported by Hubbard and May (19) would reduce the strength of the geomagnetic effect in telepathic experiences rather than artifactually evoke it.

Despite these interesting questions concerning the degree of variability in the spatial homogeneity of geomagnetic activity, Hubbard's and May's argument (19) is not relevant to this study. Because all the Maimonides data were collected in the same place, the problem of different geomagnetic measures at different locations has questionable significance. Similarly, most of the cases for the Gurney, Myers, and Podmore collection occurred within 100 km (the reason our analysis originally was performed) of the sensor that was used for the calculation of the aa values and during a period when human-caused electromagnetic noise would have been much lower than today. The fact that the geomagnetic pattern was similar in both shape and amplitude in two clusters of telepathic experiences that were separated by several thousands of kilometers and by a century challenges the validity of the over-concern with geomagnetic indices.

The issue of cultural electromagnetic signals within the intensity and frequency range of geomagnetic activity, an important component of Hubbard's and May's approach, (19) may be useful for the isolation of the mechanism by which the geomagnetic effect occurs. They postulated that a geomagnetic-telepathic effect could be negated because signals generated by a direct-current train system (BART) within the San Francisco Bay Area can exceed background geomagnetic activity by an order of 1 to 3, depending on proximity to the system. (23, 24) What Hubbard and May did not state is that (a) the characteristics of these transient signals are markedly different in both form and temporal structure from those associated with geomagnetic storms, and (b) these humanly manufactured signals are effectively absent during the early-morning hours (0100 to 0500 local time) when traditional spontaneous psi experiences tend to occur most frequently. Indeed, the presence of human-made electromagnetic signals and determination of the degree of their similarity to natural patterns may allow innovative approaches to the study of how both classes of stimuli affect the occurrence (suppression or facilitation) of traditional telepathic experiences.

The importance of the absolute value of the geomagnetic activity (or its relative, sudden decrease) as a facilitator of spontaneous or experimental telepathic experiences would argue strongly in favor of on-site measurement as suggested by Hubbard and May. Careful analysis of these records might isolate optimal parameters in the temporal structure of local field variations. Although the daily average geomagnetic measures over months between stations are highly correlated, latitude-specific local hourly variations (especially during solar quiet periods), local human-caused electromagnetic noise, and natural anomalies (e.g., buried ore deposits) are sufficient to affect the local expression of global geomagnetic activity. On-site monitoring and consequent correlation with indices of planetary activity may further reveal the local signatures that modulate the hourly variations in the occurrence and accuracy of telepathic experiences.

REFERENCES AND NOTES

1) Gurney, E., Myers, F.W.H., Podmore, F. (1886) *Phantasms of the Living* (2 vols.). London: Tribner.
2) Persinger, M.A. (1987) "Spontaneous telepathic experiences from Phantasms of the Living and low global geomagnetic activity." In: *Journal of the American Society for Psychical Research* 1987;81:23-36.
3) Sidgwick, H. (Mrs. E.M.). (1922) "Phantasms of the living." In: *Proceedings of the Society for Psychical Research* 1922; 33: 23-429.
4) Arango, M.A. (1988) *Spontaneous Crisis-Evoked Telepathic Phenomena from the Sidgwick Collection of 1922 and Low Global Geomagnetic Activity*. Ontario, Canada: Laurentian University. Unpublished fourth-year thesis.
5) Persinger, M.A. & Schaut, G.B. (1988) "Geomagnetic factors in subjective telepathic, precognitive, and postmortem experiences." In: *Journal of the American Society for Psychical Research* 1988; 82: 217-235.
6) Schaut, G.B. & Persinger, M.A. (1985) "Subjective telepathic experiences, geomagnetic activity and the ELF hypothesis. Part 1. Data analyses." In: *Psi Research* 1985;4(1):4-20.
7) Adams, M.H. (1986) "Persistent temporal relationship of ganzfeld results to geomagnetic activity, appropriateness of using standard geomagnetic indices." In: *Proceedings of Presented Papers: The 29th Annual Convention of the Parapsychological Association* 1986: 471-485.
8) Tart, C.T. (1988) "Geomagnetic effects on GESP: Two studies." In: *Journal of the American Society for Psychical Research* 1988; 82: 193-216.
9) Haraldsson, E. & Gissurarson, L.R. (1987) "Does geomagnetic activity affect extrasensory perception?" In: *Personality and Individual Differences* 1987;8:745-747.
10) Ullman, M. (1987) "Telepathy and dreams." In: *Experimental Medicine and Surgery*. 1969; 27: 19-38.
11) Ullman, M. & Krippner, S. (1970) *Dream Studies and Telepathy: An Experimental Approach* (Parapsychological Monographs No. 12). NY: Parapsychology Foundation.
12) Ullman, M. & Krippner, S. (1978) "Experimental dream studies." In: Ebon, M. (Ed.) *The Signet Handbook of Parapsychology*. NY: New American Library; 1978:409-422.
13) Child, I.L. (1985) "Psychology and anomalous observations: The question of ESP in dreams." In: *American Psychologist* 1985; 40: 1219-1230.
14) Mayaud, P.N. (1973) "A hundred-year series of geomagnetic data 1868-1967." In: *IAGA Bulletin* 1973; 33. Dream ESP Experiments.

15) Bubenik, D.M. & Fraser-Smith, A.C. (1977) "Evidence for strong artificial components in the equivalent linear amplitude geomagnetic indices." In: *Journal of Geophysical Research* 1977:82: 2875-2878.
16) Persinger, M.A. (1974) *The Paranormal* (2 vols.). NY: MSS Information.
17) Matsushita, S. & Campbell, W.H. (Eds.) (1967) *Physics of Geomagnetic Phenomena* (2 vols.) NY: Academic Press.
18) Becker, R.O. & Selden, G. (1985) *The Body Electric: Electromagnetism and the Foundation of Life.* NY: William Morrow.
19) Hubbard, G.S. & May, E.C. (1986) "Aspects of measurement and application of geomagnetic indices and extremely low frequency electromagnetic radiation for use in parapsychology." In: *Proceedings of Presented Papers: The 29th Annual Convention of the Parapsychological Association* 1986; 519-535.
20) Ahlborn, A., Albert, E.N., Fraser-Smith, A.C., Grodzinsky, A.I., Marron, M.T., Martin, A.O., Persinger, M.A., Shelanski, M.L., Wolpow, E.R. (1987) *Biological Effects of Power Line Fields: New York State Power Lines Project Scientific Advisory Panel Final Report.* Albany: New York State Department of Health.
21) Persinger, M.A. (1988) "Increased geomagnetic activity and the occurrence of bereavement hallucinations: Evidence for melatonin-mediated micro-seizuring in the temporal lobe?" In: *Neuroscience Letters* 1988; 88: 271-274.
22) For examples, see Mayaud, P.N. (1980) *Derivation, Meaning and Use of Geomagnetic Indices* (Geophysical Monograph 22). Washington, DC: American Geophysical Union.
23) Fraser-Smith, A.C. & Coates, D.B. (1978) "Large amplitude ULF electromagnetic fields from BART." In: *Radio Science* 1978; 13: 661-668.
24) Ho, A.M.H., Fraser-Smith, A.C., Villard, O.G., Jr. (1979) "Large-amplitude ULF magnetic fields produced by a rapid transit system: Close-range measurements." In: *Radio Science* 1979: 14: 1011-1015.

> *Peter Bancel and I have seen that the structure in the Global Consciousness Project (GCP) data correlates with global events, but the details are instructive. Data collected around the times of major earthquakes (Richter magnitude 6 or greater) show anomalous effects only when these quakes occur in populated areas. No structure is found if they occur in the oceans, implying that the effects must be linked to human consciousness. What is even more intriguing is that changes in our data begin some hours prior to the main temblor. This suggests some form of reverse causation, or more boldly put, precognition.*
>
> *--- Roger Nelson*

CHAPTER 25   SONIC RESONANCE — with J. ALTER

Cheri Quincy, DO

Cheri Quincy has been practicing internal medicine for over thirty years. She received her BA from the University of Pacific in Liberal Arts (1967), took pre-medical classes at UC, Berkeley, and graduated in 1976 from the Texas College of Osteopathic Medicine (TCOM). She completed 4 post-graduate years, both as Residency in Internal Medicine and a Fellowship in Geriatrics and Aging. She served as Associate Professor of Medicine at NTS TCOM for 5 years, and was a founder of one of the first preventive health curricula for medical students in 1982. She left to develop a more eclectic practice that was more responsive to the many different kinds of patients seeking a path to health. She has lectured to professional groups across the country, and presented talks on shamanism, death, dying, reincarnation, menopause, and human sensory systems. She has been interviewed by New Dimensions Radio, KQED in SF, and WBAI Radio in NY (*The Positive Mind*). She organized seminars on aging, death and dying, and life transitions.

Dr Quincy and her husband Dr Joel Alter moved to CA in 1986. They practiced together at the Santa Rosa Medical Group until he retired. They facilitated behavioral change and found many alternative methods of healing (including sound) that have been used for hundreds of years in other cultures.

In 2006, Dr Isaac Eliaz invited her to be the Medical Director of the Amitabha Medical Clinic and Healing Center in Sebastopol, CA. She is a specialist in internal medicine, and her practice includes deep medical evaluation and a broadly integrative treatment of health problems ranging from hormone issues (menopause), to fibromyalgia, IBS, Parkinson's, and cancer.

http://www.dreliaz.com/ - information@amitabhaclinic.com

THE INTERACTION OF SONIC RESONANCE WITH THE DYNAMICS OF CEREBRAL SPINAL FLUID RELATIVE TO FOCUS OF ATTENTION AND ALTERNATE STATES

Cheri Quincy, DO
Joel Alter, DO

The drum, rattle, gong, bell, and other instruments have played a large role, through the ages, in the healing of humans. Shamans, medicine men or women, healers, used these instruments as sonic drivers to heal their patients. We propose that the dynamic responses to sonic (mechanical) resonances by the structures of the cranium, brain, and cerebrospinal fluid have a significant and profound effect on individual states of consciousness and our ability to "tune" or focus attention.

The predictable and reproducible subjective effects of some sounds may be mediated through their mechanical, vibratory and/or resonant actions on the structures of the human body. In particular, certain states of consciousness may be elicited or "permitted," according to the resonant qualities of the cranial bones, and spine, and the vibrations of the intracranial membranes.

Since the cranial bones have been noted to be in a state of oscillation with a period of 6-12 cycles/minute, the interaction between this pulsatile, low pressure, irregularly shaped elastic balloon, within a flexible boney chamber, and external mechanical/sonic vibratory stimuli must be complex. The resulting effects of intersecting waves depend on many factors which include angle of interaction, medium, energy, relative wave lengths, time, etc., but account for phenomena from holography to polarized lenses and rainbows.

What then happens when sonic driving (a drum) is applied to the human skeletal structure and brain and how can these effects be explained: Furthermore, does the state of the body's structure (e.g., inflexibility, old injuries, asymmetries) impede or redirect this process? Can we purposely select or encourage the development of certain "mental" states by altering the flexibility of the craniosacral mechanism?

The cranial concept was first described by Dr William Garner Southerland (1873-1954), an osteopathic physician. He observed and studied the bones of the skull. The edges of the bones were beveled or designed like hinges and pivots, indicating to him that they were formed to permit slight movement. This led to the observation of five physiological phenomena:

1. The inherent motility of the brain and spinal cord.
2. The Auctuacion (tidal flow of movement) of the cerebrospinal fluid.
3. The mobility of the reciprocal tension membrane (dura mater) within the skull and spine.
4. The articular mobility of the cranial bones.
5. The involuntary mobility of the sacrum between the ilia.

It is the harmonious function of all of these units of the Primary Respiratory mechanism which can be characterized as system in motion that maintains health. The craniosacral system is characterized by rhythmic, mobile activity which persists through life. The craniosacral motion occurs in man, other primates, canines, felines and, probably, all other vertebrates. It is distinctly different from the physiological motions which are related to breathing and cardiovascular activity. It may be the underlying mechanism related to the Traube-Herring phenomenon, which has been observed but not yet adequately explained. Craniosacral rhythmic motion can be palpated most readily on the head and, with practice, it can be preceived anywhere on the body.

The normal rate of craniosacral rhythm in humans is between 6 and 12 cycles/minute. (This is not to be confused with alpha rhythm from the brain, which is between 8 and 12 cycles per second.) Calculations of the range of physical displacement occurring in the cranial bones predict that it is on the order of a few microns. This is in agreement with dial gauge measurements which, with the tips of the gauge tightly compressed against the parietal bones, yield values of 10 to 25 microns side displacement of these bones.

There remains a considerable gap between values of the free motion of the cranium that physicians feel during a cranial examination for mobility and those of the constrained motion measured by a mechanical dial gauge. The ratio of the two sets of values is about a hundred to one and this is explained by the special morphology of the cranial bones. The skull bones are joined by soft-tissue sutures and the architecture of the comples is such that a small angular motion of each of the bones, which are subjected to internal pressure changes, yields a side displacement component, the integral of which is noticeable and measurable. This is what the physician feels as motion of the cranium and its rhythmicity—the cranial rhythm. The normal amplitude, identified at the parietal bone, may reach I to 1.5 mm.

Changes in frequency have been noted to correlate with psychiatric syndromes and normalization with improvement or cure. Various practitioners have reported changes in speed and amplitude with varying states of physical and mental health. For example, hyperkinetic children have been observed to have abnormally rapid craniosacral rhythmic rates, as have patients suffering from acute illnesses and fever. Moribund and brain-damaged patients will often have abnormally low rates. As the clinical condition improves, the rhythmic rates move toward the normal range. Under normal circumstances, the rate of the craniosacral motion is quite stable. It does not fluctuate with cardiovascular or respiratory rates (e.g., in response to exercise).

Under reasonably normal circumstances, the rhythmic activity appears at the sacrum as a gentle rocking motion about a transverse axis located approximately one inch anterior to the second sacral segment. The rocking motion correlates rhythmically to a broadening and narrowing of the transverse dimension of the head. As the head widens, the sacral apex moves in an anterior direction. This phase of motion is referred to as flexion of the craniosacral system. The counterpart of flexion is extension. During the extension phase, the head narrows in its transverse dimension. The sacral base moves anteriorly while the sacral apex moves posteriorly.

During the flexion phase of the craniosacral motion cycle, the whole body internally rotates and broadens. During the extension phase, the body rotates internally and seems to narrow slightly. A complete cycle of the craniosacral rhythmic motion is composed of one flexion and one extension phase. A low amplitude of craniosacral rhythm indicates a low level of vitality in the patient; that is, the patient's resistance is low and hence the susceptibility to disease is high. In fact, lack of symmetry in the craniosacral rhythmic motion throughout the body is an indicator, which can be used to localize pathological problems. The craniosacral system provides the "internal milieu" for the development, growth, and functional efficiency of the brain and spinal cord from the time of embryonic formation until death.

Since men/women first drummed or sang or chanted together, we have been aware of the myriad effects of sound upon the human psyche. But before melody and harmony existed, man first paid attention to rhythm. Without hearing, Beethoven composed several symphonies and, reportedly, sank his teeth into the piano to "hear" his music. Bone conduction of sound is well described in medicine. The impact of sound as rhythm has long been appreciated in such diverse situations as military or "martial" songs, the cadence of marching, the repetitive rhythms of popular music (especially when produced within large closed "auditoriums"), and other percussive or vibratory phenomena. We believe that the effects of such stimuli are not mediated by the neuro-auditory apparatus alone, but profoundly affect the entire neuro-physiological milieu directly through their effects on the craniosacral mechanism, the reciprocal tension membrane, and the tide and flow of the cerebrospinal fluid (csf). The production of interference patterns or the redirection of fluid flow, and perhaps the production of new harmonics or resonances, can be hypothesized to contribute to the profound effects of sound on the state of consciousness of the individual receiving it. Awareness of these effects is apparent in the phrase "sonic driving," used to describe the effects of shamanistic drumming or rattling on trance subjects. Felicitas Goodman (1986) quotes Lex (1979: 110-111), in summarizing what is known about the neurobiology of the "ritual trance" or "ritual altered state of consciousness" (RASC). According to Lex, sonic driving functions either by blocking sequential processing of the left hemisphere, by promoting trophotrophic dominance, and/or by affecting motor activity in such a way as to result in intense activation of the ergotropic system. Goodman has found that the sound of her rattle does induce a reproducible change in consciousness. When coupled with selected "primitive postures" or specific body positions, the experience can be fine-tuned to produce very specific perceptions (Goodman, 1986). The exact mechanism is unknown.

We propose that sonic driving interacts with the craniosacral mechanism in a mechanical, vibratory way to produce its effects. In addition, posture acts to direct the flow of the resonances, in much the same way as osteopathic cranial manipulation to release, direct, and/or augment the effects of the external vibratory, sonic energy. Other external sonic or oscillation fields may interact with this primary neurophysiological mechanism as well. Research has yet to explain the mechanism by which electromagnetic fields affect biological systems or how geologic frequencies interact with human behavior. Perhaps the interaction between the external vibratory environment and the internal resonant environment, mediated by the flexibility and structure of the antenna (our bodies) may help to explain the production of naturally occurring "alternate states."

We believe that the combination of cranial osteopathy-subtle adjustment and balancing of the craniosacral mechanism affects the rhythm played by the reciprocal tension membrane, in the way that frets tune a guitar. The synchronistic application of structural tuning and a clear carrier wave achieved through sonic driving can be beneficial when applied to individuals who are in various states of health. One can change one's response to stress, discharge energy or amplify it, can tune to frequencies of vibrations not yet heard (i.e., overtones), and may allow states of consciousness, restricted previously, resulting in healing.

REFERENCES

1) Goodman, Felicitas D. (1986) "Body posture and the religious altered state of consciousness: An experimental investigation." *Journal of Humanistic Psychology.* Vol. 26, No. 3 (Summer 1986): 81-118.
2) Lex, B.W. (1979) "The neurobiology of ritual trance." In: *The Spectrum of Ritual: A Biogenetic Structural Analysis*, ed. E. d'Aquili. NY: Columbia University Press.
3) (1986) This article was originally published in the *Proceedings of the Third International Conference on the Study of Shamanism and Alternate Modes of Healing.* For more information about this journal, see http://www.shamanismconference.org/

* Photograph of Dr Cheri Quincy during a shamanic session by Millay.

SECTION VI

MATHEMATICAL MODELS

*Copyright © 1994 www.ScienceCartoonsPlus.com.
Sidney Harris

SECTION VI

MATHEMATICAL MODELS

Mathematics, Science and Understanding: The Power of Numbers

Mathematics is not some mysterious process but is based on logic and reason. It is a language that helps us understand and describe the universe. It is the tool that allows us to bring together, synthesize and better comprehend what we experiment with and observe. Applied mathematics helps us design and construct bridges, freeways and skyscrapers. Mathematics, tools and labor allowed the Egyptians to construct their pyramids, the Mayans their calendar, Archimedes the Archimedean screw and it is assisting us in describing the brain of humans that creates mathematics! Note that the word *logic* comes from the ancient Greek logos, or the word, and the reason comes from ratio, or relationship.

Mathematics acts as a formulator and descriptor of scientific theory and law. The scientific method can be applied to any body of knowledge one wishes to understand. Are consciousness studies and in particular psi a science? Yes, if the scientific method is applied. Science is knowledge ascertained by observation and experiment, critically tested, systematized and brought under general principles or laws. Historically, considered as nonscientific is the concept of mystical experiences. Mysticism is the belief that the most reliable source of knowledge or truth is intuition, rather than reason or the scientific method. Immediate and true knowledge is attained through a direct experience that does not depend on systematic mental activity or sense impressions. Yet, many scientists have based their understanding of nature and their own observations on the basis of that "flash of insight," for example: Tesla's inspiration for the alternating generator; Kekulé's insight that benzene was a ring molecular structure to form the correct ratio of hydrogen to carbon; the double helix of DNA. In fact many significant advancements in the understanding of scientific principles and relationships that lead to new fundamental concepts involve the diligent collection and analyzing of data and the inspiration and intuition about their connectedness.

As one of the fathers of nuclear and atomic physics put it:

> *Experiment without inspiration, or imagination without recourse to experiment, can accomplish little, but, for effective progress, a happy blend of these powers is necessary.*
>
> --- Ernest Rutherford in the 1930s.

In Aristotle's time, the heavens were thought to be the domain of perfect spheres. The moon was a perfect sphere, yet even with the naked eye, patterns can be seen and with binoculars or a low power telescope, craters can be observed. What are these pockmarks on the face of the moon? Observation, analysis and theory demonstrate they are meteoric impacts and we can even calculate the likely date and the rate at which these impacts took place. The development of mathematical models gives us the power to land explorers on the moon, Mars and elsewhere in our solar system. Mathematics is the basis for modern physics, chemistry, biology, engineering and other fields of human endeavor. Mathematical expressions express the fixed relationship between constancy and change.

The two aspects observed about the world, <u>constancy</u> and <u>change</u>, are the basis of the scientific law. Also in the Vedic literature, there are three Gunas: growth and decay (change) and balance (constancy). Scientific law is an expression of the constant relationship between variables and constants. This constant relationship is expressed by an equal sign. Probably one of the best-known equations is Einstein's relation $E = mc^2$, which expresses the equivalence of mass and energy, and where c is the constant velocity of light, which is one of the universal constants of nature.

Many aspects of life seem to be like the shifting sands, i.e., ever changing. The watch or chronometer can measure time but, really, time is a measure of the change in matter and energy. Going to a high school reunion after 20 years and seeing the changes is most evident.

What item can we find that is constant? One aspect of constancy may be expressed as constants, and the constant relationship between variable and constant, such as in geometric relations, or $C = 2\pi r$ = the circumference of a circle: C is related to its radius r by the magical number $\pi = 3.1416$. This number pi (π) is the same for all circles. This was not always understood. A number of years ago one state legislature passed a law to make $\pi = 3.0000$! Later the "law" was repealed.

Eugene Wigner, a well-known physicist, was curious about mathematics and its meaning, and like many physicists, he has put forward the idea that some of the most important concepts in physics, including that of quantum and relativity theory, owe their success to mathematical systems that have been devised without any idea about how they might be applied in the future. Wigner wrote *"It is difficult to avoid the impression that a miracle confronts us here."* (In: *Unreasonable Effectiveness of*

Mathematics in Natural Science. E. Wigner, 1960.) He agreed with Targ and me in the 1970s, that the fundamental nature of consciousness could only be comprehended in its nonlocal nature using the description I developed at that time. This is a macroscopic description of a mathematical model in hyper-dimensions (e.g., greater than the usual three dimensions of space and one of time). In the late 1940s, Albert Einstein suggested that the spatial dependence of psi should be studied as spatial and temporal effects of psi might give clues about its nature.

> *A human being is part of the whole called by us universe. A part limited in time and space. He experiences himself, his thoughts and feelings, as something separated from the rest... a kind of optical delusion from his consciousness. This delusion is a kind of prison for us, restricting us to our personal desires and to affection for a few persons nearest to us. Our task must be to free ourselves from this prison by widening our circle of understanding and compassion to embrace all living creatures and the whole of nature and its reality.*
> --- Albert Einstein

--- Elizabeth A. Rauscher

Elizabeth Rauscher, PhD

Elizabeth Rauscher received her BS (1962), MS (1964) and PhD (1979), from UC Berkeley, in chemistry, physics, nuclear engineering, nuclear science, and astrophysics. For 19 years (1962-1981), she taught and conducted research at UC and the Lawrence Berk. National Lab. (LBNL). For 2 years (1974-1976), she conducted remote perception and theoretical research at SRI International Radio Physics Lab. and developed a multidimensional model that reconciles consciousness with the main body of physics. She taught at the physics graduate school at UNR in Reno, NV (1991-1995), and started and chaired the Fundamental Physics Group (FFG) at LBNL on topics related to experimental and theoretical models of physics and consciousness research (1974-1978). From 1971 on, she continues to research theoretical complex geometry. She was awarded three Navy grants: (1) to work on multidimensional astrophysical models (1971-1974); (2) to work on the complexification of Maxwell's equations (1983-1984); (3) to work on measuring space shuttle signatures in the ionosphere and earthquake precursor detection (1991-1992). She and her late husband William Van Bise studied earthquake precursor signatures on an ongoing basis from 1979-1994. Dr Rauscher is continuing this now with the Global Coherence Initiative www.glcoherence.org. a project under the Institute of HeartMath www.HeartMath.org. For three years (1982-1985), she worked with the NASA space shuttle team, increasing the integrity of the weldments on the main hydrogen oxygen tank. From 1979-1984, she was a delegate to the UN on long-term energy sources. She holds 3 US patents on medical devices and an extremely sensitive magnetic field detector. She has published 4 books and 280 scientific papers. http://www.elizabethrauscher.com/.

LONGITUDINAL COMPARISON OF LOCAL AND LONG-DISTANCE REMOTE-PERCEPTION PHENOMENA

Elizabeth A. Rauscher

I have examined those aspects of human perception that appear to fall outside the range of well-understood perceptual processing capabilities. Of particular interest is a human information accessing "channel" termed *remote perception* (RP) or remote viewing (RV). This phenomenon pertains to the ability to access and describe by means of direct mental processes, information sources blocked from ordinary perception, which is secured against sensory access by distance, time, or shielding. I use the term remote perception rather than remote viewing because other sensory experiences, such as those involving smell, feeling, and hearing, have also been shown to arise from distant stimuli. However, both terms are used here.

The research reported here involves the investigation of the remote-perception process. The experiments are designed to eliminate classic sensory modalities and enhance the reliability of the phenomena. On the whole, the experiments conform to the protocol described below. Some of these experiences were focused on the parameters of the physical setups, and some were designed to test specific psychological or paranormal conditions. (1-5) An important finding was that subjects appeared to be capable of learning to develop and improve their remote-perception capabilities. A learning curve seemed to be evident in that later experimenters were more statistically significant. As in other complex scientific experiments, the experimenters may undergo a learning process as well.

PROJECTS, CO-RESEARCHERS, AND SUBJECTS

In 1974, I convened and conducted the "Fundamental Fysiks Group" (FFG) at the Lawrence Berkeley National Laboratory (LBNL) to study remote-connectedness concepts such as Bell's nonlocality theorem. The group also discussed the possible existence of remote perception (RP) phenomena and other "nonlocal" attributes of consciousness. Some of the FFG participants (G. Weissman, S. P. Sirag, F. Capra, G. Zukov, N. Herbert) and I developed an interest in performing our own remote-perception experiments. (1) The FFG grew to over 40 participants and continued to 1978.

At the same time, in response to criticism that remote perception is incompatible with the established theories of physics, I developed a complex hyper-dimensional (N>4) geometry to reconcile RP and precognition with accepted science. This work gained acceptance in refereed physics journals. My motivation in developing a multidimensional model was twofold: [A] to reconcile the psi database with the main body of physical theory, and [B] to theoretically describe some of the spacetime-independent features of RP. (2-11)

As a test of this theory, over a period of many years, I conducted local real-time remote-perception experiments in which target location and subject were within half an hour's driving time of each other. To further test the model, we undertook experiments that were both long-distance (thousands of kilometers) and precognitive. I participated in some of these trials when I became a consultant to the SRI International research group of R. Targ, H. Puthoff, and I. Swann. In addition to the long-distance and local RV experiments with the SRI staff, I also worked with others from the FFG (B. Rubik, B. Mayfield, J. Mishlove, A. Webster, D. Hurt [SRI], and J. Houck.) (1, 3, 5, 12)

PROTOCOL

The phenomenon my co-researchers and I investigated is the ability of a person (subject) to "view" or perceive geographical locations (targets) from several kilometers to several thousand kilometers distant from the perceiver's physical location.

The following is a summary of the major elements in our experimental protocol.

1. A person acting as a target selector (not otherwise connected with the experiment) [a] scouts for a pool of targets within a specified distance of the laboratory, [b] writes detailed traveling directions for the outbound experimenter, [c] places each set of directions in a sealed envelope and the set of envelopes, which are numbered randomly and placed in a locked box. This person has no further involvement in the experiment.
2. Laboratory room.
3. Remote-viewer (subject).
4. Monitor with recorder and pad of paper in the lab room with the remote-viewer.
5. Target pool (target locations in sealed, numbered envelopes).
6. A random-number generator (RNG) is used to select target. The number from the RNG will correspond to a number on the sealed envelope by the target selector.
7. Outbound experimental team with a recorder and camera.

Features of the method include the following:

1) From where the subject sits, s/he knows only the identity of the person or team visiting the location—the outbound experimenters.

2) The outbound team drives several blocks away from the laboratory, uses the RNG to select a target envelope, opens the sealed envelope containing their destination, and proceeds to the target and experiences the target location for fifteen minutes.

3) The monitor assists the subject in recording and clarifying impressions that are received during the designated period when the outbound team is at the target site. The monitor does not know either the specific target location for the particular trial or the pool of possible locations.

4) The subject receives feedback on the same day as the experiment when s/he is taken to the experimental target after the completion of the experiment.

5) Judging is conducted by a person(s) who is independent of the other participants in the experiment. Judging also can be performed by computer, using feature extraction and analysis. For example, Jahn and Dunne at Princeton (13) developed a matching system using an "alphabet" of 30 similarity descriptors such as indoors versus outdoors, dark versus brightly lighted, and hectic or chaotic versus inactive or homogeneous.

The outbound team typically took 3 photos of different aspects of the remote target environment and tape-recorded their impressions while they were at the site. This information, especially the time-sequencing of events and of transitory motion, was recorded for post hoc analysis. These photos and tapes were included in the judging package along with those tape-recorded responses and drawings made by the subject in the laboratory at the same time. Our experiments involved a series of six individual test sessions. The outside judges attempted to match subject transcripts to photographs and taped descriptions of target sites.

In addition to real-time local experiments, precognitive and distant experiments were conducted. In connection with the time-and-distance-independent results from the experiments I conducted, I have developed a detailed mathematical model of RP and other forms of psi. (Chapter 26.)

EXAMPLES OF REMOTE-PERCEPTION EXPERIMENTS

Typical examples of remote-perception responses are given in **Figures 1- 6**. The subjects generated taped narratives and drawings of their perception of remote locations; however, we found that drawings were better descriptors of the targets than the narrative transcripts.

Figure 1.
Location of target: Vallombrosa Center, Menlo Park, California
Subject: Engineer G. Langford
Monitor: H. Puthoff
Outbound Team: E. A. Rauscher and H. A. M.

Summary of subject's comments:
Looking up to the blue sky. Looks like Elizabeth was looking up at something — a pole or steeple associated with this place, Elizabeth kneeling — Hope is also kneeling; it's something swirling with straight tentacles extending from it — objects whirling around — hazy, swirling — partly man-made and partly natural — they are placed; that's the man-made aspect.

The outbound experimenters had first looked up at the yellow plastic church steeple and then knelt and put their hands into the swirling sprinklers. The outbound experimenter's comments at the site during the last two minutes:

The last two minutes we walked back to the church area ... I put my arms around one of the cement pillars and hugged it. I noticed that it looked like the kind that had been wrapped with some kind of thing that the concrete was poured into.

Subject's comments on the last two minutes on his tape:

Not your average pole.... It looks like that pole was concrete, like an extruded pipe. It has lines that are marked.

Local Remote-Perception Target and Response for the Vallombrosa Center

 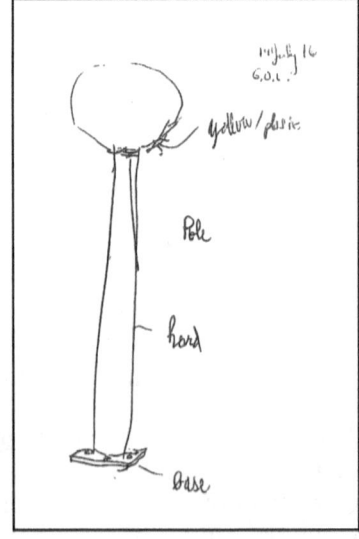

Figure 2.

Location of target: Highway underpass at University and El Camino Real, Palo Alto, California
Location of subject: Huntsville, Alabama
Subject: Engineer G. Langford
Monitor: None
Outbound Team: E. A. Rauscher and H. Puthoff

Summary of subject's comments:
I feel like you are inside a tunnel... an outbound experimenter is leaning against a wall of some sort [true]... it is a dim-to-light effect. You can still see everything though ... Hal may be leaning over an edge with an archway opening [true] ... describing the passageway under El Camino on University Avenue.

Outbound experimenters had walked down ramp to enter El Camino and University Avenue underpass, leaned against walls and leaned over railing looking at traffic. (Note: Subjects are usually instructed to look for forms and shapes and not to attempt to name the site, as some past experiments appeared to show that this might cause guessing. Hence, the subject said he resisted naming the site.) This experiment was one of a series. (2) [Rauscher was the monitor with the same subject for the Superdome target reported by Targ in Section I Chapter 1.]

Long-Distance Remote-Perception Target and Response for
The Underpass at University at El Camino Real, Palo Alto, CA,
while the subject was in Huntsville, Alabama

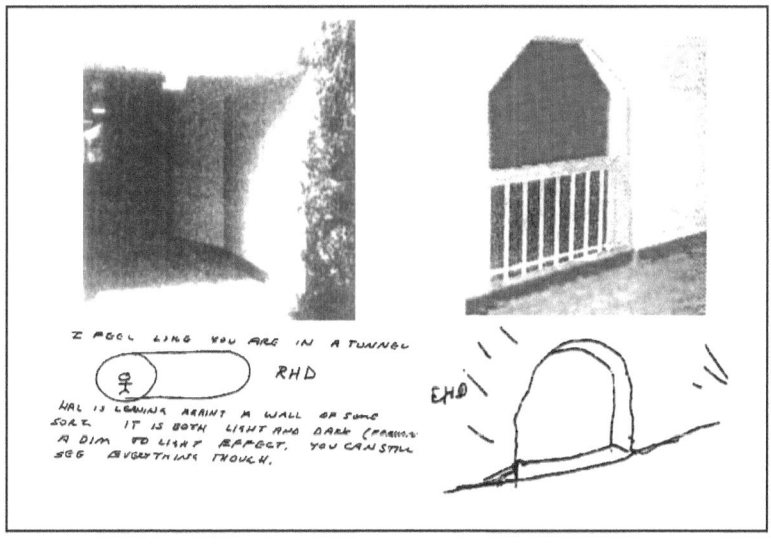

Figure 3.

Location of target:	BART (Bay Area Rapid Transit) station on Shattuck Avenue, Berkeley, California
Subject:	Physicist E. A. Rauscher
Monitor:	None. A free-response place and time were set within a three-hour time period
Outbound Team:	A. J. M. and B. M. Experiment designed by E. A. Rauscher

The subject, a meditator, knew that the outbound team would choose their target and go there for fifteen minutes some time between 2 P.M. & 5 P.M. The subject was to turn on the tape recorder and identify the time and place when the team arrived at the randomly chosen geographical location. Drive time could be anytime up to two hours and forty-five minutes.

The subject recorded the arrival time at the target as 2:40 P.M. (the actual time of arrival was 2:45). The site was also accurately reported. The subject said later upon receiving feedback (two and one-half months later, after the whole experimental series was analyzed) that she "knew" where the outbound team was ("Shattuck Avenue") and would have named the cross street but could not remember it. The subject mentioned a strong conviction about her choice even though feedback came several months later.

The subject reported during recording:

new brick ... raised circular brick ... slopes up ... could be on Shattuck around trees (planter boxes).

(This author started out as an objective researcher, but became a subject in this and other experiments.)

Remote-Perception Target and Response for the BART Station on Shattuck Avenue, Berkeley, California

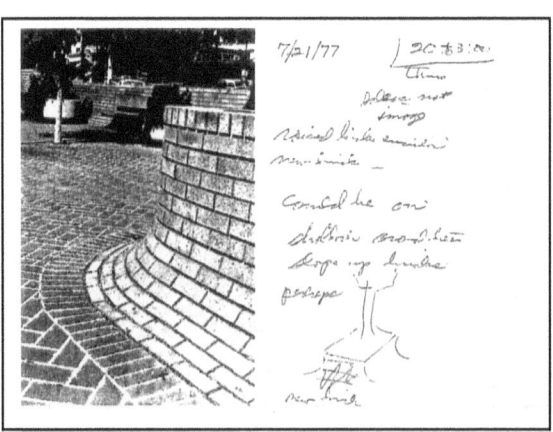

Figure 4.

Location of target:	United California Bank, Plaza and Underground Parking Stairwell
Location of subject:	Huntsville, Alabama
Subject:	A systems analyst
Monitor:	None
Outbound Team:	E. A. Rauscher, H. Puthoff, and A. J. M.

In this long-distance remote-perception experiment, the subject described cement planter boxes, with flowers inside, which were gray on a brick patio area. He also described a cement depression, which is a fountain and an underground space unavailable to the outbound experimental team. This underground space could be reached by a well with a railing around the top that the experimenters were standing near. All these responses by the subject were correct.

The subject wrote these words:
> *grey ... area is greyish, and grey in color.*

(The underground stairwell is constructed of gray concrete.) He wrote:
> *standing in a very confining space, like walls are close.*

(The stairwell is tight confining space.) He said an outbounder
> *can look up and see out.*

(From the first flight of stairs, one can see out by looking up.)

Long-Distance Remote-Perception Target and Response for The Bank Plaza and Underground Parking Stairwell in California, while Subject was in Huntsville, Alabama

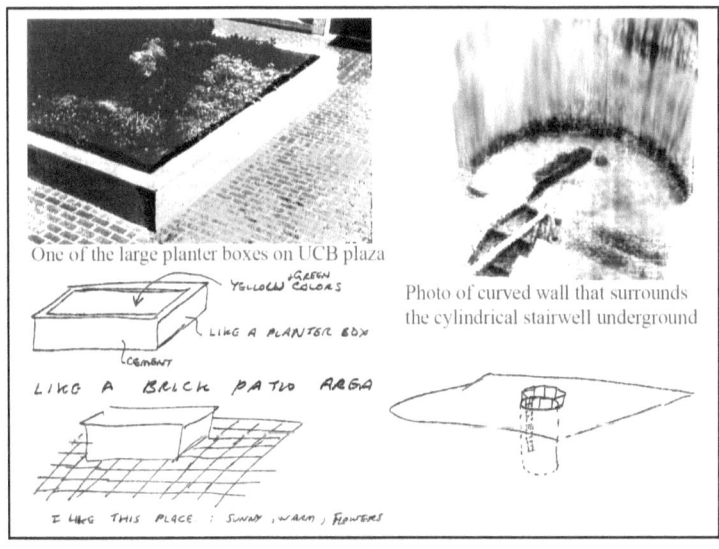

Figure 5.

Location of target:	House in France within 100-mile radius of Paris
Location of subject:	1,000 miles away
Subject:	Astrophysicist E. A. Rauscher
Monitor:	C. B.
Outbound Team:	O. Costa de Beauregard (nuclear physicist)

The subject was able to distinguish her intuitive impression from the guessed impression. She reported that if the target location was in Paris, it would be crowded with red tile roofs, but she reported on her *"flash"* impression that the target (a house) was in an uncrowded area, a quiet location, and had a brown shingle roof. She also reported that it was two stories tall and white stucco (it was actually white stone); that a metal railing around the upper-story windows had been newly painted brown (true); and that there was a large oriental rug in the living room (true). No apparent major erroneous data were reported. (I was the subject in this long distance experiment.)

Long-Distance Remote-Perception Target and Response for the House in France – Subject was 1,000 miles away

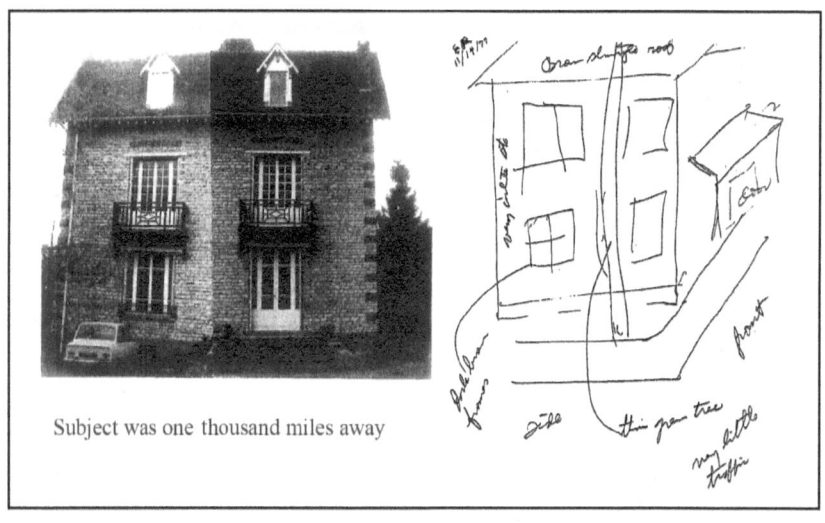

Subject was one thousand miles away

Figure 6.

Location of target:	Macy's shopping center
Subject:	Artist Hella Hammid
Monitor:	Physicist Russell Targ
Outbound Team:	Physicist Elizabeth Rauscher

We believe that a subject with a monitor can describe a remote target site before it has been randomly selected from the target pool. The following is an example of the accuracy that can be obtained:

4:30 P.M. Subject and monitor went into laboratory
 (secluded from outside contact).
4:30 P.M. E. A. R. left lab, went to car and waited fifteen minutes.
4:45 P.M. Subject made 15-minute tape recording and sketches.
5:00 P.M. Subject and monitor stopped tape recording.
5:04 P.M. E. A. R. threw die, opened selected envelope, and drove to site.
5:15 P.M. E. A. R. arrived at site — Macy's Department Store.
5:30 P.M. E. A. R. left site, returned to laboratory and
 contacted subject & monitor.

**Precognitive Remote-Perception Target and
Response for Macy's Shopping Center**

In experiments of this type, there are three significant conclusions: First, we have established that it is possible to obtain a significant amount of descriptive information about remote locations. The descriptions contain accurate and relevant information that is frequently accompanied by incorrect and irrelevant statements (or noise). Second, the physical distance separating the subject from the scene to be perceived, even thousands of kilometers, does not seem to affect the accuracy of perception. Third, the theory of relativity has led to the general acceptance of the concept of a symmetry between spatial and temporal events. In the experiments, we found instances in which a subject was able to describe a remote location before the outbound team had arrived at the site; in a few cases, the subject gave a correct description even before the target location was randomly selected. The time sequence for an example experiment in a precognitive mode is listed in **Figure 6.** We did not select the target site until after the end of the subject's fifteen-minute narrative.

The target pool consisted of the following targets from which the actual target was chosen randomly:

1. Center for Personal Growth—low, modern buildings that are basically dark brown and yellow. Rectangular shapes are prominent with extensive garden areas.
2. Busy traffic intersection — concrete and macadam with metal fencing, basically gray colors.
3. Concrete plant — an industrial site consisting of several concrete, wood, and corrugated iron structures. There were giant semi-triangular metal bins holding the various grades of gravel.
4. Large shopping center with court yard — a red brick building with large white arches. A large parking lot lies in front. (This was the chosen site. The subject's drawing matches the arch and refers to the brick, not part of any of the other possible targets.) The subject described a large brick building with a big archway a carriage could drive through. There is a stream with trees to the left (all true). The cupola in the subject's drawing on top of the building was an artifact and did not exist at the site. Upon returning to the laboratory, I was extremely impressed with Hella Hammid's response and joked, *"If you can see 15 minutes into my future, what about the rest of my life?"*

SUMMARY RESULTS AND ANALYSIS

To assist in objectifying the evaluation of remote-perception phenomena, I have developed a 7-point scale, shown below. The scale gives results similar to those of other judging procedures. Although some of our experiments had results at chance expectation, most of our results were statistically significant with a chance probability, or p value, $< .05$. Some of our experiments had highly significant results with p values of $<10^{-6}$ or a million-to-one odds against having such a result by chance.

7-Point Evaluation Scale for Target-Transcript Correspondence

7. Excellent correspondence, including good analytical detail (e.g., identifying the site by name) with essentially no incorrect information
6. Good correspondence with good analytical information (e.g., naming the function of the site) and relatively little incorrect information
5. Good correspondence with unambiguous, unique, matchable elements but some incorrect information
4. Good correspondence with several matchable elements intermixed with incorrect information
3. Mixture of correct and incorrect elements but enough of the former to indicate viewer has made contact with the site
2. Some correct elements but not sufficient to suggest results beyond chance expectation
1. Little correspondence
0. No correspondence

We applied the transcript–to–target comparison-rating scale for both geographical targets in third dimensions and abstract targets in two dimensions.

In 1975, we conducted a series of eight real-time local (RTL) remote-perception experiments that were judged to be nonsignificant by five judges matching transcripts to targets without using the point-evaluation scale. Using the scale, some positive correspondence between transcript and target was found, but the overall results were nonsignificant. (1)

In 1980, we conducted a series of 12 experiments in which subject and target locations were long distant in the north-south direction. In this series, we used the Princeton 20-point feature-matching protocol and achieved significance with a single-tailed p value of $-.01$. (3, 4) Using the point-evaluation scale yielded a slightly higher significance, but the difference in the two p values generated by the two judging methods was not significant. All other RTL, real-time long distant (RTD), and local pre-precognitive (LP) results were plotted separately, and in the other RTD experiments, the subject and target orientation was in the east-west direction, and were highly significant.

Figure 7 shows data plotted for the 20 RTL and 20 RTD remote-perception experiments over a 6-year period. In addition, one LP experimental data point is given. The axes represent a plot of R_s versus t_D, where R_s is the rating scale for target-to-transcript comparison and t_D is the time or date the experiment was conducted plotted in month intervals. Subject transcripts and drawings were matched to the target for correspondence to evaluate remote-perception success. All targets were geographical locations. In most cases, the outbound experimenter recorded an audiotape and took photographs during the experiment.

From **Figure 7**, we can generate a trend analysis in terms of the relative slope or change in R_s versus time, to, and we see that the slope for the RTL experiments yields a value of .4 and the slope for the RTD experiments yields a value slightly less of .3. For the RTD data, both north-south and east-west orientations are grouped together.

The overall average value of the 20 RTL experiments yields $<R_s> = 4$, where <> is a symbol for average, and the overall average value of the 20 RTD experiments yields $<R_s> = 5$. For all the RTL, we have p approximately equal to .001, and for the RTD, we have a p value equal to approximately .0001. Note that the horizontal line $<R_s> = 2.5$ represents chance expectation. The results from all our experiments lie on or above this line.

Figure 7.

Remote Perception Experiments Conducted Using Geographical Targets
Comparison of relative slopes of least — squares fits shows accuracy and learning in local vs distant remote perception.

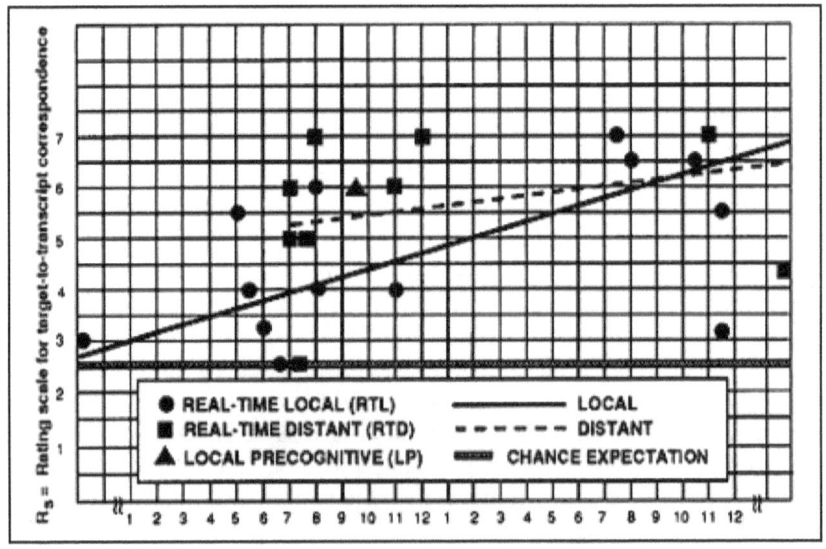

tn = The date experiment was conducted in one-month intervals
(Note discontinuities between 1975-76 and 1977-80)

We interpreted the positive slope as a learning curve for both the principal investigators and the subject-participants. Some experimenters were new to remote perception; some were experienced. Nearly all subjects were novices in remote perception before this experiment.

I worked with many subjects and other researchers, but all subjects and researchers participated in at least three experiments conducted under my guidance.

It is apparent from my research in psychic phenomena as well as from research I conducted in accelerator physics that there is an "experimenter effect." In some standard physics experiments, some researchers are not able to obtain the results obtained by other experimental groups even when the apparatus and methods used are identical. (13)

There is no attenuation of remote perception over the distance we measured. In fact, we see that the opposite appears to occur; that is, the long-distance experiments are more significant than the local experiments. A possible confounding factor is that some of the local experiments were conducted first, and hence the learning effect appears to dominate over any effect of distance.

GROUP EXPERIMENTS AND EXPERIMENTS USING GEOMETRIC TARGETS

In addition to the experiments analyzed in **Figure 7**, which used geographical location targets, we conducted another series of 20 experiments that involved two- and three-dimensional geometric targets, and we used most of the same subjects in 1976 and in 1977. These experiments had an overall significance with $<R_s> = 6$ and were significant at a p value .000001, or 10^{-6}.

To gain more data and examine intersubject interaction, we conducted six group experiments in which we had a group of subjects view the same target at the same time. Four group experiments used abstract targets (ATs); two used geographical locations (GLs) as targets.

In 1971, with 56 student volunteers through UC Berkeley, we obtained a p value of .00001 using ATs. In 1972, through the UC Stanford Linear Accelerator, 201 students using ATs obtained a p value of approximately .001. In 1973, with 16 students at the UC Berkeley Extension who used ATs, chance results of nonsignificance were obtained in 1977, through a UC Extension workshop, 35 students with ATs produced chance nonsignificant results.

In 1978, with 44 subjects, and in 1979, with 32 subjects, using GL we performed experiments with the CA Psychical Study Group with low average results, significant at .01. However, this study did include a few very accurate responses All experiments except the 1973 UC Berkeley experiment (which was a precognition experiment) were RTL experiments.

Even in the nonsignificant experiments, some interesting subject response correspondences occurred: It appeared that some subjects generated noise in the signal channel of other subjects; that is, specific incorrect subject responses acted as senders and were picked up and repeated by other subjects.

Note that I reported the results of *all* the experiments I conducted and in which I participated. The overall significance of the results of these experiments from independent probabilities is many millions-to-one against chance or random expectation. It is important to have obtained significance for both RTL and RTD experiments to test our theoretical hypothesis comparing spatial and temporal properties of the remote-perception phenomenon. At least terrestrially and for precognitive temporal intervals of several hours, there appears to be no attenuation in the significance of the effect, which is consistent with my theory presented here in Chapter 15. (6 -11, 14 - 18)

MORAL IMPLICATIONS OF SPACETIME – INDEPENDENT PSI MODELS

Our experiments as well as others of their kind show the interconnectedness of people with one another and with all aspects of the environment over great distances. How easily we seem to influence one another and to share thoughts, perceptions, and feelings. There are thus potentially an infinite number of ways to tune into and perhaps affect events and people across space and time. (14 -18)

In considering the practical applications of the various abilities we find emerging among people connected with psi research, we must consider the matter of the morality of the uses to which these human capabilities might be put. How can this capacity be used for good? How can we avoid a future in which it could, or would, be used for harm? Knowledge and ethics must go hand in hand. To quote Albert Einstein, *"We shall need to substantially change our manner of thinking in order to survive."*

We consider a multidimensional geometrical model that appears to reconcile precognition and causality in a self-consistent theoretical framework. This complex physical variable model tested for its consistency with the main body of physics and also may demonstrate a fundamental relation between relativity and electromagnetic phenomena. Remote connectedness of events appears contiguous in the hyper-dimensional complex space. With this model, a precognitive advantage can be calculated. The limits of a simple Lorentz invariant model of precognition are also examined. It is possible to demonstrate that psychic phenomena is not denied by the structure of physical law but is compatible with Poincaré invariance and causality. (7)

APPENDIX I

Principles of Physics and Their Suggested Relation to Psychic Phenomena

Principle	Poincaré Invariance	Analyticity	Unitarity
Brief Statement Of Principle	Homogeneity of spacetime	Causality	Conservation of probability
Physical theory Related to the Principle of Physics and Psychic Phenomena	Complex geometry and remote connectedness and Bell's Theorem	Complex geometry	Entropy and vacuum state polarization
Psychic Phenomena	Remote perception	Precognition	Psychokinesis

REFERENCES AND NOTES

1) Rauscher, E.A., Weissmann, G, Sirag, S.P, Sarafatti, J. (1975) "Remote perception of natural scenes shields against ordinary perception." In: *Advances in Parapsychology*. Metuchen: NJ Scarecrow Press.

2) Rauscher, E.A. & Mullins, A.J. (1977) "The scientific investigation of direct perception across space and time." In: *Mind Space*.

3) Rauscher, E.A. & Houck, J. (1985) "Los Angeles area to San Francisco Bay Area remote perception experiment." In: *Psi Research*. 1985; 4:48.

4) Houck, J, Nelson, R.D, Rauscher, E.A. (1986) "Addendum to Los Angeles area to San Francisco Bay Area remote perception experiment: A reevaluation." In: *Psi Research*. 1986; 5:108.

5) Gough, W.C, Rauscher, E.A, Houck, G.B.L, Gruye, V. (1981) The status of research on the physics of consciousness: Working models and experiments. Staff report of the Committee of Science and Technology, U.S. House of Representatives. 97th Congress, 1st session, Serial G; 1981.

6) Rauscher, E.A. (1976) "Some physical models potentially applicable to remote perception." In: *Bulletin of the American Physical Society*, 1976; 21:1305–1306.

7) Rauscher, E.A. (1979) "Some physical models potentially applicable to remote perception." In: *The Iceland Papers: Frontiers of physics conference; Select papers on experimental and theoretical research on the physics of consciousness*. Amherst, WI: Essentia Research Assn. 1996; pp. 49-93. 2nd edition. PACE, Ottawa, Canada.

8) Ramon, C & Rauscher, E.A. (1980) "Superluminal transformations in complex Minkowski space." In: *Foundations of Physics*. 1980; 10, 661.

9) Rauscher, E.A. (1983) "The physics of psi in space and time, Part I: Major principles of physics, psychic phenomena, and some physical models." In: *Psi Research*. 1983; 2:65.

10) Rauscher, E.A. (1983) "The physics of psi phenomena in space and time, part II: Multi-dimensional geometric models." In: *Psi Research*. 1983; 2:93

11) Rauscher, EA. (1978) "Complex coordinate geometries in general relativity and electromagnetism." In: *Bulletin of the American Physical Society*. 1978; 23:84-85.

12) Mishlove, J. (1979) *Interdisciplinary Sciences*. Berkeley: UC Ph.D. Dissertation.

13) Jahn, R.G, Dunne, B.J, Jahn, E.G. (1989) "Analytical judging procedure for remote perception experiments." In: *Journal of Parapsychology*. 1980; 3:231.

14) Rauscher, E.A. (1993) "Longitudinal comparison of local and long distance remote-perception phenomena." In: *Silver Threads: 25 Years of Parapsychology Research*. Kane, B, Millay, J, Brown, D. (Eds.) 1993; pp. 64-77.

15) Puthoff, H.E. & Targ, R. (1976) "A perceptual channel for information transfer over kilometer distances." In: *Proc. IEEE* 64, March.

16) Rauscher, E.A. (1993) "A theoretical model of remote-perception phenomenon." In: *Silver Threads: 25 Years of Parapsychology Research*. Kane, B, Millay, J, Brown, D. (Eds.) 1993; pp. 144-155.

17) Rauscher, E.A. & Targ, R. (2002) "Why only four dimensions will not explain the relationship of the perceived and perceiver in precognition." In: *Journal of Scientific Exploration*. 2002; 16:655-658.

18) Rauscher, E.A. & Targ, R. (2001) "Speed of thought: Investigation of a complex space to describe psychic phenomena." In: *Journal of Scientific Investigations*. 2001; 15:331.

We cannot solve the problems that we have created with the same thinking that created them.

--- Albert Einstein

INVESTIGATION OF A COMPLEX SPACE-TIME METRIC TO DESCRIBE REMOTE PERCEPTION AND PRECOGNITION

Elizabeth A. Rauscher
Russell Targ

Abstract. For more than 100 years scientists have attempted to determine the truth or falsity of claims that some people are able to describe and experience events or information blocked from ordinary perception. For the past 25 years, the authors of this paper – together with researchers in laboratories around the world – have carried out experiments in remote viewing. The evidence for this mode of perception, or direct knowing of distant events and objects, has convinced us of the validity of these claims. It has been widely observed that the accuracy and reliability of this sensory awareness does not diminish with either electromagnetic shielding, or with increases in temporal or spatial separation between the percipient and the target to be described. Modern physics describes such a time-and-space independent connection between percipient and target as nonlocal.

In this paper we present a geometrical model of space-time, which has already been extensively studied in the technical literature of mathematics and physics. This eight–dimensional metric is known as "complex Minkowski space," and has been shown to be consistent with our present understanding of the equations of Newton, Maxwell, Einstein, and Schrödinger. It also has the interesting property of allowing a connection of zero distance between points in the complex manifold, which appear to be separate from one another in ordinary observation. We propose a model that describes the major elements of experimental parapsychology, and at the same time is consistent with the present highly successful structure of modern physics.

INTRODUCTION

Scientific research into extrasensory perception (ESP) has made enormous progress since the founding of The Society for Psychical Research in 1882 by a distinguished group of Cambridge University scholars. The society's purpose was to examine allegedly paranormal phenomena in a scientific and unbiased manner – the first organization of its kind in the world. Now in the twenty-first century, the evidence has become overwhelming that our thoughts and bodies can be directly affected and influenced by the thoughts of another person, or by events and activities at a distant location blocked from ordinary perception. Although we do not presently understand the detailed mechanisms underlying psychical abilities, thousands of experiments have been carried out successfully in dozens of laboratories around the world establishing the existence of some form of ESP. We present here a theoretical model to elucidate some of the phenomena underlying the remote perception ability, while remaining consistent with modern physics. For example, our model is in good agreement with these ideas presented in the recent physics book *The Nonlocal Universe,* by H. Stapp. (1)

> ... The universe on a very basic level could be a vast web of particles, which remain in contact with one another over any distance, [and] in no time. (1)

This paper is about connecting our awareness to the universe and to each other through the use of our psychic abilities. These abilities, known collectively as "PSI" (from the Greek word for spirit, or soul), reveal numerous kinds of connections–mind to mind (telepathy), mind to body (distant healing), mind to the world (clairvoyance), precognition of future events, and what some mystics have called one-mindedness. Even though we lack an understanding of psi, we have learned a great deal about its psychology, and procedures to make these elusive phenomena appear with ever increasing reliability in laboratory experiments. For example, in today's remote viewing (RV) experiments, we can often describe and experience places thousands of miles away. These have demonstrated ten times more statistical reliability, or effect size, than those of J. B. Rhine's original "ESP" card-guessing experiments seventy years ago at Duke University. (2) These new remote perception results have been published by: R. Targ and H. Puthoff in *Nature* (3) and (4) in *The Proceedings of the Institute of Electrical and Electronics Engineers (IEEE);* by D. Bem and C. Honorton in *The Psychological Bulletin* (5); by Utts in *The Journal of Scientific Exploration* (6); by Puthoff, Targ and E. May in the *Proceedings of the AAAS* (7). In addition, highly significant double blind clinical studies in distant healing have been published in *The Western Journal of Medicine by*

F. Sicher, E. Targ, et al (8) and in *The Annals of Internal Medicine*, by W. Harris, et al. (9)

The laboratory evidence from more than one hundred years of parapsychological research makes it clear that we sometimes obtain information about the future, the past, and distant locations, which is not available to us by ordinary means, or through logical inference. This observation of precognition or paranormal foreknowledge has puzzled thinkers since the time of the Oracle at Delphi. However, mystics have known from the earliest Hindu *Vedas* of 2000 BC in India that "separation is an illusion," because our consciousness transcends our ordinary understanding of both space and time. In *The Sutras of Patanjali*, (10) from AD 500, we are given detailed instructions for looking into the distance and the future, in a manner strikingly similar to recent decades of psi research practice at laboratories such as Stanford Research Institute, (SRI) International, (11, 12) and Princeton University's Engineering Anomalies Research Laboratory (PEAR Lab). (13)

With practice, people become increasingly able to separate out the *psychic signal* from the *mental noise* of memory, analysis, and imagination. Targets details as small as 1 mm can be sensed. Moreover, we have seen that accuracy and resolution of RV targets are not sensitive to variations in distance. In 1984 Targ organized a pair of successful 10,000-mile remote viewing experiments between Moscow and San Francisco with famed Russian healer Djuna Davitashvili. Djuna's task was to describe where an SRI colleague would be hiding in SF at a specific time. She had to focus her attention 6,000 miles to the west, and two hours into the future, to correctly describe his location. These successful experiments were performed under the auspices and control of the USSR Academy of Sciences.

Ten years earlier, in 1974, Targ and Puthoff carried out a demonstration of psychic abilities for the CIA in which Pat Price, a retired police commissioner, described the contents and activities inside and outside of a secret Soviet weapons laboratory in the far reaches of Siberia. He was given only the geographical coordinates of latitude and longitude for a reference (with no on-site cooperation from a person at the target).

This experiment was such a stunning success that physicists Targ and Puthoff were forced to undergo a formal Congressional investigation to determine if there had been a breach in National Security. Of course, none was ever found, so the government supported the research into psi functioning for another fifteen-years. During these experiments at SRI, Pat Price made the sketch in **Figure 1** to illustrate what he psychically "saw" at the target site – a giant gantry crane that rolled back and forth over a building.

Data from formal and controlled SRI investigations were highly statistically significant (thousands of times greater than chance expectation) for each series of trials, and were published in the world's leading journals.

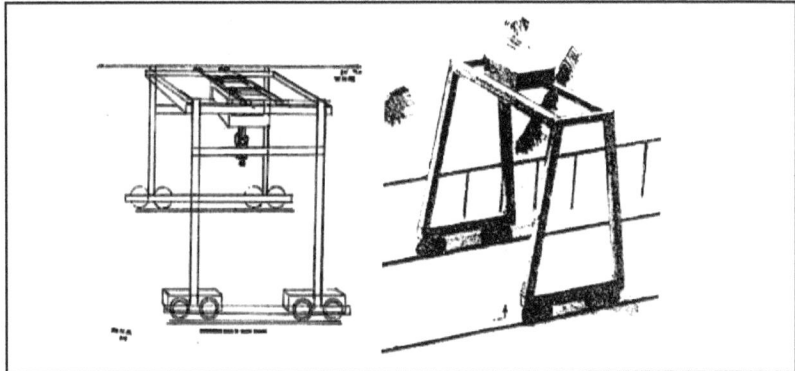

FIGURE 1. Above is Pat Price's drawing of his psychic impressions of a gantry crane at the secret Soviet research and development site at Semipalatinsk, showing remarkable similarity to a later CIA drawing based on the satellite photography shown below. Note, for example, that both cranes have eight wheels.

FIGURE 2. Here is a CIA artist tracing of a satellite photograph of the Semipalatinsk target site. Such tracings were made by the CIA to conceal the accuracy of detail of satellite photography at that time.

During one experiment, while Russell Targ was working with Pat Price at SRI International, the highly psychic retired police commissioner did not arrive for the scheduled trial.

> So, in the spirit of the show must go on, I [Targ] spontaneously decided to undertake the remote viewing myself. Prior to that, I had been only an interviewer and facilitator for such trials. In this series we were trying to describe the day-to-day activities of Hal Puthoff as he traveled through Colombia, in South America. We would not receive any feedback until he returned, and I, therefore, had no clues at all as to what he was doing. I closed my eyes and immediately had an image of an island airport. The surprisingly accurate sketch I drew is shown in Figure 3. What we learned from this trial is that even a scientist can be psychic, when the necessity level is high enough.

The purpose of our present investigation is to make use of the remote perception and precognitive database in order to deduce the relevant physical principles and laws governing paranormal functioning. One of the most common objections to the existence of psi is that it appears to be in conflict with the laws of physics, because we have not yet found the mechanism for such information transfer.

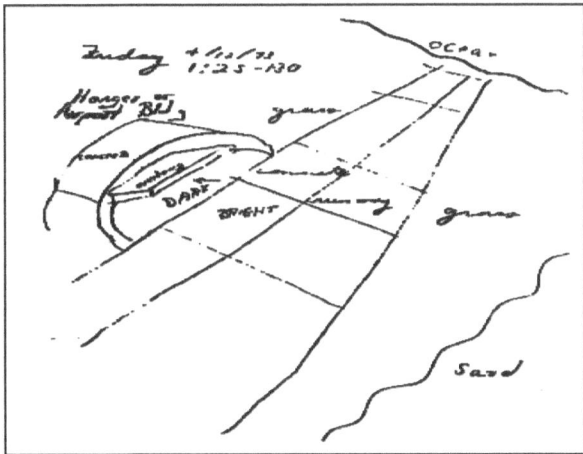

FIGURE 3. Sketch produced by physicist Russell Targ, when he spontaneously took the role of remote viewer in the absence of psychic Pat Price.

FIGURE 4. This photograph shows the target, which was an airport on an island off San Andreas, Colombia. Targ correctly saw *"Ocean at the end of a runway."*

In our investigation we attempt first to demonstrate the compatibility of psi phenomena with the laws and content of physics, and then to develop a theoretical model, which is descriptive of the nonlocal properties of psi. In this paper we present a detailed theoretical model describing the properties of psychic phenomena, which we have demonstrated to be in agreement with the main body of physics.

Specifically, we have examined a complex eight-dimensional Minkowski space, which is consistent with the foundations of quantum mechanics, Maxwell's formalism, and the theory of relativity. This is a purely geometrical model formulated in terms of space and time coordinates, in which each of the familiar three-spatial and one-temporal coordinates is expanded into its real and imaginary parts, making a total of six-spatial, and two-temporal coordinates. (14, 15, 16, 17)

The metric of this complex eight-space is a measure of the manner in which one physically or psychically moves along a world line in space and time. This movement can be as mundane as meeting a friend tomorrow at 4:00 PM on the corner of Forty-Second Street and Broadway, or as cosmic as experiencing oceanic oneness with the universe. Essentially, real-time remote viewing demands the ability for the awareness of the individual to be contiguous with a specific target at a distant location. This ability to nonlocally access information or produce an effect requires that the experienced distance between the subject and the target can be zero. Similarly, for precognition one is contiguous in awareness with the future event that is sensed. The complex eight-space described here can always provide a path, or world line in space and time, which connects the viewer to a remote target, so that his awareness experiences zero spatial and/or temporal distance in the metric. It appears that for consciousness there may, or may not be any separation, depending on one's intention. Although this paper deals principally with the physics underlying psychic abilities, we think it is evident that these abilities are fundamental to our understanding of consciousness itself. In fact, psi functioning may be the means that consciousness uses to make itself known in the internal and external physical world, and to our own awareness.

EXPERIMENTAL FOUNDATION

The fact that the future can come into our awareness at an earlier time indicates that we misapprehend both everyday causality and the nature of the very space and time, which we take so much for granted. The existence of precognition is a serious problem for contemporary science, as well as those who interpret their experience in terms of linear time, but we consider the data to be overwhelming.

Precognitive dreams are the most common psychic event to appear in the life of the average person. These dreams give us a glimpse of events that we will experience in the future. In fact, it can be said that precognitive dreams are often *caused* by the experience that we actually will have at a later time. If one has a dream of a hearse passing in front of one's window, and then wakes up the next morning and observes a funeral procession led by an hearse going down the street, we could say that last night's dream of a hearse was caused by the experience of seeing the hearse the next morning. This is an example of the future affecting the past. There is an enormous body of evidence for this kind of occurrence, which we cite below.

What cannot happen, we believe, is a future event changing the past. It appears that nothing in the future can cause something that has already happened and is known and agreed upon to have not occurred. This is the so-called intervention paradox, illustrated by the theoretical example in which one, in the present, kills his grandmother when she was a child, and therefore he ceases to exist. That kind of paradox is interesting to think about, but there is no evidence of its occurrence. The data strongly suggest that, although one can see his grandmother in the past, and obtain information about the past, there is no possibility for physical intervention. Relativity theory calls this a closed time-like loop, and it is strictly forbidden. These issues are discussed at length in Robert Brier's monograph, *Precognition and the Philosophy of Science: An essay on backward causation*. (18)

From our research, we have found that in order to know that a dream is precognitive, one has to recognize that it is not caused by the previous day's mental residue, one's wishes, or anxieties. We find rather, that precognitive dreams have an unusual clarity, but also often contain bizarre and unfamiliar material. Dream experts like to speak of *"preternatural clarity."* Again, these are not wish fulfillment or anxiety dreams. For example, if one were unprepared for an exam, and dreams about failing it, we would not consider this to be precognition. On the other hand, if one has had hundreds of uneventful plane flights, and then has a frightening dream about a crash, one might like to re-consider his travel plans. One might ask, *"How can I dream about being in a plane crash, if I don't actually get to experience it?"* The answer is that one dreams about the real crash, and then dramatizes the events to include oneself in it.

For example, a government contract monitor of the SRI work had a vivid dream about being in a plane crash, and then after canceling his flight, saw a plane crash at quite close range the next day. Since he was supposed to have been on that very plane, he had no trouble putting himself on the plane in his dream the previous night. We would say that the frightening crash that he experienced in the afternoon was the cause of his earlier dream. This is called retro-causality, and it may be the basis of most precognition. It is evident that precognition occurs, and from the laboratory data we consider it important to note that it is *just as successful and reliable as real time PSI*. (19) These experimental data from Princeton demonstrate that psi performance is not a function of temporal distance.

A well-conducted experiment involving remote viewing over intercontinental distances demonstrated that the quality of psychic functioning is the same across the street, or half a world away, which is independent of spatial distance. In one such series, experienced viewer and anthropologist Marilyn Schlitz planned to replicate those SRI RV experiments. She wanted to conduct RV experiments at much greater distances than had been published in any of the SRI papers. To carry out this experiment she enlisted the aid of her friend Elmar Gruber, a European parapsychologist who was traveling in Italy. [20] Each day for ten days in November of 1979, Schlitz, at home in Detroit, Michigan, would attempt to experience and describe the place in Rome where Gruber would be located at 11:00 AM Michigan time. Gruber, for his part, had made a list of 40 different target locations in Rome. These included both indoor and outdoor sites at parks, churches, the airport, museums, the sports arena, and the Spanish Steps. Could Schlitz, 3,000 miles away, describe each target place with enough accuracy to allow a future judge to match each description with that day's target? In addition, could she do it without any feedback for each target as she attempted this psychic investigation?

An example taken from one of Schlitz's successfully matched remote viewing transcripts is as follows:

> *Flight path? Red lights. Strong depth of field. Elmar seems detached, cold.... outdoors. See sky dark. Windy and cold. Something shooting upward.... Not a private home or anything like that – something – a public facility.... He was standing away from the main structure, although he could see it. He might have been in a parking lot or field connected to the structure that identifies the place. I want to say an airport, but that just seems too specific. There was activity and people, but no one really close to Elmar.*

In fact, the target site was the Rome International Airport, where Gruber had been standing on a hill to the side of the terminal building. Schlitz's transcripts and Gruber's descriptions of his hiding places were sent to Hans Bender, a German researcher who undertook to arrange the judging for the experiment. Five judges examined the material, and their job was to go to each of the ten target sites. At each site they read Gruber's comments about what his activities were at the site. While there, the judges were to decide which of Schlitz's ten transcripts was the best match for that particular site, which one was the second best, etc. The results revealed that out of Schlitz's ten transcripts, six were matched correctly in first place to the target that

Gruber visited on the day the transcript was created. The probability of that happening by chance is less than 6 in 10,000.

This experiment was included in K. Ramakrishna Rao's book *The Basic Experiments in Parapsychology,* (21) which is like the *"Hall of Fame"* for parapsychology experiments. Since the first 1974 publication of the RV protocol (3) there have been at least twenty-three successful replications of this work, from laboratories throughout the world. (22)

In a summary of research data from 1935 to 1989, for what we call paranormal foreknowledge, C. Honorton and D. Ferari studied 309 precognition experiments that had been carried out by 62 investigators. (23) More than 50,000 participants were involved in more than 2 million trials. Thirty percent of these studies were statistically significant in demonstrating that people can describe future events, where only five percent would be expected by chance. This gave overall significance of greater than 10^{20} to one. This body of data offers very strong evidence for confirming the existence of knowledge of the future. R. Jahn, B. Dunne, and R. Nelson at Princeton University conducted a very comprehensive laboratory examination of precognition in the 1980s. (24) They conducted 227 formal RV experiments in which a viewer was asked to describe their impressions of where one of the researchers would be hiding at some pre-selected later time. They discovered, much to their surprise, that the accuracy of the description was the same whether the viewer had to look hours, days, or weeks into the future. The overall statistical significance of the combined experiments departed from chance expectation by 1 in 10^{11}. These research findings are among the best evidence for the reality of precognition. (24)

In the laboratory, we know that if we show a frightening picture to a person, there will be a significant change in his or her physiology. Their blood pressure, heart rate, and skin resistance will all change. This fight or flight reaction is called an "orienting response."

Dean Radin demonstrated that this orienting response is also observed in a person's physiology a few seconds *before* s/he directly observes the scary picture. [See Section I Chapter 2] In Radin's comprehensive book *The Conscious Universe,* (25) he describes balanced, double-blind experiments, which show that if one is about to see scenes of violence and mayhem one's body will steel itself against the insult, but if one is about to see a picture of a flower garden, then there is rarely such strong anticipatory reaction. Fear is much easier to measure physiologically than bliss. We could say that this is a case in which one's direct physical perception of the picture, when it occurs, causes one to have a unique physical response at an *earlier* time. Again, in this research protocol, one's future is affecting his past. We are all familiar with the idea of a premonition, in which one has inner knowledge of something that is going to happen in the future – usually something of emotional significance. There is also an experience called presentiment, where one has an inner sensation, a gut feeling that something strange is about to occur. An example would be for one to suddenly stop on a walk down the street, because he felt "uneasy," only to have a flower pot then fall off a window ledge and land at his feet, instead of on his head. That would be a useful presentiment.

In the 1950s, parapsychologist William Cox carried out a study of much longer time-span presentiment. He wanted to know whether people used their precognitive abilities to avoid accidents. (26) Cox conducted an investigation of twenty-eight documented train wrecks between 1950 and 1955. He found that in every case fewer people rode the trains that crashed or were wrecked, than rode similar trains, which did not crash. These data were analyzed for weather conditions, and rider-ship on the previous and following day, week, and month. At odds of greater than 100 to 1, it appears that hundreds of people awakened in the morning, and for some reason, known or unknown, decided not to take their usual train. Thus, it would seem that one does not have to experience a future that appears to be unattractive or hazardous, to have it appear in one's subconscious processes.

It is far more probable to precognize a possible future than to produce a major change in the precognized outcome. Consider an analogy to the river of time: If Huckleberry Finn is drifting down the Mississippi River, he might determine whether he goes to Arkansas or New Orleans, just by dipping his little finger into the swirling water, *if he is far enough up stream.* What is required here is intention or information – not necessarily energy. If he were already in the delta leading to New Orleans, it would require a miracle for him to wind up in Arkansas.

It is as though we live in an interconnected spider web of space-time, in which the future is an attractor pulling the present toward itself. Since our awareness is nonlocal, the past may also act as such an attractor. It appears that the universe cannot be causal in the usual sense. That is, the likely future is already determined, to the extent that our precognition is successful. What this may indicate is that we do not lose our free will, but rather, we may use our premonitory information to make even more informed decisions about what we should be doing. We propose that the utilization of our ability to "toggle" our awareness between local four–space and nonlocal eight–space is what leads to our concept of free will. Additional precognitive and psi information allows us to choose and experience a different world line. The existence of psi creates for us a world of dynamic consequences, which depend on our state of awareness (i.e. in either four–, or eight–space).

SOME THEORETICAL MODELS
AND THEIR SHORTCOMINGS

In recent years physical models have been proposed to describe psychic abilities, in order to reconcile the psi database with the current understanding and interpretation of modern physics. Douglas Stokes has summarized and examined more than 40 theoretical models of psi phenomena. He categorizes these models, and discusses the objections from physics and the inadequacies for psi of each of the models presented. (27) We briefly address here the more compelling ones that have been proposed, such as extremely low-frequency waves (ELF), advanced electromagnetic waves, and faster than light particles called tachyons.

Beginning in the 1920s there was a prevailing view that psychic abilities were a kind of radio communication between minds. The widely read book *Mental Radio*, by the visionary author Upton Sinclair, stimulated this concept. (28) The book includes a favorable preface by Albert Einstein. Sinclair describes the highly successful experiments in mind–to–mind communication that he carried out in cooperation with his psychic and discerning wife Mary Craig Sinclair. The illustrations show the self-evident strength of hundreds of psychic matches between Sinclair's target pictures and his wife's drawn responses. The mental radio metaphor is still with us today, more than 70 years later, even though it is well understood that radio waves lose their intensity as the square of the distance from the source, and no such fall off is seen in experimental psi data. Furthermore, the data from SRI show clearly that accuracy and reliability of RV are equally significant from inside or outside an electrically shielded Faraday cage.

In the 1960s and 1970s there was intense interest in psi phenomena in the USSR. The distinguished Russian physicist I. M. Kogan put forward the concept that information transmission under conditions of sensory shielding was mediated by extremely low-frequency electromagnetic waves (ELF) in the wavelength region of 300 to 1000 km. The idea is that for separation distances of less than 1000 km, the percipient would still be in the induction field (near field) of the source, and would therefore experience less than Inverse Square fall off in signal strength. (29) Although this model has received repeated investigation – with regard to permissible bit rates and signal propagation – it fails to provide any explanation for precognitive psi, which as we have stated has the same reliability and efficacy as real time psychic perception.

This apparent time reversal, in which the event of perception seems to precede the cause or stimulus, is often viewed as paradoxical. However, in ordinary electromagnetic theory, one is cautioned not to automatically discard the mathematical solutions that suggest time reversibility. J. A.

Stratton, in his graduate text *Electromagnetic Theory*, discusses (30) so-called advanced waves and their surprising consequences:

> The reader has doubtless noticed that the choice of the function $f(t - r/c)$ is highly arbitrary, since the field equation also admits the solution $f(t + r/c)$. This function obviously leads to an advanced time, implying that the field can be detected before it is generated by the source. The familiar chain of cause and effect is thus reversed, and this alternative solution might be discarded as logically inconceivable. However, the application of 'logical causality' principles offers a very insecure footing in matters such as these. And we shall do better to restrict to the theory of retarded action, solely on grounds that this solution alone conforms to present physical data.

Such caution is justified, by the example, in the early 1920s, of Dirac's development of a mathematical description of the relativistic electron. That also yielded a pair of solutions, one of which was discarded as inapplicable until the discovery of the positron by C. Anderson in cloud chamber photographs in 1932.

The advanced wave, like the tachyon particle proposed by physicist G. Feinberg, is an information carrier that appears to travel faster than the speed of light. (31) This could allow one to experience a distant event before the corresponding light signal reached him, appearing to provide paranormal foreknowledge. However, the gain in temporal advantage would be only one nanosecond per foot of distance, whereas the data for precognition show that events are frequently described and experienced hours or days before the occurrence of an event. The advanced wave or tachyon would provide an hour's warning, only for events at a distance of 10^9 miles or greater. All electromagnetic or radio wave descriptions of psi suffer from these same limitations.

Based on the shortcomings of the above models, we have investigated a geometrical model of psi functioning, and have outlined it here. This geometric approach is very consistent with physicist John A. Wheeler's statement that our understanding of physics will *"come from the geometry, and not from the fields."*

INTRODUCTION TO THE PHYSICS OF NONLOCALITY

The physics of nonlocality is fundamental to quantum theory. The most exciting research in current quantum physics is the investigation of what physicist David Bohm calls quantum-interconnectedness or nonlocal correlations. First proposed by Einstein, Podolsky, and Rosen (EPR) in 1935, (32) as evidence of a defect in quantum theory, and later formulated as a mathematical proof by J.S. Bell, (33) it has now been repeatedly experimentally demonstrated that two quanta of light given off from a single source, and traveling at the speed of light, in opposite directions maintain their connection to one another, so that each photon is affected by what happens to its twin, many kilometers away. (34, 35)

John Clauser recently described his impressions of these nonlocality experiments to us. He said that quantum experiments have been carried out with photons, electrons, atoms, and even 60-carbon-atom Bucky balls. He said that it might be impossible to keep anything in a box. Bell emphasizes, *"No theory of reality compatible with quantum theory can require spatially separate events to be independent."* That is to say, the measurement of the polarization of one photon determines the polarization of the other photon at their respective measurement sites. This surprising coherence between distant entities is called nonlocality. In writing on the philosophical implications of nonlocality, physicist H. Stapp of UC Berkeley states that these quantum connections could be the *"most profound discovery in all of science."* (36) Nonlocality is a property of both time and space. The concept of nonlocality is very reminiscent of the data dealing with identical twins, separated at birth and reared apart, who nonetheless show striking similarities in their tastes, interests, spouses, experiences, and professions, beyond what one could reasonably ascribe to their common DNA.

The data from dream research such as J. W. Dunne's experiments with time, (37) and from the RV research at both SRI and PEAR, provide evidence that our minds have access to events occurring in distant places – and into the future or past. Immanuel Kant states that space and time are but modes of human perception, and not attributes of the physical world. These modes are powerful filters of our own invention, and often serve to limit our experience.

We know from the experimental data of psi research in our own laboratory at SRI, that a viewer can focus his or her attention at a specific location anywhere on the planet (or off of it) and reliably describe what is there. (3) We know, also, that the viewer is not bound by present time. In contemporary physics we call this ability to focus attention on distant points in space-time, nonlocal awareness. From data of the past 25 years, we believe that an experienced remote viewer can answer any question that has an answer about events anywhere in the past, present, or future.

Bohm argues that we greatly misunderstand the illusion of separation in space and time. In his physics textbook *The Undivided Universe,* (38) he defuses this illusion as he writes about the quantum-interconnectedness of all things. Bohm says *"The essential features of the implicate order are, that the whole universe is in some way enfolded in everything, and that each thing is enfolded in the whole."*

This is the fundamental statement of the metaphor of the holographic ordering of the universe. It says that, like a hologram, each region of space-time contains information about every other point in space-time. This metaphor was inspired by the indications of nonlocality in Bell's theorem.

And our data indicate that this information is available to our awareness. Bohm continues:

> ...All of this implies a thoroughgoing wholeness, in which mental and physical sides participate very closely in each other. Likewise, intellect, emotion, and the whole state of the body are in a similar flux of fundamental participation. Thus, there is no real division between mind and matter, psyche and soma. The common term psychosomatic is in this way seen to be misleading, as it suggests the Cartesian notion of two distinct substances in some kind of interaction.

In Bohm's holographic universe, there is a unity of consciousness, a *"greater collective mind,"* with no boundaries of space or time. Our mathematical model that describes such an interconnected universe is below.

Bohm goes on to describe the famous *"Wheeler delayed choice experiment."* He writes that experiments *"can be designed to show that, according to quantum theory, the choice to measure one or another of a pair of complementary variables at a given time can apparently affect the physical state of things for considerable periods of time before such a decision is made."* Such complementary variables are typically momentum and distance, or in Wheeler's experiment they refer to the dual wave and particle nature of light, as observed in a two slit interference apparatus.

DESCRIPTION OF THE EIGHT-SPACE METRIC

The purpose of our investigation is to make use of the current database of remote perception experiments, and to deduce the relevant principles and laws governing paranormal functioning. One of the common objections to the existence of psychic abilities is that they appear to be in conflict with the laws of physics. In what follows, we demonstrate the compatibility of psychic phenomena with the laws and content of physics, and develop a model, which well describes the properties of psi. In physics, we call this a "correspondence principle," so that in modeling psi, we do not create a model that is in conflict with observed physical law. We hypothesize that the data of parapsychology may even usefully inform us about some of the current questions in modern physics.

We have specifically dealt with the following areas of physics: First the major principles of physics and their relationship to, and reconciliation with, psychic phenomena; second, examination of higher-dimensional complex coordinate geometries with regard to the resolution of the questions of precognition and causality; and third we have developed a comprehensive physical model of the properties of the nonlocality exhibited in psi functioning. It is determined that the complex eight-space model not only demonstrates the consistency of precognition with causality, but also shows a fundamental relationship between Maxwell's equations, quantum theory and general relativity. (39, 40, 41) The so-called EPR paradox appears to be fundamentally related to our space-time picture, also, and is certainly an example of nonlocality in physics. The complete success of Newton's laws and Coulomb's laws occurs only in the case of two body interactions. Three body problems are solved primarily through approximations. Similarly laws of cause and effect are imprecisely defined except in the simplest cases. It is much more appropriate to describe the *effect* that one event has on another event, independent of which event appeared to come first in time. The rising of the sun has great explanatory power with regard to the increase in traffic across the bridge, but it would be obviously incorrect to say that the sun was the cause of the traffic.

Three major universal principles are used to determine the structure and nature of physical laws, and act as constraints on physical phenomena. These are *Poincaré invariance*, and its corollary, *Lorentz invariance* (which expresses the space-time independence of scientific laws in different frames of reference), *analyticity* (which is a general statement of causality conditions in the complex space), and *unitarity* (which can be related to the conservation of physical quantities such as energy or momentum). Since it is not evident that energy occupies any role in the nonlocality of psi phenomena, unitarity is not dealt with in this paper. These principles apply to microscopic as well as to macroscopic phenomena. The quantum description of elementary particles has led to the formulation of the analyticity principle in the complex momentum plane. (G. Chew, 42) Complex geometries occupy a vital role in many areas of physics and engineering. Analyticity relates to the manner in which events are correlated with each other in the space-time metric—that is, causality. When we apply this critical principle to the complex eight–dimensional space we can reconcile psi (especially precognition) with physics, without violating causality. It has been mathematically demonstrated that the equations of Newton, Maxwell, Einstein and Schrödinger are consistent with the eight–dimensional complex space described here. (15, 43)

Quantum causality, unlike classical certainty, is limited by the well-known Heisenberg uncertainty principle. Quantum systems must obey linear superposition for *both* actualized and nonactualized states. This probabilistic feature ($\Psi^* \Psi$) leads to the fundamental stochastic or statistical nature of quantum measurement. Bell asserts that this stochastic nature holds whenever quantum theory applies experimentally, and nonlocality exists as expressed in his theorem. The universality of this principle is termed the completeness theorem of quantum mechanics, and leads to the universality of nonlocality. The measure of the success in a psi experiment is also determined in terms of stochastic criteria. Statistical methods are rigorously applied in order to analyze the success rate in any psi research.

The principle of nonlocal connections in quantum theory has been applied over kilometer distances, as we described. (44, 45) Eugene Wigner stated that there may be a macroscopic nonlocality that comes out of the complex Minkowski space that could yield a metrical description of the quantum theory, which does not presently have such a description (Wigner, 1981 private communication). We term this fundamental stochastic nature and universal nonlocality *stochastic causality*. That is, events are statistical aggregates of their many causes, rather than the direct effect of a single cause or linear causal chain. This principle may explain why psi is not always successful, and also why quantum processes are only predictable statistically. However, in spite of its statistical nature, quantum mechanics is able to successfully predict the optical wavelength of light emitted in spectra of atomic transitions, accurate to eight significant figures.

Here, we present a brief description of our eight-space model. The complex metrical space includes the three real dimensions of space, and the usual dimension of time, and also includes three imaginary dimensions of space, and one imaginary dimension of time. These imaginary components of space and time are real quantities multiplied by the imaginary number $i = (-1)^{1/2}$. The interesting property of i is that $i^2 = -1$, a real number. Thus in a complex space, the square of an *imaginary* distance becomes a negative distance squared. In the eight-space, the real components comprise the elements of the space defined by Einstein and Minkowski. This is actually a four-dimensional representation of what we have been taught about right triangles in high school, which is the well know Pythagorean theorem. That is, the square of the distance between the corners of the right triangle opposite the ninety-degree angle (the hypotenuse) is equal to the sum of the squares of the other two sides. This distance when measured in the complex Minkowski space is still represented by the squares of the sides of the now complex hyper-dimensional triangle. This expanded space is constructed so that each real dimension is paired with its imaginary counterpart. In the complex space, for any hypotenuse defining the space-time distance between two points we can always find an apex angle of the triangle, such that the sum of the squares of the sides, $x^2 + (iy)^2$, can be zero. That is, in the complex Minkowski space-time, *there can always be found a path of zero distance connecting any two points on the real plane.*

The standard Minkowski metrical space is constructed so that all spatial components are real. But, the square of the temporal component differs by a $-c^2$ that is formulated from ict_{Re}, yielding a component $-c^2 t_{Re}^2$. In constructing the "mirror" imaginary four-space, each spatial component has an ix_{Im} component, yielding the square component $-x_{Im}^2$. The corresponding temporal component is $+c^2 t_{Im}^2$. This is the basis upon which the eight–space allows apparent zero spatial and temporal separation.

The lowest number of dimensions that have the property of nonlocality and which is consistent with Poincaré invariance or Lorentz invariance is eight–dimensions. In this space, each physical *spatial* distance has an imaginary *temporal* counterpart, such that there is a zero spatial separation in the higher dimensional space. We hypothesize that this path is what awareness accesses in real time remote viewing. Likewise for every real physically *temporal* separation, there is a counterpart imaginary *spatial* separation that subtracts to zero on the metric, allowing awareness to access precognitive information.

Obviously nonlocality does not require the sun and the earth to be congruent or coincident with each other. This is because physical space has the attribute of force fields and the impenetrability of matter, which dominates most physical processes. This property yields the locality aspect of the physical world with which we are familiar. But, as we have described above, not all aspects of the physical world obey this locality, such as in the case of Bell's theorem nonlocality experiment. Hence, both nonlocality and locality are coexisting properties of the physical world. The physical universe is neither completely local nor nonlocal, but has attributes of both, depending on the phenomena being observed. This is a manifestation of four–logic, which we describe in the next section.

How does consciousness access this higher dimensional space? We believe it does so through the process of intentionality, which is fundamental to any goal-oriented process, including retrieval of memory. In fact, the universality of nonlocality is *just there*, filling all of space and time. That is, it is available to be accessed at will. With regard to causality, events that appear to be determined in ordinary four–space may be more amenable to the operation of our free will in the complex eight–space. In the complex space, the causal chain is multi-valued rather than linear, offering us access to a greater number of possibilities.

FOUR–LOGIC AND NONLOCALITY

Certain apparent paradoxes may not be solvable within the framework of Aristotelian two–values logic. This logic system is basic to western analytical thought. Other logic systems have been suggested in Buddhist writings such as *The Prajnaparamita*. (46) In the second century AD, the Buddhist master teacher Nagarjuna introduced a four–logic system (47, 48, 49) in which statements about the world can be [1] true, [2] not true, [3] both true and not true, and [4] neither true or not true (which Nagarjuna believed was the usual case). The four–logic system appears quite outside western consideration and thought. A seeming paradox in physics that may well find its resolution in four–logic, or at least an expansion of the restrictions of two–logic is the so-called wave/particle paradox. This may be resolved or better understood in the context of four–logic principles. It is well known that, under the conditions of various experimental arrangements, light displays either wave-like or particle-like properties. But, what then, is the essential nature of light? This question may not be amenable to the usual two–logic, and may be better addressed by four–logic or some form of expanded logic system. We might say, for example, that light is: [1] a wave, [2] not a wave, [3] both a wave and not a wave, or most correctly, [4] neither a wave nor not a wave.

Another example that is very interesting to consider, is the famous "Schrödinger cat paradox." The key to this paradox is linear superposition in quantum mechanics, which states that the unobserved cat in the box is the sum of two wave functions, ($\Psi_{alive} + \Psi_{dead}$), which represent both alive and dead conditions. Clearly this statement is not consistent with two–logic, but appears formulated in terms of the third– and fourth– of four–logic.

We hypothesize that higher dimensional spaces, such as complex eight–space may *require* four–logic at least for certain circumstances. Specifically, in treating causality conditions, we find that certain cause and effect relations may be amenable to Aristotelian logic in ordinary four–space, but phenomena such as precognition might appear paradoxical when they occur in eight–space. For example, it appears that one's future is neither determined, nor not determined, depending on whether or not one's awareness has access to eight–space.

We could state that a possible future, which has been precognized, is neither true nor not true, in the four–logic of eight–space. In ordinary four–space, the precognized event must be either true or false, as described in two–logic, creating a seeming paradox. Time passage determines the truth or falsity of a future precognized event, and this appears as standard statistical analysis that weights the possible future outcomes. What we termed "stocastic causality" is observed as such in two–logic in ordinary four–space.

The eight–space model, which involves greater degrees of freedom than four–space, may allow for what is usually termed "free will" in this space, which may appear as "deterministic" accurate precognition in ordinary four–space. The additional perceived information acquired through the sense's awareness of eight–space allows greater degrees of freedom of choice, so that what may appear deterministic because of precognitive phenomena may not be deterministic in the higher dimensional eight–space. Additional "degrees of freedom" may allow for a broader or more global concept of free will, one in which greater information and awareness allows greater choice.

That is to say, what appears to be deterministic as an either/or condition may have greater "degrees of freedom" or choices in eight–space. Precognitive awareness may allow additional choices so that either and/or conditions can exist for temporal periods in eight–space before they become fixed as either this or that in four–space (i.e. appeared determined in this space). If one has access to psi through the existence of higher dimensional spaces, one has greater opportunities to increase awareness and increase one's options and hence more free will choices. Metaphysically, instead of crawling along the four–spacetime line at 1 sec/sec, one can expand one's awareness, and learn to reside off the timeline.

For us to have access to nonlocal events in the eight–space manifold, the familiar world line of four–space becomes a point for awareness, by utilizing the additional imaginary components. Therefore, we can see that causality will manifest through the apparent past and the apparent future, which are both pulling on the apparent present. Living in eight–space guarantees that our awareness is governed by four–logic, the two appear to be inseparable. Four–logic would say that we are neither free, nor not free. Intentionality and purpose allow us to manifest our free will, and overcome the apparent deterministic limitations of four–space. We will experience free will or determinism in our lives, depending on our intentions and awareness. Our orientation and perspective in eight–space always allows us to find a path of zero distance, and often inform us usefully of the future.

FORMALISM OF THE COMPLEX EIGHT–SPACE

We will now present our formalism, which follows along lines of the detailed formalism of Hansen and Newman (17) expressed in general relativistic terms, but we express our generalized complex eight-dimensional metric in special relativistic terms because gravity appears not to occupy a role in psi phenomena. The general relativistic formalism is relevant in astrophysics and where strong gravitational fields are present. In that case, we must utilize Reimannian (curved) geometry. For our purposes here, we will utilize the line invariant element expressed in Einstein's special relativity theory. Hansen and Newman demonstrate, in their extensive paper, (50) that the complex eight–space metric yields the proper solutions to Einstein's field equations only in the condition asymmetrically flat Euclidean geometries for the case of low gravitational fields. Thus, this formalism approximates, in very general terms the conditions described by special relativity.

Einstein used a three dimensional geometric figure termed the light cone to represent the usual four–space metric or Minkowski metric in a two dimensional plane, based on the conic sections diagrams developed by the ancient Greeks. This geometric picture is formed from a figure with two axis, the ordinate is time, t and the abscissa is formed from the three dimensions of space as one axis $X = x, y, z$. The speed of light forms the sides of the two cones apex to apex (which represents "now" time) with the t axis in the vertical direction. The purpose of this picture is to define the relationship between events in four-space. For events connected by signals of $v < c$, where "c" is the velocity of light, events occur within the top of the light cone (forward time) or bottom (past time). These are termed time-like signals. Event connections outside the light cone surface $c = c$ are connected by $v > c$ and are called space-like signals and are not addressed in standard physics. As we demonstrated before, even this "elsewhere" does not give us precognition.

In defining the conditions for causality in the usual four-space, distance ds^2 is invariant and given as $ds^2 = g_{ab}dx^a dx^b$ where the indices "a" and "b" run 1 to 4. We use the metrical signature (+, +, +, -) for the three spatial and one temporal component in the metric g_{ab}. This metric is expressed as a sixteen element four by four matrix, which represents a measure of the form and shape of space. This is the metric defined on (within) the light cone, connecting time-like events. This is to insure Einstein's postulate that $v \leq c$ for any given velocity of event connection. It is clear that precognition demands more than the relaxation of the time-like event connection for $v > c$, that is, no space-like signal will yield the observed precognitive advantage in any four-space.

Rauscher (14, 15, 16), Newman, et al. (17) construct a second intersecting light cone identifiable with the four imaginary dimensions. We express the complex eight-space metric as M_4 because it represents the complexification of four space-time dimensions. The complex space is expressed in terms of the complex eight space variable Z^μ, where $Z^\mu = X^\mu_{Re} + iX^\mu_{Im}$, and $Z^{*\nu}$ is the complex conjugate of Z^μ so that $Z^\nu = X^\nu_{Re} - iX^\nu_{Im}$. We now form the complex eight-space differential line element $ds^2 = \eta_{\mu\nu} dZ^\mu dZ^{*\nu}$ where the indices run 1 to 8. The generalized complex metric in the previous equation is analogous to the usual Einsteinian four-space metric in the above paragraph. In our formalism, we proceed by extending the usual four-dimensional Minkowski space into a four-complex-dimensional space-time. This new manifold (or space-time structure) is analytically expressed in the complexified eight-space.

Here X_{Re} is represented by x_{Re}, y_{Re}, z_{Re} and t_{Re} i.e. the dimensions of our usual four space. Likewise, X_{Im} represent the four additional imaginary dimensions of x_{Im}, y_{Im}, z_{Im}, and t_{Im}. Hence, we represent the dimensions of our complex space as Z^μ or $x_{Re}, y_{Re}, z_{Re}, t_{Re}, x_{Im}, y_{Im}, z_{Im}$, and t_{Im}. These are all real quantities. It is the "i" before the x_{Im}, etc. that complexifies the space.

Now we write the expression showing the separation of the real and imaginary parts of the differential form of the metric: $dZ^\mu dZ^{*\mu} = (dX^\mu_{Re})^2 + (dX^\mu_{Im})^2$. We can write in general for real and imaginary space and time components in the special relativistic formalism.

$$ds^2 = (dx^2_{Re} + dx^2_{Im}) + (dy^2_{Re} + dy^2_{Im}) \qquad (1)$$
$$+ (dz^2_{Re} + dz^2_{Im}) - c^2(dt^2_{Re} + dt^2_{Im}).$$

Note from now on we use lowercase x and t for the three dimensions of space and one of time. Now let us represent the three real spatial components dx_{Re}, dy_{Re}, dz_{Re} as dx_{Re} and the three imaginary spatial components dx_{Im}, dy_{Im}, dz_{Im} as dx_{Im} and similarly for the real time component $dt_{Re} = dt$, the ordinary time and imaginary time component dt_{Im} remains dt_{Im}. We then introduce complex space-time coordinates as a space-like part x_{Im} and time-like part t_{Im} as imaginary parts of x and t.

Now we have the invariant line elements as
$$s^2 = |x'|^2 - c^2|t'|^2 = |x'|^2 - |t'|^2 \qquad (2)$$
again where we choose units where $c^2 = c = 1$ which is usually made for convenience

$$x' = x_{Re} + ix_{Im} \qquad \text{and} \qquad (3)$$
$$t' = t_{Re} + it_{Im}$$

as our complex dimensional components. *(Feinberg, private com. - 1976)* Then

$$x'^2 = |x'|^2 = x^2_{Re} + x^2_{Im} \qquad \text{and} \qquad (4)$$
$$t^2 = |t|^2 = t^2_{Re} + t^2_{Im}$$

Recalling that the square of a complex number is given as
$$|x'|^2 = x'x'^* = (x_{Re} + ix_{Im})(x_{Re} - ix_{Im}) \qquad (5)$$
where
$$|x'|^2 = x^2_{Re} + x^2_{Im}$$

where x_{Re} and x_{Im} real numbers. This is a very important point, as we can only measure events described in terms of real numbers. Therefore, we have the eight-space line element where spatial and temporal distances are taken from the origin.

$$s^2 = x^2_{Re} - c^2 t^2_{Re} + x^2_{Im} - c^2 t^2_{Im} \qquad (6a)$$
$$s^2 = x^2_{Re} - t^2_{Re} + x^2_{Im} - t^2_{Im} \qquad (6b)$$

Causality is defined by remaining on the right cone, in real space-time as

$$s^2 = x_{Re}^2 - c^2 t_{Re}^2 = x_{Re}^2 - t_{Re}^2 \qquad (7)$$

using the condition c = 1. Then generalized causality in complex space-time is defined by

$$s^2 = x_{Re}^2 - t_{Re}^2 + x_{Im}^2 - t_{Im}^2 \qquad (8)$$

where the coordinates in complex eight space can be represented by $x_{Re}, t_{Re}, x_{Im}, t_{Im}$ on two generalized light cones eight dimensional space. (40, 41) Let us calculate the interval separation between two events or occurrences, Z_1 and Z_2 with real separation $\Delta x_{Re} = x_{Re,2} - x_{Re,1}$ and imaginary separation $\Delta x_{Im} = x_{Im,2} - x_{Im,1}$. Then the distance along the line element is $\Delta s^2 = \Delta(x_{Re}^2 + x_{Im}^2 - t_{Re}^2 - t_{Im}^2)$ and it must be true that the line interval is a real separation. We now consider spatial and temporal distances that are generalized, that is, are not taken only from the origin, but from any two points in space and time. Then,

$$\Delta s^2 = (x_{Re,2} - x_{Re,1})^2 + (x_{Im,2} - x_{Im,1})^2 - (t_{Re,2} - t_{Re,1})^2 - (t_{Im,2} - t_{Im,2})^2 \qquad (9a)$$

Or we can write equation 9a as:

$$\Delta s^2 = (x_{Re,2} - x_{Re,1})^2 + (x_{Im,2} - x_{Im,1})^2 - (t_{Re,2} - t_{Re,1})^2 - (t_{Im,2} - t_{Im,1})^2 \qquad (9b)$$

In equation 9b, the upper left diagonal term $(x_{Re,2} - x_{Re,1})^2$ can be offset or "cancelled" by the lower right diagonal term $-(t_{Im,2} - t_{Im,1})^2$ and the lower left diagonal term $-(t_{Re,1} - t_{Re,1})^2$ is off set by the upper right diagonal term $(x_{Im,2} - x_{Im,1})^2$.

Because of the relative signs of the real and imaginary space and time components and in order to achieve the causality connectedness condition between the two events, or $\Delta s^2 = 0$, we must "mix" space and time. That is, we use the imaginary time component to effect a zero space separation. We identify $(x_{Re,1}, t_{Re,1})$ with a subject receiver remotely perceiving information from an even target $(x_{Re,2}, t_{Re,1})$.

The remote perception experiments consist of a subject receiver in a laboratory room with an experimenter monitor who elicits a response about an outbound experimenter's location, which can be a few thousand kilometers distant from the laboratory. Correlation of the subject's response is made to the outbound experimenter's activities at the remote site and the nature of that geographical location. The experiment involves a real physical separation $\Delta x_{Re} = x_{Re,2} - x_{Re,1} \neq 0$ and can either involve a current time observation such that $\Delta t_{Re} = t_{Re,2} - t_{Re,1} = 0$ or a precognitive time interval $\Delta t_{Re} = t_{Re,2} - t_{Re,1} > 0$. The case where there is no precognitive time element $\Delta t_{Re} = 0$, the simplest causal connection then is one in which $\Delta x_{Im} = 0$, and we have

$$\Delta s^2 = 0 = (x_{Re,2} - x_{Re,1})^2 - (t_{Im,2} - t_{Im,1})^2 \quad (10)$$

These conditions are illustrated in **figure 5.** In figure 5a we represent a generalized point P (x_{Re}, t_{Re}, t_{Im}), displaced from the origin, which is denoted as P1. This point can be projected on each dimension x_{Re}, t_{Re} and t_{Im} as points P2, P3, and P4 respectively. In Figure 5b, we denote the case where a real–time *spatial* separation exists between points P1 and P2 on the x_{Re} axis, so that $\Delta x_{Re} \neq 0$, and there is no precognition, so that $t_{Re} = 0$.

Because our awareness has access to imaginary time t_{Im}, it can access the P1 to P4 interval, so that $\Delta t_{Im} \neq 0$. Then, our metric gives us $\Delta s^2 = 0$, where awareness experiences contiguity between P1 and P2 by its ability to access the path to P4. By using this complex path, the physical spatial separation between P1 and P2 becomes equal to zero, allowing direct awareness of distant spatial locations, as we observe in remote viewing of distant locations. Figure 5c represents the case where precognition occurs between P1 and a future perceived event, P3 on the t_{Re} axis. In this case, no physical spatial separation between observer and event is represented in the figure. Often such separation on the x_{Re} exists. In the case where $x\, t_{Re} = 0$, then access to precognitive information, along t_{Re} can be achieved by access to the imaginary temporal component, t_{Im}.

The light cone metric representation may imply superluminal signal propagation between subject and event in the real four–space, but the event-receiver connection will not appear superluminal in some eight–space representations.

We can consider that our ordinary four–dimensional Minkowski space is derived as a 4–D cut through the complex eight–space. (16)

We have examined causality conditions in four–space with superluminal signals and the problem of closed time loops posed by G. Feinberg's classic "Tachyon" paper. (31) These problems appear to be resolved by considering a space of higher than four dimensions.

We believe that remote perception and awareness are manifestations of non-energetic phenomena, and arise from our nonlocal nature, rather than as information "sent" from one location to another.

Location of Four Events in a Complex Plane

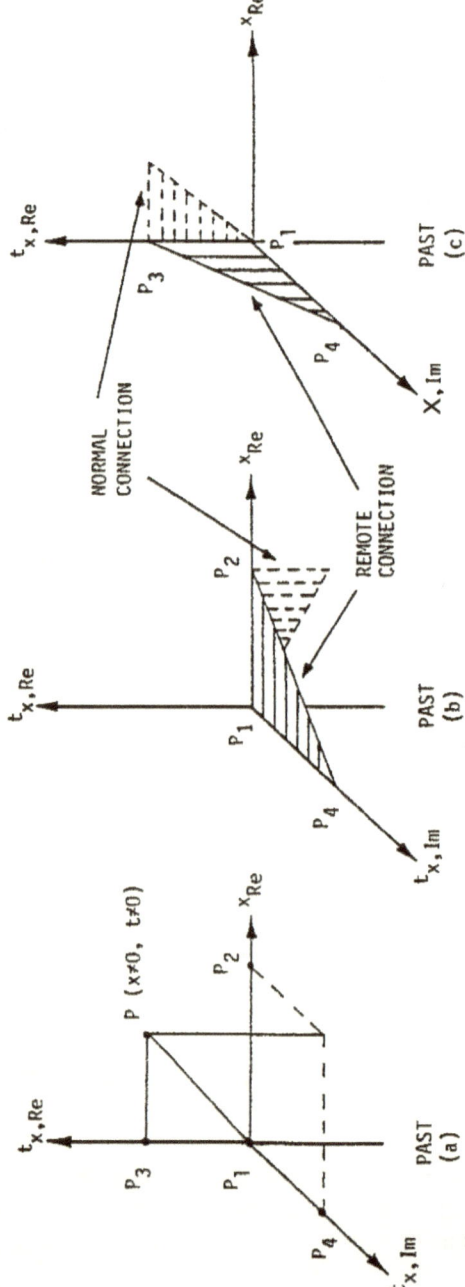

FIGURE 5. Showing the location of four points in the complex manifold. In figure 5a, point P_1 is the origin, and P is a generalized point, which is spatially and temporally separated from P_1. In figure 5b, the Points P_1 and P_2 are separated in space but synchronous in imaginary time. This could be a representation of real-time remote viewing. In figure 5c, points P_1 and P_3 are separated temporally and spatially contiguous in imaginary space. This represents a precognitive perception.

ADDITIONAL CONSIDERATION OF THE
COMPLEX EIGHT–SPACE

The complex eight–dimensional Minkowski (M_4) space metrical formalism is relevant and fundamental to a number of branches of physics. Hundreds of papers on complex eight–space by a number of researchers have been published in refereed journals, some of which are cited above. Some of this research has demonstrated the compatibility of M_4 space and standard modern physics; others have utilized complex Minkowski to better describe the foundations of physics. Some of these theoretical research papers describe the role of M_4 space in unifying the various branches of physics. Some researchers have expressed the opinion that this M_4 space may yield great contributions in unifying field models. We will briefly describe the utility of several approaches, utilizing complex eight space models, in various branches of physics.

Using general relativistic formations of Maxwell's equation, Newman has formulated Maxwell's equations in complex eight–space. (50) He demonstrates that the principle of Poincaré invariance holds and that the useful Kerr metric comes out of this formalism, and is basic to the Einstein–Maxwell field equations. Solving the non-relativistic and relativistic forms Maxwell's equations in complex eight–space yields some new and testable predictions. These predictions are detailed in Rauscher. (40, 43)

Some of the predictions of the complexification of Maxwell's equation are [1] the need for modified gauge invariant conditions, [2] short range non-Abelian force as well as the usual abelian long range forces, [3] finite but very small rest mass of the photon, [4] a magnetic monopole–like term, and [5] longitudinal as well as transverse magnetic and electromagnetic field components.

We should mention that the complex eight–space and classical mechanics are self-consistent. The form (invariance) of Newton's law of universal gravitation and Newton's laws of motion are not modified by the conditions of the complex eight–space. Essentially, as is usual in Lorentz transformation, a linear shift in axis may occur just as, for example, for time. Introducing a "–t" yields an axis shift but no changes of the form of the equations. For "t" real "+t" or "–t" both yield "t^2" which produces no changes in "t^2" in the metric, leaving the matrix unchanged and Newton's laws unchanged. The formalism of the complex eight–space is incorporated into the current Grand Unification Theories (GUT theories), supersymmetry models, and string theory that describe particle physics and the current models of the universe.

CONCLUSIONS

It appears then that there is a human perceptual modality in which distant space-time events can be accessed. The remote perception phenomena may imply, in a certain sense, that space and time are not primary physical constructs. In the words of Albert Einstein, 1941, *"time and space are modes by which we think and not conditions in which we live."* In a similar vain A. S. Eddington said, *"time is a mental construct of our private consciousness...physicists construct the concept of a world wide time from a string of subjective instances."* (1923)

The fundamental nature of nonlocality is expressed in the universe through quantum physics, in psi phenomena, and in the universality of consciousness. We have developed and presented a theoretical model, the complex Minkowski space, which expresses the nonlocal aspect of our observed reality. Not only does this model describe the data for psi, but also is consistent with the main body of physics as we presently understand it. As the data for psi become stronger and more coherent, we have the opportunity to construct physical models, which can increasingly well describe these observations.

The psi database and the properties of nonlocality in physics lead us inexorably to the conclusion that the speed of thought is transcendent of any finite velocity. Because precognition of an event is experienced prior to its apparent cause, the speed of thought appears to be instantaneous, or any other velocity one chooses. The speed of thought is therefore undefined in meters per second. Since consciousness can access the complex eight–space as though it is contiguous, space-time distances are nonexistent for mind-to-mind, or mind-to-target awareness. Separation of consciousness is an illusion. The compelling data for precognition make it appear that the future is unalterably determined. This fatalist point of view maintains that our awareness moves inexorably along the time line at a rate of one second per second. But, this seeming limitation of our free will is only a four–space perception. We believe that the higher dimensional space described here gives additional degrees of freedom, which are available to our awareness, allowing us to have greater access to possible futures.

We recognize that every ontology is perishable, and that one day it may be found that complex Minkowski space is not the best model for psi. However, we are confident that two factors will remain: namely that these phenomena are *not a result of an energetic transmission, but rather they are an interaction of our awareness with a nonlocal hyper-dimensional space-time in which we live.*

We must re-examine our concepts of time and causality, as well as determinism. Partial time symmetry, and retro-causality appear to be necessary to explain precognition, and our ability to move forward and backward in time. In our complex eight–dimensional space we are able to avoid the problems of closed time-like loops and multi-valued nows.

Certainly, the nature of psi is about our mental access, and our awareness of the truth. Ethical issues about truth also arise from the experimental and theoretical research presented here, and in many other teachings. If there is, in fact, only one of us here in awareness, we should always choose compassion over "justice," since we can always recognize compassion, but it is often difficult to discern justice from injustice. This is why the practice of compassion, and the teaching that separation is an illusion (nonlocality) are always found together in Buddhist writings. Compassion follows logically from life in a nonlocal universe.

ACKNOWLEDGEMENTS

The authors wish to express their gratitude to Dr Dean Brown for his invaluable contributions to the ontological stance presented in this paper, fruitful discussion with Dr Feinberg, and to Mike Coyle for his diligence in locating difficult to find references for our research.

REFERENCES AND NOTES

1) Stapp, H. in Nadeau, R. & Kafatos, M. (1999) *The Nonlocal Universe: The New Physics And Matters Of The Mind*. Oxford University Press.

2) Rhine, J.B, et al. (1940, 1966) *Extrasensory Perception After Sixty Years*. Bruce Humphries Publishers, Boston.

3) Targ, R. & Puthoff, H.E. (1974) "Information transfer under conditions of sensory shielding." In: *Nature*, 251, 602-607.

4) Puthoff, H.E. & Targ, R. (1976) "A perceptual channel for information transfer over kilometer distances: Historical perspective and recent research." In: *Proc. IEEE*, Vol. 64, no. 3, 329-254.

5) Bem, D. & Honorton, C. (1964) "Does psi exist? Replicable evidence for an anomalous process of information transfer." In: *Psychological Bulletin*, January.

6) Utts, J. (1996) "An assessment of the evidence for psychic functioning." In: *J. Sci. Exploration*, 10, 2, pp. 3-30.

7) Puthoff, H.E., Targ, R. & May, E.C. (1981) "Experimental psi research: Implications for physics." pp. 37-86, In: Jahn, R. G. *The Role of Consciousness in the Physical World*, AAAS Selected Symposium #57, Westview Press, Boulder, CO.

8) Sicher F, Targ, E., Moore, D. & Smith, H. (1998) "A randomized double-blind study of the effect of distant healing in a population with advanced AIDS." In: *Western Journal of Medicine*, 169, December 1998, pp. 356-363.

9) Harris, W.S., et al. (1999) "A randomized, controlled trial of the effects of remote intercessory prayer on outcomes in patients admitted to the Coronary Care Unit." In: *Archives of Internal Medicine*, 159, 2273.

10) Patanjali. *Sutra*. In: *How to Know God*. Prabhavananda, Swami & Isherwood, Christopher, (1983) Trans. Hollywood, CA: Vedanta Press.

11) Targ, R. & Katra, J. (1998) *Miracles of Mind: Exploring Nonlocal Consciousness and Spiritual Healing*. New World Library, Novato, CA.

12) Katra, J. & Targ, R. (1999) *The Heart of the Mind: How to Experience God Without Belief*. New World Library, Novato, CA.

13) Jahn, R.G. (1982) "The persistent paradox of psychic phenomena: An engineering perspective." In: *Proc. IEEE*, 70, 2, 136-170.

14) Rauscher, E.A. (1979, 80, 2003) "Some physical models potentially applicable to remote perception." In: *The Iceland Papers: Frontiers of Physics Conference*. pp. 50-93, Essentia Research Assocs. Amherst, WI. (1979). 2nd ed., The Planetary Associates for Clean Energy, Ottawa, Canada. 1996.

15) Rauscher, E.A. & Targ, R. (2003) "The speed of thought: Investigation of a complex space–time metric to describe psychic phenomena." In: *J. of Sci. Investig*. 15, 331.

16) Ramon, C. & Rauscher, E.A. (1980) "Super-luminal transformations in complex Minkowski space." In: *Foundation of Physics*. 10, 661 (1980).

17) Newman, E.T. (1976) "H-Space and its properties." In: *Gen. Rel. and Grav*. 7, pp. 107-111; Newman, E.T., Hansen, R.O., Penrose, R. & Ton, K.P. (1978) "The metric and curvature properties of H-space." In: *Proc. Royal Soc. Lond*. A363, 445-468. (1978); and Kozamah, C.N. & Newman, E.T. (1983) "A non-local variable for general relativity." In: *Proc. Third Marcel Grossman meeting on general relativity*. pp. 51-55, ed., Ning, H. Science Press and N. Holland Pub. Co.

18) Brier, R. (1974) *Precognition and the Philosophy of Science: An Essay on Backward Causation*. Humanities Press, NY (1993).

19) Jahn, R.G. & Dunne, B. (1987) *Margins of Reality: The Role of Consciousness in the Physical World*. Harcourt, Brace, NY.

20) Schlitz, M. & Gruber, E. (1980) "Transcontinental remote viewing." In: *Journal of Parapsychology*, 44, 305-317. The critical community examined this experiment. Since Schlitz and Gruber were friends, they may have been similarly affected by world events, though they did not communicate during the experiment. Gruber's comments about each target might contain words or ideas similar to those that might contaminate Schlitz's transcripts. As a result of this far-fetched, but not totally invalid criticism, the judging was repeated, omitting Elmar's comments. The significance of the study was re-calculated to 16 in 10,000—still remarkable for only 10-trials.

21) Ramakrishna Rao, K. (1984) *The Basic Experiments in Parapsychology*. McFarland & Co. Jefferson, NC.

22) Targ, R. & Harary, K. (1984) *The Mind Race, Understanding and Using Psychic Abilities*. Villard Books, NY.

23) Honorton, C. & Ferari, D. (1989) "Future-telling: A meta-analysis of forced-choice recognition experiments." In: *Journal of Parapsychology*, 53, 281-209.

24) Jahn, R.G., Dunne, B.J. & Nelson, R.D. (1987) "Engineering anomalies research." In: *Journal of Scientific Exploration*, 1, 21 (1987); Dunne, B.J., Jahn, R.G. & Nelson, R.D. *Precognitive Remote Perception*, Princeton Engineering Anomalies Research Laboratory (Report). (1983).

25) Radin, D. (1997) *The Conscious Universe*. Harper Collins, NY.

26) Cox, W.E. (1956) "Precognition: An analysis II." J. In: *ASPR*, 30, 99-109.

27) Stokes, D.M. (1987) "Theoretical Parapsychology." pp. 77 – 189. In: Krippner, S. (Ed.) *Advances in Parapsychology – 5*, McFarlane & Co., Jefferson, NC.

28) Sinclair, U. (1930 & 2000) *Mental Radio*, reprint - Hampton Roads, Charlottesville, VA.
29) Kogan, I.M. (1963) "The information theory analysis of telepathic communication experiments." In: *Radio Eng.* 23, p. 121.
30) Stratton, J.A. (1941) *Electromagnetic Theory*. McGraw Hill, NY.
31) Feinberg, G. (1967) "Possibility of faster-than-light particles." *Phys, Rev.* 159, 1089, and private conversation.
32) Einstein, A., Podolsky, B. & Rosen, N. (1935) "Can a quantum mechanical description of physical reality be considered complete?" In: *Physical Review*, 47, 777-780.
33) Bell, J.S. (1966) "On the problem of hidden variables in quantum theory." In: *Rev. Mod. Phys.* 38, 3, p. 447; Bell, J.S. (1964) "On the Einstein, Podolsky, Rosen paradox." In: *Physics*, 1, 195-200.
34) Freedman, S. & Clauser, J. (1972) "Experimental test of local hidden variable theories." In: *Physical Review Letters*. 28, 934-941.
35) Aspect, A., Grangier, P. & Roger, G. (1992) "Experimental tests of Bell's inequalities using time–varying analyzers." *Physical Rev. Letters.* 49, 1804-1907.
36) Stapp, H. (1999) In: Nideau, R. & Kafatos, M. *The Nonlocal Universe: The New Physics and Matters of Mind.* Oxford University Press.
37) Dunne, J.W. (1927) *An Experiment with Time*. Reprint by Hampton Roads, VA.
38) Bohm, D. & Hiley, B. (1989) *The Undivided Universe*. pp. 382–386, Rutledge.
39) Rauscher, E.A. (1981) "Coherent solutions of the Schrödinger equation in complex eight–space." In: *Proc. 10th Internl. Conf. on Science,* II, ICF Press, NY 1407.
40) Rauscher, E.A. (1983) *Electromagnetic Phenomena in Complex Geometries and Hertzian Waves.* Tesla Book Co. Millbrae, CA. (2005) 2nd ed., Noetic Press, CA.
41) Newman, E.T. (1973) "Maxwell's equations in complex Minkowski space." In: *J. Math Phys.* 14, 202-203.
42) Chew, G. (1964) "The analytic S-matrix, frontiers of physics." Benjamin, SF & private communication.
43) Rauscher, E.A. (2002) "Non-Abelian gauge groups for real and complex amended Maxwell's equations." In: *Vigier 2000 Symposium, Vigier III,* UC Berkeley, Kluwer Press; Dordrecht, Boston, London.
44) Gisin, N., Tittel, W. J., Brendel, J. H. & Zbinden, H. (1998) "Violation of Bell inequalities by photons more than 10 km apart." In: *Phys. Rev. Lett.* 81, 3563-3566.
45) Gisin, N., Brendel, J., Tittel, H. & Zbinden, H. (1998) II. "Quantum correlation over more than 10 km." In: *Optics and Photonics News* (Highlights in Optics 1998).
46) Hixon, L. (1993) *Mother of the Buddhas: Meditation on the Prajnaparmita*. Quest Books, Wheaton, IL.
47) Hayes, R.P. (1994) "The philosophy of Nagarjuna, Nagarjuna's Appeal." In: *Journal of Indian Philosophy,* 299-378.
48) Garfield, J.L. (1995) "The fundamental wisdom of the middle way." In: *Nagarjuna's Mulamadhyamakakarika,* Oxford University Press (1995)
49) Targ, R. & Hurtak, J.J. (2006) *The End of Suffering: Fearless Living in Troubled Times.* Hampton Roads, Charlottesville, VA.
50) Hansen, R.O. & Newman, E.T. (1995) "A complex Minkowski space approach to twistors." In: *Gen. Rel. and Grav.* 6, 361-385.

SECTION VII

PHYSICS

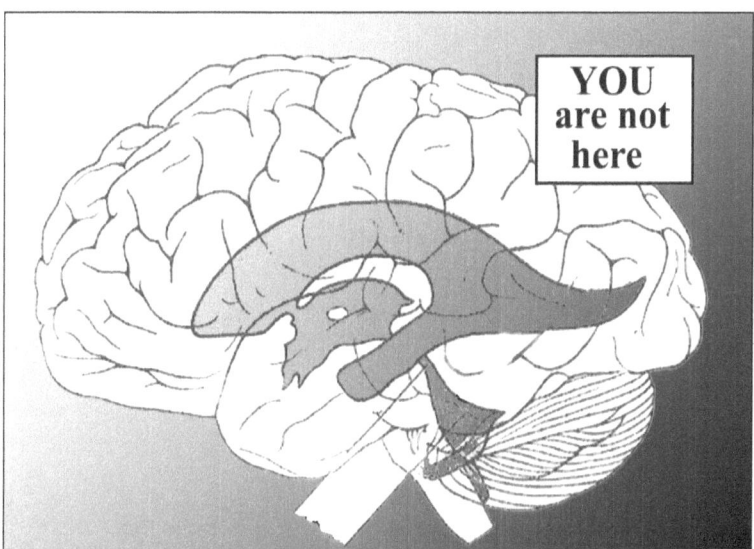

* Apologies to Tim Eagan and *"The Collected Subconscious."*

* Apologies to Harrell Graham & EarthSpace, Redmond, Oregon

SECTION IV

PHYSICS

The five physicists represented in this section have in common a deep interest in the nature of consciousness and the possibility of bringing it into the orbit of physics by way of quantum theory.

Herbert and Sirag have known each other since 1973, when they met at the Institute for the Study of Consciousness in Berkeley, and have been discussing ideas about physics and consciousness ever since, especially at Esalen physics conferences (1) and the *Consciousness Theory Group*. Herbert and Sirag got to know Rauscher in 1975 during their participation in her weekly seminar called *"The Fundamental Fysicks Group"* (FFG) at the Lawrence Berkeley Laboratory.

The main topic of discussion was Bell's theorem and its implications. Burns became acquainted with Sirag, Herbert, and Rauscher in the early 1980s in meetings of the *Consciousness Research Group,* which she cofounded in 1987. They all met at various meetings of the *Parapsychology Research Group* during this period.

It is perhaps striking that Sirag does not mention psi, and Herbert mentions psi only to say that his quantum approach to consciousness will not explain telepathy. It has long been the strategy of Herbert and Sirag to try to explain consciousness in a physical theory in such a way that psi phenomena might find a natural home.

There have been many suggestions (e.g., Walker) that quantum connectedness (Bell's nonlocality) might account for telepathy. (2) Herbert, who is an expert in this aspect of quantum theory, comes down decisively against it. His argument should be carefully considered. If he is right, telepathy will require a broader theory than quantum mechanics.

Within physics itself, we know that a broader theory than quantum mechanics is necessary. Such a theory is the goal of what used to be called unified field theory and is now called the theory of everything. Such a theory would contain both quantum theory and general relativity (Einstein's theory of gravity) as subtheories.

Sirag's approach is to propose that such a supreme theory is necessary to account for consciousness. He assumes that in such a theory a place for psi is more natural, but he does not develop this idea here. The most startling consequence of current approaches to theories of everything is that they require spacetimes of at least 10 dimensions. It is hardly novel to suggest that hyperspace (a space of more than three dimensions) might provide scope for consciousness theory. Such an idea only becomes interesting when the details are provided. Sirag's strategy is to fit mathematical structures in the hyperspace physics to aspects of consciousness such as cognition and volition. This is only a raw beginning. One might think that affect is still untouched by this approach.

Herbert suggests, *"Subjective experiences consist of the feelings that accompany quantum changes."* In other words, the quantum change is an outer manifestation, whereas the subjective experience is an inner manifestation of the same event.

The words inner and outer may be more than metaphor. They suggest the possibility of a geometric approach.

In the geometry of the supreme theory, the quantum jumps correspond to jumps from one discrete point to another in a set of discrete points, making a symmetrical structure in a certain hyperspace that Sirag calls reflection space because the jumps are a kind of mathematical reflection. The points are not states but correspond to states. Rather, the points are, in a sense, the inner manifestation of the states. Here we have an "inner" and "outer" that may match up with the inner and outer aspects of quantum jumping to which Herbert refers.

As has been emphasized by prominent quantum theorists such as Weyl and Wigner, symmetry plays a deep role in physics. By symmetry we mean a change in a system that leaves some aspect of the system unchanged. In effect, the quest for a theory of everything is a quest for the deepest symmetry. We want to know what remains invariant under the widest possible set of transformations. With reference to consciousness, this is perhaps what we mean by the self, something that remains the same through all the changes of a lifetime and perhaps even remains invariant beyond the change called death.

One important aspect of supreme theories today is the concept of broken symmetry: A system that is highly symmetrical at one level may be much less symmetrical at a lower level. The difference in levels may correspond to differences in dimensionality.

With this idea, we can make contact with the main theme of Burns' paper, *"The Arrow of Time."* Ordinarily, in basic theories of physics, time is symmetrical. The theory remains the same even if we switch the direction of the time arrow in the description of some phenomenon. If we make a movie of the phenomenon, we can run the movie backward and the theory will still provide a perfectly good description.

Some of the supreme theories have a way of introducing a time asymmetry by symmetry breaking, and this time asymmetry corresponds to the expansion of the universe.

This is not discussed in my chapter, and I mention it here because it may be relevant to Burns' chapter. She considers a combination of quantum theory and thermodynamics as a larger theory and finds it necessary to go beyond this larger theory to explain certain psi data (psychokinesis PK, dice experiments). She points out that the problem of the arrow of time – the basis for time asymmetry – is an unsolved problem with many proposed solutions. She discusses these proposals and favors the idea that the collapse of the quantum wave function may be the fundamental basis for time asymmetry. Although the evolution of the wave function is time symmetric, the collapse that occurs during any measurement is a change from a host of possibilities to one actuality. Because this one actuality is selected randomly, the collapse process is not time reversible. However, citing Walker's discussion of PK as the ability of a subject to select the actuality in a quantum collapse process, she points out that this would violate the second law of thermodynamics. This implies that a larger theory than quantum theory plus thermodynamics is necessary to embed a theory of consciousness sufficient to include psi.

Burns, in her discussion of thermodynamics, is concerned mainly with the second law, which she describes in some detail. It is useful to mention the first law, the fact that energy is conserved. This relates to the discussion of energy by Sirag that he presented in a panel discussion at the Parapsychology Research Group. The relevance of energy conservation here is that energy conservation can be derived from the time translation symmetry: the fact that a basic physics experiment does not depend on when it is done. This connection between energy and time derives from the definition of action as the product of energy and time and the law of least action, which plays a basic role in classical mechanics and becomes even more important in quantum mechanics. (3, 4)

Note that the time symmetry discussed in Burns' chapter is time reversal symmetry, which is a different matter. Broken time reversal symmetry corresponds to entropy increase. Unbroken time translation symmetry corresponds to energy conservation. This suggests that there must be some connection between energy and entropy, and there is: The second law states that entropy always increases. Another way to state this law (in addition to the statements in Burns' chapter) is that the availability of energy always decreases. (4) Moreover, quantum uncertainty also ties energy and time together: The uncertainty in energy times the uncertainty in time must be greater than or equal to Planck's constant, which is in units of action. It is because Planck's constant is in units of action that the law of least action plays such a fundamental role in quantum theory.

Rauscher's paper explores the possibility of explaining paranormal phenomena by invoking faster-than-light connections. These tachyonic connections are not based on quantum nonlocality and are consistent with

Einstein's theory of special relativity. Although special relativity forbids superlight speeds for particles of ordinary matter, it would require that a particle with imaginary rest mass always move faster than light speed. Such hypothetical particles of imaginary rest mass are called *tachyons*. The word imaginary here means that the rest mass is multiplied by the factor i, equal to the square root of minus one. This factor occurs naturally in the context of complex numbers z, which are ordered pairs of real numbers (a, b); that is, $z = a + ib$. Thus the natural framework for such a theory is not spacetime but complexified spacetime. This is an eight-dimensional real vector space formally equivalent to the four-dimensional complex vector space C^4.

Physicists have investigated the properties of complex spacetime in the context of the *twistor theory*, which is a major approach to quantum gravity. (5) In fact, a twistor can be regarded as a complex two-plane in complex spacetime. The set of all these two-planes constitutes the set of points that make up a space called *projective twistor space*. It is these points, rather than spacetime points, that are regarded as fundamental.

To provide a possible link between Rauscher's complex spacetime and Sirag's formalism, I might mention that complex spacetime is implicit in the group algebra C(OD). Embedded in this algebra is the unitary group U(2) X U(2), which could be given the name complexified *conformally compactified spacetime*. This is exactly the form of spacetime needed for twistor theory. (5) Moreover, there are profound connections between twistor theory and superstring theory, which is the other major approach to quantum gravity. (6)

I should mention that superstring theories are beset with tachyons, and great ingenuity is required to get rid of these pesky beasts because they wreak havoc with causality. Rauscher's approach to tachyons implies that perhaps some of them may be tame enough to account for strange, acausal psi phenomena.

Johnston seeks to clarify the concept of quantum wholeness (usually expressed as "nonlocality" or "entanglement"). He proposes a limited definition of wave-particle duality in which evolution of a system between measurements is always wave-like. He regards the wave as primary, and thus individuality, as distinct from wholeness, arises only upon measurement. It must be noted that quantum waves are waves of fluctuating probabilities for detecting particles. The experiments, which have sought to clarify entanglement, have led to the development of applications, such as, quantum cryptography and computers. These experiments are also widely cited by researchers in consciousness and parapsychology.

These remarks should suggest the interconnectedness and unity of ideas in physics and may perhaps help to explain the feeling that even consciousness must somehow be entailed in the basic structure of physics, especially as this structure underlies a supposed "theory of everything." It usually is thought that this program of physics is reductionistic. Perhaps it is, but notice that it is a reduction accompanied by a countervailing expansion of mathematical ideas. Moreover, the manner in which the mathematical ideas interlock would seem to be a holism of vast proportions.

··· Saul-Paul Sirag

REFERENCES AND NOTES

1) Krypal, J.J. (2007) *Esalen: America and the Religion of No Religion*. Chicago, IL: University of Chicago Press.
2) Walker, E.H. (1979) "The quantum theory of psi phenomena." In: *Psychoenergetic Systems*.
3) Wigner, E.P. (1979) *Symmetries and Reflections*. Woodbridge, CT: Ox Bow Press.
4) Feynman, R. (1965) *The Character of Physical Law*. Cambridge, MA: MIT Press.
5) Penrose, R. & Rindler, W. (1985) *Spinors and Space-Time Vol 2*. NY: Cambridge U. Press.
6) Peat, F.D. (1988) *Superstrings and the Search for the Theory of Everything*. Chicago: Contemporary Books.

CHAPTER 28 — ENERGY AND HYPERSPACE REFLECTIONS

Saul-Paul Sirag

Saul-Paul Sirag was born to missionary parents in Borneo, where he spent three years in Japanese prison camps in Java during WW II. He was raised in an orphanage near Philadelphia. He studied theology at Prairie Bible Institute in Alberta. Subsequently he went to UC Berkeley to study mathematics and physics. He served as president of the PRG between 1987-1989. He is a theoretical physicist, who has published papers on cosmology and unified field theory, especially as these topics relate to consciousness. He was a research associate at the Institute for the Study of Consciousness, in Berkeley (1973-1977). As cofounder of the Physics Consciousness Research Group, he led seminars in various California locations (1975-1976). He founded and led the Consciousness Theory Group (1977-1979). He has been a seminar leader of the annual physics conferences at Esalen, Big Sur, CA (1978-1988). He has lectured on physics and consciousness at UC Berkeley, Stanford, Georgetown, and the University of OR (Eugene). For many years he has been working on a hyperspace theory of consciousness, based on the mathematics of the unification of the four known physical forces: Electromagnetism, the weak and strong nuclear forces, and gravity.

Sirag's most detailed paper so-far is called "*Consciousness: A Hyperspace View*" and can be found on Jeffrey Mishlove's website:

http://williamjames.com/Theory/Consciousness.pdf.

CHAPTER 28

ENERGY

Saul-Paul Sirag
(With the PRG group)

Saul-Paul Sirag: I want to talk about something perhaps more mundane, which is *energy*. *[1] The reason for this is that Russell [*Targ*] has been complaining about people's use of the word "energy." At least he complained once to Jean [*Millay*] about somebody using the term *psychic energy*, and so I thought that it might be a good idea to give a brief presentation on what physicists mean by energy and how energy came into the physicist's lexicon and how that might relate to explanations of psi or non-explanations of psi, as the case may be.

So I studied up a little bit on the history of energy in physics, and actually I was quite surprised. I brought with me an old physics book—I collect old physics books. Whenever I see one, I buy one. This is quite old, published in 1837, and one of the most interesting things about it is that the word energy doesn't occur anywhere in this book *[audience laughter]*. Now that corresponds to the fact that there wasn't a physics of energy in 1837. You might think that this is just a book that was at a high school level, and so it wasn't really up with the current physics of even 1837. But actually how energy came into physics is an amazing story.

Newtonian mechanics is, in a sense, the beginning of real physics. Of course, the Greeks talked about physics—they invented the word, they invented the concept, and so on—but there wasn't really a mathematical body of theory. There were some mathematical formulas that the Greeks knew, but they didn't amount to much. We really think of physics as starting with Newton's equations.

One of the interesting things about Newton's work for us here—and it's frequently overlooked because ever since Fritjof Capra's book came out, Newton has been made sort of the bad guy *[audience laughter]* who made the world mechanistic and deterministic, and in the twentieth century quantum mechanics comes along and rescues us from all that *[audience laughter]*—that's the short version of the Capra book *[loud audience laughter]*. Capra wasn't the only one saying that; lots of people

---

*[1] More mundane than the highly metaphysical discussion of reality in the first part of the panel discussion at this May 1988 meeting of the Parapsychology Research Group.

have said that, but he said it very eloquently, and so a lot of people have that view of the history of physics.

But as a matter of fact, Newton's equations were, in a sense, a very magical set of equations because there was really no model, there was no *mechanism* whatsoever in Newton's equations. Newton's equations imply instantaneous action at a distance. He was severely criticized for this in his day, and it was in that context that he very angrily said, *"I don't make hypotheses."* Of course he made hypotheses, but he meant that he didn't have an underlying model. *"There are no strings attached between the moon and the earth; how in the world can the moon affect the tides?"* That's what people said. In fact, the French described Newton's theory as an *occult* theory for that reason because he had an occult force that acted at a distance instantaneously.

Actually, Newton realized that that was a lack in his theory, that there wasn't any underlying mechanism whatsoever. What he really believed and what he said was that space is God's sensorium. So in other words, his explanation for why the equations worked was that God made them work, so it was totally magic. However, people became familiar with those equations, and what happens when you become familiar is that the very familiarity makes it seem ordinary, makes it seem unmagical.

So it became sort of the paradigm of a mechanistic theory, and as I say, it's not mechanistic at all. However, the aspect of it that is important, which is what really impressed people, is that it was completely *deterministic*. That is to say, if you knew the positions of the planets at one point in time, then you knew the positions of the planets at any point in time. You just had to crank through the equations and you would get the position. Of course, you couldn't do it very far into the future in those days because they didn't have computers yet, but with computers and with improved mathematical techniques, we can do that quite handily.

But those are just details. The important thing is the matter of principle. The theory was, in principle, deterministic. So at first, there was a kind of worship, an awe of Newton, once people got over the shock of how magical the equations were. There was a kind of awe at the determinism, the perfect determinism of the equations, and of course, they were very successful. There were even books published that were the analog of Capra's book in the sense that they said that Newton's equations were a way of seeing the mind of God. In other words, physics at that time was being used as a way of supporting certain religious ideas. Newton himself thought of his equations that way, and other people did very much.

After about a hundred years of that, a reaction started setting in due largely to poets and philosophers like Blake who were objecting to the stifling feeling that came from the philosophy of determinism, the idea that everything was set from the word go, so to speak. Blake wrote many lines of poetry about Newton—I think he has a long poem called *Newton*, in which he asks to be saved from Newton's *sleep*. I think it was, *"God save us from single vision and Newton's sleep."* What Blake meant by that was an opposition to the supposed determinism of the universe. Determinism portrays the universe as merely clockwork—that was the catchword for Newton's theory. Newton himself didn't say that, of course, because Newton was all too aware that there wasn't any clock-like mechanism. A clock is a beautiful mechanism, whereas the planets are not. The only analogy that is valid there is the fact that a clock is deterministic and Newton's laws regarding the planets are deterministic, but otherwise, the analogy totally breaks down. The clockwork is kind of like a dead thing because once it's wound up, it just goes on until it winds down, and that's the end of the world, presumably.

A reaction set in, among the romantic poets especially, and an interesting thing is that out of this romantic reaction to Newton's determinism, the word energy started being bandied about, particularly among these philosophers and romantic poets.

Psychologist A: Did Newton use the word "energy"?

Saul-Paul Sirag: No, Newton never used the word "energy."

Physicist A: When was kinetic energy invented? (1)

Saul-Paul Sirag: I'm gonna tell about that! *[audience laughter]* No, there's no kinetic energy in Newton's work. It's all a matter of force; F=MA, and the force of gravity obeying the inverse square law. That's essentially Newton's theory of gravity, and it's not a field theory. It's an action-at-a-distance theory.

Actually, "energy" wasn't at first used in the physics context, that's the point I'm making. It was used in a personal context, that is to say, a personal freedom context, the romantic context, literally.

Physicist B: What did the word mean?

Saul-Paul Sirag: *Ergon* means *work*, and energy is the ability to do work. It's the feeling of being able to move freely. It's the opposite of the feeling of determinism, I suppose. And it's a feeling of vitality.

Physicist C: Like he says, *"Energy is pure delight."*

Saul-Paul Sirag: Yes, that is from Blake. The term really arose in that context, and the only scientists, who were thinking along the lines of an energy paradigm, you might say, were really fringe scientists in that period.

There was a German doctor named Mayer who is supposedly the discoverer of the conservation of energy. But the way he discovered it was, as you might guess, by paying attention to food, feeding rats, and weighing things. Of course, it was a rough kind of measurement that he could do in that way at that time, and he did crude little experiments that improved a little bit over the years. But he had a hard time getting that work published. When...his paper was published in 1842, that explains why there's no "energy" in here *[tapping old 1837 physics book]* whatsoever—hardly anybody knew that the thing *[Meyer's work]* was published. It wasn't published in the major journals at that time; several major journals turned down his paper.

Then in England, Prescott Joule, a self-taught amateur experimenter, was also independently trying to understand energy. One of the things that was also the impetus for his work was the development at the time of machinery that used energy in our terms today, like the steam engine, which was an important machine. But you see, the steam engine was invented by James Watt, who knew no physics whatsoever. I mean, these were just inventors, they were really fringe people; they didn't know Newton's equations. Newton's equations wouldn't have helped them one iota anyway. Knowing Newton's equations, you couldn't build a steam engine. There's nothing in there that helps you. Nothing about heat.

In other words, the concept of energy arises in the context of thinking about heat. And the problem with heat is that it's subjective before you have any equipment, before a thermometer is invented, let's say. Heat is a feeling, after all—you feel hot, you feel warm. You can have two people in the same room—one guy says it's hot, and the other guy says it's cold *[audience laughter]*. You know that problem—one guy wants the window open, the other guy wants it closed. So how can you make a science out of something so subjective as temperature—the feeling of heat?

So energy was gradually brought into the realm of physics by people like Mayer and, especially, Joule. By the way, our unit of energy in the metric system is the joule, which is one watt-second, if that means anything to you. It's not a large amount of energy, if you think about how many kilowatts of electricity you use in a day.

What Joule was able to do was to make energy respectable by doing a simple, ingenious experiment that showed an exact correspondence between the amount of heat energy and the amount of mechanical energy. In other words, he was able to define a notion of mechanical energy. He did several kinds of experiments, but I suppose his most important experiment along that line was just having a paddle moving very slowly in water or oil and measuring the change in temperature of the water as the paddle rotated a certain number of times. These were long, laborious experiments that he did, and you can imagine that the statistics on them were poor. He had to do many, many runs. It was very much like an ESP experiment *[audience laughter]* in the sense that he did many runs and he got wildly different numbers and he just averaged them to come out with these equivalences.

Hardly anybody was interested in that work. It just seemed too far off the beaten path. Joule read his paper at a scientific meeting, and no one was interested in his first experiment. So he got permission to read another paper a couple of years later when he'd improved his experiments a lot. And since there hadn't been any interest in his first paper, they were only going to give him ten minutes to read this paper in the midst of a lot of other papers being given. Fortunately, in the audience of that second paper of his was an up-and-coming 23-year-old physicist, a guy who became Lord Kelvin later on, and he saw the significance of this paper. He gave Joule a lot of feedback from the audience and then went off and did his own experiments and really developed the whole field of heat. So we have the Kelvin temperature scale, and the unit of heat in absolute units is the Kelvin.

Now the point of all this is to show how physics is a kind of a living being in a sense—it feeds on ideas and it grows. There are lots of prejudices in it, of course, but new ideas come into it, many times from the fringes of physics. A new idea comes in and gets calibrated in some way that makes sense to the rest of physics when it makes contact with some existing part of physics—not necessarily with all of physics because physics, especially at that time, was compartmentalized.

For instance, there were at the same time in the early 1800s important developments going on in electricity and magnetism. It was in 1820 that Oersted first discovered that electricity and magnetism had something to do with each other. In fact, this book, published in 1837, this is after 1820, ends with a short section on electricity and a short section on magnetism, and there's not the slightest hint that the two have anything to do with each other. So this book is quite behind the times *[audience laughter]* so far as electricity and magnetism are concerned but . . .

Psychologist B: Saul-Paul, I found a school textbook while I was looking for science textbooks that didn't seem to think that they had anything to do with each other, either. They had different sections on each one, and there was nothing that would pull the whole electromagnetic spectrum together even in this textbook recently published for junior high school students.

Saul-Paul Sirag: Well, this book came long before Maxwell's electromagnetic spectrum was invented in the late 1800s. Oersted's work was quite startling, and it took a long time for it to get into the textbooks, obviously, but the point I'm making here is that energy didn't immediately have to hook up with electromagnetism—it wouldn't have helped it much to hook up immediately with electricity and magnetism because that was a pretty far out field anyway. It had to hook up with something that was absolutely staid and established, which was mechanics, Newtonian mechanics.

It was then, in thinking about heat that the idea of kinetic energy comes in. You see there was a theory developed about that time called the *kinetic theory of heat*. This was the idea that heat is due to the random motion of atoms or small particles of some kind, that is, due to the random kinetic energy of those particles. So really kinetic energy comes into the picture first by way of heat and then it gets generalized by way of the work of Joule. That is to say, the notion of energy gets generalized, so that it includes not just kinetic energy but potential energy. That's how energy comes into the discussion of gravity, by way of potential energy.

Physicist A: When did that happen?

Saul-Paul Sirag: In the early 1800s. Joule and Kelvin had a lot to do with that. For instance, I can give this book a charge—people talk about charging—giving something an energy charge, maybe by staring at it—a flaky use of the word energy—but I can give this thing a charge simply by lifting it *[lifts book off table]*. Now it has more potential energy than it had down here on the table because I lifted it in the gravitational field. Now, Newton didn't have the notion of a gravitational field. Remember Newton's idea was that gravity worked totally by action at a distance. There's no field involved, so the field idea comes in by way of the energy idea. It actually comes in by way of potential energy, and what we say is that the potential energy is actually stored in the gravitational field. So when I lift it up, this thing here has potential energy because of where it is in the gravitational field. Now, if I drop it *[clunk]*, that potential energy is, we say in physics, transformed into kinetic energy.

So the field idea became useful in physics with the idea of potential energy being transformed into kinetic energy and doing work with that kinetic energy, and gradually, the field idea took over physics, especially in the hands of Maxwell. In the late nineteenth century, he used the field idea—the electric field idea and the magnetic field idea—to understand light itself.

Now, the first person to apply the field idea to electromagnetism wasn't Maxwell. It was Faraday, who drew lines of force explaining electrostatic fields and magnetic fields, but he was being influenced by the field thinking of the energy paradigm, you might say, that was going in that period. Now in the twentieth century, one could say that the field idea in physics is the predominant one and the particle idea is secondary.

For a while, one could say that the field idea was in a kind of abeyance or eclipse because in making the field idea consistent with quantum mechanics, tremendous difficulties were encountered because of the infinities due to the self-action of particles like an electron in a field. That was partly solved by Feynman (in the late 1940s) for electromagnetism. But the field idea didn't seem to work for other forces, such as the weak force and the strong force—the nuclear forces in other words—until the late sixties and early seventies when Weinberg and Salaam and Glashow worked out the field theory for the weak force and other people worked out a field theory for the strong force.

And, of course, Einstein conceived a beautiful field theory for gravity—the definitive field theory for gravity around 1915. Now all the forces are understood in terms of fields—you might say "energy" fields.

So the point of this history is simply that an idea that seemed flaky at first became the key idea in all realms of physics. One can't predict exactly what the future of physics will be. It could even happen that some better idea will come along and eclipse the field idea, but right now, it looks like that idea is very solid and will be here to stay.

Let me just stop there. There are lots of different things that can be said, but I'll answer some questions.

Physician: Saul-Paul, what about the curvature of spacetime explaining gravity rather than its being a force? Is that something you would recognize as already eclipsing the field idea?

Saul-Paul Sirag: Well, no, that *is* a field idea. It's a strange kind of field, a curvature field, let's say. Let me define what a field is. That's one thing that people find mysterious, this use of the word "field" in physics. A field is sort of what it sounds like—it's a spread-out, smooth structure. In other words, it's a smooth assignment of a quantity to every point of some space.

For instance, the simplest possible example, I suppose, is a temperature field, where every point in this room has a temperature associated with it and the temperature changes smoothly from one part of the room to any other part of the room. If I measure the temperature as I move along any line in the room, the temperature will change gradually. It will change at different rates, going on different paths throughout the room, but it will change gradually. Now that's an example of what we call a *scalar field* because we're simply assigning a different number, namely the temperature, and a single number is a scalar.

If we assign sets of numbers, then we might have a *vector field*. An electric field is an example of a vector field. We assign three numbers to each point in spacetime for the electric field and three numbers for the magnetic field. So, to answer your question about gravity, the way gravity is thought of in Einstein's theory is that every point of spacetime has associated with it a set of numbers that correspond to the curvature of space at that point, and that curvature in effect is the gravitational field. That's an example of a *tensor field*. The electromagnetic field is also a tensor field.

Physicist A: Saul-Paul, let me give you an example of a problem with what we mean by an *explanation*. You've given us several physically correct descriptions of gravity. You've had a number of things to say, all of which are understandable in terms of contemporary physics about gravity, but that nonetheless somebody might find unsatisfactory at a deeper level. I'm obviously not criticizing what you said because what you said is correct.

But if some child comes home from school and says, *"We were taught today about how God runs the universe."* All the parents would throw up their hands and say, *"That's terrible! How could your teacher say that?" "Well, I asked the teacher why the moon controls the tides and the teacher said, Well, the moon exerts a force on the water. And I* [the child] *wanted to know how that works? And the teacher said, All particles of matter attract one another—it's called the law of universal gravitation. Each atom in the universe has a property that exerts a force on every other atom. That's the nature of matter, that all material objects attract one another. And I* [the child] *asked, well, why is that?* And the teacher said, *Well, God made them that way, that's how we know what matter is, the fundamental property of matter, that all matter attracts all other particles of matter."*

There are many things that we would like to have described in the most infinitesimal description, the point where you run out of answers that you can give meaningfully to questions beginning with *"why."* That's why children get beaten up by their parents, *[audience laughter]* because every question that can be answered can be followed by another question at a smaller level: *"Yes, but why is that so?"* That may be one of the problems we're having describing psychic functioning.

Steve Braude, who's a philosopher, is challenging the so-called small-is-beautiful theory of description when he says that you may not find ultimate elementary psi particles that explain how psi functioning works. Psi just may not have that level of description, the same way we haven't found elementary particles of time that explain how time works. I think that this is the problem with describing gravity—we all feel we understand how gravity works, we can write descriptions of gravity and we don't ask why it is that these particles attract each other.

Saul-Paul Sirag: But we do! You see the thing is that physicists are never satisfied with the answers that we have. I mean we have to defer answers to the future all the time. Certainly Einstein, for instance, wasn't satisfied with Newton's answers about gravity, and one of the main reasons that he wasn't satisfied is simply that Newton's theory ...

Physicist A: ... didn't give the right answer!

Saul-Paul Sirag: That's not the main reason. That's just a clue that there's something wrong with the theory. There was only one discrepancy that was known when Einstein was first working on gravity, and that was that the revolution of the perihelion of Mercury wasn't correctly predicted by Newton's theory. But there was also something philosophically unsatisfying about it for Einstein, which is this action-at-a-distance business. So Einstein was trying to come up with a theory of gravity that wouldn't have that terribly unattractive feature about it.

However, we're not completely satisfied with Einstein's theory, or any theory. We do keep asking these questions, *"Why?"* If a theory says that there are just all these forces—and that's what our theories do say, they say that there are four forces—we attempt to unify the forces. (3) The reason we're trying to unify the forces is because we're not satisfied with just an answer that says there happen to be these four forces, and they happen to have these particular properties.

You see we want to go to the next level, which is exactly what the kid wants to do. Theoretical physicists actually play six-year-old kid—that's really what we're doing, we're playing that particular game. So we ask, why do these forces work the way they seem to want to work, why do they have the characteristics they do? As Einstein put it, he wanted to know whether God had any choice in the matter, which is his way of saying that he wouldn't really be satisfied with an ultimate theory of physics unless the theory could be shown to be so unique that that was the only way to do it. He never got close to that, but that was the goal, that was his vision. We're still attempting that, and yet we may never reach there.

Psychologist B: I'm really interested in all this, but one of the reasons I particularly wanted you to discuss energy is because of our original argument about energy: When spiritual healers say that they are going to "put energy through" somebody, the physicists say no, no, that's not what energy is. I really wanted to talk about the semantics problem between physics and the psi realm. People who do spiritual healing or people who are exploring these realms seem to be quite at ease with using the word energy. What word should they use instead?

Saul-Paul Sirag: Well, maybe you're misunderstanding me. I'm not saying that they shouldn't use the word "energy" at all. I'm just saying ...

Psychologist B: ... a lot of people tell me I shouldn't use that word...

Saul-Paul Sirag: ... what I'm saying is that you shouldn't use the word "energy" in that context and think that you necessarily mean the same thing the physicist means by it.

Psychologist A: How would we discriminate between those two concepts, the physics concept and the New Age concept?

Saul-Paul Sirag: Well, you have to make the point I just stated. But there's another point I want to make that I think is equally important. Remember, Newton didn't discover energy, smart as he was. All the people who were contemporary with him were smart too, and they didn't discover the notion of energy. One of the peculiar things about the notion of energy and one of the reasons that the idea of energy was discovered so late in physics is that it's invisible, it's a behind-the-scenes kind of thing, and ...

Physicist B: They just called it "work." Work is force times distance. They had energy back then, it was just a different name.

Saul-Paul Sirag: Well, energy is related to work but it's different. (4)

Psychologist B: When *[Physicist C]* was quoting Blake's equating energy with pure joy, we saw that Blake was using "energy" in the psychological sense before physicists came along and grabbed the word away from us.

Saul-Paul Sirag: Well, we used the word heat in a psychological sense before physicists gave precise notions of heat by inventing thermometers. But the point I want to make here is that the principle of the conservation of energy is interesting from the point of view that you're raising. Healers talk about putting energy into things. One thing that you have to realize is that we in physics use principles like conservation of energy to discover new forms of energy because we can use it as a bookkeeping criterion. If we do an experiment in a confined region, which means that we're able to keep track of all the energy flows, so to speak, and we find that our numbers just don't add up, that there's something missing, then we suspect that there's something going on in there that we haven't identified.

The best example of this that comes to mind is in radioactive decay. This is kind of like an alchemical change in which one type of atom changes, or decays, into another type of atom. What happens typically is that a fast electron, called a *beta particle*, that's measurable, comes out. However, there's always a tiny mass discrepancy, and there's also a discrepancy in spin. That was our first clue that there might be some overlooked type of particle, which was proposed by Pauli—he and Fermi called it the neutrino around 1930.

Now at that time, Bohr wasn't willing to countenance such a strange particle that would have no charge, no mass, but just a half unit of spin—that's it—and that would account for the energy going off. Instead, Bohr was willing to give up the principle of conservation of energy. He said that maybe on a subatomic level the principle of conservation of energy is just approximately obeyed. But most other physicists clung to the notion of conservation of energy. And by hanging on to that principle, they were able to deduce—not prove, mind you, just deduce—that there must be some other type of particle.

Now, it was more than 20 years after that—it wasn't until 1956—that the neutrino was actually shown to exist. So for 20 years there was a great deal of doubt as to whether the principle of conservation of energy even held at the quantum level or whether it was just a classic notion.

Now, the reason I'm bringing this up is that it may be that what New Age people are calling "energy" may in fact be some unusual kind of energy that we don't know about yet in ordinary physics. If that's the case then, there must be some kind of experiment we can do in which we do all of the bookkeeping on the energy flows involved, and low and behold, there's a little bit missing. Now, chances are that would be a difficult kind of experiment. But I'm just thinking that in principle, if these people are using the word energy in some way that relates to the physics of energy, then that's the sort of thing one would expect in the long run, however long the long run is.

Psychologist C: What can you say about the historical concept of the luminiferous ether with respect to energy fields—and healing—inasmuch as it may have some mass effect?

Saul-Paul Sirag: The luminiferous ether was invented by nineteenth-century physicists who established the wave theory of light. It got its more or less definitive form in Maxwell's equations. The ether was simply invented to answer the question of what is waving in a light wave, and in Maxwell's case, what is waving in the electromagnetic wave. The problem with Maxwell's luminiferous ether was that it had properties that were, to say the least, contradictory. But people lived with that because in physics, there are always conundrums going on. That was the great conundrum of the late nineteenth century, the luminiferous ether.

Then a crucial experiment was done by Michelson and Morley, who attempted to find out the velocity of the earth with respect to the luminiferous ether. Maxwell's equations implied that that was possible. In fact, Maxwell himself proposed the experiment—he was aware that that's what his equations implied. As you know, they came up with a negative result; that is to say, they came up with the result zero. Einstein explained that result by saying that there isn't any luminiferous ether. And Einstein explained the relation between electromagnetism and ordinary mechanics by the special theory of relativity.

Now, one might say that in quantum mechanics, a kind of ether has been reinvented, called the *quantum vacuum*, which has many properties of the old luminiferous ether and many new properties, properties that are magical in the quantum mechanical sense. For one thing, the quantum mechanical vacuum is exceedingly active. It's just seething with stuff going on, and we picture particles and fields coming in and out of the vacuum all the time. That's the big mystery of the late twentieth century, you might say, the quantum mechanical vacuum. It's playing the role, in a sense that the luminiferous ether played in the nineteenth century and nobody knows what the result is going to be. But some "Einstein" might come along and get rid of that too in some magical way, and that would undoubtedly create a profound change in physics. What that may have to do with psi and healing who knows? But it's a fundamental thing.

NOTES

1) In 1807, Thomas Young proposed the name "energy" for the older term *vis-à-vis*, mass times velocity squared. However, "energy" was considered too disreputable a term by most physicists until the 1840s.

2) The four known types of forces are the electromagnetic, gravitational, weak atomic nuclear, and strong atomic nuclear.

3) The idea of *force times distance* as an independent concept called *work* (and other names) was introduced in the 1820s after "energy" was proposed for *mass times velocity squared* (1807). Cf. Thomas Kuhn, *The Essential Tension*. Chicago; 1977:84.

Paranormal phenomena seem unusual because the spacetime projection provides only a partial view of the hyperspace events.

--- Saul-Paul Sirag

HYPERSPACE REFLECTIONS

Saul-Paul Sirag

The idea that space is more than three-dimensional is at least as old as Plato, who, in his Parable of the Cave, suggested that we usually identify ourselves with our three-dimensional shadows rather than with the higher-dimensional beings we really are. (1) This idea was rejected by Aristotle and subsequent generations of physicists. Recently, however, theoretical physicists working on unified field theory have found it necessary to postulate the physical reality of hyperspace, defined as a space of more than three dimensions (3-d). These proposed physical hyperspaces are 10-d or 26-d or even higher-dimensional spaces. (2)

Mathematicians began describing abstract (nonphysical) hyperspaces in the nineteenth century. They could do this because the ideas of classical geometry of 2-d and 3-d could be extended in various ways. For instance, a coordinate system can be set up in a 2-d space so that any point can be located by two numbers (e.g., latitude and longitude on the 2-d surface of the earth, or the x-y axes of a 2-d plane). Thus, by extension of this idea, three numbers would locate any point in a 3-d space, and n numbers would locate any point in an n-d space.

All 2-d spaces are either flat or curved, and this distinction can be generalized to any number of dimensions. Roughly speaking, a curved space of any dimension is a space that cannot be flattened without tearing. The unsuccessful attempt of mapmakers to construct an untorn, undistorted flat map of the Earth's surface led to this fundamental distinction between flat and curved.

Thus ordinary 3-d space and 4-d spacetime seem to be flat and were believed to be flat by physicists until Einstein's theory of general relativity (1915) proposed that gravity corresponds to curvature of 4-d spacetime. This implied that 3-d space could be curved and might form the 3-d sphere S^3 when viewed as a whole, that is, at the cosmic scale.

An ordinary globe or sphere is called a 2-sphere or S^2. The area of a 2-sphere is $4\pi r^2$ and is finite if the radius r is finite, whereas the area of the flat 2-plane of high school algebra extends to infinity and is thus infinite in area. A finite-size space such as the 2-sphere is called a compact space.

It is an open question whether the 3-d space in which dwell the planets and galaxies is a (flat) 3-plane of infinite volume, a sphere S^3 of finite volume $2\pi^2 r^3$, or some other curved space (of finite or infinite volume). This is a question to be answered by observational cosmology—the telescopic study of distant galaxies—in conjunction with theoretical cosmology, which is the mathematical description of the large-scale structure of space and time in accordance with Einstein's (1915) theory of gravity, called the general theory of relativity.

Einstein's theory says that gravity is not a force acting at a distance (as in Newton's theory), but rather controls the movement of particles along the geodesics (straightest possible paths) in a curved 4-d spacetime. The curvature of spacetime, which is allowed to vary over every point of spacetime, is an expression of particle masses and energies.

The fact that spacetime carries properties of 4-d distance (called interval) and curvature makes it clear that spacetime is a space, in fact a hyperspace, from the point of view of geometry.

The precedent set by general relativity suggested to physicists that it might be possible to bring other forces into the geometrical picture by increasing the dimensionality of the physical hyperspace.

In the 1920s, Kaluza and Klein proposed a unification of general relativity and electromagnetism by introducing a 5-d hyperspace generated as a product of spacetime (4-d) and a circle (1-d)—just as spacetime is a product of 3-d space and 1-d time. They showed that particles moving on geodesics in the 5-d hyperspace project down to paths of particles moving in 3-d space under the combined action of gravity and electromagnetism. This projection is the 5-d analog of the ordinary projection of a 3-d body onto a 2-d shadow. Shades of Plato! The reason we don't see the fifth dimension is that, as Klein calculated from quantum-theoretic considerations, the circle is very tiny—around 10^{-30} cm. In other words, we would have to be smaller than this size to be able to move around in the extra dimension. Not even a proton, which is around 10^{-13} cm, could explore this region.

This unification of gravity and classical electromagnetism was an astounding achievement. It was praised by Einstein, who could see its beauty and the possibility of applying it to the problems of quantum mechanics. It was, however, forgotten for many years because it did not account for the nuclear forces, which occupied the attention of most theoretical physicists in the 1930s and 1940s.

The Kaluza-Klein scheme has recently been revived by physicists seeking to unify all the forces. (3) In these new hyperspace schemes, the hyperspace is a mathematical structure called a *principal fiber bundle*: a space of **B + F** dimensions, where **B** is the dimensionality of a base space (e.g., spacetime) and **F** is the dimensionality of a fiber, a copy of which is attached to each point of **B**. There is a projection of the fiber space down to the base space such that all the points of a single fiber project onto a single point of the base space. Moreover, the fiber is not only a space, but also a set of symmetry transformations called a Lie group (after the nineteenth-century mathematician Sophus Lie). The symmetry transformations act on the fiber. In other words, the Lie group acts on itself. It does this by moving its points along geodesics in the fiber. In unified field theory, spacetime is considered the base space.

A geodesic path is a "free-fall" path, which means that an object traversing a geodesic feels no force. A skydiver (before opening his parachute) and an astronaut floating in orbit are in free-fall and do not feel any force, except the electrical and nuclear forces holding the atoms and molecules of their bodies together. General relativity teaches that gravity is not a force, but consists of the movement of particles in free-fall paths (geodesics) in curved spacetime. The Kaluza-Klein scheme generalizes this idea to include all the so-called forces. To do this, the correct fiber bundle must be chosen from the myriads of fiber bundles available in mathematics.

The path of a particle moving along geodesics in the hyperspace of the fiber bundle can be projected to a path in the base space (i.e., spacetime). The spacetime path will not be a geodesic, but a path seemingly acted on by a force (or set of forces) characterized by the structure of the fiber. Given the fact that the geodesics occur in the hyperspace (i.e., the fiber bundle), it is only natural to assume that this hyperspace is the true reality of the theory and that the occurrences in the base space are only appearances.

It is necessary not only to choose just the right fiber (i.e., symmetry group) to make this scheme describe the real physical world, but also to choose the right spacetime.

It has been discovered that spacetime must be at least 10-d to make the theory consistent with both the rules of general relativity and the rules of quantum mechanics. (3) Moreover, the most popular scheme, called *superstring theory*, replaces the point particles of quantum field theory with vibrational modes on tiny lines, called strings, which can be closed (like circles) or open (like threads). This scheme requires a 10–d spacetime: The 1–d strings move in a 9–d space, and as they move, they sweep out a surface in a 10-d spacetime. From the Kaluza-Klein point of view, the fiber (i.e., symmetry group) in the most popular version of superstring theory is the $E_8 \times E_8$ Lie group, which is 496–d. This group is generated by a 16–d structure that I call a "reflection space," which possesses symmetry properties that facilitate the cancellation of "anomalies" that would otherwise make the theory inconsistent.

These symmetry properties correspond to the packing of hyperspheres in 8–d space. The closest possible sphere-packing in 8–d space is 240 7–d spheres around a central 7–d sphere. This 8–d space is the reflection space of a group called E_8, whose dimensionality is 240 + 8 = 248. The full symmetry group of the standard superstring theory is a product of two of these groups, $E_8 \times E_8$, whose dimensionality is double that of E_8, that is, 496–d, with a 16–d reflection space. Note that when we form product spaces the dimensions add: The product of a 1–d space and a 1–d space is a 2–d space. The word product is justified by the fact that metrical content multiplies; for example, 2 cm along x and 3 cm along y (assuming an x,y–axis system) defines an area of 6 cm. (2)

Incidentally, I use the term reflection space because, as will be explained below, a kind of mathematical reflection takes place in such a space, which technically is called the "dual space of a Cartesian subalgebra of a semisimple Lie algebra."

Much of the current work in superstring theory is devoted to explaining how four of the spacetime dimensions expand in accordance with the currently favored big-bang theory of cosmology, whereas the other six dimensions remain small (about 10^{-30} cm in radius) and thus become internal dimensions. Other work is devoted to reducing or extending the standard 496–d fiber in various ways. But it would seem that physical hyperspace is here to stay.

Evidence for the physical reality of hyperspace could come from predictions made from superstring theory, especially as it relates to the earliest stage of the universe—at the Planck time 10^{-43} seconds after the start of the big bang. For example, various exotic particles may have been constructed at this time, some of which may still exist.

The strategy of this chapter is to assume the reality of the hyperspace (in particular, the reflection space) and to use this assumption to speculate about the nature of consciousness in the context of the mind-body problem. Verifiable consequences of this strategy will provide indirect evidence for the reality of the physical hyperspace.

The mind-body question can be posed as follows: Are the mind and body fundamentally different entities? If so, how do they interact? (This is the problem of dualism.) If not, why do they seem so different? (This is the problem of monism.) In 1637, Descartes defined a kind of dualism of mind and matter by defining matter as *res extensa* and mind as *res cogitans*. (4) This has made the problem of interaction acute, for, it is argued, how can matter, which is extended in space, interact with mind, which is not extended in space? To answer this criticism of Cartesian dualism, psychiatrist J. Smythies, (5, 6) following the lead of philosopher C. D. Broad, (7) has proposed a non-Cartesian dualism: Mind *is* extended in a spacetime that is connected to but different from ordinary physical spacetime. If we reduce 4-d spacetime to a 2-d spacetime, we can picture this as two sheets of paper (each representing a 2-d spacetime, one mental and one physical) that intersect each other in a line. In general, when two spaces intersect, we call the space that the two spaces have in common the intersection space. The dimensionality of the intersection space depends on the dimensionalities of the two intersecting spaces as well as on the manner of intersection.

The Broad-Smythies scheme is not a model of mind-body interaction, but provides a general framework for such a model. My approach is to look for a unified-field-theory hyperspace structure that entails the intersection of two spaces. It is clear that this intersection structure must be a special kind of space. In fact, I propose that it is the reflection space of the unified field theory itself.

A reflection space is a mathematical concept inspired in part by Lewis Carroll and in part by the kaleidoscope. Alice in Carroll's *Through the Looking Glass* assumed that she could go from the world in front of the mirror to a similar world behind the mirror. We smile at this childish naiveté and know that no such thing is possible in the physical world of ordinary mirrors. Mathematicians, however, have discovered abstract reflection spaces that function much as Alice imagined her world to function. (8, 9)

To understand the mathematician's reflection spaces, we shall first describe an ordinary kaleidoscope and then describe the mathematical reflection spaces abstracted (and generalized) from it. If you set two ordinary physical mirrors in 3-d space at 60 degrees to each other and stand between them, you will see four extra mirrors as reflections of these mirrors, so that you will see five copies of yourself, that is, six images including yourself. This is similar to the way a kaleidoscope works. To see this, set up two mirrors at 60 degrees to each other, with their edges resting on the floor. (A pair of hinged mirrors works best.) The part of the floor between the mirrors is called the *fundamental region*. Place some pattern in this fundamental region. When looking down at the fundamental region from above, we see the pattern reflected five times, making six images of the pattern, thus deriving a hexagonal (snowflake) design. A toy kaleidoscope is nothing but a miniature version of our hinged mirrors mounted in a tube with bits of colored glass in the fundamental region of the viewing screen.

To abstract a mathematical reflection space from the physical kaleidoscope, we regard the 2-d viewing screen of the kaleidoscope as a 2-d mathematical reflection space. In general, an n-dimensional reflection space with n basic mirrors can be defined.

We can describe the mathematical definition of a reflection as follows: A reflection is a transformation of all the points in the reflection space from one side of a mirror plane to the other side and vice versa. This transformation must reverse the direction of all the vectors attached at 90 degrees to either side of the mirror. This transformation also must leave the mirror fixed and leave the measure of distance in the space unchanged. This definition of reflection requires a mirror to cut the space in half. Moreover, repeating a reflection restores the original space just as if it had not been transformed. We write $r^2=1$, where r is a reflection and 1 is the identity transformation, which is to say, "do nothing."

The reflections that correspond to the mirrors bordering the fundamental region are the basic reflections. Any possible reflection in a particular reflection space is merely a combination of some or all the basic reflections in some particular order. In fact, the set of all possible combinations of basic reflections in a given reflection space form an algebraic structure called a *reflection group*.

Each reflection group acts in its own reflection space, which is defined by the placement of mirrors, each of which bisects the reflection space. A line in a plane has two sides, but a line in 3-d space has an infinity of "sides." Therefore, a line cuts a 2-d space into two parts, whereas it takes a 2-d plane to cut a 3-d space into two parts. Similarly, a 3-d hyperplane cuts a 4-d hyperspace into two parts. This means that the mirrors of various n-dimensional reflection spaces will have to be hyperplanes of dimension **n – 1**. To describe the mutual orientations of the mirrors with respect to each other, we make use of a mirror vector (of unit length) attached to each mirror at a right angle. We attach these mirror vectors at the point where all the mirrors intersect.

For the kaleidoscope viewing screen, setting the mirrors at 60 degrees to each other makes the mirror vectors point 120 degrees away from each other. In generalizing the kaleidoscope viewing screen to n-space, we shall consider only the case of the n basic mirror vectors set at 120 degrees to each other.

We define these reflection spaces as spaces generated by basic mirror vectors separated by 120 degrees. There are other reflection spaces known to mathematics, but these kaleidoscopic reflection spaces with basic mirror vectors set at 120 degrees to each other are the simplest and the most useful. (10)

It is known that there are three types of these simple reflection spaces, called **A, D,** and **E**. A and D constitute two infinite series of reflection spaces. For each dimension n, there is an A_n type—A_2 being the ordinary kaleidoscope 2-d viewing screen. For each dimension n beyond 3, there is a D_n type. The type **E** is called exceptional because within this category, only reflection spaces E_6, E_7, and E_8 exist. Moreover, all these reflection spaces are hierarchical in the sense that the A_n reflection space contains the $A_n - 1$ reflection space; D_n contains $D_n - 1$; and E_8 contains E_7, which contains E_6. Also, D_n contains $A_n - 1$ whereas E_n contains both $A_n - 1$ and $D_n - 1$.

Now there is a deep sense in which one of these reflection spaces (with all its lower-dimensional embedded spaces) must be the kaleidoscopic "viewing screen" for the physical world.

According to quantum mechanics, the only observable quantities in the world are certain numbers called *eigenvalues* of observation "operators." A unified field theory supposedly describes all the basic eigenvalues and observation operators of the world. Reflection spaces are central to this task because the observation operators form a basis for a reflection space, whereas the eigenvalues are sets of numbers in the reflection space that define the mirror vectors and their "duals." In this by now standard scheme, the force particles correspond to the mirror vectors.

The matter particles correspond to dual vectors that can be derived from these mirror vectors by a certain nonreflection transformation of the reflection space itself. (Technically, the mirror vectors are called "roots" and the dual vectors are called "weights.") (11)

Note that observation is an aspect of consciousness. In this context, it is significant that mathematician John von Neumann and physicist Eugene Wigner have proposed that consciousness be the ultimate repository of quantum observations. (12) One consequence of the nonlocality of quantum mechanics, as proved by Bell's theorem, is that this consciousness as theorized by von Neumann and Wigner must be a universal consciousness. (13, 14) Thus it becomes plausible to regard some appropriate reflection space as the space of universal consciousness.

In 1974, the A_4 reflection space was used by Georgi and Glashow to unify three forces. (15) The four dimensions of the A_4 reflection space were allocated as follows: electromagnetism **(1–d)**, the weak force **(1–d)**, and the strong color force **(2–d)**. [Their theory usually is called the **SU(5)** grand unified theory because **SU(5)** is the continuous symmetry group—or the fiber as described above associated with A_4.]

To bring gravity into the unification scheme, much larger reflection spaces seem to be necessary. This is related to the fact that a **10-d** spacetime is required. Hundreds of physicists are working on superstring theory in which the reflection space of $E_8 \times E_8$ (described above) is the repository of observable charges. (16-18) This scheme is plausible only because of the hierarchical structure embedding the A_4 reflection space in that of E_8.

I have been working on an alternative route to unified field theory in which I introduce a finite group called the octahedral double group **OD**, whose **48** elements provide an explanation for the three families of matter particles. (19–22) Accounting for these families is considered the deepest problem of unified field theory. So my strategy has been to start with the deepest problem, rather than to deal with this problem after an enormous mathematical machinery is in place.

In quantum field theory, a set of n particles generates an n-dimensional space. Because the 48 elements of the **OD** group can be given particle labels, they will generate such a space. Moreover, this space will be an algebra, because the 48 elements are group elements. This is the **OD** group algebra, written as **C[OD]**. This is a linear algebra that has a "regular" representation consisting of 48 X 48 matrices. This group algebra has a **10–d** subalgebra that could play the role of a **10–d** spacetime for a version of superstring theory. Seven of these 10 dimensions form another subalgebra that can be identified with the E_7 reflection space because of an amazing theorem that makes a one-to-one correspondence between the **A-D-E** reflection spaces and the symmetries of certain Platonic structures: (23)

A$_n$ corresponds to the symmetries of an **(n + 1)**–sided polygon.

D$_n$ (n greater than 3) corresponds to the symmetries of an **(n - 2)**–sided polygon, assuming we can turn the polygon over.

E$_6$, E$_7$, and **E$_8$** correspond to the symmetries of the tetrahedron, octahedron, and the icosahedron, respectively.

McKay's theorem implies that the entire 133–d Lie algebra E_7 (generated from the E_7 reflection space) intersects with the 48-d group algebra **C[OD]** in such a way that the E_7 reflection space is the overlap region (called C_7). In analogy with the Broad-Smythies hypothesis that mental spacetime and physical spacetime are partially separate spaces that interact by way of the *intersection* between them, I propose that:

E_7 is universal mind (both consciousness and "the unconscious");

C[OD], since it includes spacetime, is universal body;

C^7, the E_7 reflection space, which is the intersection between E_7 and **C[OD]**, is universal consciousness.

In this theory, the physically observable charges reside in the E_7 reflection space C^7. In the standard superstring theory, these charges would reside in the 16–d reflection space of E_8 X E_8. In the standard theory, however, one projects immediately down to the reflection space of E_6, skipping over E_7 for certain technical reasons. The E_6 reflection space is contained in that of E_7, whereas the E_7 reflection space is contained in that of E_8. The main problem of the standard theory is making appropriate contact with the "low energy" particle structure – the charges residing in the A_4 reflection space – that describes the three (non-gravity) forces well known to physics. This means that one has to provide a role for the other charges in the E_6 reflection space. This role could be a mental one if a different strategy for a unified field theory were used.

My strategy is to use the E_7 reflection space C^7 as a bridge to the "low-energy" particle structure described by the group algebra $C[OD]$. All the charge structure in the reflection space is a structure of observable quantities, hence the connection with consciousness.

Because C^7 is universal consciousness, it is necessary to describe how individual conscious entities emerge from this theory. To describe this, we must first describe how ordinary spacetime couples to C^7. The ordinary spacetime of this theory is a substructure of the universal body $C[OD]$. The 3-d part of spacetime is the sphere S^3, whereas time is in C^7, or rather in a space written as C^7/W, where W is the E_7 reflection group acting in C^7. In other words, all the reflections acting in C^7 generate C^7/W as a new 7-d space that has special features. Most important, C^7/W is time plus the 6-d control space of a "catastrophe structure." (24–26)

A *catastrophe* is a structure with a dynamic system and a set of control parameters on which the dynamic system depends in such a way that a small change in one or more of the control parameters corresponds to a large change (perturbation) in the dynamic system.

We can consider a path in C^7/W to be the path of an individual consciousness. Because of the structure of the intersection between E_7 and $C[OD]$, every point of S^3 can be considered a copy of C^7/W.

Movement in S^3 is correlated with movement along a path in C^7/W. Moreover, a small change along such a path can correspond to a large change in S^3. Hence a small change in consciousness can correspond to a large change in a body that is a subspace of S^3.

The six control parameters correspond to the six internal dimensions of the 10-d superstring space of this theory. This implies that every point of ordinary spacetime has access to six control parameters. A body is a subspace of S^3, and a brain is a means of accessing, in a richly interconnected way, a large number of paths in C^7/W.

Many more aspects of C^7 seem suggestive of aspects of consciousness. For example, the E_7 mirror vectors generate an error-correcting code – the Hamming-7 code – which is well known to communication engineers. The dual vectors generate the E_7 quantizing scheme (i.e., analog–to–digital conversion). (26) There also is the E_7 "contact" structure and the E_7 "quiver." The list goes on and on.

The richness of these reflection-space structures can be surmised from a proposition of Russian mathematician V. I. Arnold: *"To easily checked properties of one set of associated objects correspond to properties of the others, which need not be evident at all. Thus the relations between all the A, D, E – classifications can be used for the simultaneous study of <u>all simple objects</u>, in spite of the fact that the origin of many of these relations (for example, of the connections between functions and quivers) remains an unexplained manifestation of the mysterious unity of all things* [emphasis added]." (31)

Because the **A-D-E** classification structure is hierarchical, higher-dimensional objects contain the lower-dimensional objects. This suggests that if the E_7 reflection space corresponds to consciousness, there are higher and lower realms of consciousness. In this regard, E_6 and E_8 are especially interesting, since these three are the only exceptional structures in the **A-D-E** scheme. And these exceptional structures are the link to nonsimple structures. (25, 26)

In 1864, Maxwell unified electricity and magnetism in such a way that he produced an electromagnetic theory of light. This unification made the startling proposal that visible light is merely a tiny part of the electromagnetic spectrum.

Similarly, because we today are unifying all the forces, something new, analogous to light, should come out of our endeavors. I propose that a theory of consciousness should emerge and that such a theory should imply that "ordinary" consciousness is but a small part of a spectrum of realms of consciousness. Because, through Arnold's work, the **A-D-E** classification is itself a small part of a vast scheme that deals with nonsimple mathematical objects – for example, chaos – there are many realms for us to explore. (25, 26)

UPDATE (2007)

In 1995 Edward Witten (27) unified the five competing string theories into a single overarching theory he called M–theory, where M (according to Witten) stands for *"magic, mystery, or membrane – according to taste."* M-theory itself is an 11–d spacetime theory, whose symmetry group is E_7 – with the 7 hidden dimensions being the 7–d torus structure of the maximal commutative subgroup of E_7. This development was very exciting to me, since I had made E_7 central to my approach (as in the title of reference **20**). However, it is clear that all the **A-D-E** Coxeter graphs must be seen as a unified whole, since the higher dimensional graphs contain the lower dimensional graphs as substructures. Each mathematical object classified by the **A-D-E** graphs provides a separate window into a vast underlying structure, which I take to be reality in all its complexity. So I call this approach to the unification of reality ADEX-theory, where the X stands for the vast underlying structure of reality. (See the table below.)

UPDATE (2009)

In 2002, the University of London physicist Bernard Carr gave his presidential address to the Society for Psychical Research. Under the title *"Worlds Apart? Can Psychical Research Bridge the Gulf Between Matter and Mind?"* he presented in great detail a hyperspace approach to the mind-body problem. This has now been published as a 96-page paper in the *Proceedings of the Society for Psychical Research* (Vol. 59, Part 221).

The A-D-E Coxeter graphs (Dynkin diagrams)
ADEX-theory: the study of all the A-D-E-classified objects

Label:	Coxeter graphs:	Compact Lie groups:	Total no. of mirrors:	McKay subgroup of SU(2): no. of elements:
An:	•–•-...-•	$SU(n+1)$	$(n^2 + n)/2$	Cyclic: Z_n: $(n+1)$
Dn:	•–•–•-...-• | •	$SO(2n)$	$n^2 - n$	Dihedral double: Dd_n $2n$
E6	•–•–•–•–• | •	$E(27)$	36	Tetrahedral double: TD 24
E7	•–•–•–•–•–• | •	$E(56)$	63	Octahedral double: OD 48
E8	•–•–•–•–•–•–• | *	$E(248)$	120	Icosahedral double: ID 120

Note: These graphs classify many mathematical objects of great importance in physics (especially unified field theory, string theory, and M-theory). Thus they provide a way to transform from one type of object to another. These objects include:

Lie algebras (and Lie groups): Gilmore (10), Georgi (11).
Kac-Moody (infinite–d) algebras: Kaku (28), Kac (29).
Coxeter (reflection) groups: Coxeter (8,9), Grove & Benson (30).
McKay groups (finite subgroups of SU(2): McKay (23).
Hyperspace crystallographies: Coxeter (8), Conway & Sloane (31). 6-2008.
Sphere-packing (root) lattices); error-corr. codes: Conway & Sloane (31).
Quantizing (weight) lattices; analog-to-digital changes: C. & S. (31).
Conformal field theories (living on 2–d string world-sheet): Kaku (28).
Gravitational instantons (cf twisters): Kronheimer (32) Ward & Wells (33).
Arnold-Thom catastrophes: Thom (34), Arnold (26), Gilmore (35).
Singularities of differentiable maps: Arnold (25).
Heisenberg algebras (in various hyperspaces): Kostant (36).
Kortweg de Vries hierarchy of nonlinear equations: Julia (37).
Generalized Braid groups (cf. knots and links): Kauffman (38), Birman (39).
Quivers: Derksen & Weyman (40).

REFERENCES

1) Plato. *The Republic*. In: Hamilton, E. and Cairns, H. (Eds.) *The Collected Dialogues of Plato*. Princeton, NJ: Princeton University Press, 1961:747-749.
2) Duff, M.J. (1986) "Recent results in extra dimensions." In: Piran, I. & Weinberg, S. (Eds.) *Physics in Higher Dimensions*. Singapore: World Scientific, 1986:40-91.
3) Appelquist, T., Chodos, A., Freund, P.G.O. (1987) *Modern Kaluza-Klein Theories*. Menlo Park, CA: Addison-Wesley.
4) Descartes, R., cited in Gregory, R.L. (Ed.) (1987) *The Oxford Companion to the Mind*. Oxford.
5) Smythies, J.R. (Ed.) (1967) "Is ESP possible?" In: *Science and ESP*. London: Routledge & Kegan Paul, 1967:1-14.
6) Smythies, J.R. (1971) "Aspects of consciousness beyond reductionism." In: Koestler, A. & Smythies, J.R. (Eds.) Boston: Beacon Press, 1971:233-257.
7) Broad, C.D. (1927) *The Mind and Its Place in Nature*. London: Routledge & Kegan Paul.
8) Coxeter, H.S.M. (1973) *Regular Polytopes*. (3rd ed.) NY: Dover.
9) Coxeter, H.S.M. (1991) *Complex Regular Polytopes*. (2nd ed.) NY: Cambridge U. Press.
10) Gilmore, R. (1974) *Lie Groups, Lie Algebras, and Some of Their Applications*. NY: Wiley–Interscience.
11) Georgi, H. (1982) *Lie Algebras in Particle Physics*. Reading, MA: Benjamin/Cummings.
12) Wigner, E.P. (1979) *Symmetries and Reflections*. Woodbridge, CT: Ox Bow Press.
13) d'Espagnat, B. (1983) *In Search of Reality*. NY: Springer-Verlag.
14) Herbert, N. (1985) *Quantum Reality*. Garden City, NY: Doubleday, Anchor Press.
15) Georgi, H.A. (1981) "Unified theory of elementary particles and forces." In: *Scientific American*. April 1981:48-63.
16) Green, M.B. (1986) "Superstrings." In: *Scientific American*. September 1986:48--60.
17) Green, M.B., & Gross, O.J. (1986) *Unified String Theories*. Singapore: World Scientific.
18) Peat, F.D. (1988) *Superstrings and the Search for the Theory of Everything*. Chicago: Contemporary Books.
19) Sirag, S.P. (1982) "Why there are three fermion families." In: *Bulletin of the American Physical Society*. 1982: 27:31.
20) Sirag, S.P. (1986) "An E_7 unification scheme via the octahedral double group." Contributed paper at *23rd International Conference on High Energy Physics*. Berkeley, CA.
21) Sirag, S.P. (1993) "Consciousness: A hyperspace view." In: Mishlove, J. (Ed.) *Roots of Consciousness*. Tulsa, OK: Council Oak Press.
22) Sirag, S.P. (1996) "A mathematical strategy for a theory of consciousness." In: *Toward a Science of Consciousness: The First Tucson Discussions and Debates*, pp. 580-588 Stuart R. Hameroff, Alfred W. Kaszniak & Alwyn C. Scott (Eds.), Cambridge, MA: MIT Press.
23) McKay, J. (1980) "Graphs, singularities, and finite groups." In: *Proc. Symp. Pure Math.* 1980;37: 183-186. (See also: John McKay (2001) *A Rapid Introduction to ADE Theory*.) http://math.ucr.edu/home/baez/ADE.html.
24) Gilmore, R. (1981) *Catastrophe Theory for Scientists and Engineers*. NY: Wiley-Interscience.
25) Arnold, V.I. (1981) *Singularity Theory*. Cambridge University Press.

26) Arnold, V.I. (1986) *Catastrophe Theory*. Berlin: Springer-Verlag.
27) Witten, E. (1995) "String theory in various dimensions." In: *Nuclear Physics*.1995; B433, 85-126.
28) Kaku, M. (1999) *Introduction to Superstrings and M-Theory*, 2nd ed. NY: Springer-Verlag.
29) Kac, V.G. (1985) *Infinite Dimensional Lie Algebras*, 2nd ed. Cambridge University Press.
30) Grove, L.C. & Benson, C.T. (1985) *Finite Reflection Groups*, 2nd ed., NY: Springer-Verlag
31) Conway, J.H. & Sloane, N.J.A. (1988) *Sphere Packings, Lattices and Groups*. NY: Springer-Verlag.
32) Kronheimer, A. (1989) "Torrelli-Type theorem for gravitational instantons." In: *Journal Differential Geometry*. 1989; 29:685-698.
33) Ward, R.S. & Wells, R.O. (1990) *Twistor Geometry and Field Theory*. Cambridge U. Press.
34) Thom, R. (1975) *Structural Stability and Morphogenesis*. Reading, MA: Benjamin.
35) Gilmore, R. (1981) *Catastrophe Theory for Scientists and Engineers*. NY: Wiley.
36) Kostant, B. (1984) "On finite subgroups of SU(2), Simple lie algebras, and the McKay correspondence." In: *Proc. Natl. Acad. Sci.* USA. 1984; 81: 5275-77.
37) Julia, B. (1985) "Supergeometry and Kac-Moody algebras." In: *Vertex Operators in Mathematics and Physics*, pp. 393-409. J. Lepowski, S. Mandelstam & I.M. Singer (Eds.) NY: Springer Verlag.
38) Kauffman, L.H. (1991) *Knots and Physics*. Singapore: World Scientific.
39) Birman, J.S. (1974) *Braids, Links, and Mapping Class Groups*. Princeton University Press.
40) Derksen, H. & Weyman, J. (2005) "Quiver representations." In: *Notices of the AMS*, Feb. 2005; 52:2, 200-206.

Western science is approaching a paradigm shift of unprecedented proportions, one that will change our concepts of reality and of human nature, bridge the gap between ancient wisdom and modern science, and reconcile the differences between Eastern spirituality and Western pragmatism.

--- **Stanislav Grof**
--- *Beyond the Brain*, 1985

CHAPTER 30   QUANTUM REALITY AND CONSCIOUSNESS

Nick Herbert, PhD

Nick Herbert graduated in engineering physics from Ohio State U (1959), received his PhD from Stanford (1967), worked as Senior Physicist at Memorex and Smith-Corona in Silicon Valley on the physics of magnetic, electrostatic and photographic media as well as helping to develop early versions of the now-ubiquitous ink-jet printer. For a dozen years with Saul-Paul Sirag he led invitational seminars on physics foundations at Esalen Institute, Big Sur, CA. He is the author of *Quantum Reality* (1985); *Faster Than Light* (1988); *Elemental Mind* (1993); and a chapbook *Physics on All Fours* (2000).

Dr Herbert devised the shortest proof of Bell's Theorem to date, and he had a hand in the Quantum No-Cloning Theorem. He invented the "Metaphase Typewriter" and is currently obsessed with a new way of connecting with the world, which he calls *Quantum Tantra*.

Recently, he discovered a brand new law of nature while exploring a new FTL signaling scheme, which is "A pair of quanta cannot be wed." See http://lanl.arxiv.org/abs/0802.1536. He was a frequent speaker at the Parapsychology Research Group meetings with Saul-Paul Sirag. In 1990, he amazed the group with his description of his proposal for "Building a Quantum Mind Link" based on some ideas that regarded consciousness as a quantum effect that evolution has managed to insinuate into the brain's meaty microstructure. He had also presented these ideas at the Ars Electronics Festival in Linz, Austria, where the motto was "One World is Not Enough."

He maintains a blog at http://quantumtantra.blogspot.com/.

QUANTUM REALITY AND CONSCIOUSNESS

Nick Herbert

Speculations concerning the origin of inner experience in humans and other beings have been few, vague, and superficial. They include the notion that mind is an "emergent property" of active neural nets, (1) or that mind is the "software" that manages the brain's unconscious "hardware." To these soft speculations I would like to add my own: the conjecture that mind is not a rare phenomenon associated with certain complex biological systems, but is everywhere, universal in nature, a fundamental quantum effect more akin to the mass and charge of the electron than to complicated computer operations.

The notion that consciousness might be a quantum effect is not new. In 1924, Alfred Latka, one of the founders of modern theoretical biology, guessed that the then-new physics of the quantum might someday account for the phenomenon of human awareness. (2) Neurobiologist Sir John Eccles recently proposed that a nonmaterial mind gains control over the matter of the human brain by way of quantum mechanical acts performed on certain intrinsically inefficient neural synapses. (3) World-class mathematician John von Neumann (4) and Nobel laureate Eugene Wigner (5) claim that quantum theory is actually formally incomplete and that the least drastic way to make quantum theory mathematically consistent is to introduce consciousness as the necessary accomplice of every quantum jump. Despite its support by certain prominent physicists and biologists, no serious experimental program has yet been conceived, let alone carried out, to test the quantum consciousness hypothesis. (11)

What is quantum theory in a nutshell? (6) The oddest thing about quantum theory is that it describes the world differently, depending on whether you look at it or not. When you don't look, the theory treats objects not as real things, but as "vibratory possibilities," oscillating opportunities for something real to happen.

On the other hand, when an object is observed, it always looks ordinary, taking on just one of its previously numerous possibilities. During the act of observation, the quantum description shifts from a spread-out range of possible attributes (unlooked-at object) to single-valued actual attributes (looked-at object). This sudden observer-induced switch of descriptions is called the "collapse of the wave function" or simply the "quantum jump." The nature of the quantum jump is the biggest mystery in quantum physics: Does this abrupt shift in quantum description correspond to an actual change in the real world, or is it a mathematical fiction like the International Date Line, a purely conventional discontinuity? The quantum model of consciousness holds that quantum jumps are real and that all conscious beings live at some location where quantum possibility turns into actuality. Our subjective experiences consist of the feelings that accompany that quantum change in some part of our brains. In a sense, the business of consciousness is to actualize possibility. Our inner experience during each quantum jump is our reward for this job.

Half-baked attempts to explain consciousness, such as mind as software or mind as emergent property, do not take themselves seriously enough to confront the bare experimental facts; our most intimate database – how mind itself feels from the inside. One piece of suggestive evidence for a quantum model of mind is that our experience of ordinary sentience is somewhat congruent with what quantum theory says is happening during an observation. Looking inside, I do not feel like "software," whatever that might mean, but indeed like a shimmering center of ambiguous possibility around which more solid perceptions and ideas are continually precipitating. This rough match of internal feeling with external description could be utterly deceptive, but it at least shows that a quantum model of mind can begin to successfully confront the introspective evidence in a way no other mind models even attempt.

What other aspects of quantum theory besides the sensation of the quantum jump might we look for in human consciousness? Three features of quantum theory seemed so strange to Albert Einstein that he refused to accept them: They are randomness, thinglessness, and interconnectedness.

Quantum randomness means that the quantum jumps occur at random, with no discernible physical cause. The quantum consciousness assumption proposes that the causes of quantum jumps do indeed lie outside of physics. They are psychological in origin, the results of the inner intent of some immaterial mind. A key part of quantum consciousness research will be learning to distinguish conscious matter from unconscious matter by looking for deviations from ordinary quantum statistics. Conventional quantum theory represents the default statistics for unconscious matter. Minds are able to violate these statistics, usually unintentionally, in the same way that thoughtfully we can violate the English language statistics that loosely govern our speech. For instance, there's a novel, *Gadsby*, by Ernest Vincent Wright that does not contain a single instance of the letter "e." (7)

Quantum thinglessness refers to the state of a quantum system when it is not being observed. I described the unobserved state as a bundle of possibilities. But the real situation is much more ambiguous. Quantum possibilities are not well defined like dice possibilities, but depend on the measurement context. The quantum state is like a set of blank dice whose faces are assigned only after the gambler has decided which game he wants to play. Depending on the game chosen, the blank dice will take on numbered faces, playing card faces, or colored faces, just as a quantum system takes on momentum or position possibilities, depending on the measuring instrument used to investigate it. Because of their sensitivities to the measurement context, quantum systems possess a deeper kind of uncertainty than that of classical systems. Quantum systems are not only random like dice but, unlike dice, they do not even know what game they are playing until the observer makes that choice for them.

If consciousness is a quantum effect, we might expect it to possess this double level of uncertainty also, a deeper form of doubt than simple ignorance concerning which preexistent possibility might manifest. Soviet physicist Yuri Orlov mathematically described one possible model of a type of "deep doubt" that might arise in a quantum kind of mind. (8) Given a quantum situation with only two possible outcomes, such as the polarization attribute of light, the observer's freedom to choose a different measurement context expands the number of conceivable measurement outcomes to a two-fold infinity of polarization pairs. Instead of a simple yes-or-no situation, the range of doubt concerning a photon's polarization spreads out onto the surface of a sphere. Orlov proposes that ordinary two-valued human uncertainties – *"Did I see a 'wolf' or a bundle of 'wool' in the twilight?"* – may be similarly expanded, under some circumstances, into a spherical form of ignorance. So far, Orlov's model of mind (smuggled out of a Soviet prison camp) has made no connection with the way humans actually experience the ambiguous background out of which clear choices emerge and present themselves to the will.

Quantum connectedness is also a more complex type of interaction than its classical counterpart. A classical connection must be "local," that is, mediated by fields that fall off with distance and transmit forces at light speed or slower. Quantum connections, on the other hand, are unmediated, unmitigated (no degradation with distance), and immediate (faster than light). The quantum connection, alas, is also invisible: It never shows up as a statistical change in the pattern of many quantum jumps but acts only on the level of individual jumps. Any superluminal message sent via the quantum connection from one person to another cannot be deciphered by its human recipient because it is scrambled by quantum randomness, masked by an unbreakable code to which only Nature and her subquantal sentient representatives hold the key. Although this superluminal linkage can never be directly observed, the real presence of the quantum connection has been verified in an indirect but undeniable way by way of Bell's theorem and the associated Clauser-Aspect experiments. (9) Because of its statistical invisibility, this peculiar connection would not be of much use in explaining telepathy – direct mind-to-mind transmission of statistically stable patterns. But it might account for certain far-flung harmonies between like-minded people, such as the remarkable concordance in the behaviors of identical twins raised apart (10) or, manifesting as lucky, one-of-a-kind events, create "fortunate coincidences" that put us in touch with people, ideas, and things helpful to our development.

The quantum theory of mind is one tentative approach to the solution of the mind-body problem. It suggests that the essence of subjectivity is the intentional transformation of deeply ambiguous possibilities into concrete actualities. Furthermore, this activity, although conditioned by physical laws, does not arise from physical causes: Our choices are truly free, from physical determinism at least. In addition, our minds may be connected by inner non-telepathic links that coordinate human action into a larger harmony than that produced by external forces.

REFERENCES AND NOTES

1) Minsky, M. (1985) *Society of Mind.* NY: Simon & Schuster.
2) Latka, A. (1956) *Elements of Mathematical Biology.* NY: Dover reprint.
3) Eccles, J.C. (1986) "Do mental events cause neural events analogously to the probability fields of quantum mechanics?" In: *Proceedings of the Royal Society.* 1986;227B:411.
4) von Neumann, J. (1955) *Mathematical Foundations of Quantum Mechanics.* Princeton, NJ: Princeton University Press.
5) Wigner, E. (1967) *Symmetries and Reflections.* Bloomington: University of Indiana.
6) Herbert, N. (1985) *Quantum Reality: Beyond the New Physics.* NY: Doubleday.
7) Wright, E.V. (1939) *Gadsby: A Story of Over 50,000 Words Without Using the Letter "E."* Wetzel Publishing Co.
8) Orlov, Y.F. (1982) "The wave logic of consciousness: A hypothesis." In: *International Journal Theoretical Physics.* 1982; 21:37.
9) Herbert, N. (1988) *Faster Than Light: Superluminal Loopholes in Physics.* NY: American Library.
10) Tellegen, A., Lykken, D.T., Bouchard, T.J., Jr. (1988) "Personality similarity in twins reared apart and together." In: *Journal Personality and Social Psychology* 54:1031.
11) Dick Bierman (2006) at University of Amsterdam performed a series of experiments to test whether consciousness collapses the wave function. His results were inconclusive. Bierman, Dick J. & Whitmarsh, Stephen: "Consciousness and quantum physics: Empirical research on the subjective reduction of the Statevector in the emerging physics of consciousness." Jack A. Tuszynski, (Ed.) Springer.

CHAPTER 31   TIME, CONSCIOUSNESS AND PSI

Jean Burns, PhD

Jean Burns received her PhD in physics from the U of Hawaii in 1970. Her multidisciplinary interests are included in her publications: thermodynamics and the nature of entropy; consciousness and free will and their relationship to presently known physical laws; parapsychology and the relationship of psi phenomena to presently known physical laws. Dr Burns is also a founding Associate Editor of the *Journal of Consciousness Studies*, which publishes research on consciousness from multidisciplinary perspectives. She was president of the Parapsychology Research Group (PRG) between 1995-1998.

Dr Burns believes in the importance of networking for research in consciousness, so people from a number of fields can interact. In 1990 she and Ravi Gomatam (a researcher in the philosophy of science at the Bhaktivedanta Institute, Berkeley, CA) founded the *Consciousness and Science Discussion Group*, which presented talks on the subject of consciousness in SF, CA, over a period of twelve years. Researchers from a variety of fields (such as biology, physics, psychology, artificial intelligence, and parapsychology) gave presentations at these meetings. Dr Burns has also participated in some of the annual *International Conferences on the Study of Shamanism and Alternate Modes of Healing*, organized by Dr Ruth-Inge Heinze in San Rafael, CA.

For more information about these topics, visit her website: http://www.mindspring.com/~l.o.v.e.r/JBurns.html.

TIME, CONSCIOUSNESS AND PSI

Jean Burns

One might suppose that the conscious experience of time can be described solely in terms of properties of the physical world. Indeed, a great deal of empirical data in neurophysiology demonstrates a dependence of the content of conscious experience upon encoding in the brain. (1) And a great deal of empirical data in psychophysics demonstrates that the content of visual, auditory, and other sensory experience has a correspondence with the physical quantities it represents. (2) Furthermore, psychophysical experiments show that our experience of time intervals is dependent on encoding in the brain. For instance, for very short time intervals, a subject may know that two events have occurred but be unable to specify which came first; thus we are limited in temporal discrimination by encoding in the brain. (3)

However, time in the physical world has two aspects, clock time and the arrow of time, which are not described in the same way by physical laws. Therefore, if we are to ask what the relationship is between the conscious experience of time and physical time, we should ask this question with respect to each aspect of physical time.

In order to explore this relationship, a comparison must be made between the description of conscious experience and the description of the physical world (i.e., physical laws). We should note that not all qualities characteristic of conscious experience correspond to known physical properties. For instance, the quality of awareness is fundamental to conscious experience, yet this quality does not appear in any known physical law. Therefore, the conscious experience of time, and time in the physical world, do not necessarily correspond in all respects.

In making a distinction between the description of consciousness and the description of the physical world, no ontological relationship, such as physicalism or dualism, is implied herein. Physicalism holds that consciousness arises out of the physical world, and a quality of consciousness, which is different from known qualities of the physical world, can be described as *emergent*. (4) Dualism holds that consciousness is an independent realm, and a quality of consciousness, which is different from known qualities of the physical world, is described as *independent*.

However, there is no known empirical way to distinguish between an emergent quality and an independent quality. (5)

In order to make a comparison between the conscious experience of time and its physical aspects, we will first describe physical time, in both its aspects. We will see that the fundamental nature of the arrow of time is not well understood and discuss some competing hypotheses about its nature. We will then discuss the relationship between the conscious experience of time and physical time. We will see that our experience of the relative duration of time and of the temporal ordering of events probably derives from encoding in the brain and corresponds to clock time in the physical world. However, the hypothesis that consciousness can do processing independently of the brain, made in a number of recent models of consciousness, suggests that our understanding of the arrow of time should be broadened. (6) Finally, we will discuss the relationship of psi to the arrow of time; we will see that data in parapsychology may have profound implications for our understanding of the arrow of time.

THE NATURE OF TIME IN THE PHYSICAL WORLD

In the physical world time intervals can be described by readings on a clock, and in this respect the description of time is fairly simple. However, the conception of time in the physical world is made more complicated by the time reversibility of the dynamical laws which describe physical processes, the block universe of relativity, and the nature of irreversible processes, as we will see.

Time Reversibility of the Dynamical Laws of Physics

The state of a system in the physical world can be described by dynamical laws (classical or quantum mechanical), with time occurring as a parameter in these laws. All the dynamical equations of physics are time reversible; this means that for a given trajectory, which is a solution to a dynamical equation, the equation is satisfied regardless of the direction in which the particle travels the trajectory. For instance, a planet can travel around the sun in either direction.

The fact that the dynamical equations are time reversible could also be interpreted to mean that a particle can traverse a dynamical trajectory either forward or backward in time. We suppose that particles travel only forward in time because backward travel is contrary to common experience, not because this idea is incompatible with the dynamical laws.

If we suppose, in accord with common experience, that there is an arrow of time, i.e., that all physical processes move forward in time, the dynamic laws provide a simple concept of clock time: It specifies the number of times a periodic cycle, such as the swinging of a pendulum or the orbiting of a planet, has been completed, and thereby measures the duration of time between different events. However, the concept of clock time is made more complicated by considerations from relativity.

The Block Universe of Relativity

In relativity the dimension of time occurs as a geometric parameter, similar to spatial dimensions, and the physical world described by relativity is sometimes called the *block universe*. Two sorts of separations between events in space-time can occur, those that are "time-like" and those that are "space-like." Two events that have a time-like separation can always be viewed, from a suitable reference frame, as taking place at the same spatial location. Alternatively, this idea can be expressed by saying that events which occur in the history of any individual object will always have a unique ordering in time, such that the sequence of events occurring to that object will be the same in any reference frame. For that reason, the history of an object can be viewed as being on a "worldline" in four-dimensional space-time.

On the other hand, if space-time events are so far separated spatially that light, which travels at a finite velocity, cannot travel from one event to another in the time between the events, the events have a space-like separation, and there is no unique temporal ordering between them. Therefore, according to the laws of relativity, it is not possible to classify all events as happening either before or after any given reference event.

Thus the time-reversible dynamical equations and relativity together describe a universe which is in a state of being, i.e., the states of its constituent particles are specified at each point of time, and no deviations from these specified states are allowed for. Even a random process can be represented as a series of predetermined events on a worldline in such a universe. However, this view is not consistent with the idea that the universe as a whole exists at a particular time, "Now," and is evolving from present moment to present moment. For that reason, Einstein, in letters to friends, wrote, *"For us who are convinced physicists, the distinction between past, present, and future is only an illusion, however persistent,"* and *"You have to accept the idea that subjective time with its emphasis on the now has no objective meaning."* (7)

In an alternative view, Stapp has proposed that the physical world is characterized by two kinds of time – Einstein time and process time. Einstein time is the time part of the space-time continuum, and process time describes events in a uniquely ordered sequence. (8) In order to be compatible with the relativistic restriction that events with space-like separations cannot have a unique temporal ordering, the theory provides that an ordered sequence of events can only occur in a bounded region of space-time. Thus, as Stapp described it,

> ... the actual is represented not by an advancing, infinitely thin slice through the space-time continuum, but rather by a sequence of actual becomings, each of which refers to a bounded space-time region.

In another alternative view, Moon, Spencer, and Moon have proposed a modification of special relativity in which universal time can occur, i.e., events on different worldlines can evolve simultaneously. (9) Relativity theory as developed by Einstein holds that the velocity of light is the same in each reference frame. Moon, Spencer and Moon, in analyzing the possible conditions in which universal time could occur, have shown that only one postulate about the velocity of light can predict the possibility of universal time for all reference frames in arbitrary translational motion; in this postulate the velocity of light depends on the velocity of the source. They pointed out that binary star data, which were considered to have established the validity of Einstein's postulate, are equally well explained by their formulation.

The Arrow of Time

Because the dynamical laws of physics are time reversible, a molecular system cannot move toward any preferred microscopic state. However, everyday experience shows that many physical processes do show a preferred direction: For instance, heat transfers from hot to cold, but not the reverse; at a given temperature and pressure, chemical reactions proceed in a given direction; if an egg is dropped, it breaks, but a broken egg does not spontaneously recombine. Processes such as the above can serve to define an arrow of time. However, because such processes are inconsistent with the dynamical equations, there has been a continuing discussion in physics during the last century over their fundamental nature. We will discuss time asymmetric processes with respect to molecular interactions, the collapse of the quantum mechanical wave function, the expansion of the universe, the decay of the neutral K-meson, and quantum randomness. We will see that, in spite of numerous attempts to understand the arrow of time, there is no consensus as to its fundamental nature.

Molecular Interactions

Processes involving molecular interactions can be readily observed, on the macroscopic level, to move toward an equilibrium state. Thus one would expect that, using kinetic theory, it would be possible to model molecular action on the microscopic level, and average over this action to describe irreversible processes (those which take place in only one direction) on a macroscopic level. Indeed, an equation derived by Ludwig Boltzmann more than 100 years ago is often used for this purpose; however, the

Boltzmann equation includes an *ad hoc* term, the "collision term," and the modeling of irreversible processes comes from this term. Many attempts have been made over the years to resolve the question of what the collision term represents. As Davies has reviewed, the hypothesis that under repeated collisions, the velocities of molecules are reshuffled at random, together with some other simple assumptions, can be used to derive a detailed expression for the microscopic collision term. (10) An averaging shows that on the macroscopic level, a function (the H function) derived from the latter expression is irreversible. However, the time symmetry of this function is not compatible with time reversibility, and one of the assumptions made in deriving it presupposes that molecular states after collision are different than before collision, and hence presupposes irreversibility. (10)

As Zeh has reviewed, attempts have been made not only in kinetic theory, but also in statistical mechanics, to find the relationship between microscopic processes and irreversible macroscopic processes. (11) In statistical mechanics, a quantity is averaged over all possible microscopic configurations, given macroscopic constraints on the system (such as the total energy). However, even in statistical mechanics the H function will not show irreversibility unless a "coarse-grained" average – which takes into account only macroscopically available information, instead of complete information about microscopic states – is used. (11) Irreversibility is sometimes described as a phenomenon which is statistical and solely macroscopic in nature: Under repeated collisions, particles change energy and momentum and thus occupy many different microscopic states, and an equilibrium state can be described as the most probable macroscopic state (the macroscopic state which corresponds to the most microscopic states). Thus, using the results of the "coarse-grained" average, irreversibility is sometimes characterized as a phenomenon in which processes are reversible on a microscopic level, but tend to their most probable state. However, the view that irreversibility is solely a macroscopic phenomenon is unsatisfactory in that it provides no explanation as to how a macroscopic process, which lacks time symmetry, can derive from microscopic processes, which are symmetric in time (this point is called Loschmidt's objection). Also, we have no explanation as to why irreversibility cannot be derived from ordinary averaging, but only from averaging in which information about the system is left out.

Quantum Mechanics and the Collapse of the Wave Function

Zeh, in examining the possibility that irreversibility has a quantum mechanical origin, has noted that quantum statistical mechanics has an inherent difference from classical statistical mechanics because a quantum system contains correlations between its parts, and is therefore nonlocal, whereas a classical system is inherently local. (11) Nevertheless, as Zeh has discussed, in quantum statistical mechanics, as in classical statistical mechanics, an irreversible process cannot be described by averaging over a system which follows time-reversible dynamical laws, but can be predicted for macroscopic variables if one does not take into account the full microscopic description.

An alternative possibility is that the arrow of time might be associated with collapse of the quantum mechanical wave function. This "collapse" can be described in the following way: There is a difference in description of events between that given in quantum mechanics and that of ordinary reality. In quantum mechanics events are described in terms of a wave function that describes mutually exclusive possibilities. However, ordinary reality is characterized by definite events. Although there is no formal resolution of this discrepancy in descriptions, it is usually supposed that a quantum system makes a transition to a definite state by "collapse" of the wave function. (12)

Zeh has proposed that collapse of a wave function, which describes macroscopic variables, is an irreversible process. (11) He showed that collisions of very low energy photons with a system would destroy the quantum correlations of the system (because of the lack of correlation of the photons) and thus could be viewed as causing continuous collapse of the wave function; he also showed that such interactions would be associated with a net increase in entropy. (Irreversible processes are characterized by an increase in entropy; we will discuss entropy in more detail in another section.)

Zeh has noted that opinions differ as to whether collapse of the wave function is an irreversible process, associated with an increase of entropy, or is characterized by a gain of information, associated with a decrease in entropy. (11) Walker (13) and Goswami (14) have proposed that collapse of the wave function is not a physical process, but is produced by the action of consciousness, and they also disagree on the latter point: Goswami has proposed that collapse produces irreversibility, whereas Walker has held that it is associated with a gain of information to the physical system involved.

Expansion of the Universe

If the universe is assumed to be homogeneous on a large scale and to be in uniform expansion from an initial point event (the big bang), an observer in a co-moving reference frame (a frame which moves with the expansion) can associate events with the sequence of states that the universe passes through. (10) The time scale defined by the expansion, called *cosmic time*, can be viewed as no more than a parameter in the block universe. However, if for all events with a space-like separation, an absolute temporal ordering is specified to be the ordering determined by the co-moving frames, then cosmic time could be associated with irreversibility. Thus it has been proposed that cosmic time provides the master arrow that determines the direction of all other time asymmetrical processes. (11) Since no molecular processes are completely isolated from cosmological-related processes such as the production of energy at the center of stars, the arrow of time for all such processes could be linked to the cosmic arrow. (11)

The equations of general relativity that describe the expansion of the universe are time symmetric, although the universe could expand indefinitely or recontract, depending on the curvature of space. (10) Thus if the universe were completely homogeneous, expansion could not lead to thermodynamic nonequilibrium. If a master arrow is associated with expansion, a seed of inhomogeneity must have been present from the beginning, or else a spontaneous breaking of the symmetries of homogeneity and time isotropy must occur at later times. (11)

With regard to the latter point, Hawking has proposed that the universe can be described by two kinds of times, ordinary time and *imaginary time*. (15) By doing a quantum mechanical analysis (a sum over histories) with imaginary time, he showed that if the early universe had no more inhomogeneity than the minimum allowed by the uncertainty principle, amplification of this initial fluctuation could account for all of the inhomogeneity of the present time. Hawking's imaginary time was constructed as a mathematical artifice to solve a computational problem; (15) it is akin to Einstein time and is not proposed to be related to irreversibility. However, because a master arrow must be associated with inhomogeneity in the universe, the latter result suggests that the arrow of time might be intrinsically associated with quantum uncertainty.

Decay of the Neutral K Meson

Only a single exception is known to the rule that the dynamic laws are time symmetric, and this is one of the decay modes of the neutral K meson, also called the K-zero meson. This particle is only produced at very high energies, and it is unstable, with a very short lifetime. Thus there are probably very few of these particles in the universe, and consequently they probably interact very little with the rest of the matter in the universe. It is not known how or whether this decay mode might be related to the arrow of time associated with ordinary physical processes.

Being Versus Becoming

A system in which irreversible processes take place can be described by an entropy function, i.e., a function that increases monotonically in time and specifies an equilibrium (attractor) state. (16) It is known that the evolution of any dynamical system along a well-defined trajectory, such as the orbiting of a planet around the sun, has zero entropy change. Thus

Prigogine has proposed that dynamical systems may not always have well-defined trajectories. (16) He has further proposed that trajectory and entropy are complementary quantum mechanical qualities, with a detailed formulation that defines entropy as a quantum mechanical operator.

Prigogine has characterized the states associated with these complementary qualities as *being*, the state in which the trajectory of a system is known, and *becoming*, the state in which the evolution of the system is not predetermined. (16) Prigogine's formulation produces the conclusion that a system can be described by two sorts of time: the clock time of the dynamical equations and *internal time*, a quantum mechanical operator whose eigenfunctions describe the system at a sequence of times, from the far past to the distant future, and whose eigenvalues specify the age of the system. (16) (Eigenfunctions and eigenvalues are mathematical functions and quantities, respectively, which describe quantum mechanical states.) The reversible aspect of a system is described by all eigenfunctions of the internal time, but the contribution of these eigenfunctions to the irreversible aspect is modified by a function which decreases monotonically from 1 in the far past to 0 in the distant future. (17) Thus, the irreversible aspect of a system contains contributions from the past and the nearby future, but no contributions from the distant future.

As we noted earlier, one view of molecular irreversibility holds that it is a macroscopic phenomenon only, which occurs as a consequence of a "coarse-grained average" used in making observations of a system, although objections can be made to this view. Prigogine differs from this view by holding that randomness occurs at a microscopic level. (16, 17) He has pointed out that many dynamical systems, including any three-body system, are characterized by weak stability, a condition in which the trajectories of neighboring points diverge by arbitrarily large distances after sufficient time, and he has proposed that irreversibility is produced by such diverging trajectories. However, even in such a system, any given trajectory is deterministic, so irreversibility is still not accounted for.

Quantum Randomness

To understand the possible relationship between quantum randomness and the arrow of time, we should first discuss the uncertainty principle. In quantum mechanics a particle does not have definite attributes, but rather has collection of possible, mutually inconsistent attributes; for instance it might have a fairly definite position, but a spectrum of possible momentum values. The particle only attains definite attributes upon "measurement" (also described as "collapse of the wave function"), but the nature of this measurement process is not understood. (12) And the uncertainty principle places a limitation on how well certain attributes, such as position and momentum, can be simultaneously known.

It is known that a probabilistic process, i.e., a process in which information about past history is not preserved, produces an increase in entropy. (17) Therefore, it is possible that irreversibility derives from probabilistic processes at the microscopic level. The dynamical laws do not describe such processes. However, if quantum uncertainty not only limits our knowledge about a system but also introduces randomness into it, then irreversible processes could be produced by the cumulative effect of quantum uncertainty in molecular collisions.

The latter idea represents an extension of the usual view of the uncertainty principle. However, this hypothesis answers a number of questions that have come up in the various attempts to derive irreversibility from the dynamical laws. For instance, as we have seen, irreversibility can be explained in kinetic theory by making the assumption that molecular velocities are reshuffled at random under collision. This assumption is not consistent with the dynamical laws, but it is consistent with the hypothesis that quantum uncertainty produces random change during collisions. Similarly, in both quantum and classical statistical mechanics irreversibility can be explained by using an average in which information about microscopic trajectories is dropped; in a random process information about past history is in fact lost. This idea is also consistent with the idea that the arrow of time is associated with expansion of the universe through inhomogeneities produced by quantum uncertainty. We will return to the hypothesis that irreversibility is associated with quantum randomness in our discussion of parapsychological data.

TIME AND CONSCIOUSNESS

The conscious experience of time measured in psychophysical experiments has to do with duration of time, as measured by a clock, rather than with irreversible processes. Thus it seems reasonable to suppose that our experience of time duration derives from clock time in the physical world, via encoding in the brain.

It is true that the subjective experience of time duration can be expanded, such that time appears to "slow down." However, an expansion effect can also be seen in other sensory experiences. For instance, in comparing colors one ordinarily compares one category of color with another: This color is red and the other is blue. But in comparing different shades of blue, say, one can become aware of many shades of blue, all slightly different from each other. In this respect, an expansion in scale is not unique to time. So even with respect to the "slowing down of time," it is reasonable to suppose that our experience of time duration is associated with encoding in the brain, and derives from clock time in the physical world.

Consciousness and the Second Law of Thermodynamics

The second law of thermodynamics has several different, equivalent formulations. Basically it states that irreversible processes can be described by an entropy function. As we noted earlier, an entropy function increases monotonically in time and specifies an attractor (equilibrium) state. Alternatively, entropy can be described in terms of the degree of disorder of the components of a system, with the equilibrium state corresponding to maximum disorder. (16) At the molecular level entropy describes the degree of randomness in the distribution of positions and velocities of the molecules in the system, and the equilibrium state corresponds to the maximum disorder possible, for given external constraints such as temperature and pressure. The second law was originally formulated for systems near equilibrium. However, it can be readily observed that any physical system, even if far from equilibrium, will tend toward an attractor state. For instance, at a given temperature and pressure a chemical system, even if far from equilibrium, will proceed in a definite direction, toward an attractor state. Thus the second law is now used in descriptions of systems far from equilibrium. (16)

The reason for discussing the second law at this point is that a number of researchers have proposed that consciousness can do processing independently of the brain. (6) The types of processing proposed are free will and holistic information processing; free will would make a selection from alternative programs in the brain, and holistic information processing would correlate, modify and/or activate encoding in the brain. (6) Such independent processing could occur even if all of the content of conscious experience is encoded in the brain. (6) However, it has been shown by several researchers that independent processing by consciousness violates the second law of thermodynamics. (6)

Reasoning for the above conclusion can be given as follows: Although the brain is an open system, far from equilibrium, physical processes will nevertheless tend toward their attractor states. However, if an independent process is to affect encoding in the brain, through activation and/or modification, then some physical process in the brain must move in a different direction from that in which it would otherwise have gone. Thus the second law must be violated. (18) Following a somewhat different line of reasoning, Jahn and Dunne have pointed out that holistic information processing must contradict the second law because such processing can organize information. (19)

Thus, if independent processing exists, the state of becoming described by Prigogine must be associated both with increasing disorder through processes in the physical world and with increasing order through processing by consciousness. Although the decrease in entropy associated with the latter action is, in principle, measurable, it would probably be very small and not in reach of present measurement. If it were not for data in parapsychology, we would have to consider the possibility of independent processing by consciousness as pure speculation. However, such data can provide an important means for exploration of the nature of becoming and the arrow of time.

PSI AND TIME

The various phenomena of extrasensory perception (remote viewing, telepathy, precognition, etc.) violate the second law of thermodynamics, because they consist of the introduction of order (information) where it did not previously exist. With regard to precognition, Prigogine's theory predicts that the description of an object in its aspect of becoming depends on its entire past and the near future, but not the distant future. Some studies suggest that precognition falls off with increasing time lapse between the prediction and the event; however, not all researchers agree that such attenuation occurs. (20) Thus not enough is known about precognition at the present time to provide any evidence relevant to the above theory.

As has been discussed by several researchers, psychokinesis (PK) also violates the second law. (18, 19, 21, 22) (The arguments are similar to those given above for consciousness.) The results of a study by Rauscher of material (metals and crystals) that was bent or broken by PK are consistent with this view. (23) The material showed more movement along crystal boundary dislocations, as compared to that bent or broken in a comparable way by normal means, and the microstructure of the material subject to PK appeared to be annealed. PK appeared to release stress in the material, and to increase the ordered crystal pattern array.

Analyses of PK experiments on traveling cubes are also relevant to hypotheses about the nature of irreversibility. Walker showed that initial shifts in the angular orientation of a cube are amplified on each successive bounce and that even when these initial shifts are extremely small, they produce a sideways deviation of macroscopic size fairly quickly. (24) He proposed that PK-induced sideways deviations could be accounted for by shifts within the limits of the uncertainty principle in the initial orientation of the entire cube. A more detailed analysis by the present author later showed that shifts of the entire cube, with its macroscopic mass, were too small to account for experimental results. (25, 26) However, if the trajectories of air molecules are shifted within the limits of the uncertainty principle, such that their trajectories are ordered, the impact of only about 10^5 ordered molecules could provide a sufficient change in the cube's initial orientation to account for the experimental results. (26)

The experiments (27) on which these analyses were based were performed more than 40 years ago, and should be carried out with more modern techniques, in order to confirm the experimental results. (26) However, these results are consistent with the view that PK can order the randomness associated with quantum uncertainty. Because such an ordering process would be a counterpart of irreversibility (which produces disorder), this view suggests that irreversibility and the arrow of time are connected with quantum randomness. (28)

SUMMARY AND CONCLUSIONS

In order to describe time in the physical world, one must describe not only clock time, which is associated with the time-reversible dynamic laws and the block universe of relativity, but also the arrow of time, which is associated with irreversible processes and the second law of thermodynamics. The physical nature of the arrow of time is not presently understood, and it is not known whether irreversible processes are macroscopic or microscopic in nature.

It is likely that clock time is common to consciousness and the physical world. However, independent processing by consciousness inherently produces order in the physical world, whereas irreversible processes produce disorder; thus these processes act in opposite ways.

Psi, like independent processing by consciousness, violates the second law of thermodynamics, and in this respect it follows properties of consciousness, rather than those of the physical world. Thus data about psi can be an important tool in exploring the nature of consciousness and the arrow of time. In particular, PK-induced deviations in the trajectories of tumbling cubes can be explained in terms of the ordering of quantum randomness. This result implies that PK and irreversible processes are counterparts; one producing order and the other disorder, and thereby suggests that irreversible processes occur at the microscopic level and that the arrow of time is connected with quantum randomness.

REFERENCES AND NOTES

1) Blakemore, C. (1977) *Mechanics of the Mind.* NY: Cambridge Univ. Press.
2) Gescheider, G.A. (1985) *Psychophysics: Method, Theory and Application.* Hillsdale, NJ: Lawrence Erlbaum.
3) Uttal, W.R. (1978) *The Psychobiology of Mind.* Hillsdale, NJ: Erlbaum Assoc; 978:420.
4) Gregory, R.L.(1981) *Mind in Science: A History of Explanations in Psychology and Physics.* NY: Cambridge University Press.
5) Burns, J. (1990) "Contemporary models of consciousness: Part I." In: *Journal of Mind and Behavior.* 1990;11:153-172.
6) Burns, J. (1991) "Contemporary models of consciousness: Part II." In: *Journal of Mind and Behavior.* 1991;12:407-420.

7) Prigogine, I. (1980) *From Being to Becoming.* NY: W.H. Freeman 1980:203.
8) Stapp, H.P. (1986) "Einstein time and process time." In: Griffin, D.R. (Ed.) *Physics and the Ultimate Significance of Time.* Albany: State U. of NY Press; 264-270.
9) Moon, P., Spence, D.E., Moon, E.E. (1989) "Universal time and the velocity of light." In: *Physics Essays.* 1989;2:368-374.
10) Davies, P.C.W. (1974) *The Physics of Time Asymmetry.* Berkeley: UC Press.
11) Zeh, H-D. (1989) *The Physical Basis of the Direction of Time.* NY: Springer-Verlag.
12) Herbert, N. (1985) *Quantum Reality.* NY: Doubleday.
13) Walker, E.H. (1979) "The quantum theory of psi phenomena." In: *Psychoenergetic Systems.* 1979;3:259-299.
14) Goswami, A. (1989) "The idealistic interpretation of quantum mechanics." In: *Physics Essays.* 1989;2:385-400.
15) Hawking, S.W. (1988) *A Brief History of Time.* NY: Bantam Books.
16) Prigogine, I. (1980) *From Being to Becoming.* NY: W.H. Freeman.
17) Prigogine, I. (1986) "Irreversibility and space-time structure." In: Griffin, D.R. (Ed.) *Physics and the Ultimate Significance of Time.* Albany: State U. of NY Press; 1986:232-250.
18) Burns, J. (1986) "Consciousness and psi." In: *Psi Research.* 1986;5(1/2):166-205.
19) Jahn, R.G. & Dunne, B.J. (1987) *Margins of Reality.* NY: Harcourt Brace Jovanovich.
20) Stokes, D.M. (1987) "Theoretical parapsychology." In: Krippner, S. (Ed.) *Advances in Parapsychological Research, Volume 5.* Jefferson, NC: McFarland; 1987:77-189.
21) Mattuck, R.D. & Walker, E.H. (1979) "The action of consciousness on matter." In: Puharich, A. (Ed.) *The Iceland Papers.* Amherst, WI: Essentia Research Associates; 1979:112-159.
22) Rush, J.H. (1976) "Physical aspects of psi phenomena." In: Schmeidler, G.R. (Ed.) *Parapsychology: Its Relation to Physics, Biology, Psychology and Psychiatry.* Metuchen, NJ: Scarecrow Press.
23) Rauscher, E.A. (1983) "The physics of psi phenomena in space and time: Part I: Major principles of physics, psychic phenomena, and some physical models." In: *Psi Research.* 1983;2(2):64-88.
24) Walker, E.H. (1975) "Foundations of paraphysical and parapsychological phenomena." In: Oteri, L. (Ed.) In: *Quantum Physics and Parapsychology.* NY: Parapsychology Foundation; 1975:1-53.
25) Burns, J.E. (2003) "The tumbling cube and the action of the mind." In: *Noetic Journal.* 2002;3(4):318-329.
26) Burns, J.E. (2002) "The effect of ordered air molecules on a tumbling cube." In: *Noetic Journal.* 2002;3(4):330-339.
27) Forwald, H. (1959) "An experimental study suggesting a relationship between psychokinesis and nuclear conditions of matter." In: *Journal of Parapsychology.* 1959;23:97-125.
28) For further discussion see Burns, J.E. (2006) "The arrow of time and the action of the mind at the molecular level." In: Sheehan, D.P. (Ed.) *Frontiers of Time.* Melville, NY: American Institute of Physics; 2006:75-88.

INDIVIDUALITY AND WHOLENESS IN QUANTUM PHYSICS

James R. Johnston

In a 1980 pilot project involving telepathy and interpersonal brainwave phase synchronization (see Chapter 22), a first sense of the importance of individuality and wholeness in both our psychic knowing and in quantum physics was noted.

Individuality and wholeness are important aspects of human existence. Examples include the Constitutionally designed tension between individual states and the federal government, and personal individual freedom versus any kind of government restriction – the needs of the individual vs. the needs of society. In his book on ecology, (1) Al Gore describes our tendency to focus on the individual aspects of nature instead of Earth as a whole, and our own individual needs rather than the Earth and its inhabitants as a whole. While this is a common issue in a general sense, specific examples may be very different. In quantum theory this issue is intimately related to wave-particle duality, setting it apart from other examples.

The perspective presented here began with criticism of the inappropriate use of the concept of point-particle photons in description of the electromagnetic field, presented at three consecutive NSF Summer Institutes on "Macroscopic Quantum Coherence." (2) Macroscopic quantum coherence is an arena that relates to wholeness in the physical realm. The measure of coherence in laser radiation (3) and the measure of "global coherence" for superfluidity (4) are the same. (5) Special care is required in thermodynamic treatment of superfluid (coherent) states because of their global coherence. (5) Fritz London's description of superfluidity and super-conductivity focuses on the superfluid component as a globally coherent part of the wavefunction, representing a kind of wholeness. (6)

This perspective leads to nice analogies between superfluidity and aspects of consciousness (including nonlocality). I have chosen to not consider any such analogies for several reasons. Within a monistic perspective there has been a strong tendency to assume that mind, or consciousness, is explainable via physical and/or biological mechanisms. In an unbiased monism, causation may be in either direction, or more likely both. We currently know little about consciousness itself – especially individual vs. collective aspects thereof! I prefer, for now, to not model from mechanism, but to focus on the laws that govern or the patterns that exist in each arena.

Individuality vs. wholeness is an issue in consciousness and in physical "nonlocality," and is relevant to significant conceptual errors in the common lore of quantum wave-particle duality. The purpose of this chapter is to present the quantum physics part of this perspective for both physicists and those interested but not trained in physics. In order to do so, the reframing of misconceptions identified herein needs to be justified.

There are two sources of confusion in the lore of quantum physics. The concept associated with the word "particle" is not carefully defined, allowing it to represent simultaneously something capable, and also something not capable, of interference. Also, "wave-particle duality" is applied both: 1] to the association of wave frequency with physical dynamical properties such as energy and momentum, and 2] (erroneously) to long wavelength vs. short wavelength phenomena (where the latter seems like beams or particles). In clearing up this confusion, it is shown that Heisenberg uncertainty is a simple, direct consequence of the equations of wave-particle duality, independent of disturbance-due-to-measurement, and also there is a fundamental change in the nature of the fundamental dimensions used to describe dynamics.

There are two kinds of change involved in quantum theory (7) namely: 1] Mathematically described smooth evolution of a system between measurements, and 2] probabilistic discrete changes involved in measurement events. The first, the evolution of a system, is wave-like and capable of interference; the second involves discrete exchange of energy/momentum quanta. <u>Concepts and pictures applied to each need to be distinct.</u>

Attention to basics leads to the view that evolution of systems between measurements is a purely wave-like wholeness, from which individual object-like "measurement events" manifest. Also, "entangled" states have a blatant quality of wholeness called "nonlocality." Application of concepts of object-likeness (individual particles) to evolution of systems invariably leads to nonsense. Three significant examples are provided.

(This perspective does not consider particle physics, wherein one does not picture space-time evolution between measurements. Also, while there is an unavoidable epistemological aspect to quantum probability, that aspect is "side-stepped" here. The perspectives herein should have relevance regardless of that issue.)

Basics – Language, Particles and Waves

Quantum mechanics purports to be a description of physical reality, which deliberately eliminates from theory all features not demanded by experiment. That there should be any need at all for special efforts to accomplish this obviously sensible aim is partly due to a peculiar feature of human language.

Language has been largely fashioned after macroscopic models. For example, if the word "particle" is used as a subject to which various physical properties are attributed, one notices the subversive effect of language when one tries to completely avoid the surreptitious use of some mental image of a "particle" between measurements. However, to refrain from using inappropriate mental modes is just the kind of intellectual asceticism demanded by quantum mechanics.

--- F. A. Kaempffer (8)

First, there are matters of language. The word "particle" can refer to entities with enduring attributes (e.g. mass or charge) that are constant within nonrelativistic quantum theory. "Particle" can also refer to a highly localized entity: a "point-particle." The latter meaning, referred to by Kaempffer, is used herein, and is considered an aspect of "object-likeness." The word "photon" refers to the minimum quantum of energy-momentum exchanged in the interaction between the electromagnetic (EM) field and matter. It often refers to a point-particle (supposedly the epitome of the quantum EM field), sometimes a wave or wave-packet.

We need to be very careful about the specific meaning of the word "particle" as a localized entity:

1. A "point-particle" has no extent in space, and is thus not capable of interference.
2. When the word "particle" (or "photon") applies to a wave or wave packet (i.e., has extent in space), it can participate in interference phenomena.
3. If, as with Bohm, (9) a point-particle is associated with, embedded in, a wave or wave-packet, then interference is related solely to the wave or wave-packet. The role of the ("inert") point-particle becomes relevant only in the process of detection.

With lack of care with these concepts (e.g., moving from one to another in the same context), illogical statements or questions will likely arise. This is evident in the history of experiments proposed and done to help us better understand quantum theory.

For clarity, the word "interference" refers to situations where intensity fringes occur due to "constructive" and "destructive" interference. The word "diffraction" refers to the wave-like variation in intensity near edges where waves are blocked by an object, or inversely, are passing through an opening. In a finite opening like a single slit, or a finite width collimated beam, the diffraction pattern has interference fringes. Interference fringes are sufficient but not necessary to demonstrate wave behavior. Matching the shape of a central (or only) lobe of a diffraction pattern is sufficient, as was done using diffraction of a slow neutron beam by a knife edge (a "half-slit"). (10)

In any system governed by a wave equation, wave-like interference or diffraction is not seen when the wavelength of the wave is small compared with objects it interacts with. Short wavelength behavior (e.g., light being refracted or reflected by lenses or mirrors) is derivable from the wave equation governing its behavior. In quantum physics, particle-like tracks in cloud or bubble chambers, etc. are predicted by the Schrödinger wave equation. (11) (The quantum wave at its first interaction with matter [e.g., a bubble] collapses into a localized wave-packet there, and the next interaction with matter occurs on a line parallel to the momentum vector from the first interaction.) (12) <u>Quantum wave-particle duality must refer to something other than long versus short wavelength behavior of a wave.</u>

The wave-likeness that dominates quantum theoretical description of the dynamics of particles and fields becomes a challenge to our sense of objective reality. David Bohm (9) extended an idea of Louis de Broglie to frame an "ontological quantum theory" in which a particle is embedded in a pilot wave, and is "pushed" by that wave during evolution of the system. This point-particle is an "inert passenger" in the wave until a measurement event occurs. While Bohm's perspective may give a partial sense of relief for those who believe there needs to be an underlying object-like reality, there is an unavoidable nonlocal character to quantum theory (discussed below) that also disturbs our object-like sense of reality.

Looking into our language, we find that the definitions of the words "objective" and "objectivity" fall into two categories: 1] having to do with "truth-value," relating to reality independent of our prejudices, fancies, etc., and 2] being: A} a distinct object, and, B} separate from self. It is clear that the physical (and related) sciences in the past have obtained the first (objectivity = "truth-value") by dealing solely with the second (object-like systems, separate from self), in concept and in empirical practice. Discrimination between these two distinct categories often becomes blurred, since objectivity (truth-value) becomes strongly associated with empiricism based on object-likeness and separateness from self.

The recognition of distinct objects moving in smooth trajectories is wired into our brain during the early months of our neonate development. (13) Even when our mind is embracing abstract notions about reality, there is a part of our intuition that tends to associate those abstract notions with a reality that is composed of distinct objects. <u>Objectivity does not require object-likeness.</u> The perspective presented below favors a more abstract view as a way to avoid ways of thinking, or intuition, that lead to ill-formed questions.

A well-known story *("Sometimes a system behaves like a particle, sometimes like a wave..."* – supposedly an example of quantum wave-particle duality) assigns wave-likeness to passage through a double slit while assigning particle-likeness to passage through a single slit. It is patently false. There is a wider, not always discernible, diffraction pattern – with fringes – behind the single slit. One telling of that story (14) included a diagram that showed a diffraction fringe (a side-lobe) behind a single slit – while assigning particle-likeness to the beam in that situation. The rounded main lobe of the diffraction pattern was explained as being due to some particles being bounced off the side of the slit. The side-lobe was ignored. This is a vivid example of the "surreptitious," "subversive" effect of our stories: ignoring what is in plain sight. (Pedagogical question: How is it that this erroneous view, regarding single and double slit diffraction and interference, has remained so long in quantum lore?)

Figure 1. (14) Double and single slit interference are evident in a story about wave-particle duality, where particle-likeness is attributed to the single slit.

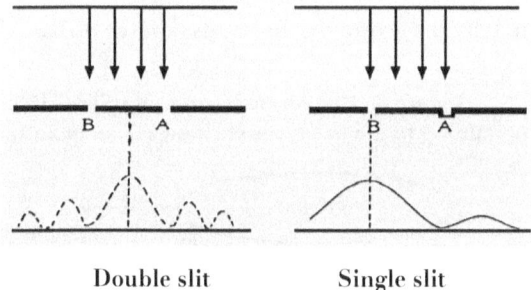

Double slit   Single slit

This conceptual error, and the view that the passage of a particle through multiple (e.g., double) paths is a criterion for wave-likeness, is common in historically important experiments designed and performed to probe the nature of quantum reality.

Figure 2. (15) Interference from individual detections.

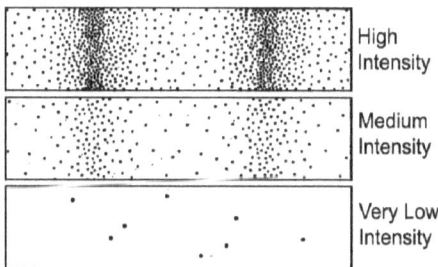

Usually, interference is indicated by intensity patterns found in accumulations of single detections. Also, generally, the statement that "sometimes a system behaves like a particle and sometimes like a wave, depending on the experimental situation" is false. In this example, both individual detections, and interference patterns in the accumulations thereof, are clearly present in the same experiment.

The original meaning of "wave-particle duality" came from the recognition that quantum systems have a wave character (frequency) directly associated with properties such as energy and momentum formerly attributed to particles. (See the "Basics" section, below.) This remains true no matter what kind of experimental setup is used.

Individuality and Wholeness (1)

In quantum theory we do not "make measurements" in the classical sense. We set up an apparatus, and individual detections occur "of their own accord," (i.e., probabilistically). A measurement result, except in very special cases, does not represent a property possessed by the system prior to measurement. (In this sense, the word "measurement" is very poor.) The dynamics of a system, how it moves/evolves in space and time, is very different from how its existence becomes known to us via measurement events.

Figure 3. (16) "Abstract" and "Manifest" layers,
pertaining to the two types of change (7) in quantum theory

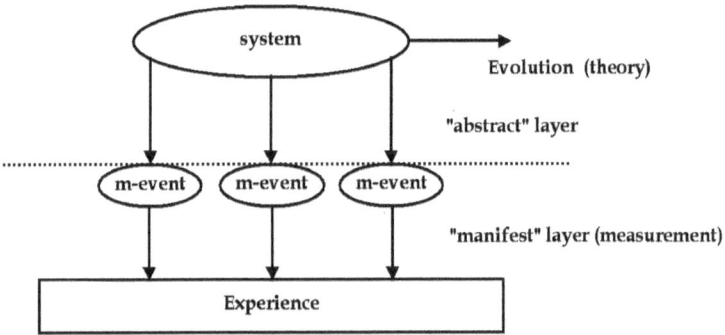

The "abstract layer," represents the continuous causal evolution of the representation of state, distributed in space as described by the Schrödinger wave equation. The "manifest layer" represents the discrete probabilistic measurement events ("m-events") involving exchange of quanta, manifestations in space-time, by which we become aware of physical reality. These two "layers," or "arenas," represent "construct" and "sense" (16) in a classical perspective. But, the "manifest layer" here may contain some elements of construct (and inference) in some interpretations of measurement events.

(Here, we focus on individual quantum measurement events involving exchange of few quanta, or accumulations thereof. And, quantum probability is simply related to statistical results of measurement, (17) without making any deeper inquiry or assumptions. However, c.f. Stapp. (18)

The "abstract" layer represents hypothetical constructs regarding the quantum system, (19) and its dynamical equations of motion. It is abstract in the sense that all things that we attribute to reality (including, e.g., tables and chairs), are according to Einstein, (20) *"in no way immediately given to us,"* and are not logically deducible from the data of our senses. Rather, they come to us by *"the way of conscious or unconscious intellectual construction, which proceeds completely free and arbitrarily."* These intellectual constructs have value to the extent they *"stand in a relation of 'correspondence' with our sensations."* (There are more sophisticated, nuanced, philosophies; but Einstein's comments serve well here.) <u>Since objectivity does not require object-likeness, lack of such does not prevent this layer from representing an "objective reality."</u>

Concepts or pictures appropriate to the discrete changes involved in measurement events in the manifest layer should not be applied to the abstract layer, and vice versa; doing so leads to ill-formed questions and associated experiments. The concept of discrete photons is useful only in the manifest layer (as quantum exchanges).

Basics – Wave-Particle Duality, and Heisenberg Uncertainty

As indicated previously, quantum wave-particle duality does not relate to long wavelength vs. short wavelength behavior of the quantum wavefunction. It is defined by the Planck-Einstein-DeBroglie equations relating energy and momentum to frequencies,

$$E = h \cdot f_t, \quad p_x = h \cdot f_x.$$

("E" is energy and "f_t" its temporal frequency; "p_x" is momentum in the x direction and "f_x" spatial frequency with respect to position x; and "h" is Planck's constant). Simply stated, energy and momentum are proportional to temporal and spatial frequency, respectively. (21) The pairs of variables E and t, or p_x and x (and others), are called "canonically conjugate" variables; they play a fundamental role in the description of dynamics, a role that is affected by wave-particle duality.

In **purely mathematical** wave theory there is a kind of inverse relationship between frequency and location leading to a well-known uncertainty relation between the two:

$$\Delta f_t \cdot \Delta t \geq 1/4\pi \quad \text{(temporal)},$$
$$\Delta f_x \cdot \Delta x \geq 1/4\pi \quad \text{(spatial)} \qquad \text{(pure math)}$$

where Δ is "uncertainty in" (standard deviation). These represent the fact that it takes a wide band of frequencies to have a more precise location, and it takes a large spread in location to have a more precise frequency. Multiplication of these purely mathematical uncertainty relations by Planck's constant h, and simple substitution from the equations of wave-particle duality, yields equations in physics: (22)

$$\Delta(hf_t)\Delta t = \Delta E \Delta t \geq h/4\pi,$$
$$\Delta(hf_x)\Delta t = \Delta p_x \Delta x \geq h/4\pi. \quad \text{(physics)}$$

This simple derivation is presented to show the intimate, direct relationship of the Heisenberg uncertainty relations to wave-particle duality, *without any reference to disturbance-due-to-measurement*. <u>The Heisenberg uncertainty relations are, fundamentally, specific statements about the wave-likeness of quantum states. Disturbance-due-to-measurement plays no role here; it is neither causative nor explanatory for the Heisenberg uncertainty relations.</u> (And, it is not essential to complementarity.) (23)

(As a corollary, since quantum states violating Heisenberg uncertainty are mathematically impossible, measurements producing such are impossible.)

In classical physics, these canonically conjugate pairs of variables (E & t, or p_x & x, etc.) serve as fundamental <u>independent</u> dimensions for the description of dynamics. Using them as axes of a graph (a "Cartesian grid") provides a "phase space" on which the dynamics are represented by trajectories. With quantum wave-particle duality, these graphs become <u>frequency vs. location graphs</u>: The formerly independent classical variables for the axes (grids) are now non-independent, non-Cartesian dimensions. (A point on that graph is a mathematical impossibility. The use of classical phase space is replaced by the use of Wigner functions, e.g., ref. 24.) Bohm and Hiley (25) argue that the "Cartesian grid" describes essentially a local order, and that a new kind of order is needed: one that is nonlocal. This shift in the nature of the fundamental dimensions of dynamics indicates the need for a drastically new intuitive sense of the nature of physical reality, one that is fundamentally wave-based.

Bohr's concepts of "complementarity" (7) are wide ranging, and hard to pin down. Given an ingrained classical bias toward the perspective of canonically conjugate variables as independent dimensions of dynamics, the lack of independence between the two (frequency-location) canonical variables in quantum theory would understandably give rise to concepts akin to complementarity.

The issue of ontological vs. epistemological interpretations of quantum probability have been side-stepped herein. There are good reasons to associate quantum probability with human knowledge. (e.g., ref. 18). But, it is hard to imagine what role the phase of the quantum probability amplitude (responsible for interference) plays with respect to human knowledge. And, it would seem prudent to consider Eastern empirical study of consciousness, especially aspects that involve nonlocality and other aspects of quantum theory that currently challenge our understanding.

The challenge of understanding quantum theory is likely to remain until we find a more essential, intuitive way to understand wave-particle-duality. (The lack of a "simple statement" of the "central idea" of quantum theory is what drove Wheeler to pursue delayed choice experiments, described below.) (26)

In the Einstein-Bohr debates (that included Bohr's statements on complementarity), disturbance due to measurement was often used to debunk attempts to get around Heisenberg uncertainty. This led generally to an inappropriate sense of importance for disturbance-due-to-measurement (e.g., ref. 23).

The Photon

In the second paragraph of his 1905 paper on the photoelectric effect, (27) Einstein indicated that photoelectric phenomena relate primarily to the "emission and transformation of light" involved in its interaction with matter. But, in the next paragraph, he indicated his conclusion:

> ... The energy of a light ray spreading out from a point source is not continuously distributed over an increasing space but consists of a finite number of energy quanta which are localized at points in space, which move without dividing, and which can only be produced and absorbed as complete units.

This new concept of "quanta" of light, later named "photon," was applied by Einstein to that which evolves, as well as its interaction with matter, contrary to his earlier comment. The lack of distinction between dynamic evolution and interaction with measuring instruments was noted immediately (e.g., by Planck's assistant Max von Laue, (28) and since, e.g. refs. 29, 30). However, consistency with the exchange of quanta requires, not traveling particles, but quantized energy levels in the field.

Einstein's postulated exchange of quanta in measurement events was foundational in the development of quantum theory. But, the unneeded, erroneous concept of traveling point-particles has remained in the common lore of quantum physics, contributing to ill-formed questions and associated experiments.

Examples: Photon Concept Failures

First, early experiments designed to demonstrate the existence of evolving photons (31) predicted that there should be no coincidence counts from a low intensity field. (A point-particle photon cannot be in two places at once, and chance for two simultaneous photon detections would be very low in a weak field.) The experimenters were surprised to find that the coincidence counts were not only greater than zero, but twice what they expected from a simplistic classical view, ignoring fluctuations. (32) The experiment went through many changes, including attenuation so that, supposedly, only one photon would be in the apparatus at any given time. (33) Success was claimed, finally, when an entangled state (described below) was used to guarantee a sharp only-one-photon field that showed lack of coincidence counts. But, this lack of coincidence is demanded by conservation of energy in a field with an excitation level of unity. Anticoincidence (in this experiment) does not discriminate between field and traveling photons.

Second, a well-known two-laser experiment (34) was set up to test a statement by Paul A. M. Dirac: (paraphrasing) Photons interfere only with themselves, never with each other. (35, 36) Two independent lasers, side-by-side, were aimed so that their beams would overlap at a moderate distance. The experimenters pictured each of the two lasers emitting a distinct photon, so that evidence of interference in a place where the two beams overlapped would indicate interference between the two photons – thereby disproving Dirac's statement. Interference was observed in this experiment. That was supposed to disprove Dirac's statement; but then the picture was changed. A new, "sum-over-paths" perspective was taken (involving a quantum theoretic use of Huygens' principle from classical wave theory), consistent with electromagnetic waves radiating from each laser, having a wave-like interference pattern where they overlapped, and from that a single photon being absorbed at the detector. Thus, the conceptualization shifted from traveling photons to only one photon involved in the process of detection. Interference was within the field, not between photons. The experiment was empty. The picture of distinct particles, photons, evolving through space toward the detector led to an ill-formed question, and an empty experiment.

Also, they did a second version of their experiment with a highly attenuated field, (34) claiming that there was only one photon at a time, on average, in the apparatus. Since interference was involved, a localized "photon" has to refer to a wave-packet. The cross-coherence of the two independent lasers, at the time data were taken, indicated the presence of coherent wave-packets at least (roughly) 6000 meters long. (37) For a nominal optical path length between laser emission and detection (one meter, say), the field had to have something of the order of 6000 very long overlapping single-photon wave-packets in the apparatus in order to meet their criterion of one photon count per transit time through the apparatus. The picture of such a large overlapping of individual wave-packets seems like an awkward way to describe a field.

The simplest and most reliable way to picture this situation is to view each laser emitting into a wave-like electromagnetic field, with absorption of a quantum from the field at the detector.

Third, in 1978, John Archibald Wheeler proposed several "delayed choice" experiments to probe our lack of understanding of quantum theory. (26) In his own words:

> We search here, not for new experiments or new predictions, but for new insight. Experiments dramatize and predictions spell out the quantum's consequences; but what is its central idea? A pedant of Copernican times could have calculated planetary positions from the equations of Copernicus as well as Copernicus himself; but what would we think of him if his eyes were closed to the main point, that the 'Earth goes around the Sun'?
>
> In the absence of an equally simple statement of its central idea, quantum theory appears to many as strange, unwelcome, and forced on physics as it were from the outside against its will.

Wheeler's choice to explore "delayed choice" with traveling photons was motivated by the debates between Einstein and Bohr. (38) An experiment, done with a more practical beam splitter instead of double slits, (39) as described by Abner Shimony, (40) was used to see if a photon could make its "choice" to go through only one, or both, split beams – after it had already passed through the beam splitter.

Wheeler was very careful in the language he used (26) for this temporally paradoxical situation:

> 'No phenomenon is a phenomenon until it is an observed phenomenon.'
> In other words, it is not a paradox that we choose what shall have happened after 'it has already happened.' It has not really happened, it is not a phenomenon, until it is an observed phenomenon.

Figure 4. Delayed choice interferometer. (40) The fast switch chooses continuation of split path A, <u>or</u> path B, while (supposedly) a single photon is in the apparatus.

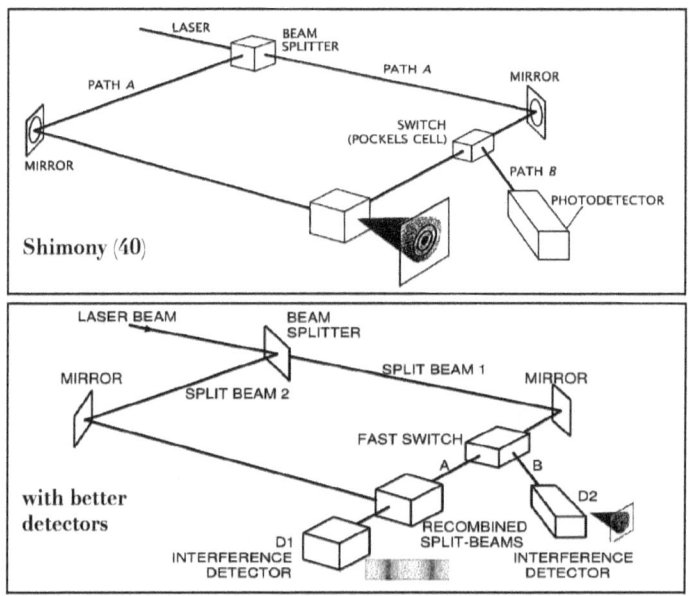

In the conventional description (top diagram, Figure 4) particle-likeness is attributed to the split-beam that is incident on the photodetector. But, accumulations of fine-resolution photodetections in that path [B] would reveal a diffraction pattern due to the collimation of the split-beam (a high density circle with circular fringes around it, represented roughly in the lower diagram of Figure 4, above).

The error here is the projection (back in time from a measurement event) of the classical concept of a point-particle photon going through two paths (or any subset of paths available to the wavefunction). How could a point-particle do that: have extent?

The patterns of photo-detections (diffraction in the single split-beam or interference in the recombined split-beams) are predicted by the local intensity of the electromagnetic field at the detectors. Any consequence, on the system as a whole, of a measurement event (such as the "collapse" of a wavefunction consistent with a specific subset of paths) is considered <u>instantaneous and nonlocal</u>, as discussed in the next section. The temporally paradoxical description by Wheeler is indicative of the construction of the issue: As a consequence of detection, the classical notion of a photon's "choice" of a subset of paths is projected backwards in time. It is inappropriate to attribute "choice" to an (imagined) object in the field due to consequences of, and prior to, a specific detection.

This beautifully intricate line of questioning demonstrates how a more classical sense of reality creeps in when the concept of point-particles is introduced into the realm of wave propagation. Our challenge is to understand more deeply the wave nature of quantum theory. <u>The concept of a traveling point-particle photon led to the misguided temporally paradoxical questioning of "delayed choice."</u>

Helmuth, et al., performed this experiment and got the predicted results. (39) Also they reported (ref. 39 - p. 2540):

> ... Wheeler ... noted that it was just 'bad use of language' which got us in the dilemma of deciding whether the photon 'shall have come by one route, or by both routes' after it 'already has done its travel'.

(This leads one to wonder if he was referring to Kaempffer's comment – ref. 8.)

The conceptual errors in these three examples are related solely to the imagined point-particle photon in the realm of wave propagation. These errors do not occur when the concept of particle is used carefully (as in Bohm's view), or is applied solely to the process of detection.

INDIVIDUALITY AND WHOLENESS (2)

The familiar wave-like nature of the electromagnetic field, described nearly the same in both quantum and classical physics (3, 41), presents no issues. However, the quantum electromagnetic field has introduced deeper problems: Infinities associated with vacuum fluctuations, and incompatibilities between quantum theory and relativity. (The latter includes the fact that "before" and "after" are not the same in all relativistic frames of reference, while quantum theory treats time, not as a quantum variable, but as an "axiomatic referent" as the basis of change.) Also, we do not understand the nature of quantum probability, nor the relationship between that and human consciousness. (Quantum probability seems to be both epistemological [subjective] and ontological [objective]; assumption of solely one or the other leads to difficulty.) With this challenge, it is imperative that we clear misconceptions from current perspectives. Addressing these issues in a fundamental way will require the kind of "asceticism" championed by Kaempffer. (8)

In a recent article, (42) David Albert and Rivka Galchen present a remarkably clear exposition of the issues that need to be resolved in order to approach understanding of the nature of the reality that is addressed by quantum theory and relativity. Quantum nonlocality is a central theme in that discussion. Herein, a quality of "wholeness" (involving nonlocality) is attributed to the quantum wave-function generally, and to entanglement in quantum states in particular. The word "wholeness" is used because the most conflict-free perspective seems to be one in which "wholeness" is in some sense "ontologically prior," with object-likeness arising out of that wholeness.

Much has been written about quantum theoretical "entangled states." The following is a very simplified description, hopefully faithful to the issue. The entangled states usually discussed involve two photons (or electrons with intrinsic spin, etc.) combined in a quantum state for which the properties of the whole are determined as precisely as is allowed in quantum theory. But, because of wave-particle duality, the dynamic properties of the individual constituents of these entangled states are completely indeterminate. The individual properties are not determined until a property (or properties) of one of the constituents is determined via measurement, and the corresponding property or properties of the other may be calculated from conservation of energy, momentum, angular momentum, or intrinsic spin, etc.

In a classical system such as a single stationary object (e.g., a cannonball in space) that explodes into two halves, there is no issue. The dynamic properties of the two individual halves are determined by the explosion (in accord with conservation of energy and momentum, etc.). But, the individual properties of either half are unknown until the properties of one of the halves are measured, from which the properties of the other can be calculated. This is a good example of epistemological (subjective) probability, described by an ordinary probability distribution representing certainty-uncertainty in our knowledge. However, this explanation is not consistent with quantum theory. Treating the constituents as a pair of distinct localized objects, possessing their individual properties prior to measurement, unavoidably leads to predictions contrary to quantum theory. (43) No matter how wide the separation between the constituents, the determination of an individual property of one of them via measurement determines, instantaneously, the corresponding individual property of the other – even though (contrary to criteria of Einstein, et al. – ref. 43) the constituents could not have possessed these individual properties prior to that measurement. This phenomenon is given the name "nonlocality" (c.f., 42). This situation is another robust example of how the assumption of distinct local objects in that-which-evolves-dynamically — that which we use to model reality — leads to unavoidable inconsistency with quantum theory.

The 2-body entangled state represents a kind of wholeness out of which individual properties manifest in measurement events. Part of the attraction of the concept of traveling photons is that it seems to explain how it is that a field distributed in space can discretely give up locally a quantum of energy and momentum to a detector, and instantaneously adjust itself for that loss globally throughout space. This is, loosely, a one-body version of the nonlocality found in entangled states. With entangled states, the two measurements involved provide solid confirmation of nonlocality. Both the 1-body and 2-body versions involve a not yet fully understood quality of "wholeness" in quantum theory.

FINAL COMMENTS

The assumption of particle-likeness in the realm of quantum wave propagation permeates the common lore of physics (e.g., ref. 44), resulting in ill-formed questions. Quantum theory's representation of physical dynamics involves a wave-like wholeness that manifests in discrete measurement events. The concept of object-like point-particles is incompatible with the evolution of quantum systems. For some, dropping this concept might create a kind of vacuum; a loss of old conundrums ("old friends"), and for most of us, deep mystery. With the inevitable introduction of consciousness to quantum theory, the mystery will become even deeper, and wider. We need even more to distance ourselves from old tales that do not fit, learn more about consciousness from within and from without – and play in the depths of "not knowing."

In the perspective regarding psychic knowing described here, information from a perhaps timeless wholeness manifests in our individual consciousness. There seems to be the same kind of mystery in both physical and psychic domains. In these mysteries (and that regarding the nature of the monism that encompasses both realms, as well), finding well-formed questions is essential.

The resolution of these mysteries likely will require exploration of states of consciousness, a combining of the empirical tools and perspectives appropriate to both inner and outer realities, and many practices involving direct observation of consciousness/awareness. The study of consciousness from within requires different tools for objectivity (requiring, e.g., clarity, and cultivation of subtle discernment and discrimination in mind – not an easy task). Methods for developing consensus (e.g., ref. 45) regarding subjective and objective experience, within and across individuals, will be important. Issues of individuality and wholeness are likely to be relevant in both domains.

The study and practice of psychic phenomena hopefully will contribute to shifts in and exploration of consciousness, and inform our perspective in both domains. (Exploration of brainwave feedback as a tool to explore one's attention, etc., is a current interest for me.)

Of the three essential aspects of quantum reality spoken to by Nick Herbert in Chapter 30, "randomness, thinglessness, and interconnectedness," this discussion has focused on the second two; "thinglessness" (letting go of the concept of individual objects possessing their dynamic attributes) and "interconnectedness" (a quality of "wholeness" that is responsible for "nonlocality"). (Note that "interconnectedness" implies connections between individuals. "Wholeness" is not constructed from individuality; it is here assumed to be ontologically prior to manifestation of individuality.)

REFERENCES AND END NOTES

1) Gore, A. (1992) *Earth in the Balance.* NY: Houghton Mifflin Company.
2) National Science Foundation Summer Institute in "Macroscopic Quantum Coherence." San Diego State College (now University), 1969-1971.
3) Glauber, R. (1963) "The quantum theory of optical coherence." In: *Phys. Rev.* 130, 2529; "Coherent and incoherent states of the radiation field." In: *Phys. Rev.* 131, 6, p.2782. (Glauber's fully quantum theoretic description of coherence and noise in radiation becomes applicable to classical theory by replacing quantum correlation functions with their classical counterpart.)
4) Yang, C.N. (1962) "Off-diagonal long-range order." In: *Rev. Mod. Phys.* 34, 694. For superfluid helium: Penrose, O., & Onsager, L. (1957) In: *Phys. Rev.* 108, 1175.
5) Cummings, F.W. & Johnston, J.R. (1966) "Theory of superfluidity." In: *Phys. Rev.* 151, 105;164, 270(E) (1967). See also Johnston, J.R. (1970) "Coherent states in superfluids: The ideal Einstein-Bose gas." In: *Am. J. Phys.* 38, 516-528). Since the measure of coherence in superfluidity and lasers applies also to the classical electromagnetic field, that also could be considered an example of macroscopic quantum coherence.
6) London, F. (1961) *Superfluids.* (Vol. 1, *Superconductivity)* NY: Dover; 1964 (Vol 2 *Superfluidity)* NY: Dover.
7) Bohr, N. (1928) "The quantum postulate and the recent development of atomic theory." In: *Supplement to Nature.* 580-590.
8) Kaempffer, F.A. (1965) *Concepts in Quantum Mechanics.* NY: Academic Press p.1.
9) Bohm, D. & Hiley, B.J. (1993) "The undivided universe." NY: Routledge. Chapter 2; Bohm, D. (1952) *Phys. Rev.* 85, 166-93.
10) Abundant data were tightly packed on the theoretical curve. As remembered, this was published in a Canadian journal, which I read in the late 1960s in the physics library at Dalhousie University, Halifax, Nova Scotia. The author would be grateful to anyone that could find that reference.
11) Schiff, L.I. (1955) *Quantum Mechanics, Second Edition.* NY: McGraw-Hill Book Company p. 209; (p. 335 in the third edition).
12) Photons do not cause tracks because they do not possess enduring properties. (Sciamanda, R.J. (1969) "Dirac and photon interference." In: *Am. J. Phys.* **37**, 11, pp. 1128-1130). Photons represent excitation of the field, and may be considered "absorbed" at detection.
13) Bower, T.G.R. (1971) "The object in the world of the infant." In: *Scientific American,* 225, (October).
14) Adapted from "story" of wave-particle duality accompanying Gleidman, J. (1983) In: *Science Digest* 91, 74 (June), p. 78).

15) Illustration from Morse, P.M. & Feshbach, H. (1953) *Methods of Mathematical Physics Vol 1.* NY: McGraw Hill Book Company, 225.

16) The diagram presented here uses only the interface between "sense" and "construct" that was the central aspect of Margenau's more elaborate diagram of the "C-field" and "P-field." (Margenau, H. (1950) *The Nature of Physical Reality: A Philosophy of Modern Physics.* NY: McGraw-Hill, 106.)

17) Margenau, H. (1958) "Philosophical problems concerning the meaning of measurement in physics." In: *Phil. Sci.* 25 1 (Jan), 23-33; *Phys. Rev.* 49 240. In general, physicists are not this careful, but safely in most cases.

18) Stapp, H. (1999) "Attention, intention and will in quantum physics." In: *Journal of Consciousness Studies* 6. Henry Stapp's admirable approach for combining physical material, body, and mind in a single quantum representation is based on "The Copenhagen Interpretation," in which quantum probability does not represent the behavior of physical systems, but our knowledge of that behavior (it is epistemological, not ontological). This would require consideration of both individual and "collective" aspects of consciousness.

19) Bohr, op. cit., p. 581. "Radiation in free space as well as isolated particles are abstractions."

20) Albert Einstein's letter in Samuel, H. (1952) *Essay in Physics.* NY: Harcourt, Brace and Company. Note that in Einstein's reference to "free intellectual constructs," "free" is meant in a logical sense only. This is a simple, but valuable, distinction between "sense" and "construct."

21) For non-sinusoidal modes (e.g., a high frequency square-wave), the frequency used would be the weighted average of the sinusoidal frequencies involved in the non-sinusoidal mode.

22) This is an informal derivation. Use of non-commuting operators in a Hilbert space (in a Fourier representation) for the derivation of the purely mathematical uncertainty relations would emphasize the simplicity of its introduction into quantum theory. However, the energy time relationship requires special treatment because, in quantum theory, time is not an ordinary physical variable; it is an "axiomatic referent" for change.

23) Englert, B-G., Scully, M.O., Walther, H. (1994) "The duality in matter and light." In: *Scientific American* (December) p. 86; Scully, M.O., Englert, B-G., Walther, H. (1991) "Quantum tests of complementarity." In: *Nature* 351, No. 6322, 111-116.

24) Holger, M. & Schleich, W.P. (2003) "A photon viewed from Wigner phase space." In: *Optics & Photonics News (OPN Trends)*, S-28 – S-35 (October).

25) Bohm, D. & Hiley, B.J. (1993) *The Undivided Universe.* NY: Routledge 351 (section 15.1). In the last chapter ("Quantum theory and the implicate order"), Bohm and Hiley introduce new ideas: Letting go of the "Cartesian notion of order," *"unbroken wholeness"* as a quality common to relativity and quantum theory, implicate order as a way to explore "an order appropriate to wholeness," and discusses the sum over paths as a Huygen's construction so that "matter is now analyzed in terms of quantum fields."

26) Wheeler, J.A. (1978) In: *Mathematical Foundations of Quantum Mechanics*, edited by A.R. Marlow. NY: Academic Press 9-48. (Quotation from p.14.)

27) Einstein, A. (1905) In: *Ann. Physik* 17, 132. Translation Arons, A.B. & Peppard, M.B. (1965) *Am. J. Physics* 33, 5.

28) Max von Laue to Albert Einstein (June 2, 1906) *Collected Papers of Albert Einstein*, vol. 5; cited in Overbye, D. (2000) *Einstein in Love*. NY: Viking.
29) Lamb, W.E., Jr. (1995) "Anti-photon." In: *Appl. Phys. B* 60 77-84.
30) Muthukrishnan, A., Scully, M.O., & Zubairy, M.S. (2003) "The concept of the photon – revisited." In: *Optics & Photonics News (OPN Trends)*, S-18 – S-27, October 2003. See S-25.
31) Greenstein, G. & Zajonc, A.G. (1997) *The Quantum Challenge*. Sudbury, MA: Jones and Bartlett Pub., Inc. 26-35. This is an excellent, comprehensive description (aimed at students) of historical experiments done to learn more about the nature or wave-particle duality, nonlocality, etc., in quantum theory, a good representation of the "common lore." Grangier, G. Roger & Aspect, A. (1986) "Experimental for a photon anticorrelation effect on a beam splitter." In: *Europhysics Lett.* 1 (4) 173-179.
32) Glauber, op. cit., Correction of this misunderstanding led to Glauber's Nobel prize-winning quantum theoretical description of all orders of coherence in the electromagnetic field, and a novel use of fluctuations for stellar interferometry. (Hanbury Brown & Twiss (1956) "A test of a new type of stellar interferometer on Sirius." In: *Nature* 178 1046.)
33) From the perspective of a field, it is clear that attenuation would affect only the counting rate, not the relative fluctuations or relative coincident counting rates (Glauber, op. cit.).
34) Pfleegor, R.L. & Mandel, L. (1967) "Interference of independent photon beams." In: *Phys. Rev.* 159, 1084. Pfleegor, R.L. & Mandel, L. (1968) "Further experiments on interference of independent photon beams at low light levels." In: *J. Opt. Soc. Amer.* 58, 946.
35) Dirac, P.A.M. (1958) *Quantum Mechanics*, 4th ed. London: Oxford U Press, p. 9.
36) The concept of a photon interfering with itself refers to the electromagnetic field interfering with itself. (The common description of laser radiation being generated from an emitted photon being in-phase with the emitting photon is quantum theoretically incorrect. Laser radiation is generated by atomic emission into, thereby raising the excitation of, the stimulating mode of the field.)
37) The auto-coherence length of each wave packet must be at least as long as the cross-coherence length of the two lasers; otherwise, the two lasers could not be considered independent.
38) Bohr, N. (1949) "Discussion with Einstein on epistemological problems in atomic physics." In: *Albert Einstein: Philosopher-Scientist*, Ed. Schilpp, P.A. Evanston, IL: Library of Living Philosophers 199-241.
39) Hellmuth, T., Walther, H., Zajonc, A. & Scleich, W. (1987) "Delayed-choice experiments in quantum interference." In: *Phys. Rev. A*, 35, 2532-2541. See also Alley, C.O., Jakubowicz, O., Steggerda, C.A., & Wickes, W.C. (1983) "A delayed random choice quantum mechanic experiment with light quanta." In: *Proceedings of the International Symposium on the Foundations of Quantum Mechanics – Tokyo*, Kamefuchi, S. (Ed.) (Physics Society of Japan), 158-164.
40) Diagram taken from Shimony, A. (1988) "The reality of the quantum world." In: *Scientific American* 258, 1 46-53).
41) Wheeler, op. cit., pp. 15-16. Wheeler, citing Heisenberg and Pauli, presents an argument supporting the use of a classical treatment of the electromagnetic field that can later become quantum theoretical when appropriate annihilation and creation operators are inserted.

42) Albert, D.Z. & Galchen, R. (2009) "A quantum threat to special relativity." In: *Scientific American* (March), 32.

43) Bell, J.S. (1964) "On the Einstein Podolsky Rosen paradox." In: *Physics* 1, 1964. This was John Bell's response to the famous "EPR" paper: (Einstein, A., Podolsky, B. and Rosen N. (1935) "Can quantum-mechanical description of physical reality be considered complete?" In: *Phys. Rev.* 47 777-780) that was based on the assumption that physical reality is composed of independent objects that possess their dynamical attributes. (These are the historic first papers.)

44) Hilmer, R. & Kwiat, P. (2007) "A do-it-yourself quantum eraser." In: *Scientific American*.

45) Stoyva J. & Kamiya J. (1968) "Electrophysiological studies of dreaming as the prototype of a new strategy in the study of consciousness." In: *Psychological Review*, Vol. 75, 192-205. This was a resolution of a battle between proponents of the superiority of objective data (EEG/REM) vs. subjective reports in the study of dreams. That "convergence" takes place, to some extent, naturally within individuals — making that process more conscious may be useful.

> *In some sense man is a microcosm of the universe; therefore what man is, is a clue to the universe. We are enfolded in the universe.*
>
> --- David Bohm

SECTION VIII

DIMENSIONS OF SPIRIT

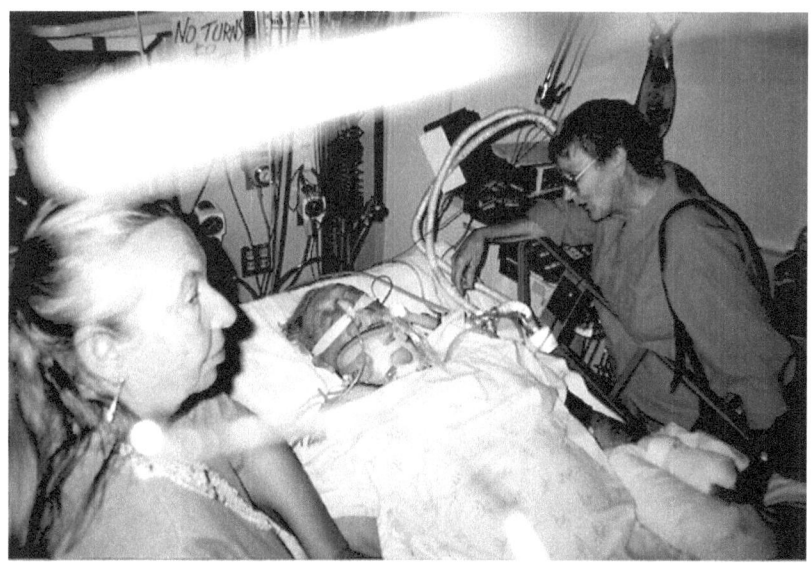

Nip Neilson was seriously injured. His wife Deana stayed beside him, and her constant presence was a very important part of his recovery. He could walk again and he lived several more years to the age of 89. Millay felt a presence over her head—the spirit of her great-grandmother—who was also Nip's grandmother. Notice the series of circle lights that seem to start from the bottom of the picture (where Millay is holding his hand), and continue up to her shoulder.

(Photo of *"Gramma's Spirit"* © 1997 by Echo Penrose)

SECTION VIII

DIMENSIONS OF SPIRIT

When existential emergencies occur and show overwhelming dimensions, when politicians lose the confidence of their constituency, when priests do not consider the needs of their community, when physicians and psychotherapists treat the symptoms and not their patients, because they don't have the time or they feel constrained by "scientific" considerations, when underlying imbalances in an individual's physical, emotional, mental/moral, social, and spiritual systems remain unattended, then the search for spiritual help begins and will, at times, produce new shamans.

In sum, shamanism is very much alive today. It has stayed accessible whether we look without or within. Shamans ritualize the processes of transformation. Shamans have been and are called to serve and to restore the connections between the sacred and the profane.

The need to come into the presence of the spiritual is deeply rooted in the human soul. Over thousands of years those seeking a spiritual connection developed different methods and disciplines to come "to know God." In each culture, spiritual disciplines are available to those who look for them. Many, however, have neither the inclination nor the time for "spiritual practice"; they seek, instead, mediators who have developed the ability to access spiritual energies and who can manifest the spiritual in visible form.

--- Ruth-Inge Heinze [1]
--- (1919 – 2007)

---

[1] Heinze, R-I. 1989 (Excerpts from) "Who are the shamans of the twentieth century?" In: Heinze, R-I. (Ed.) *Proceedings of the Fifth International Conference on the Study of Shamanism and Alternate Modes of Healing*. Berkeley, CA: Independent Scholars of Asia. (Proceedings are available at: http://www.shamanismconference.org.)

INTRODUCTION

Sondra Barrett believes that the activity of the cells in our bodies provides spiritual lessons for us all. (Chapter 33)

"A Healer's Journey" in Chapter 34 is a fascinating report about the process of becoming a healer. Osteopath Joel Alter began his practice as a surgeon, but he gave that up many years ago to study and practice the less invasive techniques of alternative medicine. After one serious accident injured his spine, and later another one broke his neck, he became disabled and confined to a wheelchair. Nevertheless, his extensive knowledge of the human body, the mind, its resonance in nature, and his spiritual energy, continued to bring healing comfort to those who always counted on him to ease their pain.

Stephan Schwartz writes a moving account (from his own direct observation) of an amazing healing by the Native American medicine man Rolling Thunder in Chapter 35.

The director of the Institute for Transpersonal Psychology (ITP) Arthur Hastings has created a supportive environment for those suffering intense grief, so they might communicate directly with the spirit of a lost loved one. His report of the results of this project in Chapter 36 is inspirational.

Ruth-Inge Heinze continues to teach us about the freedom she experiences as a disembodied spirit. She and other teachers of consciousness have asked Millay to channel information about their existences in the other dimensions. Jack Stucki provided us with a photograph of a woman who received a heart transplant from a man who had been killed in an accident. Included in the same photo is the spirit face of the donor. The ancient Native American Mountain Spirit (MS or "the Chief") also provided valuable information about the Spirit World. He called Hosteen Nez to be his apprentice medicine man many years ago, and Nez has agreed to share some especially significant transmissions.

> *Out of a startled mass of earth and water,*
> *we arise,*
> *with the first breath,*
> *surprised*
> *for having done it.*
> *and with the second,*
> *forgetting why we came.*
>
> *--- Shoshi Morginn*

CELLS AND THE SACRED

Sondra Barrett

What if you were given a laboratory and told to discover the coding for normal cells and malignant cells? Where would you start? What strategies could you learn to quiet your racing mind to listen to other ways of knowing? And how in the world do you leap into the great unknown with only a microscope in hand?

My decoding prowess began as I looked at human white blood cells with a microscope seeking clues to growth patterns, normal and not so normal. Trained in observation I reacted to that first blip into my consciousness – normal cells revealed predictable patterns of form while abnormal leukemic cells showed chaotic shapes. My mind tried to make sense of this, concluding that form followed function – abnormal cells functioning in an unpredictable fashion looked disorganized and misshapen compared to normal healthy functioning cells.

To quiet and sooth my ever questioning mind I studied a variety of traditions – shamanism and aikido, qigong and Buddhism, astrology and creative expression. One thing became clear from my merging mental and metaphysical meanderings with microscopic journeys: Our cells can be our teachers in living well and our molecules hold clues to their divine design. Here I will attempt to make a short discourse into the wonders of the invisible realm that are lessons or messages from our cells that far surpass the messages in water.

Carl Jung, the great psychologist from the last century, gave us a reverence for the power of symbols and a universal unconsciousness. He called the patterns that structure our imagination "archetypes." They shape matter and mind. These elemental patterns and images are in every culture.

So where do cells and molecules fit into the idea of archetypes? I posit that the architecture of life and the structure of our molecules served as templates for essential teachings throughout the ages and can be discovered by looking at sacred art. Do cells carry spiritual intelligence? Can they teach us how to live?

Our oldest living ancestors have much to tell us of the evolutionary journey from cell to SELF. Each of us is a community of cells, trillions of microscopic individuals merged to create sanctuary for one human soul.

Within and **beyond** the scientific paradigm, the microscopic universe reveals an invisible world that carries meaning beyond physical form. I promise a fascinating exploration into our inner nature that will transform your experience of science, art, and your own divinity.

We'll close the gap between science and religion by taking a brief peek into the essence and archetypes of the cellular universe. Bringing together science, art and spirituality this practical understanding of the wonders of our sacred cellular nature starts with ten lessons from our cells. To unearth this story, perhaps a brief glimpse into its author will help you enjoy the adventure.

As teller of this tale, I call myself Sondra Barrett cellular archeologist, though in truth I was trained as a biochemist and medical researcher into the nature of disease. My unconventional leaning, while being a bona fide academic faculty member at the UC Medical School, had me also exploring the nontraditional medicine of the shaman, energy practitioner and creative arts therapist. My penchant for connecting disparate points of view had me seeing cells in Native American pictographs, molecules as mystical, and interpreting cell form and function as lessons about life.

So in this tale that celebrates our cells as sacred we start with creation. What else? In order for life to survive, it needed a place. And so over eons, molecules formed and eventually merged to shape the sanctuary for life. That sanctuary, with poetic license omitting all the permutations it took to arrive at a human cell, was created by the embrace of molecules. Imagine that! The great Jesuit theologian Teilhard de Chardin wrote that because of the propensity for molecules to unite, love exists in us. (8)

> If there were no internal propensity to unite... in the molecule itself, it would be physically impossible for love to appear higher up, with us. By rights... we should assume its presence... in everything that is.
>
> --- Teilhard de Chardin, *The Phenomenon of Man*

And so we have the first lesson from our cells, the essentials to life – embrace. Molecules cannot form without uniting with another. Newborn babies will not survive without being touched or embraced by another. And we humans thrive when we embrace love. A question that our cells may ask – what else do you embrace? What is important for your life; what gives you meaning? What touches you?

As the cellular scientist, searching for how cells grew and matured, what made them choose life or death, maturity, or the same old repetitive pattern, answers came again in the hidden structures of the cell.

Inside our cellular sanctuary is a vast shimmering fabric constructed of gossamer strings, long tubes and thin filaments. The fabric, named the cytoskeleton, may, in fact be the seat of consciousness and the actual intelligence of the cell. Dr Donald Ingber (3, 4) at Harvard Medical School discovered that the tension placed on this cellular webbing influenced whether the cell made carbon copies of itself, changed the program and matured, or switched to the ultimate recycle and died a gentle death. Pulling on the tension of the cell changed its genetic expression. Taut and stretched out, attached to a surface, the cell repeated its genetic program, making more of the same self. Yet when the cell let go of some of those attachments, it shifted to a pattern of maturity. Letting go of attachments allowed maturity to develop? Sounds like a Buddhist teaching to me. And when the cell fully let go, it was time to surrender into the great unknown. Often the trigger for fully letting go was the "altruistic" need for limited resources that are then made available for the younger cells.

A few lessons come from our cells – what do I attach myself to, what do I need to let go of, and what permits my maturity? Ingber showed that our cells can be regulated mechanically. Thus, along with mind or consciousness-altering messages of the cell, bodymind practices may enhance our experience. When we stretch in yoga we shift our cells' tensions. Physical exercises handed down from ancient Mexican sorcerers and taught by Carlos Castaneda were said to change consciousness and help a person shape-shift to another form. Castaneda called these tensegrity practices. Interestingly, from the architect and biologist's points of view, changing tension on a structure to maintain its integrity is called – you guessed it – tensegrity.

This very basic property of our cells to change their state through mechanical forces and movement is mirrored in many physical and spiritual healing practices like yoga and shamanic dance. Scientists have learned even more about the shimmering cytoskeleton; its strings and strands vibrate in order to change shape, its structures can respond to sound and energy. The centriole, one unique tubular construction within the cell, guides cell division. It also "reads" infrared energy and according to scientists Roger Penrose (5) and Stuart Hameroff, (2) it moves electrons and is the seat of human consciousness.

Our cellular wisdom tells us to create sanctuary, embrace and attend to what we attach to, let go of whatever prevents our maturity. We do this from our molecules on up.

Another set of properties of our cells is their ability to recognize self and other, to communicate. And of course, the cell asks us how do we recognize our self and communicate with others.

The final cellular or universal law I'd like to discuss here is the law of three. Our basic genetic code is built from a threesome of the four nucleic acid bases, nicknamed ATCG. A genetic codon is something like ATA, CCC, CAT. Threesomes are everywhere in biology. Three embryonic layers form once the egg is fertilized egg. These layers, the ectoderm, mesoderm and endoderm, give rise to a living being. We have a triune brain — the reptilian brain stem, the emotional limbic brain, and the thinking cerebral cortex. At a human level, threes are also very popular — maiden, wife, crone; father, mother, child; beginning, middle, end. And let's not forget the threesomes in spiritual traditions; the Christian Father, Son, and Holy Spirit; Jesus, Mary, and Joseph. In Hebrew, we have the three mother sounds SH, MM, AH of the most sacred prayer, and the three forms of God — Yahveh, Shekinah, Ruach. The Hindus have their triad — Brahma, Shiva and Vishnu. And so it goes on and on. Do the ever-present philosophical threesomes have their roots in our biology, in our molecular codes for life and consciousness?

And to make this information practical, think where we enjoy threesomes in everyday life — ready, set, go. We can put the threesome into action. Imagine attaching your attention to an intention, moving and stretching with it, and letting it go into the action or goal you want manifested. Simple as one, two, three.

There's a lot more to say about the sacred messages from our cells and the exquisite beauty of our molecules and their metaphysical stories. The full essay *Cells and the Sacred: from Cell to Soul* is on my website. (9)

Finally, though modern scientists discovered the functioning of our cellular domains, perhaps the ancient artist and seeker saw them and made them holy. This idea is not unprecedented. Leonard Shlain in *Art and Physics* (7) offers a convincing story that the artist's work preceded the physicist's discoveries. To me, it is compelling to interpret our cells as divinely inspired, that their teachings and designs have been carried through the ages. I will end with three final impressions for you. A few visuals may help clinch these ideas.

The ten lessons or messages our cells offer us may help us sustain a fulfilling life. Ancient cave paintings hold some of those mysteries. This ninth century **Medicine Wheel** convinced me that the ancients saw inside, and it was good.

DNA? This is a cave painting by the Sinagua people. Palakti ruins, AZ

Ninth century Medicine Wheel.

Compare those images to my drawing of a cell. Maybe this wheel of life stood for the essence of our lives – the cell as well as the universe. And just maybe its image originated in the inner vision of the ancient peoples.

CELL DRAWING

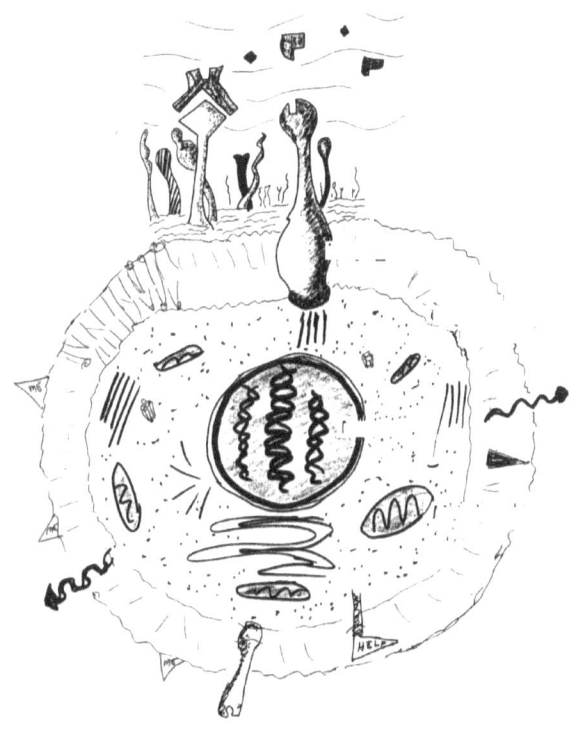

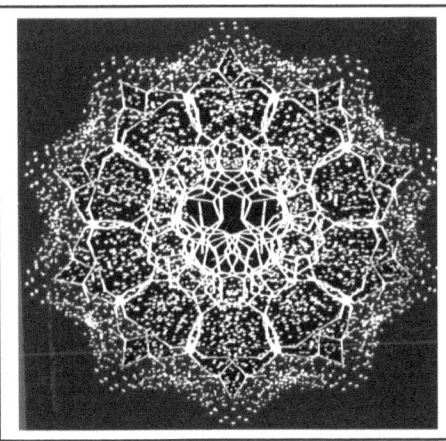

A Tibetan mandala? No.

Take a look at this mandala of DNA as well as what I interpret as strands of DNA on that same cave wall as the medicine wheel painted a thousand years ago.

This computer graphic of DNA is shown here with the compliments of:

Robert Langridge, PhD.

LESSONS FROM OUR CELLS

Embrace
Recognize
Respond
Move
Communicate
Create
Repair, Recycle, Rest
Energize
Remember
Purpose

REFERENCES:

1) Denton, Michael. (1998) *Nature's Destiny: How The Laws Of Biology Reveal Purpose In The Universe.* Simon & Schuster
2) Hameroff, Stuart & Penrose, R. (1996) "Consciousness, the brain, & spacetime geometry." In: *J. Consciousness Studies* 2:36–53.
3) Ingber, D.E. (1998) "The architecture of life." In: *Scientific American* Jan. 278: 48-57.
4) Ingber, Donald. (2004) "The mechanical cell." In: *Dream, the Magazine of Possibilities.*
5) Penrose, Roger. (1994) *Shadows of the Mind.* NY: Oxford University Press.
6) Rensberger, Boyce. (1998) *Life Itself.* NY: Oxford University Press.
7) Shlain, Leonard. (1993) *Art & Physics: Parallel Visions in Space, Time & Light.* William Morrow
8) Teilhard de Chardin, Pierre (1961) *The Phenomenon of Man.* Harper Torchbook edition.
9) Barrett, S. *Cells and the Sacred: From Cell to Soul.*

Website: www.SondraBarrett.com

> *Molecules awoke one morning to find that atoms were inside them, enfolded in their very being. Cells awoke one morning to find that molecules were actually inside them, as part of their being. And you might awake one morning and find that nature is a part of you, literally internal to your being.*
>
> *--- Ken Wilber*
> *--- "A Brief History of Everything"*

Joel Alter, DO

Joel Alter earned his degree as doctor of osteopathy (1964) and completed his internship (1965) from Kirksville College of Osteopathic Medicine. Between 1965 and 1968, he was the resident in general surgery at the Osteopathic Hospital in Fort Worth, TX. Later, he became the director of the Texas College of Osteopathic Medicine (TCOM), and worked as general surgeon and medical educator there for twenty years. Shortly after 1980 when he received tenure there, he decided to practice hands-on osteopathy instead of the very invasive surgeries. That is when he and his wife Cheri Quincy moved their practice to Santa Rosa, CA, and established the SR Alternative Medical Clinic. He continued working for some time even after he broke his neck, but eventually, that, combined with returning problems of older injuries, confined him to a wheelchair at home. He is still an important healer in his community, as his friends and clients will testify, though his healing practice has evolved to a deeper spiritual level.

Dr Alter held medical licenses in four states, has been a member of many professional societies, serving as chairman on seven of them, and has also served on the board of directors of the American Cancer Society in Terrant County, TX. He has conducted several medical research projects and has published numerous papers. These include "Evaluation of breast lesions," "Surgical treatment of diseases of the spleen," (1976) "Geriatric surgery," (1983), all in: *Osteopathic Annals*; and "Anesthetic considerations in surgery of the aged," in: *Amer. College of Osteopathic Anesthesiologists*, October 1985.

A JOURNEY
ONE HEALER'S STORY

Joel Alter

For some people in my life, October 17, 2009 signified that I'd been working on my 69th year. For me, however, it meant that perhaps I'd make it to next October, when I will celebrate 70 years of age, which is significant for me, since I can't believe that I'm almost there. I spent most of these years trying to find out who I am and learning more of what would make me better. When I ask myself, *"What am I making better?"* the answer always comes, *"It's this thing inside of me that desires to come out and be present, to be recognized and accepted. To further use my abilities to help others."*

I certainly have had a number of names added on to my given name. Each name denotes just what degrees I have earned or services that I have to offer. None of them really speaks to all that I am, all that I do or have been able to achieve in this world. Professionally, I've been called a doctor, a surgeon, and an educator—ultimately a father and grandfather. (I'm sure, I've been called a host of other things that just might be a bit derogatory too.) Several weeks ago after I treated a member of the clergy, he spoke out, saying, *"I know who you are! You're a holy man."* Maybe that's what I've become? I do sit on a hill, in a temple, praying, meditating, and administering to the needs of others—if those are the qualifying marks.

For years I've run away from any kind of labeling. In fact, most of the labels that I have tried on haven't fit very well. Certainly being a surgeon, a doctor, and an educator had entranced me. When I wore those labels, they defined a big part of myself.

At the time I was wearing those labels, I was one of the founders of the medical school in Fort Worth, Texas. I became its first clinical dean and its first chairman of the surgical department. I had spent a large amount of time developing new curriculum for doctors and experimented with computerized medical education and records in the latter '70s and early part of the '80s. My colleagues and I developed an entire medical school curriculum based on preventive medicine. We were among the first to do so.

During that time, I also helped develop an institute of human fitness and brought and developed a marathon, called the Cow Town Marathon, to Fort Worth, Texas. In my professional life I was operating on 15 people per week. I was an innovator and brought new procedures to my hospital such as colonoscopy, laparoscopy, surgery for obesity and hyper alimentation. I was constantly introducing better methodology for better and more successful surgeries. I certainly thought of myself as an academic practitioner and wrote and presented numerous articles and case studies before the College of Surgeons. (1-4) In the fields of general and trauma surgery I became certified in, and a fellow of, the American College of Osteopathic Surgeons.

While doing all this I participated as a father raising four children who demanded (and got) a lot of my attention.

Occupied with so many things, in my late 30s, I became uncomfortable with who I was. And I began reading a great deal about psychology in men going through their middle life moment. Since I was at the medical school, I gathered a team to study what was happening to others and me.

In a very short time, I found out that I was in the midst of a transition called "the male midlife crisis." I created a survey and analyzed over 1,000 doctors. The goal was to find other doctors who were going through a male midlife crisis. I wrote an article about this that was published in major psychological and professional journals. The study attempted to find out whether other men my age were going through a period in their lives called the middle life crisis, and whether they recognized it or not.

The study showed that men between the age of 36 through 50 went through a cycle in their lives, where they began looking at a shift, a change in who they were. Forty percent of men, going through the male midlife crisis changed their way of being significantly. Another 40% went through this phase, looked at who they were, and didn't change anything. Then there was this group of approximately 10%, who had found out they were participating in a life that didn't belong to them, and proceeded to change their life so significantly that they became unrecognizable to those who knew them before.

Through this process of studying men very similar to myself, and then writing about it, inevitably I sat down and examined my own self. What I found was that I was an impostor. I had played many roles, to great acclamation and applause, but none of them were *"Me."* I had lied to myself and even forgotten that I was lying. I had tucked my real feelings inside of spaces so deep that I was afraid I would never find them or ever be able to find out who I really was. I had never given myself a chance to become myself. From the time I was a child I had been remodeling myself, as I put it, to look like and be like everybody else. I had no idea what it was to look like and be like *"Me."*

I had run off from the tenements in the Bronx, and landed in Missouri to learn how to be a physician. I left the New York scene and immersed myself in study to find out how to be a doctor. Certainly, the model of doctor that I saw was not a Park Avenue specialist. I had already committed myself to going west. But, it was very strange to me! Modeling myself to look like a student, graduate, intern, then practicing physician, had made me one of the top surgical residents of that era.

It was at this point that I met and began spending time with Judy, my wife to be. Somehow I had wrangled myself into the upper echelons of osteopathic society in the mother of all schools. Here I was associating with the inheritors of the founders of Osteopathy, those who had descended from the founder, Andrew Taylor Still, MD. Being with Judy had allowed that. Her father was the president of the Chicago College of Osteopathic Medicine. He was one of the people who had brought that school from the very depths of education to one that was very well admired. He and the people he associated with were preserving the original tenets of osteopathy. Although I didn't realize it then, I had moved myself into the security of power and Christianity.

During my internship, I met the scrub nurse Mary Delaware, the first Native American I ever knew. I was intrigued with her and we soon became friends. One day, I asked her what she was doing for the weekend and she said that she was going home to Oklahoma for some ceremonies of her tribe. I asked if I could come along. She replied, *"I'll have to ask my brother if you can come."* I had no idea what an Indian ceremony was like but I had always known that I was supposed to see one. Perhaps, it was the movies of my youth that had stirred me.

Bob Delaware called back the next day to say that I could come. On Friday morning we went to Anadarko onto the Indian Reservation of the Delaware tribe, which is southwest of Norman, Oklahoma. Within short order, I was attending my first sweat lodge and was immersed into this foreign, yet so indigenous way of being. Inside the sweat, chants and songs were sung through four rounds of hot stones, steam, heat, sage, and herbs. Everybody sang and knew the prayers of the rounds except me. I know my consciousness disappeared in the heat and smoke. I had been terribly frightened as no one that I met was white or spoke English. Fortunately, or serendipitously, Bob Delaware was the leader of the sweat and he strangely made me feel comfortable.

There seemed to be no other white people on the reservation that day. Miraculously, I had defied my hysterical mind, in which I had created scenarios of Western movies, with me the white sacrificial animal, tied to a post, being burned by the Indians dancing and howling around me. Here I was instead, in the middle of a large sweat lodge, participating in something that I had never seen before nor thought about. Sitting among the naked braves was quite a dimensional shift. At one time I thought I saw a big bird flying in the middle of the smoke. It came to me, looked at me, and fanned me with his wings. Another time I saw a face of an old Indian in the middle of the hot rocks. The image was showing his hands to me. I was astonished, and amazed.

After leaving the sweat we all soaked ourselves in a cold river. Bob invited me to the dancing and I was asked to participate in some very rhythmic communal dancing. Again nothing like I had seen before. The men and women danced together in short scuffling rhythmic steps. They would gather together to the center where ten men played a large drum. Everybody was singing and dancing and moving in and out and around in a circle and I found myself included in the hypnotic dance and song. Afterwards the leader of the dance came to me and spoke in the Athabascan dialect. He thanked me for coming and honoring them. (Another dancer Jane interpreted for me.) He looked into my eyes and said: *"You are of the healing way and must follow it."* I didn't think too much about what he had said, at that time, for I was sure that he knew that I was a doctor. I went on back to Missouri and kept on with my work.

Years later while finishing my surgical residency, I was invited by a local veterinarian to hop onto an airplane on a medical mission to the Tarahumara Indians in Copper Canyon, Chihuahua, Mexico. There were a group of doctors who flew their own little planes on these missions and they called themselves *DoCare*. We flew into this huge canyon that I never heard of, and I was amazed at its size. Copper Canyon defied my imagination. These Indians were quite primitive and lived in caves and shacks throughout the area. I worked in a small hospital run by the Catholic Church for a month. I found these Indians could run for at least 50 miles kicking a ball. They were really quite amazing. Although I was told that they were not very friendly, I seemed to get along well with them. After saving one of the local chief's sons from an acute appendicitis, I was invited to my first peyote ceremony and introduced to the visions of the medicine space. It was not the first time that I had taken peyote. I had ingested it once before in Greenwich Village when I was 17, after I had seen the pictures of the healer Maria Sabina in *Life* magazine. Something inside of me knew that this was my way.

Although the ceremonies and visions were pertinent, I put them to the side and went back to Fort Worth, Texas, to build a large surgical practice. I forced myself to stay away from things that I thought were abnormal, and eating bitter cactus, as I had in Mexico, was said to make one go crazy. I watched my colors change just as a chameleon. I dressed in cowboy jeans and leather boots. My voice began to talk with a twang and I had four children and a wife who all talked in a Texas way. I walked into another dream world. Any time a vision would come my way or a voice would appear I would dismiss it so that I would stay on the path that looked "right."

Somewhere I adopted the characteristics of the landowner and began planting beautiful gardens that attracted me. Along the way I decided to plant some azaleas. These plants needed cottonseed meal and I went out to the local cotton gin and picked up a 100-pound sack. Somewhere in moving that sack from one place to another I developed a complete compression of my spinal cord. Of course I wouldn't admit to the pain until my legs went into spasm. I even tried to do surgery with a spasm until I fell down and then I submitted to examination by neurologists and neurosurgeons.

One day, I found myself going to the Mayo Clinic for spinal cord surgery. I was rushed into the emergency room, then x-rayed, and then seen by the neurosurgeon attending. He was a rather plaintive man dressed in any surgeon's cap and gown. He told me in a clear and decisive voice that my spinal cord was almost pinched in half and that I would have to be operated on immediately. He told me that my condition was extremely dangerous and I had a very good chance of ending up totally paralyzed and in a wheelchair for the rest of my life. I had a small chance of escaping this by being operated on. I took a chance and escaped this fate for a while.

Coming out of surgery I remember a voice speaking to me, telling me that I had to run, and run hard to stay away from the wheelchair. So I did. It was while running my many marathons that the voices of the Tarahumara Indian shaman came to me. He told me to go on in the holy work and eating the sacred food again. Practicing running over many months threw me into profound states of meditation and for a short while, clarity engulfed my life.

I soon began reading books on mysticism and the ancient arts of alchemy and divination. As I grew in my understanding of shamanic knowledge, my wife and I became philosophically incompatible and we could not stay together any longer.

Later, I fell in love with my present wife and the mystery went deeper. One of my teachers introduced me to Ecstasy (MDMA), and through several sessions, the artificial barriers that I had built up around myself began to be torn down.

These barriers had engulfed me for many years. I was thoroughly captured by the imposters that I had built up to act out the various personas of my life. In short, I was an impostor to myself and to others. I was a good one and I had even fooled myself. I went on a mission to find my self. I was quite fortunate that this had occurred when I was going through the middle crisis of my life.

My 17-year-old memory of the picture of the great curendera Maria Sabina in the *Life* magazine story by Gordon Wasson returned. I desired to heal people in the ways she did, to take the sacred medicine and let it teach me how to heal people.

So that's what I did: I left traditional medicine and went to be with traditional indigenous healers utilizing the mushroom, the San Pedro cactus, and the Mimosa hostilis. In each of these plants I have found spirit helpers to open up energy vortices that course through me into my patients and heal them. Becoming this type of healer was very difficult. I did not have a traditional native, tribal format to learn from. I was never bestowed with knowledge or awards acknowledging this aspect of my life.

I don't know how I decided that there were rules or acknowledgments on how to be a healer except to heal people.

Then I went to work in Santa Rosa, in a clinic with my wife Cheri Quincy. I decorated a room to maintain sacred space and created an altar with a variety of symbols on it.

As patients began coming in I silently prayed for each of them as I was putting my hands on them. People told me that they saw spirits in the room and colors floating around me. They tried to label me as a shaman and a worker of energy. I refused both of those names and just kept working. There were times when I touched 28 people a day and all of them went away satisfied. I pray that I've worked well for all.

In considering what it is, or has been to be a healer, I must say that I'm sure that all of us are such. If one has special talents, then they will stand out. I'm sure that I had the ability to heal people since the time of my birth. The difficulty was in activating and assuming the mantle of a healer. It is extremely challenging in this society to find out that one is a healer. In my case I was fortunate enough to have chosen the medical profession so that I could access those talents in a reasonably accepted way.

The ultimate is to be recognized and accepted by one's patient. Then the healer must accept all things that surround or interact with that patient's injury, persona, and life pattern.

Over the years I've acquired extensive medical experience through practice as a surgeon and a hospital physician. I've also practiced in the realms of psychology and general practice so that I'm able to see people through a number of their screens and their conditions.

I've had my share of personal injury to overcome such as gun shot wounds along with third-degree burns and breaking my neck along with three spinal surgeries. The result is that now I am in a wheelchair, and yet I continue to heal people from this state of being.

I use my hands to work on people by placing them on the body. I let go of all my thoughts and go to a profound meditative state. At that moment, I feel I am in contact with my spirit helpers and the great mystery. I ask my spirit helpers to facilitate the well-being of the patient I am interacting with and this invariably happens.

I feel that in order to do this I must make a heavy commitment to interact with the spirit world through ritual practice on a regular basis. I do this with a heavy commitment to the use of the entheogens, and a heavy commitment to the sacredness and profundity of this kind of work.

I am grateful to all: My wife, my children, my close friends in our men's group and to my patients for they reinforce my own spiritual practice. And I am grateful to be allowed to continue to practice this way for this time. And I am grateful to my little dog—the embodiment of unconditional love.

REFERENCES

1) Alter, J. (1971) "Endometriosis." In: *Journal of the American Osteopathic Association.*
2) --------- (1983) Cefizoximine sodium, the effects of beta lactamase resistance with colonic bacteria. (SkF Grant.)
3) --------- (1985) "Endoscopy for the general surgeon." *Texas College Osteopathic Medicine.*
4) --------- (1985) "Lasers in surgery." *Laser Course for Practitioners*, Fort Worth, TX.

ADDENDUM

In 2006 I began examining vibration for loosening and moving the muscles of my own body, since astronauts were already using vibration for exercise in space. A pure sinusoidal waveform is possible only if the acceleration for a platform did not exceed one earth's gravitational field G.

A motor vibrating anywhere from 30 Hz to 75 Hz (over varying time levels) was placed underneath the osteopathic treatment table. While the subject was lying on this table, his/her body could become aligned with gravity after a small amount of time. All subjects experienced improved relaxation with varying levels of consciousness.

All muscles are lined up in right angles whether on the microscopic level or on a gross anatomical view. These triangles form successively larger structures: First they form columns, then tubes, and then larger structures, which can be named — all the way from tendons to the actual structure of the muscle. Ligaments, and groups of muscles are included in larger areas, which work together.

I feel that energy flows within the center of these triangles and when they are disturbed, they suffer dis-synchronous motion. When the usual waveform becomes distorted and painful, it sets off all kinds of electrochemical reactions causing a variety of symptoms of disorders that may eventually cause diseases. Since the structure of the human body is based on right-angled triangles, the distorted structure is difficult and painful to move. However, by utilizing various methods of osteopathic therapy and massage, combined with the vibrating table, it is possible to restore a system of health in the human body.

Stephan Schwartz

Stephan A. Schwartz is a Research Associate of the Cognitive Sciences Laboratory and previously founder and Research Director of the Mobius laboratory, and Director of Research at Rhine Research Center. Schwartz is part of the small group that created Remote Viewing, and the principal researcher studying the use of RV in archeology. In addition to more than 40 papers and technical reports he has written four books: *The Secret Vaults of Time*, *The Alexandria Project*, *Mind Rover* and, most recently, *Opening to the Infinite*. His submarine experiment, Deep Quest, determined nonlocal perception is not an electromagnetic phenomenon. He also created the ARV (Associated/Associational Remote Viewing) protocol. Other research focuses on creativity and Therapeutic Intent. He is the columnist for the journal *Explore*, and Editor of the daily www.schwartzreport.net. Schwartz was an editorial staffer of *National Geographic*; Associate Editor of *Seapower*; Senior Fellow at The Philosophical Research Society; Special Assistant to the Chief of Naval Operations; member of the MIT/Secretary of Defense Discussion Group on Innovation, Technology and the Future; and Staff Writer for *The Times Herald* and the *Daily Press*. He has produced and written numerous national television programs. His magazine work has appeared in *OMNI*, *Harpers*, *Smithsonian*, *American Heritage*, *American History*, *Parabola* and other publications; newspaper writing includes work for *The Washington Post*, *The New York Times*, *The Washington Star*, and many other newspapers. He is listed in *Who's Who in America*.

THE MIST WOLF

Stephan A. Schwartz

We are standing in a parking lot in gathering twilight – maybe 20 of us, including half a dozen physicians and several scientists. Standing there, leaning in, watching a Shoshone shaman, Rolling Thunder, attempt to heal the wound of a teenager boy lying on a massage table. It is a painful wound, torn into the muscle of his leg, and the boy is clearly in discomfort, and just as obviously medicated. He got this wound through some kind of accident, and it is not healing properly. This is what has brought him to this Virginia Beach parking lot at the back of Edgar Cayce's old hospital. It is now the headquarters of the ARE, the organization founded in 1931 to preserve Cayce's readings, discourses given from a state of nonlocal awareness while Cayce lay seemingly asleep. It seems fitting to be standing here, a generation later, watching for signs of another nonlocal phenomenon: therapeutic intent expressed as physical healing. For many reasons Edgar Cayce should be acknowledged as the father of complementary and alternative medicine. His observations about health and his therapeutics are today so fully integrated and general as no longer to be associated with him. They are part of the paradigm. But the therapeutic intent about which Cayce spoke, the idea that the consciousness of one person can therapeutically affect the well-being of another (still controversial in some quarters today) was beyond the pale in 1968, when I and the others witnessed this.

A small log fire, which I had built earlier at Rolling Thunder's request, flickers on the ground at the boy's head. I am here as a journalist. This ceremony is taking place in the middle of my interview with Rolling Thunder. Part of my income, while I complete a program of study to prepare for my goal of doing research into the nature of consciousness, comes from writing for the *Virginian-Pilot* about unusual people who come to Virginia Beach, which mostly means to the ARE.

Hugh Lynn Cayce, its Executive Director, called late on Monday afternoon to say a shaman, a medicine man, as he explained it, was coming. If I wanted to interview him I could pick him up at the Greyhound station, and talk to him that afternoon. Saturday he would be doing a traditional Native American healing ritual, which I was welcome to attend. That's how I first heard about Rolling Thunder. [His photo is on page 9.]

Of course I accept, and he gave me the time. Four o'clock. I have to check the location, it seems so improbable, *"The Greyhound...bus station...in Norfolk?"*

"The same," Hugh Lynn replies.

I had done a number of these interviews, and was thinking of doing a book of them. Although there were some other journalists, and a few scientists amongst this number, most of the people I had met through Hugh Lynn put themselves forward as spiritual teachers and shamans and were accepted, by at least some people, as being the genuine article. Having spent hours talking to these men and women, listening to their stories, their answers to my questions, their affect, how they dressed, how they stood, their eyes, what I can only call their *beingness*, I have begun to develop some discernment. It is clear to me that authenticity is in part a measure of the continuity between the public persona and private personality. To the degree they are not one and the same that person seems diminished.

About a month before, Hugh Lynn had alerted me to an Indian of another type, a Hindu priest from India. He arrived in a Cadillac accompanied by an entourage. In the trunk of the car was the food he would eat, and the pans it would be prepared in, and the dishes upon which it would be served.

"The master is so evolved, he is barely in touch with the physical plane anymore," an acolyte explained to me as he brought out the boxes of the guru's portable kitchen.

"Wow," I thought. *"This man must be in a truly exalted state of consciousness."* I looked forward to hearing him speak later that night.

In the event, however, he was quite disappointing. He had beautiful diction, but spoke almost nothing but platitudes and slogans. By the time he was through I realized I was dealing with shtick, whether consciously contrived or not I couldn't tell. But it taught me a lesson I never forgot: If an expert is someone from more than 100 miles away with a briefcase, a holy man may be only someone from a distant land, practicing an unfamiliar faith, with a different set of altar ornaments.

This is still very much in my mind on a hot summer afternoon as I drive down to the Greyhound station. The Norfolk iteration of this cultural institution comes complete with the usual: Sailors BSing one another, Marines playing a game of black jack, old black ladies, sitting patiently cooling themselves with paper church fans. And leaning up against the snack counter is a middle-aged Indian, with an unblocked cowboy hat, an old tweed jacket, and a bolo tie with a turquoise slide. He is eating some cheddar cheese Nabs, and drinking a coke. He smokes a pipe, I can see. It is sticking out of the breast pocket of his jacket.

We introduce ourselves, and he picks up a small bag and we walk out to the car. Twenty minutes later we are driving down Shore Drive, which parallels the coast, and he asks me to stop at a super market. Would I go in and buy two steaks? Sure. In those days I was a vegetarian, really a vegan, and buying steaks for a powerful shaman seems very odd. I am such a naïf. Hospitality demands his request be honored, so I go into the market and buy him two of the best Porterhouse cuts they have. A mile further and Shore Drive cuts through a state park, and suddenly we are in beach wilderness such as 16th century colonists would have seen, and it runs on for several miles. We are about midway through when Rolling Thunder asks me to pull over. Reaching for his bag, he opens the door and gets out of the car, asking me when he is supposed to be at the ARE. I think he wants to take a leak. But no. He clearly intends to leave me. *"About seven p.m.,"* I say. He thanks me, asks me to build a small fire where he is to work, and turns and walks down the bank and into the woods. *"Don't forget the steaks,"* he calls out as he walks away. He is completely natural in all of this. It is not being done for effect and, as it is happening, it seems the most obvious and appropriate thing for him to be doing. Only, as I watch him vanish into the trees, does it become clear how unusual this is. Presumably he is going to sleep in the woods. Rolling Thunder reminds me of a Polish sergeant I had when I was in the Army. So thoroughly secure in his esoteric skills, that what seemed improbable he did with effortless competence. I realize they are just different kinds of warriors.

The next afternoon I go up to the ARE with the steaks in a cooler. Someone has moved a massage table out into the parking lot. Not quite sure where the fire should be I gather wood from the forest that borders the back of the parking lot, and set it up near the table, then leave for an early dinner. When I get back just before seven a crowd has gathered. I get the cooler out of the car, and go over and light the fire. Hugh Lynn comes over, wearing a windbreaker and an ironed white shirt, without a tie. He always reminds me of a prosperous small town banker, not the youngest son of one of the most famous clairvoyants in history. In fact he has the mind of a Medici, and is the most interesting person I have met doing these interviews. He introduces me to two of the doctors, then goes over to the vans parked nearby, and talks with two women. They are the mothers, who have accompanied their sons. Inside each van one of the boys to be healed lies quietly in the back. It is twilight now and I can see them framed in the overhead light in the vans. Another physician, almost in silhouette, moves between them.

Precisely at seven Rolling Thunder, looking just he had the day before, walks out of the woods holding his small bag. He goes up to Hugh Lynn who, seeing him coming, calls everyone together. He says a few words of introduction, and while he does this Rolling Thunder kneels down and pulls out from the bag what I can see, from maybe three feet away, is the breast and extended wing of a crow or raven. The pinion feathers are spread. Seeing me he thanks me for the fire, and asks if I have brought the steaks. I go over to the cooler and bring them over. He takes one, and tears off the plastic wrap, and the paper tray, handing this back to me. He walks the few feet back to the fire and drops the steak into the gravel and dirt, next to the little fire ring of stones I have made. It is the strangest thing he has done yet, but like walking into the woods, it just seems the thing to do.

He gestures to Hugh Lynn, who goes over to one of the vans, and the boy within is brought out on a stretcher, and placed on the massage table. As Rolling Thunder talks quietly to the boy, he seems to be having trouble at first focusing on what is being said, probably because the move has caused him additional pain. But gradually he calms, and lies still, his eyes closed. His mother comes over and stands to one side. While this is going on, by unspoken consensus we observers have been slowly shuffling forward until we reach an acceptable compromise between intruding and being able to closely observe. It turns out this is an arc about eight feet away from the boy on the table.

Rolling Thunder begins a soft slow chant. I cannot make out the words, just the rhythm of the rising and falling sound. He begins making slow passes over the boy's form using the wing and breast of the raven, moving it just an inch or two above his body. I can see the feathers spread slightly against the air pressure as his arm sweeps along – long graceful strokes. Every second or third stroke he flicks the wing tip down towards the steak on the ground. As it grows darker the fire becomes more prominent, and the boy and the man drift into shadow.

It goes on monotonously. Everything else is silent. Suddenly, I notice that there is a white mist-like form taking shape around and in front of Rolling Thunder's body. Sometimes I can see it, sometimes not. But it becomes stronger, steadier, until it is continuously present. It is almost dark now, but the fire gives enough light to see. Then it takes form, slowly at first, but as if gathering energy into itself it takes form. I can clearly see the smoke-like form is a wolf. Rolling Thunder moves as rhythmically as a clock. Sweep. Sweep. Flick. Sweep. Sweep. Flick.

After about 30 minutes the form begins to fade, first losing shape, then becoming increasingly insubstantial. Finally, it is nothing more than a chimera, there and not there. Then it is gone. Rolling Thunder straightens up, and stops. He makes a kind of gesture, and somehow we are released to come forward. The boy is very peaceful. His mother steps up to him and leans over him, kissing his forehead.

The wound is completely healed. It looks like your skin does when a scab falls off leaving smooth unlined pink skin, shiny in its newness. I am astonished. Clearly so is everyone else. I go over to Hugh Lynn who is in animated conversation with a British scientist, Douglas Dean, who has come down from New Jersey to see this. Hugh Lynn asks me, *"What did you see?" "Yes, what... ?"* Dean says. I tell them, and when I say the mist took form, they exchange a look, and Hugh Lynn says, *"What shape?"* When I tell them I saw a wolf, another look passes between them, and they tell me that they have seen the same thing.

There is a kind of break. People go to the bathroom, get a drink of water. Half an hour later we gather again. The second boy is brought out. I cannot see anything wrong with him. His mother, however, is very attentive, so something is wrong. Hugh Lynn says it is a broken bone, which will not heal. Rolling Thunder asks for the second steak, and I go back to the cooler to get it. This one he also drops to the ground. He says nothing to me, and I know better than to say anything to him.

The chanting begins, and all appears to be headed towards what it once was. The mist, it seems about 2 inches thick, begins to form. It grows stronger, stops flickering, but, just as it begins to take form, it stalls. It happens once. A second time. A third. This time, I look around and my eyes are drawn to the mother. I have no idea how I know this, but I know it is the boy's mother. She is blocking this.

As Rolling Thunder is beginning a fourth attempt he suddenly stops. He straightens up, turns and walks over to Hugh Lynn. He says, *"I cannot do this. The mother will not permit it. She has a mother's love, and it is very powerful."*

"Yes. I noticed. I'll talk to them."

Hugh Lynn goes over and talks to the doctor for a while, then the mother and the son. I can't hear them. Then he comes over to where Dean and I are standing, and says, *"He was drifting away from her, now he is dependent once again. She is conflicted about giving that up."*

Rolling Thunder goes over and sits on the cooler that held the steaks. The evening is clearly over. People start drifting away. I can hear cars starting and, in the glare of their headlights, I go over and kick out the fire. Rolling Thunder is there before me. He reaches down and I can see the steaks. Both are withered and gray. One of them hardly looks like meat at all.

"You put whatever is wrong into the steak?"

"That's right. The fire will purify and release it"

He throws the steaks into the hot coals. The fat crackles and catches fire. The two of us stand there in silence. It doesn't take long, and they are gone. During those minutes I don't know what Rolling Thunder is thinking. I am reconsidering how the world works.

CHAPTER 36 — AN APPROACH TO BEREAVEMENT

Arthur Hastings, PhD

Arthur Hastings is one of the founders of the Parapsychology Research Group (PRG), and he has been president of the Association for Transpersonal Psychology and the Institute of Transpersonal Psychology (ITP) in Palo Alto, CA, where he is professor and Director of the William James Center for Consciousness Studies. He received his PhD in communication from Northwestern University.

Dr Hastings' publications include articles on informal logic, transpersonal theory, scientists' resistance to belief, and the use of hypnosis in evoking nondrug altered states. He has conducted research on telepathy, remote viewing, hypnosis, dreams, stress, and bereavement.

In chapter 28, he reports his pioneering work on healing bereavement using a form of restricted sensory environment, a quiet booth called a psychomanteum that provides a period of inner reflection for persons who are grieving the loss of a loved one. The process appears to allow people going through the experience to release distress and sadness and to increase feelings of connection with the deceased. Assessments before and after the experience show highly significant changes in bereavement for almost all the participants.

Dr Hastings is the author of *With the Tongues of Men and Angels: A Study of Channeling*. He is the senior editor of *Health for the Whole Person*, an award-winning book on holistic medicine. He is also a coauthor with Russel Windes of *Argumentation and Advocacy*.

The website for the Institute of Transpersonal Psychology (ITP) is: www.itp.edu.

RESEARCH ON AN APPROACH TO BEREAVEMENT USING A PROCESS WITH A PSYCHOMANTEUM

Arthur Hastings

During the past several years, a team of colleagues, doctoral students, and myself have developed and researched an experiential process for addressing bereavement, using a technique called a psychomanteum. For almost all of the participants in the research, this process has been effective in lowering the levels of grief, sadness, guilt, anger, and other effects of bereavement for the deaths of others. (9) This chapter reports on the process that has been developed, and the results of the research.

A PROCESS FOR HEALING BEREAVEMENT

Approaches to healing of bereavement for the death of a person include activities such as personal comforting, counseling, support groups, psychotherapy, funeral and memorial services, and actions by the survivor such as mourning, prayer, talking to the deceased, and writing letters to the deceased. In addition to the social and personal support for bereavement, it appears that there are inner processes that naturally occur and are opportunities for healing, such as recalling memories of the deceased, feeling the person's presence, emotional expression, tears, grieving, cognitive processing, and the reduction of feelings of loss through passage of time. Medications may be prescribed that reduce the intensity of the experience of loss. These are all influenced by culture, social customs and implicit worldviews. Any of these approaches can be helpful in reducing bereavement, and of course, the result is dependent upon the situation and the bereaved person. There are many configurations of bereavement, because people who die are unique, and so are the people who survive them. The surviving persons are left with relationships having only one side, and empty spaces in the fabric of their lives.

THE PSYCHOMANTEUM AND BEREAVEMENT

The approach that we have developed to assist with bereavement was somewhat unconventional, as it was not therapy, counseling, medication, or a support group. It was a three hour long, structured process of remembering the deceased. It included writing about the deceased, telling recollections, expressing emotions, and having a period of reflection, which allowed the participant to review thoughts, feelings, and memories, with the potential to form a new relationship with the person who has died. It provided an experience that seemed tuned to the participant by the participant's own needs, and that potentially resulted in a shift of bereavement feelings. Integrated in this procedure were assessments for before and after measures of bereavement, and for reports on the qualitative feelings and experiences.

The reflection period took place in a psychomanteum. This was a quiet, dimly lit, curtained booth, with a chair for the participant and a mirror to focus attention. The mirror was tilted so one's reflection was not seen. The booth sat inside a windowless, somewhat soundproofed room. It is 8' feet long, 7' high, and 5' wide, made from PVC pipe and covered with black theater curtain cloth. Sitting in the booth as part of the bereavement process created a mild altered state; (20) our study allowed subjective experiences that are conducive to resolving feelings about the deceased, and sometimes even sensing the presence or having a conversation with the person who has died. The name "psychomanteum" means theater of the mind and was suggested by Moody, (12) who was attempting to facilitate apparitions similar to those experienced by surviving spouses, relatives, and friends of deceased persons. (17) Moody (12, 14) reported that 25% of his early participants had some kind of apparitional experience, with the percentage increasing in later sessions. Further he noted that the participants' bereavement distress was reduced after their sessions. Roll (18) also reported reductions in bereavement in a study using a psychomanteum in a workshop format. Radin (16) did not address bereavement in his study, but found that subjective apparitional phenomena were correlated with physiological effects such as heart rate and skin conductance, and environmental events such as room temperature and electrical fields. So far as we know, our work has been the only research to systematically collect data on changes in bereavement, with before and after ratings, and to investigate the content of the subjective experience.

Our research was explicit in that it offered participants an opportunity to explore a possible contact or connection with a person who has died. There was no promise that this would occur, or that any experience would occur, or that any experience of a deceased person would be valid. In the information to participants, it was stated that in psychomanteum research some of the participants reported contact with the deceased. This was based on the studies of Moody (12) and Roll. (18) It also stated that we did not interpret these experiences, but left it to the judgment of the participant. Almost all of the participants who volunteered had this in mind, that is, interest in contact with a deceased person and in one case with a pet.

Communication with the deceased is a controversial issue, yet the topic appears to be less taboo (and less dismissed) than even a decade ago. It is well documented that 50% or more of surviving widows cross-culturally experience a visual or other contact with a deceased spouse. (6, 8, 17) Surveys show that about 70% of the US population believe in life after death. (5, 15) This experience has its own acronym of ADC (after death communication). There are books that have compiled personal experiences of ADCs (1, 7) with varying degrees of investigation. Contacts with the deceased have also been reported by Botkin, (2) using the clinical technique of Eye Movement Desensitization Reprocessing (EMDR). Some professionals and bereavement counselors will believe that this research fosters superstitious and delusional perceptions of death and life after death. However, this is not a closed issue. In the scientific field there are thoughtful attempts to define methodology and examine evidence seriously, such as the investigation and documentation of apparitions and post-death contact, apparent memories of past lives, near-death experience, hidden information, and the philosophical issues involved. For overviews and examples, see Braude, 2003 (3); Fontana, 2005 (4); Kelly, Greyson, & Kelly, 2007 (11); and Stevenson, 1974 (19).

THE EXPERIENTIAL FORMAT

To date, we have conducted a pilot and two formal studies using this experiential process. [1] The procedure was based on Moody's format. (12, 13, 14) He took individuals one at a time and held long discussions with them about the deceased person, perhaps as long as a full day. He had the participant bring mementos of the sought person to talk about. Then the person sat in his psychomanteum, a room (rather than a booth) with dark walls, a mirror and chair, with a dim light. We adapted the process for research purposes (with questionnaires and self-reports) and time constraints (fitting within a 3-4 hour process), still hoping to retain the individual support and personal attention. [2] The process involved 6 stages.

Stage 1. Initial Pre-Questionnaire. The participant completed a questionnaire asking information about the person who had died, and the feelings and reactions of the participant. The participant rated how he or she felt regarding 21 effects of bereavement using a 1 – 7 scale, with 7 meaning "strong or always." These items included grief, missing the person, guilt, fear, sadness, love, anger, and other elements of bereavement. The questionnaire was a measure of the person's feelings at the beginning of the process and was completed before coming to the session. It also was a way to evoke and open the feelings such as those mentioned above and questions such as *"Are there any unfinished feelings about this person's death?" "What would you like to say or express to this person?"* and *"What would you like to hear from this person?"*

Stage 2. Initial Interview. The participant was then interviewed in a counseling room by the facilitator, who asked the participant to tell about the deceased, and talk about memories, feelings, regrets, and intentions for the process. We felt it was important to keep the participant remaining in the feelings about the death and the relationship, letting go of defenses against experiencing and showing them. This was not psychotherapy in the usual sense, and facilitators did not analyze or advise. Rather, they listened empathically and asked questions to facilitate the participants' remembrance. At the end of the interview, participants were invited to use art materials (pastels, colored pencils, crayons, clay) to express feelings and reactions in a nonverbal mode. Most of the participants did this.

Stage 3. Sitting in the Booth. The facilitator then led the participant to the psychomanteum booth in another room. The participant sat in a recliner chair, looking at the mirror's reflective surface. A dimmer control for the night-light was on a table with a box of tissues. The facilitator sat in an outer room, where the participant could be heard if he or she wanted to come out before the 45-minute time was up (this never happened, however). The instructions were to gaze at the mirror, adjust the light to be comfortable, and reflect on feelings and thoughts about the deceased. If the participant had something to say, it could be said mentally or aloud.

Stage 4. Post-Interview. After 45 minutes the facilitator re-entered the room and brought the participant out to the same counseling room. The facilitator asked the participant to tell about the experience in the booth: about the perceptions, thoughts, feelings, and events. At the end of this interview, the art materials were again offered.

Stage 5. Post-Questionnaire. Staying in the same room, the participant then filled out the post-questionnaire, reporting on the experiences in the booth, and repeating the rating of the effects of bereavement. At this time we supplied the participant with snacks and bottled water, as this had been a long and usually intense experience.

Stage 6. Follow-Up. Four weeks after the session a follow-up questionnaire was sent to the participant, asking about the impact of the experience on the life of the participant, and another repeat of the rating of bereavement effects.

This was not a mechanical process, but in our view required careful facilitation and respect for the person participating. The intention of the carefully sequenced protocol was to create an opportunity for a state of mind and experience that would allow a shift in bereavement, and that would come in response to the participant's own needs. This could include a shift in perspective, a new understanding or insight, an apparent conversation with the deceased, mental or external images, or some other form. It was not possible for facilitators to predict what kind of experience would assist the participant. There was simply an assumption that when there was an opportunity, the self would move toward healing.

THE PSYCHOMANTEUM EXPERIENCE

Twenty-seven participants were taken through the process. Of these, thirteen reported that they felt a contact with the deceased. Two of them believed that they visually saw the deceased, and others had mental conversations, felt touches, or reported that they sensed the presence of the person who had died in some way. Here are examples from the written post-questionnaires of the participants.

Expressions of gratitude were given by one participant:

Conversation with my father. Feelings of wanting to connect, love, gratitude, release. Throughout peace. Expressing sorrow for way he died. Thanks for his life. Big shift was releasing him after I experienced angel behind and over me. . . . I felt a connection with my father. Hard to say at time of talking to inner sense of father or to father "out there." (P30.)

Participant 34 sought her uncle, and had physical sensations:

There was an intense warmth (physically, spatially) around me. My uncle's presence was felt but it was slight and somewhat guarded. He repeated, "Don't worry" and "Do what is best for you," which somehow I can't hear enough of. (Unpublished data, P34.)

Visual sensations were common, including lights and imagery, either in the mirror or space of the booth:

I saw flowers – big red, yellow, white, Georgia O'Keeffe like flowers, and several animal faces. . . . I didn't see the person but experienced a dialogue that led to a resolution. It wasn't a major issue, but I'd say it was the only upsetting issue we ever had that I remember. (Unpublished data, P21.)

One participant sought her grandmother:

I quickly intuited that the love that my grandma had for me was within me, and that was the place to discover unconditional love. There was purple coming out of the mirror entering my heart, healing sadness. . . . I saw a person on a flying trapeze cross the mirror. . . . I feel as if I got a message from my grandma: To look within myself to fly high with abandonment and also outside facilitation and guidance from [spiritual teachers] as well. (Unpublished data, P17.)

One participant wished to contact Blackie, her cat.
She wrote that she did not know if she contacted her cat
or if it were her bringing bring this forth, or both:

I prayed that God would let Blackie manifest if he wanted to and then I saw white swirling energy. I felt like this may be Blackie trying to show himself. I watched this a while and then drifted into sleep, where I dreamed I was Blackie chasing a rabbit. The dream was so vivid that I woke up.
(Unpublished data, P19.)

Participant 37 wished to connect with her spiritual teacher
who died ten years before in an accident. She wrote
of receiving detailed instructions from him:

Alternative waves of light and dark, silence and sound, and internal energy waves. Feelings of connection w/S. [the teacher] Series of intense memories of past experiences w/him. Clear instructions about contacting his son and family _today._ Clear message about my future work as a teacher and mentor, especially to young people. (Unpublished data, P37.)

Participant 23 had an experience that appeared similar to meditative
and transcendent states, including love and peacefulness:

Overall: Being held in the heart of the Mother. Floating in the Void, which is empty and full, close and spacious. Swimming in peace and serenity. Letting go. Timeless. Floaty unconsciousness. (Unpublished data, P23.)

Participant 17 sought a friend who had died three years before. She wrote
that her friend communicated in a "gentle, slightly devilish way":

At one point I had a sense that [my friend] stood just to the right of the mirror. I had the impression that he said something like "Come on, Maria. As if I am going to show upon the mirror." I found this _very_ funny. Followed by approx. 10 minutes of simply feeling love. (Unpublished data, P17.)

Here is a similar message but with a different feeling:

I experienced some mental "knowings," and my friend chided me for resorting to such trappings in order to contact her. She "said" (internally) that she did not want her energy used for my amusement. If I really wanted to contact her I could be more connected with the part of her that lives on in her sister who is alive. (Unpublished data, P26.)

The subjective experiences with the deceased persons included messages, memories, advice, answers to questions, explanations, and reassurance. The most common modes of communication were conversations and dialogs in the mind, movements of lights in response to questions, responses of touch, and reviews of memories.

Participants in the study reported experiencing lights moving in the mirror and through the booth, imagery in the mirror and the mind, visions of the starry night sky, physical touches, odors, and sounds. Some of these sensory phenomena were felt to be associated with the deceased. However, a contact with the deceased or having sensory phenomena was not a necessary condition for a participant to have a shift in the level of bereavement. At the same time, some of the individuals who did not experience a contact had feelings of disappointment at the lack of communication.

Table 1. Statistically Significant Changes in Bereavement Ratings from Pre-Questionnaire to Follow-Up Questionnaire. (n=27) (Hastings, et al., 2002)

Item	Wilcoxon z	p value (2 tailed)
I have unresolved feelings.	2.68	0.007
Unresolved issues with this person affect my ability to carry out daily activities.	1.96	0.05
I miss this person.	3.14	0.05
I need to improve my relationship with this person.	2.84	0.004
I feel good about the status of my relationship with this person.	2.17	0.03
Grief	2.63	0.009
Missing the person	2.30	0.02
Guilt	2.08	0.04
Sadness	1.83	0.005
Loss	2.35	0.01
Need to communicate	3.36	0.0008
Fear	2.02	0.04

STATISTICAL ANALYSIS

The before and after ratings on the bereavement effects were analyzed by comparing means to see group changes. For the Hastings, et al., study, all of the 21 bereavement effects showed reductions in the group means for distressing effects (some items were reversed, such as "love," and showed increases). A Wilcoxon Signed Ranks test was used to analyze each of the 21 bereavement items individually, e.g., the total changes of the before and after ratings for "grief" for the participants. The Wilcoxon test analyzes both the direction of any change and also its magnitude. The 2002 study compared the pre-questionnaire ratings with the long-term follow-up ratings. Twelve of the 21 items showed statistically significant changes, with p values ranging from 0.05 to 0.0008. See Table 1.

DISCUSSION

The statistical analysis showed that the bereavement process had a strong effect on reducing the distress and emotional intensity of bereavement. This corresponds to the observations of the other studies. (12, 18) The follow-up data indicate that the changes continue over time.

In the format used here, the process requires a sequenced protocol, more than one room, and well practiced facilitators. For this reason, the sessions were scheduled during weekends when facilities and personnel were available. This may be a difficult arrangement to use for individual bereavement treatment and individuals who are grief counselors. However, there are some facets of the process that may be useful for any approach to grief. We found that empathic and attentive listening, without advising or therapeutic advice, was beneficial for participants. Also helpful was to ask the questions that were illustrated earlier. From participant reports, simply having the time to sit and reflect on memories and feelings evoked during the process was helpful in resolving feelings. The structure of the process appeared to serve as a container for holding the bereavement and not having it overpower the participants.

The experiential component has similarities to the experiences of after-death communication that are reported by friends and relatives of the deceased. This research suggests that persons who have these experiences should be reassured that this is natural and personal to them, and they should be allowed to interpret them for themselves. The comfort and reassurance of such events is supported by our participants. However, a caution is that the expectation of such contacts in everyday life for survivors may lead to disappointment if one does not occur. Another caution is that this research was done with self-selecting volunteers. It does not seem likely that it will be effective unless the person is desirous and ready for the experience.

Some, perhaps most of the participants who reported the presence of the deceased, accepted that the experience was real, that the sought person had been present. Others accepted the experience, but wondered if it was being constructed by their minds. The research was primarily designed to assist the resolution of bereavement, not prove life after death. Thus there was no data collected on validity of messages, or information that would have been known only to the deceased. In any event, it was important for the process and the participant for the context to acknowledge the possibility of life after death and that messages from some surviving aspect of the deceased were not dismissed as fantasy, wish fulfillment, or grief driven hallucination.

There is no doubt that the protocol, which we used, encouraged the participants to develop expectations for a possible connection, and to prepare them emotionally for the situation. Hood and Morris (10) using a sensory isolation condition (floatation tank) were successful in instructing participants to generate religious imagery during the sensory isolation period. Terhune and Smith (21) found that suggestions for anomalous experiences such as voices and images tended to produce such phenomena in a psychomanteum setting. This does not necessarily mean that contact experiences in our research or in spontaneous cases are hallucinated or are constructed by the individual's mind. In the research reported here, the suggestions were intentional and implicit in the process, assuming that they would facilitate whatever process was occurring, whether from an external or internal source. It is possible that further research designs, brain science, and conceptual analysis will illuminate this issue further.

Although a psychomanteum chamber has been used here, and by Moody, Roll, and others, it is not clear what properties it has. It could be just a quiet, dimly lit room, where the mind, free of distractions, can sort out feelings and obtain resolution. Or could it be like the spirit cabinets of the 1800s that the spiritualists (some fraudulent, some more respectable) used to contact the dead, claiming that the cabinet gathered energy in the dark for contact with the dead? Does it create a condition that somehow allows persons to go beyond their ordinary conditioned senses? And, would any quiet, peaceful room serve perhaps as well?

At the very least, the role of the psychomanteum in our work was to provide a state of consciousness in which cognitive thinking and analysis were reduced, and the intensity of bereavement could be open to shifts in feelings and emotions. It may be that such a state of awareness could also heighten sensitivity to some aspect of another self that survives the experience of death. In any event, for persons who are ready, the process seems productive for supporting healing shifts in bereavement.

REFERENCES

1) Arcangel, Diane (2005) *Afterlife Encounters: Ordinary People, Extraordinary Experiences.* Charlottesville, VA: Hampton Roads.
2) Botkin, A.L. (2000) "The induction of after-death communications utilizing eye-movement desensitization and reprocessing: A new discovery." In: *Journal of Near-Death Studies,* 18(3), 181-209
3) Braude, S. (2003) *Immortal Remains: The Evidence for Life After Death.* Lanham, MD: Rowman & Littlefield.
4) Fontana, D. (2005) *Is There an Afterlife?: A Comprehensive Overview of the Evidence.* C. Ropley, Hants: O Books.
5) Gallup, G. (1985) *Religion in America: 50 years 1935-1985.* In: *The Gallup Report.* Princeton, NJ: Princeton Religious Research Center.
6) Greely, A. (1975) *The Sociology of the Paranormal: A Reconnaissance.* Beverly Hills, CA: Sage.
7) Guggenheim, B. (1996) *Hello from Heaven.* NY: Bantam Books.
8) Haraldsson, E. (1985) "Representative national surveys of psychic phenomena: Iceland, Great Britain, Sweden, USA, and Gallup's multinational survey." In: *Journal of the Society for Psychical Research,* 53(801), 145-158.
9) Hastings, A., Hutton, M., Braud, W., Bennett, C., Berk, I., Boynton, T., Dawn, C., Ferguson, F., Goldman, A., Greene, E., Hewett, M., Lind, V., McLellan, K., Steinbach-Humphrey, S. (2002) "Psychomanteum research: Experiences and effects on bereavement." In: *Omega: Journal of Death and Dying,* 45(3), 195-212.
10) Hood, R.W. & Morris, R.J. (1981) "Sensory isolation and the differential elicitation of religious imagery in intrinsic and extrinsic persons." In: *Journal for the Scientific Study of Religion,* 20, 210-211.
11) Kelly, E.W., Greyson, B., & Kelly, E.F. (2007) "Unusual experiences near death and related phenomena." In: E.F. Kelly, E.W. Kelly, A. Crabtree, A. Gauld, M. Grosso, & B. Greyson. *Irreducible Mind: Toward A Psychology for the 21st Century.* Lanham, MD: Rowman and Littlefield.
12) Moody, Raymond (1992) "Family reunions: Visionary encounters with the departed in a modern-day psychomanteum." In: *Journal of Near-Death Studies,* 11(2), 83-121.
13) Moody, Raymond (1999) *Into the Light and Through the Tunnel and Beyond.* Atlanta GA: Hinshaw Productions. (Video) (DVD 2004).
14) Moody, Raymond, with Perry, P. (1994) *Reunions: Visionary Encounters with Departed Loved Ones.* NY: Ivy Books.
15) Newcott, B. (2007 September & October) "Life after death." In: *AARP Magazine.* Retrieved 3/12/09 from: http://www.aarpmagazine.org/people/life_after_death.html?print=yes.
16) Radin, D. (2001) "Seeking spirits in the laboratory." In: J. Houran, & R. Lange. *Hauntings and Poltergeists: Multidisciplinary Perspectives,* (pp. 165-174). Jefferson, NC: McFarland & Company.
17) Rees, W.D. (1971) "The hallucinations of widowhood." In: *British Medical Journal,* 209-222.
18) Roll, William G. (2003) "Psychomanteum research: A pilot study." In: *Journal of Near-Death Studies,* 22(4), 251-260.
19) Stevenson, I. (1974) *Twenty Cases Suggestive of Reincarnation.* 2nd ed. rev. Charlottesville, VA: University of Virginia Press.

20) Suedfeld, Peter E., & Borrie, R.A. (1978) "Altering states of consciousness through sensory deprivation." In: A.A. Sugerman & R.E. Tarter (Eds.) *Expanding Dimensions of Consciousness* (pp. 226-252). NY: Springer.
21) Terhune, D.B. & Smith, M.D. (2006) "The induction of anomalous experiences in a mirror-gazing facility: Suggestion, cognitive perceptual personality traits and phenomenological state effects." In: *Journal of Nervous and Mental Disease*, 194(6), 415-421.

ENDNOTES

1) The pilot research and the first study were published in Hastings, et al. (2002), and is the source for this article. Some unpublished cases from the first study are included in this report. The second study is being analyzed at this time.

2) William Braud was a consultant on the design of the research and the analysis. Michael Hutton developed the facilitation training. Arthur Hastings directed the research. The studies were carried out by doctoral students trained in the conduct and facilitation of the research. Funding and other support was received from private individuals, the Bernstein Brothers Parapsychology and Health Foundation, and the Institute of Transpersonal Psychology with curriculum and facilities.

Dying is the process

of becoming

predominantly aware

of the relationship

between radiance and density.

Focus on the radiance

and become it.

Then the transition

can be pure joy.

— *Ruth-Inge Heinze*
— (*Transmitted through J. Millay*)

MESSAGES FROM SPIRIT FRIENDS

Different Spirits
Different Transmissions

INTRODUCTION

Do spirits really talk to us, or is it just our imagination? Years of research have encouraged some believers while the doubters may never be convinced. That is because the beliefs we hold are part of the experiences we create for ourselves. From my own investigations of other cultures, where spirit communication is fundamental to their beliefs, the interpretation of what that "spirit energy presence" seems to be is both culturally defined and at the same time very personal.

Spirits may attempt to contact us directly, but unless we are psi sensitive, we may not be consciously aware of it. We may have a dream, or just wake up in the morning with the answer to a problem, blithely unaware that our loving grandmother, grandfather, or spirit guide is protecting us. When we meditate or create a profound silence within, we can ask for advice or request communication. Some have complained to me that they asked, but did not get an answer. A common problem is that a person may continue to ask (repeating the question over and over), but is not silent long enough, or really open enough to "receive" the answer. Hold the question in your mind, and let it go. The spirit guide already knows what you need to know. Over the years, our spirit friends have given us specific information as well as general advice.

Just because a person has graduated from Earth School, and now exists totally as a spirit, there is no guarantee that s/he can tell you more than you already know, especially if s/he chose to remain ignorant while alive. Sometimes a spirit may need help and love from us. At the time one makes the transition from life to pure spirit, one may feel lost, and choose to stay close to loved ones or to a familiar environment. To demonstrate this, we are privileged to have an example captured in a Polaroid image with the help of the "Luminator."[*2] The *Instrumental transcommunication* (ITC) research began in the 1950s to capture spirit voices on radio, etc. The Luminator is a recent addition. We don't yet know how or why it works.

[*2] A photo of Jack Stucki with his Luminator is in Mark Macy's book. (2006) *Spirit Faces: Truth About the Afterlife*. SF, CA: Red Wheel/Weiser, LLC.

CAPTURING IMAGES OF SPIRITS

Over the years attempts to capture images of spirits on film has had mixed results. Often the image seemed to be just a shimmering light, as in the illustration on page 407. Lately, there is an interest in photographing "orbs," which are round lights that seem to hover over cemeteries, and power spots. (1) However since Jack Stucki (a music therapist) and Mark Macy have begun to use the "Luminator" to find the shadows of spirits, sometimes something remarkable appears on Polaroid film. (2) A fuzzy image of Dr Heinze (1919 – 2007) appeared beside Millay in a photo (after she had channeled her at a Council Grove meeting), but it was not clear enough to publish. However, Stucki recently captured a very strong image of a heart transplant patient with the face of the spirit of the heart donor in front of her. Stucki wrote the following:

The woman was referred to me, by her regular physician, because she was having trouble with the anti-rejection medications used for the new heart. I did a biofeedback evaluation with her using surface EMGs and fingertip temperature. These parameters indicated that she pretty much kept herself in a state of hyper-vigilance — even when she was asleep. There were severe abuse issues from when she was a baby through her teenage years. She thought she had dealt with these issues well enough on her own to obtain her education at the master's degree level and gainful employment.

A real turning point in her therapy was when we did the 4:00 am session. The reason I had to see her that early is because we wanted to try to make an audible contact as well. I was told by a discarnate that it was much easier for them to use the shortwave radio as a means to communicate audibly when there was less RFI (radio frequency interference) in the air. So I tuned an analog shortwave radio to a Japanese station with a female announcer reading the news. Like Mark Macy, I turned the tuner knob slightly off the station so there was some static-type noise. Then we heard the Japanese woman's voice change to suggest to us that: "She needs to heal waveform (why she needed the heart transplant) or will take to next life – more difficult to deal with."

Once the woman saw the donor's face and heard the voice come through telling her she needed to "heal the wave form" she suddenly released a load of repressed emotions. We were able to deal with that and so gradually she was finally able to release the muscle tension so the blood could flow easily to warm her hands and feet.

Stucki took the Polaroid images on the following page in color. The originals had a better definition. However, the black and white translation is still clear enough to show that the face is definitely a semi-transparent man's face over the woman's face.

She agreed that we could publish these pictures, if her name was changed to protect her identity.

Many photos taken by Macy and Stucki seem so blurry, that it is difficult to convince nonbelievers that they are anything but just "double exposures." However, one cannot take a double exposure with a Polaroid camera. One click, and the picture pops out of the camera. Then it takes a minute for that one exposure to develop enough to see the image.

Figures 1, 2, and 3. The Luminator image of a woman with the face of the spirit of the heart donor included.

Figure 1. Photo of Ms Jones by Stucki during the 1st session to discuss the possibility of the presence of the spirit of the donor.

Figure 2. Photo of Ms Jones by Stucki with the same camera in the same room – the Luminator reveals the face of the heart donor.

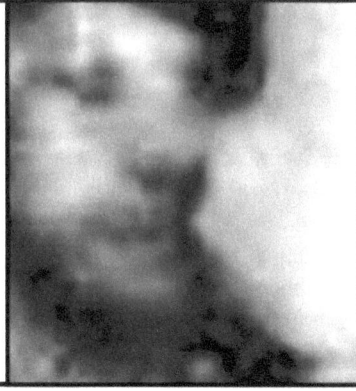

Figure 3. An enlargement of the man's face that appears over the face of Ms Jones in figure 2.

The shadow under her nose becomes his eye, but his nose, mouth and chin are clearly in front of her face.

The heart donor had been killed in a motorcycle accident. After the heart transplant, Jones developed a curiosity about "Harleys" and also a slight craving for Budweiser beer that she didn't have before the transplant.

When the spirit-consciousness leaves the body at death, the evidence of its presence (brainwaves, heart beat) also leaves. The consciousness of the spirit may then experience (for a time) whatever its belief system expects to experience. Marge King (1921-2002) channeled this to her sister Jean: *"You perceive what you believe – that is because you project your own memory and belief system onto the universe of possibilities."* Ruth-Inge Heinze agreed that the consciousness of the spirit still identifies with its most recent personality, which it helped to form out of brain/body/mind through the imprints and memories that spirit brought to the body before, during and after birth. At a later time, Marge continued,

> ...I found that after a time of exploring spacetime travel at the speed of thought (which is faster than light), I realized that my earlier concepts were quite limited, and that beyond them I could explore anything.

Even though the spirit might have memories of its own past lives, and know that the soul is eternal, it may choose to stay to help its loved ones as spirit guide, when those still living are aware and open to receive it. The famous spiritual healer Olga Worrall (Chapter 7) said her late husband Ambrose continued helping her with healing work as a spirit. (3)

It is sad that so many disembodied spirits are not yet aware that they are no longer limited by the four dimensions of spacetime. One reason is the misinformation about the afterlife given by fundamentalist religious organizations that are attached to the same control trips used in the Middle Ages (i.e. *Obey only our laws during this life, and you can go to Heaven – forever. If you break any of our rules, you will burn in Hell – forever).* While some religions allow a trial period in purgatory before final placement, the choices are still only very limited. None of it even hints at the richness of the afterlife that spirit friends have described to us. Millay encountered a spirit during a séance who had no intention of being stuck forever in either place – neither heaven nor hell appealed to him – and he didn't know about any other beliefs of the afterlife. He'd had such a good time as an entertainer in a speakeasy during prohibition (before he was shot by a jealous lover), he refused to leave the club where he continued to enjoy all the drinking parties still held there. Suggestions offered to him, from others in the same séance group, to "go into the light" were firmly rejected. (4) Apparently, we still have free will as a spirit, but to exercise it fully, we do need to know what all the choices are. That is why we have asked several spirit friends to share their afterlife experiences with us.

Ruth-Inge Heinze, PhD

When Ruth-Inge Heinze was taken to the hospital, I (Millay) drove the 250 miles over the mountain to visit her. We discussed her imminent transition, and her deep understanding of the Spirit World. It is because of this knowledge, that she devoted 23 years of her life to organizing those extraordinary conferences on shamanism. (5) She felt intensely the need for both the atheist materialists and the Bible fundamentalists to evolve beyond the limited ideas that each advocates, because their highly emotional conflict continues to foster hostility and dangerous instability, not only in our political situation, but also in the world.

A few days after I returned home, Gail Hayssen called to say that Ruth-Inge was still in the hospital therapy center, but she could no longer speak. She became so angry at the way she was being treated that she woke me from sleep, though I was many miles away. Her voice and accent was very strong when I clearly heard her shout, "*I vant to go home!*" I called Gail, and Bett Martinez, who were among those who lovingly cared for her, to tell them. Eventually, they were able to arrange the paperwork to move her to a more comfortable hospice. She still spoke to me to tell the others, so I used the computer to catch most of it directly, though she spoke faster than I can type. Dots are used to show where I missed something. The italics are the words I could capture. The smaller words in brackets are those I remembered later and added to catch up, to join a discontinued thought, or to explain when she was talking to those beside her, instead of to me:

I am determined to pass the information that I have gained during this terrible experience in the hospital and therapy center. You did your best, but there needs to be new ways of supporting the dying process... a new consciousness about it.... It was so humiliating to be talked to by hospital staff as though I was an imbecile, and to be poked and pushed – my back was too painful. My anger response was unrestrained, unleashed, strong. I was not ashamed of expressing it. I enjoyed it. For me it [anger] *was an experience of high energy and insight.... I only wanted to go home to die peacefully, not in this unholy environment – torturous. But the anger was useful, after all. Since it led to this moment of peacefulness with you.* [Here "you" refers to the group of caring women beside her at the hospice. I can "see" them and "feel" them through her.]

There were things I wanted to communicate about the work we all love and that you have helped to accomplish. I hope you find the will to continue the study of shamanism and healing.... Mind needs to be known for its essential power. The two [Mind and Matter] *are interconnected naturally... when Mind is released from Matter it is called spirit or soul... some beliefs define them differently. But spirit may still have an attachment to local identity* [or most recent personality] *... and soul is an extension into the timelessness of many identities, which can hold and continue a drama through lifetimes – until resolved and then it can become identified with all beings, with Oneness.*

I have practiced mind over matter for many years now, with the pain in my back getting worse. I was proud of my ability to exert mind over matter. 'Mind over matter, mind over matter' was my mantra. My dedication to the work kept me alive this long. You all have helped me so very much, and I bless you for that. But few who have been through what I have just experienced have been able to live long enough, or remained conscious enough, to talk about It. [Or complain to the hospital.]

The laws, the big pharmaceutical companies and the established medical system take over to suppress the spiritual needs of the people. The society itself becomes insane here – out of balance. The religion that would save life's 'Matter,' in spite of the wishes of its own sacred 'Mind,'

> *has lost touch with the higher spirit of the source of life itself – LIGHT AND LOVE – dying is the process of becoming predominantly aware of the relationship between radiance and density. Focus on the radiance and become it. Then the transition can be pure joy.*

After her transition, Ruth-Inge spoke to me again. The computer helped me to catch most of it directly, though some was too fast, as usual.

> *It can be NOW for the shamans of the world, who keep the knowledge of the soul's journey in consciousness, to come forward with their sacred information. All our statements to 'explain' the LIGHT (and its power to others) need to be carefully considered in the world where poverty and hatred tend to create darkness... where great wealth is created by the exercise of that darkness... where the extreme interpretation of heaven vs. hell... has been used as a dark power.*
>
> *Through understanding of mind and spirit, earth's needs and the real material needs of the* [currently kept poor] *inhabitants can be created –* [the kind of work that provides clean air, water, food, and maintain earth's needs as well.] *Life is timeless.... Whatever supports life will support it, and some form no matter how bizarre may choose to 'electrify' its own environment with its growth. A religion that* **prevents** *people from controlling their own reproduction is interfering with human, animal and Earth's balance. This is where shamanism, meditation, education for creativity, self-esteem, and a direct experience with how our own electrical energies blend into nature and each other can help. A psi sensitive woman can 'communicate' with the unborn. The women must take charge of honoring the Great Earth Mother... and not burden her with too many people... to the destruction of its life giving habitats. Global warming is caused by overpopulation.*

Even as a spirit, she attended the 24th *International Conference on the Study of Shamanism and Alternate Modes of Healing*. There she transmitted love nonverbally directly to the hearts of those at the conference. She also transmitted information to them directly, and verbally through me, which was recorded on CD. (6) (As one can hear on the CD, sometimes her voice is dominant and sometimes it seems we are having a conversation, as we used to do about these issues. I stay as clear as I can, but I do not choose to be completely possessed, which would mean becoming unconscious as Espiritista mediums do in Brazil. To stay in that state safely, one must be able to trust the assistance of devoted helpers.)

Ruth-Inge was determined to communicate the importance of learning as much as we can about the afterlife. So much of our present life attachments to negative attitudes continue in consciousness, unless we learn about the importance of the love that crosses all barriers between life and death. She also was very concerned about the young soldiers at war:

> *When soldiers die on the field of battle, the military chaplains pray for all of them during their pain and after their death. But I believe that some of the dead are reincarnated to live on the mean streets of major cities,*

> because they are still in the mode of battle — to kill or be killed. The violence of children, while caused by gangs, peer groups and unhealthy environments, also might be traced to the passions of hate and terror carried over from a violent past life. The survivors of the horrors of war who continue to suffer mental disturbances and experience unbearably gruesome memories and dreams are currently diagnosed with Post-Traumatic Stress Syndrome [PTSD]. However, the spirits of the enemies they killed may have taken hostile possession of some of them. Even the spirits of friends they reached out to save [but were unable to do so] might follow them home, out of fear of abandonment in that field of death. (7)

Mediums have reported that people who died in such extreme pain took the memory of the pain with them. The person channeling such a spirit will feel that pain in her own body, and will help the spirit to remove it from both of them. Ian Stevenson has reported that children who remember their last incarnation may actually have marks on their bodies in the same place as the serious wound that killed them. (8)

When Rolling Thunder spoke to an audience of young war protesters at CSUS in 1975, (9) he told of the "cleansing ritual" that the medicine man and elders performed for those returning from battle. He said that in his culture, this purification ceremony was essential before any warriors were allowed back into the community. The lingering energy of the violence and death that remained in their biofields must be released before such energy could exert a harmful influence on sensitive mothers and children causing them to have nightmares or to become sick.

<u>A purification ceremony is needed in our own civilization.</u> How shall we create a new one through our increased understanding of the Spirit World? Today when our soldiers come home with PTSD, there is very little help for mental and/or physical problems, (10) and there is even less attention paid to the need for spiritual cleansing. (11) Without that, our veterans may turn to the types of drugs that bring about stupor or actual unconsciousness in order to block out ghastly memories. Alcohol also plays a major role in this effort to ease the spiritual pain – the soul sickness that the war itself causes. (12)

In ancient times, those men, among the warrior class trained in hand to hand combat, would be proud of the number they had slaughtered in battle. The people would praise them (the "great" Caesar wiped out a million Gauls), and the priests claim "The Gods are always on our side." Today, our "civilized" society legislates to "save life" (animals, humans and zygotes), teaches peace, and in many states condemns the death penalty, even for a mass murderer. When women and men from such a society discover the real issues of war – blood, hate and death – they are totally unprepared psychologically for this major conflict in their spiritual values. Soul sickness overwhelms them and can devastate their loved ones.

The Ancient Native American Mountain Spirit of Nevada

This Mountain Spirit (MS) visited me (Hosteen Nez) at the house I built on top of a high hill (formed from an extinct volcanic plug). This had been a favorite meditation spot for MS, and I learned to listen to his sage advice about many things. MS liked the new entheogens I was developing, and declared me to be his apprentice in finding healing plants and medicines. He also liked the young forest of a few hundred pine trees that I had planted near the house, since I had included his favorite pine nut trees. MS said that there were trees there when he was here in bodily form, so it made him feel "at home."

The following are a few of the messages from the Mountain Spirit (MS) to me from about 1970 to the present 2009. (13) MS told me what it is like when I call him up when we wish to merge. During one of these first meetings or mergings as he liked to call them, I told him that I was sorry I had dug him up and that I had reburied him down the hill. (While digging for the swimming pool, I had found a cache of small finger bones.) He laughed and said that was really funny from his perception and although he appreciated my effort, it wasn't necessary because he had no use for the bones or any other part of him. He said:

> *Your priests have taught you this reverence for dead bodies that the spirit (consciousness) is all done with. This is because they do not see a differentiation between the spirit and the body; all they can see is the body and when it is dead they want you to make more fuss over it than when it was alive. Also your priests have instilled in you a great fear of dying and they use that fear to control you in many ways. Dying is nothing more than going to sleep and when you awake you are on the other side and many of your friends whom you knew in the past, and who have crossed over, are there to greet you and again you have the greater knowledge of the universe, which you largely lost when you took human form. You will not think of your body or possessions you left behind because where you will be is so much more than the earth bound spirit knows.*

He identified himself as a medicine man that had come here to die a long time ago. He chose this place since he had come here often before. It was one of his power spots or places. There is a very large flow of energy from Mother Earth to the surface and beyond. He told me that he had been a medicine man's medicine man (a very heavy-duty person). He could not be specific about when he lived here, because on the 'other side' there is no time, as we know it here. However I felt from this and several other communications that it was between 500 and 800 years or more. I did find that he was a member of the Washoe tribe, a small peaceful group who lived on this side of the Sierras mostly south of what is now Reno, NV.

I will add a few words here about what the communications or mergings (as he calls them) are like. It is necessary for me to be in a calm, quiet space and generally sitting although sometimes walking. If I wish to merge with him for a particular reason, I go into a meditative state and just call him up. I speak to him by thinking to him because he is right in my head. There is no vocalization by me and no so-called automatic writing, just communication in its purest form (telepathy). He speaks to me not so much in words, but in entire mental concepts. The communications are quite short, from less than a minute to just a few minutes. Later on when I began writing down the content of these events, it would take up to an hour to write it all down. Sometimes the Mountain Spirit comes by and if I am busy, he will stuff some concept into my consciousness without my even being aware of it and then during the ensuing days and weeks the concept is thought through, digested, mulled over and eventually assimilated and integrated into my awareness; then I have all this new knowledge or understanding without having to read or study.

At first I did not question him hardly at all about various things – I just listened to what he transmitted to me. Later on when I started to ask specific questions he seemed delighted to respond in great detail. Sometimes I think of a question for him between contacts, and on the subsequent merging he reminds me of the question and gives the answer because often he is around or present without my being aware of him.

In 1984 the Mountain Spirit told me he was going to be gone for a while and that I should not be concerned on account of his absence. He said he was going to leave a small part of himself here as sort of a watchman but he would not be available for mergings as before. I asked him where he would be and what he was going to do. He said that he was going to explore for another place to incarnate again sometime in the future when he was finished here. He said that I could handle anything that came up as I had learned a great deal in the years of our friendship.

In May 7, 1985, I had the first good contact since his leaving several months ago. He said he was assembling himself from the expedition as he had divided himself up into many smaller units to better look at more places. He gave an analogy of several small radios each making some sound in widely scattered locations and when you get them all together they make a much louder noise. It sounded like a hologram to me and he could divide up into smaller units each having all the imagery of the whole. He said he had been to marvelous places and he would tell me about them later when he was fully assembled. When asked where he had been, the reply was *"exploring complex solar systems (many dozens of planets) around very large solitary stars outside of our galaxy and not part of other galaxies."* I asked him how he had gotten that far in so short a time, considering that the closest star in our galaxy is four light years away. He said I already knew the answer and reminded me of a book I had read (*The Dancing Wu Li Masters* – ref. 14) that explained Bell's Theorem. Scientists had found that electrons were communicating with each other at speeds that made the speed of light look like it was standing still. He told me:

> *A thought has no limits. There are not that many entities on the 'other side' around Earth as one might expect so you just don't bump into them much and they are all busy assisting the people they are working with. You don't take much of my energy as some others do. We communicate with as many people as we can; it is necessary to be selective, as not everyone is ready for this learning. It is good to be back, as there is much to do that was neglected during my absence.*
>
> *There was one thing that I had not seen before, it was a rather smallish planet around this solitary star, and it was all liquid from the center to the upper atmosphere. The liquid at the center was quite dense, but not as much as one might expect, and it gradually got lighter and thinner all the way to the upper-most part. Its composition was all the same, very clear and its rotation made the planet slightly flattened. All of the life forms (of which there were myriad) swam in some fashion as do fish on earth. The smallest thing seemed to be vegetable life of some sort, which the larger swimmers consumed, and the animal swimmers did not eat other swimmers, just the vegetable things. Many of the animal swimmers were of enormous size some larger than your whales; they could not go as close to the surface as the smaller ones. Some were almost bird-like and could go the highest of any into the thin liquid (or thick gaseous) atmosphere. There was no distinction between the thinner and thicker liquids, which were all the same composition. There was a gradual gradient from one to the other with no boundary. The entire drop of liquid hanging in space was luminous even at the center although somewhat less there. Due to the rotation, the luminosity changed with the side that was closer to its sun. The variety of colors and shapes of the inhabitants was nearly endless. Some were nearly transparent like jellyfish all the way to tough walrus type skins. There were no shellfish, as you know them. It seemed to be a marvelous ecosystem and everything was in balance. I did not get a chance to study the reproductive method much as all the species seemed to be long-lived, perhaps since others weren't eating them in order to live. It was a very interesting planet and from a distance appears to be a soft luminous silver ball floating in space.*

MS gave it a lot of thought when I once asked him what he was like on the other side and after some time, he said:

> *Imagine a great number of electrons arranged in a lattice or matrix-like manner and being able to store or remember all manner of things and to be able to move about at will. Now take away the electrons and just leave a tiny bit of thought or consciousness where each electron had been. That is very much like you have in your head (brain) except it is imbedded in what you like to call gray matter and this makes the handling of thoughts*

much slower than with me. That is about as close as I can get; when you are over here you will understand more fully.

I felt that his explanation was good and it gave him a reasonable concept of what he was and what he could do and why he could do it all so fast like the space exploration he described. When I asked him about enlightenment, he explained:

You do not have to clean up everything before attaining a state of enlightenment. Only those things that you have chosen to do. Those things which you may not be consciously aware of, but that which your intuition or inner voice tells you; you have to listen very carefully.

People who have spent many lifetimes on this earth and who are getting closer to being enlightened are closer to the source and have some experiences of breaking through briefly. This makes it difficult for them to fit in well with so-called society because they see that the enculturation is mostly just so much "nonsense" and they do not participate. Therefore people around them think they are strange, weird, different, etc. You can see it yourself; even at an early age your parents and relatives felt you were different except for two (your grandfather and one aunt). They knew you were different and recognized themselves in you and liked it.

REFERENCES AND NOTES

1) Sweet, L. (2005) *How To Photograph the Paranormal*. VA: Hampton Roads Pub.
2) Macy, M. (2006) *Spirit Faces: Truth About the Afterlife*. SF, CA: Red Wheel/Weiser, LLC.
3) Olga Worrall, famous spiritual healer. (Personal communication. She told Millay that her husband Ambrose continued to help her heal the sick as a guiding spirit.)
4) Millay, J. (1990) "What happens to a spirit after death?" In: *Proceedings from The 7th International Conference on the Study of Shamanism and Alternate Modes of Healing*. Heinze, R-I. (Ed.) Falls Village, CT: The Bramble Co. 1990. pp. 275-283.
5) Heinze, R-I. (1984-2005) Heinze published all the presentations for 23 years in the proceedings. These are now available from www.shamanismconference.org.
6) All CDs are available from www.shamanismconference.org.
7) Millay, J. (2007) Channeled information from Ruth-Inge Heinze at *The International Conference on the Study of Shamanism and Alternate Modes of Healing*. Heinze, R-I. (Ed.) Falls Village, CT: The Bramble Co. 1990. pp. 275-283.
8) Stevenson, I. (1993) "Birthmarks and birth defects corresponding to wounds on deceased persons." In: *Journal of Scientific Exploration*. Vol.7.No.3, p.403. 1993.
9) Rolling Thunder (1975) Personal notes from his talk at CSUS.
10) Government Report on the Veterans Hospital conditions
11) Paulson, D.S., Krippner, S. (2007) *Haunted by Combat: Understanding PTSD in War Veterans, Including Women, Reservists, and Those Coming Back from Iraq*. Westport, CT: Praeger Security International.
12) Fiore, E. (1987) *The Unquiet Dead: A Psychologist Treats Spirit Possession*. NY: Ballantine
13) Nez, H. Conversations with the Ancient Mountain Spirit.
14) Zukov, G. (1979 – 2001) *Dancing Wu Li Masters*. NY: Harper Collins Publishers, Inc.

SECTION IX

DIMENSIONS OF CONSCIOUSNESS

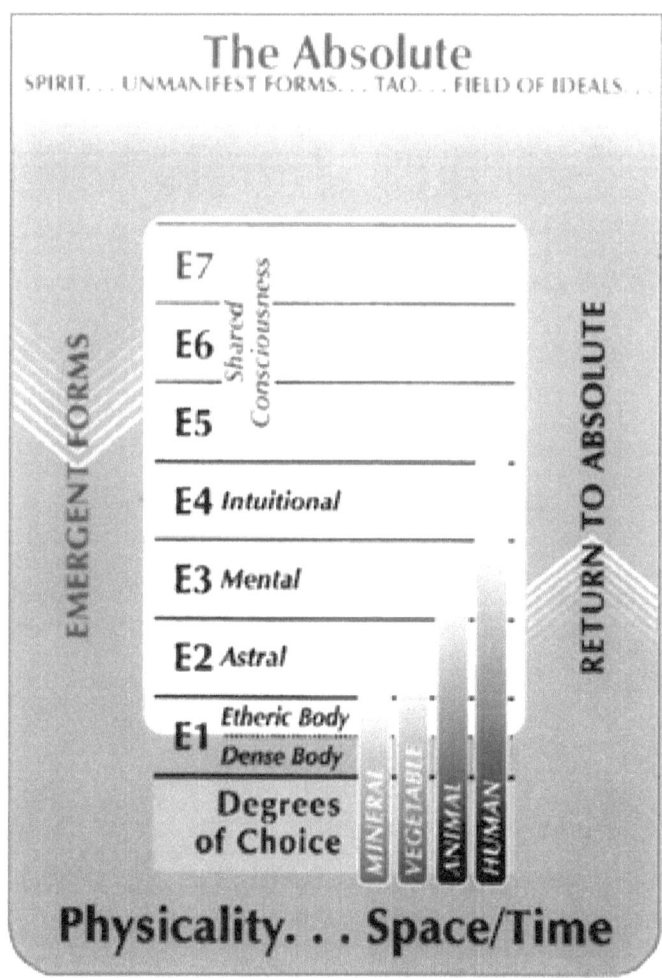

* **Figure 1.** Drawing of the Absolute as conceived by William C. Gough and Dean Brown, PhD, and illustrated by Bob Boudreaux. See page 461 of Gough's chapter for full explanation.

SECTION IX

DIMENSIONS OF CONSCIOUSNESS

Dean Brown was a key player in the innovations and advanced thinking of our time. He was also one of the editors of *Silver Threads*. His last major book *"Cosmic Law: Patterns in the Universe,"* which he coauthored with his wife Wenden Wiegand, provides a solid contribution to our understanding of the multiple dimensions of the world we live in. He graduated from earth school before this revision of *Silver Threads* began; yet the essence of his work guides the direction of our collective discussions here. William C. Gough, a cofounder of the *Foundation for Mind/Being Research,* had known and worked with Brown for over two decades, and agreed to make this important understanding available on their foundation website: http://www/fmbr/org/cosmiclaw/index.htm. We are grateful to Gough for providing in Chapter 38 a short version of the essence of Brown's fundamental understanding of all the dimensions of consciousness.

Roger Nelson has advanced the work of the Global Consciousness Project (GCP), to demonstrate another previously unknown dimension of our world—the effect that the thoughts of millions of people can exert over matter (Chapter 39). The results from years of research on this project suggest what we might accomplish if millions of people chose to think positively about peace at exactly the same time. First consider the study done by Hagelin mentioned in the introduction to Section II. He was able to demonstrate successfully that 4,000 meditators were able to lower the crime rate in Washington, DC, by 25% during the time of the meditation. Suppose we ask a major science organization to make a first class documentary with top video expertise and equipment, covering the relationship between the frequencies of the electromagnetic energies of the sun, earth and life. To attract a worldwide audience, include popular performers who can inspire through music and laughter the deep experiential understanding that we are all connected. Include also inspiring images of nature, plants, animals and peaceful people working together for peace and understanding. This event could demonstrate, to those who choose to wake up to the astounding possibilities, the solid scientific evidence of the power of mind coherence.

Finally, a no-nonsense look at the UFO question, Jacques Vallee has studied the UFO phenomena objectively for over 30 years. In Chapter 40, Vallee and Eric Davis provide a 6-level model to classify the different types of reports over many years. Much of what they have analyzed from the reports of competent witnesses fits with the concepts about the existence of "other dimensions" discussed in Sections VI and VII—Math and Physics.

Vallee and Davis prefer to use the term "Unidentified Aerospace Phenomena" (UAP) to avoid the pre-determined ideas about the phenomena adhered to by "UFO cults." (Materialistic scientists automatically reject sightings as hallucinations — one government official called a sighting to be "only *the rising crescent moon of the planet Venus"*).

These three chapters here provide a map for the expansion of scientific study beyond the biases that the current limited concepts of the world have demanded. In the last two centuries, the practiced separation of realms into "materialistic science" and "religious faith" is no longer even logical. There is no matter without the underlying energy that is part of its existence. Now we can experience the growing recognition of the importance of "energy medicine" along with the power of mind over matter. (For more about energy medicine, see www.issseem.org.)

We must also take a serious look at the needs of education. Our children must understand the energies that bombard them in their world of electronic toys, tools and media hypnosis dominated by large corporate financial interests. Education must be a top priority. In the next section, several innovative teachers have provided directions, outlines and even lesson plans, to guide this knowledge into the conscious awareness of the children of the world: We are all connected in energy.

--- Jean Millay

Big Mind is something to express,
not something to figure out.
Big Mind is something you have,
not something to seek for.

--- Tarthang Tulku
--- Time, Space and Knowledge, 1977

CHAPTER 38   THE ESSENCE OF DEAN BROWN'S COSMIC LAW

William C. Gough

William C. Gough graduated from Princeton U with BS and MS degrees in electrical engineering and is a registered professional engineer (nuclear). At Harvard University's Kennedy School of Government, he did research and studies on the Interaction Between Science and Public Policy. Gough was a manager at the US Atomic Energy Commission's controlled fusion research program, where in 1968, he co-invented the Fusion Torch concept that would produce sustainability for the material world (www.FusionTorch.com). He has written two papers with George Miley, U of Illinois, on the application of the Fusion Torch concept to close the materials cycle from use to reuse, and for the production of hydrogen from water. These papers were presented at meetings of the American Nuclear Society in 2008. See Gough's 2008 paper *A Route to Ecological Sustainability* at http://www.fmbr.org/papers/ecological_sustainability.pdf. Later he was the manager of the fusion power program for the electric utility industry at the Electric Power Research Institute (EPRI), and then the US DOE site manager for high-energy physics and synchrotron radiation at the Stanford Linear Accelerator Center (SLAC). His published works appear in *Scientific American*, *The Environmental Engineer's Handbook*, and other publications.

In 1980, he cofounded a nonprofit organization—the Foundation for Mind-Being Research (www.fmbr.org). Since 1988 he has pursued his study of the science of consciousness, and has assisted in the evolution of consciousness studies in an effort to bring this field into wider recognition as a bona fide science. The complete *Cosmic Law* book by Dean Brown and Wenden Wiegand is available at http://www.fmbr.org/cosmiclaw/index.htm.

THE ESSENCE OF DEAN BROWN'S COSMIC LAW

William C. Gough

INTRODUCTION

Dean Brown's passion was physics, the study of Nature. As Dean's life progressed he concluded that the fundamental structures of the world of matter, the world of the mind, and the world of the abstract were identical and interwoven. He then began his quest for the set of patterns in the universe that were truly invariant. Invariant means that which everyone can agree upon from all possible different viewpoints. They represent patterns in Nature that are observed to be invariant under all transformations. The result of this search was published in his 2002 book, *Cosmic Law: Patterns in the Universe*, which he jointly authored with his wife Wenden Wiegand. (1)

Thus, these laws represent the unchanging organizing principles of the universe. Dean found eight unchanging laws in the universe, which he named *"Cosmic Law."* Dean believed that these eight fundamental axioms underlie the evolutionary process in Nature. He concluded that survival is not the sole criterion for evolution, but rather there exists an inherent drive in every living creature, in business, in society, and in the cosmos to do better. Dean defined wisdom as a practical understanding of cosmic law (the dynamic invariants) and the skill in applying the law (intention). Wisdom is what remains after state-dependent, culture-dependent, and time-dependent realities have been subtracted. It is wisdom that shows one how to live a good life.

A MODEL OF THE COSMOS

Before we discuss the LAWS of the cosmos, let's review the model that Dean and I felt represented how the cosmos operates. (8) (9) Dean believed in a domain of unbounded potential, the Absolute, from which all emanations arise. The Absolute constitutes the source of everything in the physical world. The science of the Absolute has evolved from the ontologies developed by past cultures. These ancient traditions represent a universal wisdom since they have within them aspects that are invariant through time.

Figure 1. The Model of the Absolute as Conceived by William C. Gough and Dean Brown. Illustrated by Bob Boudreaux.

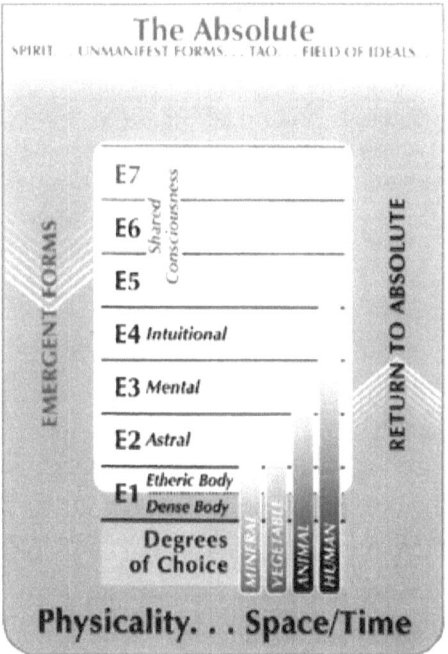

The Absolute is the source of the physicality of space-time. In the Absolute, space and time have no meaning. The left-hand side represents the emergence of form into the physicality of spacetime. The right-hand side represents the return over time of everything that is in the physical back to the Absolute. The physicality of space-time is divided into seven levels that constitute a subset of the Absolute. The "dense body" (the physical world of common experience) is shaded and the remainder is not shaded. This indicates that we are normally unaware of most of space-time. Everything in the material world is a multilevel, multidimensional object whether it be cells, plants, the Earth or us. The degree to which a living system is **consciously aware** of the different multilevels of the universe creates the difference between the mineral, plant, animal, and human "kingdoms."

In addition, such a postulate for a creative source appears necessary in modern science for two reasons: First, the creation of the universe via the "big bang" violates the conservation of energy—a law at the foundation of modern physics. Second, all life began in nonlife; therefore, every living thing could not have evolved from an ancestor. This is true since the universe started from "nothing." Since life started from matter, and all matter came from nothing, i.e., from a nonphysical domain, life must have started from "nothing" also. A well-known scientific concept for addressing this issue is Dr David Bohm's "implicate order," an order of undivided wholeness. (4)

The model presents the Absolute as unchanging and timeless, but time exists in the physical world time. Some have said that time is God's way of not having everything happen at once. But there is a deeper meaning; we can't have change without time. In fact, time is nothing but change. (3) Time is the mechanism by which Nature creates differences. Without time we would only have the perfect patterns of the Absolute. With time come imperfections! Nowhere in all Nature are any two things found to be exactly alike. By Nature, Dean means that which gets born, whether it be a galaxy, a planet, a plant or a person. In Nature we perceive patterns but they are always in flux—everything is vibrating. Science agrees that everything in the universe is vibrating; therefore all forms and patterns must have a wave spectrum associated to them.

The phenomenon of wave resonance depicts the mechanism for the interaction of physical Nature with the nonphysical Absolute. (7) Since the Absolute has no time, past, present, and future are one. Modern physics has a similar characteristic. In the fundamental equations of physics, i.e., electromagnetic, relativity and quantum, the backward and forward directions in time are not distinguishable—there is a symmetry of time. It is only when we consider the physicality of three-dimensional space from the engineering perspective of thermodynamics that time has an arrow. If one accepts relativity theory, light has "no time" since at the speed of light clocks effectively stop, and time has no meaning. It is the manifest world that gives time a meaning; in the Absolute time has no meaning, it is always the Now. **Figure 1** is a schematic representation of this model in which a cosmology of multiple (seven) levels or fields of waves, related to each other, not causally, but by reflecting a common pattern. The basic model's roots go back into antiquity but the specifics could be said to start a century ago with the work of C. W. Leadbeater, the Theosophist, (11) and from more recent extensions made by Elmer Green, PhD, of the Menninger Foundation. (10)

THE MEGA–LAWS OF THE COSMOS

So what are these eight mega-laws of the cosmos? Dean divided the eight Laws into two groups. The first four Laws are laws of form, static, grounded in the timeless Absolute. They are the eternal invariants. The second four Laws are laws of process. They are dynamic and operate in Nature. They deal with flow and with life in its most elemental essentials.

The second set of four Laws of Nature are isomorphic to the first set of four Laws of the Absolute, i.e., "as above, so below."

LAWS OF THE ABSOLUTE

LAW I: The first Law is the law of Nothingness. Dean considered this the greatest Law of all! Empires, galaxies, love affairs, languages, people come and go, leaving not a trace. There is a lot of comfort in this – whatever we mess up is erased and forgotten. In the long run, nobody knows or cares. Time heals, then forgives and finally forgets, forgets all.

The Nothingness is where we encounter the domain of eternal form. It is in the Nothingness where we can achieve "effortless effort," and "actionless action," and "purposeless purpose." The Nothingness is a Vedic concept, from which derives Plato's field of ideals, Jung's archetypes, and Theilhard de Chardin's noosphere. Timeless forms of aesthetics, ethics, logic, mathematics, and humanity reside here. Meditation returns us to this source of rejuvenation and creativity. When we are centered in this quite empty place, our perceptions are clearest, our hang-ups are diminished, and true essences come into focus. The quiet center of Nothingness is the place of infinite potential.

LAW II: The second Law is the Law of the Progression of Contraries. This Law underlies the existence of paradox. For example, we have the interplay of Male and Female, Good and Evil, light and darkness, chaos and order, finite and infinite, knowledge and wisdom, love and romance, etc. Each attribute should be in harmony and in balance with its complement. Dean considered love as the substrate that holds the universe together. A feeling that applies to the whole world – "Love thy neighbor." Romance is in the moment, where you are caught up in the experience of cosmic beauty and "rightness."

LAW III: The third Law is the Law of Concealment. Without concealment there would be no enlightenment, no learning, no process, no evolution. All would be known, static. Dead. It is at the heart of the life force to have a passion for the hidden, the occult, for all of us, children, storytellers and scientists alike. It is the business of art and science to tease truth from our mother, Nature. It is her business to reveal herself *gradually*, so as not to overwhelm, but to progressive revelation.

The ultimate wisdom hides herself. The concealed generates both energy and drive for the evolution process—our curiosity. Have you ever had an experience where everything appears clear to you at once? Then the fog closes in and everything becomes fuzzy again. Even when it remains clear to you, it cannot be communicated to someone else if they don't already know! Ultimately everyone has to discover for himself.

Concealment results in imperfection in the physical world. Dean stated that the power of forgiveness is based upon the fact that imperfection represents a cosmic principle of God. Therefore, we need to accept and love the inherent imperfection in everything and everybody. Imperfection is eternally with us. Not in all of nature are any two things alike. Ancient societies have honored the importance of imperfection. For example, (2) the sacred rugs of Persia are always made with a deliberate imperfection in recognition of the inherent imperfection that god has created into Nature.

LAW IV: The fourth Law is the Law of Revelation. Revelation comes through grace alone as the words of the ever-popular hymn "Amazing Grace" illustrates. By grace, eventually that which was concealed will be revealed. However, there exists a family of different subtle depths of perception. They result from different degrees of intention and cognition. For example, the testimony of several people who witness a car wreck will be different—sometimes in very substantial ways. Who is right? There will never be complete agreement among them, no matter how much new data are collected.

The progression toward Truth is always incomplete. Therefore, how can we know that we are on the right path? We know that we are on the right track if the revelation is progressively more beautiful—beauty is truth, truth is beauty. We have all had at one time or another a breakthrough in our perception. It occurs when we flash upon the deep meaning of an expression or an event and it becomes an *"aha"* experience. No amount of wishful thinking or logic or persuasion can bring you to this *"aha."* It just comes when it comes, and it brings with it certainty. Sometimes it comes after a serious personal crisis such as a heart attack. The doors of perception are cleansed and things appear as they really are.

Dean knew that the Law of Revelation placed a limitation of our "scientific understanding" of the reality of Nature. The underlying issue is that all our scientific instruments that we use to "measure" our world have limitations. They can only measure real numbers that are rational. Real numbers that are irrational can only be approximated and imaginary numbers are not measurable at all. The rational numbers are an infinitesimal part of the total real numbers, and say nothing about the "imaginary spaces." In physics this is known as the "measurement problem." The deeper implication of this limitation is that all measurements are tentative. Between any two measured points an infinite number of possibilities may occur. Every theory, every model, every ontology, is always superseded by a more refined one. The more we know, the less we know—science unfolds by progressive revelations. Yet each individual through direct experience can explore undiscovered realities of the Absolute. These realities are beyond our space and time but often have been described by mathematics—they are realities that the limited physical instruments of science can never measure. (6)

LAWS OF NATURE

The laws of Nature deal with flow, and with life in its most elemental essentials. Nature is a process of ever-flowing im-balance. There are four stages. We are conceived and born, we attain the crest of our careers, we descend into old age, and we die and reform, preparing for rebirth.

LAW V: The fifth Law is the Law of Emanation, the Law of Becoming. Its essence is birth, creating, causing, and emergence—meaning emerging from the complexities of Natural processes. The basic idea is to birth something from the abstract Absolute realm into the tangible world of the relative. The emphasis is upon bringing forth, emanating, and manifesting.

From time to time we all have a "primal urge." We are born with these impulses and carry them throughout our lifetime. One has the impulse to be a lawyer, another a nurse, another a musician, another a scholar, another a mechanic. The word urge comes from the Greek *"erg,"* meaning energy. Other primal urges include sex, ego identity, altruism, survival, hunger, and friendship. These are all creative energies that promote emergence, emanation, the bringing forth of Life in general, and of your personality, of your unique individuality in particular.

Everything that now exists in manifestation was once just a fresh-formed idea, weightless and without energy. Words are the ultimate reality. The magic word *"abracadabra"* means *"I create as I speak"* in Aramaic. Not only does Nature manifest itself from the Absolute, you and I create by the same process. We cast a *spell* to invoke magic. We are one, one with everything. To approach the universe, understand it, play with it—produce effects through your pure center. Life becomes active and joyful. Just be centered, then you become nothing/everything—you are in the "emptiness" of the Absolute, the domain of infinite potential.

LAW VI: The sixth Law is the Law of Sustenance. Everything that is living at this moment is living by the grace and the nourishment of Providence! Our food, our air and water, our care and attention – all are undeserved gifts from an abundant and loving Nature. We are truly too poor and helpless to manage anything by ourselves. We are too innocent to take care of even our most humble affairs. The future is an infinite path, unwinding slowly ahead of us, and we are just beginning to creep along its way. The only sensible course is one of **absolute trust**, just as the newborn trusts its mother. This leads us to a great cosmic principle, **Expect Nothing**. Why should we trust Nature? Providence is abundant. The Universe has an unlimited bank account reserved in your name, particularly to be used for your enjoyment. But to draw on it you must write the check!

This brings us to the topic of love. In a treatise on Cosmic Law, love enters under the Law of Sustenance. Love sustains. "God is Love." Love is unconditional. It cannot be defined. It can only be experienced. It is the ultimate nourishment. Love is the demonstration of supply increasing demand and demand increasing supply—if love for one increases, then love for all increases.

LAW VII: Law seven is the Law of Dissolution. Everything that has a beginning has an end—ashes to ashes, dust to dust. That which has form will return to the formless. Graceful de-construction is a blessing. It is necessary to clear our "history" and wash the slate clean. Successes as well as failures, equally, become limitations to further growth and evolution. Plan for the end of an enterprise before beginning it. As the Sufis say, die before you die. Compose a good life, and then compose a good death. One of the most satisfying feelings is the sense of having attained full closure on a project or a lifetime. If we were completely deprived of the sense of completion, life would become pointless and sour. Completion of life is the time to turn over all the karma, good and bad alike, to the Universe.

LAW VIII: The eighth Law is the Law of Return. Dean believed in reincarnation – that we are impelled into the Absolute, from which rebirth emanates. He considered this the most creative part of your spiritual journey, where you re-member yourself back into another existence, another rebirth. In the domain of the Absolute, time does not exist, only Spirit. Since we are in Eternity, rebirth can be emanated into manifestation at any time and culture, past, present, or future, according to our choice. Here is where we choose our parents, our bodies, and our lifetime's mission. It is also where we fold our previous lifetimes' experience back into fresh new innocence, with the memories we choose to bring with us. Some of these things are eternal and carry forth from lifetime to lifetime. There is a transcendence of love over death – for sweethearts, for family, for friends.

Reincarnation research implies the possible existence of a spirit world as Dean Brown put forth in developing Cosmic Law. Dean has good company regarding a belief in reincarnation: Plato, Virgil, and Pythagoras among others. Modern physics and cosmology often hypothesize the possibility of realities outside of our physical space-time. Dean, as a quantum physicist, was well aware of these theories. He also understood the impressive research of Ian Stevenson, PhD, a psychiatrist at the University of Virginia, who over his lifetime compiled thousands of cases involving children who remembered past lives in detail. These cases sometimes included the physical appearance of wounds that were consistent from lifetime to lifetime. (13, 14)

Here is an interesting story about Dean. Philosophy was Dean's great love. He considered philosophy to be his most important field of study. He would talk about the work of C. S. Peirce, his favorite philosopher, with deep respect. Walter Semkiw, MD, was doing reincarnation research to demonstrate that facial features, personality traits and even linguistic writing style remain consistent from lifetime to lifetime. Dr Semkiw would hypothesize a past-life match, often with the assistance of the famous medium Kevin Ryerson, and then check it out using historical documentation. He did this for Dean Brown and provided evidence that he was the reincarnation of C.S. Peirce! Compare the pictures published in Semkiw's book, and you will be impressed by the similarities between the facial features of Dean and Peirce. (12)

CONCLUDING REMARKS

I have known Dean Brown for over two decades. He frequently spoke at our Foundation for Mind-Being Research meetings and contributed editorials to the FMBR Newsletter. Dean and I would get together at either his home or mine and talk science and philosophy for hour upon hour. I treasured these discussions; we spent hundreds of hours together and I taped many of our dialogues. Together Dean and I wrote two papers that discussed the mysteries of the Absolute.

In writing the *Essence of Dean's Cosmic Law* I used Dean's words directly from his book and other writings. There are no quotes around the excerpts since there are too many, and some have been edited, combined, or condensed. However, I believe they accurately reflect Dean's insights. If any do not I hope Dean will forgive me. I encourage each of you to go to the original source of Dean's writings and enjoy the full wisdom of this inspiring man.

REFERENCES

1) Brown, D. & Wiegand, W. (2002) *Cosmic Law: Patterns in the Universe*. Alamo, CA: Self-published. Available on the web at http://www.fmbr.org.
2) Brown, D. (2002) "Importance of imperfection." In: *FMBR Newsletter,* Available on the web at http://www.fmbr.org/editoral/edit01_02/edit8_may02.htm.
3) Barbour, J. (1999) *The End of Time: The Next Revolution in Physics*. NY: Oxford U Press.
4) Bohm, D. (1980) *Wholeness and the Implicate Order*. London/Boston: Routledge & Kegan Paul.
5) Gough, W.C. (2006, January) "Reincarnation." In: *FMBR Newsletter*. Available on the web at http://www.fmbr.org/editoral/edit05_06/edit4-jan06.php.
6) Gough, W.C. & Brown, Dean. (2001, May) "Measurement & reality." In: *FMBR Newsletter*. Available on the web at http://www.fmbr.org/editoral/edit00_01/edit8-may01.html

7) Gough, W.C. & Brown, D. (2001) "Resonance, coherence, and us." In: *Proceedings of the 18th International Conference on the Study of Shamanism and Alternative Modes of Healing*, San Rafael, CA, Sept. 1-3, 2001. Available on the web without illustrations at http://www.fmbr.org/papers/resonant.php.
8) Gough, W.C. & Brown, D. (2002) "Domain of unbounded potential: The science of the Absolute." In: *Proceedings of the 19th International Conference on the Study of Shamanism and Alternative Modes of Healing*, San Rafael, CA, Aug 31 – 9/2/2002. Available on the web without illustrations at http://www.fmbr.org/papers/absolue.php.
9) Gough, W.C. & Shacklett, R.L. (1999) "What science can and can't say about spirits." In: *Proceedings of the 16th International Conference on the Study of Shamanism and Alternate Modes of Healing*, San Rafael, CA, Sept. 4-6, 1999. (Also published as a three part series in *The Journal of Religion and Psychical Research*, July & October 2000, Vol. 23, No. 3, pp. 124-132 & No. 4, pp.208-217, and January 2001, Vol. 24, No. 1, pp.48-57). Available on the web without illustrations at: http://www.fmbr.org/papers/abut_spirits.php.
10) Green, E. & Green, A. (1989) *Beyond Biofeedback*. Ft. Wayne, IN: Knoll Publishing Co., pp. 30-31.
11) Leadbeater, C.W. (1975/1902) *Man Visible and Invisible*. Wheaton, IL: Theosophical Publishing House, Quest Book, p. 11 (First published 1902).
12) Semkiw, Walter. (2003) *Return of the Revolutionaries: The Case for Reincarnation and Soul Groups Reunited*. Charlottesville, VA: Hampton Roads Pub. Co.
13) Stevenson, Ian. (1975,1977, 1980, 1983) *Cases of the Reincarnation Type: Vol. 1 India, Vol. II Sri Lanka, Vol. III Lebanon and Turkey, Vol. IV Thailand and Burma*. Charlottesville, VA: University Press of Virginia.
14) Stevenson, Ian. (1996) *Reincarnation and Biology: A Contribution to the Etiology of Birthmarks and Birth Defects, Vol. I & II*. Westport, CT: Praeger Publishers.

Individuality is only possible if it unfolds from wholeness.

--- David Bohm

CHAPTER 39   THE GLOBAL CONSCIOUSNESS PROJECT

Roger D. Nelson, PhD

Roger Nelson was coordinator of research at the Princeton Engineering Anomalies Research (PEAR) laboratory, Princeton University, from 1980 to 2002. He is the Director of the Global Consciousness Project (GCP), which he founded in 1997. He is an experimental psychologist. His broad interests in psychology, physics, philosophy and the arts generated opportunities to collaborate with creative interdisciplinary teams at PEAR and elsewhere, developing technologies and experimental applications to study consciousness, intention, mind-matter interactions, and anomalous information transfer. In 1993, building on years of laboratory experiments, Nelson began using random event generator (REG) technology in the field to register correlations of data with special states of group consciousness. This work led naturally to the GCP, a global network designed to test the hypothesis that effects of globally shared emotions or states of consciousness might be seen in correlations of REG data with major world events.

Dr Nelson is committed to scientific research of the highest quality, embodying both skepticism and an open mind, and to a balance of science and aesthetics. After a decade of increasingly persuasive evidence from the GCP analyses, he has shifted focus toward public presentations about the research and its implications about the nature of consciousness.

The Global Consciousness Project
http://noosphere.princeton.edu/

THE GLOBAL CONSCIOUSNESS PROJECT:
Can a Meeting of Minds Structure Random Data?

Roger D. Nelson

> *Now, if the cooperation of some thousands of millions of cells in our brain can produce our consciousness, a true singularity, the idea becomes vastly more plausible that the cooperation of humanity, or some sections of it, may determine what Comte calls a Great Being.*
> ---- J.B.S. Haldane

OVERVIEW

The remarkable evolutionary biologist Haldane proposed an analogy between human communities and brain cell networks that suggest we might look for extended manifestations of shared ideas and collaborative efforts. (6) Many visionary thinkers have proposed similar notions describing something we can call a *"global consciousness."* In the middle of the twentieth century, Teilhard de Chardin (23) envisioned the next stage of our evolution as a sheath of intelligence for the earth that he called the *"noosphere."* That term seems to have been coined, with much the same meaning, by Vernadsky (24) earlier in the century.

This possibility of a communal intelligence, along with some more explicit and tractable questions about the behavior of networked random sources, has guided the development of the Global Consciousness Project (GCP), an international collaboration of about 100 scientists, engineers, and researchers. We record continuous data from a world-spanning network of electronic random sources, and we ask whether special states of "global consciousness" defined by major world events will correspond to anomalous structure in the data. To flesh out the meaning of such correlations, we ask about linkage with other variables, especially social measures such as polling data or variations of news intensity.

The GCP network has nodes in some 60 locations around the world, hosting devices that generate random data continuously and send it for archiving to a dedicated server in Princeton, New Jersey. Subsequent analyses determine whether nonrandom sequences occur during the global events we identify. According to standard physical theory, there should be no structure at all in these random data, but we find significant deviations from statistical expectations during many of the events we examine.

The anomalous patterning is subtle, however, so that repeated tests on similar events are required to develop reliable statistics. Nevertheless, the composite result over 10 years of the project indicates a highly significant effect, with odds against chance of more than 10 million to one. The research implies that standard physical models are incomplete, and it provides evidence for meaningful interactions of consciousness with the physical world.

INTRODUCTION

The Global Consciousness Project (GCP) is an international collaboration of researchers interested in the developing frontiers of consciousness research. We use technology designed for assessing the effects of conscious intention in laboratory research (7, 8, 5), and later exploited to look for effects of group consciousness. (14, 15) The GCP application is designed to register similar effects of consciousness on a global scale. We record a continuous time series of parallel data sequences from calibrated physical random sources located in a wide geographic distribution. The resulting database can be used for various purposes, but our focus is on correlations with special states of an operationally defined *"global consciousness."* The idea is that when great events engage the attention and emotions of large numbers of us, there will be an interaction of our communal consciousness and the physical world. As in the laboratory and field experiments, we predict that this interaction will affect our network of physical random sources. One of the most intriguing possibilities for this project is that it may be capable of detecting faint glimmerings of global consciousness as a coalescing layer of intelligence for the earth—Teilhard de Chardin's Noosphere. (23)

Although this is an attractive metaphor, it isn't likely that we will be able to find direct evidence for it. However, we do predict a correlation of nonrandom structure in our data with human consciousness responding to world events. We can look for modulation of these correlations by physical, geophysical and cosmic variables, and assess direct correlations of the data with social indices such as stock market fluctuations, polling data, or gauges of news intensity.

We maintain a network of detectors located around the world in about 60 host sites, from Alaska to New Zealand. These devices generate random data continuously and send it for archiving to a dedicated server in Princeton, New Jersey. The data are vetted and subjected to rigorous standard procedures to ensure they are free from defects (for example, from mechanical or electrical failures). Background tests establish that any nonrandom behavior cannot be attributed to mundane sources such as electrical grid stresses, mobile phone activity, or ordinary electromagnetic fields.

The data are analyzed to determine whether the sequences of nominally unpredictable random values contain periods of structure that may be correlated with major events in the world. We use a replication model, conducting a series of hypothesis tests where all parameters are defined *a priori*, that is, before the data are examined. The formal procedure is scientifically rigorous, with careful controls and multiple observers. It includes independent statistics, which complement and support each other. These analytical formalisms provide a statistical framework that is reliable and transparent, and which provides confidence in the results.

The bottom line is that we find patterns in data that should be random, and the patterns are related to events of importance to humans. According to standard physical theory, there should be no structure at all in these random data. Yet, many of the global events we look at are associated with striking patterns in the data. Special times like the celebrations of New Years, natural disasters like the Indian Ocean tsunami, and tragic events like the terror attacks on September 11, 2001, tend to show departures from random expectation. The changes are apparently correlated with shared periods of deep engagement or widespread emotional reactions. The evidence suggests that the anomalous structure we see is somehow responsive to periods of coherent focused human attention generated by extraordinary events.

BACKGROUND

Extensive experiments at the Princeton Engineering Anomalies Research (PEAR) laboratory have demonstrated that intentions can affect random processes of several different kinds. In 12 years of controlled research, the accumulated data from over 1000 experiments using a variety of electronic, mechanical, and other random devices show a correlation with intentions that is highly significant. (8) The overall probability against chance fluctuation as the explanation for the results is on the order of 10^{-13}. The largest subset of these tests uses an electronic random event generator (REG), which is based on quantum processes that are truly random.

Miniaturized versions of the REG allow us to take the research into the field to look for effects of group consciousness. Data collected in situations that foster strong communal feeling show statistically significant departures from expectation on average. These "FieldREG" experiments indicate that interpersonal coherence or resonant engagement can affect physical random event generators, even in the absence of intentions focused on the device. (14, 15)

The REG experiments are part of a corpus generated over decades by dozens of researchers, providing evidence from controlled experiments for an interaction of mind and matter. (20, 21) The field-oriented experiments also were immediately and successfully replicated. (2,22,16) But the next step is a big one. How do we make the leap from local experiments in laboratories and small groups to a world-spanning network testing for signs of a "global consciousness"? This requires an unambiguous nonlocality of effects that extends the lab and field paradigms into little-tested realms. How could there be any effect of a New Year's celebration, or the beginning of a war, or a billion people watching a funeral ceremony, on REG devices placed in far corners of the world?

Invoking a metaphor, it may be helpful to envision a "consciousness field." David Bohm's "active information field" provides a useful analogy. (4) We can imagine a faint radiance of information extending out indefinitely from each mind, with a wavelike interpenetration creating tenuous interference patterns that differ depending on our intentions and our degree of engagement. Most of the time we are busy with our individual thoughts, and the relationship of our consciousness fields would be random. But if we share experience and emotions, the patterns might constructively interact and reinforce each other, as resonant sound waves meld into a chord. Remember that this is a metaphor; there is no physical energy field that we can directly measure generating such an interaction. Yet, there appears to be something like a field, carrying information representing the coherent aspects of our consciousness, which can interact nonlocally with other similar fields and potentially with random physical systems as well. It is conceivable that this may be responsible for the anomalous effects in studies with REGs. The future state of a truly random physical REG is undetermined; perhaps that makes it a potential receiver for structuring information present in a consciousness field.

EXTRAPOLATION TO A GLOBAL NETWORK

The field REG studies suggested new questions. For example, would multiple devices produce different or stronger results? Does the distance from the apparent source of the anomalous effect matter? After *ad hoc* trials with a dozen or more REGs in Europe and the US showed positive results for a broadly organized global meditation event called "Gaiamind," (9) and for the funeral services of Princess Diana in September 1997, (13) we decided to create a permanent, world-spanning network to collect data continuously so that we could monitor the effects of great events on the world stage. A core group of researchers including several who contributed data to the prototype Gaiamind and Diana efforts developed plans and began assembling resources to create the infrastructure for the Global Consciousness Project. The GCP network was designed to capture or absorb the subtle effects of a communion similar to that described above, speculating that major events might create or manifest interacting fields of thought and emotion all over the world. As we will see, the data gathered over the intervening years show that we are able to detect structure in otherwise random data when large numbers of people become attuned to a common interest and feeling.

Friends and colleagues around the world with interest in the questions posed by the GCP are willing to set up a computer to host an "Egg"—one of our REG-based instruments. (The term derives from the acronym *EGG*, which stands for *ElectroGaiaGram,* an early name for the GCP.) Figure 1 shows the network of Egg host sites. This is a live Google map on the GCP website, providing detailed information about the host sites, including location, equipment, history, and who is responsible for each of the Eggs.

Figure 1.
GCP Eggs are located around the world, from Alaska to Fiji, on nearly all continents and in most time zones. There were approximately 60 operational nodes in 2008.

We collect data at the rate of one trial (a sum of 200 random bits) per second at each node, day and night, month after month, generating a history of parallel, synchronized readings from all over the globe. We thus have random data corresponding to every moment, and naturally covering every momentous occurrence on the world stage from August 1998 to the present time. These data are the same kind as used in the PEAR laboratory and field experiments showing what appear to be nonlocal correlations with human intentions and emotions. Our central archive is thus a database that contains a complete record of responses that might be registered as detectable structure in the nominally random GCP data when a major event stimulates an unusual coherence of thought and emotion anywhere in the world.

PICTURING OUTCOMES

With the data in hand, we ask what happens during a global event. The measures we use are designed to identify small signals in what is typically a very noisy background of random numbers. Even tiny changes from what's expected, if they are consistent, can become statistically significant indicators of a real effect, providing we are patient and are able to replicate the tests many times for independent events. We interpret departures from expected behavior in our data as a measure of something related to consciousness, following principles developed over decades of laboratory research (8, 20, 21) indicating that human intentions and special states of consciousness can affect the randomness of such devices. To show how the analysis we use can reveal structure, we will look at some special cases that illustrate how graphs of the data represent the correlations we are interested in, and help impart meaning to the formal statistics.

The database contains many cases where the data show a departure from expectation that might be interpreted as evidence for a burgeoning global consciousness. It is important to acknowledge that there may be other causes or explanations, such as an effect of the experimenters' strong interest, but we are sure at this point there is no mistake – the data show real anomalies. It is also important to remember that the effects are too small to be found reliably in single instances. However, we select some especially clear cases to illustrate what might ideally happen (or what shows up on average).

For example, the scale and nature of the effects is evident in a six-hour period centered on the beginning of NATO bombing in Kosovo, March 24, 1999. This action was judged by the Western nations and the US in particular to be the only choice available to stop the ethnic war in Yugoslavia. It was a shock to the world, even though it was not unexpected. The formal hypothesis test for this event specified just one hour, beginning at the moment of the bombing, and the result was marginally significant with 1-tailed p-value of 0.045. Figure 2 shows this one-hour period in the context of six hours of surrounding time. We plot the cumulative sum of deviations from expectation in the sequence of squared composite Z-scores across Eggs, which is a measure of variance in the network. The GCP data appear to be markedly different before and after the beginning of the bombing. For the three-hour period leading up to the first explosion, the trace is a classic random walk, with no noticeable trend. (Truly random data will show a raggedly varying but basically level trace.) Then, beginning abruptly at the time of the bombing, the trace changes; the next three hours no longer look random.

This is, of course, a picture of statistical quantities, and as a single instance, does not answer the question whether focused attention and emotion may affect the GCP network. But it is not a lone example. It turns out that about two thirds of our formal tests have a positive trend supporting the hypothesis, and almost 20% are statistically significant at the level where we expect 5% by chance. Such results begin to add up to a persuasive case, even though the effects we seek to capture are subtle.

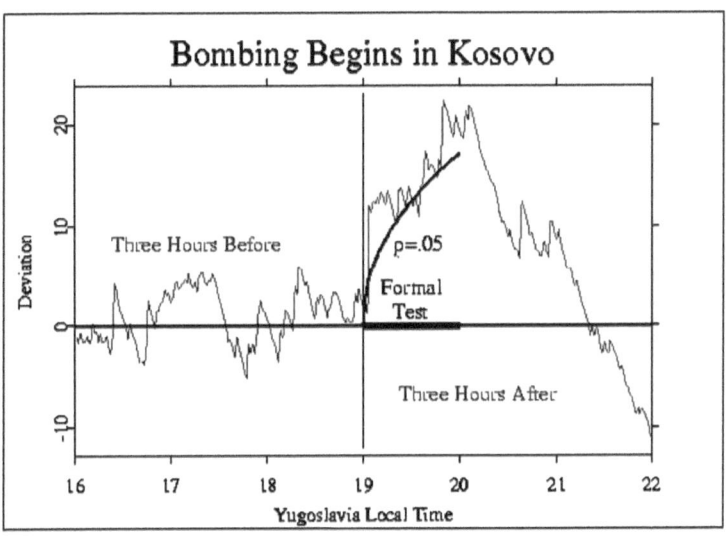

Figure 2.
Cumulative deviation of squared Stouffer Z across Eggs for GCP data during three hours preceding and three hours following the beginning of bombing in Yugoslavia. Adapted from a figure by George deBeaumont.

TERROR AND TRAGEDY

Many other cases of violent disruptions of the social fabric have been assessed, and most, though not all of them show the predicted effects. The clearest of these cases was the terrorist attack of September 11, 2001, where we see extraordinary departures of the data from expectation. The formal test specified a period of a little more than four hours, and it did yield a significant result ($Z = 1.873$ and $p = 0.031$). However, this limited view did not reflect the full impact of the 9/11 attacks and the worldwide reactions to them. In *post hoc* explorations, we took a broader perspective in order to learn as much as possible about the effects a powerful event might have on the network. Simply put, we found strong deviations in a number of measures. The results reflected the intensity of this event, which, without question, affected our global consciousness deeply.

This was an extreme instance of a global event such as we hypothesize should affect our measures, and we looked at it from every angle, with results detailed in several publications. (10, 17, 18) The graphs in Figure 3 give an idea of the kind of departures found in the data on September 11. **Figure 3a** shows the network variance (squared Stouffer Z), which was significantly high relative to expectation for more than two days following the attacks. The persistence and strength of this response is extraordinary. **Figure 3b** traces the variability among the 37 REG devices reporting on September 10, 11, and 12.

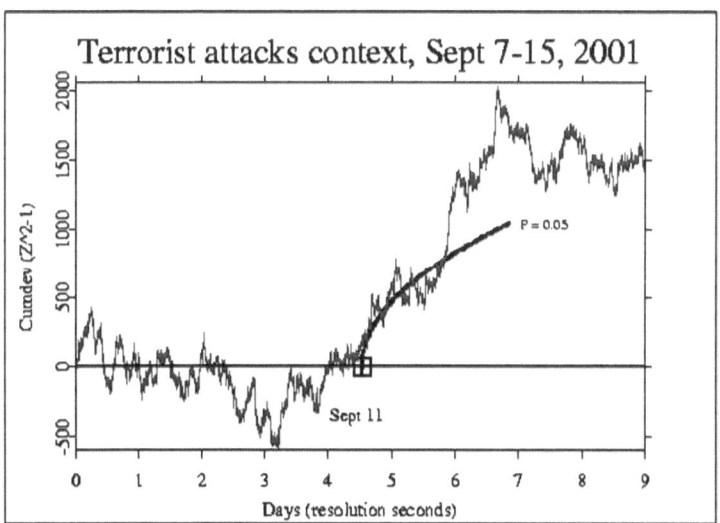

Figure 3a.
Network variance (squared Stouffer Z) shows a random walk until Sept 11 2001, but then takes on a significant trend that persists for two days before returning to normal.

On the 10th we see the expected, more-or-less level random walk – variance was in the normal range. But early in the morning of the 11th, between 4:00 and 5:00, the Eggs began showing consistently large variance to an extreme degree, and that tendency continued until about 11:00 or a bit later. After the second tower fell, the variance became extremely compressed and remained smaller than usual until early evening. This is a remarkable figure in many ways. The peak departure on September 11 has odds of less than one in 10 thousand, and is essentially unique; no other day in the four years of data to that time shows such a large deviation. There is also a startling but clear indication that the Egg network began to react well before the first plane hit the World Trade Center. There may be a more mundane explanation (even chance fluctuation is possible, though extremely unlikely) but this looks as if our global consciousness somehow registered a precognition or a presentiment (3) of the terrible events to come.

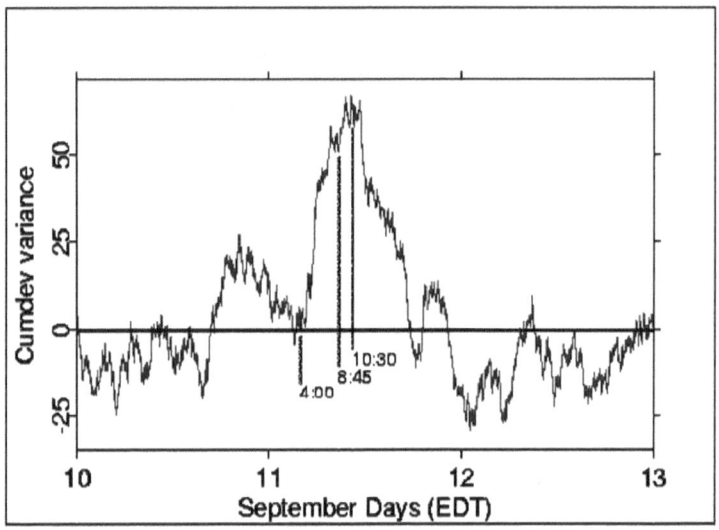

Figure 3b.

The EGG data show highly significant aberrations in the device variance before and during the attack. The cumulative deviation of second-by-second variance across Eggs shows a large spike on the 11th compared with other days.

RELIGION AND RITUAL

The intuition that there is a deep sharing of emotion during big events on the world stage leads to asking more general questions about what states of consciousness might have manifestations in our data and under what range of circumstances. An event that attracted a great deal of media attention and was followed with positive regard by people everywhere was the week-long pilgrimage in March 2000 of Pope John to the Middle East, to sites that are regarded as the sacred locus of origin for three of the world's major religions. The data showed a persistent trend over the six-day period that certainly did not look random, and culminated in a significant departure ($p = 0.009$). The Muslim Ramadan, the Indian Kumbh Mela, and other major religious celebrations also tend to show deviations commensurate with the participation of millions of people.

Organized meditations also seem to affect the Egg network, albeit in a different way. Several cases have shown persistent reduced variance (opposite to our standard prediction). The effect is shown in Figure 4, which summarizes 14 hour-long group meditations by advanced Siddhi practitioners of Transcendental Meditation, gathered to meditate together twice daily over the summer of 2006. The odds of such strong and consistent deviations are greater than 100 to 1 against chance even considering a compensation for multiple analyses. Other organized meditations show a similar outcome. For example, a synchronized global peace prayer/meditation on May 20, 2007 brought half a million people to a common focus. The data again show a significant reduction of the network variance.

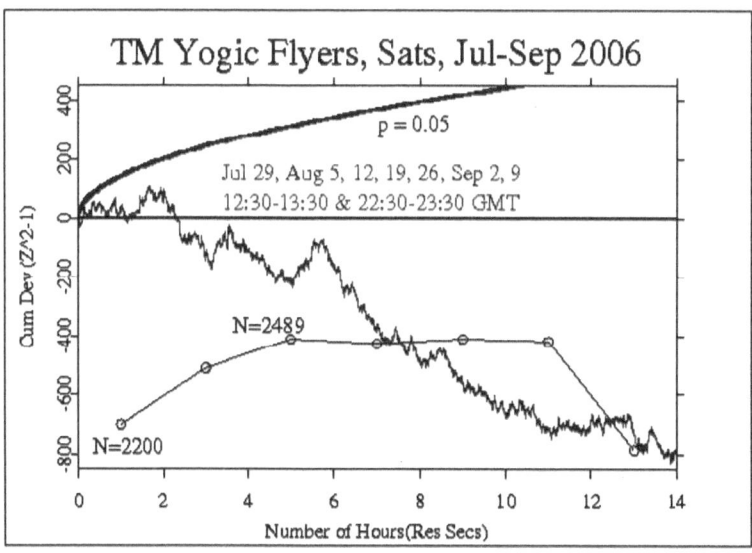

Figure 4.
Nearly 2500 TM Siddhi meditators gathered in Washington, DC, and Fairfield, IA, for daily meditations during the summer of 2006. Data for two sessions each Saturday were assessed. The network variance was consistently and significantly small. The points on the black line plot the number of meditators, which shows modest correlation with the size of the deviations.

CONCERN AND COMPASSION

In early 2003, concern about a possible war in Iraq was at the forefront of world news, and a focal issue for so many in the US and around the world that it seemed likely to provide other opportunities to test for the presence and activity of our hypothetical global consciousness. There were a number of major demonstrations in the US and in other countries. Many thousands or hundreds of thousands of people participated, and probably millions watched and joined in the shared feelings of concern. On the 15th of February, enormous numbers (literally millions) of people in the great cities of the world came together in demonstrations aimed to show worldwide support for peaceful resolution of the conflicts in Iraq and elsewhere in the Middle East. The GCP network seemed to respond. The data shown in the following figure are clearly random for the first few hours of the GMT day, but around 11:00, when people were assembling for major demonstrations in Berlin, Rome, and London, the composite measure departed from expectation with a steep trend that continued for the rest of the day.

Taking a careful scientific stance, we recognize that the deviation could be just a chance variation, but the timing and the strength of the trend are striking. In the context of similar outcomes for other events with global social impact, it seems justifiable to interpret the correlation at least tentatively as an effect of many millions of people expressly sharing their concern and compassion. Again, we must acknowledge that while there may be evidence of a subtle effect on the REG network, the forces of politics and economics driving world events remain far more powerful. Nevertheless, it is fair to say that these results support the intuition people have had from the beginning of culture that prayer and intention matter; that they can affect what happens in the world.

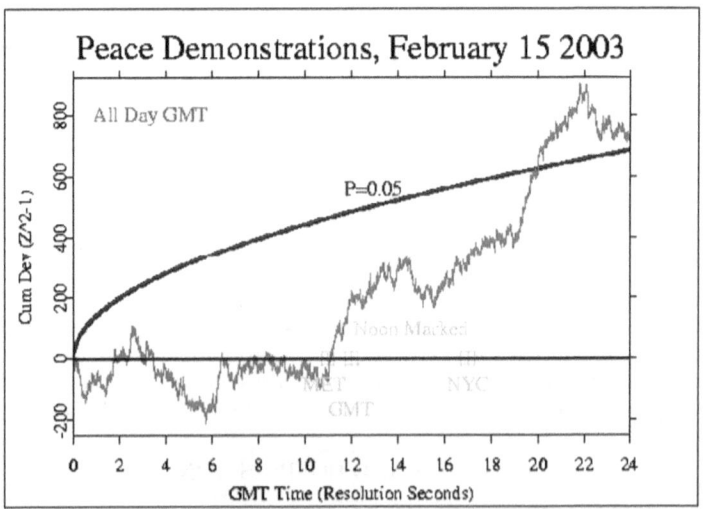

Figure 5.
Gathering great numbers to show opposition to the Iraq war, and support for peaceful solutions to political crises in the Middle East. A strong trend in the cumulative deviation begins at midday, corresponding to the timing of the major demonstrations.

CELEBRATIONS

Perhaps the most obvious global event for which widespread engagement can be predicted ahead of time is the celebration at New Years, in which there always is great interest and participation practically everywhere in the world, albeit with special intensity in the west. One of the first items entered in the GCP Hypothesis Registry was a prediction of nonrandom patterns in the data to be collected during a period of 10 minutes surrounding the midnight transition from 1998 to 1999. New Year celebrations are a time of shared thought and feeling. People feel relaxed and easy in groups whose focus is on friendship and on an optimistic vision of the future. We proposed to look for changes around midnight in each time zone, especially where there are widespread celebrations, using epoch averaging across all the time zones to compute statistics.

We now have 10 New Years for which we can test the hypothesis of correlated structure in the GCP data. One of our predictions is that the variance among the Eggs will decrease as midnight approaches, then, after midnight, will return to normal. There are some years with unimpressive results, but the composite outcome is persuasive. Averaged over all time zones and all years, the data show a pattern conforming to our prediction. There is a visually compelling decrease in variance centered on midnight, and it is statistically significant.

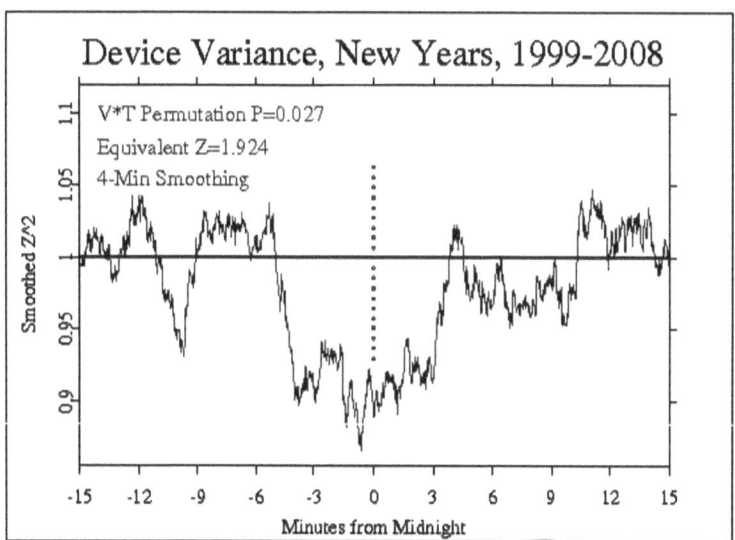

Figure 6.
Changes in the variance across Eggs during the New Year transition. The midnight epochs in 37 time zones are signal averaged for each year. The figure shows the composite of 10 New Years from 1998-1999 to 2007-2008.

Figure 6 shows this structure, and permutation analysis yields an estimated $p = 0.027$ that chance fluctuation accounts for the depth and proximity to midnight of the variance drop. The fact that this structure is linked with a *physically abstract* but *socially immanent* transition through a moment in time is worth noting. I think this distinction makes it clear that the effects in GCP data are associated with consciousness on a global scale, as it focuses and gathers into a coherent form.

POLITICAL PRESENCE

We have looked at a number of political events, which tend to show weak responses in the GCP data. But the 2008 presidential campaign, and to a lesser degree that in 2004 and 2000, did provide noteworthy results apparently reflecting tremendous, widespread interest. There are especially notable moments in Barack Obama's campaign. Our data show impressive deviations when he won the Democratic nomination ($p = 0.015$) and during his Denver acceptance speech ($p = 0.021$). The formal GCP event representing the national election was pre-defined as the 24-hour period beginning at 3 pm EST Nov 4. It also was positive though not statistically significant ($p = 0.164$). However, the period beginning with the closing of polls in the eastern US and growing certainty of a Democratic victory is striking. Figure 7 explores this defining moment.

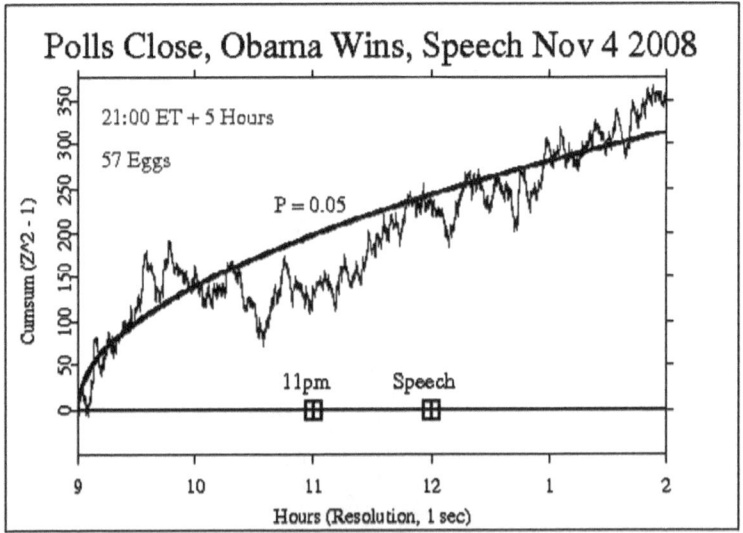

Figure 7.
November 4th 2008. Obama wins US Presidential election. Last polls close at 11 pm EST. Obama gives acceptance speech at about midnight to crowd of 100,000 in Grant Park.

The graph displays a five-hour period starting when it was clear that Obama had won the election, continuing through the official declaration at 11 pm EST and through Obama's Grant Park speech, followed by two more hours of celebration, which news reports showed was worldwide.

MULTIPLE PERSPECTIVES

The search for explanations and for causal relationships remains ahead of us, but work toward that end already yields interesting results. Over the past several years, the GCP analysis has benefited from applying an array of sophisticated and powerful statistical tools. (1) This work also constitutes an independent perspective confirming the original analyses. It begins with a rigorous normalization using empirical estimates for the mean and variance for each of the Eggs (this ensures that the results cannot be affected by the slight variations that are expected from real-world devices relative to theoretical randomness). Given the normalized data, it is possible to create new and very informative pictures, for example, visualizing long-term changes and structure. In addition to the event-based analysis, we can look at overall trends and at correlations of the data with external variables representing social issues and conditions.

In an earlier analysis from this perspective, we found that correlations among the Eggs are generally stronger when an independent measure of "news intensity" is high. (18) When we look at the database as a whole, we find that a long and steady trend begins late in 2001, and it can be established through analysis of statistical models that this trend is significant. This is a strong indication that our long-running database of physical random numbers is affected by external factors, which, if we can identify them, will richly inform our understanding. It seems especially appropriate to consider psychological or social measures with a global reach. Here we explore an interesting candidate measure, namely presidential approval ratings. The raw polling data over the past nine years are shown in Figure 8a (upper trace), with the GCP network variance during the same period for comparison. There is similarity in the overall trends, and suggestive matching of details. Figure 8b shows a simple model of the polling data that attempts to fit the GCP data and the parallel structure is striking. Not surprisingly, the parametric correlation is significant.

Thus, the overall variation of the long-term GCP data trace is correlated with a sociological measure, presidential approval rating, registered in repeated polling samples over the years. Again, this apparent relationship may very well be coincidental, but it is thought provoking. We also note that presidential approval rating is a US-centric measure, but the world-wide effects of decisions by the US president in the world make the polling data a useful window into the global state of consciousness.

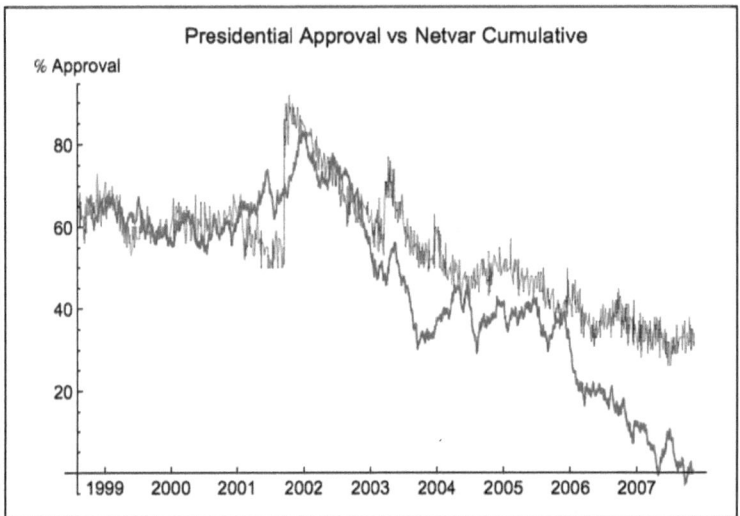

Figure 8a.
The full database network variance shows distinct trends that are not random fluctuations (lower dark trace). The upper trace shows raw presidential approval rating in multiple polls (lighter, jagged fluctuations). Both traces show more than 9 years of data.

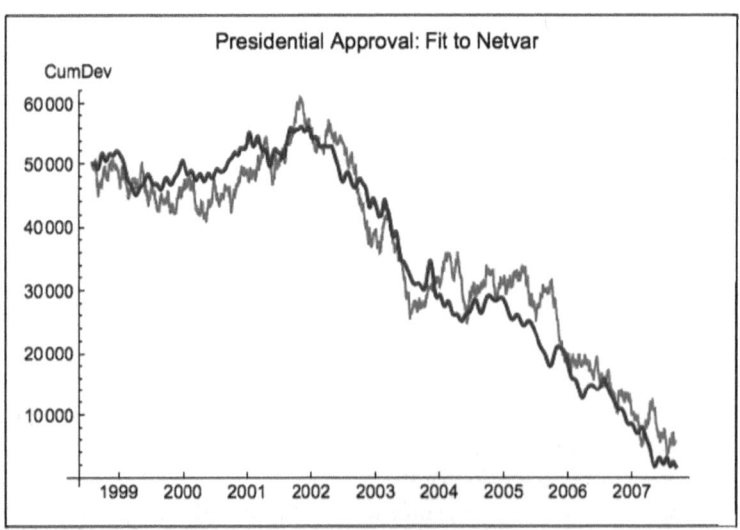

Figure 8b.
The trends in GCP data may be correlated with social measures such as presidential polling data, as suggested in Figure 8a. This figure compares a simple model of the polling data and GCP data; the smoother, dark curve is the from the polling data model, which uses only 2 parameters but provides a good fit. Analysis of both figures are by Peter Bancel.

Our ongoing work seeks to establish linkages with other indicators of broadly shared perceptions and emotional states. Although ratings and assignments are necessarily subjective and have intrinsic variability, it is possible to sort the 260-plus events into categories that represent various questions. For example, we can estimate the numbers of people engaged by the events and sort them into small, medium, and large categories with sufficient reliability to make useful comparisons. Simple t-tests of differences in effect size reveal that large events contribute most of the anomalous effect in the database; the difference between large and small is significant ($p = 0.017$, two-tailed). This accords with most observers' intuitions; it makes sense and acts like comparisons of a similar nature in psychology and sociology.

It is perhaps more interesting to look at emotions represented in the events. Doing so, we find that events categorized as having a high level of emotional impact are much more likely to affect the GCP network than those rated as medium or low in their emotional content (two-tailed $p = 0.004$ and 0.002, respectively). When we ask about types of emotions, we find that both negative and positive feelings (e. g., fear and love) are associated with strong effects in the GCP data at roughly the same level. Looking at specific emotions, we find that some stand out. For example, those events that evoke or embody a high level of compassion have a much larger effect size than those with a low rating (two-tailed $p = 0.025$). To summarize the findings in such investigations of the GCP data, it appears that our hypothesized global consciousness responds to events in ways that are recognizable, indeed quite familiar to us as individuals. (11)

THE BOTTOM LINE

In the first 10 years of the GCP, we have identified two or three major events every month, well suited for testing the notion that we may be able to detect effects of a shared state of consciousness. Some results are as striking as the pictures of New Year celebrations or September 11, while others show no suggestion at all of departures from expectation. As of December 2008, we have made 267 formal predictions. From these, it is possible to generate a bottom line assessment of the project's basic hypothesis that there will be a correlation of patterns in the REG data with special moments of widespread engagement of human attention by major events.

We might be able to ignore the data from a few such cases, or argue that if we look long enough we must find an occasional remarkable pattern in random fields, but structure appears in the random data more often than it should, and we have found that it does so in meaningful correlation with global events. Though we have more work to do, it is already clear that these correlations are material from which we can derive insights into the far-reaching capabilities of consciousness. The grand, composite result, shown graphically in Figure 9, represents the repeated confirmation of our simple hypothesis, and it clearly isn't just a chance fluctuation. The graph shows the cumulative departure from chance in more than 260 tests of the hypothesis that major global events will correlate with structure in data that should be truly random. It summarizes over 10 years of experience with the GCP network responding slightly but with statistical reliability during events of importance to people around the world. The odds that such a large accumulated departure from a random relationship would occur by chance are less than one in 10 million.

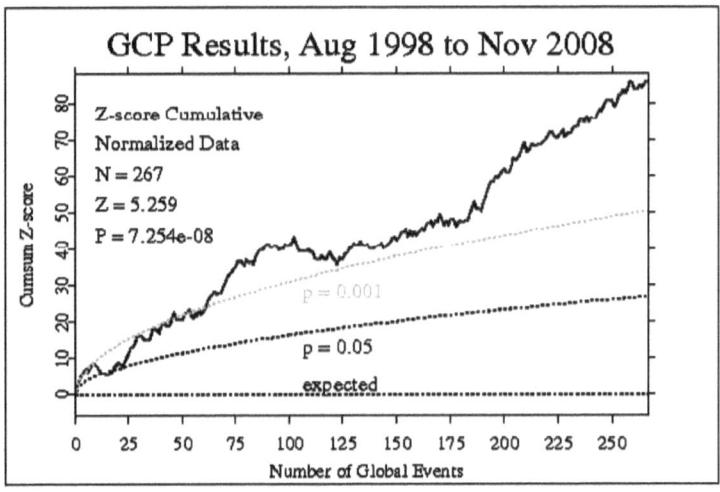

Figure 9.
Cumulative total deviation of results for 267 formal hypothesis tests. The dotted smooth curves show the 5% and 0.1% significance criteria. A truly random trace would fluctuate around a level trend at zero on the ordinate.

MEASURE AND MEANING

Defining global events is necessarily somewhat arbitrary, though there are cases that most people readily agree upon. For the sake of rigorous hypothesis testing, the basic requirement is that the event be chosen, the parameters set, and the analysis specified prior to examination of the data. The formal series of 267 global events all meet this standard. In addition, there are more general ways of assessing the data to see if there is any unexpected structure. The news intensity and long trend examples show that although our original analysis was focused on major events, we don't need to identify the events specifically, or even to know about them; correlated structure exists in any case. Retrospective analyses of classes of events are also possible, given the permanent archive of continuous data.

For example, we identified all major earthquakes of magnitude 6 and greater, dividing the 600 quakes found over the time we have been collecting data into those on land where people are affected, and those in the oceans. The quakes that affect humans show significant structure in the corresponding data; while the ocean quakes have no effect on the GCP network. (12)

Our primary results are based on correlating specially chosen moments, usually drawn from world news headlines, with data taken at the same time by the Egg network. When we assess the correlations carefully, we find a tendency for the data to be different from what is expected of random data, leaving only a few possibilities to consider. It may be that the interest and desires of the people involved in the project produce what is called an "experimenter effect" which is registered by the network. But the long-term trend linked with social measures, correlations among independent statistics, and retrospective findings like the earthquake differentiation are inconsistent with any simple version of an experimenter effect. There are several lines of convergent evidence that, although it may contribute, an anomalous experimenter effect is unlikely to be an adequate explanation for the structure found in our data.

It may also be that the nature of the question we ask somehow shapes the outcome, and there may be subtle contributions from other sources. The results are remarkable in any case, but I think it is fair to say that the pattern of correlations shows a primary influence linked with the events themselves. While we cannot at this point claim that "global consciousness" is the responsible agent, my detailed experience with the complete database leads me to believe it is a good candidate for a major role. That is, I think the deviations are most clearly and most strongly related to the important world events and human reactions to them as the main source of the effect. Overall, it is arguably simplest to interpret the anomalous trends in the data as evidence that something like our hypothesized global consciousness exists in a faint but detectable form and that it can affect our measurement system. But there are a number of challenging issues to address before drawing that conclusion as a final interpretive model.

We can be quite sure these results represent a genuine anomaly, but at this point, we cannot offer a definitive explanation. There are suggestions that might begin to explain these effects, although these remain speculative. One of the most promising physical models is drawn from David Bohm's theory of active information. (4) In his terms, this form of virtual information is nonlocal, extending indefinitely throughout space and time. Active information can be envisioned as a potential field interacting in and helping to guide manifestations from the implicate order into the physical world. Active information is thus virtual, but when a "need" for it exists, the need actualizes the information by creating (or being) a repository for it. In such a model, the question we ask in the Global Consciousness Project plays the role of a need for information, making it possible for the inchoate meaning of a major event resonating in human consciousness to manifest as subtle changes in the behavior of our detectors. The REG devices have an undetermined and hence labile future; in our context, they "need" information that will determine what happens. They manifest that information as nonrandom correlations or structure associated with the events that engage our thoughts and emotions.

Another promising, albeit metaphorical approach to a theoretical model is based on extrapolations of the principle of entanglement that is basic to quantum theory. Particles such as electrons that once have interacted remain entangled, so that even when great distances separate them, changes in the state of one of them will be found to correlate with changes in the other. Dean Radin develops this model in his book *Entangled Minds*, (19) and provides argument that although most of the evidence for entanglement is in the quantum domain, new findings show it occurring in complex atomic and molecular structures, and suggest that it may be a general feature of the world. Thus, even macroscopic objects and living beings, including humans, are entangled, though the evidence for this may be subtle and difficult to detect. Radin notes:

> Some scientists suggest that the remarkable degree of coherence displayed in living systems might depend in some fundamental way on quantum effects like entanglement. Others suggest that conscious awareness is caused or related in some important way to entangled particles in the brain. Some even propose that the entire universe is a single, self-entangled object.

This holds promise as a functional model to explain the existence of global consciousness.

Suggestions of a universal mind, made in many intellectual and cultural traditions, appear to have a modicum of support in the GCP results. The idea of a large-scale group consciousness, potentially engaging whole populations, gains some credence. At the very least, these results are consistent with the idea that a subtle linkage can exist between widely separated people, and that we may be interconnected on a grand scale by consciousness fields. It is interesting to consider that the GCP is itself the product of a sequence of unlikely "chance" meetings and connections. There is a reflexive irony in this, for the database produced by the collaboration allows us to examine distortions of chance itself, apparently wrought by consciousness reaching out to generate interconnections in the material world.

What should we take away from this scientific evidence of interconnection? If we are persuaded that the subtle structuring of random data does indicate an effect of human attention and emotion in the physical world, it points to a creative quality of consciousness. One implication is that what we envision may be slightly more likely to happen; a cooperative intent can have real consequences. This confers both a possibility and a responsibility on us for shaping our future as participants in a conscious evolution. A global consciousness will surely strive for evolution and spiritual growth, and will seek personal and planetary wellness. We must hope so, for it is clear that our future holds challenges of planetary scope, demanding a unifying and ultimately unitary view. We will want to be of one mind.

ACKNOWLEDGEMENTS

The Global Consciousness Project would not exist except for the immense contributions of Greg Nelson and John Walker, who created the architecture and the sophisticated software. Paul Bethke ported the Egg software to Windows, thus broadening the network. Dean Radin, Dick Bierman, and others in the planning group contributed ideas and experience. Rick Berger helped to create a comprehensive Web site to make the project available to the public. Peter Bancel has been a major contributor to the analytical program. The project also would not exist but for the commitment of time, resources, and good will from all the Egg hosts. Our financial support comes from individuals including Charles Overby, Tony Cohen, Reinhilde Nelson, Michael Heany, Alexander Imich, Richard Adams, Richard Wallace, Anna Capasso, Michael Breland, Joseph Giove, J. Z. Knight, Hans Wendt, Jim Warren, and major donations from an anonymous contributor. We also gratefully acknowledge donations via PayPal from many individuals. The Institute of Noetic Sciences provides logistical support as a nonprofit home for the project, and the Lifebridge Foundation has provided generous support for documentation of the GCP. Finally, there are very many friends of the Egg project whose good will, interest, and empathy open a necessary niche in consciousness space.

> *Observations of this kind banish to the historical archives the myths of mechanistic science that portrays consciousness, life, and creative intelligence as epiphenomena of matter and as insignificant accidents in the evolution of the universe. In light of the new data, consciousness appears to be an equal partner of matter or even a principle supraordinated to it.*
>
> --- **Stanislav Grof**
> --- *When the Impossible Happens*

REFERENCES AND NOTES

1) Bancel, P.A. & Nelson, R.D. (2008) "Rigorous exploration of GCP data: Correlations, structure, implications." In: *J. Scientific Exploration*, 22;3, pp. 309-333.
2) Bierman, D.J. (1996) "Exploring correlations between local emotional and global emotional events and the behavior of a random number generator." In: *J. Scientific Exploration*, V.10;3, pp. 363-374.
3) Bierman, D.J. & Radin, D.I. (1997) "Anomalous anticipatory response on randomized future conditions." In: *Perceptual and Motor Skills*, 84, 689-690.
4) Bohm, D. (1980) *Wholeness and the Implicate Order*. Boston: Routledge & Kegan Paul.
5) Dunne, B.J. & Jahn, R.G. (1992) "Experiments in remote human/machine interaction." In: *J. Scientific Exploration*, V.6;4, pp. 311-332.
6) Haldane, J.B.S. (1932) "Essay on science & ethics." In: *The Inequality of Man and Other Essays*. London: Chatto and Windus.
7) Jahn, R.G., Dunne, B.J., Nelson, R.D. (1987) "Engineering anomalies research." In: *J. Scientific Exploration*. V.1;1, pp. 21-50.
8) Jahn, R.G., Dunne, B.J., Nelson, R.D., Dobyns, Y.H., Bradish, G.J. (1997) "Correlations of random binary sequences with pre-stated operator intention: A review of a 12-year program." In: *J. Scientific Exploration*, V.11;3, pp. 345-368.
9) Nelson, R.D. (1997) "Multiple field REG/RNG recordings during a global event." In: *The Electronic Journal for Anomalous Phenomena (eJAP)*.
Originally published at http://m0134.fmg.uva.nl/-djb/psi/ejap.
Now available at http://noosphere.princeton.edu/ejap/gaiamind/1997_2.html.
10) Nelson, R.D. (2002) "Coherent consciousness and reduced randomness: Correlations on September 11, 2001." In: *J. Scientific Exploration*, 16;4, pp. 549-570.
11) Nelson, R.D. (2008) "Emotions in global consciousness." In: *Proceedings of the 7th Symposium of the Bial Foundation*, Porto, Portugal, in press.
12) Nelson, R.D. & Bancel, P.A. (2006) "Anomalous anticipatory responses in networked random data." In: *Frontiers of Time: Retrocausation — Experiment and Theory*, (Ed.) Daniel P. Sheehan, AIP Conference Proceedings, Vol. 863.
13) Nelson, R.D., Boesch, H., Boller, E., Dobyns, Y.H., Houtkooper, J., Lettieri, A., Radin, D.I., Russek, L., Schwartz, G., Wesch, J. (1998) "Global resonance of consciousness: Princess Diana and Mother Teresa." In: *The Electronic Journal for Anomalous Phenomena (eJAP)*.
Originally published at http://m0134.fmg.uva.nl/-djb/psi/ejap.
Now available at http://noosphere.princeton.edu/ejap/diana/1998_1.html.
14) Nelson, R.D., Bradish, G.J., Dobyns, Y.H., Dunne, B.J., Jahn, R.G. (1996) "FieldREG anomalies in group situations." In: *J. Scientific Exploration*, V.10;1, pp. 111-141.
15) Nelson, R.D., Bradish, G.J., Dobyns, Y.H., Dunne, B.J., Jahn, R.G. (1998) "FieldREG II: Consciousness field effects: Replications and explorations." In: *J. Scientific Exploration*, V.12;3, pp. 425-454.
16) Nelson, R.D. & Radin, D.I. (2003) "FieldREG experiments and group consciousness: Extending REG/RNG research to real-world situations." In: Jonas, W. & Crawford, C. (Eds.), *Healing, Intention and Energy Medicine*. London: Harcourt Health Sciences.
17) Nelson, R.D., Radin, D.I., Shoup, R., & Bancel, P.A. (2002) "Correlations of continuous random data with major world events." In: *Foundations of Physics Letters*, 15, 6, 537-550.

18) Radin, D.I. (2002) "Exploring relationships between random physical events and mass human attention: Asking for whom the bell tolls." In: *J. Scientific Exploration*, 16;4, pp. 533-548.
19) Radin, D.I. (2006) *Entangled Minds: Extrasensory Experiences in a Quantum Reality*. NY: Paraview Pocket Books, Simon and Shuster, Inc.
20) Radin, D.I. & Nelson, R.D. (1989) "Evidence for consciousness-related anomalies in random physical systems." In: *Foundations of Physics*, V.19;12, pp. 1499-1514.
21) Radin, D.I. & Nelson, R.D. (2003) "Meta-analysis of mind-matter interaction experiments: 1959 - 2000." In: Jonas, W. & Crawford, C. (Eds.), *Healing, Intention and Energy Medicine*. London: Harcourt Health Sciences.
22) Radin, D.I., Rebman, J.M. & Cross, M.P. (1996) "Anomalous organization of random events by group consciousness: Two exploratory experiments." In: *J. Scientific Exploration*, V.10;1, pp. 143-168.
23) Teilhard de Chardin, P. (1959) *The Phenomenon of Man*. NY: Harper & Row, Publishers.
24) Vernadsky, V.I. (1926, 1986) *The Biosphere*, first published in Russian in 1926. English translation: Oracle, A.Z., Synergetic Press.

> *As the GCP demonstrates, a major incident can amplify the emotions of millions of people around the world to have an effect on random event generators, whether it be the shock of disaster or the joy of success. The media reporting the incident uses the EM frequencies of basic electricity (50Hz or 60Hz). In addition, TV uses either VHF (very high frequencies) or UHF (ultra high frequencies). The same sound bites and flickering images of the event are shown by the media continuously to amplify the hypnotic effects.*
>
> *What if those millions of people choose to turn OFF their TVs at the same time, and instead focused all of their emotions of love and compassion on our planet? Earth frequencies are in the ELF (extremely low frequency) range—longer and slower than VHF, at 7.4HZ to 7.8Hz. We now know that the frequencies of our hearts and minds are more attuned to these slower vibrations.*
>
> *--- Jean Millay*

Jacques Vallee, PhD

Jacques F. Vallee was born in France, where he received a BS in mathematics at the Sorbonne (1959) and an MS in astrophysics at Lille University (1961). He came to the US as an astronomer at the U of Texas, where he codeveloped the first computer-based map of Mars for NASA (1963). He later moved to Northwestern U where he received his PhD in computer science (1967). He went on to work on information technology research at SRI International and the Institute for the Future, where he directed the project to build the world's first network-based conferencing system as a Principal Investigator for the groupware project on Arpanet, the prototype network for the Internet (1973-76).

Dr Vallee has been a venture capitalist since 1984, and has served as an early-stage investor and director of many companies. Apart from his work with information technology and finance, he has had a long-term private interest in astronomy, in writing and in the frontiers of research. His most recent book *The Heart of the Internet* is available free of charge on Google Books. He was awarded the Jules Verne Prize for a science fiction novel in French. Among his major books are *Anatomy of a Phenomenon* (1965), *Challenge to Science* (1966), *Messengers of Deception* (1975), *Passport to Magonia* (1969), his "Trilogy": *Dimensions, Confrontations, Revelations* available from Anomalist Books and his Journals, entitled *Forbidden Science* (volume I and II). He was always a favorite speaker at PRG meetings.

Website: http://www.jacquesvallee.com/

CHAPTER 40   A CHALLENGE OF HIGH STRANGENESS

Eric W. Davis, PhD

Eric W. Davis earned an AA in Liberal Arts from Phoenix College (1981), a BSc in Physics-Mathematics (1983) and PhD in Astrophysics (1991) from the University of Arizona. He is a Senior Research Physicist at the Institute for Advanced Studies at Austin and the CEO of Warp Drive Metrics. His research specializations include breakthrough propulsion physics, general relativity theory, quantum field theory, the search for extraterrestrial intelligence, and interstellar spaceflight. He was a technical contributor and consultant to the NASA Breakthrough Propulsion Physics Program (1997-2002). His professional experience includes aerospace phenomenology research at NIDS/Bigelow Aerospace Co. (1996-2002); research associate at the Voyager Ultraviolet Spectrometer Experiment Group (Voyager 1 & 2 missions to the outer planets) (1985-1991) and research assistant at the Infrared Astronomical Satellite Group (1984-1985), University of Arizona. He taught at the University of Maryland University College (1995-1996), Pima College (1991-1995), and the Community College of Southern Nevada (2004).

Dr Davis is a Fellow of the British Interplanetary Society, Associate Fellow of the AIAA, member of the New York Academy of Sciences, member of the American Astronomical Society, and member of the American Institute of Beamed Energy Propulsion.

INCOMMENSURABILITY, ORTHODOXY AND THE PHYSICS OF HIGH STRANGENESS: A 6–LEVEL MODEL FOR UNIDENTIFIED AEROSPACE PHENOMENA

Jacques F. Vallee
Eric W. Davis

National Institute for Discovery Science
Las Vegas, Nevada [*1]

ABSTRACT

The main argument presented in this paper is that the continuing study of unidentified aerial phenomena ("UAP") may offer an existence theorem for new models of physical reality. The current SETI paradigm and its "assumption of mediocrity" place restrictions on forms of nonhuman intelligence that may be researched. A similar bias exists in the ufologists' often-stated hypothesis that UAP, if real, must represent space visitors. Observing that both models are biased by anthropomorphism, the authors attempt to clarify the issues surrounding "high strangeness" observations by distinguishing six levels of information that can be derived from UAP events, namely (1) physical manifestations, (2) anti-physical effects, (3) psychological factors, (4) physiological factors, (5) psychic effects and (6) cultural effects. In a further step they propose a framework for scientific analysis of unidentified aerial phenomena that takes into account the incommensurability problem.

[*1] Based on a presentation at the Forum on *"Science, Religion and Consciousness"* held at the University Fernando Pessoa, Porto (Portugal), October 23-24 2003.

THE CHALLENGE OF HIGH STRANGENESS

The rational study of reported cases of Unidentified Aerospace Phenomena (UAP) is currently at an impasse. This situation has as much to do with the incomplete state of our models of physical reality as it does with the complexity of the data. A primary objection to the reality of UAP events among scientists is that witnesses consistently report objects whose seemingly absurd behavior "cannot possibly" be related to actual phenomena, even under extreme conditions. Skeptics insist that intelligent extraterrestrial (ETI) visitors simply would not perpetrate such antics as are reported in the literature. This argument can be criticized as an anthropocentric, self-selected observation resulting from our own limited viewpoint as twenty-first century Homo sapiens trying to draw conclusions about the nature of the universe. Nonetheless, the high strangeness of many reports must be acknowledged.

Advocates of UAP reality, on the other hand, generally claim that the Extra-Terrestrial Hypothesis (ETH) centered on interstellar travelers from extra-solar systems visiting the Earth is the most likely explanation for the objects and the entities associated with them. This argument, too, can be challenged on the basis of the witnesses' own testimony: Ufologists have consistently ignored or minimized reports of seemingly absurd UAP behaviors that contradict the ETH, by selectively extracting data that best fits their agenda or version of the ETH. Thus the ETH, just like the skeptical argument, is based on anthropocentric self-selection. (18) Here we are witnessing an interesting overlap between the SETI and UAP paradigms: Each excludes consideration of the other when laying claim to the legitimate search for and contact with potential nonhuman intelligence.

In the view of the authors, current hypotheses are not strange enough to explain the facts of the phenomenon, and the debate suffers from a lack of scientific information. Indeed, from the viewpoint of modern physics, our Cosmic Neighborhood could encompass other (parallel) universes, extra-spatial dimensions and other time-like dimensions beyond the common 4-dimensional spacetime we recognize, and such aspects could lead to rational explanations for apparently "incomprehensible" behaviors on the part of visitors to our perceived continuum. As it attempts to reconcile theory with observed properties of elementary particles and with discoveries at the frontiers of cosmology, modern physics suggests that mankind has not yet discovered all of the universe's facets, and we must propose new theories and experiments in order to explore these undiscovered facets. *This is why continuing study of reported UAP events is important: It may provide us with an existence theorem for new models of physical reality.*

Much of the recent progress in cosmological concepts is directly applicable to the UAP problem: Traversable wormholes (3-dimensional hypersurface tunnels) have now been derived from Einstein's General Theory of Relativity. (7, 19) In particular, it has been shown that Einstein's General Theory of Relativity does not in any way constrain spacetime topology, which allows for wormholes to provide traversable connections between regions within two separate universes or between remote regions and/or times within the same universe. Mathematically it can also be shown that higher-dimensional wormholes can provide hypersurface connections between multi-dimensional spaces. (10, 5) Recent quantum gravity programs have explored this property in superstring theory, along with proposals to theoretically and experimentally examine macroscopic-scale extra-dimensional spaces. (11) Thus it is now widely acknowledged that the nature of our universe is far more complex than observations based on anthropocentric self-selection portend. In this respect, ufologists and SETI researchers appear to be fighting a rear-guard battle. Both suffer from identical limitations in the worldview they bring to their own domains, and to their antagonism.

ANTHROPOCENTRIC BIAS IN THE *SETI* AND *UAP* PARADIGMS

The anthropocentric biases in the SETI program are evident in the present search paradigm. Historically the founders of SETI defined the search paradigm from a series of complex arguments and assumptions that led to the creation of a "SETI orthodox view" of interstellar communication while applying the "assumption of mediocrity" to our known present technological capabilities. (8)

This approach was predicated on the notion that it was economically cheaper and technologically easier to generate and receive radio-wave photons for interstellar signaling rather than engage manned interstellar travel or robotic probes. Indeed the latter was considered economically and technologically improbable within the "SETI orthodox view." This has led to four decades of the SETI program following a dominantly radio/microwave (RMW) oriented search scheme.

Given the failure of this initial approach, in the last two decades alternative SETI programs have been proposed. They exploit coherent laser optical/IR (COSETI), holographic signals and worldwide web detection schemes, as well as ideas to search for ETI artifacts (SETA, or astroarchaeology) and visiting probes (SETV, V=visitation) in the solar system or on Earth. (13)

There are new proposed search schemes based on the application of high-energy (particle) physics detection, such as modulated neutrino beams, X-rays, gamma rays, and cosmic rays, etc. Other search schemes propose looking for artificially generated excess radiation emissions from astronomical bodies in space or for high-energy radiation starship exhaust trails (Matloff, personal communication, 1998).

These new programs have been at odds with members of the dominant RMW-SETI program, possibly because of concern over having to share scarce resources or compete with other non-RMW programs for the very limited private funding available for overall SETI research.

The community of UAP researchers is also driven by its own orthodoxy, which is only violated at great personal risk to the critic who proposes a deviant view, and by its own "principle of mediocrity" when attempting to categorize and hypothesize explanations for the phenomenon. For this reason we prefer to use the term "UAP" rather than the more common "UFO," which is immediately associated with the idea of space visitors in the mind of the public and media. Yet a bridge could be formed between the disparate SETI and UFOlogy communities if both would only recognize a simple fact: *No experiment can distinguish between phenomena manifested by visiting interstellar (arbitrarily advanced) ETI and intelligent entities that may exist near Earth within a parallel universe or in different dimensions, or who are (terrestrial) time travelers.*

Each of these interesting possibilities can be manifested via the application of the physical principle of traversable wormholes since they theoretically connect between two different universes, two remote space locations, different times and dimensions. (1) Traversable wormholes are but one example of new physical tools that are available or on the horizon for consideration of interuniversal, interstellar, inter-dimensional or chronological travel.

This leads the present authors to speculate that a new synthesis can be found by examining the full context of the UAP phenomenon — including its apparently "absurd" characteristics — in terms of a six-level model. The model uses the framework of the incommensurability problem and concepts borrowed from semiotics.

UAP - THE NEED FOR A UNIFIED APPROACH

What we present here is a new framework for UAP analysis that takes into account the lessons from SETI. In any scientific question it must be possible to ascertain to what extent a hypothesis, when tested and proven to be true, actually "explains" the observed facts. In the case of UAP, however, as in physics generally, a hypothesis may well be "proven true" while an apparently contradictory hypothesis is also proven true. Thus the hypothesis that the phenomenon of light is caused by particles is true, but so is the opposite hypothesis that it is caused by waves. We must be prepared for the time when we will be in a position to formulate scientific hypotheses for UAP, and then we may face a similar situation.

The framework we present here is based on such an apparent contradiction, because we will argue that UAP can be thought of both as physical and as "psychic." We hope that it will prove stimulating as a unified approach to a puzzling phenomenon that presents both undeniable physical effects suggesting a technological device or craft *and* psychic effects reminiscent of the literature on poltergeists and psychokinetic phenomena. Here we use the word "psychic" in the sense of an interaction between physical reality and human consciousness.

The feeling of absurdity and contradiction in these two aspects is not worse than scientific puzzlement during the particle/wave or, more recently, quantum entanglement and multi-dimensional transport controversies. The contradiction has to do with the inadequacy of our language to grasp a phenomenon that defies our attempts at classification.

THE SIX LEVELS OF UAP ANALYSIS

Let us consider the characteristics of the sightings that are not explained by trivial natural causes; we can recognize six major "levels" in terms of our perceptions of these characteristics, as they can be extracted from earlier works about UAP phenomenology (16, 17) or from the current NIDS database.

Level I: First of all is the **physical level**, evident in most witness accounts describing an object that

- occupies a position in space, consistent with geometry
- moves as time passes
- interacts with the environment through thermal effects
- exhibits light absorption and emission from which power output estimates can be derived
- produces turbulence
- when landed, leaves indentations and burns from which mass and energy figures can be derived
- gives rise to photographic images
- leaves material residue consistent with Earth chemistry
- gives rise to electric, magnetic and gravitational disturbances

Thus UAP, in a basic physical sense, are consistent with a technology centered on a craft that appears to be using a revolutionary propulsion system.

Level II: For lack of an adequate term we will call the second level **anti-physical**. The variables are the same as those in the previous category but they form patterns that conflict with those predicted by modern physics: Objects are described as physical and material but they are also described as

- sinking into the ground
- shrinking in size, growing larger, or changing shape on the spot
- becoming fuzzy and transparent on the spot
- dividing into two or more craft, several of them merging into one object at slow speed
- disappearing at one point and appearing elsewhere instantaneously
- remaining observable visually while not detected by radar
- producing missing time or time dilatation
- producing topological inversion or space dilatation (object was estimated to be of small exterior size/volume, but witness(es) saw a huge interior many times the exterior size)
- appearing as balls of colored, intensely bright light under intelligent control

Level III: The third level has to do with the **psychology** of the witnesses and the *social* conditions that surround them. Human observers tend to see UAP while in their normal environment and in normal social groupings. They perceive the objects as nonconventional but they try to explain them away as common occurrences, until faced with the inescapable conclusion that the object is truly unknown.

Level IV: Physiological reactions are another significant level of information. The phenomenon is reported to cause

- sounds (beeping, buzzing, humming, sharp/piercing whistling, wooshing/air rushing, loud/deafening roaring, sound of a storm, etc.)
- vibrations
- burns
- partial paralysis
- extreme heat or cold sensation
- odors (powerful, sweet or strange fragrance, rotten eggs, sulphurous, pungent, musky, etc.)
- metallic taste
- pricklings
- temporary blindness when exposed to the objects' light

- nausea
- bloody nose and/or ears; severe headache
- difficulty in breathing
- loss of volition
- drowsiness in the days following a close encounter

Level V: The fifth category of effects can only be labeled **psychic** because it involves a class of phenomena commonly found in the literature of parapsychology, such as

- impressions of communication without a direct sensory channel
- poltergeist phenomena: motions and sounds without a specific cause, outside the observed presence of a UAP
- levitation of the witness or of objects and animals in the vicinity
- maneuvers of a UAP appearing to anticipate the witness' thoughts
- premonitory dreams or visions
- personality changes promoting unusual abilities in the witness
- healing

Level VI: The sixth category could be called **cultural.** It is concerned with society's reactions to the reports, the way in which secondary effects (hoaxes, fiction and science-fiction imagery, scientific theories, cover-up or exposure, media censorship or publicity, sensationalism, etc.) become generated, and the attitude of members of a given culture toward the concepts that UAP observations appear to challenge. The greatest impact of the phenomenon has been on general acceptance of the idea of life in space and a more limited, but potentially very significant, change in the popular concept of nonhuman intelligence.

POSSIBLE NATURE OF UAP TECHNOLOGY

A framework for scientific hypothesis on the UAP observations can be built on the identification (admittedly very coarse) of the six major levels of UAP effects. If we must formulate a view of the problem in a single statement at this point, that statement will be:

> UAPs are the product of a technology that integrates physical and psychic phenomena and primarily affects cultural variables in our society through manipulation of physiological and psychological parameters in the witnesses.

This single statement can be developed as follows:
The phenomenon is the product of a technology. During the

observation, the UAP is a real, physical, material object. However, it appears to use either very clever deception or very advanced physical principles, resulting in the effects we have called "anti-physical," which must eventually be reconciled with the laws of physics.

The technology triggers psychic effects either purposely or as a side effect of its manifestations. These consciousness phenomena are now too common to be ignored or relegated to the category of exaggerated or ill-observed facts. All of us who have investigated close-range sightings have become familiar with these effects.

The purpose of the technology may be cultural manipulation — possibly but not necessarily under control of a form of nonhuman intelligence — in which case the physiological and psychological effects are a means to that end. But the parapsychologist with a Jungian framework may argue that the human collective unconscious is also a potential source of such effects — without the need to invoke alien intervention.

THE INCOMMENSURABILITY PROBLEM

Many SETI workers now realize that we cannot be so presumptuous as to assume that ET cultures, possessing a cognitive mismatch with us, will behave as humans do in the twenty-first century. Specifically, there is no reason to restrict them to radio-based communications technology and to exclude travel through interstellar space or the sending of automated probes. Thus the SETV/SETA program overlaps ETH-based UFOlogy. Both are dedicated to detecting nonhuman intelligence on or near the Earth, demonstrating a paradigm shift away from the "SETI orthodox view" and principle of mediocrity.

The view that ETs and humans may have such divergent ways of conceptualizing the world that there can be no mutual understanding is referred to as the "Incommensurability Problem" in the SETI literature. (15) (D. A. Vakoch, private communication, 1999.) The cognitive mismatch or Incommensurability Problem between human and ET cultures will guarantee that the latter will develop communication techniques other than radio. ET cultures may be sending radio and optical signals to Earth now but they may also be sending signals in a variety of other forms such as holographic images, psychic or other consciousness-related signals, modulated neutrinos, gamma ray bursters, wormhole-modulated starlight caustics, signals generated by gravitational lensing techniques, modulated X-rays, quantum teleported signals, or some quantum field theoretic effect, etc. The Incommensurability Problem even applies to the problem of understanding UAP manifestations within the framework of the ETH.

At the core of the Incommensurability Problem is the view that no intelligent species can understand reality without making certain methodological choices, and that these choices may vary from civilization to civilization. (15) If ETs and UAP entities have different biologies and live in considerably different environments from humans, they may well have different goals for their science, and radically different criteria for evaluating the success of their science. Their explanatory mechanisms, their predictive concerns, their modes of control over nature might all be very different, and their means of formulating models of reality should be expected to differ drastically from ours. (9)

In this regard, there is one additional feature that needs to be mentioned in support of alternative SETI paradigms. The SETI program's encryption/decryption emphasis on pictorial images or messages is predicated on the assumption that ETs have sight like humans vis-à-vis the "SETI orthodox view." (8) We observe that this emphasis is not so much a reflection of the primacy of vision in humans, but rather a reflection of the philosophical assumptions about the proper means of gaining knowledge. Hence, anthropocentric self-selection becomes manifest within the SETI and UFOlogy "orthodox view."

Michel Foucault asserts that human reliance on science is based on studying visible characteristics of objects. (2) The belief that true knowledge must be acquired from sight originated in the seventeenth century. This emphasis on sight led to eliminating the other senses as potentially valuable sources of scientific information.

Without even raising the question of whether ETs or UAP entities can "see," we may be wise not to overestimate the importance of pictorial representations for them. The same applies for ET/UAP transmissions to us. We can see and gain knowledge by sight, but ET/UAP signals potentially bombarding the Earth could be misunderstood, unrecognized or undetected because we are not employing paradigms involving our other modalities, such as psychic functioning. Many examples of this are found in interactions between humans from different cultures. (4)

Because we cannot be certain of the nature of ET/UAP recipients of our deliberate messages and they cannot be certain of our nature when sending us their messages *a priori*, it is difficult to construct pictures that will be unambiguous. To some extent, ET/UAP viewers of our pictograms may project characteristics from their own species-specific experiences onto our messages, and we certainly project our own species-specific experiences onto their messages. The former may be the cause for the lack of detected ET signals (save for those 100+ radio and optical signals which were not false positives but also not repeated by their source) while the latter can be the cause of the current impasse in the study of UAP phenomena.

SEMIOTICS

In his analysis of the communication problem SETI Institute psychologist D. A. Vakoch has advocated the application of semiotics, the general theory of signs (D. A. Vakoch, private communication, 1999), where a sign is something that represents something else — the signified. For example the words "the coin" might represent the object you hold in your hand.

In interstellar messages, in terms of classical information theory, there is no innate relationship between the form of the message and the content borne by the message. Once the information of the message is decided upon, an efficient means of encoding it is sought. In this approach, there is a purely arbitrary connection between content and form of the message. Semiotic-based messages have a wider range of possibilities for relating form and content.

Semioticians categorize signs according to the ways that the sign and signified are related to one another. In the association between the sign "the coin" and its signified object, this relationship is purely arbitrary. The sign for this object could have well been "the poofhoffer." This is a purely conventional association. In semiotics, when the association between sign and signified is arbitrary, the sign is referred to as a symbol. With symbols, there is no intrinsic connection between the form of expression (the sign) and the content that is expressed (the signified).

There are alternatives to the arbitrary connection between sign and signified that are seen in symbols. One alternative is the icon, a sign that bears a physical resemblance to the signified. With icons, the form of the message reflects its contents. For example, the profile of the man on a modern American quarter is an icon for a specific man who was the first President of the United States. We can also represent the same man with the symbol "George Washington." In the former case, the image of Washington is an icon because it physically resembles the signified. Icons can also be used when the signified is less concrete. For example, the scales of justice icon represents the concept of justice because there is similarity between the sign (scales that balance two weights) and the signified (concept of justice, which involves a balance between transgression and punishment).

It is also helpful to realize that icons are not specific to the visual sensory modality. It is possible to have a sign that physically resembles the signified in a nonvisual way. For example, the fly Spilomyla hamifera beats its wings at a frequency very close to the wing-beat frequency of the dangerous wasp Dolichovespula arenaria. As a result, when one of these flies is in the vicinity of a group of these wasps, the fly gains some immunity from attack by insect-eating birds. The fly's mimicry of the wasps occurs within the auditory modality. It is not attacked by would-be predators because it sounds like the wasps. In short, the fly's defense strategy is based on producing an auditory icon, in which the fly's wing-beating (the sign) physically resembles the wing-beat of the wasps (the signified). (D. A. Vakoch, private communication, 1999.)

Icons could function in any sensory modality. Given that we are not sure which sensory modality will be primary for ETs/UAP, a sign for communication that is not reliant on any particular sensory modality would be preferable. In SETI/CETI, electromagnetic radiation is used as an iconic representation, allowing a direct communication of concepts (Earth chemistry, solar system organization, human DNA, math, geometry, etc.) without encoding the message into a format specific to a particular sensory modality. In using icons, the message's recipients are pointed directly toward the phenomena of interest, and not toward our models of these phenomena.

From a more complete perspective, the sign and the signified are in a triadic with the interpreter of the relationship. Thus, the similarity that exists between an icon and its referent does not exist independently of the intelligence perceiving this similarity. Although in iconicity there is a natural connection between the sign and the signified, this connection cannot exist without intelligence to observe the connection.

Ultimately, the problem of iconicity is that similarity is in the eye of the beholder. And because we do not know what ETs/UAP are really like, we cannot be sure that what to us seems an obvious similarity will be seen as such by an intelligence with a different biology, culture, and history, possibly originating in a different universe. Thus, judgment of similarity is not purely objective, but is influenced by a variety of factors that impact conventions of interpretation.

THE UAP AND ABDUCTION PROBLEM

The aforementioned behavior of UAP is not really so absurd. This "absurdity" is merely a reflection of the cognitive mismatch or the "Incommensurability Problem" that exists between humans and the phenomenon.

In this particular case, UAP are sending the message and we are the recipients. The message(s) they are sending to us are icons. These icons are fashioned by the phenomenon and sent to us via various sensory modalities. The difference between our respective cultures, biologies, sensory modalities, histories, dimensional existence, physical evolution, models of nature and science, etc. is directly responsible for our lack of understanding of the phenomenon and its message. We cannot see what UAP believe to be (iconical) similarities in the message that is intended for us. These stated differences directly impact our conventions of interpretation in such a way as to impair our recognition of the "similarity" between the sign and the signified contained within the icons of the UAP message, further impairing our ability to "see and understand" the potential message.

The difference between the sensory modalities of UAP entities and humans is responsible for our inability to properly detect the UAP message (icons) and correspond with them. This difference may also prevent us from correctly interpreting what their icons are if we do in fact recognize them. In this regard, recall that we will project our own species-specific experiences onto their icons (messages) thus manifesting the appearance of "absurdity" during the human-UAP interaction.

UFO abduction cases may exemplify this, in the sense that the "absurd" activities (or scenes) concurrent with abduction events could merely be the iconical defense mechanism deployed by the UAP to protect itself from the victim/subject much like the way Spilomyia hamifera protects itself from insect-eating birds by mimicry.

Kuiper (6) and Freitas (3) suggest that Ets/UAP visiting Earth would find it necessary to hide themselves from our detection mechanisms until they have assessed our technological level or potential threat and hazards. They would employ an adaptive multi-level risk program to avoid danger. Low observable stealth such as simple camouflage through mimicry, which works well in nature, may be the technique of choice for visiting UAP/ETI experienced in surveillance. (12) Examples of mimicry techniques are UAP/ETI entering the atmosphere with either the look or trajectory of a meteor or hidden within a meteor shower, behaving like dark meteors without the associated optical signature, hiding within an artificial or natural cloud or a satellite reentry, behaving as pseudo-stars sitting stationary over certain regions, or mimicking man-made aircraft's aggregate features. (13) Another possibility is mimicry techniques employed for the manipulation of human consciousness to induce the various manifestations of "absurd" interactions or scenery associated with the encounter.

CONCLUSION

Modern engineering has made us familiar with display technologies that produce three-dimensional images with color, motion and perspective through physical devices. We speculate that UAP are analogous to these display technologies but utilize a wider range of variables to operate on the percipients and, through them, on human culture. The long time scale and the global nature of the effects make it difficult to test hypotheses involving such cultural effects.

Science fiction has familiarized us with the concept of machines (or beings) projecting an image of themselves that systematically confuses observers. One could imagine that UAP represent physical craft equipped with the means to interact both with the surrounding atmosphere and with the senses of observers in such a way as to convey a false image of their real nature. One could argue that such an object could use microwave devices to create perceptual hallucinations in the witnesses (including messages that are heard by a single individual in a group).

Even such a complex scheme, however, fails to explain all the reported effects and the subsequent behavior changes in close-range witnesses. We must assume something more, the triggering of deep-seated processes within their personality. The question then becomes: To what extent are these effects evidence of a purposeful action of the operators? To answer this question, and to test more fully the hypothesis that UAP phenomena are both physical and psychic in nature, we need much better investigations, a great upgrading of data quality, and a more informed analysis not only of the object being described, but of the impact of the observation on the witnesses and their social environment.

REFERENCES

1) Davis, E.W. (2001) "Wormhole-Stargates: Tunneling through the cosmic neighborhood." In: *MUFON 2001 International UFO Symposium Proceedings*, Irvine, CA, pp. 32-50.
2) Foucault, M. (1966) *The Order of Things*, trans. by A. Sheridan. NY: Random House.
3) Freitas, R.A., (1980) "A self-reproducing interstellar probe." In: *J. British Interplanetary Society*, 33, pp. 251-264.
4) Highwater, J. (1981) *The Primal Mind: Vision and Reality in Indian America*. NY: Meridian.
5) Kaku, M. (1995) *Hyperspace: A Scientific Odyssey Through Parallel Universes, Time-Warps, and the 10th Dimension*. NY: Anchor Books Doubleday.
6) Kuiper, T.B.H. & Morris, M. (1977) "Searching for extraterrestrial civilizations." In: *Science*, 196, pp. 616-621.
7) Morris, M.S. & Thorne, K. S. (1988) "Wormholes in spacetime and their use for interstellar travel: A tool for teaching general relativity." In: *Am. J. Phys.*, 56, no. 5, pp. 395-412.
8) Oliver, B.M., et al. (1973) *Project Cyclops: A Design Study of a System for Detecting Extraterrestrial Intelligent Life*. NASA-Ames Research Center, CR 114445, pp. 177-181.
9) Rescher, N., (1985) "Extraterrestrial science." In: *Extraterrestrials: Science and Alien Intelligence*, E. Regis Jr. (Ed.) Cambridge UK: Cambridge U. Press.
10) Rucker, R. (1984) *The Fourth Dimension: A Guided Tour of the Higher Universes*. Boston: Houghton-Mifflin Co.
11) Schwarzschild, B. (2000) "Theorists and experimenters seek to learn why gravity is so weak." In: *Physics Today*, 53, no. 9, pp. 22-24.

12) Stride, S.L. (1998) "SETV - The search for extraterrestrial visitation: Introduction to a heterotic strategy in the search for ETI." Submitted *JSE* manuscript, Fall, 1998.
13) Stride, S.L. (2001) "An instrument-based method to search for extraterrestrial interstellar robotic probes." In: *J. British Interplanetary Soc.*, 54, no. 1/2, pp. 2-13.
14) Tough, A. (2000) http://members.aol.com/AllenTough/strategies.html. University of Toronto, Canada.
15) Vakoch, D.A. (1995) "Constructing messages to extraterrestrials: An exosemiotic approach," Paper IAA-95-IAA.9.2.05 presented at the *SETI: Interdisciplinary Aspects Review Meeting*, 46th *International Astronautical Congress*, Oslo, Norway.
16) Vallee, J.F. (1975a) *The Invisible College*. NY: E. P. Dutton.
17) Vallee, J.F. (1975b) "The psycho-physical nature of UFO reality: A speculative framework." In: *AIAA Thesis-Antithesis Conference Proceedings*, L.A, CA pp. 19-21.
18) Vallee, J.F. (1990) *Confrontations: A Scientist's Search for Alien Contact*. NY: Ballantine.
19) Visser, M. (1995) *Lorentzian Wormholes: From Einstein to Hawking*. NY: AIP Press.

> *Although I am among those who believe that UFOs are real physical objects, I do not think they are extraterrestrial in the ordinary sense of the term.*
>
> *In my view they present an exciting challenge to our concept of reality itself.*
>
> --- *Jacques Vallee*
> --- *Dimensions: A Case Book of Alien Contact*
> --- 1988-2008

SECTION X

Page 509

EDUCATION:
INCREASING INTELLIGENCE
Through Understanding and Application of
The Dimensions of Consciousness

We discover that each of us conducts enough electricity to activate the Skin Conductance Response machine (SCR). Two who don't touch have sensors attached to their fingers, so everyone else in the circle has to touch to complete the circuit that "turns on" the SCR feedback sound. We are all connected in energy. This image was adapted from an illustration in *Biomeditation*. *[1]

---

*[1] Payne, B. & Reitano, C.T. (1977) *Biomeditation*. Brookline, Mass: Institute of PsychoEnergetics. Original illustrations by Alex Grey and Gaetani Frenier. See also Payne's *The Biofield* at: www.buryl.com.

SECTION X

EDUCATION:
Increasing Intelligence Through The Understanding and Application of the Dimensions of Consciousness

INTRODUCTION

> *Education is the kindling of a flame,*
> *not the filling of a vessel.*
> — Socrates

Master teacher and philosopher Dr Dean Brown believed: (1)

> *Education is the most important activity there is, was, and ever shall be. All else depends upon it. Education is imperative, primary. The purpose of living is to learn and teach.... The most crucial part, the part where we most often fail, is content. What shall we teach? Thoughtful people agree: first and foremost <u>teach learning how to learn, the metaprocesses</u>. After that, teach reverence for the material. After that, all that remains to do is to share the zest for learning — at the highest level of discrimination and the intellect.*

Dedicated scientists have provided us with a rich collection of ideas, based on solid research, and these ideas substantiate what caring and devoted teachers have been writing about for the last 30 years (or for a few thousand if we count Socrates). Our children have an urgent need to be able to apply this information to the challenges of their lives as the environment and the world rapidly change.

Developmental optometrist Dr Raymond Gottlieb wisely observed: (2)

> *The present educational paradigm is rooted in the assumption that the only questions worth dealing with are ones for which we already know the answers. If education condones only answerable questions, where can one learn to live with the uncertainties of the real world? Uncertainty is the rule. Insecurity is inescapable. The issue is not how we avoid insecurity, but how we learn to live most comfortably with insecurity.... Our perceptions need to be flexible so they don't become restricted automatically from habit when we encounter the unexpected in life.*
>
> *Mastery describes the process of doing any task with optimal expenditure of energy, performing with confidence and clearness of mind. There is rhythm, ease of flow, awareness, ...energy and breath. There is readiness for the unexpected.... Mastery should become the basic goal of early learning experience, and the major part of that is the development of the sensory-motor responses in the first few grades.*

We asked experienced teachers from different disciplines to tell us what specific changes need to be applied to public education. Alpha Quincy introduces us to The Problems in Chapter 41. She understands them well. She has spent most of the 20th century totally involved in public schools—as a young girl in a one-room rural school in the 1930s, as a classroom teacher in a large elementary school, as one of the first women hired to be an elementary school principal, and as president of a school board. She fought tirelessly for the rights of students against the political and economic demands for lower budgets; while the once first class educational system of California deteriorated into crowded classrooms, increased regimentation and lower standards of achievement.

Dr Stanley Krippner outlined important concepts to be applied for Solving The Problems. (3) Teachers and therapists sharing his humanistic values enthusiastically participated in this first graduate program in humanistic psychology.*[2] Teachers, who were applying these concepts of holistic education that we read in Krippner's outline, describe their successful applications in Chapter 42. The first concept addresses the primary need for children to "Learn How to Learn." Gottlieb outlines visual training exercises, and provides lesson plans for using body movement in rhythm to improve self-confidence and focus of attention. The second concept explains the need to educate the intelligence of all the senses. Parents and their children can play the few games suggested here (or create their own) to improve their ability to identify smells, tastes, textures and sounds. (4) Since for most of us, vision forms a dominant part of the information we receive from the senses, the major focus of these lessons is on developing the language needed to communicate what we see (both externally and envision internally). Lesson plans to encourage a child to scribble, and later to draw from life are included. A psi sensitive can "receive" information from any or all of the senses by remote perception (RP), so being able to identify and communicate them is useful. The third concept explains the urgent need for classes in *Self-Discovery Science,* (5) which utilizes several forms of bio/neurofeedback and HeartMath™. Physiological feedback shows us just how thoughts, emotions, and sound affect our bodies directly. Therapists have used physiological feedback for over 35 years to alleviate ADHD and stress. At the same time, simple feedback tools have been used successfully in the classroom and the school counseling office. New computer feedback games are being developed to enhance focus of attention. Some can also

---

*[2] Humanistic Psychology Institute (HPI) was established in 1970, in SF, CA, to be the educational arm of the Association for Humanistic Psychology (AHP). Eleanor Criswell, PhD, then president of AHP, helped to make this happen. By 2010, HPI had evolved into Saybrook University with 3 colleges. www.saybrook.edu.

reveal the reactions of our bodies to TV, music, the environment and to any alterations that drugs or electronic gadgets attached to our ears might impose. The fourth concept suggests ways to highlight students' natural creativity and psi sensitivity. These are best practiced in a calm stable environment. Therefore, students of all age groups need exercises that are <u>c</u>arefully <u>a</u>rranged to <u>r</u>elease <u>e</u>motions <u>s</u>afely (CARES games). Different types of exercises for different age groups are suggested. Students of all age groups are encouraged to think of ways to express those released emotions. After the activity of the CARES games and the creative responses to them, the teacher helps the class to settle down by counting each breath for one minute. When students are ready to focus, remote perception games can begin.

Chapter 43 provides statistically significant evidence of the value of holistic teaching methods. A formal study of holistic techniques applied in a fifth grade classroom verified that these students achieved a greater advance in academic achievement, emotional maturity, and self-confidence, than those in other classes that used the standard curriculum. Some expensive private schools do use some of these holistic methods to expand intelligence. Surely, public school children have the same needs.

REFERENCES

1) Gottlieb, R. (1979) Excerpt from: "Training for mastery – Education for mystery." In: *AHP Newsletter—A Glimpse Into the Future of Education.* May, pp. 16-17. Guion, C. & Millay, J. (Eds.).
2) Brown, D. (2001) Excerpt from: "Hardware: What a computer can do has no limits. What a mind can do has no boundaries." In: *AHP Perspective.* Erickson, E. (Ed.).
3) Krippner, S. (1979) "The influence of consciousness research." In: *AHP Newsletter—A Glimpse Into the Future of Education.* May, pp. 11-12. Guion, C. & Millay, J. (Eds.).
4) Ali Akbar (1979) "Education and Music." In: *AHP Newsletter—A Glimpse Into the Future of Education.* May, pp. 22-23. Guion, C. & Millay, J. (Eds.).
5) King, M., Millay, J. & Mayo, M. *Self-Discovery Science.* www.fmbr.org.

> *I believe I can make a solid case for the existence and potential of a superior intelligence within everyone, a mind born of brain but existing apart from brain, a mind with extraordinary, unacknowledged potency and range of powers.*
>
> *--- Barbara B. Brown*
> *--- New Mind, New Body, 1974*

The Megacorporations As Educators Of The Divine Child *1
--- Laura Huxley*

Children Are Our Ultimate Investment

They are also the ultimate investment of the:

- Nicotine pushers—every day in America 3,000 young people become regular smokers; the average smoker starts at age 14 and becomes a habitual smoker by the age of 18!
- Powerful alcohol conglomerate. In 1996, the total cost of alcohol use was $52.8 billion.
- Gun merchants. More children are killed by guns than by all other causes.

Parents Are Losing Control Over Their Children
--- Ralph Nader*

It is time to realize that the alienation of young people from their parents, from society, and from themselves is increasing despite the wealth of our country.... The omnipenetrating hucksterism of companies...[use] large sums of capital, lobbyists, child psychologists and communications specialists...to stimulate and exploit their anxieties fears, loneliness, and sensual drive in order to sell.... *2

Love Is The Best Policy
--- Aldous Huxley*

Let us steal a bit of energy from our need to achieve and give it to our need for loving. Love is as necessary to human beings as food and shelter.

NOTES AND REFERENCES

*1 Huxley, L. (2001 Excerpts) "Megacorporations as educators of the divine child." In: *AHP Perspective*. Erickson (Ed.). SF, CA: Assn. for Humanistic Psychology.

*2 [Editor's Note: Corporations that control major media outlets use the TV "light in motion" with repeated phrases to hypnotize children into becoming consumers of an unsustainable lifestyle. The meanings of patriotic catch phrases are twisted to "sell" political ideas favorable to corporations—for their own power and profit. Democracy itself is threatened by such media control and the cost of elections. Real freedom of speech is denied without equal access to the media.]

EDUCATION: THE PROBLEMS

STUDENTS ARE NOT MACHINE PARTS

Alpha Quincy[*3]

The Problems

Machine parts can be honed to the same size, making them interchangeable with other parts when assembling machines on an assembly line. Students cannot, and should not, be honed to standards of exactness. The more precisely we attempt to measure student learning the less certain we can be of the accuracy of our results. The more easily the skill, ability, or knowledge can be measured, the less important to learning it is likely to be. The more important learning is more difficult to measure. There is a false sense of security in reporting a numerical measure of an objective, standardized, multiple choice test, and yet, decisions that affect lives are often made on the basis of such tests.

Since the publication of *"A Nation At Risk"* in 1983 and later writings decrying the decline of public education, everyone wants to get into the act of helping improve education. By trying to fix education, many proposals, with the best of intentions, have made the problem worse. These new programs often leave a growing pile of unintended consequences. Should we expect high standards of teaching? Yes. Should we expect standardization of students? No.

"No Child Left Behind," the *"Race to the Top,"* and *"Closing the Gap"* are titles of new programs intended to help educate students. We can all agree with the statements expressed in the program titles, but the unintended consequences of each are many. If the students and schools in the national NCLB program have not achieved their annual yearly progress (AYP), and are not at or above average, or at 100% proficiency by 2014, punitive sanctions can be imposed on the school and staff. Schools can be

---

[*3] Alpha B. Quincy was twice elected president of the school board of Contra Costa County, CA, (1991 and 1995). She was one of the first women to become a school principal in a large school district, and is now the president of the Retired School Administrators of two counties. She has taught every grade from pre-school to graduate school and has served the State of California as a member of the Curriculum Development and Supplemental Materials Commission.

closed, staff fired, and students moved to other schools. Compliance is weighted heavily on the results of standardized objective tests in reading and math. And I needn't mention the mathematical definition of average that precludes all students reaching "above average." If all do not win the "Race to the Top," it is possible to lower the top until they do, though that is not the intent. "Closing the Gap" between high and low achieving students is a program intended to raise the scores of lower achieving students. The gap can be narrowed, if not closed, by ignoring the high achieving students and pushing the lower level students to raise their test scores. Such tactics can result in a loss of interest in learning in both groups, though I doubt that is the intent of the program. Think of the metaphor of a three-foot hurdle. If all students are to be tested in their ability to jump a three-foot hurdle, those who can clear it easily should be challenged with a higher mark. Those who repeatedly try and fall against the hurdle will soon tire of trying. Each student should be challenged to reach one's highest level of ability, wherever that might be.

WYTIWYG, the acronym for *What You Test Is What You Get*, is apt for looking at what happens to the curriculum for students and schools judged on the results of high stakes tests. Since machine scoreable tests are not appropriate for measuring achievement in the arts, music, or physical education, those subjects tend to get short shrift in favor of allocating classroom time for test preparation. The subjects of the high stakes tests, primarily reading and math, are also narrowing to focus instruction on those standardized skill areas that will be tested. In order to put more emphasis on science, history, and the social sciences, should more testing be placed there? Little instructional time is left to guide student exploration or discussion in depth for real understanding in any subject.

Approaching A Solution

<u>The Teacher</u>, first and foremost, is the most important factor in student learning. Teachers must be recruited from the top echelon of university students to build the prestige for a profession that will, in turn, attract more top students. Schools of education must look for both intelligence and ability in the students they enroll and provide them education in the science and art of teaching. Income level is also a factor in building the prestige that attracts the best and the brightest, and must be considered when seeking to improve education.

As professionals, teachers at all levels work with students and make the decisions that advance learning. Learning occurs when the teacher and student know and appreciate each other and work together. When you remember your own high school years, do you remember the course work or the teacher? *"I had Mr. Armstrong for math,"* you might say, or advise an incoming student, *"Do take Mrs. Baker's English class. You'll like her."*

<u>The Environment</u> must be arranged to allow for good teaching and learning. Unless one student and one teacher occupy each end of a log (Socrates), numbers of students must be grouped for instruction. Students learn best when they have a place to belong and where they know that someone cares. Teaching and learning is best when the teachers and students can know and appreciate each other and work together. Class sizes, schools, and school districts should be small enough so students and teachers don't become anonymous in large systems that sometimes number in the thousands. Polls have repeatedly shown that a community supports the schools in their neighborhood, but disdains all the "other schools" out there that they don't know.

High schools today are structured for madness. They have become the Procrustean bed of education, built without considering the human needs of the student. They are the unintended consequence of modeling them after the successful assembly lines used by manufacturing companies in the last century. Fortunately, there are new ideas of ways to change the madness that are showing promise. The Bill and Melinda Gates Foundation is experimenting with smaller schools. The George Lucas Educational Foundation (clef.org) is also funding ideas that put students in a more human environment. Some large high schools are dividing their total enrollment into groups of smaller numbers that remain with the same teachers all four years Some districts and schools are instituting smaller schools designed as Career Technical Education with a focus on one career, such as medicine, business, media, etc. with all academic studies woven into classes focusing on that career.

Students in both elementary and high school today are digital natives. Everything they want to know they can find on a small electronic instrument most carry with them in a pocket. Instruction must adapt to the new way of accessing knowledge. Should teachers admonish: "Now turn them off and bring your eyes to the front of the room"? I think not. Google, Twitter, Facebook, and YouTube are valuable learning tools and should be included in instruction, taking their place along with the library and books. Students must learn how to discriminate between fact and opinion, to recognize sources, and to fact check. Google's first five choices are only the most popular answer to the question, not necessarily the most appropriate or useful. New rules of plagiarism must be devised.

Students must learn to work in groups and share knowledge, solve real world problems, and reach for broad goals, rather than focus on discrete bits of knowledge for testing.... Short tests are OK for the teacher to find out what needs to be taught... but not for a nation to use as the basis for judging the whole of learning.

EDUCATION: SOLVING THE PROBLEMS

Stanley Krippner [*4]

OUTLINE FOR CHANGE

The influence of consciousness research includes such areas as altered states, biofeedback, video feedback, hypnosis, acupuncture, relaxation, meditation, yoga, the "body therapies," creativity and parapsychology.

I have published accounts of my work with hypnosis and poor readers, and my notions as to how biofeedback and parapsychology could be used in education. (1, 2, 3, 4) I also feel that there are associations between creativity and parapsychological phenomena that we have barely begun to explore.

We now know that altered states of consciousness are characterized by shifts in factors such as perception, cognition, time sense, and body image. However, disabled learners often manifest one or more of these changes in their everyday behavior. We might do well to think of poor learners in terms of the states of consciousness in which they exist and to study the literature for clues as to how learning is best attained for people in those states.

For exceptional children who are gifted and talented: The literature abounds with cases in which creative products emerged from dreams, reverie, hypnosis, and relaxation states.... This is not the only milieu in which creativity develops, but it is one virtually ignored by our educational system. There is no reason why properly trained teachers could not make use of children's dreams or give opportunities for "classroom periods of reverie and relaxation" after which artistic, scientific, or technical materials are made available.

[Consciousness research also] has provided some successful alternatives to drug treatment for hyperactive or neurologically impaired children.... In addition to sensory-motor training (5) and megavitamin treatment, parents could investigate special education techniques (e.g., behavior modification); changes in life style (e.g., less television and more

---

[*4] Krippner, S. (1979) Excerpts from "The influence of consciousness research." In: *AHP Newsletter—A Glimpse Into the future of Education.* May, pp. 11-12. Guion, C. & Millay, J. (Eds.).

active sports); family counseling (e.g., the child whose hyperactivity represents "acting out" behavior in a frustrating family situation); alterations in the classroom (e.g., the child whose hyperactivity is the result of boredom with academic material that is not challenging); and other aspects of orthomolecular psychiatry. In addition to megavitamin treatment, the child should be tested to see if he or she is allergic to items such as food additives or dairy products or if the hyperactivity is a reaction to a diet that includes too much white sugar or flour.... Researchers need to find ways to match the hyperactive child to the optimal treatment.

At the present time, no one knows with certainty which treatment is best for which child. I advise parents to educate themselves about every available treatment, hopefully with the help of a knowledgeable physician, educator, or psychologist. They should then...start with the least expensive approaches available and the one, which, if nothing else, will do the child no harm. (6) ... I am a firm advocate of children's rights and believe that the child's wishes should play an important part in the decision making process. In fact, I would not object to letting some children make the decision themselves as to which alternative to accept, once they have examined the available facts....

If a youngster cannot learn a skill in a traditional way, there may be a nontraditional way better suited for that child. We need to discover what unused senses and affective states can assist learning, what undiscovered cognitive modes could enhance development and what educational environment is most conducive for a particular child. Educators, parents, specialists, and the children themselves can work together in reshaping education so that it is finally prepared to meet the needs and develop the potentials of all our children.

REFERENCES AND NOTES

1) Krippner, S. (1971) "On research in visual training and reading disability." In: *Journal of Learning Disabilities*, 1971, 4, 6-17.

2) Krippner, S., Dreistadt, R., & Hubbard, C.C. (1972) "The creative person and non-ordinary reality." In: *Gifted Child Quarterly*, 1972, 16, 203-234.

3) Krippner, S. (1971) "The use of hypnosis and the improvement of academic achievement." In: *Journal of Special Education*, 1971, 4, 451-460.

4) Krippner, S. (1975) "An alternative to drug treatment for hyperactive children." In: *Academic Therapy*, 1975, 10, pp. 433-439.

5) Krippner, S. (1971) "On research in visual training and reading disability." In: *Journal of Learning Disabilities*. 1971, 4, 6-17.

6) Krippner, S. & Fischer, S. (1973) "A study of neurological organization procedures and megavitamin treatment for children with brain dysfunction." In: *Journal of Orthomolecular Psychiatry*. 1,121-132.

EDUCATION: SOLVING THE PROBLEMS
1) LEARNING HOW TO LEARN

Ray Gottlieb

TRAINING THE INSTRUMENT

We must act now if we are to keep up with the demands of the fast-paced changes and international competition we face. We know enough about brain function, medicine and psychology to make fundamental improvements in education and how we train our children. Over 100 years ago, William James warned about our widespread "habit of inferiority to our full self." He urged educators to discover and optimize each student's unique set of powers and teach them to maximize their energy. James wrote:

> The human individual lives usually far within his limits; he possesses powers of various sorts which he habitually fails to use. He energizes below his maximum, and he behaves below his optimum. In elementary faculty, in coordination, in power of inhibition and control, in every conceivable way, his life is contracted like the field of vision of an hysteric subject – but with less excuse, for the poor hysteric is diseased, while in the rest of us it is only an inveterate habit – the habit of inferiority to our full self – that is bad.
>
> We ought somehow to get a topographic survey made of the limits of human power in every conceivable direction, something like an ophthalmologist's chart of the limits of the human field of vision; and we ought then to construct a methodical inventory of the paths of access, or keys, differing with the diverse types of individual, to the different kinds of power.
>
> --- **William James** (1)
> --- *The Energies of Men* (1907)

I have seen little evidence that James' suggestions have impacted mainstream education. Not that there hasn't been a surge of interest in educational reform and a growing awareness that schools must become brain and health enhancing rather than degrading. Indeed, brain scientists, computer programmers, psychologists, educators, clinicians, business leaders and parents have joined their interests and talents to form multidisciplinary departments at major universities. Brain and learning organizations offering websites, conferences, books, videos and computer games are popping up like wildflowers in the early spring. Word is spreading quickly except for shortsighted politicians who bury their heads in the sand, to look in wrong places in order to save money by gutting education funding to leave our students and our future far behind.

As Mark Twain saw it: "*In the first place God made idiots. This was for practice. Then He made School Boards.*"*[5] He despaired about the irrationality of American education, and referred to the amazing achievements of Helen Keller: The methods used in the asylums (deaf and blind schools) are rational. The teacher exactly measures the child's capacity, to begin with; and from thence onwards the tasks imposed are nicely gauged to the gradual development of that capacity, the tasks keep pace with the steps of the child's progress, they don't jump miles and leagues ahead of it by irrational caprice and land in vacancy — according to the average public-school plan.

I'm reminded of the analogy about the optometrist who wrote his patients' eyeglass prescription before he measured their eyes. When they returned complaining of blurred vision and headaches he told them, "*Too bad, you get an F.*" Children learn and develop in individual ways and mature at different rates.

When skills and information are taught in a haphazard way without regard for the unique psychophysiology and perception/cognition of each child, learning blocks are the likely result. Stressing students by assigning unachievable goals according to preconceived lesson plans based on abstract norms risks negative health, self-confidence, motivation and learning outcomes. When demands on students over-exceeds their capability, chronic physical and mental tension results.

The incidence of nearsightedness has been correlated with academic success and high levels of myopia increase chances of ocular pathology later in life. It doesn't have to be this way. Visual skills can be trained properly. **If children are taught to see twice as much, in half the time, with half the effort, imagine how quickly and easily they could be taught to master reading.**

How we learn is more important than how much we learn, especially in the early years. Teaching meaningless details or sticking to the lesson plan is secondary business compared to the student's state of mind.

I have studied and practiced vision therapy and training for over thirty years. The following is offered in the hope that the educational system will evolve.

---

*[5] Twain, M (1899) *Following the Equator: A Journey Around the World*. V.2, Ch, XXV, 293. NY: Harper & Brothers Publishers.

VISION THERAPY/TRAINING

Vision allows us to be active participants in our world, continually moving through it and molding it to our needs and desires.

--- **Sue Berry**
"Stereo Sue" (2)

I practice vision therapy optometry. This is not the optometry of prescribing lenses and medications or selling glasses and contact lenses. It's more than a 100-year-old optometric specialty that focuses on expanding human visual performance capacity. For nearly 40 years I've been working to eliminate learning/reading dysfunction; rehabilitate the after-effects of brain and body trauma; straighten and improve cross-eyed, wall-eyed, and lazy-eyed vision; reverse myopia and presbyopia and enhance athletic, acting and music performance. I've worked with low, normal, and gifted achievers, with the young children, teens, adults and the elderly, and in hospitals, schools, gyms and offices. My foremost influences have been William H. Bates, (3) ophthalmologist, the father of natural practices for preventing and reversing vision problems, Robert Pepper, (4) optometrist, who invented the Stress-Point learning approach described below, H. Riley Spitler, (5) optometrist and medical physician, who invented Syntonic Optometry, a method of colored light therapy delivered through the eyes, Kurt Goldstein, (6) neuropsychiatrist, whose holistic insights about human behavior were derived through working with brain-injured solders, Karl Pribram, (7) neuroscientist, whose insights on brain function provided a framework for my thinking, and, of course, William James. (1)

Vision therapy/training is aimed at increasing the binocularity, ease, flexibility, accuracy, stamina, speed and automaticity of visual processing of environmental clues. As we coach patients to improve their eye movements, stereo awareness, peripheral vision, visual attention, timing and information processing, we train the brain and its myriad of visual connections. Vision is a complex process. Vision therapy/training is also complex and many facetted. It is an evolving art that combines scientific knowledge with empirical insights and employs many tools and approaches. The ultimate aim of visual training is to develop or rehabilitate an individual's ability to select appropriate goals and then to marshal working memory, attention, and inhibitory control for the purposes of planning and executing actions to achieve the goal. Frontal cortical dysfunction, depending on the exact location of the deficit, leaves specific cognitive abilities and general intelligence largely intact but greatly impairs planning, self-monitoring, attention, and responsiveness to impending reward or punishment.

STRESS-POINT TRAINING

Below is a brief description of a unique therapy that I specialize in that was developed by optometrist Robert Pepper. My favorite part of Pepper's "Stress-Point Training" approach uses rhythm, movement, and multi-tasking exercises to improve learning, thinking, and performance skills. Patients bounce on a small trampoline while performing visual/cognitive tasks of increasing complexity in tempo with their bounces. (A few example exercises are described below. If you don't have a trampoline, you can clap your hands or use a metronome without trampoline.) This not only increases the speed and accuracy of eye movements and visual information processing but also improves motor intelligence, attention, memory, motivation, emotional control, communication, self-confidence and, of course, learning. The following is a brief summary of Stress-Point Training principles.

Flow-State Learning: The guiding principle and ultimate outcome is flow-state consciousness. (10) This is an active, engaged meditative state where senses are fresh, instinct guides action, and the past, present and future merge into NOW. Optimal learning is an altered state and it is this state that we should be teaching, especially for the very first learning experiences. Unless children are trained to mastery levels, where performance is not merely accurate but is automatic, graceful and expressive, they never learn flow-state learning consciousness. Unless they know how good it feels they won't become attracted, addicted to it.

Pepper's Five Questions: These important goals must be achieved to insure mastery. Can I do it? Can I do it well? Can I do it well every time (whenever I want to and for as long as I want to)? Can I accept change (do it at different speeds, with different information, in different circumstance - in front of an audience)? And finally, the fifth question: Can I do it in the flow state (creatively, artistically, inventing, and experimenting on the go)? Most people feel complete if they can answer yes to question one. Unfortunately educators and parents stop too soon. They don't teach beyond competence. They leave children with half-baked brains.

Process Learning: In Stress-Point Training, the process of how one learns is emphasized. Students are too product oriented. They're so focused on the reward that if they don't succeed right away, it means they are stupid. When challenged at the stress-point, they quickly become anxious, lose motivation and run away. Learning stops. Too often children are praised for the product of their effort rather than for the effort. When they're told "You're so smart" to reward their good work they come to equate being stupid when they don't succeed. Much better is to praise the quality of their effort and to coach them on the process. **The development of self-confidence is much too important to be left to chance.**

Rhythmic Learning: The trampoline is fun and children love bouncing. It's like a big metronome with the jumper as the pendulum with a steady beat. Rhythmic learning primes the brain to be more open to incoming information, develops precise, rapid and graceful neural processing, and organizes action plans for goal attainment.

Expressive Learning: Attention problems are hidden and can't be corrected unless the learning process is active and outwardly expressed. Most education, unfortunately, is passive. Most people aren't aware when their mind wanders. For example, when you listen to a lecture, watch a movie or read silently, you daydream without knowing and can't remember what just occurred. Expressive learning provides instant feedback for when attention wanders. The error detection brain senses our mistakes even before they happen to train effective recovery of attention. This is the key to improving learning ability. Catching yourself before you make an error early enough to recover (precovery) trains a broad range of neural networks across many parts of the brain.

Stress Point Learning: Start with easy tasks to warm up for the greater challenges to come. Gradually increase difficulty to match and then just exceed ability. For example, spell a word aloud by saying the letters at a given tempo (see exercise #3). More difficult would be to spell a whole sentence by saying letters on the beats but making a silent beat to mark the spaces. The trainer gradually increases the demand — speed, word length, and complex rules — to find that point of stress that challenges the student, that takes effort, but it is in the student's reach to accomplish. In the effort to succeed, learning blocks, normally hidden beneath the student's comfort threshold, are revealed. Once out in the open, the embedded negative responses (such as the frustration, avoidance, poor recovery, confusion) can be identified and replaced by positive ones. As harder tasks are mastered, awareness sharpens and ability grows. Thus learning deficits are eliminated.

Completion of an exercise requires more than calling out correct letters at the right time. Students are held to the task until a flow-state is mastered. Learning to rise to the occasion, give up old patterns, release conscious control and to flow through the experience from beginning to end becomes the new normal. In flow the voice becomes fuller, confident, and more precisely on the beat. The eyes, face and body look alert and aligned with present action. The strategy is to activate the flow-state, strengthen it and then work on the disabilities. **In this open and flowing state, breakthrough learning and new brain connections occur.** Students integrate new abilities into a unified whole rather than by closing down and adding just another splinter skill. The trainer's job is to carefully choose the tasks that help students attain and increase flow strength. With a success-oriented, nonjudgmental attitude, the teacher coaches the students' awareness and strategies. Students learn to confront real world challenges enthusiastically and objectively.

William James gets right to the point:

> Since [habit], under any circumstances, is what we always tend to become, it follows first of all that the teacher's prime concern should be to ingrain into the pupil that assortment of habits that shall be most useful to him throughout life. Education is for behavior, and habits are the stuff of which behavior consists.
>
> We must make automatic and habitual, as early as possible, as many useful actions as we can, and as carefully guard against the growing into ways that are likely to be disadvantageous. The more of the details of our daily life we can hand over to the effortless custody of automatism, the more our higher powers of mind will be set free for their own proper work.

--- **William James** (8)
--- *Talks to Teachers* (1899)

Soon, I hope, individualized training and sophisticated technology will usher in a new education based on James' principles. Attention, memory, balance, eye-hand and gross body coordination, vision and auditory development, flow, spatial intelligence, decision-making, effective self-regulation, thinking and planning skills must be intentionally trained and made automatic and habitual rather than leaving them to develop haphazardly, by luck on their own. This new focus in the early years would diminish learning disabilities and children would emerge self-directing, mentally, personally, and socially healthy with creativity and productivity far beyond present norms and expectations. We must act now to navigate the looming storms that darken coming days if we are to survive more fit, free, and capable than we are today. (9)

EXERCISES FOR TRAINING THE INSTRUMENT

Exercise #1 – Bilateral Multi-Tasking

Face a large chalkboard standing with your nose about six inches away. Draw a line on the board that is level with your nose tip and add an "**X**" in the middle of the line. Hold a stick of chalk in each hand. The task is to write the numbers 1–10 with both hands, while staring at the "**X**." Reach as high and stretch as far to each side as possible. Simultaneously with both hands, write 1 and then directly below that write 2, then 3 and so on to 10 in two parallel columns. Look at the "**X**" all the time. Don't rush. Take time to do a good job. Write the numbers, starting and finishing the left and right hand at the same time. When finished, check your work. Are any numbers missing? Are they all correct or is one side written backwards? Are the lines parallel (they should be) or do they converge toward the bottom? Erase and repeat the exercise several times working for simultaneous awareness of the right and left sides.

More advanced tasks: Repeat the above while counting by twos, spelling a word, or saying the sum of the numbers as you add one more to the list. Try writing 1-10, top to bottom with one hand and at the same time from the bottom up in reverse order 10-1 with the other. Write the numbers one to five with one hand and the letters "A" to "E" with the other. Work for bilateral self-awareness, automaticity, poise, energy and steady breathing.

Exercise # 2 – Rhythm

Clap your hands in a steady tempo. One or two claps per second. Can you keep the beat? If not, use a metronome or get a helper to clap with you. You can use a trampoline and clap at the bottom of the bounce. (Write these numbers quite large on a white or black board.) When you can sustain a steady tempo, read them out loud in time with your claps.

7 4 3 9 5 6 2 9 4 7 2 3 8 6 1 4

Some can do this easily on their first attempt but others have to work at it. If you don't have success after several attempts, make the task easier. Use fewer digits or skip a beat between reading the numbers. Too easy? Increase the speed; read backwards or forwards. For more complexity try these: Clap on every number but say only every second number; say each number and clap on every other number; don't clap on even numbers but clap on the odd ones; or say the alphabet between the numbers.

At some level you'll reach that point of stress, which blocks your learning and causes you to make errors. That is where you may become aware of attention problems or emotional behaviors. Can you bring your attention back when your mind wanders or do you get anxious, tighten, and stop? Are you continually distracted by thoughts such as: *"This is easy,"* or *"I'll never make it through"*? Do you reverse, skip or call out wrong numbers? Do you falter at the start or lose focus near the end? Can you catch errors yourself or must someone point them out? As you become conscious of your errors, then you can learn to correct them yourself.

Exercise # 3 – Sentence Exercise

The trampoline is a consciousness-feedback device for improving attention, memory, movement skill, and emotional/motivational learning behaviors. Anxiety and self-doubt can distort timing, speed and flow. Anxious people speed up and lose control without realizing why.

The trampoline's strong internally generated rhythm improves time perception, integrates the senses and organizes planning and learning.

Performing in tempo requires a more organized brain. Adding complexity to tasks while performing complex movement patterns moves the brain toward multi-tasking perceptual/motor fluency (e.g., moving arms in circles and legs alternate in and apart 'jumping Jack' style).

An example: Write a sentence on the board in large letters. Say each letter on one bounce and indicate the space between the words with a silent bounce.

WE ARE PART OF THE ENERGY OF THE EARTH

Too easy? Say the consonants; be silent on vowels and clap for spaces. This would be a mid-level task—easy for some, a stretch for others, and much too difficult for others. (You can do this without trampoline if you don't have one.) Try it backwards, or do it from memory.

Exercise #4 – Application To Life Situations

The final goal of the training is to transfer flow state learning to real world learning. This requires self-understanding and the patience to embrace difficulties with a sense of strategy and play, without self-criticism. Students learn to apply stress-point principles by breaking any new task into appropriate-sized modules and to work to achieve flow.

In this way improved learning capacities and habits are integrated into the functional organization of the brain and into the world beyond the training environment. In the end, perception expands; self-awareness grows, while stress and fear decrease. The individual becomes more creative, confident, and capable of navigating toward higher quality success.

> *In life, uncertainty is the rule. Insecurity is inescapable. The issue is not how to avoid insecurity, but how to learn to live most vitally and productively with insecurity.*
>
> *--- Raymond Gottlieb*

REFERENCES AND NOTES

1) James, W. (1907) "The Energies of Men." In: *Science*, N.S. 25 (No. 635), 321-332.
2) Berry, S. – "Stereo Sue" (2009) *Fixing My Gaze*. NY: Basic Books.
3) Bates, W. H. (1921) *The Cure of Imperfect Sight by Treatment Without Glasses*. NY: Central Fixation Publishing.
4) Pepper, R. & Nordgren, M.J. (2008) *Stress-Point Learning: A Multi-sensory Approach to Processing Information*, OEPF, Inc., Santa Anna, CA.   Find it at: http://oep.excerpo.com/index.php?action=show_details&product_id=3190.
5) Spitler, H. R. (1941) *The Syntonic Principle*.   The College of Syntonic Optometry. www.oepf.org and www.syntonicphototheray.com.
6) Goldstein, K. (1939) *The Organism, A Holistic Approach To Biology Derived From Pathological Data In Man*. NY: American Book Company.
7) Pribram, K. (1971) *Languages of the Brain*. NY: Prentice Hall.
8) James, W. (1899) *Talks to Teachers*. http://www.des.emory.edu/mfp/james.html#talks.
9) Gottlieb, R. (2005) *Attention & Memory Training: Stress-Point Learning on the Trampoline*, OEPF, inc., Santa Anna, CA. Optometric Extension Program. See websites: www.withoutglasses.com and http://oep.excerpo.com/index.php?action=show_details&product_id=3078.
10) Csikszentmihalyi, M. (1991) *Flow: The Psychology of Optimal Experience*. NY: Harper Collins.

Risk brings its own rewards: The exhilaration of breaking through, of getting to the other side, the relief of a conflict healed, the clarity when a paradox dissolves. Eventually we know deeply that the other side of every fear is a freedom. Whoever teaches us this is the agent of our liberation.

--- Marilyn Ferguson
--- The Aquarian Conspiracy, 1979

EDUCATION: SOLVING THE PROBLEMS
2) LEARNING THE LANGUAGE OF THE SENSES
To Improve Communication of Nonverbal Intelligence

Jean Millay

> My great-grandmother, who was a healer, taught me how to interact with all my senses, because the senses cross over. She did things to teach me how to hear with my hands, and hear with my eyes and see with my hands, and caress with my eyes, and listen with my hands, to touch a person and be able to hear what their body is telling me. She always told me that the mind should be able to work on six tracks instead of one track, that you should be able to do many things simultaneously. (1)
>
> --- **Oh Shinna**
> (Healer and teacher who integrates
> Apache, Mohawk and modern traditions)

Any one, or all, of the senses might be involved in dreams or remote perception (RP). Can you discriminate internal impressions of sounds, smells, tastes, feelings or images well enough to communicate them to others? To Oh Shinna's great-grandmother and other Native Americans, the senses were a fundamental channel of information about good food, healing herbs, and how to live on the earth in awareness of the human place within the whole biosphere.

However, in our time, much of our food and medicine is synthesized. Our knowledge of the world and how to live in it comes largely from flickering lights across the flat screens of computers or television sets. Schools above all teach reading and writing (on flat pages) to prepare them for tests—tests that compare their "intelligence" to pre-determined "norms." With little or no experience in the dimensional world of nature, any direct sensory information that is available may be limited or distorted. Our sensory systems can be trained to provide independent information even from nonlocal spacetime. Classes to learn the languages of all the senses are not included in overburdened school curriculums, which would then require more attention from overburdened teachers, as well. However, sensory games can be fun for both parents and children, as they learn to identify different smells, tastes, or textures, and then try to do it while blindfolded, or perhaps try to identify what another family member might be smelling, or tasting by remote perception.

GAMES TO ENHANCE SENSORY AWARENESS

These games are designed to enhance discrimination of sensory information. There should be no grades given, nor should "right" or "wrong" answers ever be used to judge anyone. All responses are learning tools for improving awareness. The mood is "just for fun." The important part is the opportunity to learn through our interaction with different people how we all "think" differently. A good cook can discriminate subtleties of smells and tastes better than I can. I chose to study art because I "think" in pictures (mother tried to teach me to play music, to no avail, though I do enjoy listening). One friend "thinks" in words (continually using word puns that I miss), and another friend "feels" all the emotions in the room. How many families ever stop to ask such questions about each other? The question "How do you think?" is a good place to start.

Some of my students took days to figure out how to answer that. One student complained, *"Teachers always told me what to think, but in 15 years of school no one ever asked me how I think."*

SMELLING AND/OR TASTING

Begin by isolating several smells or flavors with their correct labels, so the participants can learn to identify them. After that, can anyone identify a smell or taste while blindfolded? Can anyone correctly identify what another is tasting or smelling by remote perception (RP)?

Once at a PRG meeting, we attempted an exercise in RP of smell. Ten different smelly things were secretly placed in small film cans, and tossed into a square tissue box. They were placed in a room down the hall (away from the meeting room), along with ten sealed envelopes with the target pictures. The "sender" went there, picked one film can with a target smell, and one envelope with a target picture. Back in the meeting room, the PRG members began to RP both targets—the image and the scent. As the group independently began drawing, we heard a cry for—*"HELP"*—down the hall. I rushed to check it out. One of the cans had leaked a drop of fingernail polish remover (weak acetone). Its unique aroma now dominated the official target—menthol. I had to dispose of the acetone immediately. When I returned to the meeting room, the group had completed their RP responses, which we shared. In spite of the disturbance, some drawings included definite similarities to the target picture. However, the only person who had perceived the smell was Joanne Kamiya (her excellent cooking is legendary). She had drawn rows of rectangular windows on a 3-story building. Under that was a dark rivulet she described as a *"toxic waste is leaking out."* While her drawing had no similarity to the target picture, her building had the same proportions as the leaky tissue box, with the same number and arrangement of windows as the rows of small flower pictures on the box—plus, of course, the toxic leak. We all laughed.

Some of our very early RV–RP experiments just didn't go according to plan. Yours may not work out at first, either. Learn to laugh about the errors. Humor is a very important part of the learning process.

HEARING

When it comes to training the sense of hearing, I asked musicians. They seem to relate everything to rhythms and sounds, and they really do "think" differently than I do. Once I asked the world famous musician Ali Akbar Khan why the ancient North Indian music he had just played had never been written down, he replied, (2)

> Music is a sound, and when you want to play this sound, you don't need to train your eyes, you need to train your ears. And therefore if you start with the children by putting the printed notes in front of their eyes, they take the whole thing in reverse; the whole idea has changed....
>
> I started to play music when I was three years old. My father never actually forced me to sit down and take the instrument. But maybe for one minute...he would give me one note and say, 'All right say this. Say this word, and make the sound like this.'

Music and the wide range of emotional effects it has on consciousness has been well documented, since music can entrain brainwaves. Using music for an RP exercise can be fun, though as far as I know, very little has been done in a controlled study of sound transmission to provide statistics.

> Once I was able to "hear" a recording that my children were playing in LA, while I was in NYC (3,000 miles away). We had agreed ahead of time on a list of 10 albums that we had at both places, and we agreed on the one we would play at the same time in both places to "tune in" for the experiment. After that, the children danced and sang to the music they chose to play in LA. Unfortunately, it was a special song on a new album they were excited about. It was not on my list, nor had I heard it before. Nevertheless, I correctly identified the group of musicians, because I could "hear and feel" their rhythm and style by RP, and I reported that it must be a song I had never heard before. That too was correct.

When attempting formal RP experiments for hearing music or non-musical sound, dynamic music (classical, jazz or rock) familiar to both may work well. When using music to establish contact for remote touching, soft music (i.e., for meditation, romance, or a lullaby) may work better, so it won't distract one's focus on the "feeling" of the remote touch.

MUSIC TO ENHANCE REMOTE TOUCHING

When bonded couples (or parents and children) are lonesome because they have to be separated by work or emergencies, they might try the exercises described on the next page. While there are no statistical studies on this, those who did try this have reported to me that they both actually "felt" the presence of each other and both enjoyed the experience.

1) **SUGGESTIONS FOR CHOOSING THE RIGHT MUSIC.**
   Choose a musical CD that has special meaning to you both ahead of time. Have it ready in the player to turn on at the right time, or download it to play at the same time. This helps to "tune in" to each other, for closeness, and/or to "feel" remote touching.

   a) Between parents and children choose familiar happy music, perhaps a favorite sing-along, or special "goodnight" music, so they can both "feel" the exchange of the usual goodnight hug and kiss.

   b) Couples that are just beginning to practice RP for the purpose of improving their focus on "feeling love and/or healing" for each other may prefer romantic music. Some may prefer to choose those melodies without words to focus more on the sensations of touch.

2) **CHOOSING THE BEST QUIET TIME TO ESTABLISH CONTACT.**
   Both would need to agree on this. On a short budget one might call the other, let the phone ring twice and hang up as a signal to begin. (The expansion of communication technology does provide other ways to begin, though the communication that depends on a machine stuck to your ear can miss important subtleties of touch.)

3) **CLEAR YOUR MINDS.**
   Take the first five minutes to get comfortable, and the next five minutes in meditation to clear your mind of other thoughts.

4) **START THE MUSIC AS YOU FOCUS ON EACH OTHER.**
   If one starts the music a minute or two before the other, don't worry. Focusing on each other is more important than exact timing. After all, RP is said to take place in nonlocal spacetime, anyway. The music helps to focus in present time, the memory of touching in past time, in order to re-create the actual experience of it even though you are no longer close enough to share the same space.

5) **SHARE YOUR INDIVIDUAL EXPERIENCES AFTER EACH EVENT.**
   This helps to improve what might not have been communicated as planned, and to amplify what did work. Congratulate each other on the best of the experience. Positive feedback increases your understanding and success. Since we "think" differently, we often interpret sensory experiences differently, even though we both "felt" a deep sense of sharing together.

6) **AVOID NEGATIVE FEEDBACK, BECAUSE IT DIMINISHES SUCCESS.**
   Never complain to your partner that s/he did not "receive" or interpret your "message" the way you intended. Criticisms may limit some openness of the relationship. Share your different experiences of this exercise, also, to improve your understanding of each other.

SEEING

Most of my studies as an artist and a psi sensitive have involved visions. More importantly, as an art teacher, I have seen that the language of vision is seriously neglected. Learning to draw what you see is learning to see more when you look, and it is learning to express the language of vision in a concrete form. This is essential for the accurate transmission of a distant image, or to illustrate a dream or a visionary experience.

This practice in drawing what you see might even be included in the science curriculum. Even though high density colored photos are readily available in books and on the web (including films), scientists need to be able to discriminate the details of the actual bugs, birds, rocks, trees, grasses, animals, in their full multisensory dimensions.

However, life-drawing exercises need not take the place of the classes in "art," which may have a different focus—such as the study of design, color, layout, free expression and emotional impact.

> It saddens me to see elementary teachers pass out copies of the same pumpkin or valentine to all the young children to color (or to add pasted lace)—and call that an "art" class. The children will take this "pretty" thing home to please momma, and momma will say she is pleased.

That is a common ritual, but it is not education. Children need to express themselves freely with their own lines, shapes and colors. They also need to learn to see and think by drawing what they see and think about the world around them.

PERCEPTIONAL DEVELOPMENT

Rhoda Kellogg (3) was able to collect and study a million drawings made by young children around the world while she was working with the United Nations. She found a sequence to motor development, hand-eye coordination, and types of imagery, which evolve naturally, regardless of cultural differences. She found that children the world over seem to enjoy aesthetic sensitivity from the first free scribbles right up to the emergence of images from the external world.

Children need the freedom to scribble until they have developed their own internal sense of the head and body. (4, 5) Scribbling is a biofeedback device for the observation of the brain's perceptual organization as it develops. Young children need to develop their own relationship between the 2-D of the paper and the 3-D world they live in before they are locked in to the flat world of reading, writing, television and computer screens.

When the child is drawing, s/he is establishing the space-frame that s/he inhabits. (4) While sitting, that frame begins with the nose, extends to the hand holding a crayon, and ultimately stops at the crucial point of interaction between the crayon and the drawing paper. The eyes are then focused on the paper and the marks being made with the motion.

The motor activity is an essential part of the perception, as the child enjoys the body sensations while the whole arm moves, and the body changes. The child must be allowed to scribble. The word here is "allowed," because parents or "sitters" must make scribbling possible by providing space and materials—toddlers should be allowed paper, pencils, crayons, and even colored pentels, water colors and finger paints, though these need to be supervised, naturally, to save the house and the child. Children rarely need to be encouraged to scribble. It is a natural activity. (If the parent can play classical music during this activity, especially Mozart, there may be an extra advantage to brain development.) (2, 6)

The natural sequence of visual development, as seen through the scribbles of children around the world, (3) and those of my students, children and grandchildren, evolves more or less like this:

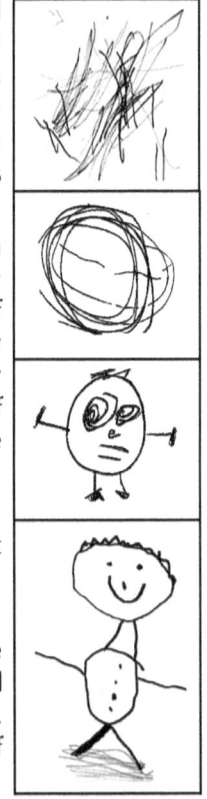

1. At first there are attempts to hold a pencil and make a few marks. The child explores the pencil and the paper and often stabs at the paper, and then is surprised at the mark. Then the child will make many marks and want to share the delight. (This may be between 16 and 28 months old, but the time to start is at any age the child becomes interested in the activity.)

2. Soon the child discovers that the hand and arm move easily in circles, and s/he will draw circles many times, both for the fun of seeing them and for the fun of the body movement. It is important to have lots of paper and always put the new one up on the wall (or refrigerator). This may go on for weeks. You may tire of seeing scribbles hung on the wall, but be patient—these efforts are part of the development of visual intelligence.

3. After the child discovers the square and the circle, eventually the circle becomes a face with two straight lines coming out of the head for arms and two for legs. Arm lines now might include hands.

4. Then two circles emerge, one for the head and one for the body, and perhaps some scribbles will be added to suggest hair on the head, or buttons on the clothes. The child may then identify the drawing as a picture of daddy or mommy.

5. Please do not provide children with ordinary coloring books! Most cheap coloring books use heavy black line drawings or cartoons that distort the child's natural relationship to the 3-D world of form and space. Let the child explore color freely for its own sake. Some children accept

those black outline drawings as "better" than their own (because adults buy such books and approve of them). Consequently, those line drawings often create a perceptual distortion between the 3-D and 2-D spaces, which can cause children to lose self-confidence in their own early attempts to draw. At that point they may lose interest in attempting to draw from life, and shift completely into flat, symbolic representations. Even at age forty or more, people will still draw the same cat or rabbit in exactly the same way that they learned to draw it from the coloring book or from the first-grade reader. It is not a picture from nature. It is only a memorized word-picture-symbol. Symbols have their place in our education, but they should not overwhelm the development of sensory intelligence that is potentially available and more direct. When people mainly focus on symbols, which can be manipulated, the original meanings can be and are often distorted to stir emotions for political gain, as well as for profit.

6. However, a coloring book with mandalas can be useful. They can help organize vision with concepts of symmetry, balance and centering. Begin with those that are small, easy and simple to complete, and if the child enjoys this type of exercise, more elaborate ones are available. (7)

Designs that are created using the proportions of the Golden Section can also help build an inner sense of balance. (Some of the mysterious crop circles have been reported to include such designs.) (8) Otherwise, just make color and paper available, and most children will be happy expressing their own "free will."

7. Once a child has scribbled enough to establish the body image and motor activity in her drawings, when the internal imaging has been completed, then the child can begin to "see" outside of herself and start drawing from life, with or without parental encouragement. Those first efforts to draw from life are crucial to the development of perception. Any direct attempt to draw from life is educational and wonderful, no matter what it looks like to an adult. Children and adults don't "see" or interpret the world in the same way. These drawings are not to be thought of as exhibition art, except on the family wall. They are personal, internal exercises to develop the visual intelligence system. Pure sensitivity to shape and color should be allowed to dominate. This is not the time to pressure the child "make it better," or to compete for some prize. Just encourage the process, and make the supplies available.

A precocious four-year-old painted this portrait of her two-year-old brother in bright colors with large shapes. She added outlines last to emphasize solidity.

8. Modeling clay is an excellent way for a child to respond directly to the 3-D world, and to the way solid objects in space look and feel.

On the right is a six-year-old child's model of a chair with feet and hands made with ceramic clay, which was fired in a kiln by an adult. It was glazed by the child, and fired again. Other types of materials are available that are easily fired by parents in an oven at home. Some clay comes in an assortment of colors that never get hard, and can be used over and over again.

9. Creating sculptures with found objects can also be fun and useful for brain development and for enhancing creativity. Take ordinary objects. Then arrange them and paint them to look like something else altogether.

VISUALIZATION

This is a major educational exercise for problem solving and for increased creativity. Teaching children all the potential power of their visual systems today is as important as teaching all of us to read and to understand our Bill of Rights. Being open to inner vision encourages the development of creative ideas. Visualizing pure light can help release pain.

One simple exercise is to show the children a simple object. Then ask them to close their eyes and to visualize it. Open their eyes and look again; did their inner image match, or did they miss some parts? Did they see the color, or details? Then ask them to visualize something they left at home, a dog, cat or toy. Can they draw a picture of it when they open their eyes? This may be easy for some, but for those who "think" mostly in words, this may be difficult, so you might ask them to describe it verbally.

Can they visualize something by remote perception that another child is holding in a different room? Do they "see" something they saw on television instead, because it was already dominant in their memory?

The Pervasive Influence Of Television On Memory

Many problems with the development of visual intelligence are caused by television, which has the potential for implanting trance-induced suggestions with the use of flickering lights and repetitious sound bits. People who are susceptible to hypnotic suggestion will likely be stuck with unwanted memories for the rest of their lives. (9, 10) They can process their emotions and psychological reactions to them, but the actual memory will still be around. I still remember the melody and the words to an advertisement that I heard over and over again on the radio 75 years ago.

> One student in my study of telepathy had watched TV all during the winter holiday, and whatever he watched influenced all of his telepathic responses. Even though he had drawn the shape and color of each target accurately, his written comments included *"...like what I saw on TV."*

Our first memories and the first time that we learned something new are always there in the form that we learned them. That moment is precious. Those memories will be around for a very long time. Letting the children watch cartoons on Saturday morning so the parents can sleep in is a common practice. However, the first words they learn may be those from repetitive advertisements for plastic toys easily broken. This may not be the type of education the parents had in mind for their children, but it is the one they will receive when there is no supervision.

Another visual problem with TV is the after image, which affects your eyes even though you may not pay any attention to it. (12, 13) Try this: When you have watched TV for an hour or more, turn it off. Notice what you see. Then turn the room lights off, or go outside, and notice that wherever you look, a television screen-sized shadow is superimposed over everything. When you close your eyes, it is still there, but lighter. What color is it? Ask others to describe how their own after image looks to them. Keep track of how long it takes for the haze of the afterimage to fade from your vision.

Our visual system is a true form of intelligence in itself, independent of the verbal and symbolic mental processes. It can be expanded and developed through interaction with the dimensional world, as we attempt to respond to it directly. Children need the opportunity to play in and fully experience the wonders of the natural environment.

REFERENCES

1) Oh Shinna (1979) "Educating the whole child on a whole earth." An interview in: *AHP Newsletter—A Special Issue on Education*. C. Guion & J. Millay (Eds.) SF, CA.
2) Ali Akbar Khan (1979) "Education and music." An interview in: *AHP Newsletter—A Special Issue on Education*. C. Guion & J. Millay (Eds.) May pp. 22-23. SF, CA.
3) Kellogg, R. (1969) *Analyzing Children's Art*. Palo Alto, CA: Mayfield Publishing Co.
4) Pasto, T. (1964) *The Space Frame Experience in Art*. NY: A. S. Barnes & Co.
5) Millay, J. (1962) *An Approach to the Discovery and Education of the Visually Oriented Student*. Thesis submitted for teaching credential from UC Berkeley.
6) Campbell, D. (1997) *The Mozart Effect: Tapping the Power of Music to Heal the Body, Strengthen the Mind, & Unlock the Creative Spirit*. NY: Avon Books.
7) Geometric designs for coloring at www.mindwareonline.com.
8) Andrews, C. with Spignesi, S.J. (2003) *Crop Circles: Signs of Contact*. Franklin Lakes, NJ: New Page Books, a division of the Career Press, Inc.
9) Mander, J. (1976) *Four Arguments for the Elimination of TV*. NY: Morrow Quill.
10) Enzenberger, H.M. (1975) *The Consciousness Industry*. NY: The Seabury Press.
11) Millay, J. (1999) *Multidimensional Mind: Remote Viewing in Hyperspace*. Berkeley, CA: A Universal Dialogues Book, North Atlantic Books.
12) Ott, J.N. (1973) *Health and Light*. Old Greenwich, CN: Devin-Adair.
13) Wurtman, R.J. (1975) "The effects of light on the human body." In: *Scientific American*. July 1975; 69-77.

EDUCATION: SOLVING THE PROBLEMS
3-A) SELF-DISCOVERY SCIENCE
(Reports From Two Teachers)

BIOFEEDBACK AND NEUROFEEDBACK

Marge King *[6]

One of the most important purposes of education is to put all children in complete possession of their abilities and talents. To date, those abilities and talents have been defined without reference to the autonomic nervous system. Biological feedback introduced into the school curriculum brings an understanding and control of the nervous system to children before they become habituated to unhealthy reactions to the stresses commonly experienced today in so many educational environments.

There have been decades of research on the therapeutic uses of bio/neurofeedback (BFB) and (NFB). This "Medical Model" has worked successfully to alleviate many health problems, especially for those patients ensnared in old habits of stress. Now it is time to introduce the "Self-discovery Model" of bio/neurofeedback to children before similar unhealthy reactions to stress become habits for them as well. Consider the economic savings in healthcare for adults if they had learned to manage stress early in life, and thus were able to avoid many health problems. The evolution of healthcare in the 21st century should follow our best research, which has created the technology of **energy medicine**, and the tools for learning self-regulation of the autonomic nervous system.

Most of us grew up believing "the doctor knows best," even those who (in these days) spend very little time talking to us. After one very brief look at our chart, some will automatically prescribe expensive (and sometimes harmful) pills. At this writing, we all suffer from this inefficient system,

---

*[6] Marjorie Beers King, MS (1921 - 2002), graduated from high school when she was 16. Her opportunity for higher education came during WWII, when she served in the Navy Waves as a Lieutenant. After marriage and four children, she became their sole support, so she worked for the aerospace industry as a "literature chemist," until they grew up. After earning a teaching credential, she taught math, chemistry and science in high school and college. Her work was among the first to achieve success with difficult students using physiological feedback. This chapter includes excerpts from her major contributions to *Self-Discovery Science*. Available free at www.fmbr.org.

because of its emphasis on the old allopathic model of healthcare, that has been corrupted by large pharmaceutical companies that "buy" political benefits from politicians, and "advise" FDA administrators. Medical schools rarely mention the healing power of good nutrition or herbs that have been used for healing for centuries, *7 and doctors rarely prescribe neurofeedback for pain instead of pills; the insurance doesn't cover it.

We propose the introduction of free and voluntary biofeedback into public school science classes beginning with ten-year-olds. In a short time, these students and their parents could begin the shift of emphasis from allopathic medicine to energy medicine, saving millions of dollars in healthcare (even with the new "healthcare law"). In that way, we could bypass the difficulties now firmly entrenched in the present system. BFB and NFB therapists have proved over many years that these methods work to give the power back to the patient and alleviate ADD and ADHD. *8 Only children with extreme cases actually need the kind of dangerous drugs doctors prescribe for them. When learned early enough, NFB and BFB can be instrumental in increasing the intelligence of students of all ages, since the ability to focus attention is a key to intelligence. Students can also use BFB to enhance sports performance.

By demonstrating to students how their own electrical and magnetic frequencies are related to those of the sun and the earth, children also find that we are all connected to everything. This is good science, especially as we struggle with the problems of climate change and expanding renewable energy. Learning about electromagnetism (EM) is fundamental for all of us now. The current educational system only provides classes in EM for those college-bound high school students who may take a class in physics. But we have demonstrated that ten-year-olds in our BFB classes can understand the basics of it easily as their own electrical physiological responses are fed back to them. More importantly, they will see if their increasing use of electronic gadgets has an effect on their energies.

The *"Self-Discovery Model"* of biofeedback demonstrates the way our bodies respond to our own thoughts and to other people. This information provides the power to change our reactions voluntarily as needed. With this self-control, we can discover also the innate power of our own multidimensional consciousness. In 1975, Leary predicted that students in the future would learn to **"Dial and tune their nervous systems to produce a quantum leap in intellectual efficiency and emotional equilibrium."** *9 The technology of bio/neurofeedback is making that happen. It has

---

*7 Personal communication from interviewing several doctors.

*8 Green, G.H. *The A.D.D. Quest for Identity: Inside the Mind of Attention Deficit Disorder*. Reno, NV: The Biofeedback Center Press. 1997. www.stresslesslife.com.

*9 Leary, T. (1975) "Seeds of the Sixties." *Spit in the Ocean*, Kesey, K. (Ed.).

become inexpensive enough for school use, and is especially useful as well as for personal use at home.

Buryl Payne, PhD, developed the first portable GSR machine to provide sound for feedback (now called SCR for Skin Conductance Resistance). His book *Biomeditation* describes how students invented their own SCR games that they really enjoyed. He wrote:

> One instrument can be connected to a whole group of people if they hold hands or touch each other on the skin. We have connected more than 100 persons to one instrument.... Yelling, deep breathing, chanting, or any of the exercises and experiments, which have been done with the GSR individually, can be done with a group. (See illustration on the first page of Section X, p. 509.)

If anyone stops holding hands, the feedback sound will stop. If two of them tap hands, the feedback sound will match the rhythm. Students directly experience the reality of their electrical connection to each other.

Since the 1970s, health professionals have proved the benefits of NFB and BFB for the prevention or relief of many stress related illnesses. During this same time, quietly without fanfare, and with little or no funding, teachers in different parts of the country have brought **BFB** and **NFB** into their classrooms. Some have used it for lessons in:

1. SCIENCE
   a. To study the electricity and magnetism of the body,
   b. To demonstrate the relationships between brain/body frequencies and those of sun, earth, and sound,
   c. To show physical reactions to thoughts.
2. STRESS MANAGEMENT
   a. To demonstrate ways of releasing emotional tension. (SCR)
3. WAYS TO MODIFY A LEARNING DISABILITY
   a. Brainwave and/or SCR training can be used to help alleviate Attention Deficit Hyperactive Disorder (ADHD / ADD).
4. EXPLORING ANY EFFECT ON THINKING CAUSED BY FOOD OR DRUGS
   a. Do you feel your thinking changes when you are hungry? How?
   b. How do your brainwaves change when you have used any of the following substances? – lots of sugar, greasy food, colas, coffee, high fructose corn syrup (HFCS), Aspartame, or other?
   c. How does your energy level change, and for how long?
5. SELF-DISCOVERY FOR THOSE WHO NOTE THEIR OWN REACTIONS
   a. What changes occur in the energy signals from my body and/or brain when I think about different ideas?
   b. Can I learn to increase my ability to focus attention?
   c. Will my hands and feet get warmer if I just think about warm things?
   d. If my heart is beating rapidly, will it slow down when I focus on breathing slower and more evenly? (Use heart rate feedback.)
   e. Can I learn to stop a headache by relaxing tense muscles?

USE OF COMMON NEUROFEEDBACK INSTRUMENTS

Some are available in portable machines that are inexpensive. Others use sensors with a computer that are operated by a program on a disc.

1. **SKIN CONDUCTANCE RESISTANCE (SCR)** – [It was originally called GSR.]

    This tracks emotional responses by measuring amounts of sweat on your fingertips. Exercise causes sweat, but when the hands are clean and dry, emotional reactions also cause the skin to produce minute amounts of sweat, and this changes the electrical conductance of the skin. Feedback from the SCR can demonstrate a direct relationship between emotions and health.

    Exercise: Each student could keep a record of those thoughts that cause the sound of the SCR to change to a higher or to a lower sound (i.e., thoughts that cause his/her skin to "talk").

2. **SKIN TEMPERATURE (TEMP)** – [The Skin Temperature thermistor and the SCR can be used together. They are both inexpensive.]

    This feedback machine provides a sound that is quite helpful for registering minute changes in skin temperature. A thermistor often comes with the SCR package. Tense muscles will cause the hands and feet to be cold constantly, so the EMG is also useful here, and might be used together with the SCR.

    Exercise: Tape a thermistor to your fingertip to see if you can learn to raise or lower the temperature of your hand. Keep notes on what thoughts help you to do this. (If there is no feedback machine, use a thermometer.)

3. **ELECTRICAL ACTIVITY OF MUSCLES (EMG = ELECTROMYOGRAM)** – [It is slightly more expensive than the SCR.]

    The electrical signals of <u>tense</u> muscles are stronger than the signals of <u>relaxed</u> muscles. With this type of feedback, students can discover for themselves how to relax tight muscles, or how to tighten loose ones after an illness.

    Exercise: Tight muscles in the forehead and neck often cause headaches. When students keep a record of what they do as they learn to relax, they can practice at home without the EMG instrument. This technology can also be used to enhance sports activity.

4. **ELECTRICAL ACTIVITY OF BRAIN (EEG = ELECTROENCEPHALOGRAM)** – [The Electrodes are placed on the scalp to measure the electrical energy from the brain (called EEG or brainwaves). The EEG is more complex and expensive. However, Millay's 5th grade students, and King's continuation high school students learned to use the machines easily as they were also connected to the brainwave light sculpture — illustrated on p. 249.]

    Every thought, feeling or emotion we have is accompanied by electrical signals in our brains. We can learn voluntary control of them using EEG neurofeedback equipment. Measuring brainwaves requires more complex computer analysis, because muscle and eye movements could interfere. If brainwave analyzers are available, however, they have the potential to teach students specific ways to focus attention. Brainwave neurofeedback is used in clinics to alleviate some forms of ADHD. (See www.stresslesslife.com.)

Exercise: Discover the differences in your brain's electrical signals between your thoughts of joy, anger, anxiety, stress, relaxation, or creative insight. It is possible for students to learn how to maintain steady brainwaves in fast or slow frequencies for longer periods of time. This becomes an exercise in learning to increase intelligence. **1)** Form a clear intention. **2)** Practice extending your ability to sustain a steady focus of attention on that intention. **3)** To achieve phase coherence, stop thinking in words while you focus a light or a steady "OM" ("AUM") sound in the center of your head. After such a sustained focus in phase coherence, an idea or a way to solve a problem may arise in your thoughts. (See Appendix A, pages 250-251 in Section 5.)

5. **HEART RATE RHYTHM, ENTRAINMENT AND COHERENCE** – HeartMath Freeze Framer™ and other companies are developing new BFB toys. You can also find a wealth of information about Biofeedback on Google.]
(Mayo's report about student use of heart feedback is on pp. 544-548.)

OTHER FORMS OF SELF-DISCOVERY FEEDBACK

6. **VIDEO FEEDBACK (VF)** – [Most schools have video cameras for teacher use.]

With proper use of VF, students can learn to improve their speaking ability. Students form small groups to talk about a class project (or a subject they choose). A video camera is stationed on a tripod in a corner, where the operator can zoom in on students as they are involved in their discussions. (Those who just look at the camera are ignored.) Before the class ends, the teacher will stop the discussion in time to provide students with that session's feedback. Most students discover that they did much better than they expected. Train the camera operator to find the best moment for each one to enhance his/her self-confidence. Students will discover their own unconscious habits (nervous twitching, mumbling, dominating the conversation or interrupting others) and change them, even when others are not allowed to comment.

7. **DISCOVERING THE DIFFERENCES IN HOW WE THINK AND REMEMBER.**

Ask students simple questions such as, *"Think of a number from 1 to 10."* The actual answer to such a question is not important. <u>How</u> the answer arrived in the mind is important. Did they see it, hear it, or how? What is important is for the students to realize how everyone thinks in different ways.

8. **FEEDBACK OF BODY CHEMISTRY** –

Simple pH test strips can be found at pharmacies or vitamin stores. Their colors show us

ACIDIC		ALKALINE
6 pH	7 pH	8 pH

whether the body is in balance at **7** pH, acidic at **6** pH, or alkaline at **8** pH. When students make a list of those foods that are more alkaline, and which are more acidic, they have more information about how to be more responsible for their own health. Medical studies have suggested that one might be more susceptible to illness if one's body is out of balance because of being highly acidic most of the time. Increasing healthcare costs demand more education about how to take care of our selves and our family.

SUCCESS STORIES

Years ago, when I began teaching science at a continuation high school, I discovered that the students usually only attended school because it was a requirement for staying out of juvenile hall. That is why I developed the "Self-Discovery Model" to use biofeedback as a science lesson. Below is a summary of my students' responses on the final exam:

FINAL EXAM: WHAT DID YOU LEARN IN SCIENCE THIS YEAR?

1) "I've learned a lot from this class. I've always hated science and only took it when I had to, but I heard some people talking about your class so I went and got enrolled. It was hard at first sitting still for five minutes. And dreams, well, I just didn't dream! But I learned different. I could remember my dreams and start to control who or what I dreamed about. The nightmares didn't come as often and dreams with meaning started coming.... I could watch my thoughts and not get involved. Problems that were in my mind got solved easier because I was not involved. This has been the best class I've ever been in. I wish I'd started earlier. I feel a lot better about my mind and body because I know more about it now."

2) "One of the things I think it did for me was to mellow me out. And from being mellow, I have found it much easier to relate to people.... It has also helped me to cut down on using drugs. In the morning I meditate instead of smoking."

3) "I'm understanding how to really have control over my being."

4) "I've learned a lot about bodily functions – how the heart, eyes, lungs, muscles and glands work. I really understand how they work. Not a textbook paragraph of which I can quote but a real understanding. I can now explain in my own words how they work in detail. I've also gained a lot of self-control and a better understanding of people. I've learned to improve my memory, how to relax, meditate, and I can identify all (practically) of my emotions."

5) "When my right hand was eight degrees colder than my left hand, I couldn't get either of them to change. You found a tight muscle in my right shoulder. I used the EMG and got the muscle to relax, so my hand warmed up. A few days later, I found out why my right hand was so cold the other day! Last night my Dad was yelling at me again and after I went to my room, I realized that my shoulder muscles were all tight, because I wanted to hit him. After that, I pretended I was using the temperature trainer and right away relaxed."

Student comments after using the brainwave light sculpture. (p. 249)

6) "I'm in beta when I add, I'm in theta when I'm mad, therefore I can't add when I'm mad."

7) "I'm in alpha when I float with the music, I'm in beta when I listen to the words, and I saw theta flashes on the downbeat in time with the music."

CHAPTER 42 in 4 parts

EDUCATION: SOLVING THE PROBLEMS
3-B) LISTEN TO YOUR HEART TALK *[10]

Mara Mayo

The equipment for this study is called the Freeze-Framer™ program, (1) and it is available through HeartMath, ® Inc. I used a Dell laptop with a sensor hook up that attaches to a finger. The sensor measures heart rate variability from the pulse. Data are collected and analyzed to create graphs and percent of relative coherence. The heart actually produces much higher amplitude of magnetic energy than the brain. This "field" influences the rest of the body in very profound ways. Because it is controlled by feelings and not so much by thought, the feedback is more relevant for working with students with specific learning disabilities, as well as those with severe emotional disturbances. We can bypass the linear thought, and go straight to feelings. It is possible that "Heart Intelligence" might have evolved before the logical brain.

Students who get "hooked up" to it initially get to see their pulse appear on the computer screen (which they all want to try). Then I switch them to a split screen that shows current heart rate variability, three bars that sort the % of coherence, and a graph of "the Zone." The first bar is red which represents low coherence (frustration, anger, intense attention). The second bar is blue which represents medium coherence (mild relaxation, meditation, possibly with alpha brainwaves). The third bar is green, which represents a high level of coherence (feelings of pure joy, gratitude, connectedness). Timed trials are printed out and saved for future comparisons with past data. The program comes with the ability to graph progress as well as look at power spectrum information on each trial (reported in Hz).

---

*[10] *Mara Mayo, M.F.M.C., C.S.A.C., began working as a high school therapist in 1994. She had used other biofeedback instruments before, but most of the students who were sent to her office were initially too nervous or hostile to use them. However, with the HeartMath program, most could relate to the idea of controlling changes in their heart rhythms. The program was quite successful, and was later used with adults for drug abuse prevention. Later she retired to spend more time on her farm, with her exotic birds, plants and animals. These can be seen on her website: www.maramayo.com along with her fine art work.*

According to 2000 census, Pahoa High and the Intermediate school is the most culturally diverse school in the USA. It is located on the Big Island of Hawaii in the Puna district. I worked as a school based behavioral therapist, with a caseload of Disthymic Disorder, Conduct Disorder, Intermittent Explosive Disorder, ADHD, PTSD, ODD, and MR clients. Additionally, some are also poly-substance abusers.

The average reading level is 3rd–5th grade. Half of my caseload is in need of day treatment, but there is none available on this island. Students who come into my office have different communication styles as well as different understandings about what they hear. The local dialect is a "Pidgin English" that incorporates words from the Hawaiian, Japanese, Chinese, Filipino and Portuguese languages. The structure is similar to the original Hawaiian language with subject, object, verb order reversal and varying intonation. It is a heart-based culture, originally from an oral tradition with no written language. Traditional school has failed these children, as it does not address the challenges of the various learning styles. Combine that with postcolonial identity confusion and poverty, and this creates many situations of domestic abuse. Most of these kids come to me with the belief that OTHERS make them mad! They have no concept or experience of emotional self-control. Most don't believe that it is possible.

The Freeze-Framer™ program allows them to experience their own heart in a different way. It gives them the opportunity to see that they do have control of their feelings, and how that ultimately affects their body. Sessions with this tool become part science lesson, part self-discovery and part therapy. I am always pleased with the results. Even if the students cannot relax at first, or even identify how they feel, a door has been opened for a new perspective.

SUCCESS STORIES

Some successes include a 9th grader, who has had behavior problems historically since early grammar school. He was able to move into a fully self-contained classroom. He started on the Freeze-Framer™ in November 2001. By February, he could take five deep breaths and become calm. In the classroom he progressed from a reading level of l.9 to nearly 3rd grade level in just months. Best of all, he takes more responsibility for his own behavior.

A 10th grader who used to come in here and explain how *"so and so made me so mad, I had to hit him."* Later he came to me when he wanted to see how "amped" he was so he could bring it down. He knows that it is up to him to control it!

For the most part, the fully self-contained classes used me as a way to de-escalate students who are out of control. I like to help them realize when they assign fault for their feelings to someone else, that they are giving their power away.

Another success was a 17-year-old boy, who had serious problems with peers and attendance. After biofeedback practice, he started coming to school every day. He found something that he can do well, and that gave him some positive recognition. Other students began competing to see how well they could do at controlling their heart and mood. This form of self-discovery, through biofeedback, gives a measure of personal power back to the student. The benefits can be exponential. The benefits of learning some voluntary control <u>before a crisis</u> is demonstrated below.

A thirteen-year-old girl had previously learned to establish some voluntary control over her heart rhythms. But one day she ingested some speed and an unknown substance. The teacher who sent her to my office described her behavior as "silly" and "off the wall." Her heart rate was wild and dangerous (**Chart 1**) with rates shifting between 59 bpm to 136 bpm (bpm = beats per minute).

Chart 1 = Heart rate is 59 bpm to 136 bpm

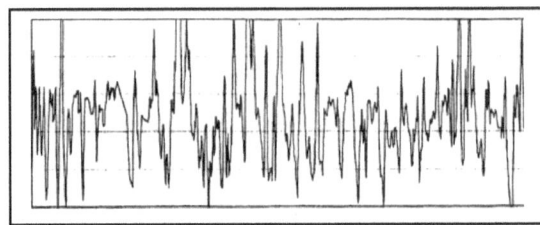

After two and a half hours, she was able to bring her heart rhythms back from the total chaos of extreme variability to a relatively calmer rate between 68 bpm to 110 bpm. **Chart 2** below shows at least some improvement in her heart rate, but it was still not as good as the more coherent rhythm she had been able to do before mixing speed-type drugs. Fortunately, she was able to do much better the next day.

Chart 2 = Heart rate is 68 bpm to 110 bpm

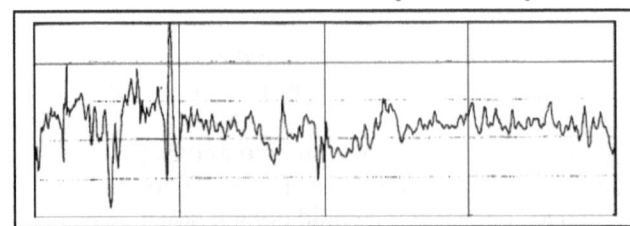

Chart 3 (next page) shows what a coherent heart rate looks like. Compare it with the two charts from the student above. The Freeze Framer™ biofeedback devise was also used at Lokahi treatment center

(2004-2009) with adults with good success to provide an alternative to drugs for control of emotions and anger, and to empower a feeling of self-control and well being. *[11]

After I had practiced some time on this equipment myself, I was able to bring about the coherent heart rhythms shown below. On that day, I was totally there with empathy for my students

Chart 3 = My own coherent heart rhythm on a good day

REFERENCES AND NOTES

1) The following is quoted from the Freeze-Framer™ User's Manual:

The Freeze-Framer™ was developed based on research findings conducted by the Institute of HeartMath® *under the direction of Doc Childre, PhD, & Howard Martin, PhD, in Boulder Creek, CA. It embodies the successful merging of the latest scientific findings on physiological balance. IHM's research indicates that a person's state of heart, or heart entrainment, is integrally linked with state of mind, emotions and physiology. Learning how to enter and maintain the heart entrainment mode results in coherence which uplifts the mind and body, and results in clearer thinking, improved problem solving skills, increased concentration, and an overall more peaceful outlook....*

When people...sustained sincere positive feelings like appreciation, the heart adopts a more coherent mode of function in its rhythmic beating patterns and can pull other biological systems into entrainment with it. In this state there is harmonious balance between the two branches of the autonomic nervous system and our physiological systems operate with increased efficiency ... * www.heartmath.com.

2) Students from Phyllis Gagnier's project with the Tohono O'odham Tribe wrote about their HeartMath experiences:

Ashley, age 12 – *HeartMath is special and fun. It gets you in your heart. Makes you do better in school and feel better for the rest of the day. It helps you focus and it helps me get along with friends. After I get out of the HeartMath class, I go to science and I feel better for the rest of the day.*

---

*[11] [Editor's note: The billions wasted on the "drug war" could be diverted to supplying bio/neurofeedback programs and trainers directly to the schools across the country. All are suffering from similar problems.

Kyle, age 12 – *HeartMath helps me try harder in school. When I shift to my heart, I feel good.*

Gordon, age 12 – *I show other kids how to do the Freeze-Framer™ so they learn to get in the heart. Being in your heart relaxes you. It feels good.*

Jesse, age 13 – *This HeartMath stuff is about learning more about your heart. How to get in it and listen to what it is telling you, because your mind can sometimes tell you bad things to do, like hurt people. The heart gives you good thoughts. I like the Freeze-Framer because I can see my heart rhythm. It will tell if you are getting into your heart or just in your mind. Sometimes, I practice getting in my heart when I'm in my room alone. I can be more relaxed alone.*

Jonathan, age 11 – *I like to shift to my heart when my friends make me mad. Shifting to my heart helps me get along better with my friends.*

We are at a critical juncture where children and adults need to be empowered to be their own heroes and healers as much as possible... not only could biofeedback serve our children as means of approaching behavioral problems that consistently plague our schools today, it could prevent the development of these problems and in fact free up energy and creativity for significantly greater gains.

--- *Stephen Wall, PhD*
--- (2001) bri@7hz.com, Cotati, CA

EDUCATION: SOLVING THE PROBLEMS
4) EXPLORING THE DIMENSIONS OF SELF *[12]

Sola Patricia

First we must realize that children are full-grown spirits in little bodies. There is no need to talk down to them or use a baby voice. And they don't have to be taught to be psi sensitive, they were born that way, and they could feel and respond to the emotions of others before they could talk.... They don't have to be taught how to see auras, read minds, see possible futures, and communicate with trees, insects, birds, or flowers. They already know and would just like for these talents to be accepted and respected.... Young children do seem to be telepathic, which accounts for how quickly they pick up language, as well as the positive and negative traits of their parents. Before the age of two some children recall their past lives. Some children have psychokinetic abilities. Some learn to connect with animals easily. Much of this ability diminishes with age and exposure to our culture, which generally doesn't reinforce them.

How are children to be taught these wonderful talents in the classroom? ... The aim of good education is to help children retain the talents they were born with. The goal is to possess freedom of movement, of emotions, of mental activity, psychic skills, and appreciation and respect for other people and all living beings.... As a teacher it's easy to make games out of these talents, and encourage their use.... (1)

--- Buryl Payne

Gail Hayssen's psi ability was encouraged in her childhood. As an adult, her substantial ability as a remote viewer has provided significant information that enriched the studies of consciousness (pages 608-611). Young people who grow up in a milieu where unique experiences are accepted and openly discussed are more liable to become what Aldous Huxley (2) has called "full blown human beings" than are those whose self expression is criticized and repressed.

---

*[12] Sola Patricia has over thirty years experience as an innovator and teacher of many holistic programs – from preschool through college level. As co-founder of the *Jefferson Economic Development Institute*, she was awarded the *Distinguished Educator Award* in 1993 by the CA Dept. of Ed. for her *"LifeWorks! Pathways to Success Program."* Sola's *"Conversations with God"* TV show interviewed guests on their direct psi experiences and it was awarded the *Swan Award* for best new TV show in Ashland, Oregon in 1994. At the PRG, she often guided group meditation circles.

Elders in many Native American traditions would observe the children carefully, and listen to their dreams. A child, who was particularly sensitive, compassionate and aware, would be trained very early to become a healer. Oh Shinna, a healer and teacher who integrates modern practices with the Apache and Mohawk traditions learned from her great-grandmother, describes her childhood experiences for us:

> My great-grandmother used to take me into the towns, take me to a street corner and put her hands over my eyes. After 18 seconds or so she'd remove her hands, let me take a look around, and then make me close my eyes and describe to her everything I saw. She wanted me to... read the people to describe their attitudes.... Also [while she was] doctoring she'd bring a person into the room and have me look at him. [Later] she would... ask me what I saw, what I thought was wrong with him. She started me on all of this when I was about two years old. She did hand exercises, little hand games, to sensitize my hands, to feel the energy between them. Then she took me from feeling my own energy to the animals. She showed me how I could help make the animals get better by certain energy manipulations. She would blindfold me and put things into my hand, and make me tell what they were. It got kind of intense when I was about four. Up until then it was like games, but when I was four, she really got serious about it... *[13]

CARES GAMES

There are a variety of exercises that a teacher can use to enhance the awareness and development of students' innate sensitivities. Among them are the CARES games (which are <u>C</u>arefully <u>A</u>rranged to <u>R</u>elease <u>E</u>motions <u>S</u>afely). CARES games need to be carefully selected to fit developmental age, culture, and current emotional awareness level of the class.

GUIDELINES:
1) Create a safe environment with open space and establish agreements for nonviolent communication.
2) Provide clear and simple instructions, and include a demonstration.
3) Begin rhythmic music and encourage the students during the exercise.
4) Provide time for students to reflect on their experiences quietly.
5) Support students to choose their own creative expressions which can be private or shared in a circle — draw, paint, write a story, dance, sing or keep a journal for personal reflection.
6) It is essential to have solid safety nets available, since some students may need to deal with their emotions privately first, or with a counselor. The SCR is also useful for understanding and releasing one's emotions.

---

*[13] Oh Shinna (1979) Excerpts from "Educating the whole child on a whole earth." In: *AHP Newsletter – A Glimpse Into the Future of Education.* May, pp. 20-21. Guion, C. & Millay, J. (Eds.) SF, CA.

MOVEMENT AND DANCE TO EXPRESS EMOTIONS

To begin, the teacher will ask the students to help clear the space for active movement. Students then stand apart from each other, while the teacher directs them to begin deep even breathing. As the musical rhythms begin, the students individually explore different ways to move with it (teacher can suggest movements like jump, shake, dance, wiggle, jiggle, shake fingers, or just let go of muscle tension). When any emotions arise, students are encouraged to release it through the movement. (3, 4)

Use the music to follow the energy level of the class, finally tapering the volume and rhythm to a gentle softness. Invite the students to find a quiet resting place for a time of personal reflection. Guide the students in becoming aware of their breathing and consciously slowing the breath towards a calm state. As students relax, the teacher provides art tools for personal creative expression of their experience.

CREATIVE EXPRESSION

After the students have decided in what way they want to express their thoughts and feelings during the exercise, they may come into a circle. Here they have option of sharing, or just listening to the experiences of others. Listening guidelines are important to allow the speaker to share without evaluation, interruption or feedback. After this sharing is complete it is time for a recess. When class resumes, a minute of silence can precede the next activity. My experience has shown students' ability to focus attention increases significantly after the CARES games. (5)

CONFLICT RESOLUTION

Older students need different methods to release anger and thereby gain relief and control. Individuals or groups having difficulty resolving disagreements may call for a Youth Council with the clear guidelines already established. Students play the roles of judge, jury and attorneys. Allow each side the same short amount of time to state the problems in quiet voices (no shouting). This may be enough to clarify a misunderstanding. If not, a "trial" will be held. The jury will recommend remedies to the judge for actions to be taken to re-establish harmony within the learning environment.

Allowing the emotions to be expressed in the classroom in a formal setting has a better chance of keeping them manageable, rather than ignoring them until they erupt in violence in the schoolyard. The Youth Council promotes self-responsibility and learning as well as creative activity. Students write papers about the experience, and may suggest ways of improving the conflict resolution process. As students take more responsibility in managing their own class, they are empowered.

COMMUNICATION WITH NATURE

Children need to become acquainted with nature. In a big city, even a small park can provide an opportunity to practice communicating with growing things. Little children usually know that the world is actually alive, and if they don't know it yet, they are usually happy to find out. Encourage children to listen quietly and to imagine what the plants are communicating to them. When a group plays with imagination in this way, it can be fun for both teachers and students, especially when they share their experiences, to see how similar or different their experiences are. Children may try to "experience" the tree, with their backs touching it, and their eyes closed. They might try to "feel" the roots going into the ground, and the branches reaching to the top of the tree. Trees actually vibrate between 7.4 – 7.8 cycles per second, which is also in the range of frequencies used by the heart and brain. (See Chapter 23 and reference 8.)

HEALING

Small children usually enjoy group healing. When a child is hurt, a group healing can be formed, using hands-on healing, while each individual focuses an intention that a healing take place. If one student is upset, ask the class to visualize a light around her/him. This will help to add positive energy to the sad person's biofield.

Older students who live with heavy emotional problems at home may need different approaches. For example: The teacher can suggest that if one student has a pain in her hand, that student could visualize a healing light in that spot. At the same time, the teacher (or a friend) can put a hand lightly on each side of the other's pain and focus a healing light between them. If they both can visualize the light at the same moment in time, their brainwaves can become synchronized for that moment, and when both "feel" that the light connects, a small pain will usually go away. (6) The power of visualization has been the subject of many books, and educational programs that foster visualization, intuition, healing and self-exploration of human potential. (p. 537 and ref. 5) For serious illnesses, spiritual healers call on their spirit guides and/or the higher powers of the cosmos that connects all of us in the light of healing love.

REMOTE VIEWING FOR CHILDREN

The practice of remote viewing for children and adults begins with a clear mind. Old memories, especially emotional ones, can become a source of error in the interpretation of a remote perception, so for optimal results in any type of RV experience begin with an exercise to clear the mind of emotional material. The use of feedback technologies to bring phase-coherence to the heart rhythms, or to the brainwaves is a useful way to clear the mind of its busy dialog. The age-old standard practice used to clear the mind is meditation. Then there are numerous classes that teach different methods of RV–RP–ARV–CRV. They are listed in the website of the International Remote Viewing Association (www.irva.com), and so are the websites of their various members.

The games presented here are designed to help children clear their uncomfortable memories, so they can "see" beyond them and to be more open to their own psi sensitivity – however it manifests to them. Those children, who needed to be released from unhealthy memories, and were encouraged to find creative ways to become free of them, can more fully enjoy the exploration of the multidimensions of their own consciousness. The games presented in Chapter 42-2 are also useful to learn the language of the senses. When the mind is clear, the senses can provide information from anywhere. Can we communicate an inner vision, a sound, or a smell to others when we experience it?

SUMMARY

When children are honored and respected for what they already feel and know, they are more likely to be inspired to learn more. Each individual naturally holds precious and unique gifts that can resonate with others, as well. Each person is but one string of a harp, yet when all the strings are skillfully played together, celestial harmonies sing beyond the Earthly ear. As we experience the joy of this harmony together, we also appreciate and respect all people and all living beings.

REFERENCES AND NOTES

1) The authors wish to thank Dr Buryl Payne for the extensive contributions he has made to the field and to this chapter especially.
2) Huxley, A. (1962) *Island*. Harper & Row.
3) Pesso, A. (1973) *Experience in Action: A Psychomotor Psychology*. NY: New York University Press. [Note: Albert Pesso is the founder of *Psychomotor Therapy*.]
4) Lowen, A. (1969) *Bioenergetics: The revolutionary therapy that uses the language of the body to heal the problems of the mind.* www.bioenergeticpress.com/.
5) Patricia, Sola (1988) *LifeWorks! Pathways to Success*. Self-Sufficiency Curriculum for Jefferson Economic Development Institute.
6) Millay, J. (1994) Personal communication. Casual and random observations over the years of doing this "visualization for pain relief" have depended on the simultaneous presence of the EEG phase comparator, the healer and the person with a pain. A definitive study could be made of this healing process with the modern equipment.
7) Caddy, Peter (1980) Organizer of *Gathering of the Ways*. This was a series of seminars with international leaders of consciousness studies — the youth program part of this series — "Childlight" was directed by Sola Patricia at Stewart Springs, Mt. Shasta.
8) Payne, B. (2010) *Discovery of the biofield: A different type of magnetism?* (Manuscript in preparation.) For more information see his website: www.buryl.com.

HOLISTIC EDUCATION:
A STATISTICALLY SIGNIFICANT STUDY

--- V. Louise Crawley Sample

Louise Sample, MA, taught middle school for 30 years. She served as an instructor at JFKU in Orinda, CA. She developed seminars on biofeedback, learning styles, multiple intelligences, cooperative learning, self-esteem, and brain research. She was a board member of the Institute for Integrative Learning and Teaching, a developer and trainer for Project REACH, *a consultant to school districts, and a trainer for the* TRIBES *program among others, as well as a coauthor* of The Heroic Journey: A Rite of Passage for Adolescents.

ABSTRACT

This pilot study investigated the effects of holistic educational techniques in jr. high English classes. Five classes and two teachers were involved. Pre-post CTSS reading tests were administered to 141 students. Pre-post personal assessment questionnaires were administered to 162 students. The same curriculum was presented to all students. However, students in the control classes were taught in the traditional mode, using units and materials designed for specific ability levels. In the experimental classes, all students were given the materials designed for the gifted level, and holistic teaching methods were used. These included cooperative learning, multi-modal and multi-intelligence processes, accelerated learning, and biofeedback for relaxation and stress reduction.

Statistically significant improvements of the experimental group over the control group were recorded in all areas tested in this study:

(1) Vocabulary;
(2) Reading comprehension;
(3) Self-esteem;
(4) Positive attitude increase.

On the CTBS, the experimental group showed a mean **gain of 15.3** months growth, as contrasted with a mean gain of **9.2** months growth for the control group **(P < .002)**. The experimental group also demonstrated an average of **10% overall increase** in positive attitude/self-esteem responses above the control group. **This pilot study validated use of the holistic educational techniques, which increased learning, self-esteem and positive attitudes.**

SECTION XI

REFLECTING ON PARAPSYCHOLOGY

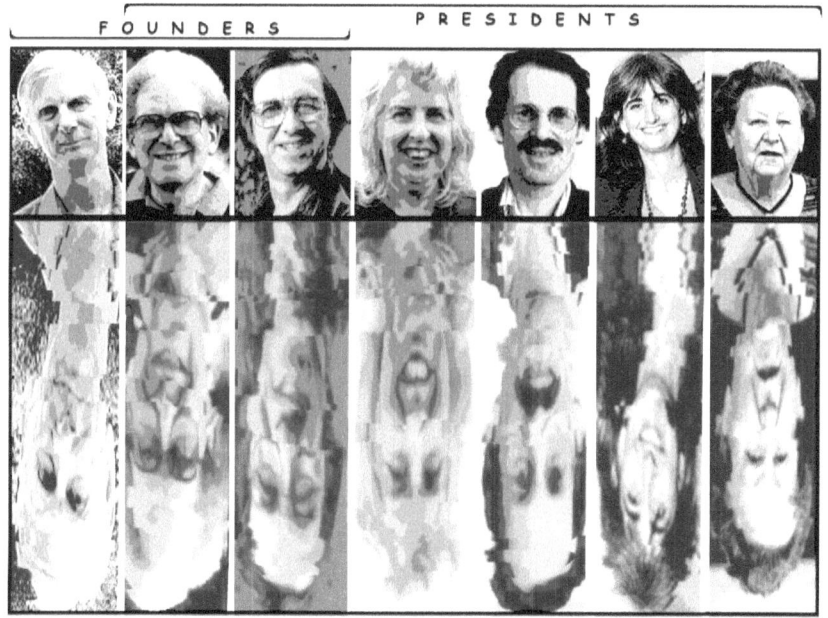

* See Timeline for additional founders and presidents

SECTION XI

REFLECTING ON PARAPSYCHOLOGY

When PRG members chose to research the field of the paranormal, we also found that we chose a life of criticism, derision, and for some of us, difficulty getting the college degree we studied for, and/or finding a job. However, it is from the last forty years of the persistent research by this brave group, along with others around the world, that today the reality of psi events are better known. Most of the milestones listed below are those our members and their colleagues had accomplished by publication date in 1993. (A few notes have been added that were overlooked at that time.)

MILESTONES IN THE HISTORY OF THE PARAPSYCHOLOGY RESEARCH GROUP

The first PRG Anthology from 1963 to publication in 1993

1963 Jeffrey Smith, professor of religion and philosophy at Stanford, gives a talk at the university about his own psychic experiences.

1964 Charles T. Tart, Arthur Hastings, Russell Targ, David Hurt and others meet in Jeffrey Smith's home to begin discussions of parapsychology.

1965 The political and cultural climate in northern California, characterized by the civil rights, free speech, peace movements, and the psychedelic subculture provides a legendary milieu for revolutionary and creative thinking.

1966 *The Parapsychology Research Group* (PRG) is founded in January. The first board of directors consists of Frederick Domeyer, David Hurt, Walter Neumeyer, Jeffrey Smith, Russell Targ, and Charles T. Tart. Also present at that time were Charles Schulz and Anthony White. Russell Targ was elected president at the first official meeting in February.

1966 Charles T. Tart, assistant professor of psychology at UC Davis, publishes "Models for the Explanation of Extrasensory Perception" in the *International Journal of Neuropsychiatry*.

1968 Joe Kamiya reports in *Psychology Today* that subjects in his studies gain "Conscious control of brainwaves." (His study of EEGs during dreaming, which began in 1958, stimulates research among parapsychologists as well as medical scientists. His discovery of EEG biofeedback—later called neurofeedback—gives rise to bio/neurofeedback societies around the world. The operant conditioning models that follow grow into the next new field of psychoneuroimmunology.)

1968 Stanley Krippner and Montague Ullman begin to teach and publish their groundbreaking work at Maimonides Medical Center in Brooklyn, New York in dream telepathy, which began in 1964.

1969 Charles T. Tart publishes the influential book *Altered States of Consciousness: A Book of Readings*.

1970 *Psychic Discoveries Behind the Iron Curtain* by Shelley Ostrander and Lynn Schroeder stirs up new interest in psychic research. Limited funding for research becomes available in some areas.

1971 David Hurt and Russell Targ create the multiple-choice extrasensory perception (ESP) teaching machine. *[1]

1971 Tim Scully and Jean Millay develop the *First Stereo Brainwave Biofeedback Light Sculpture* with grants from her parents (George and Grace Beers) and from Stanley Krippner.

1972 Summer – Stanley Krippner and James Hickman travel to the USSR to meet Soviet parapsychologists mentioned in *Psychic Discoveries behind the Iron Curtain*. On their return, they sponsor *The First Western Hemisphere Conference on Biofeedback, Acupuncture, Kirlian Photography and the Human Aura* in NYC.

1972 Fall – With a grant from the US government, Targ and Puthoff establish a parapsychology research lab at SRI International in Menlo Park, CA. They carry out successful experiments in remote viewing (RV). Ten years of research follows.

1973 Astronaut Edgar Mitchell founds the Institute of Noetic Sciences (IONS). Later, Willis Harman becomes president.

1973 Spring – Charles T. Tart organizes a major conference on ESP at UC Davis, which was repeated at UC Berkeley.

1974 Stanley Krippner and James Hickman return to the USSR for a conference and lay the groundwork for the Soviet-American exchange program to be sponsored by Esalen Inst., Big Sur, CA.

---

*[1] In 1972, Russell Targ asked Tim Scully to redesign the ESP teaching machine and in 2009, he asked David Levitt to develop it for an iPod—now available free.

1974 Eleanor Criswell, a professor at CA State U at Sonoma (CSUS), initiates a special studies program in parapsychology attracting students from all over the country. Criswell, as president of the Association for Humanistic Psychology (AHP), helped organize its branch – Humanistic Psychology Institute in 1971– renamed Saybrook Institute in 1976. Stanley Krippner joins that faculty as professor of psychology. The institute becomes a center for students interested in parapsychology and alternative healing.

1975 Henry Dakin establishes the *Washington Research Institute* (WRI), which encourages and assists publications on consciousness research. A first one is: *Kundalini, Psychosis or Transcendence?* by Lee Sannella, MD. The WRI also sponsors activities that play a role in opening communications between parapsychologists in the US and the USSR that help to diffuse the Cold War.

1975 Elizabeth Rauscher convenes the *Fundamental Fysiks Group* at Lawrence Berkeley Laboratory with forty physicists to discuss quantum theory and Bell's remote-connectedness theorem. They also perform remote viewing experiments and continued to meet regularly until 1979.

1975 Jeffrey Mishlove receives the first and only PhD degree in parapsychology from the University of California Berkeley.

1975 William Kautz founds the Center for Applied Intuition (CAI) in SF.

1975 A successful intercontinental remote viewing session is conducted among participants at four locations: 1) the AHP conference held in Estes Park, Colorado (led by Stanley Krippner); 2) the *Congress of Sorcery* in Bogotá, Colombia, SA (led by Jean Millay); 3) the *Metatantay Foundation* in Carlin, Nevada (led by Rolling Thunder); 4) a studio in Santa Rosa, CA, where artist James Dowlen drew images that he received telepathically from all three places with extraordinary accuracy.

1978 Henry Dakin publishes *High-Voltage Photography* to aid researchers in understanding Kirlian photography as well as other methods for showing physiological and psychophysical energy interactions as visible images.

1979 Barbara Honegger becomes president of the PRG for one year while earning the first accredited master's degree in parapsychology at John F. Kennedy University. Two years later, she becomes a policy analyst in the Reagan White House Office of Policy Development.

1979 Arthur Hastings becomes dean of the Institute of Transpersonal Psychology, and becomes president from 1983 to 1984.

1980 Elizabeth Rauscher becomes president of the PRG until 1986.

1980 Willis Harman becomes a member of the board of regents of the UC until 1990. His book *Global Mind Change (1988)* is significant.

1980 William Gough and Virginia Cates established the *Foundation for Mind-Being Research* as a non-profit scientific organization.

1981 Larissa Vilenskaya, sponsored by Henry Dakin and the *Washington Research Institute*, emigrates from USSR to the US. She translates papers smuggled out of the USSR for *The Voice of America* and she produces and edits the *Psi Research Review*.

1984 Ruth-Inge Heinze inaugurates an *Annual International Conference on the Study of Shamanism and Alternative Healing* in San Rafael.

1986 Jean Millay becomes president of the PRG until 1988 and asks the group to celebrate the PRG's 20th anniversary by writing for a book called *Mind Matters*. Dean Brown agrees to be coeditor.

1988 Saul-Paul Sirag becomes president of the PRG for one year.

1988 Beverly Rubik becomes director of the *Center for Frontier Sciences* at Temple University, Philadelphia.

1989 Shelley Thomson becomes president of the *SF Tesla Society*.

1989 Jean Millay returns as president of the PRG to revive the idea of a PRG anthology, now to be a twenty-fifth anniversary volume.

1990 Beverley Kane assumes production of the PRG book. The new title is *Silver Threads: 25 Years of Explorations in Parapsychology*.

1990 Jean Burns cofounds the *Consciousness and Science Discussion Group* at UCSF with Ravi Gomatam of the Bhaktivedanta Institute.

1992 The PRG board of directors consists of Jean Millay, PhD, president; Bryan McRae, secretary; Henry S. Dakin, treasurer; Dean Brown, PhD; Jean Burns, PhD; Ruth-Inge Heinze, PhD; Beverley Kane, MD; Elizabeth Rauscher, PhD; Russell Targ; Shelley Thomson.

1992 Elisabeth Targ, MD, becomes president of the PRG.

1993 The first anthology of the PRG is published with Kane, B., Millay, J. & Brown, D. (Eds.). *SILVER THREADS: 25 Years of Parapsychology Research*. CT: Praeger. It cost $69.00 with 340-pages in hardcover.

1999 Elisabeth Targ, MD, and her colleagues found (through randomized double-blind clinical trials) significant benefit to HIV positive AIDS patients from receiving prayers from distant healers of a variety of faiths. This groundbreaking study was reported in the national news—*Time* magazine, *The Wall Street Journal*, and *The News Hour with Jim Lehrer*.

2001 Mark Cummings, PhD, became president of the PRG, when his wife Elisabeth Targ became ill. He is a physicist who studies Buddhism, but there is no picture or bio of him here, since he has been traveling out of the country for two or more years, and we have not been able to contact him for this book.

2003 Ruth-Inge Heinze, PhD, volunteered to hold meetings at her apartment in Berkeley when Henry Dakin retired and closed the *Washington Research Institute* (WRI).

2004 The PRG disbanded as an organization. The major accomplishments of our old and new members, since the last publication, are listed in each of their essays in this final anthology of this extraordinary collection of scientists called the *Parapsychology Research Group*.

2010 At the time of this publication, our members continue to explore the vast dimensions of the Great Mystery. Some have retired into private study and/or meditation. Others continue to support advanced study through their websites, which are listed in their bios. A partial list of webs below provide additional information:
- American Society for Psychical Research at www.aspr.com
- Association for Humanistic Psychology at www.ahpweb.org
- Association for Transpersonal Psychology at www.atpweb.org
- Foundation for Mind/Being Research at ww.fmbr.org
- International Remote Viewing Association at www.irva.org
- International Society for the Study of Subtle Energies and Energy Medicine at www.issseem.org
- Parapsychology Association at www.parapsych.org
- The Institute of Noetic Sciences at www.noetic.org

(Additional groups are listed among the websites of participating authors and in the biographies that follow.)

2010 The final anthology of the PRG is published, with great appreciation for the substantial help of our authors, and our family and friends.

RADIANT MINDS:
Scientists Explore the Dimensions of Consciousness

> *Parapsychology is not an anti-intellectual science. Rather, it seeks to elevate all abilities to the standard of our intellectual genius. Intelligence is neither synonymous with nor solely a function of the intellect. All modes of experience constitute a unified intelligence.*
>
> *--- Beverley Kane*

CHAPTER 44   FIFTY-FIVE YEARS IN PARAPSYCHOLOGY

Charles Tart, PhD

Charles T. Tart is the Executive Faculty at the Institute of Transpersonal Psychology (ITP), Professor Emeritus of Psychology at UC Davis and Senior Research Fellow of the Institute of Noetic Sciences (IONS). He is internationally known for his research with altered states of consciousness, transpersonal psychology, and parapsychology. His books include two that have been called classics, *Altered States of Consciousness* and *Transpersonal Psychologies*. In 1997, he edited essays by eleven major authors in the book *Body, Mind, Spirit: Exploring the Parapsychology of Spirituality*. In addition, he has published eleven other books; most of them deal with states of consciousness, marijuana intoxication and parapsychology. His 1986 *Waking Up: Overcoming the Obstacles to Human Potential* synthesized Buddhist and Sufi mindfulness training ideas transmitted by G. I. Gurdjieff with modern psychology, as did *Living the Mindful Life* and *Mind Science: Meditation Training for Practical People* (2000), further exploring the possibilities of awakening. His most recent book is *The End of Materialism: How Evidence of the Paranormal is Bringing Science and Spirit Together*. He has been a student of Aikido, Buddhist meditation, Gurdjieff's work and of other psychological and spiritual growth disciplines. His primary goals are to build bridges between the scientific and spiritual communities and to help bring about a refinement and integration of Western and Eastern approaches to personal and social growth.

More information is available on his website and on his blog: http://www.paradigm-sys.com/cttart and on http://blog.paradigm-sys.com.

FIFTY-FIVE YEARS IN PARAPSYCHOLOGY: FRUSTRATIONS, ADVANCES, DIRECTIONS, MEANING AND AN INTERESTING LIFE

Charles T. Tart

I read my first books on parapsychology as a young teenager, probably about 1950. I was a voracious reader by then, visiting the Trenton city library once or twice a week on my bicycle and checking out at least half a dozen (eight was the library's limit) adult books every time. My interests were very wide – religion, astronomy, physics, chemistry, adventure, electricity and electronics, pioneering, explosives and weapons (I was a boy, after all!), psychology, hypnosis, occultism, etc. With the wisdom of more than 60 years of hindsight, some of what I read was undoubtedly fantasy and craziness, masquerading as fact, some was very profound, but that's the self-taught information mass I started from. Among my many thoughts about parapsychology stimulated by this reading, though, there was never one that some day I would be a senior person in the field, looking back on a lifetime of research, and asked to give some wise advice to new people entering the field!

Why would a young teenage boy read about psychical research and parapsychology? Partly just plain curiosity – this was interesting and puzzling stuff – but mainly as an attempt to deal with my own developing conflicts, shared by so many in our culture, between science and religion. I was raised as a Lutheran by my loving grandmother, and as a child I accepted what I was taught. But as I grew older and started thinking for myself, while the heart of spirituality deeply appealed to me, too many other aspects of it didn't make sense, or seemed contradicted by what I was learning from my new love, science. I was thus understandably excited when I read the goals of the founders of the Society for Psychical Research. Yes, they agreed with critics, some of religion makes no sense, some may be psychopathological, and some is factually contradicted by modern science, but spirituality and religion (by which I distinguish as "religion" the complex social adaptations that started from direct spiritual experience) are where our highest human values come from.

Should we throw them out completely, as so many insisted, in favor of nothing but materialism? No, rather than be so extreme, let's apply the basic *methods* of science, the emphasis on good data, experiments, and testable hypotheses, to the area of spirituality and see if we can separate the wheat from the chaff, the real spiritual phenomena from the accumulated superstitions and social distortions.

I was inspired and took it as my personal life goal to aid in this refining process. Yes, there is some deep emotional appeal in spirituality for me, but the *method* of science (as opposed to the arrogant attitude of scientism) is indeed a good one for refining knowledge – and besides, I've always hated to be fooled about anything! Looking at the state of our world, refinement and discrimination and better understandings of the spiritual are desperately needed! More than 55 years later, I'm still working at it. My best understandings to date are in my latest book, *The End of Materialism: How Evidence of the Paranormal is Bringing Science and Spirit Together*. (45) I'm not alone in this concern. While many scientists investigating aspects of parapsychology claim to be working from pure scientific curiosity, a survey I carried out in 2001 found that about one third of parapsychologists acknowledged important spiritual motivations for entering the field. (42)

In accordance with a basic aim of this book, to give new researchers to the field some ideas of potentially fruitful directions,*[2] I will briefly mention some of the main areas I've researched in my 55+ years in the field and continuations or expansions on them that I think can be fruitful. I wish I had the time and resources to review *all* the exciting developments in parapsychology in my lifetime, not just ones I've been personally involved in, but that's too much for this work.

BACKGROUND CONSIDERATIONS

Scientific research doesn't happen in a vacuum of totally disinterested, objective observers simply indulging their curiosity, so my personal approach and personal life is an integral part of the story here. To begin, there are two important considerations as background for my work.

---

*[2] To mention just some of those I've found most stimulating and exciting, but have had little or no personal involvement in researching, with references to start the interested reader wanting to know more of that area: geomagnetic effects on psi (Persinger, 1987), effects of sidereal time on psi (S.J.P., 1997), the application of remote viewing in archeology (S. Schwartz, 2007; S. A. Schwartz, 1978), extensive studies of near-death experiences (Ring, 1984), psychic healing studies (Dossey, 2001), laboratory study of psychic dreams (Krippner, 1993), poltergeist studies (Auerbach, 1986), presentiment effects (May, 2005), the Ganzfeld technique for inducing psi (Bem, Palmer, & Broughton, 2001), reincarnation studies (Stevenson, 1974, 1997; Tucker, 2005), and Rhea White's brilliant analyses of the internal processes of talented psychics (White, 1964).

First, I've almost never tried to "prove" the existence of basic psi phenomena like telepathy, clairvoyance, precognition, psychokinesis (PK) or psychic healing. Even as a teenager, it was clear to me that the mainstream establishment's resistance to accepting psi phenomena was irrational. The methodology establishing these basic phenomena had been well refined before I came into the field, and collecting more evidence for the existence of some kinds of psi would not make any difference against the irrational resistance. The essence of this resistance, for example, was expressed all too well in a feature article in *Science* (13) where the author, a chemist, stated that no intelligent person could read the evidence for ESP and doubt that it existed, but, since we *knew* ESP was impossible, we had to conclude that all this evidence was due to error and fraud. We're not doing science when we deal with dogmatic attitudes like this.

One of the sad aspects of my career has been watching otherwise dedicated and brilliant colleagues waste time and creativity in trying to rationally prove to the pseudo-skeptics*[3] that psi is real. Hundreds of successful psi experiments have been ignored and rejected already, a few more won't make any difference. Mainstream acceptance will come when (a) there is a major paradigm shift that suddenly allows psi, and/or (b) mainstream scientists discover and deal with their irrational fears and resistances to psi, and/or (c) applied psi becomes strong enough that you can clean out a pseudo-skeptic at a game of chance whenever you feel like it. So one of my main items of advice for new researchers, if you are already personally convinced of the reality of some forms of psi, is to not waste your time in the "proving psi is real" game, focus on understanding its nature and making it work better, a theme I'll develop below.

Second, my scientific work and life has always been informed (not always adequately) by a basic spiritual attitude on my part, a conviction that there are probably higher intelligences and principles in the universe than simple materialistic greed and struggle and animal impulses, and I want to learn more about and live more in accordance with such spiritual factors. I don't think any current spiritual tradition has any monopolies or necessarily ultimate understandings of this potential reality, and I see all such traditions as attempts by limited humans (like us) to make sense of certain kinds of "mystical" or spiritual/transpersonal experiences, as well as

---

*[3] I have enormous respect for genuine skepticism and try to practice it myself. By genuine skepticism I mean a dissatisfaction that current explanations of something are adequate and a desire for better empirical and rational understanding. Pseudo-skepticism masquerades as genuine skepticism to gain respectability, but is a matter of dogmatic conviction of the total explanatory power, in the case of parapsychology, of the philosophy of materialism, motivating irrational (and often strongly emotional) attacks on those data of parapsychology, which appear to undermine dogmatic materialism.

other life experiences. Spiritual beliefs are informal theories, just like scientists formally make in attempting to understand observations. But it's a great human failing to turn these attempts at making sense into rigid dogmas, which then inhibit and distort further experiencing (data collection) and thinking. We can have, and I have personally tried to have, a more "experimental spirituality," an openness to collecting data/having experiences and working to make intelligent sense out of them, but with humility, with trying to compensate for the desires and fears that distort our thinking and experiencing. Just as the formal sciences start with relatively crude data, some of which is erroneous, but try to get more accurate observations and theorize about them in ways which can be experientially/experimentally tested, we can do the same with spiritual experiences. This is a basically scientific attitude. Make data/experience primary, theorize about it, test your theories, make more observations, and keep refining your theories and concepts against actual data.

I don't have space to expand on this approach here – some of it is outlined in Tart (45), as well as expanded on in a way that considers the possibilities of creating sciences that function in altered states of consciousness (ASCs) in my proposal for the creation of state-specific sciences (25, 38) – but this desire for personal spiritual growth that can be of benefit to others has been a steady part of my life's work. Your personal attitude is important. If you accept the possibility of psychic communication between people, the sensing of your attitudes by people you work with can have an effect on them. I'll say more about such experimenter effects later, but researchers would do well to understand their deep attitudes toward life, toward others, toward "subjects" in experiments (32), and what they do.

STUDIES OF THE "SOUL"

I know many of my colleagues will cringe at the sight of the word "soul," because of its connotations for specific religions, particularly some of the dogmatic ones that oppose science, but it's a good common-sense term for the idea that we humans have a "nonphysical" aspect that can sometimes separate from the physical body and that permanently separates from it at death. I normally use the term *out-of-body experience* (OBE, an acronym I coined) (43), but the reason I use the term soul here is as a methodological reminder. By avoiding popular terms and using more scientific-sounding ones we do indeed gain some distance from unwanted connotations, and certainly appear more scientific, but sometimes at a cost of losing touch with what actually happens to ordinary people in the real world. So be careful with terminology: If you coin a fancy new word, how much are you gaining distance and objectivity, how much are you just playing a social game of "I'm a real scientist!", and how much are you losing touch?

I carried out my first formal parapsychological study while I was a sophomore at MIT, studying electrical engineering. I had long been fascinated by the phenomena of "soul travel" or "astral projection," in which someone experiences themselves as outside their physical body, but possessing rational, ordinary consciousness (these two are the defining characteristics of OBEs), and sometimes – this is what made it so interesting from a parapsychological perspective – correctly perceiving some distant scene, i.e. using ESP of some sort. I was familiar with some older literature reporting that OBEs could often be induced by hypnosis, so, with the help of friends from our student psychical research society,*[4] I trained several students to go into hypnosis, then hypnotized them and suggested they would go out of their bodies and visit a target area in the basement of a home in a suburb of Boston. With my electronics background I had even constructed a capacitance relay at the target site to see if it would be set off by my subjects' OBE visits, but this equipment turned out to be useless, as it was constantly being set off by electrical artifacts.

With the wisdom of hindsight this first experiment was inadequate, as I had not worked out an objective way of evaluating whether the descriptions of the target given by my OBE subjects were a significant match to the target. Only a spectacular result, an obvious and highly specific correct description of the target, would have been useful. On the other hand, for a college sophomore working pretty much on his own, it wasn't a bad first start.

I went on to do five more studies of OBEs over the course of my career (39) with interesting, but mixed results. One talented OBEr, Miss Z, correctly identified a five digit randomly chosen target number on a shelf near the ceiling, while showing unusual brain wave patterns during her OBEs. Two studies with businessman Robert Monroe, well-known for his three books (8, 9,10) on his OBEs, yielded ambiguous results both in terms of ESP and physiological correlates of OBEs, and my last study with highly trained hypnotic virtuosos showed how hypnosis could definitely create out-of-body *experiences* that didn't seem to involve actually being out of body in some real sense, for while their experiences of being out were quite vivid to them, my participants' perceptions of objects in a locked target room were so poor as to not warrant formal evaluation.

---

*[4] Founding the MIT student psychical research society was also an interesting social lesson in prejudice against researching psychic material. We needed a faculty sponsor for a student club. I asked many professors, but they weren't interested. One finally suggested I contact a psychologist who was affiliated with the Student Health Center. When I saw him, I found he had assumed that I wanted to see him because I was troubled by delusions about psychic phenomena.

Why this continuing interest in OBEs? Because in terms of affecting people, the few minutes of an OBE (or the more elaborate near-death experience [NDE], which usually includes an OBE component) usually has more impact on a person's beliefs and life than almost any other human experience. A typical report from those who've had an OBE or NDE, e.g., is on the order of *"I no longer believe that my soul will survive death. I know it will! I've had the direct experience of existing outside my body."* Much of psychology (and too much of parapsychology), by comparison, seems to be about trivial aspects of behavior. OBEs and NDEs are some of the most important things that can happen to people and should be investigated much more intensely, both for their intrinsic importance and as a way of gaining more popular support for parapsychology.

FROM ENGINEERING TO (PARA) PSYCHOLOGY

After a couple of years of training at MIT, I had decided electrical engineering was not really what I wanted to do in life, I wanted to be a parapsychologist. Since that did not look like an occupation you could make a living in, or even get formal training for at that time – and is still too much the case today[*5] – I decided to become a psychologist, both because many aspects of psychology interested me anyway and because psychological factors seemed to be the most important ones affecting psi. So in the fall of 1957 I transferred to Duke University to major in Duke's high quality psychology program, but mainly because I hoped to work in Dr. J. B. Rhine's famous parapsychology laboratory. I had already met Rhine several times during some of his talks in Boston and corresponded with him.

Before moving from Boston to Durham, though, I had a most interesting summer job with Dr. Andrija (Henry) Puharich at his private research institute, the Round Table Foundation, in Glen Cove, Maine. Eileen J. Garrett,[*6] founder of the Parapsychology Foundation and a world famous medium, had told me about research she had done with Puharich, and that he had developed electrical apparatus that could amplify or

---

[*5] An article on Career Advice, for those wanting to research consciousness or parapsychology, is on my website, http://www.paradigm-sys.com/cttart/.

[*6] Mrs. Garrett's attitude toward her mediumship was quite sensible. She had read all the theories, worked with a number of investigators, and, in founding the Parapsychology Foundation, was giving grant support to parapsychological studies. Asked toward the end of her life what she thought about her personal mediumship, she responded that on Mondays, Wednesdays and Fridays she thought it was just what it seemed to be, she went into trance and spirits spoke through her. On Tuesdays, Thursdays and Saturdays she thought the psychologists were probably right, it was her subconscious mind creating imitations of spirits, with a little ESP thrown in for verisimilitude. On Sundays she tried not to think about it...

inhibit psychic functioning. Naturally this was of enormous interest to me – I had been a ham radio operator and previously worked as a radio engineer at a commercial radio station, since I had a First Class Radiotelephone license from the Federal Communications Commission – and to my fellow students in the MIT Psychic Research Society. We had Puharich lecture to the Society at MIT and visited his laboratory in the spring of 1957. Some of us were skeptical about the soundness of his results, others, including me, thought his methods basically sound. At any rate, I was interested, and I needed a summer job (at the munificent minimum wage rate of forty dollars a week, but lucky to get that in the tremendously impoverished field of parapsychology) to help work my way through college.

Puharich was already a highly controversial figure in the small community of research parapsychologists, however. He was reporting very high levels of ESP performance in many of his studies, rather than the typical statistically-significant-but-practically-trivial results in everyone else's ESP studies – so he must be being fooled by his subjects or is a charlatan! His work was ignored or condemned by other parapsychologists, and J. B. Rhine warned me, in correspondence, that if I worked for Puharich, it would demonstrate that I lacked the kind of critical judgment that was needed to be a scientific parapsychologist.

THE RELIGION OF THE .05 LEVEL

This phenomenon of colleagues' intense attacks on parapsychologists who report strong psi results has amazed and intrigued me throughout my career, as I've seen it happen a number of times. If someone researching, say, lasers, reported a method for getting ten times as strong a light beam from a laser as was usually gotten, other researchers would hasten to try it themselves. In parapsychology, by contrast, if you report really strong results, most other parapsychologists become highly suspicious and assume something is wrong with your experimental design, or that you or your subjects cheated. I've thought about it as a psychological effect of what I've long called the "religion of the .05 level." If your results are practically trivial, percipients guessing at, say, 51% correct when chance is 50%, but keeping it up long enough to become statistically significant at the .05 probability level, your results are generally accepted unless there is some obvious other problem. But if you're reporting, say, 60% success, a high resistance springs up which seems to go well beyond a rational questioning.

Partly this is a historical consequence. Parapsychologists have been subjected to such bitter and irrational criticism for so long, they want to have methodologically superior if not perfect experiments, and so are super-sensitive to possible methodological problems or flaws in experimental procedure. It's also true that sometimes really strong psi results have turned out to be due to an artifact. But the religion of the .05 level I've seen goes well beyond this, and is part of, I believe, a general problem with hidden fears of psi. I've written on this at some length (35, 36, 40, 47, 51, 52) and won't say more about it here, except to emphasize that I believe that unless we deal with these hidden fears and ambivalences problem head on, results in parapsychological studies will too often stay unreliable and practically trivial. Individual parapsychologists must deal with the fear question on a personal level, not just think of it intellectually as something that might apply to somebody else.

THE NATURE OF THE EXPERIMENTER

Related to this is the experimenter problem. In an ordinary psychological experiment where you assume a known, physical universe, it's straightforward to apparently completely control interaction between experimenters and subjects, so you can evaluate the results of your experiments in terms of formal independent variables and dependent outcome variables.*[7] If you're investigating psi, though, you are admitting to the possibility of another channel of interaction than the known physical ones, and since we know almost nothing about the characteristics of this channel, it could carry all sorts of information to participants in the experiment, such as the biases and attitudes of the experimenter, hidden purposes of the experiment, etc.

In parapsychology, we have some experimenters who consistently get positive psi results in their studies, and others who consistently get almost none, even though they seem to follow similar methods. Is there something about the characteristics of the experimenters that mediates this enhancing or inhibition via psi (as well as ordinary biasing possibilities)? I think the collective social desire/bias in parapsychology is that we want to be respected (and supported) as real scientists, real scientists are "objective," thus the characteristics of the experimenter don't matter, so if we keep ignoring the characteristics of the experimenter we will get recognition and respect as real scientists... It won't work. One of the most pressing research needs of parapsychology is to start measuring and "calibrating" experimenter characteristics and seeing how they affect outcomes. We don't know exactly what to look for yet, so this means extensive psychological testing of experimenters until we discover empirical correlations of success and failure.

I think the increased possibility for experimenter bias, once you allow for ESP, is one of the principal reasons why psychologists, as a profession,

---

*[7] Actually problems of experimenter-induced bias are rampant in ordinary psychological experiments, but psychology is not ready to acknowledge this.

tend, in my experience, to be more irrationally opposed to parapsychology than, say, physical scientists. Psi-mediated experimenter bias, if admitted to, could drastically undercut the apparent findings base of psychology – how many are actual, factual relationships and how much are artifacts caused by psi-mediated biasing? – And psychology is already low on the social hierarchy of the sciences.

ELECTRICALLY ENHANCING ESP

Going back to my summer at the Round Table Foundation, I became further convinced that Puharich's experiments in enhancing or inhibiting ESP were basically sound, although some of his more speculative approaches to explaining ESP (and some of his later work) might be questionable – I didn't have the technical background to judge. Basically, Puharich tried putting pre-selected, talented psychic subjects inside an electrically shielded enclosure, called a Faraday cage after its discoverer, physicist Michael Faraday. This is a metal-skinned box, and has the property that static electrical charges, since they mutually repel each other, all stay on the outside of the metal cage without penetrating to the inside, and radio waves similarly hardly make it through. If you are in your car and it's struck by lightning, e.g., you probably won't feel any electrical effects inside your car, for you are mostly surrounded by metal except for the windows. Puharich found that if the solid surface copper Faraday cage he used was electrically connected to the earth, grounded, ESP scores increased over ordinary room conditions, whereas if the cage was electrically "floating," i.e. insulated from the ground, ESP scores dropped below ordinary room conditions.

This made no sense in terms of conventional physics, but then ESP makes no sense in terms of conventional physics. Nevertheless it was data, it was an empirical observation, and the essence of science is that *data are always primary*. If your theories don't make sense of your data, that's too bad for your theories, not for the data.

I felt that Puharich's finding was immensely important for parapsychology. Remember that most psi experimental results were typically statistically-significant-but-practically-trivial. I started expressing it then by the analogy that parapsychology was in the same place that our understanding of electricity had been for most of humanity's history. We had lightning, big, powerful, fantastic electrical displays – but unpredictable, and over in a second, you really only had memories to study. We also had weak static electrical effects such as you might get from rubbing amber with fur and then being able to *sometimes* pick up a little feather. "Sometimes," as it often didn't work for reasons not understood at the time. Our understanding of electricity didn't progress much under these conditions. But when Volta invented the electrical battery, everything changed. It was very weak compared with lightning, but very strong and reliable compared to static effects, so you could go into your laboratory every day and study what affected electricity. In no time, compared to the long span of human history, we had a science and numerous practical applications of electricity.

The situation was the same in parapsychology back then (and, in too many instances, still the same today). We had spontaneous psychic experiences, which could convey a lot of striking information, but they were unpredictable and quickly over, so all you had to study were reports of memories. We had our "static electrical" effects, the statistically-significant-but-practically-trivial effects in card guessing tests, which worked often enough to know some kind of psi was happening but were otherwise too weak for useful functional studies of the nature of psi. What we needed was a "parapsychological battery," a process that let us go into the laboratory almost any day and be able to study the properties of ESP and build the scientific understandings we needed and the practical applications.

So perhaps Puharich's Faraday cage procedure, used with talented percipients as in his studies, was the parapsychological battery? So lots of parapsychologists built Faraday cages and tried to replicate and extend Puharich's results, yes? Reasoning that even if the results might not be true, they would be so potentially important if they were that it was worth a try?

Instead, Puharich's results were totally ignored (until I was able to do a single, partial replication years later – see below). After all, he was probably a charlatan, or was certainly too far out, wasn't he? His involvement some years later with Uri Geller, UFOs, and psychoactive mushrooms (controversial areas where he was indeed very far out) seemed to further justify the initial prejudice that he wasn't a real scientist, and could be ignored...

Many years after that summer of 1957, when I was a professor at UC Davis, I received grant support from the National Institute of Mental Health (NIMH) for hypnosis and sleep research, and I used a small part of that money to build a solid-wall Faraday cage. It was very useful for my sleep wave research, shielding out interference from power lines when I measured brain waves. But I designed it so that eventually I could ground or unground (float) it (in a double blind manner to avoid ordinary experimenter effects), and so use it to test Puharich's basic findings. I had to do the experiment with ordinary college students as percipients, though, not having the resources then to find and train psi-talented people. Nevertheless I found that while my percipients scored only at chance in the ungrounded, "floating" Faraday cage condition, they did score significantly (albeit weakly in an absolute sense) in the grounded condition, in line with Puharich's findings. (37)

Need I say that if Faraday cages in grounded conditions do indeed amplify ESP it's one of the most important things that parapsychology could research? Yet no one has followed up on this research, except to measure the radio frequency (RF) attenuation characteristics of the cage in grounded and ungrounded conditions, (5) finding no difference. Whether the RF attenuation characteristic of a cage is the relevant variable is unknown. Is the hidden psychological resistance of today's parapsychologists sufficient that they will continue to ignore this possibility?

TO NORTH CAROLINA FOR PSYCHOLOGY AND PARAPSYCHOLOGY

Returning to my story, I worked at the Round Table Foundation for the summer of 1957 and then moved to Durham to continue my college education at Duke, majoring in psychology. True to his warning, Rhine considered my being foolish enough to work for Puharich as indeed evidence that I didn't have enough critical judgment to work in parapsychology, and the part-time job he had offered me before I transferred from MIT never materialized. Indeed, friends at Rhine's laboratory (I kept quietly visiting) told me I had been put on the official list of people to be discouraged from visiting the lab. I was incensed at the time, but years later, found out that many of the people who became the most creative researchers in parapsychology had also been on that list! With much more maturity, I came to appreciate Rhine's position: He was the central leader of an under funded, irrationally rejected field, desperately trying to uphold what he believed were the standards needed for its progress, and I can see why he decided against me. Later in life he decided I did indeed have enough judgment, and we smoothed out our differences.

UNCONSCIOUS PSI

I soon married – a result of a lovely young coed at Duke coming to visit Rhine's lab after she heard him lecture, and our meeting in the lab's library – Rhine's greatest gift to me – and transferred to the University of North Carolina at Chapel Hill to continue my undergraduate, and later my graduate work, in psychology. I still wanted to do research in parapsychology. Because of my skill with electronics, I got a part-time job as a technician at the Duke Medical School with some psychophysiology researchers. They didn't think much of parapsychology, but needed my skills to keep their cutting-edge electronics equipment functioning, so I was able to do my second formal experiment in parapsychology. (21) It seemed to me that a person might react on an unconscious level to a psi event even if it didn't successfully result in a conscious perception of the event. Since unconscious reactions often had a bodily component, and I had access to some of the most sensitive (at that time) equipment for measuring such reactions, I persuaded my bosses to let me run an experiment on my own time. There had been a few similar experiments in the past, but with much less sensitive devices.

A subject – picked from Duke students who were in the Air Force ROTC, since the psychophysiology lab was primarily funded by an Air Force grant – would come in and be told by an assistant that this was an experiment in "subliminal perception," a topic in the newspapers at that time. Technically this was true, and that was important to me, as I strongly dislike lying on moral grounds – and anyway, how can you really lie to someone if you think ESP may work? The stimulus was sub-sub-subliminal, as it were.

The subject then sat for about an hour in a steel, double-walled, sound-attenuating chamber in the dark, effectively isolated from any normal sounds outside. He was told that if he thought he had received any kind of stimulation to tap on the signaling key on the arm of his chair, but otherwise relax. His brain waves, skin resistance, and blood pressure responses were continuously monitored. But the only stimuli were those hopefully transmitted by some kind of psi, occasional electrical 2-second shocks to a "sender" in another room, given at random intervals. The shock was adjusted to be the maximally painful one the sender could stand without moving or crying out. In between shocks the sender read a novel to stay calm.

I was the sender, so the experiment is a strong memory for me!

I found the subjects showed small but significant physiological responses to the shocks, reinforcing the idea that we may respond to psi stimuli, but not necessarily consciously. I'm glad to say that a number of experimenters have since carried out more sophisticated versions of this procedure, with positive results. Not only should this kind of research be expanded, but also it could be combined with training procedures to make people more sensitive to bodily responses and so perhaps bring psi under more conscious control.

EXTINCTION VERSUS LEARNING: ANOTHER APPROACH TO THE PSYCHIC BATTERY

At UNC in Chapel Hill I plunged into the study of psychology. When entering the graduate program I elected to follow the clinical track so I would be able to find employment as a clinical psychologist, knowing how difficult it would probably be to find any employment in parapsychology. I later switched to personality and experimental psychology. One of the intense courses I took after switching was on the psychology of learning, a central topic in psychology at that time, and this connected with my longstanding concern that we must develop the "parapsychological battery" for the field to move on.

At that time the typical ESP test involved guessing the order of a deck of 25 cards, made up of five symbols, the classic Zener cards. There might be a sender trying to send if it was a telepathy procedure, or no one knowing the order of the shuffled deck if it was a clairvoyance procedure, or, if a precognition procedure, the percipient had to guess the order to the deck before it was thoroughly randomized at some time in the future. Because it could invite "card counting" and so invalidate the usual statistical tests of whether a significant number of hits had been called in a run through a deck, no feedback about a particular target card's identity was given until the standard run of 25 calls was completed.

As I thought about this and connected it with basic learning theory, it seemed obvious to me that the standard "testing" procedure for ESP was actually what psychology had termed an "extinction" procedure. (22) This was repeated responding with delayed feedback, delayed enough to be confusing and ineffective in guiding behavior and allowing learning. Thinking about the internal processes involved, (31) if someone asks you to use ESP, the intelligent response is *"Huh? Do what?"* It's not a straightforward performance or variation on some well learned skill you already have, it's a venture into the unknown. So should I furrow my brow while I try to get an impression? Relax? Pray? Try real hard and tense up? Concentrate on what I want, or try to distract myself?

If you had immediate feedback of success or failure on each call, you could gradually work out more successful strategies from observing outcomes, like "If I feel X, don't give any response, pass, wait for things to change, I'm almost always wrong when I feel that way," or "If I feel Y, call out my impression, I'm right more often than chance, let me observe that feeling more closely too and see if I can refine the connection." When you don't get any feedback until after a mass of calls, though, you can't make useful observations. "I was right on the 14th trial, was that the one where I relaxed, or the one where I had the tingly feeling in my hands or...?"

So I postulated that the standard very-delayed or no feedback ESP test procedure was an extinction paradigm, and sure enough, the parapsychological literature was full of evidence for the "decline effect," a steady worsening of performance with repeated testing, extinction, until even quite talented percipients dropped to chance level scoring.

My first publication on this theory (22) was greeted with intellectual interest but also, I think, with a certain amount of implicit emotional hostility. To be a parapsychologist at that time (and still today, unfortunately) involved considerable hardship: uncertain employment, very low paid employment if you were lucky enough to get a job at all, and widespread professional rejection in the academic and scientific community. You really had to care about the field to go into it! Now here was I, this young kid in his twenties, telling dedicated parapsychologists that they had been systematically killing off the very phenomena they had sacrificed so much to study!

The positive aspect of my theory was that if you (a) provided immediate feedback to (b) a *motivated* percipient and (c) *he or she had some psi talent for this sort of repeated guessing task to begin with*, he or she ought to show learning, to gradually get better at using psi. Technically the problem of "card counting" messing up the statistics was now easily handled by using electronic ESP test machines, where every trial was totally independent of preceding ones, and I designed a couple of machines of that sort, sophisticated for that time, crude by contemporary standards. (23, 29)

I had little opportunity to put my feedback learning theory to the test for some years until I was scheduled to teach an advanced level undergraduate course in experimental psychology at UCD. "Why," I thought, *"have the students do just lab exercises, where the results are already known, when they could work as my apprentices, experience what real research is like, and make an actual contribution to new understanding?"*

We did some preliminary research on this with my experimental psychology class in 1972, constructing a special testing device, the Ten-Choice Trainer (TCT). Initial results were quite encouraging, and are reported in Chapter 3 of my book *Learning to Use Extrasensory Perception*. (29) Students were enthusiastic about doing real research and put in a lot more time than would ordinarily be required for the course's units.

Next year began an exciting two quarters of teaching and research with fuller testing of the theory. Intermixed with my lectures on research methods and constant discussions of how we were doing, practical ways to solve problems, etc., my students started looking for psi-talented percipients. They requested the last few minutes of many professors' classes and did a quick and simple ESP card guessing test. Over 1500 UCD students were screened this way. (11) Of course with lots of testing, you get lots of false positives, people scoring at individually significant levels through chance alone. To eliminate most of those who were such false positives in the first round of selection, the high-scorers were invited to my lab for individual testing on two different ESP testing machines we had, the 10-choice TCT and a 4-choice Aquarius Trainer. Those who continued to score at individual levels of significance were invited to participate in the main, 20-session Training Study. The chances of someone scoring at individual levels of statistical significance by chance twice in a row were low (about .0025), so we could assume that most of the people entering the Training Study indeed possessed some psi talent, and they had to be reasonably motivated, of course, to commit to multiple lab sessions.

The results were exciting, and have been presented in detail (11, 26, 27, 29, 35, 33, 49) in both book*[8] and journal form. Briefly, the results fit the theory. No significant declines with practice were seen, and there were some inclines suggesting learning, especially on a short-term basis.*[9] The amount of incline correlated, as expected, with initial ESP talent.

Further, a totally unexpected finding was massive precognitive missing on the one-ahead target. After controlling for possible artifacts (46) I proposed a theory of *trans-temporal inhibition* to account for it, a psi form of a general information processing algorithm (lateral inhibition) found in all sensory systems for sharpening perception. (30, 39)

I was able, with the valuable assistance of parapsychologist John Palmer, to carry out a second study (50) with a new group of student assistants and percipients a year later. The initial screening process for percipients was not as successful in yielding psi-talented participants, though, so the outcome was only partially successful, although completely in line with the theory's predictions. After that the Psychology Department no longer scheduled me to teach experimental psychology, so I did not have the resources to follow up this research.

But of course many other parapsychologists picked up this promising line of research, a method that might train percipients to manifest strong, reliable psi, and give us our parapsychological battery, yes? And the information processing mechanism I postulated, transtemporal inhibition, was thoroughly investigated by others so it could be utilized to further enhance psi performance?

Nothing of the sort happened. The lower level of results in my second study was taken by many as a sign that my learning theory was invalid, even though all the results were completely in accord with my theory. Even worse, the few people who did test for effects from immediate feedback completely ignored my repeatedly stressed point that *you had to start with talented and motivated percipients*: You can't train and reinforce a talent if it doesn't manifest in the first place. So a number of experiments were published showing feedback had no effect – in unselected, untalented percipients – and taken to mean the theory was incorrect, even though this is exactly what the theory predicts. Was the religion of the .05

---

*[8] I was very proud that the study had been done well enough that *Learning to Use ESP* was published, after detailed technical vetting, by as prestigious a publisher as the University of Chicago Press.

*[9] Too long intervals between lab sessions for some percipients probably resulted in skill losses as a delicate process was forgotten or interfered with. A detailed analysis of this is presented elsewhere (C. P. J. Tart & Redington, 1979a).

level manifesting again? As to transtemporal inhibition, it clearly needed high performing percipients to investigate, and no such study has been done. But the case for the value of feedback training is not over for, curiously, a closely related form of it is routinely used in remote viewing studies, and investigators seldom mention declines in such studies. More on this below.

REMOTE VIEWING

A very promising new development in parapsychology also distracted me from further multiple-choice feedback training work in the 1970s, namely the remote viewing (RV) protocol developed at Ingo Swann's suggestion at Stanford Research Institute (now SRI International) by physicists Hal Puthoff and Russell Targ. I was somewhat skeptical (the religion of the .05 level rubbing off on me too?) when I first heard about how good some of the results were, but after seeing a personal demonstration of it at the meetings of parapsychological researchers (PRG) I then held each month at my home in the SF Bay Area, I got very excited over its potentials, and eventually spent a year as a fulltime consultant to the SRI project.

Knowing how important the psychology of the experimental situation is, especially in parapsychology, I repeatedly asked Puthoff and Targ about their psi-facilitating psychological procedures. What did they do to get remote viewers to perform so well? They repeatedly gave me blank looks: They were physicists and they did experiments, they didn't do anything psychological. On my first visit to their lab at SRI, though, I was tremendously impressed with their implicit procedure. First you drove to this world-renowned, prestigious research center, SRI, full of leading scientists. Since Puthoff and Targ were physicists they were also way up there in the scientific prestige hierarchy, a fact bound to impress visitors. Second, since a lot of classified government research and private industrial research was done at SRI – the impressiveness continues to build! You had to sign in at a front desk and receive an identity badge, to be worn at all times. That wasn't enough, though, for third, you couldn't wander around unescorted, an SRI employee had to take you around, so Targ and Puthoff came to get me. Their lab seemed to be a ways off in a maze of buildings, but they knew shortcuts for getting there, which involved, fourth, cutting through some high-tech labs instead of the longer roundabout route through the halls. Any visitor had to know they were in The Temple of Science at the sight of the equipment in those labs! Fifth, then they showed me examples of past successes in remote viewing, and while they, sixth, presented them in a low-key, matter-of-fact way, they were very impressive! I saw the psi-facilitating induction technique now: Any visitor had to be special to be allowed into such a Temple of Science and remote viewing success was routine, let's get on with doing something interesting... Understanding this kind of "psychology of the experiment" is vitally important for encouraging psi functioning and needs much more research. Schwartz has written very fruitfully about this. (16)

The formal RV protocol has been well described in numerous places (see, e.g., 20 or 48), so I will only comment on one aspect of it here, the feedback aspect. In stark contrast to the massed trials with no feedback until after many trials of multiple choice, card-guessing tests, only a single RV trial was usually done in a day. There was no immediate feedback with the usual procedure, since the outbound experimenter had to return from the target site, and then the outbound and inbound experimenters and the viewer drove out to the remote target site to make their own comparisons (this wasn't the formal evaluation, of course) of how well the RVing had gone that day. So there was a long period before feedback, but there was no potentially interfering activity of the same type as the RVing activity to confuse the viewer as to how she had felt while doing the RVing. I think this procedure is one of the little-recognized components that led to remote viewers not showing declines with repeated experiments. The general lore among remote viewers and experimenters is not about declines but about viewers getting better with practice. If my theory is right, you could extinguish RV ability (why would you want to do that?) by doing a large number of RVings in a row before giving any feedback.

With the right viewers and the right experimenters, the RV protocol looked to be the parapsychological battery, the usually reliable, moderately strong source of psi that would allow functional studies of the nature of ESP as well as practical application. The protocol has been used practically to earn money, although to date it seems to work only the first time a group tries it, so there may be psychological barriers to be dealt with here. The classified intelligence community supported RV research for many years, and the published results demonstrate that it could be practically useful in intelligence applications. Much unpublished and still classified material further supports that conclusion. There are still difficulties to be overcome in using the RV protocol for functional studies of the nature of ESP.

In any functional study, you vary the value of some independent variable while measuring the value of the dependent variable and see if there's a relationship. With a multiple-choice guessing test, like card calling, you have a precise, quantitative outcome, the number of cards guessed correctly in a run and can, in principle, pick out small variations in performance, which may relate to the functioning of the independent variable. In RV studies, though, the usual evaluation of a series of trials is a judge's ability to blind match targets and descriptions, and this is much less precise. In a six trial RV series, for example, the viewer need give only one unique and correct item for each target and the judge will get all six correct, a statistically significant outcome. If the viewer, working, say, under different conditions, gives a dozen correct, unique items for each target, the judging outcome and statistical significance is just the same, even though much more information has been obviously picked up by ESP. You might suspect the second condition of working is more favorable for ESP, but your formal analysis can't justify that conclusion, it's the same level of statistical significance in each case.

One of the main things I worked on as a consultant to the RV research was devising a way of quantifying how much information was actually picked up in a given viewing. This turned out to be quite difficult. You could break descriptive statements down into individual items, but then you lost the gestalt information that was often important. Also, which of those broken-down items was likely due to chance and so inflating a score artifactually? In the end the best that I and others could do, a method that has been used in a number of subsequent RV studies, was have a judge give an overall subjective impression of whether a little or a lot of information came from a given viewing. Thus our ability to quantify the outcomes of the RV procedure is still crude and needs improvement.

LARGER CONTEXT – THE NATURE OF CONSCIOUSNESS

There have been other parapsychological studies in my career, but I think my main long-term contribution to parapsychology may be to try to fit it into a larger, more inclusive domain of consciousness studies.

Ever since I was a child, I have been curious about how my mind works. Why am I thinking what I'm thinking? What led up to that? And to that...way back? Why do my thoughts and feelings not always work together? Where do dreams come from? Why do people act so strangely? Are their minds like mine or different? Etc., etc., etc... When my interests started to include psychical research and parapsychology, my questions expanded to include ones like what is the nature of a mind that can sometimes reach out through space and time to read and affect the world? Does the mind survive death? If so, in what form? As my knowledge of spirituality grew beyond my local tribe's education/indoctrination of me as a child, more questions became important: What is enlightenment and spiritual growth, for example? What are these altered states of consciousness (ASCs) in spiritual traditions about? Are they insights or delusions? Evolution or escape? What is the ultimate nature of mind? How much of consciousness is brain-based and how much is something else? How do "nonmaterial" mind and material brain relate?

Thus while I generally devoted about a third of my research time to parapsychology during the first few decades of my career, the remainder was devoted to studying consciousness and ASCs. This somewhat more respectable work (than parapsychology) helped me attain tenure in my university position and so have some job security.*[10] My collection of scattered, little-known studies of ASCs in my 1969 *Altered States of Consciousness* anthology (24), for example, helped to stimulate and legitimatize the study of consciousness within psychology, and my 1975 *Transpersonal Psychologies* anthology (28) was one of the foundation documents of the field of transpersonal psychology. When forced to categorize myself*[11] nowadays, I say I'm a transpersonal psychologist. I'm interested in the ultimate nature of the mind, especially as manifested in transpersonal, "mystical," ASC experiences. Within that broad basis of transpersonal psychology (which really includes all of what we know about mind and brain, as they are part of the big picture), parapsychology is a technical specialty of mine.

I emphasize this big picture approach as some of my colleagues in parapsychology occasionally tend to get lost in the technical details of investigating statistically-significant-but-practically-trivial psi phenomena, and treat psi as an isolated phenomenon that will someday get pigeonholed into conventional physicalistic views of reality. I can understand getting wrapped up in the details like this, I have a strong "nerdish" side and get fascinated by equipment, methods and analyses too. But at practical levels of thinking and living, I am a pragmatic, scientific dualist at this point. Whatever mind is, and the psi phenomena it sometimes manifests are, will, I believe, require extensive investigation on their own terms, rather than merely being pigeonholed into current physicalistic theories. So I suspect a fuller understanding of psi will require a much broader picture of reality than we currently have, and will make our current distinction between "mind" and "matter" seem rather crude. In terms of finding support for the discipline of parapsychology, too, it's well to remember that, on the one hand, there has always been and still is enormous, partly unconscious and often emotionally based irrational resistance to it from the materialistic mainstream, and, on the other hand, that psi phenomena and its implications are not just laboratory curiosities, there are strong ties to basic spiritual ideas and they are thus quite important to real people, not just laboratory curiosities to be "explained away."

I have argued these points in detail in two major technical journal papers. In one, addressed primarily to parapsychologists (41), I develop this idea that psi phenomena are part of human's spiritual life and need to

---

*[10] Not without struggle, of course. The too typical kinds of struggles some of us in the academic world have had to go through as a result of our parapsychological interests have been sadly documented by Hess. (1992)

*[11] While trying not to let the category concept actually limit me, of course.

be addressed in this wider frame – with no lowering of methodological standards of course, and a great increase in creativity to see how to expand in this direction. In the other (44), addressed primarily to transpersonal psychologists, I show how psi phenomena provide a potential reality basis for some transpersonal experiences rather than the whole field being reducible, for those with a materialistic bias, to the study of comforting *illusions* of spirituality, and emphasize the need to interact with parapsychologists to increase the methodological rigor of transpersonal psychology. In my most recent book, *The End of Materialism: How Evidence of the Paranormal is Bringing Science and Spirit Together* (45), I deal with all this on a more individual level: How can one be both spiritually inclined *and* scientifically inclined, rather than having one's spiritual impulses stifled by the widespread, but erroneous conviction in our culture that science has shown that all spirituality is nothing but nonsense and neurosis? Yes, there is lots of nonsense and craziness going around under the label spiritual – just like there is in all areas of life. But too many people undergo unnecessary suffering by this blanket dismissal of some of the finest and highest aspects of human life.

My final line of advice to people entering the field, then, is based on my life experiences. Basically there is some sense in which spirituality is about something real and vital, although we have no shortage of distorted and crazy ideas about it, and there is lots of room for personal and societal growth in dealing with this area. As the founders of psychical research envisioned, though, it is possible to take the methods of essential science, the emphasis on open-minded and accurate data gathering, rational thinking and theorizing, *but always subjecting theory to more testing and observation*, and start to refine our knowledge of what is genuinely spiritual and what is indeed superstition and pathology. Don't be so caught up in the technical aspects of doing science that you lose touch with the human implications of our field and its importance for real people.

It's an exciting path in life and a demanding one. You have to brave irrational rejection from pseudo-skeptics who are dogmatically committed to scientism or various dogmatic creeds, including conventionally religious ones, on the one hand and, on the other, be open to learning from people who have something of whatever this "spiritual" stuff is, but may mix it with lots of hope and fear, imagination and dogma, but also love and compassion, genuine helpfulness and openness. Being human is complicated...but oh so interesting...

Berkeley, California, August 2008

REFERENCES

1) Auerbach, L. (1986) *ESP, Hauntings and Poltergeists: A Parapsychologist's Handbook.* NY: Warner Books.

2) Bem, D., Palmer, J. & Broughton, R. (2001) "Updating the ganzfeld database: A victim of its own success." In: *Journal of Parapsychology, 65*, 207-218.

3) Dossey, L. (2001) *Healing Beyond the Body: Medicine and the Infinite Reach of the Mind.* Boston: Shambhala.

4) Hess, D. (1992) "Disciplining heterodoxy, circumventing discipline: Parapsychology, anthropologically." In: *Knowledge and Society: The Anthropology of Science and Technology, 9*, 223-252.

5) Hubbard, G.S.V. (1988) "Electromagnetic measurements of the shielded room at UC Davis." In: *Journal of the American Society for Psychical Research, 82*(2), 147-152.

6) Krippner, S. (1993) "The Maimonides ESP dream studies." In: *Journal of Parapsychology, 57*, 39-54.

7) May, E., Paulinyi, T. & Vassy, Z. (2005) "Anomalous anticipatory skin conductance response to acoustic stimuli: Experimental results and speculation about a mechanism." In: *Journal of Alternative and Complementary Medicine, 11*(4), 695-702.

8) Monroe, R.A. (1971) *Journeys Out of the Body.* Garden City: Anchor Books.

9) Monroe, R.A. (1994) *Ultimate Journey.* NY: Doubleday.

10) Monroe, R.S. (1985) *Far Journeys.* NY: Doubleday.

11) Palmer, J.T.C. & Redington, D. (1976) "A large-sample classroom ESP card-guessing experiment." In: *European Journal of Parapsychology, 1* (3), 40-56.

12) Persinger, M.A. (1987) "Spontaneous telepathic experiences from 'Phantasms of the Living' and low global geomagnetic activity." *Journal of the American Society for Psychical Research, 81*, 23-36.

13) Price, G.R. (1955) "Science and the supernatural." In: *Science, 122*, 359-367.

14) Ring, K. (1984) *Heading Toward Omega: In Search of the Meaning of the Near-Death Experience.* New York: Wm. Morrow & Co.

15) Spottiswoode, S.J.P. (1997) "Apparent association between effect size in free response anomalous cognition experiments and local sidereal time." In: *Journal of Scientific Exploration, 11*(2), 1-17.

16) Schwartz, S. (2007) *Opening to the Infinite: The Art and Science of Nonlocal Awareness.* Buda, TX: Nemoseen.

17) Schwartz, S.A. (1978) *The Secret Vaults of Time: Psychic Archaeology and the Quest for Man's Beginnings.* NY: Grosset & Dunlap.

18) Stevenson, I. (1974) *Twenty Cases Suggestive of Reincarnation* (2nd ed.). Charlottesville VA: University of Virginia Press.

19) Stevenson, I. (1997) *Reincarnation and Biology: A Contribution to the Etiology of Birthmarks and Birth Defects* (Vol. One: Birthmarks). Westport, CT: Praeger.

20) Targ, R. & Puthoff, H.E. (1977) *Mind Reach: Scientists Look at Psychic Ability.* NY: Delacorte Press/Eleanor Friede.

21) Tart, C. (1963) "Physiological correlates of psi cognition." In: *International Journal of Parapsychology, 5*, 375-386.

22) Tart, C. (1966a) "Card guessing tests: Learning paradigm or extinction paradigm." In: *Journal of the American Society for Psychical Research, 60*, 46-55.

23) Tart, C. (1966b) "ESPATESTER: An automatic testing device for parapsychological research." In: *Journal of the American Society for Psychical Research, 60*, 256-269.

24) Tart, C. (1969) *Altered States of Consciousness: A Book of Readings*. NY: John Wiley & Sons.

25) Tart, C. (1972) "States of consciousness and state-specific sciences." In: *Science, 176*, 1203-1210.

26) Tart, C. (1975a) *The Application of Learning Theory to ESP Performance*. NY: Parapsychology Foundation, Inc.

27) Tart, C. (1975b) "Studies of learning theory application, 1964-1974." In: *Parapsychology Review, 6*, 21-28.

28. Tart, C. (1975c) *Transpersonal Psychologies*. NY: Harper & Row.

29) Tart, C. (1976) *Learning to Use Extrasensory Perception*. Chicago: U. of Chicago Press; currently in print through www.iuniverse.com.

30) Tart, C. (1977a) "Improving real-time ESP by suppressing the future: Trans-temporal inhibition." In: *Proceedings of the IEEE Electro 77 Convention, 1977*.

31) Tart, C. (1977b) "Toward conscious control of psi through immediate feedback training: Some considerations of internal processes." In: *Journal of the American Society for Psychical Research, 71*, 375-408.

32) Tart, C. (1977c) "Toward humanistic experimentation in parapsychology: A reply to Dr. Stanford's review." In: *Journal of the American Society for Psychical Research, 71*, 81-102.

33) Tart, C. (1978a) "Comments on the critical exchange between Drs. Stanford and Tart: Dr. Tart's reply to Dr. Gatlin." In: *Journal of the American Society for Psychical Research, 72*, 81-87.

34) Tart, C. (1978b) "Space, time, and mind." In: W. Roll (Ed.), *Research in Parapsychology 1977* (pp. 197-250). Metuchen, NJ: Scarecrow Press.

35) Tart, C. (1984) "Acknowledging and dealing with the fear of psi." In: *Journal of the American Society for Psychical Research, 78*, 133-143.

36) Tart, C. (1986) "Psychics' fear of psychic powers." In: *Journal of the American Society for Psychical Research, 80*, 279-292.

37) Tart, C. (1988) "Effects of electrical shielding on GESP performance." In: *Journal of the American Society for Psychical Research, 82*, 129-146.

38) Tart, C. (1998a) "Investigating altered states of consciousness on their own terms: A proposal for the creation of state-specific sciences." In: *Ciencia e Cultura, Journal of the Brazilian Association for the Advancement of Science, 50*(2/3), 103-116.

39) Tart, C. (1998b) "Six studies of out-of-body experiences." In: *Journal of Near-Death Studies, 17*(2), 73-99.

40. Tart, C. (1999) "Fear of psychic phenomena." In: E. Leskowitz (Ed.), *Transpersonal Hypnosis: Gateway to Body, Mind and Spirit* (pp. 1-13). Boca Raton, FLA: CRC Press.

41) Tart, C. (2001) "Parapsychology & transpersonal psychology: 'Anomalies' to be explained away or spirit to manifest?" In: *Journal of Parapsychology, 66*, 31-47.

42) Tart, C. (2003) "Spiritual motivations of parapsychologists? Empirical data." In: *Journal of Parapsychology, 67,* 181-184.
43. Tart, C. (2004a) "Credit for coining terms." In: *Journal of Near-Death Studies, 22*(No. 4), 284-285.
44) Tart, C. (2004b) "On the scientific foundations of Transpersonal Psychology: Contributions from Parapsychology." In: *Journal of Transpersonal Psychology, 36*(1), 66-90.
45) Tart, C. (2009). *The End of Materialism: How Evidence of the Paranormal is Bringing Science and Spirit Together.* Oakland, CA: New Harbinger.
46) Tart, C. & Dronek, E. (1982) "Mathematical inference strategies versus psi: Initial explorations with the Probabilistic Predictor Program." In: *European Journal of Parapsychology, 4,* 325-356.
47) Tart, C. & LaBore, C. (1986) "Attitudes toward strongly functioning psi: A preliminary study." In: *Journal of the American Society for Psychical Research, 80,* 163-173.
48) Tart, C., Puthoff, H. & Targ, R. (Eds.) (1979) *Mind at Large: Institute of Electrical and Electronic Engineers Symposia on the Nature of Extrasensory Perception.* NY: Praeger.
49) Tart, C.P.J. & Redington, D. (1979a) "Effects of immediate feedback on ESP performance over short time periods." In: *Journal of the American Society for Psychical Research, 73,* 291-301.
50) Tart, C.P.J. & Redington, D. (1979b) "Effects of immediate feedback on ESP performance: A second study and new analyses." In: W. Roll (Ed.) *Research in Parapsychology 1978.* Metuchen, NJ: Scarecrow Press, pp. 145-146.
51) Tart, C.T. (1982) "The controversy about psi: Two psychological theories." In: *Journal of Parapsychology, 46,* 313-320.
52. Tart, C.T. (1994) "Fears of the paranormal in ourselves and our colleagues: Recognizing them, dealing with them." In: *Subtle Energies.* Vol. 5, No. 1, 1994.
53) Tucker, J. (2005) *Life Before Life: A Scientific Investigation of Children's Memories of Previous Lives.* NY: St. Martins Press.
54) White, R. (1964) "A comparison of old and new methods of response to targets in ESP experiments." In: *Journal of the American Society for Psychical Research, 58,* 21-56.

> *We are in no way attacking the fundamental spirit of scientific inquiry. We are, rather, suggesting that it is time for science to take a major step in its own evolution.*
>
> *--- Willis Harman*

ADDITIONAL BIOGRAPHIES AND WEBSITES

Our first PRG Anthology *Silver Threads: 25 Years of Parapsychology Research (ST)* was published in 1993, seventeen years ago. Since then the twenty-five authors included in that book have scattered across the country and around the world. Those who are not represented in the previous chapters are included here, along with additional biographies of other PRG members to acknowledge their important contributions to the field of consciousness studies. The PRG officially disbanded 6 years ago in 2004.

Psi information has expanded because of the important research done by this group and others, so this new anthology has more than 50 participants. While the skeptics are still struggling to find ways to debunk psi, and the media over-dramatizes the bizarre, ordinary people need to be able to share their personal psychic experiences in an open-minded environment. This book is designed to shed more light and less heat on this ancient and modern discussion. Biographies of psi sensitives are in Chapter 46. They have always been among us, though they might have hidden or disguised their abilities to avoid ridicule from materialists or condemnation from religious extremists. The PRG provided a positive environment for sharing psi experiences, and for encouraging those who could to help others explore the incredible dimensions of their own consciousness.

Additional Biographies of PRG Scientists:

1) *Joe Kamiya* — He initiated EEG biofeedback research, opening new fields of study in energy medicine and education.
2) *Jon Klimo* — Author of "Channeling" in *Silver Threads*.
3) *William Braud* — Participated in a PRG discussion in *Silver Threads*. Writer, researcher, professor emeritus of ITP.
4) *Brian McRae* — PRG board and PK adept.
5) *William Croft* — Author of "PK on the PC" in *Silver Threads*.
6) *Kenneth Ring* — Author of "Near–Death Experiences" in *Silver Threads*.
7) *Barbara Honegger* — President of the PRG from 1979-1980.
8) *Charles Honorton* — Participated in a PRG discussion in *Silver Threads*. Former Parapsychologist at the University of Edinburgh, he was pursuing his doctorate at the U of Edinburgh at the time of his death in 1992. His bio and photo were not available to be included.

Joe Kamiya, PhD

Joe Kamiya *has been called the grandfather of brainwave (EEG) biofeedback, which he first developed in 1958 while on the faculty of the Department of Psychology at the University of Chicago. In 1961 he joined the faculty of the Psychiatry Department of University of California at San Francisco (UCSF), and directed a research program on the psychophysiology of consciousness at the Langley Porter Psychiatric Institute at UCSF, with biofeedback being the main tool. In the early years his wife Joanne helped develop a biofeedback program for elementary school children at the private Montessori-style "San Francisco School." This demonstrated biofeedback to be a useful part of a self-discovery educational program.*

Dr Kamiya *retired as a professor in residence of medical psychology in 1992, but remains active in the Biofeedback Society of California, the Association of Applied Psychophysiology (which he served as one of the founders of the organization, first known as the Biofeedback Research Society, then as the Biofeedback Society of America before it adopted its current name), and the International Society of Neuronal Regulation. He is a Fellow of the American Psychological Association.*

When Joe Kamiya developed a system for alpha EEG biofeedback in the late 1950s, his equipment was simple and borrowed. By the mid 1960s, it took up a whole room, cost $80,000, and had all of 16k memory.

Here Dean Radin is showing Joe the small size of the equipment he was able to use in 2005 that had hundreds of times greater capacity to collect data of all kinds.

Research expands <u>consciousness</u>.
<u>Consciousness</u> expands research.

BIOFEEDBACK IN THE STUDY OF CONSCIOUSNESS *[12]

Joe Kamiya

Consider now the potential utility of these biofeedback systems for the science of consciousness. An important step in the science is making observations of the relationships between states of consciousness and other aspects of the publicly observable world. By the very nature of this research field, a feature of some of its observations is that they are private, first person data. Here biofeedback provides a unique opportunity for the scientist to participate as a subject in the research, because the aspects of the world that are to be related to the first person observations are the very physiological activities of the person being monitored. However, the first person observations do not only have unique features because of unique individual histories, they have universal qualities as well. For example, your sadness or joy or perceptions of the same in others are the same as mine because they are based on millions of years of evolved central neural processes common to our species. This universality of private experience is not only the basis of personal interaction with others it is the basis for the science of consciousness. [#1 in footnote *12]

Fortunately the huge strides taken by the electronic and data processing industries will help. Multi-channel measures and real-time computer analyses are now routine, low cost and miniaturized. Some manufacturers are beginning to make units that will transmit physiological data by radio or light waves, so that connecting wires are not needed.

These increased technological advances will stimulate two developments. The first is that the biofeedback signal can be made to represent specific combinations of individual measures. These may be more closely related to the ongoing experience of the individual. This makes possible tailoring feedback training to the specific physiological profiles of different individuals ... for relaxation ... and for achieving a "High Learning State." The second likely development is that biofeedback training will no longer be restricted to clinics and laboratories, but will become more widely used in the daily lives of individuals....
[#2 in footnote *12]

---

*[12] Excerpts from two of Dr Kamiya's essays: [1] 1979, April/May. The AHP Newsletter special issue on "The Future of Education." SF, CA: C. Guion & J. Millay (Eds.);
[2] 2002 Biofeedback in Education—a collection of essays and lesson plans by 12 teachers, printed privately in an 80-page booklet. A one-meter long electromagnetic spectrum chart in color is included to show the relationship between the frequencies of sun, earth, and human energy. It was revised in 2007 as Self-Discovery Science—now available free from www.fmbr.org.

Jon Klimo, PhD

Jon Klimo *began his career as a poet and painter. He earned his BA and MA in 1972 from Brown U in multidisciplinary studies, creative writing and studio art. He was a professor at Rutgers U Graduate School of Education and founding director of its Creative Arts Program from 1974-1982. He earned his PhD in 1988 from Rosebridge Graduate School of Integrative Psychology. He has taught in doctoral programs for the past 34 years, and is currently in his 10th year as core faculty (now Full Professor) in the clinical program at the SF Bay Area campus of The American Schools of Professional Psychology, Argosy U. He is considered an authority on the phenomenon of channeling, based on his book* Channeling: Investigations on Receiving Information from Paranormal Sources *(1988, 1998). He and Pamela Heath, MD, PsyD, coauthored* Suicide: What Really Happens in the Afterlife? *(2006). He has published numerous articles and chapters and has given hundreds of public presentations. He has appeared on more than 20 television and 100 radio programs, including "Coast to Coast A.M." with both Art Bell and George Noory as hosts. As a lifelong multidisciplinarian, he has done extensive research, publishing, teaching, and presentations in the areas of creativity, intuition, imagination, parapsychology, consciousness studies and transpersonal psychology.*

Dr Klimo *continues to write and teach. Among his writings are: "Quantum Idealism: Propositions, Illustrations, and Operationalizations; Toward the Emerging Spiritualization of Science" (2008); "The Neo-Shamanism of Quantum Idealism: Toward an Emerging Technology" (2007); "Consciousness Engineering and State-Dependent Science" (2005); "Shamanism and the Emerging Spiritualization of Science" (2001).*

TOWARD AN UNDERSTANDING OF QUANTUM IDEALISM

Jon Klimo

My challenge and problem in this lifetime is that I have primarily chosen to be a creative artist and poet, which has often involved states of personal consciousness and energy that fall outside the norm. At the same time, I have continued to teach in doctoral programs for 35 years, chaired hundreds of dissertations, and have studied a variety of disciplines (i.e., metaphysics, physics, cognitive science and philosophy). This background has led me to take considerable liberties and poetic license with the ideas, concepts, and even the language of specific disciplines, such as quantum physics, for example. Such liberties and license on my part creates a challenge in communicating these ideas to others. Nonetheless, I continue to believe that I have something worthwhile, and important, to contribute, hopefully, to the development of an emerging interdisciplinary paradigm for our species. I feel my role is to represent inspiration and creative vision in this developmental process. Bridging the gap between the "language" of inspiration and vision and the language required to communicate with others continues to be a challenge.

I am a philosophical idealist, for whom consciousness is the primary reality responsible for all other reality, including the physical reality as our consciousness experiences it as such. My goal at present is to bring to classical and quantum physics a perspective of philosophical idealism that sees physicality (as we currently understand it) as being a subordinate emergent epiphenomenon of an underlying superordinate mental, subjective, even spiritual, field. Seeing all that exists as consciousness (and its experienced objects, contents, and events), and interacting with the conceptual framework of quantum physics from this idealist perspective, as well as from the perspective of the poet and artist I am, I have begun to develop over the past 20 years a field called "Quantum Idealism." In recent years, this perspective has allowed me to address my long-standing interests regarding what I call the "emerging spiritualization of science," and in understanding the nature of how we create our own reality. Construing all that exists as an infinite dimensional consciousness field moves me to want to play with the traditional Copenhagen interpretation of collapsing wave functions, reframing it largely as a way in which we see how we humans, sub-portions of the universal field, interact with other portions of that field, and with the field at large, thereby bringing something like local quantum decoherent systems out of an underlying nonlocal superposed quantum coherent system containing all probabilities or potentialities for local, transient, objective reality.

The full text of his papers is on his website: www.jonklimo.com.

William Braud, PhD

William Braud, PhD, began his academic work in physics, at Loyola U in New Orleans, but switched to psychology, earning his BA in psychology in 1964 from the U of New Orleans. He earned his MA in 1966 and his PhD in 1967, both in experimental psychology, at the U of Iowa. From 1967 to 1975, he taught undergraduate and graduate psychology courses at the U of Houston and conducted original research in areas of learning, memory, motivation, psychophysiology, and the biochemistry of memory. After 8 years, he left his tenured Associate Professorship to join the Mind Science Foundation (San Antonio, TX) where, for 17 years, he directed research in parapsychology; health and well-being influences of relaxation, imagery, positive emotions, and intention; and psychoneuroimmunology.

In 1992, he joined the Residential Core Faculty of the Institute of Transpersonal Psychology (Palo Alto, CA), as professor, research director, dissertation director, and codirector of its William James Center for Consciousness Studies. In 2002, he joined the Core Faculty of ITP's newly created distant learning Global PhD Program. In 2009, Dr Braud retired from his position at ITP, and was awarded the title of Professor Emeritus.

Professor Braud has published over 250 professional articles and book chapters, coauthored *Transpersonal Research Methods for the Social Sciences* (Sage, 1998), and authored *Distant Mental Influence* (Hampton Roads, 2003). He serves on Editorial Boards of several professional journals.

His website is: http://inclusivepsychology.com.

PROFESSOR BRAUD'S EXTENSIVE INTERESTS

Professor Braud is the recipient of fellowships, travel awards, federal grants, honors and awards, including a university-wide Teaching Excellence Award (U of Houston), Award for Outstanding Contribution (Parapsychological Association), and President's Award for Outstanding Service (ITP).

During his 17 years at ITP, Professor Braud taught research-related graduate psychology courses, supervised dissertations, and conducted quantitative and qualitative research studies in areas of exceptional human experiences (mystical, intuitive, peak, transformative) and their interpretations, meanings, and life impacts; personal and spiritual change and transformation; alternative ways of knowing; the development and promotion of more inclusive and integrated inquiry approaches for transpersonal studies and science in general; and examining some of the underlying assumptions of science, psychology, transpersonal psychology, and certain spiritual and wisdom traditions.

Within the areas of parapsychology and consciousness research, Professor Braud's interests focus on:

(a) Exploring the range and limits of direct intentional influences on animate and inanimate systems (including possible "backward in time" and "forward in time" influences);

(b) exploring ways in which psychic functioning might reveal aspects of reality other than those immediately evident to the conventional senses (e.g., connections, histories, future outcomes, relationships, meanings);

(c) life impacts of psychic and related experiences;

(d) novel methodological approaches to the study of survival of bodily death.

Brian McRae

Brian McRae was secretary on the board of directors of the PRG from 1989-95, and demonstrated (on video) that he could bend metal by psychokinesis (PK). He attended classes at the U of Michigan (Dearborn, 1973-76); since there were no classes in parapsychology or consciousness he began reading the subject matter on his own. After he transferred to Wayne State U in Detroit, MI (1976-83), he found that there were no such classes there, either. Nevertheless, he became more engrossed in parapsychology. When he became interested in bodywork (e.g., Rolfing and acupressure), he noticed an increase in his own psi activity and developed a feel for alternative states of consciousness — leading to an increase in hostility from the mainstream academic staff toward his ideas.

When a friend told him about the parapsychology program at John F. Kennedy U in CA, he transferred there (1986-91), where he was able to run a few psi experiments and participate in others. On the surface the school seemed liberal and tolerant, but he discovered that in spite of the name "JFK," the school was actually quite conservative. The local newspaper published an interview with one administrator who implied that the parapsychology program made the school look "flakey." McRae graduated from JFK with a BS in parapsychology and psychology, but he was denied the MS he earned, and the legal contretemps have yet to be resolved. He writes, "I spend a lot of time with psychospiritual development, alternative states, psi development systems and psycho-technology."

Brian McRae maintains his interest in parapsychology, consciousness and UFOlogy research. Next he plans to continue his studies of psi at Saybrook University in San Francisco, CA.

William Croft

William Croft is an engineer working in the field of energy/informational medicine modalities using open-source (cooperatively developed) technologies. He has evolved Dr Paul Nogier's VAS (Vascular Autonomic Signal) pulse reading technique into a general purpose bio-information readout system. The VAS connects to a level of "heart-intelligence" or wisdom knowledge about what are the most appropriate vibrational modalities and parameters to resonantly facilitate shifts in client energetics and consciousness.

He was a founding staff member at the Live Oak Center for the Healing Arts and also works with projects of the Qigong Institute. He has held research positions at Stanford University Medical Center, SRI International, and Sun Microsystems, and has developed communications network technology for over thirty years. His work is mentioned in the book *Light Years Ahead*.

At Stanford University working with the first release of the Macintosh computer, he created innovative open source software and hardware for the first campus-wide gateway system linking Mac's to the internet; the first Mac C language compiler; and the bootstrap protocol now used by all internet computers to acquire their network address / name (BOOTP / DHCP).

One of the founding staff members at Sun Microsystems, he built their diskless workstation and remote disk server software, which was a significant factor in the early success of Sun in campus and research environments.

At the Qigong Institute he cocreated the Qigong Database project, reviewing qigong scientific research worldwide.

For more information on the Lightfield Systems, see www.lightfield.com.

Kenneth Ring, PhD

Kenneth Ring published the first scientific study in 1980 of the near-death experience (NDE) *Life at Death*. The next year he helped found the International Association of Near-Death Studies, which has branches in ten countries around the world. He established *The Journal of Near-Death Studies* in 1983. In 1984, Dr Ring introduced his second book, *Healing Toward Omega*, which was concerned mainly with the after effects and evolutionary implications of NDEs. In 1992, he published *The Omega Project*.

In response to our plan for a revision of *Silver Threads* he wrote:

"I don't know if you should really bother to reproduce that article of mine. Let me count the ways...you may want to discard it.... First, I wrote the original version of that article more than 20 years ago.... I haven't worked the NDE field since 2000, and have nothing I want to write or add to it now.... I'm really busy now with other projects...concerned with the plight of the Palestinians, and that is taking a great deal of my time and energy. So...you should just leave me out of the book altogether, of course, I still wish you the very best with your book and thank you for wanting to include me in it."

Kenneth Ring's Research and Publications Made a Substantial Contribution to this Large Study:

In 2008, the *World Science* website posted this announcement:

"World's largest study of near-death experiences to start September 11, 2008, courtesy of University of Southampton and World Science staff. The University of Southampton, U.K. announced it is launching this week the world's largest-ever study on whether people have thoughts for a time while they are clinically 'dead.'

The AWARE (<u>AWA</u>reness during <u>RE</u>suscitation) study is to be launched by the Human Consciousness Project at the University, an international collaboration of scientists and physicians who study the brain, consciousness and clinical death. The study is led by Sam Parnia of Weill Cornell Medical Center in New York, with University of Southampton researchers. Following an 18-month pilot phase at some UK hospitals, the study is now being expanded to include other centers within the UK, mainland Europe and North America, Parnia said....

Barbara Honegger, M.S.

Barbara Honegger received her BA in Creative Writing from Stanford University in 1969, and did graduate work on the neuropsychology of human and nonhuman primate communication. She received the nation's first accredited Master's degree in Consciousness Studies/Experimental Parapsychology from John F. Kennedy University in Orinda, CA, in June 1981. In 1979-1980, Honegger served as President of the Parapsychology Research Group (PRG) and did research writing in SF at Henry Dakin's Washington Research Institute (WRI) in SF. She was a researcher at the Hoover Institution in the late 1970s before becoming a White House Policy Analyst and Special Assistant to Reagan's Chief Domestic Policy Adviser, and then the Project Director of the Attorney General's Anti-Gender-Discrimination Task Force, in the first Reagan Administration. Honegger's public resignation of conscience in August 1983 triggered a ten-day wave of international publicity. She again confronted controversy in May 1989 when she published her now famous book **October Surprise**, in which she documented that Reagan's vice presidential running mate George H. W. Bush and then 1980 campaign manager William Casey, soon to be Reagan's CIA Director, secretly offered the Iranians a better arms deal than Carter if they held on to the 52 hostages until after the election, which they knew would guarantee Carter's defeat. (Validated by released official records.)

In the wake of Sept. 11, Honegger published **The Pentagon Attack Papers,** detailing the evidence that the attacks were an inside job, not the act of "Al Qaeda," at www.patriotsquestion911.com. Honegger is one of 20 founding members of Political Leaders for 9/11 Truth. http://pl911truth.com/index/php?option=com_content&view=article&id=47&Itemid=53.

NOTES ON A CHARMED LIFE OF LIVING PSI

Barbara Honegger

From the time I was a small child, "things happened" – "things," I later came to understand, that didn't happen to everyone, at least not as often as they did for me, and which the adult world called synchronicity, serendipity, or just luck. By the time I became the pioneering graduate of the first ever fully accredited graduate program in Consciousness Studies and Parapsychology, at John F. Kennedy U (JFK) in CA, the phenomena behind these "things" I experienced every day had come to be called "Psi."

As a young child, I learned that my grandfather, who died not long before I was born, was a "diviner" and that my mother was afraid I'd inherit his "special abilities," not because of the abilities themselves, but because of the social repercussions they could trigger.

The first inkling of these "other abilities" I recall in my own life was a game of pretend that a friend and I were playing at our house to pass the time while our mothers were out shopping, when I was about three. We found a "magic orange" in a nearby orchard and took turns using it to "see" what was on the coffee table inside the house. The one with the orange got to run in first and arrange the things on the table to match their "vision." In the middle of this game, as I was holding the orange, I suddenly "knew" with a sense of absolute certainty that my friend's mother had just bought her a bicycle, and blurted it out. A few minutes later, our parents returned. *"Come see what I got you!"* my friend's mother called out, to which my playmate said excitedly as we raced toward the car, *"I know what you bought me, Mommy. Barby said you bought me a bicycle!"* Not long after this, this same friend and her mother took me to a bingo game, where we kids were allowed to play "just for fun." After winning two in a row and a rush of whispers that swept across the room, the M.C. announced that kids wouldn't be allowed to play after all.

Life on a Shoestring

The cognitive side of psi soon expanded to include psychokinesis, after we moved to a big ranch house in the country. I was learning to roller skate, and was excited to get in some practice on the new patio off the side porch after school. While hurriedly tightening the shoelaces on my left skate, the lace in my right hand suddenly broke. In a completely spontaneous action, I held the short piece against the broken end of the lace that was still in the shoe, closed my eyes, and squeezed them together as tightly as I could. I remember focusing my intention to a hard point, as if it were a diamond. When I opened my eyes and hand, the lace was unbroken. With a thrilling sense only of success – like the one I'd felt after successfully tying my shoelaces for the first time – and not of surprise, I went on to skate as if nothing had happened.

Years passed, and I'd been given my first car. First at the intersection one day after high school, with a string of cars behind me, I suddenly became unaware of anything around me and spontaneously focused on something that was terribly important, like the hard "diamond" feeling I'd had before the shoelace had "healed." I didn't know what it was, but was soon to find out. That night, my normally jovial father was strangely silent and serious at the dinner table. He finally broke the silence and said, *"You almost lost your father today."* A rancher, that afternoon he'd been standing, balanced, on the back of a seeder plow, pouring seeds into a funnel that dropped into the fresh furrows made by the tractor's large scythe-like blades. The tractor suddenly lurched, and he started to lose his balance. Just when he was afraid he might fall into the blades, something pulled him back – just when I was stopped at the intersection. A long leather shoelace on one of his high work boots had come untied and the hard knot at the end of the lace had become caught in a metal groove.

It wasn't until years later, with a jolt, that I realized the two synchronicities shared the same theme – of the shoestring. This realization was made possible by a detailed contemporaneous journal, which I kept for nearly two decades. In the journal, any event that seemed to stand out from "ordinary" experience as numinous, special, strange, paranormal or miraculous – for any reason – was highlighted.

As in the example of the shoestring-theme synchronicities, I soon discovered to my astonishment that these "special" events, which individually are often causally inexplicable, are linked and related to one another in a free-associational network, like the verbal "syllabic chemistry" of the deep structure of dreams uncovered by Freud. This led to the realization, which I published, that "numinous" or "miraculous" events form a pattern or network and are related via a kind of meta-causality; that when the ordinary parts of the diary are collapsed away and the special events "moved together," these special events constitute the deep structure of "waking dreams"; and that these waking dreams can be interpreted just like REM state dreams during sleep. But, most importantly, these causally "impossible" events that nevertheless take place during the waking state – like the "impossible" events of dreams during sleep – provide the "waker" with the opportunity to become lucid during the *waking* state; that this waking-state lucidity is what is known as enlightenment; and that, in the waking lucid/enlightened state, as in the lucid dream state, the waker's desires can instantly manifest themselves in what we call the physical world, or "reality." Thus, I realized, parapsychologists miss the point when they try to "explain" spontaneous psi events. It's precisely the realization that these events not only can't be explained by ordinary causality, but also *can't* actually happen in the "real" world, *and yet do*, that makes them the "Golden Door" to waking state lucidity, or enlightenment.

After graduating from Stanford University, I'd remained as a graduate-at-large studying the neuropsychology of human and nonhuman primate communication while working at the Hoover Institution, and joined the Parapsychology Research Group (PRG), of which I later became president, at the encouragement of Russell Targ, then doing remote viewing experiments at SRI. Russell became a mentor of sorts, with whom I shared many of the synchronicities I experienced, and he encouraged me to continue in the field.

The opportunity to do so soon presented itself with the founding of the world's first accredited graduate program in Consciousness Studies and Parapsychology, at JFK University in Orinda, CA. I learned of the program "by chance" one night while at a Physics and Consciousness night course in Berkeley taught by brilliant theoretical physicist Saul-Paul Sirag. A call came in for me while there, which I took in the study. Looking for a piece of paper on which to jot down a note, I picked up what appeared to be a blank sheet. It was the announcement for the new Parapsychology program, to which I immediately applied and was accepted into the first class. To move closer to JFK, I moved to SF, where I joined Henry Dakin's Washington Street Research Center (later called Washington Research Institute, or WRI) – famous for its experiments with world renowned psychics like Uri Geller and Matthew Manning, whom I met.

The JFK Parapsychology program led by John Palmer was a thrilling and historic experience. We were all aware of the paradigm-shattering nature of what we were part of for the academic world, and took it very seriously.

The *"Living on a Shoestring"* theme returned while I was living across the street from Dakin's SF lab and attending the JFK night program. My income situation had become urgent, and with the intensity of focus that had come with the shoestring "miracles," I committed to myself I would have a job by the following Monday "no matter what." The next morning, my dogs awakened me, barking far more loudly than usual. I went to the hall in time to see one of the dogs playing tug-of-war with a rolled newspaper the mailman was trying to push through the slot in the front door. He shook the paper in his teeth, flinging pieces of newsprint all over the floor. As I picked them up, "something" said to turn one of the smaller ones over. One the other side was an advertisement for what had to be the position I'd left at the Hoover Institution to attend the JFK program, which was once again open. On Monday – the self-appointed "deadline" – I drove to Stanford and slipped my resume under the door of my former supervisor at the Hoover Institution. *"Sure,"* he soon called, *"Come back and work for me."*

I did, and therein lies a life-changing synchronicity. For this wasn't just any supervisor. I'd worked before – and was now again – with Dr. Martin Anderson, soon to be tapped as Ronald Reagan's chief domestic policy adviser.

Not long after I'd returned to the Hoover Institution, Marty came into the office with a Cheshire cat grin and said, *"You have a choice. In two weeks, you can be out of a job, or you come with me to Reagan's presidential campaign headquarters and, if he wins, to the White House. What do you want to do?"* It took a nano-second to make the "choice."

And so it was that, after completing all my JFK parapsychology courses, but before completing my thesis, I was whisked off to Washington, D.C. to the highest levels of the Reagan-Bush presidential campaign. When Reagan won, I moved to the top floor of the transition team headquarters, and, on inauguration day 1981, into the West Wing of the White House, where I was a Policy Analyst and Special Assistant to the Assistant to the President – all while still a student at JFK. Not surprisingly, word got around quickly that there was a parapsychologist in what was supposed to be a conservative White House, and it wasn't long before I was asked to give a guest lecture in Smithsonian Institution and invited to tour labs where military scientists were conducting cutting edge experiments on the effects of various frequencies of electromagnetic radiation on the human brain bypassing the ordinary external sensory mechanisms.

The high point during this period was the joint 100th anniversary of the British Society for Psychical Research and 25th anniversary of the U.S. Parapsychology Association conference held at Trinity College, Cambridge, in England. I was granted leave from the White House to attend this historic conference, which was literally like stepping into a Hogwart's School of Wizardry scene from a Harry Potter movie with its medieval great hall hung with banners. The other highlight was returning to CA to receive the first accredited Master's degree in Consciousness Studies/Parapsychology at JFK's first graduation ceremony, in June 1981. This was the same ceremony at which Manley Hall received an Honorary Master's for his lifelong work.

The Feather on the Scale

By the time I entered the program, I was already well known for experiencing extraordinary synchronicities, many of which defied causal explanation, and one fellow student wanted to know whether I made them up. To find out, he'd show me a random object he'd picked up from the ground and ask if it "meant" anything. None of them did.

During this time I was independently experiencing an amazing synchronicity series surrounding the Egyptian ritual of the dead at Osiris' door, where the deceased's heart is weighed against a feather. If the heart is lighter than the feather, the soul is allowed to enter the Afterlife. If it's not, the heart is thrown to Anubis, the jackal god who guards the door. I'd already had "coincidences" while reading Budge's book on Egyptian magic involving coming into the possession of two synchronistically found "pans" that represented the scales and a lightweight piece of Styrofoam shaped like a heart. In the middle of this series, my fellow student was invited to a professor's home. While there, the professor's cat came into the room carrying a dead hawk or falcon-like bird and dropped it like a trophy in the middle of the floor. After a stunned silence, the professor shooed away the cat and removed the bird. As he walked with it out of the room, a single orange feather fell onto the carpet. The moment my fellow student saw the feather, he *did* immediately think of me, and picked it up. During a break in the next class, he showed me the feather and again asked if it "meant anything." I immediately recognized it as the last symbol needed to complete the synchronicity series about the ritual of the weighing of the heart against the feather at Osiris' door, and exclaimed, *"It's Maat's Feather!"* "How did you *know* that?" he asked in surprise. I started to explain about the ritual and that the feather belongs to the Egyptian Goddess Maat, at which he said, *"My God! I was in Professor Mott's home. So it is 'Mott's feather' – pronounced the same as Maat, but just spelled differently."* The student, who went on to earn a doctorate in anthropology, presented me with "Maat's" feather, a prized possession to this day. After explaining the methodology of his "experiment," he announced that my synchronicities appeared to be "genuine."

And so it was that I passed the "test" of Osiris' door.

It is this ritual – the weighing of the heart against a feather – that synchronistically sums up the most important thing I've learned in all the decades of experiencing "meaningful coincidences" and the hundreds of books and journal articles read in the Parapsychology program and after. When I went into the program, I was uncertain as to whether the soul/psyche/personality survived bodily death, and expected to learn the answer, or at least get closer to it. To my surprise, after knowing all the detailed numinous experiences of others and laboratory results in all those hundreds of books and articles, though I now had vastly more information than before, it still essentially divided equally on the two sides of the scale. It was then that I realized that the answer to that all-important Question is a *decision* – whether arrived at by faith or act of will – and that each of us tips our own scales, one way or the other, according to whether, and where, we choose to place a single feather.

On the Future and What I Believe

Through a combination of decades of avid reading and study, contemplation on the facts learned, and "gnosis," I have come to believe or expect the following:

- That the brain's newly named "dark" processing ("The Brain's Dark Energy," *Scientific American*, March 2010, pp. 44-49) discovered with advances in MRI technology and experimentation will prove to be the neurological substrate for the nonlocal information processes whose effects we call psi. These studies have found that the energy consumed by this "background" processing is 20 times that used by the brain when it responds to outside stimuli from "the world. This is similar to the estimated 90 percent of "dark" matter in the universe that we cannot detect with our conscious minds mediated by the electromagnetic senses, and the estimated similar high percentage of DNA whose function is currently unknown.

- That a new unified theory will be found to explain, not only gravity and quantum mechanics, but also psi phenomena, as explicated in the brilliant book by a British physicist, *Intelligence Behind the Universe*.

- That reincarnation is not only a fact, but occurs with a periodicity, like the return of comets, and thus the most important messages you can leave are to your future Self.

- That the year 2012 will involve an individual and collective breakthrough in the depth and scale of this realization about who we are, and that the trigger event will include a stunning archeological find from ancient Egypt. When I was in the White House, in the early 1980s, while studying the reign of Akhenaten and Nefertiti – about whom, along with their daughter Scotia, I have experienced profound synchronistic connections – I had a realization that the three main pyramids at Giza were intended to be and are the projection onto Earth of the three stars in the Belt of Orion. I communicated this in a letter to contacts at the United Nations. Years later, this thesis was partially explicated in a book called *The Orion Mystery*. Partially, because the book focuses only on the projection onto Earth of the stars in the Orion constellation, but leaves out *the* most important Star to the ancient Egyptians, Sirius, which by a cosmic synchronicity, the three Orion belt stars point to; and which, by another cosmic synchronicity happens to have been first seen to rise above the horizon on the very day the Nile flooded, made the High Holy Day of the ancient Egyptians, returning its life-giving water and rich soil to the land. It is the physical place on the Earth that is the projection of Sirius, not far from Giza, that will be found to be the most incredible archeological find of all time, probably including the famous Akashic Records. Those

Records probably record all major events in world history up to the opening of the Records themselves, which, if so, it must mean that, for the first time in "history," from that moment on humankind will be free to determine our own destiny.

- That this find will probably connect the Earth to Mars, as presaged by the most astounding synchronicity of my life:

In 1976, while working at the Hoover Institution at Stanford, I decided to take a walk during my lunch break. In the plaza was a "stone artist" named Jim Quackenbush who had set up a display of slices of sandstone that had the most beautiful lines and swirls in deep reds and tans – each a visual synchronicity, as if the Earth itself had painted its own future landscapes in rock laid down billions of years before. I was drawn to one small stone, that was fitted for a necklace, whose lines and swirls "painted" what looked like a red desert plain strewn with rocks with a sun surrounded by concentric rings in the distance. I purchased it and for some reason deciding to wear it when I went to sleep. Early that morning, I got an excited call from my then business partner whose main job was working with the Space Shuttle simulator at NASA's Moffett Field in Mountain View, CA. *"If you can get here in 45 minutes, I'll get you in the gate and you'll be able to see the first ever images come in live from Mars,"* he said. I was dressed and out the door in minutes and in one of the plush red seats at NASA's Moffett Field auditorium in time to see the first bits from the camera on the Red Planet projected onto a big screen.

As the pixels came in slowly, line by vertical line, there came a moment when enough of the image had formed that I suddenly realized that what I was seeing "was" the image on the Stone around my neck. *"My God!"* I whispered to my friend sitting next to me as I pulled the necklace out from around my neck, and he gasped. *"I forgot I was wearing it until this moment. I just bought this!"*

Years later, in 2009, I received an email from the artist's daughter – who wasn't yet born when I'd bought the "Mars Stone" and after he had died – saying she had found a letter I'd written her father about this incredible synchronicity, and would I mind if she included it in her master's thesis on sacred stones in the cultures of the world? I, of course, said yes, and we met in SF for the Tut exhibit, at which we stood together before carvings of Akhenaten, Nefertiti and Scotia, and the ritual at Osiris' Door.

I intend to wear the Mars Stone at The Sirius Point on the High Holy Day of the ancient Egyptians, July 23rd, in 2012. Anyone who's really Sirius about being there, too, can reach me at barhonegger@aol.com.

CHAPTER 46

Talented Psi Sensitives:
The Fundamental Energy for Psi Research.

Russell Targ has previously published reports about the outstanding remote viewing abilities of Ingo Swann. Here in Chapter 1, Targ shows examples of RV by Pat Price and Hella Hammid. Uri Geller's PK is shown in Chapter 11. While some of Elizabeth Rauscher's remote viewers chose not to be identified, their skepticism dissolved when they discovered that their own psi ability was real. Occasionally both Targ and Rauscher acted as successful remote viewers, as well.

The extraordinary psi sensitives on this list have significantly advanced the knowledge of the possible:

8) Gail Hayssen — She has demonstrated successful precognition, PK and RV during important experiments with Radin, Targ, and May. She describes herself as a *"Small Medium at Large."*

Psi sensitives may have very diverse occupations. Four of those who participated in Millay's telepathy and RV experiments are:

9) James Dowlen — He designed the cover of this book, since he is both a psi sensitive and an exceptional professional artist. His remote viewing responses extended beyond the target into the dynamics of the mind and future of the "sender," which confused the judges, since statistics have to be based on the actual randomly selected target. Yet the results were astounding and revealed how incredibly insightful psi perception can be. Examples of his RV accuracy are shown on pp. 6, 8, 9, 10, and in his bio.

10) Tom Byrne — He is a professional artist and a psi sensitive. The title page of Section I features his drawing. Other examples of his RV are on pp. 1, 6 and in his bio.

11) Mark Harris — He is a musician, teacher and psi sensitive. An example of his telepathy is on page 5. He and his teammate Russell Winkler compared their experience of interpersonal EEG alpha phase-synch (IP Sync) training in Appendix A of Chapter 22.

12) Greg Schelkun — He is a spiritual healer who was featured in a research study by Dan Wyrth on the *"Effects of Belief on Spiritual Healing."* He was also mentioned in articles in *Time*. An example of his RV accuracy of a target nearly 3,000 miles away is shown on page 7. He also describes what he felt during the IP Sync training with his wife Pricilla.

Gail Hayssen

Gail Hayssen is an outstanding psychic. Her perceptive and intuitive abilities were first recognized when, as a teenager, she did medical diagnosis in the Mind Dynamics program with Werner Erhard and Alexander Everett.

Gail Hayssen began in the late 1990s to participate in experiments with Dean Radin, Russell Targ and Ed May at Interval Research, and has continued work with Radin at The Institute of Noetic Sciences. Targ said about her, "Gail has collaborated with me in various psychic endeavors for more than a decade. She shows her remarkable abilities in formal studies of clairvoyance and precognition in our work."

Over the years, she has developed unique relationships with native people and shamans from other cultures including: the Huichol of the mountains of Mexico, the Haida of Alaska, and shamans of Mongolia, who invited her to speak at the International Shaman Symposium in Mongolia. She has shared this knowledge of the shamans with those attending The Conferences on the Study of Shamanism and Alternate Modes of Healing in San Rafael. Her papers on these experiences are found on: www.smallmediumatlarge.net.

Gail has been a subject, participant, or co-author in numerous experiments and publications. Radin said this about her work at IONS: "In another time and place, she would undoubtedly be a shaman or medicine woman. Her life has been saturated with spontaneous psychic experiences, which she has also demonstrated in the laboratory. She's been a pleasure to know, and I look forward to seeking her advice and skills in future studies of these exceptional abilities."

EXPERIMENTS AND PUBLICATIONS

Gail Hayssen is a very successful remote viewer. In this example of her work, Hayssen is facing a computer, which has a blank area where she can type or sketch (with a mouse) whatever she "sees, feels or thinks" about the future target. Her responses are recorded digitally. It will be two hours later before the computer chooses the target randomly, and displays it on the monitor. Along with the physical and visual similarities, this mosque is indeed a place with access restrictions as she described.

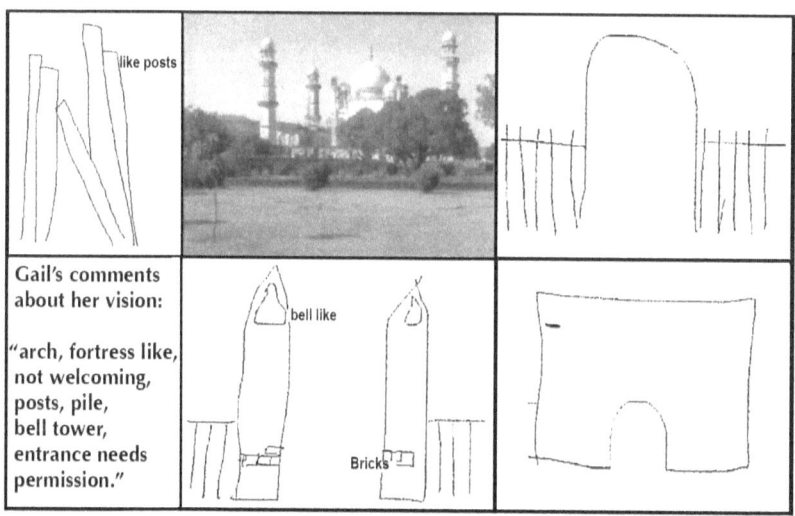

During a very different type of experiment, Hayssen was in the EM shielded room where Dean Radin had asked her to cause an effect on a photon in another room. Her first attempt showed a slight, but measurable, photon effect similar to what Dean had seen before. She asked if she could try it again, this time focusing her intent on *"blowing it up"* to impress him. Suddenly the lights went out—she was sitting in the dark room hoping she hadn't destroyed Dean's photon equipment. In fact, the entire IONS complex had lost power—something that never happens there except in violent storms. Everyone was pleased with the results.

Hayssen's publications include:

1) Radin, D., Hayssen, G., et al. (2006) "Double-blind test of the effects of distant intention on water crystal formation." In: *Explore Vol. 2 #5*, Sept./Oct. 2006.
2) Radin, D., Hayssen, G. & Walsh, J. (2007) "Effects of Intentionally enhanced chocolate on mood," In: *Explore Vol. 3 #5*, Sept./Oct. 2007.
3) Rain, D., Hayssen, G., et al. (2008) "Compassionate intention as a therapeutic intervention by partners of cancer patients: effects of distant intention on the patients' autonomic nervous system." In: *Explore, Vol. 4. #4*, July/Aug., 2008.

GAIL HAYSSEN'S EXPERIENCES OUTSIDE THE LABORATORY

Sometimes the paranormal events seem to come in waves. At the *Mind and Matter* conference at IONS in 2004, Russell Targ and Cornell Professor Dr Daryl Bem each happened to give presentations in which an item was hidden in a bag. Russell was offering an *Introduction to Remote Viewing* and asked audience members to describe the color, shape, material, or other properties of the hidden object.

Several audience members spoke up. *"It's pink." "It's metal."*

I wound up saying: *"It's one of those heavy 8-armed Shivas made of brass, with a lotus base."*

He pulled it out, and that's what it was. I had never seen this object. Russell looked more shocked than anyone, wondering how to explain this was not a joke or a trick.

An hour later, during Dr Bem's presentation—which actually was a deceptive bit of stage magic—suddenly I was sure a bag of assorted objects he was hiding contained a sand dollar, and I said so out loud. On the videotape of the session, you can hear Jeffrey Mishlove and the others sitting near me squeal as Bem then removes a sand dollar from the bag. Dr Bem is a mentalist—a magician who specializes in faking ESP, and an honest scientist. After the show, he said: *"What I was doing with this audience was 'magic.' Gail, what you did was real."*

While traveling in the remote mountains of Mexico, I dreamed my daughter Nancy was seriously ill and suddenly left the group of native Huichol peyoteros I was traveling with. When I reached my husband by phone from a switchboard in Mexico, he insisted Nancy was fine. I returned home immediately anyway. They picked me up and, on the way back from the airport, Nancy became seriously ill. At first the attending doctors thought she had the flu. But before long they realized she needed surgery. When the doctor made the incision, Nancy's infected appendix burst in his hand. She was in the hospital for ten days.

In another case I met the husband of a worker in my catering kitchen, and realized he was going to die very soon. He was a strong man with no known health problems, but my feeling made me very sure. Two weeks later he died suddenly of a rare heart disease. I never knew what to tell his wife. I catered the funeral at my expense.

While traveling through Hong Kong and China I was having a lot of precognition experiences. I would dream about things at night that then would happen the next day. I spent six weeks constantly seeing the future. I dreamed Harriet Lewis, who was in my cooking group, was writing a book. The next day when I told her, she said no one else knew she was in fact writing one. In Hong Kong I dreamt about a woman I was going to meet, I saw her dressed in a jean outfit. I met the woman the next day, dressed exactly as I had seen.

Insights were also occurring not only in the dream world, but also in my awakened world. My friend Anne discovered in the customs line at the Hong Kong airport that she had lost the key to her luggage. I immediately turned around, walked out of the terminal to the street, bent down and picked up the little key without hesitation; I was back before the customs officials could get mad. The intensity of psychic information that was flowing through me was starting to surprise everyone.

The most intense experience was during the vegetable carving class at The Town Gas Cooking School in Hong Kong. Ricky, my first sweetheart, had contracted AIDS in the early eighties. I had heard he was one of only six men in the United States who agreed to try experimental drugs to see if it would help cure the disease. I was in the vegetable carving class holding a carrot. My head started spinning and I got very dizzy. I started choking and I couldn't breathe. I had to get out of the class and out into the street immediately. I knew my old friend Ricky was dying at that moment. It is difficult to explain what an intuitive, gut-knowingness feels like, but the feeling is so strong you just know. I got in a cab and told the driver to take me to temples all over Hong Kong. I prayed in the ancient temples for his safe passing on. I called back to California, and everyone said they had not received any calls and assumed Ricky was still doing okay. But I knew otherwise.

As I ended weeks of travel, my husband picked me up at the airport. In the car he handed me a letter from Ricky's mother dated July 10th 1984. Six weeks after my Cosmic Connection with Ricky, I received my verification. Yes, he had died the day I knew he had—five days before his 34th birthday.

On one occasion a friend asked me to talk to a man whose mother had been missing for more than a week. The police were stumped. Somehow after speaking with the man for a few minutes, I found—to my astonishment—that I could see and describe the location and condition of the missing woman. The police discovered her body a few hours later in exactly the circumstances I saw.

When people contact Dr Dean Radin worried about precognitive dreams, spontaneous out of body experiences, or communication with a dead relative, sometimes he puts them in touch with "Dr Gail." If I've had an experience like theirs, I say so. And immediately the person relaxes. Suddenly they're not victims with no one to talk to, or lunatics worried that they need an exorcist. They're dealing with physical and mental states, situations and experiences—kundalini, out-of-body, clairvoyance, and psychokinesis—that many others have encountered before, and they're grateful to talk to me.

James Dowlen

James Dowlen's pen and ink illustrations and fantasy paintings of the 1970s gave him a reputable name in the SF Bay Area art world. In 1975, when Millay saw the "notes" (all pictures) he drew in her class, she asked him to participate in her RV experiments, and published some of his amazing artistic RV responses in the 1993 version of *Silver Threads*, and the full set of them in her 1999 book *Multidimensional Mind: Remote Viewing in Hyperspace*. A sample of these is included in Section I, and on the next page. He has operated his *ArtWorks* design, illustration and fine art studio for over 30 years. It is now located in the Willamette Valley, OR.

James Dowlen was chosen in 1984 to pioneer some of the earliest digital tools of the computer revolution. He was among the very first to bring digital illustrations to print media, and computerized animation to video, way before these mediums became mainstream. During this storm of new and exciting creativity, Dowlen began working for notable clientele such as WED (Walt Elias Disney Enterprises), 20th Century Fox, Lucas Film at SkyWalker Ranch, and he worked personally with Steven Spielberg at his Hollywood Studios, Amblin Productions at Universal City. Dowlen also worked extensively with legendary Art Director Chris Blum, and with Ken Nordine (the 50s Beat Poet and very familiar voice talent) creating advertisements for his famed classic Levi Jeans commercials.

Limited edition fine art prints of the cover art for *Radiant Minds: Scientists Explore the Dimensions of Consciousness* are available by visiting his website www.dowlenartworks.com

TARGET: Who Will Win The World Series? (10 days in the future)

Dowlen agreed to precognize the winner of the 1982 World Series. On October 11, he drew all these in color. The series began Oct. 12th, with the Cardinals losing the first game. To establish the precognition, I had the drawings notarized in the morning of Oct. 15th as soon as they arrived in the mail. By game 6 (Oct. 19), the Milwaukee Brewers had won 3 games, and the Cardinals had only won 2, but the Cardinals won the series 4 to 3.

ARTIST'S STATEMENT

I paint from vivid source material gathered up in my dreams and my active imagination. This often includes inspirations from the natural world and the supernatural world. I look for images that reflect a personal mythology or a truth about human endeavors. I sometimes feel that I have hand carried these images back from a very distant and exotic primal or alternate local.

--- James Dowlen, 2009

Tom Byrne

Tom Byrne is a gifted artist whose drawing on the first page of the *Dimensions of Perception* asks the important question we all have: *"Does the eye see?"* He was attending Santa Rosa Junior College at the time (1976), and he agreed to participate in a series of remote viewing experiments. His complete set of drawings for that experiment can be found in Millay's book *Multidimensional Mind: Remote Viewing in Hyperspace*.

Byrne has pursued a career in graphic design and illustration. In the 1980s he copublished a regional entertainment magazine *Music West* from Auburn, CA. For the past twenty years, he has designed exhibits for trade shows and museums. Currently he is owner/partner of SGX (Sierra Group Exhibits), located in Grass Valley, CA, a firm that provides corporate marketing and event services to companies internationally. Coincidentally, they also build, package and ship isolation tanks all over the world for Samadhi, the leading manufacturer of floating immersion enclosures, used for meditation and psychic discovery.

Figures 1c and 1e show Byrne's RV response to a target 30 miles distant from him — the Novato Airport. Figures 1a, 1b & 1d are photos taken at the site during the RV session. Whereas most of us think that a fire truck looks like the one he drew in Figure 1c, this small airport needed only a pickup truck to serve as the fire truck. He seemed to get a partial idea of a gas station, where there was *"NO LIMIT"* (during a *"fuel crisis"*). Figure 1d is of the runway lights. Later, Byrne said he had no idea what it was that he "saw," but he can draw any image in his mind, and this one had a similar size and shape. His question *"Does the eye see?"* is not totally answered, over thirty years later.

TARGET: The Novato Airport (30 miles distant)

Figure 1a. The pickup truck used at the Novato Airport for fire control
Figure 1b. The system of providing airplane fuel to small planes
Figure 1c & 1e. Tom Byrnes' remote viewing responses to the airport

Novato Airport, Fire Truck (Pickup), Gas Station, and Control Operator.

Figure 1d. Landing Lights

Figure 1e. Tom Byrne's RV response

Mark Harris

Mark (Gurumukh) Harris is a musician, a teacher, and a psi sensitive. During the time he participated in Millay's telepathy and EEG phase-sync study, he described himself as colead "White Rat." Today he would describe himself in nonpsychic terms as a maroon griot (pronounced gree-ō). Maroon is the Taino word for an African / Native-American genetic and cultural hybrid. It means in that language "wild and free." A griot is a traditional African storyteller, musician, poet, historian, diplomat, and healer. Currently employed as a college professor teaching Addiction Studies and Ethnic Studies at Lane Community College in Eugene, OR. However, his main interest is in *the liberation of the human spirit*.

Certainly the development of the 12 senses is part of that. The twelve senses are the five physical senses plus the sixth sense, which is the undifferentiated signal input of the seven classical chakras. This becomes a mishmash of noise rather than a signal, until one learns to separate the signal paths and discern where the signal is coming from. Without proper filtering through appropriate memetic constructs signal becomes noise, and noise can drive you crazy. To dampen the signal, people turn to addictive substances and processes. It's tuning and focusing one needs to learn, hence my continued research into the healing aspects of music, meditation, yoga, or simple interaction with natural systems like wind, water, silence, the desert, outer and inner space. There are many tools in the art of being and becoming more human that are more infinite and connected. The effort is worth it.

SEPARATING THE PSI SIGNAL FROM THE NOISE

Mark Gurumukh Harris

Post-Traumatic Stress Disorder (PTSD) happens to an individual. Multigenerational Trauma happens to a people and is passed on within DNA, much like instinct, though you don't necessarily know what it is. There are human ethnic genomes, which breed psi sensitives and that talent was once trained from birth. However, with war, slavery, conquest, genocide, and chemical warfare in the form of alcohol and other drugs, the psi talent, which attempts to be expressed, is pathologized as insanity.

In a crude way, LSD is the opposite of Prozac, though it competes with serotonin for receptor sites. Prozac increases serotonin to screen signal out. LSD allows more signal into the sensorium. As your mind attempts to sort the incoming data into familiar patterns you see trails and the room breathes. Thus what you see on acid is not a hallucination—you also get the screened out data. One can learn to modify this signal input at will with the proper technology. In cultures of tradition, psychedelics are used like training wheels on a bicycle. A bicycle teaches the skill of internal balance. Ritual use of psychedelics allows conceptualization of levels of reality usually screened out by neurochemical sensors, as well as whatever memes of consensus reality one has. After all Chi can be sensed and trained through martial arts training, and prana is learned through yoga. Ten-year-old children can be taught to break bricks and boards.

In Gaelic the words *"kything"* and to *"ken"* imply not only understanding of things and events beyond our ordinary experience of space and time, but also the information exchange with non-human intelligence. Certainly the phrase *"All my relations,"* as used in several Native American languages, explicitly assumes our unity with the animal, vegetable, mineral and invisible worlds.

In the original telepathic experiment we found that training in EEG interpersonal alpha synch enabled telepathic communication between the trained partners. We could send images, but the signal received is translated in one's own personal internal imagery and meaning. Since that telepathic experiment, I thought of four telepathic *"bands"* (much like radio stations). Telepathic band A includes blood relatives; B includes lovers and friends; C includes random strangers; D includes those with whom you attune like regular clients.

Conceptually, the chakra input could transcend the five senses in ways that can be replicated through experience. So think of signals from the chakras like a zip file, that you need the right experiential software and understanding to unpack. This is how you begin to separate signal from noise. If it's not immediately useful, it probably will be down the road.

Greg Schelkun

Greg Schelkun is a spiritual healer working in San Rafael, CA, for over 30 years. He graduated from Dartmouth College in the early 1970s with a degree in art history. While working for a Boston publisher, his mother, who had been ill for five years, asked him to accompany her to the Philippines in search of healing. In the Philippines she met with a healer who performed "psychic surgery" on her and she was cured. The healer also cured Schelkun of migraine headaches, which he had suffered for 17 years.

In 1973, he returned to the Philippines to document and film the healers at work. While there, a healer from Baguio City Placido Palitayan invited him to become an apprentice. Greg spent the next two years there, learning about, and developing, his latent healing gifts.

In 1975, he came to the San Francisco Bay Area, and began his individual practice. Greg has lectured and taught at schools and centers throughout the West Coast. Greg became the focus of many experiments and tests of the paranormal at institutions such as: The Institute of Noetic Sciences (IONS), the Washington Research Institute (WRI), and the University of California San Francisco (UCSF), Langley Porter Psychophysiology Lab.

Looking for physical ways to describe the attributes of the healing, Greg found the best affirmation of his work came from his patients. His primary work was and remains his individual practice.

In 2001, he was awarded "alternative practitioner of the year" by Marin County's Breast Cancer Watch, for his continuing work with women with breast cancer.

PUBLISHED REPORTS ABOUT THE SPIRITUAL HEALING BY GREG SCHELKUN

1) (1987 – December 7). "Living: New Age harmonies."
   In: *Time* Magazine.
2) (1988 – Chapter 12) "Hands on healing."
   In: *Higher Dimensions of Healing*. Rodale Press.
3) (1993) Wirth, Dan. "A Study on belief" (doctoral thesis).
   In: Harvard University's *Pergamon Journal for Social Science and Medicine*. Boston, MA.
4) (2005 - May/June) *Neimark, Jill.* "The Making of a healer."
   In: *Spirituality and Health* magazine.

   Additional reports about Greg Schelkun can be found on websites:
   http://www.spiritualityhealth.com/NMagazine/articles/php?id=1148
   http://www.yourownhealthandfitness.org/topicsAlternative.php

~~~~~~

THANK YOU, GREG SCHELKUN

Carol Guion

Greg Schelkun is a loving bear of a man. I had visited him professionally for the odd twitch or tweak, which he always managed to put right. So I knew I needed to take my increasingly demented mother up to see him, three years after I had moved her out to California. She had nursed my father through cancer, and after he died my brother died of cancer. That is when she started having small strokes.

This was back before dementia, Alzheimer's, etc. were really acknowledged as something people actually dealt with, and didn't shove into carehomes. I saw people react to her strangeness with fear, day centers tried to give her heavy tranquilizers, and a doctor I took her to couldn't even get her on a table.

My nephew Gerry came out then to help with his Gram, and we all, including my afghan hound Ayesha, went up to see Greg. I was exhausted beyond words, Ayesha had gotten into some chocolate, and Mom was, well, Mom. Greg swept us all into his office, and said he should just stack us all up on the treatment table. Mom instantly adored him, and with no trouble was lifted up, laid down, and "worked on." Calm and joy!

Greg's humor, humanity, love and skill got us all through some peculiar times, and isn't this what it's all about?

EPILOGUE

ENVISIONING GLOBAL MIND

Roger Nelson

We may be participants in an interaction similar to that of the neurons in a brain. These individual cells don't know anything about the mind or the questions we ask, or what consciousness is, but they participate anyway. They just do what neurons do. Although we could do a better job of being humans, the evidence suggests that in a similar way we are participating in a global interaction that might become conscious and self-aware, though we have no way to perceive it. We may be "neurons" in a global brain. Maybe we will wake up as a global mind.

Consciousness has a creative, productive, generative role in the world such that what we wish for is more likely than if we hadn't put our minds to it. We have good evidence that this is true, and that what we envision together will manifest in the world in a subtle way. This means that we have an enormous untapped potential to create alternatives. It is in our power to change the world to a brighter future. It just depends on coalescing into a greater consciousness.

In the Upanishads, the ancients talk about 26,000-year cycles where consciousness wakes up and then goes to sleep, wakes up and then goes to sleep. I think this is the global consciousness idea. It is being able to look at ourselves in a different way that allows us have insight into the ride we are taking on the universal wave of consciousness. So we can actually become doubly self-reflective. The truth is, most of the time we are asleep. But we can wake up a little bit. That is the promise of global consciousness: a global mind.

SECTION XII

APPENDICES

* Real Magic = Telepathic Communication, Remote Viewing, Psychokinesis, Out-of-the-Body Experiences, Channeling Information from Spirit World Entities, Energy Healing, Group Mind-Melt.

SECTION XII

APPENDICES

1) **SILVER THREADS: 25 Years of Parapsychology Research**
   (Table of Contents from the first PRG Anthology published in 1993)

Figures and Tables
Foreword: Shifting Assumptions — *Willis Harman*
Acknowledgements
Introduction

I. Foundations
1. Parapsychology, Science, and Intuition — *William H. Kautz*
2. The Nature of Personal Belief Systems — *Beverley Kane*

II. Remote Viewing
3. Dream ESP Experiments and Geomagnetic Activity — *M. Persinger & S. Krippner*
4. A Decade of Remote-Viewing Research — *Russell Targ*
5. Longitudinal Comparison of Local and Long Distance Remote Perception Phenomena — *Elizabeth A. Rauscher*
6. Exploring the Visionary Experience — *Jean Millay*

III. Physics
7. Energy — *Saul-Paul Sirag*
8. Quantum Reality and Consciousness — *Nick Herbert*
9. Time, Consciousness, and Psi — *Jean E. Burns*

IV. Mathematical Models
10. A Theoretical Model of the Remote Perception Phenomenon — *Elizabeth A. Rauscher*
11. Hyperspace Reflections — *Saul-Paul Sirag*

V. Bioscience
12. Psychoneuroimmunology—The Bridge Between Science and Spirit — *Sondra Barrett*
13. Human Volitional Effects on a Model Bacterial System — *Beverly Rubik & E. Rauscher*

14. The Evolution of Consciousness
   Intertwined with the Evolution of the
   Science of Plants — *Dean Brown*
15. Consciously Creating Conscious States — *Cheri Quincy*

VI. Psychology
16. Alternate States of Consciousness:
   Access to Other Realities — *Ruth-Inge Heinze*
17. Firewalking—A New Look
   at an Old Enigma — *Larissa Vilenskaya*
18. PK on the PC—A Macintosh Event Generator
   Based on the Princeton Engineering
   Anomalies Research Experiments — *William J. Croft*
19. Brainwave Synchronization:
   Report on a Pilot Study — *James R. Johnston*
20. Near-Death Experiences: Implications for
   Human Evolution and Planetary Transformation — *Kenneth Ring*
21. Channeling — *Jon Klimo*
22. Implications of Consciousness Research for
   Psychotherapy and Self-Exploration — *Stanislav Grof*

VII. Reflections
23. The Dilemma of Parapsychology — *William H. Kautz*
24. Truth & Science: Ethical
   Dimensions of PSI Research — *Shelley Thomson*
25. Increasing Psychic Reliability — *Targ, Braud, Schlitz & Honorton*

Reflections on 25 Years and 25 Chapters — *Charles T. Tart*

Epilogue — *Dean Brown*

Milestones in the History of the Parapsychology Research Group
Appendix: PRG Belief Survey
Selected Bibliography
Index
About the Contributors

APPENDICES

2) GLOSSARY

General Terms

CAM = Complementary and Alternative Medicine.

Cosmogenesis = A term that relates to theories about the creation of the cosmos.

DHI = Distant Healing Intention is the term used by Elisabeth Targ, Marilyn Schlitz and Dean Radin.

DMH = Distant Mental Healing is a term used by Russian physicist and researcher Alexander Dubrov, PhD.

DMILS = Direct Mental Interactions with Living Systems. This is thought to involve psychokinetic influences on physiological and cognitive activities in distant persons, and also includes physiological measures of effects of remote staring.

EM = Electromagnetic Frequencies, such as **UHF** (ultra-high frequencies) and **VHF** (very high frequency) that are used by TV. The Ionosphere-Earth wave guide frequencies are in the range of **ELF** (Extreme low frequencies). Brainwaves frequencies are analogous to Earth's ELF.

Entheogen = Derived from the Greek root word *"Theo"* meaning "God." For example, a shaman may eat a plant called an *entheogen* to evoke spiritual visions or to communicate with the Divine.

Holotropic = Developed by Stanislav and Christine Grof to describe their therapeutic sessions, which are extremely effective.
Grof writes:
> It is derived from the Greek holos meaning 'whole' and trepein, 'to move toward'; it suggests aiming for totality and wholeness. This is a technique of self-exploration that uses activation of the unconscious through a combination of controlled breathing, evocative music, and focused bodywork. Holotropic therapy mediates access to the entire spectrum of experiences that are available in psychedelic sessions and to powerful therapeutic mechanisms on the perinatal and transpersonal levels.

I CHING = The ancient Chinese Book of Changes. It is consulted as a way to find the best path to follow in a certain situation. Three Chinese coins are used, or a selection of Yarrow sticks. These are tossed randomly during a meditation on the question. The answer to my question about taking on the job of putting this book together was this: *"Perseverance Furthers."* This job took three years.

Incommensurability = ETs from UFOs or UAPs may have such divergent ways of conceptualizing the world from the way humans do that mutual understanding may not be possible.

- **ITC** = Instrumental transcommunication. This refers to the use of technology to capture images or voices or text from spirits.
- **PNI** = Psychoneuroimmunology is a field of medicine that has evolved out of the interaction of psychology, yoga, neurobiology, immunology, theology, shamanism, and the space program. The success of the "placebo" in research studies led to the realization that the mind of the patient may be stimulated to participate actively with his/her own healing process.
- **Psychomanteum** = A "theater of the mind." In 1992, Raymond Moody used this term when he was attempting to facilitate apparitions similar to those experienced by surviving spouses and friends of deceased persons. The bereaved sat quietly with only a dim light inside a small, somewhat sound-proofed, windowless, room that was covered with black theater cloth. A mirror sits on a table angled toward the ceiling. For some bereaved, an image may appear in the mirror.
- **UAP** = Unidentified Aerial Phenomena. This term is used by Vallee and Davis to separate it from the cults who already have preconceived ideas about "UFOs" and claim to know who and what they are, whereas, we have yet to learn what they really are. It is important to keep an open mind about the observed phenomena that are conscientiously reported by responsible witnesses.

Terms Commonly Used In Parapsychology

- **Akashic** = Refers to the collected knowledge of the world through the ages. This is often referred to as the *Akashic Records*.
- **Clairvoyant** = An older term for a psi sensitive who finds information about an object, place or lost person in nonlocal spacetime when there is no sender. The newer terms **RV** or **RP** cover this form of psi.
- **ESP** = Extra Sensory Perception. An older term that included various forms of psychic activity (e. g., telepathy and clairvoyance). It is still used by some parapsychologists since more people are familiar with it.
- **Noetic** = Derived from the Chardin term for *"world consciousness."* The term has been adapted by *The Institute of Noetic Sciences* (IONS), since that organization is dedicated to the advancement of the science of consciousness and human experience for individual and collective transformation.
- **Nonlocal Spacetime** = Quantum connectedness, as proved by Bell's theorem, does not degrade by distance or time, and is faster than light.
- **Noosphere** = A term used by Teilhard de Chardin to describe a coalescing layer of intelligence for the earth, with these layers: barisphere, hydrosphere, biosphere, atmosphere, and noosphere.
- **PK** = Psychokinesis. The ability to move or change objects with mind power.

Psi = This is an abbreviation for all psychic phenomena.

Psi Sensitive = A person for whom psi information is naturally available.

RP = Remote Perception. This term is preferred by some researchers over the term "remote viewing" because psi perception includes more than just the "viewing" of targets. All the senses may be active in psi including hearing, smelling, tasting, touching, and emotions.

RV = Remote Viewing, or psi activity in nonlocal spacetime. Targ, Puthoff and psychic artist Ingo Swann chose this term in 1973 to separate psi activity from the "occult" terms discredited by materialist scientists. They received a small government grant to test the process. Later, government remote viewers and the **IRVA** (International Remote Viewers Association) developed several types of **RV**, such as **ARV** (Associative Remote Viewing) and **CRV** (Controlled Remote Viewing). Both are defined by their predetermined protocols of use. For more information, see www.irva.com, and www.espresearch.com.

Telepathy = This term specifically applies to mind-to-mind communication between people or animals ("tele" = distant, "pathy" = feeling).

~~~~~~

Terms Used In Physiological Measurement

BFB and **NFB** = Biofeedback and Neurofeedback. Information is measured from a person's physiology and is translated into audible and/or visual feedback. This helps the person to learn how to alter those responses to gain voluntary control over emotions, pain or stress as needed. **BFB** refers to all forms of feedback, such as pH levels, temperature, blood sugar, weight, etc. NFB refers especially to brain and body electrical activity, to enhance meditation. (Sects. V and X.)

EEG = Electroencephalogram. This is commonly referred to as "brainwaves," since it refers to the electrical activity of the brain. (Sects. V and X.)

EGG = Electrogastrogram. This machine measures electrical "gut" activity, and was used by Radin in Chapter 2 to study emotional responses from images sent telepathically.

EKG = Electrocardiogram. This is the recording of the activity of the heart. A rapid heart rate can be calmed by steady even breathing to release emotional pain. New hand-held feedback machines have recently become available to enhance the practice of heart synchrony, which can help one to achieve a peaceful state of mind.

EMG = Electromyogram. The recording of the activity of muscles. Very tense muscles produce more electrical signals than relaxed muscles. The **EMG** feedback machines are often used by athletes to train to improve flexibility. They are also useful for recovery of muscle activity after a strain or a broken bone.

pH Strips = These provide information about the acidity or alkalinity of the body. They are easily obtained from a pharmacy or from a health food store. To use them, simply pass the end of a strip through the flow of urine, and compare the color with the color numbers on the box. Seven represents balance. Lower than 7 means the body is more acidic. Higher than 7 means the body is more alkaline.

SCR = Skin Conductance Resistance. (**SCR**) The original term used was **GSR** (Galvanic Skin Response). This machine records emotional responses by measuring minute amounts of sweat from fingertips. This sweat is related to something as simple as the name or a word that evokes a painful memory, which can cause the sweat to increase. It is possible to release one's physiological responses to the old memory, without repressing the memory. **SCR** feedback machines are the least expensive, and the easiest to use for increased understanding of self.

Skin Temperature = A machine that records and feeds back the variations in the temperature of the skin (ST). When two or more are used you can compare any differences between them. For example, put one on each hand, or one on the hand and the other on the foot. A difference of ten degrees could relate to muscle tension in the arms or legs, or to circulation. Combine **ST** with **EMG** for better muscle control, or to discover the source of an emotional response, which has caused the skin temperature to drop.

~~~~~~

Terms Used In The Global Consciousness Project

Anomalous patterning = Departures from expectation for statistics.

EGG = ElectroGaiaGram. The REG-based instrument used in GCP. This refers to the individual REGs and to the network of REGs.

Gaiamind = A global meditation event—that was a prototype for GCP.

GCP = Global Consciousness Project. A collaboration of scientists around the world to expand this frontier of consciousness research. They host network nodes, use an REG to record a time series of parallel data sequences from a wide geographic distribution. The network has nodes at about 60 sites from Alaska to Fiji, hosting REG devices that generate random data continuously and send it for archiving to a dedicated server in Princeton, NJ. The GCP data and analyses provide evidence for the meaningful interactions of consciousness with the physical world.

REG = Random Event Generator. An electronic random number generator based on quantum processes that are truly random.

Structure = Unexpected deviations of the GCP data from random statistical behavior.

www.ingramcontent.com/pod-product-compliance
Lightning Source LLC
Chambersburg PA
CBHW030327240426
43661CB00052B/1557